LAW, CHURCH, AND SOCIETY

A volume in
The Middle Ages Series
Edward Peters, General Editor

Stephen Kuttner

ROBIN ANN ARONSTAM

THOMAS N. BISSON

UTA-RENATE BLUMENTHAL

ROBERT BRENTANO

STANLEY CHODOROW

GILES CONSTABLE

JOHN H. ERICKSON

JUDAH GOLDIN

PATRICK HENRY

STEVEN HORWITZ

THOMAS M. IZBICKI

CHARLES MCCURRY

K. F. MORRISON

JOHN T. NOONAN, JR.

KENNETH PENNINGTON

EDWARD M. PETERS

ROGER E. REYNOLDS

ROBERT SOMERVILLE

BRIAN TIERNEY

LAW, CHURCH, AND SOCIETY
Essays in Honor of Stephan Kuttner

Edited by

KENNETH PENNINGTON AND ROBERT SOMERVILLE

UNIVERSITY OF PENNSYLVANIA PRESS/1977

Library of Congress Cataloging in Publication Data

Main entry under title:

Law, church, and society.

(The Middle Ages)
Includes index.
CONTENTS: Goldin, J. A short note on the
archangel Gabriel.--The Papacy: Blumenthal, U.-R.
Patrimonia and regalia in 1111. Noonan, J. T., Jr.
Who was Rolandus? Pennington, K. Pope Innocent
III's views on church and state. Tierney, B.
Only truth has authority. Izbicki, T. M.
Infallibility and the erring Pope. [etc.]
   1. Christianity--Middle Ages, 600-1500--
Addresses, essays, lectures. 2. Canon law--
Addresses, essays, lectures. 3. Kuttner,
Stephen George, 1907-   I. Kuttner, Stephen
Georg, 1907-   II. Pennington, Kenneth, 1941-
III. Somerville, Robert, 1940-   IV. Series.
BR252.L38   261   76-53199
ISBN 0-8122-7726-0

Frontispiece photograph courtesy of Steven Horwitz

Copyright © 1977 by the University of Pennsylvania Press, Inc.

Printed in the United States of America

Contents

Table of Abbreviations

The following abbreviations are used throughout the volume without further explanation.

JE   P. Jaffé, *Regesta pontificum Romanorum,* 2nd ed. (F. Kaltenbrun-
JK   ner [JK: years ?–590], P. Ewald [JE: years 590–882], S. Loewenfeld
JL   [JL: years 882–1198])

Mansi   J. D. Mansi, *Sacrorum conciliorum nova et amplissima collectio*

MGH   *Monumenta Germaniae historica*

LL   MGH, Leges

SS   MGH, Scriptores

PG   J. P. Migne, *Patrologia Graeca*

PL   J. P. Migne, *Patrologia Latina*

Potthast   A. Potthast, *Regesta pontificum Romanorum*

Well-known sources of canon and Roman law will be cited according to standard form, without bibliographical detail.

Foreword

Stephan Georg Kuttner left Germany amid the turmoil of the early thirties, shortly after he had begun his academic career in law at the University of Berlin. He found a temporary home in Italy, worked as a research associate at the Vatican Library from 1934 to 1940, and was a professor at the Lateran University from 1937 to 1940. During this period he immersed himself in the study of medieval canon law, the discipline which became his lifelong vocation. With the support of the Vatican, he published in 1937 the first comprehensive survey of manuscripts of canon law for the period from 1140 to 1234. Through this work of extraordinary industry he placed the study of the classical period of medieval canon law on a firm foundation. But the political circumstances of the times continued to affect his life, and after the beginning of the war he and his family emigrated to the United States where he was appointed visiting professor (1940–42), and then professor of the history of canon law at the Catholic University of America.

When Stephan Kuttner came to this country there were few scholars in American universities working with medieval canon law. In large part due to his enthusiasm and vigor during more than three decades, this has changed. He was the co-founder of *Traditio* in 1943, and in 1955 established the Institute of Medieval Canon Law, a research center that would foster and coordinate the study of canon law and encourage the edition of texts. His labor also is visible in the *Bulletin of Medieval Canon Law* (from 1955 to 1970 part of *Traditio,* and now a separate journal), in the volumes of the *Monumenta iuris canonici,* and in the proceedings of several international congresses on medieval canon law, two of which met in North America (Boston, 1964; Toronto, 1972). He is a member of numerous learned societies, has received more than a dozen honorary degrees, and in 1974–75 served as president of the Mediaeval Academy of America.

Stephen Kuttner's contribution to American letters can be measured, in one sense, by his publications and scholarly activities, but his life and career have other dimensions which cannot be quantified. His greatest talent is the scrupulous precision which he demands in his own work and which he can draw out of others. He is a superb textual scholar, and combines this facility with an uncanny grasp of the mechanisms by which the Church in the Middle Ages operated. As perhaps no one in modern times, he knows the sources of the Latin Church's constitutional history from the Patristic age through the Council of Trent and even beyond. His work spans and exceeds the contributions of Maassen, Fournier, Friedberg, and Schulte. To find a scholar with a comparable range of knowledge and interests it might be necessary to move back to Antonio Agustín in the sixteenth century, or to Étienne Baluze in the seventeenth. To his students in Washington, New Haven, and Berkeley, and to the many others who have sought his assistance, Stephan Kuttner has opened new channels into the life and thought of the medieval world. The student or stranger who approaches him for guidance leaves with a solution and a friend.

The articles published in this volume represent his second such tribute. A decade ago, at the time of his sixtieth birthday, four volumes of essays were published in *Studia Gratiana* as an international acknowledgment of his contribution to legal history. The present book prints essays of colleagues and friends in the United States and Canada. Most of the contributors owe much to Professor Kuttner's magisterial influence both in and out of the classroom, and the great majority, as the articles illustrate, are active in research which intersects with the concerns which have occupied his scholarly career. The categories into which the essays fall both reflect the richness and wide range of that career, and offer a schema which many medieval men would recognize as a proper order for human society: beginning with the papacy, ranging through orders and offices of the ecclesiastical hierarchy, legal procedure, the church and society, and ending with local churches. The essays assembled under these topics—and heralded by "A Short Note on the Archangel Gabriel"—are a tribute to an exceptional man, whose life and work have a gentle strength which inspires trust and emulation, and whose career has served and continues to serve "Law, Church, and Society."

The editors would like to express their gratitude to the contributors and readers who have helped in the assembly of these essays, to Robert Erwin and his staff at the University of Pennsylvania Press, to Robin Aronstam, to The Most Reverend F. Joseph Gossman, Bishop of Raleigh-Durham, and to Edward Peters, *sine quo non*.

KP
RS

A Short Note on the Archangel Gabriel

JUDAH GOLDIN

Even the ancients knew that the authors of Holy Writ occasionally had difficulty reporting phenomena for which human vocabulary was inadequate.
They said therefore that the expressions used in such instances were only ap-
proximate, figurative, or metaphorical.[1] This was indeed "the hedge the
Prophets made about their words."[2] For example, "Scripture says: 'The lion
has roared; who will not fear' (Amos 3:8)? Perhaps His voice is only like the
voice of a lion. Say then: Who gave a voice to the lion? Is it not He? But this
is the way He is described metaphorically to His creatures so that the ear be
unoffended and be able to hear."[3] Or as the companion text puts it, "But the
eye is shown what it can see and the ear is permitted to hear what it can
hear."[4]

Another example of such resort to metaphor is to be seen, according to the
Mekilta,[5] in Exod. 19:18.[6] Still another example is Isa. 42:13, where we
must understand that the Lord goes forth not just as one "mighty man," but
as more mighty than all the mighty men in the world.[7]

And still another:

> So too, Scripture says: 'And behold the glory of the God of Israel came from the east; and
> the sound of His [coming] was like the sound of many waters'[8] (Ezek. 43:2). Say then:
> Who gave a voice to the waters:[9] was it not He? But this is the way He is described meta-
> phorically to His creatures so that the ear be unoffended and be able to hear.[10]

Such is the way Version B of *Abot de-Rabbi Natan* puts it. Version A,[11] on
the other hand, is more expository and very likely making an additional emphasis of its own.

> "And His voice was like the sound of many waters; and the earth did shine with His glory"
> (Ezek. 43:2).—
>
>> The[12] *sound of many waters* refers to the angel Gabriel. *And the earth did shine with His
>> glory* refers to the presence of the Shekinah.—
>
> Now, is there not an inference to be drawn here? If Gabriel, who is but one of thousands
> upon thousands and myriads upon myriads that stand before Him, has a voice which
> travels from one end of the world to the other, how much more so the King of kings over
> kings . . . who created the whole universe, who created the beings on high and the be-
> ings below! But the eye is shown what it can see [etc.].[13]

To avoid dangerous literalness in description of the divine, one might well
be led to explain "the sound of many waters" as a reference to the angel Ga-

briel. The Septuagint, for instance, possibly its *Vorlage* too, does not speak of *His* voice as the voice (sound) of many waters in Ezek. 43:2 ("kai phonē tēs parembolēs, hôs phonē diplasiazontôn pollôn")[14] while in 1:24 the sound of the wings "like the sound of many waters, like the sound of the Almighty [Shaddai],"[15] (as the Vulgate also: "quasi sonum sublimis Dei") is reduced and adapted to the sound of their wings "en to poreuesthai auta hōs phônēn hudatos pollou."

The Targum similarly, on 43:2, creates a buffer expression: "And behold, the glory [yqr] of the God of Israel was revealed ['tgly] from the way [direction] of the east and *the sound of those who praise His name* [mbrky šmyh] [was] like the sound of many waters"; no less in 1:24: "I heard the sound of their wings like the sound of many waters, like the sound *from before Shaddai,*[16] as they walk about, the sound of *what they utter as they" praise God* is like the sound of the camp of the angels on high, and so forth.

God's voice, of course, travels from one end of the world to the other. It did so, for example, at the Revelation.[17] But other sounds or voices do the same—for example, the sun in its revolution, the tumult of the city (of Rome), the sound of the soul when it leaves the body; some say also (the cry) at childbirth, and still others say the sound of Ridya.[18] Nor is it only sounds that may be said to travel "from one end of the world to the other." When Adam was created, "his soulless lump was laid out from one end of the world to the other."[19] One of the ways in which demons resemble the ministering angels is that they travel from one end of the world to the other.[20] Not only Moses, but the righteous, can see from one end of the world to the other.[21] And many other examples are to be found in a variety of contexts. In other words, "from one end of the world to the other" is a cliché adopted to express the superlative, the extreme, the uttermost. Legend cheerfully appropriates it because legend is thereby spared the trouble of inventing fresh figures of speech each time a wonder is to be recorded. The hyperbole is so natural indeed that the pedantry of documentation is almost superfluous. There is nothing extraordinary, then, in a statement that Gabriel's voice carried from one end of the world to the other.

But what in the Ezek. 43:2 verse suggests that the voice or sound[22] of many waters is a reference to *Gabriel?* There is a tradition that Gabriel brings astonishing and good tidings.[23] Muslims may say that Gabriel brought on the choking in the Prophet as the beginning of Revelation.[24] The mystics will associate gold with Gabriel, and he is appointed messenger for this world.[25] Gabriel's outcry, as he is struck under his wings, can set cocks crowing at midnight.[26] Some men will say that a seventeenth-century messiah, to escape being taken prisoner, ascended to heaven and that Gabriel had assumed his form.[27] Much more is included from earliest times in the lore about Gabriel,[28] but still no word about Gabriel and "the sound of many waters" (whose sound God's voice surpasses), at least not in earlier sources. Where does this association come from?

It seems to me that Version A of *Abot de-Rabbi Natan* has preserved for us a midrash in the form of numerical equation, gematria; for the Hebrew consonants of "many waters," m-y-m (40-10-40) r-b-y-m (200-2-10-40) add up to the same sum as "the angel Gabriel," g-b-r-y-$ɔ$-l (3-2-200-10-1-30) h-m-l-$ɔ$-k (5-40-30-1-20), to wit, 342. (In Scripture the order of the words is, first *we-ha-ish,* then Gabriel.) "Many waters" in the verse, therefore, equals "the angel Gabriel."

Interpretation by means of gematria may sometimes be playful[29] but not necessarily so; nor need it be late, nor is it limited to rabbinic exegesis.[30] Nor is it likely to come from unmotivated reading of the biblical text. By this last sentence I mean the following: It seems to me that in connection with Ezek. 43:2 there was a (mystical? Merkabah?) tradition that the sound of many waters referred to Gabriel and that the gematria substantiated it, not, the other way around, that gematria exercises per se put the angel Gabriel into the verse arbitrarily or by chance.[31] Of course it is impossible to say definitely which came first (verse interpreted by gematria leading to discovery of Gabriel, or thoughts about Gabriel leading to discovery of him in the verse by means of gematria), or if there is such a thing as first and second with a Bible reader, particularly with a reader of Ezekiel's visions.[32] There was the text and there were traditions of interpretation,[33] and one found elements in the text that supported a particular interpretation which was part of a much larger frame of speculations and references already favored.

And having recognized how the sound of many waters refers to Gabriel, perhaps the following speculation may be allowed. Until Rabbi Isaac had publicly preached that the light which illuminated the world on the first day of Creation ("fiat lux") came from the robe ("stolē")[34] with which the Holy One, blessed be He, covered Himself, Rabbi Berekiah (fourth century AD)[35] taught (in the name of Rabbi Isaac)[36] that Ezekiel's words "and the earth did shine with His Glory" referred to the site of the Temple, that is, that the light came from there ("kabod," glory = Temple).[37] Doubtless because of views to the contrary, Rabbi Berekiah was surely *underscoring* that from Ezekiel's words one could learn at least that the Temple-site was still charged with divine sanctity. The statement is not pointless.

Similarly, the second part of our brief midrash may be emphasizing more than is at first self-evident. "'And the earth did shine with His glory' refers to the presence of the Shekinah," or, to render with a literalness indifferent to the requirements of literary translation, "'And the earth lit up from His glory [doxa]' refers to the presence [the face] of the Shekinah [pne *ha-*Shekinah]." The expression "pne Shekinah" is not uncommon and appears in a number of hortatory statements.[38] The *Mekilta* declares that whoever welcomes "the face of the sages is as though he welcomes 'pne Shekinah'."[39] In the age to come, Rabbi Simeon ben Yohai says, the righteous will welcome (greet) "pne Shekinah."[40] According to Rabbi Meir, one who carries out the ṣiṣit commandment (Num. 15:37–41) is accounted, regarded, as though he had welcomed "pne Shekinah."[41] This is not to imply that the expression "pne Shekinah" is to be taken lightly because of its relative frequency;

however, it is to imply that there was apparently no excessive hesitancy about using it for purposes of exhortation and promise of reward.

For the remainder let us confine our discussion when possible to *Abot de-Rabbi Natan*. Version A is prepared to speak of "the splendor of *the* Shekinah [zyw *h*škynh],"[42] which the righteous will enjoy in the Future, of "the wings of *the* Shekinah [knpy *h*škynh]"[43] that shelter proselytes; otherwise, "Shekinah" without the definite article.[44] Version B talks of *the* Shekinah (but immediately thereafter, of the Holy One, blessed be He) making the rounds,[45] of *the* Shekinah being revealed.[46] But "the face of *the* Shekinah" seems to be if not unique, extremely rare. It is most likely a very bold expression, and it too is almost certainly not pointless.

God's voice was more powerful than Gabriel's, and God's *doxa,* we are told, refers to the *face* of *the* Shekinah. Does this mean no more than that while the first clause (sound) refers to Gabriel, the second (light) refers to God Himself? Or does this mean that the light which Ezekiel beheld in his vision as lighting up the earth, was stronger, brighter, than that of the prince of fire?[47] Were there those who thought that the light which Ezekiel beheld did not come from the Shekinah but came from a lesser source?

University of Pennsylvania

Notes

All Old Testament references are to the Masoretic Hebrew Bible. As to abbreviations, "B." = Babylonian Talmud; "Gen. R." = Genesis Rabba; "Lev. R." = Leviticus Rabba; "M." = Mishnah.

1. On euphemism, cf. *Mekilta, Shirta* 6, ed. J. Z. Lauterbach (Philadelphia, 1933–35), II: 43–44.
2. *Abot de-Rabbi Natan* (hereafter ARN), ed. S. Schechter (Vienna, 1887), p. 7a.
3. ARN, Version B, trans. A. J. Saldarini (Leiden, 1975), p. 46, and n. 9.
4. Version A of ARN, ed. Schechter, p. 7a.
5. *Mekilta, Ba-Ḥodesh* 4.2.221; *Mekilta R. Simeon*, eds. J. N. Epstein and E. Z. Melamed (Jerusalem, 1955), p. 144, plus additional examples; *Midrash ha-Gadol, Gen.* ed. M. Margulies (Jerusalem, 1947), Intro., p. 30. Cf. Rashi on the verses as well.
6. With reference to Deut. 4:11, see also ARN, trans. Saldarini, p. 46, n. 11.
7. Cf. Version A of ARN, ed. Schechter, p. 7a, n. 71.
8. Version B of ARN does not quote the rest of the verse (see further below) and therefore does not comment on it. On the voice of one like unto the son of man as the sound of many waters, cf. Rev. 1:15. On the "rush of many waters" following God, see the hymn in J. A. Sanders, *The Psalms Scroll of Qumran, Cave 11* (Oxford, 1965), p. 89, col. 26, l. 10, and note (p. 90). In J. Licht, *Thanksgiving Scroll* (Jerusalem, 1957), p. 68, l. 16b, and p. 71, l. 27, the reference is not to God and the imagery is meant to suggest overpowering sound and strength.
9. Cf. *Zohar Ḥadash* 18d, in I. Tishby, *Mishnat ha-Zohar* (Jerusalem, 5709), I: 441, and on "the sound of the waters like the voice of Shaddai" (Ezek. 1:24), see further below.
10. Version B of ARN, ed. Schechter, p. 7a, and ARN, trans. Saldarini, p. 46. Cf. *Yalqut Shimeoni* (Salonica, 1521) on the verse.
11. ARN, ed. Schechter, p. 46.

12. Cf. n. 8, above.

13. Note how Appendix B in ARN, ed. Schechter, p. 77a (towards bottom), reads. And note how Maimonides, *Guide of the Perplexed*, 3. 9, trans. S. Pines (Chicago, 1963), pp. 436–37, makes use of the Ezek. verse, and how Albo does, *Ikkarim* 2.29, ed. I. Husik (Philadelphia, 1946), II: 188.

14. On this reading, cf. Jerome's emphasis in F. Field, *Origenis Hexaplorum* (Oxford, 1875), II: 885, n. 2.

15. And on the reading "hôs phônēn hikanou" (!), cf. Field, ibid., p. 771, and n. 64: "šdy" equated with "dy." Cf. *B. Hagigah* 12a (Resh Laquish).

16. Cf. David Quimhi on Ezek. 43:2, *Miqraot Gedolot* (Warsaw, 1865), and see also Zohar (Wilna, 1930), I: 71b, on " 'like the voice of Shaddai,' which never grows silent."

17. *Sifre Deuteronomy* 343, ed. L. Finkelstein (Berlin, 1939), p. 399.

18. *B. Yoma* 20b–21a. On Ridya, cf. Rashi on this passage, and M. Jastrow, *Dictionary* (New York-Berlin, 1926), s.v. "Ridya." On A. Kohut, *Aruch completum* (New York, 1955), VII: 257–58, cf. IX: 38 1b, s.v. *"radayya."*

19. Version B of ARN, ed. Schechter, p. 11b; Saldarini, ARN, p. 76, n. 10.

20. Version A of ARN, ed. Schechter, p. 55a.

21. *Sifre Numbers* 136, ed. S. Horovitz (Jerusalem, 1966), p. 182.

22. "qwl," the same word for both. On the name Gabriel, cf. H. L. Ginsberg, *Studies in Daniel* (New York, 1948), p. 81, n. 22. Note in ARN not just "Gabriel" but "the angel Gabriel."

23. Luke 1:18ff. For the gnostic notion in Pistis-Sophia, cf. J. Doresse, *Secret Books of the Egyptian Gnostics* (London, 1960), p. 113, n. 116.

24. Ibn Khaldûn, *The Muqaddimah*, trans. F. Rosenthal (Princeton, 1967), I: 201f., p. 261, n. 34.

25. *Zohar* II: 147a–b; II: 231a.

26. G. Scholem, *On the Kabbalah and Its Symbolism* (New York, 1965), p. 147.

27. G. Scholem, *Sabbatai Sevi* (Princeton, 1973), p. 605. Long before that there was the notion that Gabriel could assume different guises; cf. L. Ginzberg, *Legends of the Jews* (Philadelphia, 1909–38), V: 423, n. 146, VI: 34, n. 195. See also E. Rohde's reference to the Boccaccio story, in *Psyche* (New York, 1966), I: 155, n. 134. For Gabriel on the right hand of a scholar with unchaste intentions, cf. *Seder Eliyahu Rabba*, ed. M. Friedmann (Jerusalem, 1960), Additions, p. 39.

28. See, for example, B. Cohen's *Index* to Ginzberg's *Legends*, VII: 172–74, or the material assembled by Billerbeck in his *Kommentar zum Neuen Testament* (Munich, 1924), II: 89–97. Cf. Rashi on Gen. 37:15. Doresse, *Secret Books*, p. 233–34, refers to an unpublished ninth-century text, "The Investiture of the Archangel Gabriel," in which Gabriel is first in a series of angels. Gabriel is an extraordinary polyglot and even Aramaic is not beyond him: *B. Sotah* 33a and 36b (bottom).

29. "Enter wine [y-y-n = 70], exit secret [s-w-d = 70]," *B. Sanhedrin* 38a.

30. Cf. S. Lieberman, *Hellenism in Jewish Palestine* (New York, 1962), pp. 69, 72f. See also C. B. Welles on a first-century Gen. codex fragment in *Yale University Library Gazette*, XXXIX (1964), p. 8.

31. In other words, it does not seem to me that the mention of Gabriel is accidental and that all the statement means is, any angel.

32. The expression "many waters" occurs more frequently in Ezekiel (about 11 times) than in any other biblical book. The next in frequency is Psalms (6 times).

33. Cf. above, nn. 14–16.

34. With the reading of *Pesiqta Kahana*, ed. B. Mandelbaum (New York, 1962), p. 323, cf. *M. Gittin* 7.5.

35. Cf. H. L. Strack, *Introduction to the Talmud and Midrash* (Philadelphia, 1931), pp. 131 and 324, n. 5.

36. So too *Gen. R.*, Vatican, Hebrew MS 60. Cf. next note.

37. See *Gen. R.* 3.4, ed. J. Theodor and Ch. Albeck (Berlin, 1912–27), p. 20; *Lev. R.*

31.7, ed. M. Margulies (Jerusalem, 1953–60), p. 726; *Pesiqta Kahana,* ed. Mandelbaum, p. 324. On the conception of the presence of Shekinah in the first Temple only ("only in the tents of Shem"), cf. *Gen. R.* 36.8, p. 342, and Ginzberg, *Legends,* v: 193 (top); L. Ginzberg, *Commentary on the Palestinian Talmud* (New York, 1941), III: 396–97.

38. For a number of references in the Babylonian Talmud, cf. Ch. J. and B. Kasowski's *Talmud Concordance* (Jerusalem, 1972), XXXI: 247, s.v. "pny škynh."

39. *Mekilta, Amalek* 3, II: 178 (for the reading "sages," cf. S. Lieberman, *Hayerushalmi Kipshuto* [Jerusalem, 1934], p. 291; S. Lieberman in *Kirjath Sepher* XII [1935–36], 62).

40. *Sifre Deut.* 47, p. 105.

41. *Sifre Num.* 115, p. 126.

42. Italics mine. There is also "the light [ma'or] of the Shekinah" in *Sifre Num.* 41, p. 44; cf. *Sifre Zuta,* ed. Horovitz, in the same volume, pp. 247, 248, and note also *Midrash ha-Gadol, Num.,* ed. S. Fisch, (London, 1957–63), I: 156 and 154, and n. 180 ibid. In *Pesiqta Kahana,* ed. Mandelbaum, p. 4, we read that not even the chamber behind the Holy of Holies (cf. Lieberman, *Hellenism in Jewish Palestine,* p. 172), "no place is void of the Shekinah."

43. Version A of ARN, ed. Schechter, p. 27a, Italics mine. For the reading "gpy hškynh" in Version B, p. 26a (bottom), cf. S. Lieberman, *Tosefta Ki-Fshutah, Sotah* (New York, 1973), pp. 651f. For "under the wings of heaven [knpy šmym]," see, for example, Version B of ARN, ed. Schechter, p. 27a-b (according to Schechter, p. 85b, the reading of Parma MS for 27b, line 11, is "knpy hmqwm").

44. For example, greeting "pne Shekinah" in the Temple during pilgrimage festivals (ibid., Version A, p. 28a); the equal of Shekinah (43a); ten descents and ascents of Shekinah (51b); etc. Once (Rabbi Tarfon, 23a), "His Shekinah." Ditto, anonymously, 53a.

45. Ibid., p. 28a; note also p. 20b.

46. Ibid., p. 37b. On the "great sight [vision = revelation of Shekinah]," cf. *Passover Haggadah,* ed. E. D. Goldschmidt (Jerusalem, 1960), p. 46. All these examples are representative, not complete.

47. Cf. *B. Yoma* 21b (and Rashi, s.v. *"dgbry'l,"* as well as the "early commentary" in B. M. Lewin, *Otzar ha-Gaonim* (Jerusalem, 1934), VI: 84, bottom, and Ginzberg, *Legends,* VI: 202, n. 105; see also how Albo, *Ikkarim* 4.16 (IV: 147), discusses this. On Gabriel as "herald of light," *Legends,* v: 70. Was it Gabriel who came to the rescue of Tamar (*B. Sotah* 10b) because she was about to be cast into fire (Gen. 38:24)? (But in the *Targums Jonathan* and *Yerushalmi* and *Neofiti,* Michael.) Shekinah is "fire that consumes fire": *B. Yoma* 21b.

I
THE PAPACY

Patrimonia and *Regalia* in 1111

UTA-RENATE BLUMENTHAL

The spring of the year 1111 is usually seen as the nadir of the pontificate of Paschal II (1099–1118).[1] King Henry V of Germany had celebrated Christmas at Florence and soon afterwards advanced steadily and threateningly towards Rome. He came at the head of a large army to claim the imperial coronation. Under these circumstances Pope Paschal II entered once again into negotiations with his adversary. Basic agreement was reached by royal and papal legates in Rome on 4 February 1111 at S. Maria in Turri, a church of the St. Peter's complex, and Henry confirmed this agreement on 9 February, at Sutri. It stipulated that Henry would renounce on the day of his coronation (12 February 1111) investiture with ring and staff and return the territorial possessions of St. Peter to the pope. Since the time of Constantine the Great (d. 337), emperors as well as the nobility in general had enriched the church with large landholdings, from the sixth century onwards often called *patrimonium* or *patrimonia Petri,* but the donations usually remained a dead letter. The lands were hardly ever in the actual possession of the popes,[2] and Henry's promise to rectify this state of affairs was therefore very welcome indeed. Paschal, in turn, would order all bishops and abbots of the empire to return the *regalia* they held.[3] The coronation and the exchange of public declarations never took place as planned, however, and Paschal and his entourage were captured by Henry on the evening of 12 February. After two months of captivity the pope submitted to Henry, who had by then resurrected his old demand for investiture and homage. In the treaty of Ponte Mammolo (11 April 1111), the pontiff conceded investiture with ring and staff, and promised to abstain from any future excommunication of the king and to crown him in St. Peter's.[4] After the coronation on 13 April, Henry withdrew with his forces, and the Romans celebrated the return of the pope. The Latin church, however, was torn by dissent, and Paschal may have planned to abdicate.

Historians have frequently discussed and analyzed these dramatic events, and especial attention is paid to Paschal's concessions at S. Maria in Turri, in other words, the pontiff's plan to have *regalia* returned to the king. In the agreement of S. Maria it was said that:

> domnus papa precipiet aepiscopis presentibus in die coronationis eius, ut dimittant regalia regi, et regno quae ad regnum pertinebant tempore Karoli, Lodoici, Heinrici et aliorum praedecessorum . . . id est civitates, ducatus, marchias, comitatus, monetas, teloneum,

9

mercatum, advocatias *regni, iura centurionum et curtes quae* . . . *regni erant, cum pertinentiis suis, militiam et castra* [regni].[5]

It is generally assumed that Paschal advocated on this occasion apostolic poverty for a church that was overburdened by secular cares. A very thoughtful essay by Piero Zerbi is the most recent statement in this connection.[6] Zerbi translated Paschal's decision to return the *regalia* of the empire into Tellenbach's terminology, suggesting that the pontiff's promised privilege represented a "flight from the world," that is, the motif of ascetic withdrawal. At the same time, Zerbi insisted that this ascetic and rigorous demand upon bishops and abbots is a perfect continuation of the policies of Gregory VII, since it was the only means available under the given circumstances to realize the prohibition of investiture.

The present study will be concerned, once again, with the events of February 1111. It will be shown (1) that from Paschal's point of view the negotiations in Rome and Sutri were a highly successful culmination of previous papal policies concerning investiture and the papal states; and (2) that manuscript evidence eliminates arguments against the objectivity of Paschal's account in his register. This register, now fully acceptable as evidence, shows that the pontiff and King Henry V differed greatly on the meaning of the term *regalia*. Paschal had no intention to impoverish the church.

The gains made by Paschal during the February negotiations are usually regarded as limited to Henry's proffered renunciation of investiture. It is barely mentioned that the German king also promised to return the *patrimonia* of the Holy See, that is, territories, provinces, towns and islands which had been granted in previous imperial donations to St. Peter.[7] This forgotten aspect of the negotiations deserves emphasis. Papal politics, at least since the period of Leo IX (1048–54) had not only centered on reform of the church, but also on the vindication of papal temporal possessions, in other words, the vindication of the patrimony of St. Peter.

Paschal was capable of belligerence. Even when he was dying in the Castello S. Angelo in January 1118, he had war engines mounted to bombard rebels in St. Peter's.[8] At the very beginning of his pontificate he conquered Benevento to reduce the city once again to the status of a papal vassal.[9] When Ninfa was forced to submit to Paschal, the men of Ninfa had to agree to swear fealty, come to the feudal host, attend court, observe the ban, give hospitality dues, tolls and relief as well as cartage services.[10] Henry's promise of February 1111, fully to restore the papal states, would have meant that Paschal's successes at Benevento and Ninfa, for example, would be repeated throughout Italy—and not by means of hard campaigns but simply by a stroke of the pen. Paschal could have marshalled feudal service of the type required from Ninfa on a large scale. The days of political weakness and of abject poverty of the papacy would have been over.[11]

Since Paschal was greatly concerned about the restitution of papal territories, it is probably not without significance that the first discussions between papal and royal representatives in 1111 took place in the church of

S. Maria in Turri. Adjacent to the church were three bronze portals, leading to the atrium of the basilica of St. Peter, inscribed with the names of the possessions or *patrimonia* of the Holy See granted by previous emperors. The doors graphically illustrated the meaning of the promise made by Henry V at every stage of the negotiations, that is, "to grant and return the patrimony and possessions to St. Peter as had been done by Charles, Louis, Henry and other emperors, and aid the papacy to retain them as far as was in his power."[12] This declaration, part of the agreement of 4 February from S. Maria in Turri, was confirmed by an oath taken at Sutri on 9 February on behalf of Henry V by Duke Frederic of Swabia, Chancellor Adalbert and other German nobles.[13] On 12 February, Henry again swore to preserve the patrimony of St. Peter and signed a corresponding declaration at the Silver Gate leading into Saint Peter's basilica.[14] How important these promises were to Paschal is made particularly clear in April 1111 at Ponte Mammolo. Although the pontiff surrendered at that time almost everything for which he and his predecessors had fought, he insisted once again on the restitution of the patrimony. Henry swore "faithfully to aid Paschal to hold the papacy quietly and securely, . . . to make restitution of the patrimony and possessions of the Roman church and to aid in the recovery and keeping of everything else which belonged to the church by right according to the custom of his ancestors."[15] As a result of the oath to return the patrimony, Henry V abstained from an attack, already planned, on the southern Italian Normans who held parts of the patrimony of St. Peter as vassals of the papacy.[16]

For the moment,[17] Paschal must have believed that even if he had not gained a renunciation of investiture, then at least he had saved the temporal possessions of St. Peter, which was one of the objectives he had achieved during the February negotiations. In this respect, he was continuing the policies of his predecessors. Paul Fabre traced a new system of registration for papal property back to the pontificate of Gregory VII,[18] and various contributions from this period eventually flowed into the *Liber censuum*. These included the main precedents for the privileges of Henry V concerning the restitution of the *patrimonia* in 1111: Charlemagne's confirmation of Pepin's grant of the papal states of 754, the grant of Emperor Louis the Pious of 817, and the confirmation of these earlier privileges by Emperor Henry II.[19] The source for Cencio Savelli, the papal *camerarius* who compiled the *Liber censuum* towards the end of the twelfth century and later became Pope Honorius III, was, in this instance, the late eleventh-century *Collectio canonum* of Cardinal Deusdedit of the title church Apostolorum in Eudoxia (today S. Pietro in Vincoli).[20] It is easy to exaggerate connections between theory and practice, but a link between Deusdedit's *Collectio* and Roman curial activities during the pontificate of Paschal II can be postulated. Paschal prominently quoted the work, dedicated in 1086–87 to Pope Victor III, in three letters sent from the synod of Troyes (1107) to the German bishops Gebhard of Constance, Reinhard of Halberstadt, and Rothard of Mainz.[21] Canons from Deusdedit were used both at Troyes and at the Lateran council of 1110 for the prohibition of investiture.[22]

The emphasis of the reform papacy on papal territorial possessions and related rights had caused a reaction in imperialist circles embodied in the so-called *Cessio donationum*.[23] The *Cessio* formed part of the collection of forgeries originating in the 1080s at Ravenna. The forgeries were accepted as authentic by both papalists and imperialists as shown by the negotiations of Châlons in 1107 and the *Tractatus de investitura episcoporum* used for the first time in 1109.[24] In the *Cessio* Pope Leo VIII purportedly returned to Emperor Otto I all "regales res huius regni Italie" that were given to earlier popes by the emperors beginning with Charles' father Pepin. A long list of towns, duchies, islands, mountains and their towns, monasteries, fortified places and other territories follows.[25] What Paschal achieved in 1111 was in effect a cancellation of the *Cessio donationum,* and a reconfirmation of the previous imperial grants which were the basis for the papal states. These donations until then had frequently remained a dead letter, and it might be wondered that Paschal could assume that Henry V would concede to him such extensive sovereign rights and lands in Italy. It would, nonetheless, be wrong to dismiss Henry's promises as a conventional formula used on the occasion of imperial coronations. Paschal very clearly believed Henry's oath that the patrimony of St. Peter would be returned, and must have had reasons for doing so even if these are difficult to grasp in retrospect.[26]

The promise of a restitution of the *patrimonia* had, in February 1111, been combined with Henry's promise no longer to demand investiture and homage of ecclesiastics. Yet the coronation ceremony, where Henry was formally to make these declarations, was interrupted by an uproar, and the pope and his supporters were taken into custody. Although these events were described in papal and imperial official reports, it has been unclear what really happened because the two versions are contradictory. The imperial report is an encyclical of Henry V which is preserved in several chronicles, sometimes slightly altered and re-arranged, and in the *Codex Udalrici*.[27] It gives the following account:

> The king enters Rome. Although some Germans are attacked and killed, Henry pronounces and signs, at the portals of S. Peter, a promise to preserve the ancient possessions of the church. He then immediately requests the pontiff to fulfill his written promises. When the king continues to insist, all ecclesiastics and sons of the church, both on the papal and imperial side, resist the pontiff, proclaiming his decree evident heresy. If he (Paschal) had been able, he would have read the document requiring the return of the *regalia*. The document (MGH LL IV, I: 141–42) is attached.[28]

Henry is thus claiming that all those present at the coronation regarded Paschal's proposal to return the *regalia* as heretical. *Regalia* were indeed the issue which was discussed at the occasion of Henry's interrupted coronation on 12 February, but these discussions did not lead to an uproar among the assembled ecclesiastics nor to accusations that the pope's privilege was heretical. These facts emerge from the papal account, which was preserved in Paschal's register, as will be shown below. This version is much more explicit than Henry's encyclical:

After the solemn reception of Henry in Rome on Saturday, he swears on the day of the coronation [12 February] two oaths to the Roman people and is led to the steps of St. Peter's. At the top of the stairs he is received by the pope and ecclesiastical dignitaries and taken to the Silver Gate, the main entrance to the basilica. Henry reads the imperial profession and is designated emperor by Paschal. When everybody has entered the basilica, Henry and Paschal take seats at the rota porphyretica. Paschal demands from Henry the reading of the privileges to which the king had consented at S. Maria in Turri and Sutri. Henry, however, withdraws with his bishops and princes to negotiate with them. The discussions become protracted; Paschal sends emissaries to ask again for the investiture renunciation. Transalpine bishops join the pope, but soon friends of the king claim that the concluded agreement [concerning the return of the *regalia*] cannot be confirmed if authority and justice are to be maintained. Although they are answered with Scriptural and canonical citations, among them prominently 'reddenda sunt cesari quae sunt cesaris' and 'nemo militans Deo implicat se negotiis saecularibus,' they persist in their refusal to ratify the agreement. Towards evening some ecclesiastics suggest, as a compromise, that the king should be crowned that day and the other negotiations postponed to the following week, but the imperial party rejects this solution. Meanwhile the pope, the prefect, and the papal entourage are guarded by armed soldiers; Paschal is barely able to celebrate mass, and he and his companions are taken from the church. Few escape; Rome revolts.[29]

A comparison between the earlier text from Henry's encyclical and this selection reveals two basic contradictions:

(1) instead of Paschal's demand that Henry should read the privileges which he had promised to grant, the imperial encyclical claims that the ceremony began with a request by Henry that Paschal should read the document announcing the return of the *regalia*. This distinction is significant because it implies that Henry pretended that he fulfilled his own obligations when he read and signed his declaration before the Silver Gate. But the agreements of S. Maria and Sutri differed greatly from Henry's coronation grant as will be seen;

(2) according to the imperial encyclical, everybody revolts against the pope; according to Paschal's register, Henry secedes with his adherents. In the course of the day, imperial supporters begin to declare that the *regalia* decree is unjust. They also reject a compromise offered by a group of clergy. The importance here lies in the fact that (a) Paschal's proposal was by no means universally rejected and (b) that it needed Henry's persuasion to convince even his own supporters that the papal promise to return the *regalia* was unjust.

Before it is possible to draw any conclusions from these distinctions it is necessary to discuss the manuscript tradition for the papal account of the events of February 1111. Until now the papal account was thought to be biased, since—it is said, but incorrectly as will be discussed below—it omitted all documents concerning the return of the *regalia* which supposedly would have damaged Paschal's cause.[30] As a consequence, the report has been hitherto disparaged as a piece of propaganda.

The following manuscripts contain the papal account for the events of 1111:

(1) Biblioteca Apostolica Vaticana, MS Vat. lat. 1984—*Annales Romani*[31]

(2) Biblioteca Apostolica Vaticana, MS Ottob. lat. 3057—*Digesta Pauperis Scholaris Albini*[32]

(3) Biblioteca Apostolica Vaticana, MS Vat. lat. 8486—*Liber censuum*[33]

(4) Venice, Biblioteca Naz. Marciana, MS lat. XIV. 102 (2805)[34]

Most of the relevant documents are also found in the *Vita Paschalis* by Boso,[35] and the *Chronicon* of Montecassino. Boso, however, is very likely dependent on MS Vat. lat. 1984,[36] and the chronicle interpolates and distorts the documents.[37] Both traditions possess no independent value and will, therefore, not be discussed. The papal account for the events of February and April 1111 was edited by Ludwig Weiland, but at the time the manuscripts were not examined carefully. Weiland relied, instead, to a large extent on partial editions from the manuscripts which were already available in print: Augustin Theiner's *Codex diplomaticus* served instead of MS Vat. lat. 8486,[38] and Duchesne's edition of the *Liber pontificalis* was used for MS Vat. lat. 1984. A closer look at the manuscripts yields surprises.

All of the codices listed above for the 1111 account are closely related. Independently from each other, they relied upon the same source. P. Fabre showed this for the *Liber censuum* and the *Digesta* of Albinus,[39] and E. Stevenson demonstrated the same for the *Liber censuum,* Albinus and Vat. lat. 1984.[40] The common source, as will be shown, was Paschal's register, now lost.[41] Two among these manuscripts, Ottob. lat. 3057 and Marciana, lat. XIV. 102 (2805) are unfortunately incomplete. The codices just mentioned do not include the section for 12 February 1111, and, therefore, do not contain information that would be useful in the present context. Only MSS Vat. lat. 1984 and Vat. lat. 8486 with the complete series of documents for February and April 1111 are relevant here. The latter, the *Liber censuum* codex, presents the material, however, in a reorganized version, omitting the narratives that connect the documents. Thus only MS Vat. lat. 1984 remains for a closer analysis.

Duchesne reproduced various parts of this codex, just as Pertz had done before,[42] but "not in the disorder in which they are found in the manuscript but chronologically arranged."[43] Furthermore, he only edited what seemed particularly interesting. Both Duchesne and Pertz added to this "smoothed out" account the title *Annales Romani,* an identification not found in the codex. Completely unintentionally,[44] these scholars thus created the myth of a unified narrative, coining the expression *Relatio papalis,* also nowhere found in the manuscripts, for entries actually excerpted from Paschal's register for the spring of 1111, as will be shown.[45] This would not matter, however, if historians had not assumed, as a consequence, that MS Vat. lat. 1984 contains a composition analogous to the encyclical of Henry V, but written from the papal point of view.

Pertz and Duchesne had combined as *Annales Romani* different texts, which betray very eclectic interests, made during the 1120's by several hands.[46] The entries were scattered throughout Vat. lat. 1984 wherever a blank space was available. It is difficult to distinguish the hands of the scribes,[47] but Bethmann was probably correct when he claimed that a single hand was responsible for the Paschalian texts published by Duchesne as well as for some other historical material omitted in the so-called *Annales*.[48] Among these omissions are three documents from the spring of 1111, and the report about the Lateran council of 1112. They are all found on fol. 193v. Written in the tiny script of fol. 194r, they follow each other closely:

(1) Privilegium Paschalis II. pape prime conventionis inter se et H[enricum] r[egem]. Paschalis episcopus H[enrico] eiusque successoribus in perpetuum. Et divine legis . . . duos menses.[49]

(2) Conventio secunda vi extorta. Domnus P[aschalis] papa concedet . . . et imperium.[50]

(3) P[aschalis] episcopus servus servorum dei karissimo in Christo filio H[enrico] glorioso teutonicorum regi et per dei omnipotentis gratiam romanorum imperatori augusto salutem et apostolicam benedictionem. Regnum vestrum . . . et Portuensi.[51]

(4) Actio concilii contra heresim de investituris.[52]

These privileges of Paschal for Henry are the very documents the papal account was accused of having omitted. The first item, the *Privilegium prime conventionis,* is Paschal's concession of S. Maria in Turri promising the return of the *regalia*.[53] It is fortunate that the scribe even indicated that not only the documents on fol. 194r, which are included in the so-called *Annales,* but also the additional items on fol. 193v (omitted by Duchesne and Pertz) are derived from Paschal's register. The scribe added at the end of the second privilege: "Et hoc sacramentum ex parte pontificis sicut in registro residet. Eiusdem pape privilegium secundo etiam." These lines escaped the attention of all editors, Weiland included. They show that the excerpts from Paschal's register printed as part of the *Annales* were selected arbitrarily, and it can no longer be maintained that the papacy felt any need to hide the fact that Paschal promised Henry a return of *regalia* held by ecclesiastics in the empire. The register did include the corresponding privilege. The entries for 1111 in MS Vat. lat. 1984 are, it appears, reasonably complete.

As a result of this observation, the way is open for a reinterpretation of the events of 12 February 1111. The objectivity of the papal account appears vindicated, and the conclusion emerges that opposition to the return of the *regalia* was raised at first by Henry and eventually by royal supporters, but never by the adherents of Paschal II. The reason for the disagreement between the two parties is a different understanding of the concept *regalia* at the German court, on the one hand, and at the papal curia on the other. In a recent article, Johannes Fried argued convincingly that the meaning of the term *regalia* north of the Alps corresponded to the expressions found in the *Tractatus de investituris*.[54] According to this anonymous imperialist treatise, all property and fiscal rights which secular rulers had granted to the church were *regalia*.[55] Furthermore, as Fried pointed out, the empire did not distinguish royal gifts of any type from other temporal, ecclesiastical possessions.[56] The declaration which Henry signed at the Silver Gate on 12 February reflects this interpretation found at the German court. He promised to preserve for monasteries and churches "omnia quae antecessores mei reges vel imperatores eis concesserunt vel tradiderunt."[57]

The German attitude also explains the misinterpretation of Paschal's intentions in Henry's encyclical: "ecclesie decimis et oblationibus suis contentae sint, rex vero omnia praedia et regalia . . . detineat."[58] If such had been the pope's request an uproar among ecclesiastics, assembled in St. Peter's basilica, could indeed have been expected. A wealthy and powerful section of the German nobility, the ecclesiastical princes, would suddenly be forced to live on tithes and occasional gifts. There is no need to attribute cynicism to the king when he writes in the encyclical that his emissaries at S. Maria knew that it would be impossible for the pope to keep his promise.[59]

In contrast to Henry, however, Paschal distinguished between *regalia* and other temporal possessions of the church that belonged to her by hereditary rights. Henry's privilege for the papacy, as it was hammered out by royal and papal emissaries in S. Maria in Turri, reflected Paschal's views: "[Rex] dimittet ecclesias liberas cum oblationibus et possessionibus quae ad regnum manifeste non pertinebant."[60] These properties might originally have been royal gifts, but they were not inalienable prerogatives of the *regnum* and thus in the papal opinion not *regalia*.[61] Once they had been given to churches they fell under the concept of "ecclesias cum oblationibus et hereditariis possessionibus que ad regnum manifeste non pertinebant,"[62] and would forever remain in the outright ownership of the church. Paschal only agreed to request bishops to return "regalia regi et regno quae ad regnum pertinebant."[63] Public rights, duties and lands were to be given up to eliminate royal need for investiture and homage. Certainly, imperial ecclesiastics would tend to lose, in addition to regalian income, some of their influence at the Salian court;[64] but it is not certain by any means that overburdened churchmen would not have been grateful for a partial release from public service,[65] particularly if, in exchange for the return of the *regalia*, Henry would have renounced investiture and returned the patrimony of St. Peter. A precondition for such an arrangement would, of course, have been Henry's acceptance of the Paschalian definition of *regalia*. This acceptance was not forthcoming, and before the controversy over investiture could be terminated a different solution had to be found.

Vanderbilt University

Notes

1. Bibliographical references in the footnotes have been restricted to a minimum. For the general history of the period see Gerold Meyer von Knonau, *Jahrbücher des Deutschen Reiches unter Heinrich IV, und Heinrich V.*, Jahrbücher der Deutschen Geschichte XVII.6 (Leipzig, 1907), pp. 138–230 and Exkurs 1, pp. 370–90; *Handbook of Church History*, ed. Hubert Jedin, III (tr. Anselm Biggs): *The Church in the Age of Feudalism* (New York, 1969), pp. 395–97; Wilhelm Schum, "Kaiser Heinrich V. und Papst Paschalis II. im Jahr 1112: Ein Beitrag zur Geschichte des Investitur-Streites auf Grund ungedruckten Materiales," *Jahrbücher der*

Königlichen Akademie gemeinnütziger Wissenschaften zu Erfurt, N. F. VIII (1877), 189–318; Adolf Waas, *Heinrich V., Gestalt und Verhängnis des letzten salischen Kaisers* (Munich, 1967). Research for this paper was done in Rome with the aid of summer grants from the National Endowment of the Humanities, the American Philosophical Society and the American Council of Learned Societies, for which I am very grateful.

2. In general, see *Quellen zur Entstehung des Kirchenstaates,* ed. Horst Fuhrmann, Historische Texte, Mittelalter VII (Göttingen, 1968) and Peter Partner, *The Lands of St. Peter* (Berkeley-Los Angeles, 1972).

3. MGH LL IV, I: 138–39, 140–42.

4. Ibid.: 142–45.

5. Ibid.: 138–39.

6. "Pasquale II e l' Ideale della Povertà della Chiesa," *Annuario dell 'Università Cattolica del Sacro Cuore* (Milan, 1965), pp. 203–29.

7. See the references given above, n. 2.

8. For Paschal's campaigns see especially the *Vita Paschalis II* by Pandulf, ed. Louis Duchesne, *Liber pontificalis,* Bibliothèque des Écoles françaises d'Athènes et de Rome III (repr., Paris, 1955), pp. 296–310, here p. 305: "Iamque bonus pontifex ad perficiendum quod inceperat machinas et tormenta et quaeque necessaria bello incredibili agilitate per biduum per suos parari fecerat."

9. See particularly Otto Vehse, "Benevent als Territorium des Kirchenstaates bis zum Beginn der avignonesischen Epoche. I. Teil," *Quellen und Forschungen aus italienischen Archiven und Bibliotheken* XXII (1930–31), 87–160.

10. See the corresponding document from Paschal's register preserved in the *Liber censuum,* Bibliothèque des Écoles françaises d'Athènes et de Rome, 3 vols., ed. Paul Fabre, Louis Duchesne and Guy Mollat (Paris, 1910–52), I: 407–8 and n. 2.

11. See, for example, the references given in the edition of *Goffridi Abbatis Vindocinensis Libelli,* MGH Lib. de lite II: 676–700, 677 and n. 2.

12. MGH LL IV, I: 137: "Patrimonia et possessiones beati Petri restituet et concedet, sicut a Karolo, Lodoico, Heinrico et aliis inperatoribus factum est, et tenere adiuvabit secundum suum posse."

13. Ibid.: 140.

14. Ibid.: 140. See the remarks p. 15, concerning the distinctive features of this declaration.

15. Ibid., p. 144: "Domnum papam Paschalem fideliter adiuvabo, ut papatum quiete et secure teneat; patrimonia et possessiones Romane ecclesiae que abstuli restituam, et cetera que iure habere debet more antecessorum meorum recuperare et tenere adiuvabo."

16. Walther Holtzmann, "England, Unteritalien und der Vertrag von Ponte Mammolo," *Neues Archiv* L (1935), 282–301.

17. Paschal soon had occasion to complain to Henry about non-fulfillment of the agreement. See JL 6295 (PL CLXIII: 288): "Siquidem nos per Dei gratiam boni sumus, licet quidam iussioni vestrae in his, quae B. Petro restitui praecepistis, adhuc noluerint obedire, incolae videlicet civitatis Castellanae, Castri Corcoli, Monti Alti, Montis Acuti et Narnienses; nos tamen ea et comitatus Peruginum, Eugubrinum, Tubertinum, Balneum Regis, castellum Felicitatis, ducatum Spoletanum, marchiam Ferraniam, et alias beati Petri possessiones per mandati vestri praeceptionem confidimus obtinere."

18. Paul Fabre, *Étude sur le Liber censuum* (Paris, 1892), p. 9.

19. *Liber censuum,* nos. 77–79; cf. Deusdedit, *Collectio canonum,* ed. Victor Wolf von Glanvell (Paderborn, 1905), bk. 3, cc. 184, 280, 282.

20. Deusdedit, *Collectio canonum,* p. xix; *Liber censuum,* I: 9; E. Stevenson, "Osservazioni sulla Collectio Canonum di Deusdedit," *Archivio della R. Società Romana di Storia Patria* VIII (1885), 305–98, esp. 332; cf. Ibid., 333. For the relationship between Deusdedit's works and those of Anselm of Lucca see the remarks by Horst Fuhrmann, *Einfluss und Verbreitung der pseudoisidorischen Fälschungen,* MGH Schriften XXIV.2 (Stuttgart, 1973), p. 528.

21. JL 6143–JL 6145; the citations are discussed in my *The Early Councils of Pope Paschal II,* Pontifical Institute of Mediaeval Studies, Toronto (forthcoming).

22. It cannot be assumed that this was Paschal's only use of the work of Deusdedit. It is usually very difficult, though, to distinguish in new conciliar canons the use of various reform collections.

23. MGH LL IV, I: 660–78.

24. See Suger, *Vita Ludovici grossi regis,* chap. 10, ed. H. Waquet, *Les Classiques de l'Histoire de France au Moyen* âge XI (Paris, 1929), pp. 56–58, and the discussions by Robert Benson, *The Bishop-Elect: A Study in Medieval Ecclesiastical Office* (Princeton, 1968), pp. 242–44 (esp. nn. 52–53) as well as those by Alfons Becker, *Studien zum Investiturproblem in Frankreich* (Saarbrücken, 1955), esp. pp. 99ff. *Tractatus de investitura episcoporum,* ed. Ernst Bernheim, MGH Lib. de lite II: 495–504, 498: "Adrianus papa . . . Karolo magno eiusque successoribus, futuris imperatoribus, sub anathemate concessit patriciatum Romanum, et per se vel per nuncios suos confirmationem in electione vel in consecratione Romani pontificis concessit; et investituras episcoporum eis determinavit, ut non consecretur episcopus, qui per regem vel imperatorem non introierit pure et integre, exceptis quos papas Romanus investire et consecrare debet ex antiquo dono regum et imperatorum cum aliis que vocantur regalia, id est a regibus et imperatoribus pontificibus Romanis data in fundis et reditibus."

25. Cf. Johannes Fried, "Der Regalienbegriff im 11. und 12. Jahrhundert," *Deutsches Archiv* XXIX (1973), 450–528, here pp. 505–6.

26. See above n. 17.

27. The controversies surrounding the authenticity of individual letters in the *Codex Udalrici* hardly touch the encyclical because the chronicle tradition uniformly supports the readings of the *Codex.* Cf. W. Wattenbach and R. Holtzmann, *Deutschlands Geschichtsquellen* (Tübingen, 1948), I.3: 439–42, with earlier bibliography; Peter Classen, "Heinrich IV. Briefe im Codex Udalrici," *Deutsches Archiv* XX (1964), 115–29 and Robert Somerville, "Honorius II, Conrad and Lothar III," *Archivum Historiae Pontificiae* X (1972), 341–46 are two recent contributions that partially invalidate some of the findings of Franz-Josef Schmale, "Fiktionen im Codex Udalrici," *Zeitschrift für bayerische Landesgeschichte* XX (1957), 437–74.

28. MGH LL IV, I: 150–51, "De traditione vero in nos et in nostros sic se res habet. Vix portas civitatis ingressi sumus, cum ex nostris infra menia secure vagantibus quidam vulnerati, alii interfecti sunt, omnes vero spoliati aut capti sunt. Ego tamen quasi pro levi causa non motus, bona et tranquilla mente usque ad ecclesiae beati Petri ianuas cum processione perveni . . . :Ego Heinricus Dei . . . subtrahere recuso [ibid.: 140]. Hoc decreto a me lecto et subscripto, petii ab eo, ut sicut in carta conventionis eius scriptum est, mihi adimpleret. Haec est carta conventionis eius ad me: Domnus papa precipiet . . . eum habere potuero. [ibid.: 138–39]. . . . Cum ergo supradictae postulationi insisterem, scilicet ut cum iustitia et auctoritate promissam mihi conventionem firmaret, universis in faciem eius resistentibus et decreto suo planam heresim inclamantibus, scilicet episcopis, abbatibus, tam suis quam nostris, et omnibus ecclesiae filiis, hoc, si salva pace ecclesiae dici potest, privilegium proferre voluit. Paschalis episcopus servus . . . reddituri pro animabus eorum." [ibid.: 140–41]

29. Ibid.: 147–50: "Post haec idem rex Romam accessit terito Idus, id est XI. die Februarias, in sabbato videlicet ante quinquagesima. Altero die oviam ei domnus papa misit in Montem Gaudii, qui et Mons Malus dicitur, signiferos cum bandis, scriniarii, iudices et stratores. Maxima etiam populi multitudo ei cum ramis occurrit. Duo iusta priorum imperatorum consuetudinem iuramenta, unum ante ponticellum, alterum ante portam porticus Romanorum populo fecit. Ante portam a Iudeis, in porta a Grecis cantando exsceptus est. Illic omnis Romanae urbis clerus convenerat ex precepto pontificis. Et eum ex equo descendentem usque ad Sancti Petri gradus cum laudibus deduxerunt. Cum vero ad superiora graduum ascendisset, illic domnus papa cum episcopis pluribus, cum cardinalibus presbiteris et diaconibus, cum subdiaconibus et ceteris scole cantorum ministris affuit. Ad cuius vestigia cum rex corruisset, post pedum oscula ad oris oscula elevatus est. Ter se invicem complexi, ter se invicem osculati sunt. Mox dexteram pontificis tenens cum magno populorum gaudio et clamore ad portam pervenit argenteam. Ibi ex libro professionem imperatoriam fecit, et a pontifice imperator designatus est; . . . Post ingressum basilicae cum in Rotam porfireticam pervenisset, positis utrimque sedibus consederunt. Pontifex refutationem investiturae et

cetera, quae in conventionis carta scripta fuerant, requisivit, paratus et ipse que in alia conventionis carta scripta fuerant adimplere. Ille cum episcopis suis et principibus secessit in partem iusta secretarium; ibi diutius quod eis placuit tractaverunt. In quo tractatu interfuerunt Longobardi episcopi tres. . . . Cum autem longior se hora protraeret, missis nuntiis pontifex conventionis supradicte tenorem repetiit adinpleri. Tunc episcopi transalpini ad pontificis vestigia corruerunt et ad oris oscula surrexerunt. Set post paululum familiares regi dolos suos paulatim aperire coeperunt, dicentes: scriptum illut, quod condictum fuerat, non posse firmari auctoritate et iustitia. Quibus cum euangelica et apostolica obiceretur auctoritas, quia et 'reddenda sunt cesari quae sunt cesaris' et 'nemo militans Deo implicat se negotiis saecularibus', cum armorum usus, secundum beatum Ambrosium, ab episcopali officio alienus sit. Cum hec et alia illis apostolica et canonica capitula obicerentur, illi tamen in dolositate sua et pertinacia permanebant. Cum iam dies declinaret in vespera, consultum a fratribus, ut rex eodem die coronaretur, ceterorum tractatus in sequentem ebdomadam differretur. Illi etiam hoc adversati sunt. Inter haec tam pontifex quamque et prefectus et omnes, qui cum eo erant, a militibus armatis custodiebantur. Vix tandem ad altare beati Petri pro audiendis missae officiis conscenderunt, vix ad sacramenta divina conficienda panem, vinum et aquam invenire potuerunt. Post missam ex cathedra descendere compulsus pontifex deorsum ante confessionem beati Petri cum fratribus sedit. Ibi usque ad noctis tenebras ab armatis militibus custoditus. Inde ad ospitium extra aecclesiae atrium cum fratribus deductus est . . . Factus est igitur in Urbe tota repentinus tumultus, dolor et gemitus."

30. Knonau, *Jahrbücher,* VI: 183.

31. Duchesne, *Liber pontificalis,* II: 329–50, here particularly pp. 338–43; the manuscript is described pp. xxii–xxiii. The codex is now divided into two parts, MSS Vat. lat. 1984 and Vat. lat. 1984 A. For descriptions see also B. Nogara, *Codices Vaticani Latini* (Rome, 1912), III: 387–90; V. W. von Glanvell, ed., *Die Kanonessammlung des Kardinals Deusdedit* (Paderborn, 1905), pp. xxxi–xxxiii; still useful is the old description by Ludwig von Bethmann, "Die ältesten Streitschriften über die Papstwahl," *Archiv* XI (1858), 841–49. See also *Repertorium fontium historiae medii aevi* (Rome, 1967), II: 324.

32. For Albinus see *Dizionario Biografico degli Italiani* (1960), II: 11–12 (V. Fenicchia) and most recently *Repertorium fontium,* II: 324. The *Digesta* were partially edited in the *Liber censuum,* II: 87–137, here especially pp. 135–37, no. 54. For the *Liber censuum,* see above, n. 10.

33. Edited from this manuscript by P. Fabre and L. Duchesne, 2 vols., and G. Mollat, vol. 3. See above, n. 10.

34. The text ends after the first lines of MGH LL IV, I: 139: "id est Petrus Leonis." The volume consists of old parchment folios from Aquileia, collected by G. Fontanini in 1713 and mounted on paper. The 1111 text is found on p. 352, on a mounted parchment folio written in the first half of the twelfth century. Cf. Wilhelm Schum, "Beiträge zur deutschen Kaiserdiplomatik aus italienischen Archiven," *Neues Archiv* I (1876), 121–58, 130–31.

35. Duchesne, *Liber Pontificalis* II: 369.

36. Fritz Geisthardt, *Der Kämmerer Boso.* Historische Studien Ebering CCXCIII (Berlin, 1936), p. 9.

37. For the *Chronicon* see now Hartmut Hoffmann, "Studien zur Chronik von Montecassino," *Deutsches Archiv* XXIX (1973), 59–162. A detailed analysis of the numerous pertinent chronicle accounts satisfied the present author that they also are irrelevant in the present context. The analysis is here omitted because of lack of space.

38. *Codex diplomaticus dominii temporalis s. sedis* (Rome, 1861), I: 10–11.

39. *Liber censuum,* I, esp. pp. 6–7.

40. Stevenson, "Osservazioni," p. 375.

41. For traces of the register in the *Liber censuum,* Albinus and Vat. lat. 1984, see Stevenson, "Osservazioni," p. 373 n. 2.

42. MGH SS V: 468–89.

43. Duchesne, *Liber pontificalis,* II: 329.

44. See G. H. Pertz, "Bemerkungen über einzelne Handschriften und Urkundenn," *Archiv* V (1824), 80–86, and Duchesne, *Liber Pontificalis,* II: xxiii, no. 18, and p. 229.

45. Duchesne, *Liber Pontificalis,* ii: 338–43 = MGH LL IV, i: 147–50.

46. See Pertz, "Bemerkungen," pp. 80–86, and Duchesne, *Liber Pontificalis,* ii: xxiii: "On a puisé aux chroniques, aux registres pontificaux, aux collections de pièces mises en circulation par les défenseurs du pape et par les tenants des revendications impériales, et on l'a fait avec un tel éclectisme qu'il serait difficile de déterminer la cause que l'on a entendu servir. Peut-être tenait-on surtout à se renseigner." For the date see now Dieter Hägermann, "Untersuchungen zum Papstwahldekret 1059," *Zeitschrift der Savigny-Stiftung für Rechtsgeschichte,* Kan. Abt. lvi (1970), 163 n. 19.

47. The hand which Bethmann designated as no. 4 ("Streitschriften," esp. p. 842, and pp. 847–49), wrote the curial *a.* Cf. Reinhard Elze, "Der Liber Censuum des Cencius (Cod. Vat. lat. 8486) von 1192 bis 1228," *Bullettino dell' "Archivio paleografico Italiano,"* n. s. ii–iii (1956–57), 251–70, esp. p. 263, where the letter is discussed in a different context.

48. Bethmann, "Streitschriften," pp. 447–48. It is impossible to be more definite because of the poor condition of the manuscript. On some of the folios portions of the tiny script were redrawn. The conclusions drawn by Nogara, *Codices Latini,* p. 390, are very similar.

49. MGH LL IV, i: 140–42. The narrative of MS Vat. lat. 1984 at the end of the privilege is included in small print on p. 142.

50. Cf. MGH LL IV, i: 142.

51. MGH LL IV, i: 144–45 ("apostolica" MS). Again the Vat. lat. 1984 text was added in small print.

52. Ibid.: 570–74.

53. Ibid.: 140–42.

54. For the *Tractatus* see above n. 24. For the development of the concept *regalia* see Fried, "Regalienbegriff," esp. pp. 467–81, and Benson, *The Bishop-Elect,* pp. 203–50, esp. pp. 218ff.

55. See the excerpt cited above in n. 24.

56. Fried, "Regalienbegriff," p. 470, and esp. n. 64.

57. MGH LL IV, i: 140.

58. Ibid.: 150. See also Fried, "Regalienbegriff," p. 478.

59. MGH LL IV, i: 150: "nostris itidem firmantibus, si hoc . . . complesset—quod tamen nullo modo posse fieri sciebant—me quoque investituras . . . refutaturum."

60. Ibid.: 137.

61. See Gerhoch von Reichersberg, *De edificio Dei,* chap. 17 (MGH Lib. de lite iii: 149, ll. 19–22): "sic et modo inter multas aecclesiarum villas, quas partim a regibus, partim ab aliis Deum timentibus accepit aecclesia, non apparet aliquas eam villas regalis pertinentiae habere, pro quibus debeat aut fiscum regalem implere aut milites ad procinctum stipendiare." Cf. Fried, "Regalienbegriff," p. 473, n. 72.

62. MGH LL IV, i: 141.

63. Ibid.: 138–39; see also Ibid.: 141: "Tibi . . . et regno regalia illa dimittenda precipimus que ad regnum manifeste pertinebant."

64. The king could still bestow *regalia* on ecclesiastics, but not as a matter of course: "nec se deinceps nisi per gratiam regis de ipsis regalibus intromittant." (Ibid.: 141. See the discussion by Benson, *The Bishop Elect,* pp. 245–47.) See also the careful wording of Paschal's privilege (MGH LL IV, i: 140–42). Absences from the diocese are allowed for several reasons, but they ought not to be excessive.

65. For the demanding life of an ambitious archbishop see for example the recent study by Georg Jenal, *Erzbischof Anno II. von Köln (1056–75) und sein politisches Wirken,* Monographien zur Geschichte des Mittelalters viii. 1–2 (Stuttgart, 1974–75).

WHO WAS ROLANDUS?

JOHN T. NOONAN, JR.

In 1827, Johann Wilhelm Bickell, teaching at the University of Marburg, undertook an essay on the *paleae* in Gratian, and discussing them referred to a late twelfth-century manuscript in the royal library of Stuttgart whose title was *Stroma Rolandi ex decretorum corpore carptum,* a commentary on Gratian. Bickell identified Rolandus with "a most ancient interpreter of canon law cited by Stephanus of Tournai." Bickell's reference was to the *"magister ro."* cited several times by Stephanus. He did not attempt to identify Rolandus further.[1]

No witness has ever been discovered as to who Rolandus was. That is, no person known to be a contemporary of Rolandus and in a position to know of the *Stroma* has ever been found to have written "Rolandus, the author of the *Stroma,* is also ———." The entire case for the identity of Rolandus has rested on circumstantial evidence pointing to Rolandus being the later Pope Alexander III. As the evidence is circumstantial, it must be examined for its cumulative force and weighed against other circumstances pointing to a different conclusion. It must also be ascertained if any witnesses to Rolandus's identity may be discovered. I propose here to make this examination, assessment, and ascertainment. Although the identification of Rolandus with Alexander III has had scholarly acceptance for slightly over a century, it does not seem that, in a matter of this kind, prescription has any force. If all the evidence has not been looked at before, the answer to the question of identity may not be the one conventionally accepted.

Suggestions that Rolandus was Alexander III

Maassen. Bickell's discovery did not produce any ripples for thirty years. In 1851 Georg Phillips, professor of canon law at Munich, published an authoritative history of canon law without mentioning the *Stroma.*[2] Then in 1859 Friedrich Maassen, professor of law at Innsbruck, pursued the matter further. In a report to the Akademie der Wissenschaften of Vienna, he referred to manuscripts Stuttgart Cod. jur. 62, and Berlin Sav. 14, which did not contain the title, the name of the author, or the first part, but which were substantially identical with the *Stroma*'s commentary on part II of Gratian. He had no more manuscript evidence than Bickell, but he suggested that the

Rolandus named in the rubric of the *Stroma* might be Rolandus Bandinelli, who in 1159 became Pope Alexander III.[3]

The basis of Maassen's suggestion was three references to this pope by his contemporaries. Robert de Torigny, Abbot of Mont St. Michel, writing near his death in 1184, recorded in his Chronicle for the year 1182:

> Anno superiori, id est, MCLXXXI, obiit Alexander papa tertius, ad cuius litteraturam pauci de predecessoribus ejus infra centum annos attigerunt. Fuit enim in divina pagina preceptor maximus, et in decretis et canonibus et Romanis legibus precipuus. Nam multas questiones difficillimas et graves in decretis et legibus absolvit et enucleavit.[4]

Huguccio, writing sometime between 1188 and 1192, and commenting on the date MCV in Gratian, C. 2 q. 6 c. 31, said:

> Hinc potest colligi, quantum temporis effluxerit, ex quo liber iste conditus est. Sed credo, hic esse falsam literam; nec credo, quod tantum temporis effluxerit, ex quo liber iste compositus est; cum fuerit compositus domino Jacobo Bononiensi iam docente in scientia legali, et Alexandro tertio Bononie residente in cathedra magistrali in divina pagina, ante apostolatum ejus.[5]

Gervase of Canterbury, writing sometime after 1188, said of a time which he indirectly indicates to be about 1150:

> Tunc leges et causidici in Angliam primo vocati sunt. Quorum primus erat Magister Vacarius. Hic in Oxonefordia legem docuit, et apud Romam magister Gracianus et Alexander qui et Rodlandus in proximo futurus canones compilavit.[6]

Of these three witnesses, none was precisely on point or free from ambiguity. The Abbot of Mont St. Michel's statement that Alexander III "multas questiones . . . in decretis et legibus absolvit et enucleavit" was a more accurate description of the pope's official activity as judge and legislator than it was of the rather jejune commentary which constitutes the *Stroma*. At best Robert de Torigny showed that Rolandus had a reputation for teaching in theology ("divina pagina") and for making decisions in law. Huguccio confirmed the reputation for teaching theology and, with the apparent authority of a man who himself was teaching at Bologna, placed Rolandus as an earlier teacher in the same city. But he said nothing as to Rolandus having anything to do with Gratian or the sacred canons—a notable omission or slight if the pope had once been his predecessor in commenting on Gratian. Gervase, whose sources of information, like the abbot's, are unknown, had the most awkward piece of information of all. If a comma is placed after "docuit," he seems to say ungrammatically that Rolandus was Gratian's partner in Rome in the compilation of the canons. If the coma is placed after "Gracianus," he seems to say that Gratian taught at Rome and Alexander compiled the canons. On either reading it is hard to account for Rolandus taking the stance of a mere commentator on a work which he himself in his prologue ascribes completely to Gratian. Moreover, if the collaboration had taken place about 1150, when Rolandus was a coming man in the *curia,* about to be named cardinal, his subordination to Gratian would need explanation.

Maassen noted none of these problems or weaknesses in his case. What he considered established was not only an identity of first names between the pope and the author of the *Stroma* but an identity of professional concerns; for, as he pointed out, the author of the *Stroma* had been a theologian who announced at C.33 q.3 his intention of writing on penance. This coincidence of interests seemed to Maassen to make a *prima facie* case. Yet he recognized that the case could easily be overturned:

> Nach allem bin ich der Ansicht, dass die Autorschaft Alexander's III. nur dann als zwiefelhaft gelten könnte, wenn die Existenz eines zweiten Rolandus bekannt wäre, den für den Verfasser zu halten ebensowohl möglich wäre. Von einem solchen findet sich aber keine Spur.[7]

Maassen did not try to explain the *"magister ro."* of Stephanus.

Schulte. Maassen's claims had no impact upon a biography of Alexander III which must have been in progress even as he wrote. A revised edition of Hermann Reuter's massive *Geschichte Alexanders des Dritten* appeared in 1864 without any reference to the *Stroma*. He did, however, cite Gervase's information associating Alexander with Gratian in the compilation of the canons; and, as he did not challenge Gervase, he appeared to accept as accurate a piece of information very difficult to reconcile with Alexander's authorship of the *Stroma*.[8]

Historians in the mid-nineteenth century were not experts in canon law. But one canonist, Johann Friedrich von Schulte, then professor of canon law at Prague, was beginning to map out the history of canon law. Five years after Reuter had ignored the question, he reported to the same Viennese academy that Maassen addressed that the *Stroma* could be ascribed with unconditional certainty to the pope, "als nicht ein anderer Rolandus als Verfasser nachgewiesen wird."[9] His reasons were these: first, Rolandus at C.16 q.5 gave an example of the bishop of Modena holding territory in Bologna; therefore, Rolandus was closely connected with Bologna. Second, the *Stroma* at C.16 q.1 took the same position on monks paying tithes as Alexander III in the decretal *Fraternitatem tuam* to the Archbishop of York (JL 13873; 1 *Comp.* 3.16.8). Finally the *Stroma* at the end of C.27 q.2 discussed what was to be done if a *desponsata* chose a second man and had intercourse with him. The *Stroma* declared it to be "ecclesiae consuetudo" to grant her to the second man. It added, "Quae tamen consuetudo, quibus auctoritatibus defendatur, me latere non denego."—i.e., "I don't deny that I don't know what authorities justify this custom." Alexander III, Schulte noted, in the decretal *Licet praeter* (JL 14311; X 4.4.3), ruled that an exchange of present consent constituted a binding marriage, even if before carnal intercourse with the first man, the *desponsata* had intercourse with another. The pope, in short, decided the case the way Rolandus implied he would have decided it.

These three reasons were, however, less than demonstrative. The first point showed only that Rolandus might be identified with Bologna *or* with

Modena. It was necessary to determine which city the author of the *Stroma* favored. Schulte left this question unexplored.

As to the tithes, the *Stroma* followed Gratian, citing scriptural and ecclesiastical authority pro and con on the obligation of monks to pay tithes. It concluded at C.16 q.1 "quod monasteriorum quaedam sunt privilegiata, quaedam non. Dicimus ergo monasteria privilegiata in hac parte decimas nullomodo alteri largiri debere, alia vero, ut quidam dicunt, decimas dare tenentur."[10] In other words, the privileged are privileged, while some authorities say the unprivileged are unprivileged—a scarcely remarkable conclusion. The decretal *Fraternitatem tuam* of Alexander III addressed a specific situation, the extent of monastic privilege after Hadrian IV had restricted it. Unlike the *Stroma*'s "ut quidam dicunt," it showed no hesitation in treating monastic exemption as entirely dependent on papal privilege. Like the *Stroma* it reflected a belief in the pope's power to grant privilege, but this was a commonplace assumption. Like the *Stroma* it used an Old Testament argument, that the tribe of Levi did not pay tithes, but the common source of both was Gratian C.16 q.1 *post* c.41. Like the *Stroma* it evoked St. Paul, but it referred to 1 Cor. 9:11 while the *Stroma* cited Heb. 9:9. Nothing in the arguments or form of arguments was sufficiently distinctive to show that the author of *Stroma* and decretal must have been the same.

Fraternitatem tuam has not been precisely dated, and it may well reflect a standard position developed over the years of Alexander's pontificate. In contrast, by several decrees including *Referente magistro* (JL 14000; 1 *Comp.* 1.3.22), Alexander III required even fully privileged monks to pay tithes from certain types of lands.[11] The pope's policy, Constable observes, "was in some way to follow no policy."[12] Assuming that the author of the *Stroma* and the pope are the same, Constable finds the key to this eclecticism in the *Stroma*'s statement in C.16 q.1 on how old churches can be deprived of tithes: "Ad quod dicimus nihil adeo generaliter dictum, cui per speciem derogari non possit. Item cuius est auctoritas condendorum canonum, eius quoque est interpretandi."[13] A papal policy on tithes or no policy corresponds to these generalizations; or, if one prefers to describe Alexander III's approach as one which distinguished between religious orders and differing local circumstances, flexibility in the exercise of papal prerogative is the characteristic mark of the pope. But this flexibility scarcely demonstrates that Alexander III and the author of the *Stroma* were identical. At most it shows that both the author of the *Stroma* and the pope took a broad view of papal power where tithes were to be created, assigned, or limited.

As to marriage, the similarity between the *Stroma* and the single decretal *Licet praeter* was not close. The decretal held that an exchange of present consent in front of a priest or notary constitutes a marriage. It is a position which is not to be found in the *Stroma*. The decretal, moreover, was undated; it is relatively late, probably written in the 1170s. If it is supposed to reflect the same position as the *Stroma,* it presents the same problem as *Fraternitatem tuam:* why did it take the pope so long to come around to the position of the *Stroma?*[14]

In summary, the marriage teaching, which is the most specific, is not the same in the *Stroma* and in *Licet praeter;* the teaching on tithes has a similarity in *Stroma* and a late decretal of a generality too broad to be decisive; and the claimed connection of the *Stroma*'s author with Bologna is not demonstrated. Like Maassen, Schulte had shown a certain congruence between the Rolandus of the *Stroma* and the pope. That this Rolandus had become the pope was plausible but unproved.

Proof that Rolandus was Alexander III

Thaner. Friedrich Thaner, like Maassen a professor at Innsbruck, published in 1874 an edition of the *Stroma* based on the three known manuscripts—the complete Stuttgart text and the incomplete Stuttgart and Berlin texts. As the editor of what has remained the only printed version of the *Stroma,* Thaner had a closer knowledge of the work than any of his predecessors. He committed himself without reservation to the thesis that Rolandus was Alexander III, entitling his edition, *Die Stroma Magistri Rolandi nachmals Papstes Alexander III,* a public positive association of the work and the pope intended to endure.

Thaner believed that the problem of identity began with the question of whether there was any other Rolandus who could plausibly be asserted to be the author. The *"magister* ro.," cited by Stephanus of Tournai, was one such person, but Thaner treated him as Alexander III, too.[15] He did not comment on the strangeness of Stephanus writing in the 1160s never saying that the authority he was citing as *"magister* ro." was also the reigning pope.

Thaner found more formidable a document already published by Savioli in 1784 and overlooked by Maassen and Schulte. Dated 9 April 1154, the document contained the report of a judgment given by a papal delegate in a case between the abbot of S. Stefano in Bologna and the administrator of S. Stefano in Quaderna. It was signed by a "Rolandinus Bononiensium" and referred to a witness described as *"magister* Rolandus."[16] The latter could not have been the later Alexander III, who was already a cardinal, for the name of this *magister* Rolandus was preceded by the names of a bishop, an archdeacon, and another *magister*. There was, therefore, incontrovertible evidence that a man with the same name as the author of the *Stroma* was a teacher in Bologna at a time when the *Stroma* could have been written. Maassen and Schulte's conjectures no longer sufficed to show that Alexander III was the only candidate for the *Stroma*'s authorship. Specific evidence was necessary to prove that he and Rolandus the author were the same. Thaner undertook to show that that evidence existed.[17]

The heart of his demonstration was a remarkable coincidence: in the *Stroma* at C.30 q.3 c.4 on spiritual relationship as an impediment to marriage and in a decretal of Alexander III on the same subject, *Utrum autem filii* (JL 14091; X 4.11.1), there was the same serious mistake in the chronology of the popes and the same unusual doctrine on the overriding force of a later papal decretal. In both, Urban II (1088–99) was referred to as if he came *after* Paschal II (1099–1118). In both, the later decretal was taken to override an earlier papal decretal, while, according to Thaner, the ordinary doctrine was that an older authority prevailed over a more recent one. Such a repetition of the same error and the same unusual doctrine on authority could not be due to chance: it must be the same man who as *magister* Rolandus made the mistake and taught the doctrine and who as Pope Alexander III repeated the mistake and the teaching.

The passage in the *Stroma* relied on by Thaner is a commentary on C.30 q.3 c.4 and c.5, where Gratian's rubrics recognize a conflict which he does not attempt to resolve between Urban II and Paschal II. The *Stroma* in Thaner's edition based on the incomplete manuscripts of Stuttgart and Berlin says:

> Horum contrarietatem taliter fore solvendam credamus. Capitulo Urbani atque communi consuetudine ecclesiae Paschalis capitulum derogatur. Vel dicamus quaesitum fuisse, utrum filii post compaternitatem geniti possint copulari ei personae, per quam compatres existunt.[18]

Thaner took "derogare" in its standard legal meaning to imply "to repeal or qualify an existing law";[19] this usage may be found in the *Stroma* itself at C.16 q.1 as we have seen above and elsewhere as at C.25 q.2. So interpreted, it is clear that Paschal is supposed by the author to be earlier than Urban who is taken as the repealing authority.

Utrum autem filii declares:

> Utrum autem filii aut filiae ante vel post compaternitatem geniti possint adinvicem copulari canones secundum diversorum locorum consuetudines contrarii inveniuntur. Et licet primus canon exinde editus natos post compaternitatem adinvicem copulari prohibeat, alter tamen canon posterius editus primum videtur corrigere, per quem statuitur, ut, sive ante sive post compaternitatem geniti sunt, simul possint coniungi, excepta illa persona duntaxat, per quam ad compaternitatem venitur. Unde tolerabilius nobis videtur, ut secundum posteriorem canonem debeat observari: nisi consuetudo ecclesiae, quae scandalum generet, aliter se habere noscatur.

The decretal does not mention the names of the popes, but it does describe under the "primus canon exinde editus" the content of Paschal's decision and it does describe under the "canon posterius editus" the content of Urban's decision, so that it effects the same reversal of Urban and Paschal as the *Stroma*. It does not use *"derogare,"* but it says, "canon posterius editus primum videtur corrigere," so that it treats a later papal decision as controlling. Thaner's case seems established.

What are its weaknesses? The manuscript evidence is not consistent. *Sicut vetus testamentum,* a Florentine MS, unknown to Thaner, reads: "Capitulo urbani atque communi ecclesie consuetudine derogatur capitulo Paschalis."[20] The grammar of the sentence shows "capitulo urbani" and "consuetudine" as ablatives by which derogation is effected. This use of the ablative for the agent of derogation agrees with a similar usage at C.16 q.1, "generali ecclesiae consuetudine huic statuto derogatum fore." This manuscript, therefore, supports not Thaner's text, but the substance of his reading. On the other hand, as Thaner's footnote acknowledged, the complete Stuttgart manuscript, Cod. jur. 63, in the second sentence of the quoted passage reads, "Capitulum Urb. capitulo Paschalis atque communi consuetudine eccl. derogatur."[21] There is here no arguable implication that Urban follows Paschal, and the alleged chronological mistake disappears. Similarly, Worcester MS Q.70, a twelfth-century excerpt from Rolandus unknown to Thaner, reads, "cap. urbani paschalis cap. atque communi consuetudine ecclesie derogatur."[22] Again, it is Urban who is overridden by Paschal. A substantially similar reading is found in a manuscript now in Bologna, "cap. urbani Pascalis cap. atque consuetudine ecclesie derogatur."[23] Finally, Berlin MS lat. f. 462 does not have anything on the question of derogation but reads: "Pascalis uero post compaternitatem genitos copulari prohibet, si nulla est inter eos dissonantia. In hoc autem ambo concordant quod illa persona qua sunt confecti compatres spirituales filiis non potest copulari naturalibus."[24] With this manuscript tradition, there is no firm basis for Thaner's argument.[25]

Moreover, the assumption is made by Thaner that the decretal is the personal work of the pope, so that the error in the decretal in his. But over seven hundred decretals were issued by Alexander III.[26] It is reasonable to assume that the decretal was drafted in the chancery of the pope and that to some extent the drafters relied on the statement of facts and issues made by the inquiring bishop. *Utrum autem filii* is indeed a fragment of the long answer to the Archbishop of Salerno of which *Licet praeter* forms a part. It belongs to the 1170s. Must we believe that twenty-odd years after the *Stroma,* the pope personally repeated an obvious chronological blunder? Is it not more reasonable to assume that either the archbishop of Salerno or a chancery draftsman got the *primus canon* mixed with the *posterior canon?* The mistake was an easy one to make if a petitioner cited from memory and, unlike Rolandus, did not have Gratian before his eyes. Consider, for example, this gloss in the *Collectio Francofurtana,* Paris, Bibl. nat., MS lat. 3922A, fol. 175, "Hic erravit Gratianus sive Alexander cum certum sit quod Paschalis II precessit Urbanum, vel scriptoris vitium."[27] Here in an effort to correct the decretal, the glossator still has the popes in reverse order. Another possibility, as Professor C. R. Cheney has suggested to me, is that the pope knew what he was doing and deliberately reversed the contents of his predecessors' decrees in order to promote the policy he favored. In this event the reversal would have been one no mere commentator on Gratian would have engaged in. In short, the "mistake" in the decretal may not be Alexander III's or the inversion may have been intentional.

Further, the *Stroma*'s use of *derogare* is not as clear as Thaner would have it. On his reading, the repeal or qualification of Paschal takes place by Urban and "the common custom of the church." The common custom of the church must mean a practice not of a diocese but of the universal church. When Gratian speaks of *consuetudo* at D.11 *post* c.4, he introduces Augustine speaking of institutions "consuetudine roborata" and of "consuetudines ecclesiae non per scripturas a Patribus traditas" (D.11 c.5); he goes on to quote Augustine in c.8 speaking of "traditio universalis." Custom has the force of law, Gratian says at D.12 *post* c.11, "que vel universalis ecclesiae usu, vel tempore prolixitate usu roboratur." Certainly Gratian does not mean by "custom" a new practice which has recently grown up. It is hard to believe that Rolandus did either. Yet that is what Thaner's reading of the *Stroma* requires. The repeal of Paschal is not merely effected by Urban but by the *communis consuetudo ecclesiae*. Can Rolandus really be saying that a decree of Paschal has been affected by a practice that has grown up in the last thirty years and has become the general practice of the church? Such an un-Gratian-like use of *consuetudo* seems improbable. If it is rejected, then we must conclude that *derogare* in the *Stroma* is used to mean "override or qualify" a new law as well as repeal an old law. This appears to be the sense in which the term is used at C.16 q.1 in the passage already quoted using the ablative of agency; there, too, custom "derogates from" a later decree.[28] The chronological implication of the verb disappears. We are driven, I think, to the conclusion that Thaner leaned too hard on the standard sense of *derogare* and jumped too quickly to the conclusion that the author of the *Stroma* had made "einem offenbaren Verstosse in der Zeitrechnung."[29]

If *derogare* does not imply what Thaner claimed, his proof collapses, for there is left only the asserted similarity of doctrine on papal authority. On inspection, that assertion turns out to be unfounded. The *Stroma* does not teach that one papal decretal overrides another but a papal decretal plus the *communis consuetudo ecclesiae* overrides another papal decision. Trying to make the doctrine the same, Thaner has again overlooked the presence in the *Stroma* of the invocation of custom as one of the controlling authorities. *Utrum autem filii* is almost just the opposite: where it speaks of custom, it is the custom of a particular diocese, and the force of custom runs against the decision of Urban; the decretal relies for authority on the later decision alone. Thaner's argument, then, falls on its own terms.[30]

Schulte. If Thaner were looked at critically, he had failed to show Rolandus's identity. This was, perhaps, what Schulte thought when he wrote his comprehensive *Die Geschichte der Quellen und Literatur des canonischen Rechts,* published in 1875, the year after Thaner's edition of the *Stroma*. In a footnote he noted Thaner's argument without comment on its cogency. In his text he announced that there was "keinen Zweifel" that the author of the *Stroma* and the later pope were "eine und die selbe Person." For this conclusion there was "ein positiver Beweis" from Stephanus of Tournai.[31]

The positive proof was this: At C.35 q.2 and 3, Stephanus said, "Alexander differentiam canonicae et legalis computationis assignans fratres, qui et filii dicuntur, in primo gradu ponit et sic usque ad VII procedit."[32] Schulte observed, "Das entspricht nun genau der im Stroma ausfürlich entwickelten Zählung, die gerade die Unterschiede des römischen und canonischen Rechts betont."[33] Further, he noted, at C.35 q.5 c.2, Stephanus wrote, "In hoc capitulo Alexander papa quorundam errorem . . ."[34] Stephanus had, in short, twice identified Rolandus as Pope Alexander III.

The proof was overwhelming, if true. What Schulte unaccountably failed to observe was that C.35 q.5 c.2 in Gratian was a long decretal identified by Gratian as that of Alexander II. Stephanus was referring to this pope and this decretal when he began "In hoc capitulo," and the very passage quoted by Schulte made this clear, for it continued, "Horum errorem congregato concilio Alexander papa condemnavit." Stephanus could not have imagined that the pope who called this council was Rolandus, the author of the *Stroma,* because this passage "Horum errorem" was in fact a quotation from the *Stroma.*[35] Similarly, in the earlier passage on C.35 q.2 and 3, Stephanus was following Rolandus himself, who wrote "Item cum Alexander papa differentiam canonicae ac legalis computationis assignat."[36] Stephanus could not have imagined that Rolandus before his election as pope referred to himself as Pope Alexander, and of course Rolandus was referring to Alexander II and the decretal set out in C.35 q.5 c.2. Schulte in fact had offered as positive proof two passages which by their own structure and use of quotations showed they could not refer to Alexander III.

Denifle and Gietl. In 1885 the Dominican historian, Heinrich Denifle, discovered a manuscript at Nurnberg which began, "Incipiunt sententie Rodlandi Bononiensis magistri." Denifle's concern was to show that this Rolandus and the author of the *Stroma* were the same. When he had done so to his satisfaction, he took it as a well-established position that the author of the *Stroma* was the later pope, and hence the author of the *Sentences* must be the later pope.[37]

Ambrose M. Gietl, another Dominican, published the manuscript in 1891 under the title *Die Sentenzen Rolands nachmals Papstes Alexander III.* Like Denifle, Gietl concentrated on showing that the author of the *Stroma* and the *Sentences* were the same. When he had done so to his satisfaction, he could triumphantly conclude that the *Sentences* were a work "des grossen Papstes des 12. Jahrhunderts."[38] But his conclusion like Denifle's was entirely dependent on the assumption that the author of the *Stroma* was the pope. This assumption rested on the belief that "Maassen hat nachgewiesen" the identity and that Thaner had offered "neue Beweise."[39] Accepting these authorities as demonstrative, Gietl afforded no proof of his own.

Kuttner and Rathbone. In 1951 Stephan Kuttner and Eleanor Rathbone published "Anglo-Norman Canonists of the Twelfth Century." Reviewing canonistic activity in England, they noted that among the glosses on the *Decretum* in MS 676 of Gonville and Caius College, Cambridge, was a gloss referring to Rolandus as "master and pope."[40] As they already assumed that *magister* Rolandus had become the pope, they did not comment further. But they had unearthed a writer no later than the early thirteenth century who, on their reading of the reference, indicated that Alexander III had been a *magister,* and presumably then, the *magister* of the *Stroma.* For the first time there was a person who had been alive when Alexander III was alive who appeared to link the pope to the actual teaching of canon law. How the glossator knew this connection was not clear. But if his information were accurate and if he meant the Rolandus of the *Stroma,* what he wrote was a new and powerful piece of evidence.

The Caius gloss read:

> Votum autem publicum, aliud privatum; secundum Gan. votum aliud de presenti, aliud de futuro; secundum Alex., votum aliud simplex, idest sine solemnitate; istud impedit contrahendum, sed non dirimit contractum, ut ibi; aliud solemne, quod sollempnizatur in crucis susceptione, in ordine, in habitu, in manu episcopi; istud impedit contrahendum et dirimit contractum [ut] hic.

The gloss then set out the view of "H." and declared:

> Solutio: Alexander ibi non ut papa sed ut magister distinxit; vel ibi solemne, idest de presenti; simplex idest, de futuro. Quod potest colligi ibidem et capitulo *Meminimus* in fine.[41]

The strongest evidence of connection would exist if the glossator were actually referring to the *Stroma* or *Sentences* when he says Alexander "ut magister distinxit." The *Stroma* at C. 27 q. 1 declares:

> Eorum vero, qui licita vovent, alii voto solemni, alii privato. Solempne votum dicitur, quod in conspectu ecclesiae vel in sacrario in manibus episcopi vel sacerdotis expresse praestatur. Privatum vero id fore dicitur, quod solo corde vel nudis verbis tantum constare docetur, veluti cum nec in manibus episcopi nec sacerdotis vel supra altare nec interpositione sacrae rei factum est.[42]

Solemn and private vows, the *Stroma* adds, are either manifest or not. A manifest vow is one published by judicial confession or proved by witnesses. If the vow is both solemn *and* manifest, "contrahendum impedit et contractum dirimit . . . [citing authorities]. Privatum vero impedit contrahendum sed non dirimit contractum [citing authorities]."[43] *The Sentences* of Rolandus have the same teaching: "Solum ergo solemne et manifestum votum, voto quoque sollemni adnexum contractum dirimunt matrimonium."[44]

It is plain that the teaching of the *Stroma* and the *Sentences* is formally distinct from that which the gloss ascribes to Alexander. The two books lay stress on the vow being both solemn *and* public. It does not seem that the gloss is referring directly to them. This conclusion is strengthened by the gloss using only one example of a vow which is almost the same as the *Stroma*'s—the vow "in manu episcopi"; the *Stroma* speaks of what is done "in conspectu ecclesiae vel in sacrario in manibus episcopi vel sacerdotis."[45] The *Sentences* speak of "quod fit in manibus sacerdotis vel in conspectu ecclesiae vel super altare seu cruce consecrata."[46] Clearly the gloss is not quoting directly when it gives examples. But is could easily be argued that the gloss is paraphrasing the *Stroma* or *Sentences.* The gloss, however, goes on to say that distinction should be made between vows "de praesenti" and vows "de futuro," and that this distinction can be gathered "ibidem et capitulo Meminimus in fine." If "ibidem" means the *Stroma* or *Sentences,* the glossator is taking Rolandus as Alexander. But in fact in neither of the two books is there express or implicit reference to a distinction between present and future vows. "Ibidem" refers to "H.," that is to Huguccio, the authority being cited. Huguccio is not citing *Stroma* or the *Sentences,* but only the decretals of the pope.

The distinction between a binding vow and a promise "se ad religionem transiturum" can be found in fact in *Meminimus* (JL 13162; 1 *Comp.* 4.1.6; X 4.6.3); and the statement "sicut simplex votum matrimonium impedit contrahendum, et non dirimit iam contractum, ita habitus, sine professione susceptus, ne contrahatur impedit sed contractum nequaquam dissolvit," can be found in *Consuluit,* Alexander III to the Bishop of Lucca, (JL 14005; 1 *Comp.* 4.6.7; X 4.6.4). In the same decretal Alexander III speaks of profession "in manu alicuius episcopi, abbatis vel abbatissae, aut super altare" as essential to the vow which prevents marriage. The "hand" in the singular and the reference to the altar in this decretal are elements of solemn profession as summarized by the Caius gloss.

In neither of these decretals does the pope use the term "solemn" to categorize the formal, marriage-preventing vow. But by the time the gloss on Caius MS 676 was written, that category was an established term among the canonists. Rufinus, for example, had used it routinely at C.27 q.1.[47] The gloss of the French school on Stephanus of Tournai had said, "Solempne votum et impedit matrimonium contrahendum et dirimit contractum . . . simplex votum impedit matrimonium contrahendum sed non dirimit contractum. In hac opinione fuit Gratianus, Rufinus, Johannes, Alexander III et Bassianus."[48] Like this gloss, the Caius gloss analyzes Alexander III's decretals and classifies the pope as one who distinguished between a solemn and simple vow. Based on *Meminimus* and *Consuluit,* the gloss adds that this pope distinguished between present and future vows.

There would, then, be no question that the Caius gloss referred only to Alexander as pope, except for the point it makes that "Alexander ibi non ut papa sed ut magister distinxit." In the context of our search for the identity of Rolandus it seems at first blush that the glossator meant to say that Alexander had written earlier as a *magister*. What could be a plainer reference to his earlier career as a teacher? But the glossator did not have our inquiry in mind. He was distinguishing between what a named pope said in a papal capacity and what he said as a simple teacher.

The glossator was employing a distinction which the decretals had developed in commenting on Gratian at D.30 where Gratian had contrasted the juridical and teaching authority of the pope. Developing the same idea, Huguccio wrote at D.20: "In his vero quae ut expositor dixit videtur non magis ei esse credendum quia papa."[49] The crucial distinction was familiar to late twelfth-century canonists in the very terms used by the Caius gloss. Commenting on *Super eo quod* (JL 14133; 1 *Comp.* 4.11.3; X 4.11.3), the decretal of Alexander III to the bishop of Bisceglia on spiritual relationship as a bar to marriage, a gloss on the decretals of 1 *Comp.* said:

Dicit R. quod consuetudo bene facit, quod matrimonium inter istos non est. Huguccio autem dicit, hanc non est decretalem, vel si est, locutus est magister, non ut papa . . . Et nota quia hic reprehendit Huguccio Alexandrum, quia consuetudo validum impedimentum non est ad matrimonium rescindendum.[50]

Super eo quod is a decretal expressly contrary to the teaching of *Stroma* and *Sentences*. Yet Huguccio dismisses it because in it the pope spoke *ut magister*. There can be no doubt that he meant to distinguish two capacities in the pope. Similarly, the Caius gloss distinguishes between Alexander *ut papa* and *ut magister*. There is no reference to the work of Rolandus.

That the glossator does not mean Rolandus is confirmed by looking at another gloss on Caius MS 676 where the reference is to "papam Gregorium 8 antequam esset papa."[51] The time when the doctrine was taught by the man who became Gregory VIII is specified. Here the reference is not to an earlier time in Alexander's life, but to the capacity in which the pope acted.

Duggan.   In 1965 Charles Duggan continued the exploration of Caius MS 676. Besides interpreting "Alex." as Kuttner and Rathbone had done, he suggested that the abbreviation "Bandin." in several glosses referred to Rolando Bandinelli, the later Alexander III.[52] Duggan was not attempting to prove that the Rolandus of the *Stroma* was Alexander III (an identity which he assumed to be established), but his statement could be used as proof that the Caius gloss recognized Alexander III as a commentator on the canons.

If Duggan were correct it would be remarkable, for Pacaut could discover no evidence that Alexander III's contemporaries used "Bandinelli" in referring to the Rolandus who became pope. In fact, "Bandin." is not an abbreviation for Bandinelli, but for "Bandinus." This canonist is found in the *Fragmentum Cantabrigiense,* where he is cited at C.27 q.3 in contrast with a Rolandus: "Ut dicit rolandus, ea vivente non potest aliam accipere, sed ea mortua aliam accipiat; bandinus contra." Wiegrand, who printed this excerpt, described Bandinus as a Bolognese *magister,* hitherto unknown.[53] "Bandin." is not Alexander III, and the references in the Caius gloss to "Bandin." are no evidence that the author of the *Stroma* and the pope are the same.

A century and a half after Bickell's discovery, no proof had been offered that the Rolandus of the *Stroma* was Alexander III. Maassen and Schulte had shown that such an identification was plausible. Schulte had constructed one totally erroneous proof and Thaner a proof which rested on an uncertain reading and on ignoring the vital differences between the *Stroma* and *Utrum autem filii.* Denifle and Gietl had not reexamined the matter. The references noted by Kuttner and Rathbone and Duggan were to the pope. In this state of the evidence it could be said, "Identity is a matter to be proved. It has not been proved here." Yet after a century of scholarship in which the identity of the two has been taken as a matter on which "il règne parmi les historiens un accord parfait,"[54] it is necessary to go further and consider the evidence showing that the two must be distinct individuals.

Circumstances Suggesting that Rolandus was not Alexander III

The meagre manuscript tradition. Ten MSS containing parts of the *Stroma* are known. The marriage section alone has been found by Kuttner in Berlin, Staatsbibl. lat., fol. 462; Bologna, Archiginnasio, A.48; Grenoble 627; London, British Library, Royal 11.B.II; and Worcester Cathedral Q.70. The *Stroma* without Part 1 was found by Thaner in Berlin, Staatsbibl., Savigny 14 and in Stuttgart Jur. 62. Maitland found fragments C.1–C.4 q.3 and C.13 q.1–C.23, at Cambridge, Univ. Lib., Addit. 3321. Fransen found C.1 to C.26 at Liège, Grand Séminaire, 6.N.15. Stickler found a revision of part 2 joined by a hitherto unknown part 3 at Zürich, Stadtbibl., C.97.[55]

The summa *Sicut vetus testamentum,* Florence, Bibl. Naz., MS Conv. Soppr. G.14 (1736), discovered by Kuttner in 1938, contains large sections of material identical with the *Stroma;* in a number of instances its text is demonstrably more accurate than those of the manuscripts used by Thaner.[56] Only one complete MS of Parts 1 and 2 of the *Stroma* has been found, Stuttgart Jur. 63, the manuscript discovered by Bickell and used by Thaner.

Gietl edited the *Sentences* from a single MS, Nurnberg Stadtbibl., Cent. III.77. Another copy at Naples, according to Stegmüller, contains comparable matter. Clm 3525, fols. 36r–40r, of the Bayerischen Staatsbibliothek, Munich, has the marriage section of the *Sentences* minus the part on *raptus.*[57]

Did only one scribe reproduce a complete copy of the legal teaching of the strongest papal lawgiver of the twelfth century? Was only a single complete copy of his theological teaching ever made? If Rolandus had been the pope, would his work have been so slighted by his contemporaries?

The slight evidence as to the name of the author. Nine of the ten existing MSS of the *Stroma* or its parts lack the introduction and so lack the rubric which carries the ascription to *magister* Rolandus. The Florentine MS makes no reference to Rolandus. The manuscript at Bologna is labelled "Quedam somula mag. Conradi de casibus." Only Stuttgart Jur. 63 has the rubric connecting the work with *magister* Rolandus.[58]

Not only is the ascription to Rolandus confined to a single MS. The labelling at Bologna shows that there was no tradition at Bologna connecting any Rolandus who taught there with this work. Is it likely that the teaching of the first Bolognese jurist to become pope would have been so neglected at the center of the canonistic enterprise?

If we consider the *Sentences* to be written by the same author, the Nurnberg MS testifies to the work being that of *magister* Rolandus and gives the further information that the author is Bolognese; the Naples MS is anonymous;[59] so is the marriage treatise in Clm 3525. The Nurnberg ascription creates a problem if we suppose the author to be Rolandus Bandinelli. If the *Sentences* were written in 1149 or early 1150, would Rolandus be identified as "Bononiensis magister"? The future pope was not then in Bologna; he had just come to Rome from Pisa. Boso, who met him either when he arrived at the papal court or soon after his arrival, describes him merely as "natione

Tuscus, patria Senensis." He emphasizes that his reputation had been made in "the church of Pisa": "esset in ecclesia pisana clericus magni nominis et carus habebatur ab omnibus atque receptus."[60] Is it likely that a Sienese identified with the Pisan church would speak of himself as *magister Rolandus of Bologna*"? It is possible, but it does not seem probable.

It may be objected that the title of the *Sentences* was affixed by some later scribe. If that were the case, either Rolandus was the later cardinal and pope, and the scribe would have so indicated; or he was not, so the scribe referred to him as *magister;* or the scribe did not know of his later career, in which case doubt is cast on the scribe's knowledge of his early career. It is not easy to escape the inference that the title, if it is the work of a scribe, either proves nothing about Rolandus or proves that he was not the pope. If the title is the work of the author, it is not probable that he was the later Alexander III.

The date and place of composition of the Sentences. We possess little information about Alexander III before he became a cardinal, nothing at all from an eyewitness of his earlier career. Accepting Boso as the best-informed biographer, we know that he was associated with the diocese of Pisa, and we may infer that he must have been in it a period of years to have earned his high standing in it. A Sienese newcomer would not at once have gained a reputation in that proud city-state which then dominated Tuscany, nor would he have won a name in Pisa if, as Sarti speculated, he was an absentee canon of the cathedral teaching at Bologna.[61] It was, says Boso, on the basis of his standing in Pisa that he was "ad hanc romanam ecclesiam vocatus est a beato Eugenio."[62] The reputation which impressed Eugene was earned in that pope's native city among persons who must have included that pope's kin.

When Eugene called him is not certain. It has been speculated that it was in 1148 when the pope visited Pisa to dedicate the new S. Paolo a Ripa.[63] That supposes the future pope, like Nicholas Breakspear, enjoyed a meteoric two year career in the *curia;* the rank of cardinal deacon was conferred on him by October 1150.[64] During the period after the call, Rolandus had to be on the business of the curia, either on foreign missions or, more probably, wherever the papal court was. It was a period of proving himself. "Quem," says Boso referring to Alexander, "ubi Deo auctore cognovit idoneum," Eugene created him a cardinal.[65] It was only when the pope "knew him" that he could have become a candidate for the high offices Eugene bestowed upon him. When Eugene made him chancellor of the Roman church sometime before May 1153 he became a central member of the administration of a pope who had been the protege and who remained the pupil of Bernard of Clairvaux.

If Huguccio is correct, Alexander also had taught theology at Bologna.[66] Huguccio wrote two generations after the event, and his far from precise statement does not merit the uncritical trust it has received; but let us assume he is right. Taking it, then, that Alexander may have been at Bologna and probably was at Pisa and that he undeniably became cardinal deacon by fall 1150, where can we place the *Sentences* and when can we date them if he wrote them? Everyone who has written on these interrelated questions has assumed that Alexander was the author. Each has experienced a great deal of difficulty in establishing a place and time which will reconcile all the data with this assumption. The following table suggests the variety of views:

	Time	*Place*
Denifle	1138–42	Bologna
Gietl	Fall 1150–53	Given at Bologna, revised at Rome
Ehrle	1142–50	Rome
Kohlman	1140–42	Bologna
Heyer	1145–50	Rome
Bliemetzrieder	—	Bologna or Rome
Van Den Eynde	Fall 1149–Spring 1150	Rome[67]

In short in this sample, there are two votes for Bologna, three for Rome, and two combining or hesitating between Rome and Bologna, and a spectrum of years has been proposed running from 1138 to 1153. Denifle chose the early dates because the Abelardian sympathies of the *Sentences* made him believe the work must precede the condemnation of Peter Abelard at Sens in 1142; but the early dates are impossible. The *Sentences* depend upon the *Stroma,* which cites Paucapalea, who uses a decretal of Eugene III, *Justitie ratio exigit* (JL 9658), which was most probably issued sometime after 17 June 1146.[68] Time must be allowed for Paucapalea and the *Stroma* to have been completed after this date. It is difficult to believe the *Sentences* could have been finished before 1149.

At the other end of the time span, Gietl thought the *Sentences* were written after Alexander became a cardinal, but Van Den Eynde argued that he then would have been too busy with responsibilities the curial records show he had assumed by late 1152, the only time Eugene's *curia* was in Rome after his promotion to cardinal; moreover, the rubric's reference to him as *magister Bononiensis* would be unaccountable. Gietl supposed that the work was a revision of lectures originally given at Bologna; he pointed to a striking "vobis asserentibus" which seemed to refer to an audience.[69] But Van Den Eynde replied that the "vobis" was a copyist mistake for "nobis," a word which harmonized with another "nobis" in the same paragraph.[70] Gietl thought the work had been revised in Rome because of the passage, "Rationibus et auctoritatibus secundum Grecorum superius videtur probatum esse. Spiritum sanctum a Patre procedere. Nostra vero Romana ecclesia totum in contrarium teneri edocet."[71] But Ehrle observed that any Latin Christian might speak of "nostra Romana ecclesia" when he was contrasting western belief with eastern.[72] Gietl also laid stress on a second passage, "Ad hec dicimus, quod verum corpus et sanguis Christi totum et non particulariter est in altari, et totum in hoc altari et totum in illo, et totum in manu sacerdotis et in ore cuiusque, et totum hic Rome et in Jerusolimis, uno et eodem tempore."[73] Gietl asked who could use the expression "hic Rome," except a writer living in Rome? But Kuhlman observed that the second passage had not been punctuated and that a comma should be inserted after "hic"; the reference then was not to Rome but to a third place, no doubt Bologna.[74] Van Den Eynde, however, countered this argument by noting that the passage consisted in a series of pairs—body and blood, this altar and that, hand and mouth, one and the same time; if the comma were inserted, then three places were mentioned and the rhetoric of pairs broken.[75]

If "hic" does in fact mean "here at Rome," only one time exists when the *curia* of Eugene III was actually at Rome before the later Alexander III became a cardinal. This was December 1149 to the spring of 1150.[76] Stretching "hic" a bit to include Tivoli, we can add the fall of 1149 when the curia was in this suburb.[77] On this interpretation the only possible time is that selected by Van Den Eynde, Fall 1149–Spring 1150.

Such has been the course of argument on the assumption that the author was Alexander. A "vobis" is rejected and turned into a "nobis." A "hic" is turned into a geographical index in a passage of clear rhetorical intention. The words of the rubric identifying the author as a "*magister* Bononiensis" are ignored. If the *vobis* of the text is accepted, then an audience of students is contemplated. If "hic" is read with a comma, the place is not Rome. Alternatively, "hic" may be merely a term of emphasis contrasting Rome where Christ's church is governed with Jerusalem where he died. The rubric indicates an author from Bologna not Pisa or the *curia*. Once the assumption is removed that Alexander was the author, the argumentation which places the book at Rome seems dubious.

Even more suspect is the dating which put the publication of the *Sentences* at the close of Alexander's period of proof in the *curia*. As Denifle observed, the *Sentences* are the work of an Abelardian. True, as Van Den Eynde retorted, they contain nothing from Abelard which had been condemned at Sens; the *Sentences'* Abelardian Christology which later became heretical was still being taught by Peter Lombard in the 1150s.[78] But Van Den Eynde's response is not adequate to the dimensions of the problem.

The Rolandus of the *Sentences* was saturated in Abelard. He was not a slavish follower, but as Gietl shows, he was influenced by him on fundamental questions of dogmatic theology from the Trinity to the sacraments, and he was heavily dependent on him for method.[79] It is fair to think of him as an Abelardian. The question then is not, "Were the *Sentences* in heresy?" but "Would Eugene III promote to the cardinalate and then make Chancellor of the Roman church a theologian who had just published an Abelardian treatise?"

Relying on the supposed identity of Alexander III and the author of the *Sentences,* D. L. Luscombe writes of Alexander, "His attachment to the teachings of Abelard did not impede the acquisition of the highest honors and paradoxically it was he who in 1174 raised Bernard of Clairvaux to the altars of the church. Ironically too he condemned as Pope in 1177 the doctrine of Christological nihilism which as a master and under Abelard's stimulus he had himself expounded in the schools of Bologna."[80] The paradox is that the Abelardian author of the *Sentences* should have been promoted to the cardinalate by Eugene III, the pupil and protege of Bernard of Clairvaux, and promoted just after he had published his major Abelardian work. Is this not a paradox to shock the historical imagination? It is capped by the supposition that as pope the old disciple of Abelard should have canonized his master's nemesis. There is the final irony that as pope, Alexander should formally condemn the Christology he had held as a master. But paradox and irony depend on the assumption that the author of the *Sentences* became the cardinal and the pope. These surprising results are invitations to reexamine the assumption. Peter Munz writes, "Alexander roundly condemned at that Council [Sens of 1164] the posing of 'undiciplined questions.' Had he, at that moment, forgotten that he was the author of his own *Sentences* and of a *Summa?*"[81] A better question would be, "Had he *Sentences* and *Summa* to forget?"

Anyone of course may change his mind. Inconsistency per se proves nothing. But there are degrees and varieties of inconsistency which tend to suggest improbability. Here we are asked to believe that as deep-dyed an Abelardian as Rolandus made such a reputation in Pisa that he was welcomed to the *curia* by Bernard of Clairvaux's pope. We are asked further to believe that he completed his period of trial at the *curia* by bringing out an Abelardian treatise. And we are asked to believe that as pope he changed his mind to the point of treating his own major theological treatise as heretical and making Bernard a saint. These are ironies and paradoxes which may entertain the historian or alert him to the existence of an underlying mistake.

The presence of the mistake is confirmed by a completely independent set of facts. For a long time the date of Peter Lombard's *Sentences* was uncertain, so that it could be believed, as Gietl believed, that Peter wrote about 1150 and would have had no opportunity to know the *Sentences* of Rolandus. It is now clear that the *Sentences* of Peter Lombard were composed between 1155 and 1157.[82] Peter himself had been in Italy in 1154 where he had the opportunity of obtaining a copy of Gratian. In Rome he also saw for the first time the translation by Burgundio of John Damascene's *De fide orthodoxa.*[83]

At the papal court, collecting material for his own treatise, Peter Lombard apparently knew nothing of the *Sentences* of Rolandus. If he had encountered the work, would he have passed in silence over the composition of a man who was cardinal chancellor when he wrote? The argument is from silence and suffers from this weakness, but given Peter Lombard's dependence on Gratian and his use of Burgundio, it is hard to believe he would have ignored Rolandus if in fact the *Sentences* had been published in 1150. It is equally hard to believe that Rolandus would not have used Peter if he had known his work. From the mutual ignorance of each other, it may be concluded that they are roughly contemporary writings of the second part of the 1150s. The date excludes the possibility of the Rolandus of the *Sentences* being the pope.

The sympathies of Rolandus.   Commenting on Gratian C. 16 the *Stroma* put seven different cases involving prescription. These cases are not in Gratian. Thaner supposed that they reflected actual litigation which had taken place in the late 1130s and early 1140s.[84] The evidence of this actual litigation is an interlocutory judgment of Gualterius, Archbishop of Ravenna, given 27 April 1141, and a privilege issued by Eugene III on 24 November 1150.[85]

From these two documents it appears that there were two cases between the archpriest of Monteveglio, on the one hand, and the *pieve* of Ciano, on the other, involving title to two small churches, old and new S. Geminiano in the village of Gauzano. These cases may have been the inspiration of the *Stroma*'s hypotheticals. But Thaner failed to note that the *Stroma* presented seven distinct situations, not consistent argument in a single case.[86] Monteveglio was subject to the bishop of Bologna, Ciano to the bishop of Modena, so that the *Stroma* would have had their quarrel in mind when it spoke of a conflict between "the bishop of Bologna" and "the bishop of Modena"; but in the actual litigation, the archpriest and the *pieve* appear as the litigants. The *Stroma* refers to the Bolognese taking the law into their own hands; but in the actual litigation, the partisans of the Bolognese archpriest were guilty of burning and looting one of the churches.[87] The *Stroma,* recalling Gratian's text, refers to a basilica as in dispute;[88] the two S. Geminianos must have been quite humble edifices. In short, the concrete events of the conflict may have been the inspiration of the *Stroma*'s hypotheticals; but the passages on prescription in the *Stroma* are not the brief of an advocate for either party.

Thaner, however, supposed that Rolandus had written as an advocate and that he had written as an advocate for Bologna. On this ground he explained Rolandus's phrase "in limitibus," which Thaner took to refer to a church which "in der Luft hängt."[89] Such ingenious nonsense, Thaner contended, was what Rolandus's job as Bologna's advocate required.

The phrase "in limitibus," however, is used several times by Rolandus and does not support Thaner's imaginative interpretation; a church "in limitibus" is a church within the boundaries of the diocese whose name modifies "limites."[90] Moreover, as Augusto Gaudenzi, professor of law at Bologna, pointed out in 1907, a better case could be made that Rolandus's sympathies were Modenese. Although Gaudenzi repeated Thaner's error of treating Rolandus's work as actual argument in a real case, he pointed to one piece of evidence which at least suggested that Rolandus disliked the bishop of Bologna. At the climax of the seven hypotheticals where the Bolognese use self-help to gain possession, the bishop of Bologna is characterized as one of the *filii tenebrarum* who are wiser than the children of light.[91] In an age of violent city partisanship, Gaudenzi persuasively argued, it is difficult to believe that a Bolognese would apply this opprobrious scriptural term to his own bishop.[92] Gaudenzi's argument is strengthened when it is realized that this characterization is gratuitous, made in a hypothetical argument where such passion was unnecessary. To this may be added that in the seven hypotheticals, Modena wins six out of seven times. By the punitive decree of Eugene III in 1148 Modena had been suppressed as a diocese, and it was not formally restored to the status of a bishopric until sometime in the 1150s.[93] In the time of suppression in particular a man from Modena would have the motivation to structure his imagined cases to produce repeated victories for the bishop of Modena.

The argument is not demonstrative. Rolandus might have had entirely personal reasons for disliking the bishop of Bologna and favoring an imaginary Modenese; but against the background of Bolognese-Modenese rivalry, a patriotic motive for preferring Modena is more likely. If Rolandus is Modenese, he cannot be Alexander III, "natione Tuscus, patria Senensis."[94]

The treatment of Rolandus by Rufinus, Stephanus, and Gandulphus.   Heinrich Singer, the editor of the *Summa* of Rufinus, dated it by Rufinus's remarks about the *Stroma.* Rejecting as unsound Schulte's attempt to determine the date by references to papal election practice, Singer, nevertheless, confidently dated it before Alexander III's election to the papacy in September 1159 because of the insolent tone Rufinus adopted toward Rolandus: "am allerwenigsten wäre, jedoch eine solche Impietät und Rücksichtslosigkeit gegen den Träger der höchsten kirchlichen Würde mit den uns bekannten Gesinnungen Rufins vereinbar."[95]

Rufinus, in fact, does not mention Rolandus by name, but at several points he appears to jibe at the *Stroma.* Discussing spiritual relationship at C.30 q.3, Rufinus refers to Rolandus's precise teaching in this way: "Quidam tamen, ex sequenti decreto Pascalis errandi fomitem summentes in hunc modum distinxerunt, astruentes, filios ante compaternitatem genitos naturalibus filiis alterius posse coniungi, non autem eos, qui post compaternitatem suscepti sunt." He then adds, "Sed forte non errassent, si ad finem capituli oculos porrexissent."[96] Or, in other words, Rolandus was lazy.

Rolandus in the *Sentences* distinguished between the binding effect of consent *de praesenti* from a promise *de futuro* where the existence of a marriage was at issue. Rufinus, following his namesake Tyrannus Rufinus, speaks of those who make this distinction at C. 27 q. 2 in this fashion: "quidam simplicium potibus invidentes more sevorum animalium, cum pertransissent, aquas limpidas turbaverunt et hanc sacram distinctionem alto vento superbie exsufflantes novam fabulam ediderunt."[97] Rolandus, in other words, has acted like a beast and a windbag.

Rolandus's seven hypotheticals added to the discussion of prescription have been noted. In making them up, Rolandus had shown a great ability at imagining a variety of situations. With these apparently in mind, Rufinus observed scathingly at C.16 q.3, "Quot sunt ingenia legentium, tot hic surgere soleant diversitates casuum. Sed super quorumlibet opiniones stultum est sollicitum esse."[98]

At C.23 q.8, Rufinus referred to Rolandus's opinion that those who are in sacred orders may not carry arms, but that clerics in minor orders might do so at the command of prince or pope. "Quidam de antecessoribus nostris magis ebriose quam sobrie distinguere nitebantur," he wrote and went on to pulverize Rolandus's distinction and reasoning.[99]

Rolandus is lazy and pompous; he acts in the manner of a wild beast; he makes foolish distinctions, sometimes drunkenly. No wonder that Singer thought Rufinus could not be speaking of the reigning pope. But Singer never reexamined Thaner, so he did believe that Rufinus, writing after 1154, was speaking of the cardinal-deacon who was chancellor of the Roman church.

Is that credible? Let anyone who doubts read again the famous opening address of Rufinus to the Third Lateran Council.[100] Let us suppose that Alexander III could have forgiven these insults and given Rufinus the honor of opening his great triumph. Could the unctuous prelate who speaks there have so assaulted the chancellor of the Roman church? It is not believable.

The evidence from Stephanus of Tournai is of another kind, but also of relevance. He does cite a "*magister* ro.," but his references to this *magister* are few and indistinct.[101] He says nothing to connect his authority with Alexander III, the reigning pope when he wrote. Now, as Stephanus's correspondence makes clear, he enjoyed knowing members of the Roman *curia,* and he recalled with pleasure his days at Bologna.[102] If *magister* Rolandus were indeed the pope who had taught at Bologna, it would have been a matter to commemorate, not pass over. But Stephanus makes no claim that his "*magister* ro." was at Bologna in Gratian's day and is now on the throne of Peter.

Gandulphus, who wrote his *Sentences* at Bologna between 1160 and 1170, refers to Rolandus under the conventional "Quidam." He follows his views at least five times and differs from him at least once.[103] He has none of Rufinus's animosity. On the other hand, he gives not the smallest indication that he is referring to the pope in office when he wrote.

The existence of other magistri Rolandi.   Both Maassen and Thaner acknowledged that if there were other *magistri* bearing the name Rolandus who could be shown to be plausible authors of the *Stroma,* their case for Alexander III had not been proved. Maassen knew of no other Rolandus; Thaner disposed of the *magister* Rolandus who appears in the Bolognese records of 1154 by concentrating on what he took to be the demonstrative proof that Rolandus was Alexander III. Once this proof is seen as fallacious, the *magister* Rolandus of 1154 appears as a possibility. There are other Rolandi to be considered as well.

In 1159 four *magistri,* Rolandus, Petrus, Gandulfus and Guidottus, wrote to the emperor, Frederick Barbarossa, objecting to his restrictions against students from Brescia, Cremona and Milan studying at Bologna.[104] This

Rolandus, a leader at Bologna, may be the same as the man identified at the notarial act of 1154. Whether he is the same person as "Rolandus causidicus de Petro Veclo," who witnesses a land transaction in Bologna in 1159, is not certain.[105] Again, the identity is not clear of "Rolandus causidicus" who appears as a judge in a case in Bologna in 1157 between the abbot of S. Stefano and one Girardino.[106] In another land transaction of 1159 in Bologna, "Rolandus causidicus filius Rodulfi di Guarino" appears as a witness. This Rolandus was the son of an imperial judge and by 1157 was himself *iudex communis*. In 1174 and 1175 he was a consul of Bologna and in 1183 went on a Bolognese embassy to the Emperor.[107]

We may choose then between Rolandus de Petro Veclo and Rolandus Rodulfi de Guarino and possibly between the *magister* Rolandus who outranks Gandulfus in 1159 and the *causidicus* Rolandus who judges the abbot of S. Stefano in 1157. There are at least two Rolandi and there may be four. Any one of them could have written the *Sentences*. If we assume the *Stroma*'s author had also been a non-Modenese jurist with a peculiar sympathy for Modena, any one of them could have written the *Stroma*. If, as seems probable, the author of the *Stroma* was Modenese, we can exclude Rolandus Rodulfi de Guarino, who has Bolognese roots; the other possibilities remain.

Positive Identification of the Rolandus of the Stroma

To this point, the evidence suggesting that the Rolandus of the *Stroma* was not Alexander III has been circumstantial. It has also been convergent. It seems unlikely that an author little reproduced and little identified by name, disrespectfully treated by Rufinus, unknown by Peter Lombard and unacknowledged as the pope by Stephanus and Gandulphus, Abelardian in thought and method, and Modenese in sympathy, should have been Alexander III; but the possibility, no doubt, remains open unless there is positive identification of Rolandus as some other man. Does such identification exist? I believe that it does.

With his edition of the *Stroma,* Thaner published a set of *Quaestiones* which he found after C.36 in the incomplete Stuttgart MS Cod, jur. 62. He dated them as written after 1154, for they contained a decretal of Hadrian IV on tithes, and before 1179, for they had nothing from the Third Lateran. He noted that the *Quaestiones* seemed to be the work of a school, that they had a practical bent, and that they cited Rolandus the author of the *Stroma* twenty times. He also noted that they referred to Rolandus at least four times where nothing like their citations could be found in the *Stroma;* he concluded that other writings of Rolandus were being drawn on. He observed that the *Quaestiones* were done at Bologna because the example in C.1 q.3 appeared "ad captandum benevolentiae" of the bishop of Bologna.[108]

There can be no quarrel with Thaner's conclusion that a single *magister* Rolandus is referred to by the *Quaestiones,* for no attempt is made in them to distinguish the author of the *Stroma* from a second Rolandus. It is also clear that the author of the *Stroma* is the Rolandus being quoted, for there is an express reference to the *Stroma:* "reperiri potest in summa magistri Rolandi, ubi tractat de tribus generibus affinitatis."[109] But it is not clear that other writings of Rolandus are being used or that the *Quaestiones* originate in Bologna.

A number of places are referred to in the *Quaestiones.* Custom in *Lombardia* is mentioned in Case 9. In Case 27 Modena asserts prescription against Mantua. Case 35 involves a noble from Parma, the bishop of Regino, and the archbishop of Milan. Case 33 speaks of "an Apulian" coming to Bologna and Case 14 speaks of the apparently imaginary "bishop of Puglie." No consistent pattern appears. But the reference to the bishop of Bologna in Case 1 is scarcely calculated to win his friendship: it is supposed that he is someone who "semper vixit religiose," but is now accused of adultery by a twice-married witness. The witness, the author concludes, can "de rigore iuris" easily be admitted to testify against him. The bishop's posture is comical not complimentary.

Bologna, nonetheless, is the only city known to have had a center of canon law studies in the 1150s. Fried's investigations of Modena have shown that *magister* Aldricus came there from Bologna in the late 1150s, while the first law teacher in Modena, Pillius, can be placed there only in 1169.[110] Consequently, we must conclude that the *Quaestiones* were done in Bologna by a person not entirely friendly to the bishop of Bologna.

As to the existence of other writings by Rolandus, C.26 q.2 on marriage reads, "Si quaeras a Rolando . . . dicit."[111] The phrase could refer to writings or it could refer to direct report on an oral statement of Rolandus as a senior member of the school. In C.29 q.1, the *Stroma* is paraphrased on exemptions from tithes, "qui habet potestatem condendi canones, habet inde et potestatem interpretandi eos."[112] "Si quaeras ab eo an," the case continues, "quia canonici habent privilegium ut habeant decimas suae diocesis, possint petere quartam episcopi, dicit quod non, quia statuta apostolicae sedis benignius interpretandi sunt." By "eo" Rolandus is meant. The inquiry could have been directed to other of his writings; it sounds more like a direct interrogation following up the point made by his text.

Rolandus appears in these passages as a respected living authority in the school which produced the *Quaestiones.* There is no suggestion that he is now the chancellor of the church or the pope. He is occasionally criticized—e.g., C.38 q.2: "Sed hic non clare videtur videre Rolandus."[113] His teaching is amplified in C.29 q.3 with the teaching of "Metullus."[114]

In 1963, Weigand remarked on the frequent citations of a Rolandus in the *Fragmentum Cantabrigiense,* a commentary on C.23–C.35 of Gratian. He also called attention to three citations where "Rolandus dicit," as if, Weigand says, the citations were from oral memory.[115] Yet he could not believe that these quotations came from Alexander III as pope or cardinal. He raised the question if there was not a second *magister* Rolandus teaching in Bologna in the 1150s and '60s. Was not this *magister* Rolandus, he asked, also the authority so described and cited on conditional marriage by Johannes Faventinus? This Rolandus used the canon *Quicumque* which was not used in the *Stroma*.[116] This *magister* Rolandus, he suggested, was a second Rolandus in the *Quaestiones* edited by Thaner.

Gérard Fransen reviewed Weigand's suggestion in connection with an analysis of Bamberg, Staatsbibliothek, MS Can. 17 (P.I.11) and Cambridge, University Library, MS 3321, vol. 2, fols. 26v–31v, two manuscripts containing variations of the *Quaestiones* edited by Thaner. In agreement with Weigand, he concluded that the Rolandus of the oral answers in the *Quaestiones* was a second Rolandus. Looking at the phrase "Si queras a Rolando . . . dicit," Fransen observed, "Nous sommes manifestement devant des 'qq schola Rolandi disputate'." In agreement with Weigand, he identified the Rolandus of the oral answers as a second Rolandus. What was decisive in his opinion was that both the Cambridge fragment analyzed by Weigand and the *Quaestiones* cited Metullus, a canonist otherwise unknown.[117]

Weigand then analyzed Munich, Bayerische Staatsbibliothek, Clm 3525, fols. 40r–50r, which also had a set of questions containing the opinions of Rolandus. Two of the questions were identical with those already published by Thaner. Metullus appeared as an active disputant in the school. Weigand concluded that again we were in the presence of the second Rolandus. From a reference in question 6 to the practice of Ivo of Chartres, Weigand inferred that this Rolandus had French associations.[118] Like Fransen, he carefully treated him as distinct from Rolandus the author of the *Stroma* and the pope.[119] The questions in Clm 3525 immediately followed, fol. 36r to fol. 40r, the anonymous treatise on marriage which, as we have seen above, is actually the marriage section of the *Sentences* of Rolandus.

Weigand and Fransen were right in treating the second Rolandus as distinct from Alexander III, wrong in treating him as distinct from the author of the *Stroma*. That he used the canon *Quicumque* in teaching but not in the *Stroma* shows only that the teaching was later than the *Stroma*. The *Quaestiones* know only one Rolandus, the *magister* who knew France and was a disciple of Abelard and taught in Bologna in the 1150s. Implicitly by their usage, the *Quaestiones* of Thaner are eyewitness testimony to the identity of the author and teacher of the school. He is the author of the *Stroma* and the *Sentences*. He is "our Rolandus."

Of the Rolandus who became Alexander III we know that he was Sienese, that he may have taught theology at Bologna, that he was great in the church of Pisa by 1148, that he was brought to Rome by Eugene III, the protege of Bernard of Clairvaux, that in the fall of 1150 he was created cardinal deacon by Eugene III, that in 1153 he became chancellor of the Roman church, that in 1159 he was elected pope, that in 1177 he condemned the Christology of Abelard, that he in 1179 appointed Rufinus to open the Third Lateran Council and elevated Bernard to the altars of the Church, that he issued various decretals on tithes, that he took various positions on how a valid mar-

riage was formed and in one decretal seemed to require a formal witness of
the consent given, that he inclined to a strict view of the spiritual relationship which barred marriage, that he thought a solemn vow in the present
tense impeded marriage, that he treated an earlier papal decree as capable of
overriding a later one, and that he was the most renowned pope of the
twelfth century.

Of the Rolandus who wrote the *Stroma* and the *Sentences* we know that he
was Modenese or pro-Modenese, that he was a disciple of Peter Abelard, the
great enemy of St. Bernard, that he had no connection with Pisa, that he
taught theology and canon law in Bologna in the 1150s, that he was attacked
as long-winded, drunken, and beastly by Rufinus, that he was thought of little account by Stephanus in the 1160s, that he had a broad view of papal
power over tithes, that he rejected what he took to be Roman custom of the
effect of a *desponsatio,* that he inclined toward a liberal view on the spiritual
relationship which barred marriage, that he considered only solemn and
public vows an impediment to marriage, that he believed a decretal plus the
common custom of the church overrode a deviant decretal, and that his work
was little copied and his name forgotten at Bologna. He never became pope.
He can be restored as a new name among those who began the teaching of
canon law at Bologna.

University of California, Berkeley

Notes

I am indebted to Christopher Cheney, Mary Cheney, Charles Donahue, and Charles Duggan for their thoughtful reading of drafts of this manuscript and for their helpful suggestions.

1. J.W. Bickell, *De Paleis, quae in Gratiani Decreto inveniuntur, Disquisitio Historico-Critica*
(Marburg, 1827).

2. See G. Phillips, *Kirchenrecht* (Regensburg, 1851), IV: 162–65.

3. F. Maassen, "Paucapalea," Viennese Academy, *Sitzungsberichte, Philosophische-Historische
Klasse* XXXI (1859), 450–53.

4. Robert de Torigny, *Chronica,* ed. R. Howlett, Rolls Series, LXXXII.4 (London, 1889),
p. 298.

5. Huguccio, *Summa.* Munich, Staatsbibliothek, MS 10247, fol. 109r.

6. Gervase, *Actus Pontificum,* ed. W. Stubbs, Rolls Series, LXXIII.2 (London, 1880), pp.
384–85. On the probability of the sentence on Gratian and Rolandus being a later interpolation, see R. Southern, "Master Vacarius and the Beginning of an English Academic Tradition," *Medieval Learning and Literature: Essays Presented to R. W. Hunt,* ed. J. J. G. Alexander
and M. T. Gibson (Oxford, 1976), p. 281.

7. Maassen, "Paucapalea," p. 455.

8. H. Reuter, *Geschichte Alexanders des Dritten* (Leipzig, 1864), II: 443.

9. J. F. von Schulte, "Zur Geschichte der Literatur 'über das Dekret Gratians'," Viennese
Academy, *Sitzungsberichte, Philosophische-Historische Klasse* LXIII (1869), 315–16.

10. Rolandus, *Stroma,* ed. F. Thaner (Innsbruck, 1874), p. 40.

11. G. Constable, *Monastic Tithes From Their Origins to the Twelfth Century* (Cambridge,
1964), p. 301.

12. Ibid., p. 294. Charles Duggan has observed to me that he believes that Alexander

III's decisions on tithes cannot correctly be characterized as showing "no policy"; and I have amended the text to show an alternative way of viewing Alexander III's approach.

13. Rolandus, *Stroma*, p. 42.

14. Note, in contrast, *Veniens ad apostolicae,* P. Kehr, *Italia pontificia* (Berlin, 1908), III: 404 and 453, reproduced in J. Dauvillier, *Le mariage dans le droit classique depuis le Décret de Gratien (1140) jusqu'à la mort de Clément V (1314)* (Paris, 1933), p. 481, considered to have been issued early in Alexander's pontificate. There stress is put on the man giving the girl a ring "utpote solet fieri." If that has occurred, the pope declares, then the *desponsatio* so made prevails over carnal intercourse between the girl and a second man. Assuming the identity of the author of the *Stroma* and the pope, Dauvillier finds in this decretal an echo of the *Stroma,* "où Roland déplore que la coutume applique la solution contraire" (Ibid., pp. 482–83). But Rolandus does not deplore the custom so much as note its conflict with his authorities; the custom he notes relates to a second *desponsatio* followed by intercourse, not intercourse only; and in the decretal, the operative fact is one unknown to the author of the *Stroma,* the giving of the ring.

15. Thaner, "Einleitung," Rolandus, *Stroma,* p. xlvii.

16. Reproduced in M. Sarti and M. Fattorini, *De claris Archigymnasii Bononiensis Professoribus* (Bologna, 1896), II: 21–22.

17. Thaner, "Einleitung," pp. xxv–xxx.

18. Rolandus, *Stroma*, p. 146.

19. E.g., Ulpian, *Regulae* 1.3; " lex derogatur, id est pars primae legis tollitur." See generally *derogo* in *Thesaurus linguae latinae,* v. 1:1.

20. Peter Grootens, S. J., who has very kindly supplied me with his transcription of the Florentine MS, has corrected "capitulo Paschalis" to "capitulum Paschalis"; but the MS itself uses a double ablative, Florence, Bibl. Naz., Conv. Soppr. G.IV (1736), fol. 46va, as does the passage in the *Stroma,* C.16 q.1, p.43, quoted in the text.

21. Rolandus, *Stroma*, p. 146.

22. I am indebted to Richard Fraher for this transcription, and to the dean of the cathedral chapter of Worcester for making the MS available to him.

23. Bologna, Archiginnasio, MS A.48, fol. 39va. I am indebted to Dr. Gerard Achten for the transcription.

24. Berlin, Staatsbibliothek, MS lat. fol. 462.

25. At this point I have been unable to consult Grenoble MS 627 and London, British Library, Royal 11.B.11, which also contain the marriage section of the *Stroma.*

26. See JL 10584–14495.

27. I am indebted to Christopher and Mary Cheney for bringing this gloss to my attention.

28. Rolandus, *Stroma,* p. 43.

29. Thaner, "Einleitung," p. xxxvi.

30. Thaner does not argue that the *Stroma* and Alexander III have the same substantive teaching on spiritual relationship. In fact, *Utrum autem filii* clearly differs from the *Stroma* on this subject; both differ from Rolandus's *Sentences* on C.30, q.3; and all three differ from Alexander III, *Super eo quod* (JL 14133; X 4.11.3), which favors the strict rule of Paschal II. These four different teachings illustrate the difficulty of trying to establish identity through a comparison of doctrinal positions.

31. J. F. von Schulte, *Die Geschichte der Quellen und Literatur des canonischen Rechts* (Graz, 1956), I: 116.

32. Stephanus, *Summa,* ed. Schulte (Giessen, 1891), p. 254.

33. Schulte, *Die Geschichte,* I: 116.

34. Stephanus, *Summa,* p. 254.

35. Rolandus, *Stroma,* pp. 216–17.

36. Ibid., p. 215.

37. H. Denifle, "Abaelards Sentenzen und die Bearbeitungen seiner Theologia," *Archiv für Literatur- und Kirchengeschichte des Mittelalters* I (1885), 451.

38. A. M. Gietl, *Die Sentenzen Rolands nachmals Papstes Alexander III* (Freiburg im Breisgau, 1891), p. ix.

39. Ibid., p. v.

40. S. Kuttner and E. Rathbone, "Anglo-Norman Canonists of the Twelfth Century," *Traditio* VII (1949–50), 318.

41. Gloss, Caius MS 676, fol. 178vb, C. 27 *ante* c.1, s.v. *Quod voventes*, reproduced Kuttner and Rathbone, "Anglo-Norman Canonists," pp. 349–50.

42. Rolandus, *Stroma*. p. 116–17.

43. Ibid., p. 118.

44. Rolandus, *Sententiae*, p. 274.

45. Rolandus, *Stroma*. p. 117.

46. Rolandus, *Sententiae*. p. 273.

47. Rufinus, *Summa Decretorum*, ed. H. Singer (Paderborn, 1902), p. 433.

48. Gloss on Stephanus, *Summa*. Berlin, MS lat. qu.192, fol. 186, published by F. Thaner, Viennese Academy, *Sitzungsberichte, Philosophische-Historische Klasse* LXXIX (1870), 216–18.

49. Huguccio, *Summa*. fol. 18r.

50. Gloss on 1 *Comp*. at 4.11.3 s.v. "consuetudinem," reproduced in J.F. von Schulte, "Literaturgeschichte der Compilationes Antiquae," Viennese Academy, *Sitzungsberichte, Philosophische-Historische Klasse* LXVI (1870), 93–94. A comparable phrase has been kindly called to my attention by Brian Tierney from the Summa, *Et est sciendum*, Rouen MS 710, fol. 70v. at D.20 *ante* c. 1: "ubi non ut papa locutus est set ut expositor."

51. Gloss on Caius 676, fol. 134ra, reproduced in Kuttner and Rathbone, "Anglo-Norman Canonists," p. 318.

52. C. Duggan, "The Reception of Canon Law in England," *Proceedings of the Second International Congress of Medieval Canon Law*. Monumenta iuris canonici, Series C: vol. I (Vatican City, 1965), p. 375.

53. R. Weigand, *Die bedingte Eheschliessung im kanonischen Recht* (Munich, 1963), p. 123.

54. D. Van Den Eynde, "Nouvelles Précisions chronologiques sur quelques Oeuvres théologiques du XIIe Siècle," *Franciscan Studies* XIII (1953), 100.

55. S. Kuttner, *Repertorium der Kanonistik*. Studi e Testi LXXI (Vatican City, 1937), pp. 127–28; G. Fransen, "Manuscrits de Décrétistes dans les Bibliothèques liégeoises," *Studia Gratiana* I (1953), 292; A. Stickler, "Iter Helveticum," *Traditio* XIV (1958), 467.

56. See J. Noonan, "The True Paucapalea," communication to the Fifth International Congress of Medieval Canon Law, 27 September 1976, publication pending.

57. The *Summa divinitatis senteniarum omnium magistrorum*. Naples, Bibl. NAZ., VII C.43 fol. 1–90, noted in F. Stegmüller, *Repertorium Commentariorum in Sententias Petri Lombardi* (Würzburg, 1947), p. 753. Weigand discovered Clm 3525 at the Bayerische Staatsbibliothek, Munich, and described it as an anonymous work, Weigand, "Kanonistische Ehetraktate aus dem 12. Jahrhundert," *Proceedings of the Third International Congress of Medieval Canon Law*. Monumenta iuris canonici, Series C: vol. IV (Vatican City, 1971), pp. 78–79.

58. Kuttner, *Repertorium*. pp. 127–28.

59. Stegmüller, *Repertorium*, p. 753.

60. Boso, *Vita Alexandrii tertii*. in *Liber pontificalis*. ed. L. Duchesne, annotated C. Vogel (2nd ed., Paris, 1955), II: 39=PL CC: 11. On Boso see J. M. Brixius, *Die Mitglieder des Kardinalkollegiums von 1130–1181* (Berlin, 1912), p. 58.

61. Sarti and Fattorini, *De claris Professoribus*. I: 624. In the documents of the church of Pisa, a Rolandus appears as a *causidicus* in an act of 17 July 1126, N. Caturegli, *Regesto della Pisa*. Regesta Chartarum Italia XXIV (Rome, 1938). It is not unlikely that the future pope was already involved in legal work by this time. A Rolandus, listed with others as "in Dai legi discretis," appears as a deacon of the church of S. Maria in 1141; his cognomen is apparently "Papa," ibid., no. 381; a Rolandus appears as a canon of "the church of Pisa" on 20 January 1145, ibid., no. 396; and a Rolandus appears as a deacon and canon of the church of S. Maria on 16 March 1145, ibid., no. 397. Taking these several references as being made to the same

person, it could be assumed that they refer to Rolandus, the later pope. But in 1154 there is a reference to a Rolandus who is a deacon and canon of S. Maria, ibid., No. 433; and in 1158 to a Rolandus who is a canon of S. Maria, ibid., no. 457. If he is the same man as the deacon and canon of the 1140s, he cannot be the future pope. See also M. Pacaut, *Alexandre III* (Paris, 1956), pp. 62–63.

62. Boso, *Vita, Liber Pontificalis*, II: 39=PL CC: 11.

63. On Eugene III's visit to Pisa in 1148, see F. Guia, "Le Origine della Chiesa e del Monastero di S. Paolo a Ripa d'Arno in Kinzcia," *Bollettino storico pisano* XXXIII–XXXV (1964–1966), 110.

64. JL II: 20.

65. Boso, *Vita, Liber Pontificalis* II: 39=PL CC: 11.

66. Huguccio, *Summa,* fol. 109r.

67. H. Denifle, "Abälards Sentenzen," p. 590; Gietl, *Sententiae,* pp. xiv–xx; F. Ehrle, reviewing Gietl, *Zeitschrift für katholische Theologie* XVI (1892), 148; B. C. Kuhlmann, *Der Gesetzbegriff beim hl. Thomas von Aquin im Lichte des Rechtsstudiums seiner Zeit* (Bonn, 1912), pp. 392–93; F. Bliemetzrieder, "Paul Fournier und das literarische Werk Ivo von Chartres," *Archiv für katholisches Kirchenrecht* CXI (1935), 84; D. Van Den Eynde, "Nouvelles Précisions," pp. 100–110. I am dependent on Van Den Eynde for the views of Kuhlmann, and I have profited by Van Den Eynde's careful review of all these authorities.

68. P. Kehr, *Italia pontificia.* IV: 219, as supplemented by W. Holtzmann, "Kanonistiche Ergänzungen zur Italia Pontificia," *Quellen und Forschungen aus italienischen Archiven und Bibliotheken* XXXVII (1957), 46, no. 53.

69. Gietl, "Einleitung," Rolandus, *Sententiae,* p. xviii.

70. Van Den Eynde, "Nouvelles Précisions," p. 109.

71. Rolandus, *Sententiae,* p. 35.

72. Ehrle, review of Gietl, p. 149.

73. Rolandus, *Sententiae,* p. 222.

74. Kuhlmann, *Der Gesetzbegriff,* cited in Van Den Eynde, "Nouvelles Précisions," p. 101.

75. Van Den Eynde, "Nouvelles Précisions," pp. 103–4.

76. See JL II: 64–67.

77. See ibid., II: 62–64.

78. Van Den Eynde, "Nouvelles Précisions," pp. 107–8.

79. Gietl, "Einleitung," pp. xxi–xxxiv.

80. D. E. Luscombe, *The School of Peter Abelard* (Cambridge, 1970), p. 16.

81. P. Munz, "Introduction," *Boso's Life of Alexander III,* trans. G. M. Ellis (Oxford, 1973), p. 19. Munz's reference to Alexander III at the Council of Sens is dependent on *Annales Reicherspergenses,* MGH SS XVII: 471, which Munz acknowledges may not be accurate. The condemnation of Abelardian Christology occurs in Alexander III to Guillaume, Archbishop of Reims, H. Denifle and E. Chatelain, eds., *Chartularium Universitatis Parisiensis* (Paris, 1889), I: 8–9.

82. I. Brady, *Prologomena,* to Petrus Lombardus, *Sententiae in IV libris distinctae* (Quarracchi, 1971), p. 129*.

83. Ibid., p. 32*.

84. Thaner, "Einleitung," pp. xxxiii–xxxix.

85. Gualterius, "Judgment," in L. Savioli, *Annali Bolognesi* (Bassano, 1784) I, App. 197; Eugene III to the archpriest and Augustinian canons of Monteveglio, ibid., App. 221=PL CLXXX: 1428; JL 9416, Kehr, *Italia Pontificia,* V: 244.

86. The seven cases in the *Stroma,* C. 16 q. 3 and 4, begin at *Territorii nomine,* ed. Thaner, p. 46, where two alternative situations are put. At *Casum nota limes,* p. 48, two more alternatives are added. At *Nunc vero assignandum,* p. 49, a fifth possibility is imagined; at *Si vero,* p. 50, a sixth; and at *ea siquidem,* p. 50. a seventh.

87. Gualterius, "Judgment," p. 197.

88. Rolandus, *Stroma,* p. 50.

89. Thaner, "Einleitung," p. xxxviii.

90. See Rolandus, *Stroma*, p. 48.

91. Ibid., p. 54.

92. A. Gaudenzi, "L' Età del Decreto di Graziano e l'Antichissimo MS Cassinese di Esso," *Studi e Memorie per la Storia dell'Università di Bologna* (1909), I: 85. On the warfare between Bologna and Modena, see Savioli, *Annali bolognesi,* I: 218–58.

93. Kehr, *Italia pontificia,* v: 304–5.

94. Boso, *Vita Alexandrii tertii,* in *Liber pontificalis,* II: 397 = PL CC:11. The same information appeared on the Epitaph of Alexander III: "patria Tuscia, Sena Domus," *Liber Pontificalis,* III: 139.

95. H. Singer, "Einleitung," Rufinus, *Summa decretorum,* pp. cxiv–cxv.

96. Rufinus, *Summa,* pp. 463–64.

97. Ibid., p. 440. Cf. Tyrannus Rufinus, *Prologus in Adamantii quinque libros,* Corpus christianorum xx: 263. I am indebted to Professor Dag Norberg for this reference.

98. Ibid., p. 361.

99. Ibid., pp. 412–13.

100. G. Morin, "Le Discours d'Ouverture du Concile général de Latran (1179) et l'Oeuvre littéraire de Maître Rufin, Évêque d'Assisi," *Atti della pontificia Accademia romana di Archeologia,* 3rd Ser., *Memorie* II (1928), 113. Even the detractors from the liberal arts, satirized by John of Salisbury as buffoonish boors, were held back from criticizing Robert Pullen "by their deference to the apostolic see, which raised him to the office of chancellor" (John of Salisbury, *Metalogicon,* 1.5, ed. J. Giles, [Oxford, 1848]). If they would not have criticized the chancellor of the church, would Rufinus have? Professor Donahue has suggested to me that Rufinus could have been writing after the schism of 1159 and as a writer then belonging to the imperial camp not hesitated to slur Alexander III. But to accept this suggestion is to place Rufinus later than he has been now dated.

101. Stephanus, *Summa,* pp. 234–35, 253–54.

102. E.g., Stephanus to Cardinal Gratian, *Les Lettres d'Etienne de Tournai,* ed. J. Desilve (Paris, 1893), p. 57 = PL CCXI: 338.

103. Gandulphus, *Sententiarum Libri Quatuor,* ed. Joannes de Walter (Vienna, 1924). Citations are in IV: 294, 319, 353; criticism at IV: 266.

104. Their protest is excerpted in J. Fried, *Die Entstehung des Juristenstandes im 12 Jahrhundert* (Cologne and Vienna, 1974), p. 55.

105. *Chartularium Studii Bononiensis* (Bologna, 1916), III: 113.

106. Ibid., III: 107.

107. Ibid., III: 111; Fried, *Die Entstehung,* pp. 150–51.

108. Thaner, "Einleitung," pp. l–lv.

109. *Quaestiones Incerti Auctoris,* ed. Thaner (Innsbruck, 1874), p. 273.

110. Fried, *Die Entstehung,* pp. 187–88.

111. *Quaestiones,* p. 278.

112. Rolandus, *Stroma,* p. 42.

113. *Quaestiones,* pp. 281–82.

114. Ibid., p. 283.

115. Weigand, *Die Bedingte Eheschliessung,* p. 124.

116. Ibid., p. 156.

117. G. Fransen, "La Structure des Quaestiones Disputatae et leur classement," *Traditio* XXIII (1967), 519.

118. Text of question 6 in Weigand, "Quaestionen aus Schule des Rolandus und Metellus," *Archiv für katholisches Kirchenrecht* CXXXVIII (1969), 87.

119. Ibid., p. 85. Weigand finds him again under the sign "M. ro" in *Queritur cuius sint hec verba,* Leipzig MS 247, fol. 11ra, R. Weigand, *Die Naturrechtslehre der Legisten und Dekretisten von Irnerius bis Accursius und von Gratian bis Johannes Teutonicus* (Munich, 1967), p. 441.

Pope Innocent III's Views on Church and State: A Gloss to *Per Venerabilem*

KENNETH PENNINGTON

Pope Innocent III's views on the relationship between the church and the state have generated as much controversy in the twentieth century as they did in the thirteenth, but the debate has had the salutary effect of enhancing our understanding of the complex issues which churchmen and Innocent himself faced in that critical period of European history. Since 1940 when Maccarrone published his study of Innocent's policies, other historians have followed his lead and emphasized the relationship between Innocent and earlier canonistic and theological thought.[1] They have examined especially the web of canonistic theories on church and state in the twelfth and early thirteenth centuries and have attempted to fit Innocent's decretal letters into the pattern of earlier speculations about the relationship between the two powers. The result of this work has been tentative agreement among historians as to what Innocent's claims to exercise authority in the secular sphere encompassed.[2] About ten years ago, Brian Tierney and John Watt published rather similar studies on Innocent which steered a course between the two extremes of earlier opinion.[3] Innocent, they said, did make major new claims for the papacy in the secular sphere, but even his most trenchant declarations did not claim an absolute right for the exercise of papal power in secular affairs. In Tierney's words, what Innocent asserted were powers which "correspond fairly closely to those of a supreme court of judicature."[4] Thus both Tierney and Watt believe that the "dualistic" and "hierocratic" interpretations misrepresent Innocent's thought.[5]

The whole thrust of research since Maccarrone has been to emphasize the legal ramifications of Innocent's decretals, and it is not surprising that Tierney and Watt have come to approximately the same conclusions as most thirteenth-century canonists did when they glossed Innocent's decretal letters. The pope could not, said most glossators, claim all secular dignities and powers were a part of his plenitude of power, but he could exercise secular jurisdiction in a fairly large number of areas. Further, the right to interfere in temporal matters inhered in the papal office, i.e. the papal office contained both the priestly and royal powers.[6] From the lack of response to Tierney and Watt, perhaps one may conclude that either a broad area of agreement has emerged concerning Innocent's views, or that the discussion has reached an impasse—the hierocrats, dualists and a *via media* (Tierney and Watt) having articulated their respective positions find that new debate along old lines is fruitless.[7]

There is a subplot to the story as well. All parties, even the hierocrats, agree that although there were exceptions, the prevailing thought of the twelfth-century canonists was dualistic. The decretal letters of Pope Alexander III as well as the commentaries of the lawyers put up, legally speaking, a fairly rigid wall between *sacerdotium* and *regnum*,[8] and Innocent's decretals, even the dualists concede, establish important exceptions to the general rule of separation. Why, then, did Innocent III change the character of papal and canonistic thought? The dualists maintain that Innocent merely followed in the footsteps of his teacher at Bologna, Huguccio of Pisa, and never deviated from an essentially dualistic position. The hierocrats, perhaps best represented by Walter Ullmann, assert that Innocent upheld the final and inevitable superiority of the spiritual over the temporal and in doing so culminated centuries of preparation for the hierocratic position. Ullmann sees a decisive break between "Huguccio and his English and Spanish followers" and Innocent III.[9] Tierney and Watt differ on this point. Although Tierney does not explicitly say so, he seems to see a break between Innocent III and his predecessors, while Watt states that "[Innocent's] political legislation emerged logically from a decretist background," and that he was particularly influenced by his teacher, Huguccio, in his thought.[10] Yet the evidence Watt presents argues against such continuity. If Innocent was in tune with earlier canonists, he was almost alone among the thirteenth-century lawyers in interpreting the implications of his predecessors' positions correctly. Most historians agree that the decretal letter *Per venerabilem* was Innocent's most comprehensive statement on the relationship between the two powers. Yet Watt must conclude that it was only Hostiensis who "brought the canonists back to the real mind of the legislator" when he glossed *Per venerabilem*.[11] In fact, as Watt's study demonstrates, contemporary canonists did a great deal of fussing and grumbling about almost all of Innocent's decretals which touched upon church and state. The obvious question is whether Innocent's thought represented continuity with earlier, accepted canonistic thought, and if so why did the canonists refuse to see the continuity? And if he did break with past canonistic traditions, why did Innocent ride a different horse?

In order to answer these questions, I should like to take another look at Innocent's ideas on church and state from a new perspective. Innocent has usually been characterized as a great lawyer-pope who was trained at Bologna by the twelfth-century canonist, Huguccio of Pisa. Since historians have described Innocent as a lawyer, they have tended to see his decretal letters on *sacerdotium* and *regnum* as subtle, well-considered legal briefs or opinions into which Innocent poured his most profound thoughts on the subject, even though some of his letters have perplexed historians because of inexact and nonlegal terminology.[12] If Innocent was indeed schooled in law at Bologna, this would be entirely proper. A man's education does shape his thought, and nowhere is this truism more apparent than in law. Anyone acquainted with the writings of the lawyers knows that although they often disagreed—sometimes unseemly—their thought could be engagingly predictable. The modern scholar derives a sense of pleasure when he follows an intricate canonistic argument and anticipates the legal maxim with which the canonist will close his case. However, Innocent was not a doctor of laws, nor, very likely, even a polished product of the law school at Bologna.[13] Therefore instead of interpreting Innocent's most characteristic statements on the relationship between church and state as sophisticated legal briefs, we might more accurately examine them as only crude embodiments of legal principles.

The evidence for Innocent's legal training is as follows. The story that Innocent studied with Huguccio originated in Johannes Andreae's fourteenth-century commentary on the Decretals of Gregory IX. Johannes put forward this notion because he had misinterpreted an earlier gloss in which Hostiensis had pointed out that Innocent III had rejected Magister Huguccio's opinion in one of his decretals. Johannes transformed Hostiensis's statement and declared that Innocent had rejected *his* master's opinion. Later historians have depended on Johannes's text to establish that Innocent studied with Huguccio. Since there is no other source for the story that Innocent studied with Huguccio, the tradition must be abandoned.

The only evidence that Innocent studied in Bologna is the anonymous *Gesta Innocentii,* and the *Gesta* merely asserted that after studying in Rome, Paris and Bologna, Innocent surpassed all his contemporaries in philosophy and theology, but said nothing about law. Historians have concluded that, since Innocent studied with Huguccio, he must have pursued legal studies. If we disabuse ourselves of the notion that Innocent was Huguccio's student, we find that the evidence for Innocent's legal training is meager. Further, given what little we know about the chronology of Innocent's early life, it seems fairly certain that he studied in Bologna for a maximum of two years—very likely even less. Although it is most reasonable to assume that he did spend his time in Bologna studying law, it is unlikely that two years would have been an adequate period of study to learn Roman and canon law well enough to have produced some of the superb decretal letters which we find in his registers. Therefore, I think that we must be chary of characterizing Innocent as a lawyer-pope.[14]

There is no question that Innocent studied theology at Paris. Not only do we have the *Gesta's* praise of his talents, but also a number of theological works and sermons which betray clearly their Parisian origins.[15] Historians have been less kind than the *Gesta* when they have evaluated Innocent's skills as a theologian. In a recent book, Helmut Roscher remarked that he did not know how a man of Innocent's intelligence could have written such prosaic theology,[16] and anyone who takes the time to read Innocent's theological works and sermons can only concur. His theological speculations are hardly breathtaking; in fact, if one examines his sources closely, it is difficult to find an idea which is uniquely Innocent's.[17]

Yet with that said, Innocent's vision of papal monarchy which we find in his sermons and decretal letters is impressive. His conception of papal authority has both grandeur and breadth; it was his profound belief in the dignity and power inherent in the papal office that led Innocent to formulate his novel claims of papal prerogatives in the secular sphere. Innocent made original contributions to the theory of papal monarchy, and he pointed the papacy in a new direction which would have profound implications for the late Middle Ages.[18]

Not only were his letters on the relationship between *regnum* and *sacerdotium* important, but his other decretal letters had an enormous impact on the development of early canon law. His pontificate produced the first officially sanctioned collection of legislation in the west since the revival of learning in the twelfth century, and his decretal letters touched almost every aspect of contemporary law to the extent that virtually every study of twelfth- and thirteenth-century canon law must focus on legislation which Innocent's curia produced.

We even have colorful descriptions of Innocent's courtroom manner. Two Englishmen, Gerald of Wales and Thomas of Marlborough, sketched vivid portraits of the young pope presiding over the highest court in Christendom.[19] The anonymous chronicler who wrote a history of Innocent's early pontificate observed that he heard legal complaints three times a week in his consistory and dealt personally with the more important cases ("causae maiores"). He then listed eight cases which Innocent handled.[20] Not surprisingly, all of the cases were matters of importance to the ecclesiastical hierarchy: four cases treated translations of bishops which had not been authorized by the papacy; two cases determined archiepiscopal jurisdictional claims over contested bishoprics, and the last two concerned conflicting jurisdictional questions between bishops and other ecclesiastical corporations. The *Gesta*'s author praised Innocent's skill in settling these cases and his ability in bringing the litigating parties together with a just solution of their differences—a quality of his justice for which Innocent was noted. There is an example of this in the Evesham case. Thomas of Marlborough observed that since Evesham had already won the first half of the dispute, Innocent, he thought, would favor the bishop of Worcester in the second half.[21] Whether or not Thomas is correct, Innocent's relativism is not to be despised. Medieval justice often depended on compromise as a means of preventing subsequent litigation, and compromise may have been the only way to assure that distant litigants would follow papal decisions.

In his account of the Evesham case, Thomas of Marlborough described Innocent as a judge who possessed a keen sense of humor which sometimes obfuscated the legal point at hand, and as a strong-minded man who did not tolerate criticism of his actions, even when criticism might have been justified. Two anecdotes support these points. One of the key arguments in the

Evesham case centered on the issue of whether the monastery at Evesham could prescribe the rights ("iura") of the bishop of Worcester. The bishop's advocate, Robert, thought not and said to Innocent: "Holy Father, we learned in the schools, and it is the opinion of our masters, that prescription cannot run against episcopal rights." To which Innocent responded, "You and your masters drank too much English beer when you learned that."[22] What has been lost in the humor of the moment is that Innocent's remark (and that of Robert) was not an accurate description of what the lawyers thought about the prescription of episcopal rights. Some episcopal rights could not be prescribed, and Thomas subsequently gave both Innocent and Robert a fairly accurate summary of canonistic thought on prescription.[23] Immediately after this exchange, Innocent pointed out to Robert that perhaps frequent vacancies in the episcopal see of Worcester vitiated the monastery's claim of prescription. Innocent's suggestion distressed Thomas for he thought Innocent exceeded a judge's proper role, and he tells us that his tongue could not be restrained:[24] "Holy Father, you have been called in plenitude of power and all things are permitted to you, but according to civil law it is not permitted to other judges to aid advocates *de facto,* but only *de iure.*" Innocent retorted, "That is false; rather a judge may offer aid *de facto* and *de iure.*" The anecdote may reveal more of Innocent's character than it does of his knowledge of legal doctrine, but, in fact, few lawyers would have supported Innocent's—or Thomas'—dogmatic assertion. Most lawyers would have said that a judge may always offer aid *de iure,* but only sometimes *de facto.*[25]

In spite of Innocent's imperious and sometimes rash manner in the papal consistory, contempories called him "nostri temporis Salomon,"[26] and Hostiensis later named him "pater iuris."[27] Yet to argue that such a man was not a trained lawyer is neither paradoxical nor perverse. Legal history is replete with emperors, kings, lawgivers and even supreme court justices who did not themselves possess subtle legal minds but had other qualities which produced great changes in law. Innocent was a superb administrator, and this talent helped him to reshape both papal government and papal law.

When we turn to Innocent's decretal letters which deal with the problem of church and state, we immediately encounter a methodological difficulty. I have argued that we cannot evaluate Innocent's legal learning by reading his decretal letters because we cannot be certain whether these letters contain Innocent's own words and ideas or those of a canonist working in the papal curia.[28] Of course, the pope must have been the final arbiter of what his letters contained, but that is no proof that the specific ideas in any particular letter are Innocentian. When one considers the seven major letters of Innocent which bear upon the relationship between church and state and were incorporated into the corpus of ecclesiastical law, it must be admitted that they do not contain either conceptualizations or phraseology (for the most part) which could stamp them as Innocent's. Further, the legal justifications put forward in these decretals which permitted the pope to judge in the *regnum—ratio peccati, vacante imperio,* or reason of heresy—are not concepts which are derived necessarily from the work of the canonists or any other branch of learning.[29]

However, historians have usually turned to the decretal *Per venerabilem* as Innocent's most important and characteristic statement on papal power.[30] And with good reason. We have a large body of works which Innocent wrote before and after his election to the papal throne, and there are obvious stylistic and thematic correspondences between *Per venerabilem* and sections of his sermons.[31] The major literary images which Innocent used again and again are quite familiar, and most of them occur in *Per venerabilem.* He relied on the standard biblical texts which theologians and canonists commonly cited when discussing papal power—Matt. 16:18, the vicariate of Christ and papal plenitude of power—and also brought forward a novel *figura* from the Old Testament to prove his claims to exercise secular jurisdiction. The pope was the vicar of him who was represented by the order of Melchisedech, and by implication, as Christ's vicar the pope had the power of both a priest and a king as a part of his office.[32] The symbol of Melchisedech pervades Innocent's writings and occurs in *Per venerabilem* in conjunction with an obscure passage from Deuteronomy. The only "Innocentian" text which does not appear in *Per venerabilem* is Jer. 1:10, a passage which Yves Congar has shown was used frequently by earlier popes.[33] We turn then to *Per venerabilem* not only as a touchstone of Innocent's thought, but as a summary of what Innocent said about the relationship between *sacerdotium* and *regnum* in his sermons, theological works and decretal letters.[34]

Per venerabilem was sent to William of Montpellier in 1202 in answer to William's request that Innocent legitimize his bastard children so they might inherit their father's possessions and title. Innocent rejected William's plea, but asserted that the pope could grant such a request if the occasion demanded such action.[35] The decretal divides into three parts. In the first part of the letter Innocent declared that an action of legitimization was within the pope's jurisdictional competence and cited several legal precedents to support his contention. In the second, he set forth his reasons for rejecting William's specific request, and in the third he outlined a rationale and justification for papal action not only in William's case (if the pope had wished to act) but in other secular matters as well.

The legal arguments which Innocent put forward in section one are interesting, for there was no legal precedent for William's request. Whether the legal citations represent Innocent's own thought, or merely the arguments of William's lawyers, we cannot be certain. Innocent IV evidently assumed that the first part of the decretal was not really Innocent's formulation of the case, but only the arguments which could be put forward on the count's behalf.[36] In any case, the legal precedents cited in the decretal are weak. First, he noted that when a person becomes a bishop, he is exempted from *patria potestas.* If a bishop then ordains a *servus,* the latter escapes from the yoke of servitude. Further, argued Innocent, since the pope may legitimize in the spiritual sphere, he may legitimize in secular matters "quod in maiori conceditur licitum esse videtur et in minori" (what is conceded in a greater, also seems to be lawful in a minor), because—as all of his contemporaries would have admitted—the spiritual power requires greater authority and suitability than does temporal power. John Watt remarks at this point that Innocent's basic argument in *Per venerabilem* was grounded on the Roman law maxim, "in eo plus sit, semper inest minus" (the smaller is always included in the greater).[37]

The canonists were remarkably unimpressed with Innocent's reasoning, for the objections to Innocent's assertion are obvious: the Roman legal maxim which Innocent cited pertained to officials in the same jurisdictional sphere—any power possessed by a subordinate is also possessed by his superior. But few thirteenth-century canonists (not even Innocent himself) would have conceded that temporal power was merely delegated by the pope. Innocent confused two different concepts in his assertion: the superiority of the spiritual power over the temporal (the spiritual power being of a higher order) with the jurisdictional power which a superior judge could always exercise *in lieu* of an inferior. The maxim *in eo* was not the basis for Innocent's claims in *Per venerabilem,* but was an example of a logical equivocation. If the maxim had been Innocent's fundamental claim in *Per venerabilem,* then he could have used the same reasoning to justify any incursion into the secular sphere, but as we shall see, he based his right to exercise secular power on quite different grounds.[38]

Innocent's example of the *servus* who was removed from the power of his secular master when he became a priest is a poor analogy to the case in *Per venerabilem.*[39] In the ordination of a *servus,* a bishop frees the man by bringing him into the ecclesiastical hierarchy, but in *Per venerabilem,* Innocent declared that he could change a person's legal status when the person remained in the temporal sphere. In fact, Innocent IV pointed out Innocent's faulty reasoning when he glossed *Per venerabilem.* He noted that if a prince legitimized a person in his jurisdiction, a heir still could not inherit hereditary goods from someone who died intestate under another prince's jurisdiction.[40] By implication, Innocent IV denied that the pope could routinely legitimize a person in temporal matters and rejected the claims in *Per venerabilem,* as did most canonists before Hostiensis. Thus, the legal arguments put forward in section one—if they do represent Innocent's own thoughts—are neither subtle nor convincing. The canonists soon advanced much stronger arguments to justify the pope's right to legitimize in the temporal sphere. Innocent could have asserted, as Vincentius, Johannes Teutonicus and Innocent IV did, that the pope could exercise temporal jurisdiction when legitimizing if all parties concerned agreed to the action, i.e. when the pope exercised "jurisdictio voluntaria."[41] Or Innocent might have used Hostiensis's intriguing argument that the pope alone could legitimize a person—Hostiensis thought that legitimization, like marriage, should properly fall within the sphere of ecclesiastical law.[42] In either case, the canonists provided legal rationales which were lacking in section one of the decretal.

In the second part of *Per venerabilem,* Innocent gave his reasons for denying

William of Montpellier's request. He took care to show that William's situation was quite different from that of King Philip Augustus, the precedent which William had cited to support his case. The main difference between the two cases, said Innocent, was that Philip had no superior in the temporal sphere, but William did. If he legitimized William's children, Innocent would injure the rights of the French king. This he refused to do.[43]

Finally, in the last and most important section of the letter, Innocent reasserted his right to legitimize in the *regnum:*[44]

> Having been convinced by these reasons, we bestowed the requested favor upon the king; we conclude from examples drawn from both the Old and the New Testaments that not only in the patrimony of the church where we hold full power in temporals, but in other regions as well, having examined the circumstances we exercise temporal jurisdiction in certain cases.

Here Innocent did not merely claim the power of legitimization in the secular sphere, but to exercise *casualiter* secular jurisdiction, "certis causis inspectis," and turned to the Old Testament for textual support. An argument which occurs in almost all of his writing on church and state was that the pope is a priest in the order of Melchisedech. Melchisedech was a mysterious figure in the Book of Genesis who was called a priest of the most high God and king of Salem. Since Melchisedech gave bread and wine to Abraham and blessed him, biblical commentators quickly interpreted Melchisedech as being a forerunner of Christ.[45] To theologians of the twelfth century, Melchisedech represented Christ and the "order of the priesthood," a quality which was common to all priests.[46] St. Bernard was the first to connect Melchisedech specifically with the papal office, but he did so in commonly accepted theological terms. In a passage of *De consideratione,* Bernard said that the pope was a "priest in the order of Melchisedech,"[47] that is, priesthood was one of the characteristics of the papal office. Innocent connected the symbol of Melchisedech with the vicariate of Christ in *Per venerabilem,* and since Melchisedech prefigured Christ, therefore the pope—like Melchisedech—had both royal and spiritual power inherent in his office.[48]

The figure of Melchisedech was transformed into Innocent's most dramatic argument for papal monarchy. In a letter to the bishop of Fermo in 1205, Innocent wrote:[49]

> Although pontifical authority and imperial power are diverse dignities, and the royal and sacerdotal offices are distinct, because the Roman pontiff holds on earth the office of him who is the kings of kings and the lord of lords, priest forever in the order of Melchisedech, he not only holds the highest power in spiritual affairs, but truly even in temporal affairs he holds great power from the same lord.

Although Fermo was a city in the patrimony of St. Peter, Innocent's use of the Melchisedech imagery in letters which were addressed to persons outside of the patrimony makes clear that he did not intend that the pope's royal powers be confined to the papal states. *Per venerabilem* is one example. Innocent cited Melchisedech to demonstrate the royal and sacerdotal character of the papal office, and unlike earlier commentators, he emphasized Melchisedech's royalty as well as his priesthood. In *Per venerabilem* Innocent used Melchisedech with Matt. 16:18 to prove his claim that the pope could exercise temporal power outside of the papal states, "certis causis inspectis."[50]

To modern historians, Innocent's use of the *figura* of Melchisedech seems to capture the very essence of the medieval biblical exegesis. Innocent himself stated that the Old Testament had a fundamental relationship with the New Testament which could be easily demonstrated. The idea is a commonplace in medieval exegetical thought.[51] Innocent's use of Melchisedech to prefigure and to justify the temporal power of the pope seems to be an exegetical triumph. I have already shown that commentators in the twelfth century did not anticipate Innocent's explication of Melchisedech, but, as persuasive as Innocent's argument may seem to moderns, I have not found a single canonist after Innocent who cited Melchisedech to establish the pope's right to act in the *regnum*. The one notable exception to this generalization is *Eger cui lenia,* a polemical document which emanated from the curia of Pope Innocent IV, but which, as Peter Herde has shown, probably does not reflect the mind of Innocent IV.[52]

Later canonists and theologians did employ Innocent III's assertion that the pope was the vicar of Christ and exercised a plenitude of power as the successor of Christ's first vicar, Peter. However, their position raised problems which Innocent's use of Melchisedech avoided. How could the vicar of Christ claim royal power when Christ himself said that his kingdom was not of this world, and that his followers ought to render unto Caesar those things which are Caesar's? The usual answer which the advocates of papal power gave was to demonstrate the superiority of spiritual to temporal power and to cite the text of Matt. 16:18, insisting that when Christ said St. Peter could loose or bind *"quodcumque,"* that meant everything, both in the spiritual as well as the temporal realm.[53] But in the fourteenth century, Marsilius of Padua still found Innocent's arguments weighty enough to reassert the theological position of the twelfth-century scholastics: Melchisedech's royalty prefigured only Christ, not his vicar.[54] Marsilius argued the case well, but he was tilting with windmills; almost no contemporary theologian was making such an argument.

The second text which Innocent cited was a passage from Deut. 17:8–12. "It may be that some matters of law will be too hard for your unravelling, between blood and blood, case and case, leper and leper, and your own judges disagree, make your way to the place which your lord God has chosen, and to the priests of Levi's race." Again, Innocent's interpretation of this text is unusual. The Ordinary Gloss stated that, "He instructed the priests of God's church that they render ecclesiastical judgments reverently according to the power given them by God."[55] In *Per venerabilem* Innocent connects Deut. 17:8 with secular cases and with Matt. 16:18.[56] "He indeed is a priest or judge over them, to whom the Lord said in Peter, 'Whatsoever you shall bind on earth shall be bound in heaven, and whatsoever you shall loose on earth shall be loosed in heaven,' that is his vicar, who is a priest forever in the order of Melchisedech, appointed by God the judge of the living and the dead." I have found no earlier biblical commentator who uses this passage to justify ecclesiastical interference in secular cases although at least three Gregorian canonical collections did employ the text to support papal judicial power.[57] Why did Innocent choose this particular text? I suspect that the Ordinary Gloss's comment on Deut. 17:12 convinced him that the passage was admirably suited to his purpose[58]: s.v. *sacerdotis imperio.* "Of Christ who is a priest forever in the order of Melchisedech, who substituted vicars for himself, to whom he said, 'Who hears you, hears me, who spurns you, spurns me [Luke 10:16].' " Innocent undoubtedly read both the gloss and the text of Deut. 17:8–12 together, and the Gloss's reference not only to Melchisedech, but also to Christ's vicars must have persuaded him that the passage was ideal for describing the judicial powers of the papacy—Melchisedech foreshadowed the papal office and Deut. 17:8–12 foreshadowed the pope's power to judge.

Deut. 17:8 created exegetical difficulties for Innocent. He might have cited Deut. 1:17 which made the same point as Deut. 17:8 but in simpler terms. There, Moses, who could also be viewed as a forerunner of the papal office,[59] said: "if any quarrel seems hard to decide, refer it to me, and I will take cognizance of it myself." Peter the Chanter had incorporated Deut. 1:17 in his description of ecclesiastical judicial power in his *Verbum abbreviatum* and even the gloss to Deut. 1:17 seems to be more amenable to Innocent's purpose than Deut. 17:8[60]: s.v. *quod si difficile.* "Greater men ought to judge greater and more difficult things; lesser men the smaller and easier."

However, Innocent did not use Deut. 1:17, and the tripartite division of judicial cases in Deut. 17:8 caused him to have problems with his terminology. Tierney has shown that Innocent intended that Deut. 17:8 should demonstrate that both secular and ecclesiastical cases which were difficult and ambiguous ought to be referred to the pope. The canonists in Bologna certainly interpreted Innocent's words in this way. Yet the three types of judgment which the text described fit awkwardly into the legal categories of the early thirteenth century. Innocent stated that the three types of judgment in Deuteronomy were secular criminal cases, ecclesiastical criminal cases and a last category of ambiguous secular and ecclesiastical cases. Innocent declared that if difficulties arose in any of these areas, they should be sent to Rome. The divisions of legal cases which Innocent set forth are not only incomplete, but, from a legal point of view, Innocent muddled his thought by a poor choice of terms.

In his *Ordo iudicarius,* which was written slightly later than *Per venerabilem,* Tancred stated that there were four kinds of cases in ecclesiastical justice: criminal, civil, spiritual and mixed.[61] He might have observed that at least three of these categories could be applied to secular justice as well—secular courts could judge in mixed cases such as disputes which arose between lay patrons to churches but not in purely spiritual matters. There were, in other words, seven different types of cases which Innocent telescoped into his rather crude outline of ecclesiastical and secular justice. He might have alleviated the difficulty in his terminology if he had described the "causa et causa" cases referred to in Deut. 17:8 as civil cases in both secular and ecclesiastical courts, and not as "cases which were ecclesiastical as well as secular." His categories would have then had more symmetry and less confusion. Further, when Innocent described the third set of cases as "tam ecclesiasticum quam civile," he committed a blunder in terminology which I believe no one who had been trained in law would have made. "Civile" could refer to noncriminal matters such as those which dealt with money or to secular problems;[62] we find both usages among contemporary lawyers. Innocent had used "civile" to mean secular when he described cases of blood and blood, but he introduced an ambiguity into his text when he chose "civile" to describe the third set of cases (although both of the usages of "civile" in *Per venerabilem* are internally consistent, i.e. they both mean secular) because one could interpret the third set as referring to either civil ecclesiastical or just ecclesiastical cases. The canonists saw the ambiguity immediately and glossed the second "civile" as "seculare."[63] In sum, Innocent's description of justice based on Deut. 17:8 is hardly satisfying. Because of imprecise definitions, his argument has baffled both thirteenth- and twentieth-century scholars. It is not surprising that later canonists did not consider this intractable text when they wished to illustrate the relationship between papal power and secular justice. Like Melchisedech, the passage lived on in the corpus of canon law, but it was largely ignored.

Finally, Innocent cited St. Paul's first letter to the Corinthians 6:3 to prove that the pope could, in Innocent's words, judge in secular affairs because of his plenitude of power:[64] "Indeed Paul, in order to explain plenitude of power, wrote to the Corinthians and said: 'Know you not that you shall judge angels? How much more the things of the world?' " There was a tradition of sorts for the citation of this text in connection with papal judgmental power,[65] but once again, Innocent's exegesis of the passage is unusual. Twelfth-century theologians interpreted Paul's words to mean that the church could judge in spiritual matters, but they did not interpret "secularia" as meaning temporal affairs.[66] St. Paul contrasted heavenly and worldly matters, not spiritual and temporal. Although this passage was used by later papal writers—notably again *Eger cui lenia*—and led to the question of whether the pope could judge angels,[67] 1 Cor. 6:3 was not an important reference for later hierocrats.

Innocent coupled Melchisedech, Deut. 17:8 and 1 Cor. 6:3 with the *locus classicus* of papal judgmental power, Matt. 16:18 in the decretal *Per venerabilem*. He linked these biblical texts with the legal and theological concept that the pope was also the vicar of Christ. While all priests were sometimes described as being vicars of Christ, Innocent emphasized that "vicarius Christi" was a special papal title in his writings. Although Innocent often connected the vicariate of Christ with the biblical texts which we have discussed, later writers eliminated Innocent's more strained exegesis and retained his emphasis on the pope's plenitude of power and his vicariate.[68] That was his lasting contribution to the ideology of the papal office.

Innocent's conception of the papal office was both brilliant and sweeping, but his vision was not based on law or on legal arguments which some of his contemporaries were making. He might have adopted the view of Alanus Anglicus that the pope held both swords, spiritual and the temporal, and that all jurisdiction flowed from the pope. Such an argument had the great virtue of simplicity and, on its own terms, was an unassailable position. Or he might have settled on the same distinction as Vincentius Hispanus and Johannes Teutonicus: the pope could legitimize outside of the papal states through "jurisdictio voluntaria," a distinction which would have preserved a jurisdictional separation of the two powers. Innocent, however, rejected a legal solution and substituted his own "political theology."[69] *Per venerabilem* was not a product of a mind which had been honed at the law school in Bologna for, as a legal document, it was unsatisfactory and stood in sharp contrast to the lawyers' clear expositions on the relationship of the temporal and spiritual spheres. But the decretal was included in the corpus of canon law, and lawyers did have to extract what meaning they could from it. Their difficulties were similar to those which have perplexed modern commentators. If the pope legitimized a person, was that person capable of holding secular offices and inheriting temporal goods and dignities? Could the pope legitimize outside the papal states? Did *Per venerabilem* prove that the pope had ordinary power in temporals? The canonists confronted these knotty problems with mixed success. They were, of course, attempting to fit the decretal into the prevailing framework of canonistic thought.

When the combative canonist, Hostiensis, finally gave a detailed commentary to *Per venerabilem* in the mid-thirteenth century, he had harsh words for his predecessors. He was a lawyer who adhered to the letter of the law ("textus") and he bristled when he saw earlier canonists trying to vitiate Innocent III's clear intent in *Per venerabilem*. In his Gloss to the beginning of the third part of the decretal, he observed that Tancred and Vincentius erred when they said that the pope could not freely legitimize outside of the patrimony of St. Peter. Such an opinion went contrary to the clear meaning of the text.[70] He then turned sarcastic when he commented on Bernardus Parmensis's Ordinary Gloss:[71] "Behold a good gloss which says that only they who live in the patrimony of St. Peter can be legitimized by the pope, and the text says not only they." But as I have pointed out, although Hostiensis may have brought canonistic thought back to the mind of the legislator, his solution was hardly an outgrowth of Innocent's arguments.

Innocent's description of the papal right of legitimization in *Per venerabilem* was based on a series of Old and New Testament texts which were neither part of the canonistic tradition, nor, more surprisingly, part of earlier theological traditions. Innocent lived in an age which relished extravagant biblical exegesis, and he demonstrated that passages in the Old and New Testaments adumbrated his conception of the papal office.[72] Since this methodology was a standard tool of the medieval exegete, historians have seen Innocent's textual explications as having intellectual verve and, more importantly, respectability. Medieval men must have found Innocent's arguments reasonable because that is the way men thought in the Middle Ages. But this assumption is open to serious question; Innocent's biblical exegesis was not accepted by later writers although his decretals became the *loci* for canonistic commentary on *sacerdotium* and *regnum*.

How does my characterization of Innocent's thought change our view of him? In some ways very little. His pontificate was one of the two or three most important in the medieval period, and his personality and character set the tone of papal government. Since the eleventh-century reform movement, the papal office had become an ever more important element in Christian society, and Innocent brought the power and dignity of the papal office to new heights. He saw that there were problems in Christendom which only the bishop of Rome could remedy. For Innocent, the ultimate purpose of the papacy was embodied in Jer. 1:10, another favorite text. "[The pope should] root up and pull down, overthrow and lay in ruins, build and plant anew."[73] When he turned his mind to the powers and duties of the papal office, he was masterfully ingenious. He carried the idea that the spiritual power is superior to temporal power to its logical conclusion: in some cases the spiritual power might find it necessary to intervene in secular affairs. But the policies which Innocent III began inexorably led to the excesses of his successors.

We might change our views in one respect. Innocent has been pictured as a calculating lawyer, skillfully paving the way for papal monarchy. Rather I think that it was Innocent's high sense of moral and historical purpose which motivated him to formulate his policies. The older view that Innocent cleverly contrived to gain worldly dominion is belied by his obvious sincerity. At times, he may have been rash, autocratic and shortsighted, but he strove vigorously to shape a meaningful Christian society on earth. If Innocent had been more sophisticated in his thought, more contemplative, better trained in law, his decretals on church and state might have been quite different. Of course, he could rarely, if ever, render a judicial decision which touched upon the delicate jurisdictional boundary between church and state without considering the political impact of his decree. In *Per venerabilem,* Innocent did not want to offend the king of France or William of Montpellier, and he offered an imperfect solution to a complex problem. But we can better understand the man, if we understand the intellectual milieu from which he framed his answer. And what possible answers there were.

Syracuse University

Notes

1. Michele Maccarrone, *Chiesa e Stato nella Dottrina di Innocenzo III* (Rome, 1940).
2. Since Maccarrone wrote there has been a fairly abundant literature on Innocent III. The most important subsequent studies are: Friedrich Kempf, *Papsttum und Kaisertum bei Innocenz III.* (Rome, 1954); Helene Tillmann, *Papst Innocenz III.* (Bonn, 1954); Helmut Roscher, *Papst Innocenz III. und die Kreuzzüge* (Göttingen, 1969). These works contain complete bibliographies.
3. Brian Tierney, "The Continuity of Papal Political Theory in the Thirteenth Century," *Mediaeval Studies* XXVII (1965), 197–218 and *"Tria quippe distinguit iudicia . . .,* A Note on Innocent III's Decretal *Per venerabilem."* *Speculum* XXXVII (1962), 48–59. John Watt, "The Theory of Papal Monarchy in the Thirteenth Century," *Traditio* XX (1964), 179–317 which was published as a separate monograph (London and New York, 1965).
4. Tierney, "Continuity," p. 238.
5. I agree with the views of Tierney and Watt. A recent, thorough analysis of Walter Ullmann's vision of papal monarchy is Francis Oakley, "Celestial Hierarchies Revisited: Walter Ullmann's Vision of Medieval Politics," *Past and Present* LX (1973), 3–48. Ullmann, more than any other single historian, has shaped the debate about political theory. Indeed, the use of the words "state" when refering to the *regnum, forum seculare, forum civile,* or *in temporalibus* (all terms used by medieval lawyers) is anathema to Ullmann—a betrayal of gross ignorance on the writer's part. I think that when medieval lawyers do not have the precise terminology for referring to the secular sphere, the historian is justified in choosing an English word which conveys clearly the meaning intended, even if the word is a trifle anachronistic. Economic historians encounter no difficulty in describing the economic systems of the Middle Ages with anachronistic terms, why should not historians of political theory if the meaning is clear to all?
6. Watt, *Theory of Papal Monarchy,* is an excellent survey of canonistic opinion after Innocent III.
7. Recent work on Innocent III which sometimes touches on his views of papal power is: K. Schatz, "Papsttum und partikular kirchliche Gewalt bei Innocenz III.," *Archivum historiae pontificiae* VIII (1970), 61–111; Ludwig Buisson, "Exemples et Tradition chez Innocent III," *L'Année canonique* XV (1971), 109–32; John C. Moore, "Papal Justice Around the Time of Pope Innocent III," *Church History* XLI (1972), 259–306; James Ross Sweeney, "Innocent III, Hungary and the Bulgarian Coronation: A Study in Medieval Papal Diplomacy," *Church History* XLII (1973), 320–34.
8. Kempf, *Papsttum and Kaisertum,* pp. 181–230, provides a good survey of canonistic thought in the twelfth century, along with Sergio Mochi Onory, *Fonti canonistiche dell'Idea moderna dello Stato* (Milan, 1951). Alfons Stickler's detailed studies which are listed in the bibliographies of the works listed in note 2 are also valuable.
9. Walter Ullmann, *Medieval Papalism: The Political Theories of the Medieval Canonists* (London, 1949), p. 146.
10. Tierney, *"Tria quippe distinguit,"* pp. 55–56; Watt, *Theory of Papal Monarchy,* p. 34.
11. Watt, *Theory of Papal Monarchy,* p. 111.
12. E.g. Tierney, *"Tria quippe distinguit,"* p. 54.
13. The conclusions presented in the following paragraphs are taken from my essay, "The Legal Education of Pope Innocent III," *Bulletin of Medieval Canon Law,* n.s. IV (1974), 70–77.
14. How much law Innocent could have learned in two years is impossible to estimate. A student who had studied canon law for two years felt inexpert enough to ask Peter of Blois for his opinion of a legal problem, see S. Kuttner and E. Rathbone, "Anglo-Norman Canonists of the Twelfth Century: An Introductory Study," *Traditio* VII (1949–51), 279–358, at p. 286. My thanks to Paul Hyams for this citation.
15. Innocent's theological works are conveniently printed in PL CCXVII.
16. Roscher, *Papst Innocenz III.,* p. 261.

17. E.g. M. Maccarrone, "Innocenzo III Teologo dell'Eucarestia," *Studi su Innocenzo III* (Padua, 1972), pp. 341–424.

18. Cf. Watt, *Theory of Papal Monarchy*, pp. 34–49, also, Kempf, *Papsttum und Kaisertum*, pp. 194–230, examines earlier canonical theories on church and state and argues that Innocent follows earlier decretists.

19. Tillmann, *Innocenz III.*, p. 237 and pp. 40–1; 50–52, discusses both chroniclers; their anecdotes about the papal court and Innocent are well known, see R. Brentano, *Two Churches: England and Italy in the Thirteenth Century* (Princeton, 1968), p. 15–17, also Brentano, *Rome before Avignon* (New York, 1974), pp. 147–53; C. Cheney, *From Becket to Langton: English Church Government 1170–1213* (Manchester, 1956), p. 73. For Innocent's personality and wit, see Tillmann, pp. 47–55 and 234–44.

20. PL CCXIV: lxxxi–lxxxix.

21. The Evesham case is justly famous and has been given detailed accounts by G. G. Coulton, *Five Centuries of Religion* (Cambridge, 1927), II: 347–78 and D. Knowles, *The Monastic Order in England*, 2nd ed. (Cambridge, 1966), pp. 331–45.

22. *Chronicon abbatiae de Evesham*, Rolls Series, XXIX (London, 1863), p. 189.

23. Ibid., p. 190. For typical comments of the lawyers on the problem, see the ordinary glosses to C.16 q.3 c.4 s.v. *provinciam;* X 1.37.18 s.v. *de lege iurisdictionis,* and X 2.26.15 s.v. *ius episcopale.*

24. Ibid., p. 191.

25. See, for example, the glosses to D.28 c.4 s.v. *filiam* and X 1.5.3 s.v. *curavimus allegare.* For another example of Innocent acting irresponsibly early in his pontificate when he performed his judicial duties, see Cheney, *From Becket to Langton,* pp. 73–74, where the Lambeth case is discussed, one of those cases singled out by the author of the *Gesta* for praise. Also the conclusions of Sweeney in "Innocent III, Hungary," pp. 333–34.

26. Ranier of Pomposa, PL CCXVI: 1173. "Cupientes nonnulli, qui de diversis et ultimis etiam mundi partibus ad apostolicam sedem accedunt, audire sapientiam nostri temporis Salomonis, nec non et multi alii honesti viri atque prudentes, qui nobiscum praesentialiter conversantur, justitias et iudicia ipsius in scriptis habere. . . ." Salomon may have been used by intimates when they referred to Innocent, see K. Hampe, "Eine Schilderung des Sommeraufenthaltes der romischen Kurie unter Innocenz III. in Subiaco 1202," *Historische Vierteljahrschrift* VIII (1905), 509–35 and [anonymous], "Une satire contre Innocent III," *Festschrift Bernard Bischoff* (Stuttgart, 1971), 372–90, although I do not think that the evidence is overwhelming that the poem in the article is directed against Innocent. R. Brentano, *Rome before Avignon,* pp. 154–55, argues convincingly that the Subiaco letter was satirical.

27. Pennington, "Legal Education," p. 74. Late in the thirteenth century, the Franciscan chronicler, Salimbene, called Innocent a "professor iuris": "Sane iste Innocentius fuit iuris professor et totum ius, tam canonicum quam civile, sub compendio emendavit in voluminibus tertiarum et quartarum decretalium." *Cronica,* ed. F. Bernini (Bari, 1942), I: 26. If Innocent had compiled *3 Comp.* and *4 Comp.,* Salimbene's conclusion about his legal knowledge would have more weight. Certainly, Innocent was not a teacher of law. Two other thirteenth-century sources attest to Innocent's legal knowledge, but both are not reliable. Gerlac, the abbot of Mühlhausen, wrote a chronicle which centers on Bohemian affairs, and there is no evidence that he ever traveled outside of Bohemia. He writes: "Vir sicut juvenis et in utroque jure doctissimus." MGH SS XVII: 709. Gerlac ended his portion of the chronicle in ca. 1208 (although it is extant only to 1198) and died sometime before 1228. He may have been retrospectively impressed by Innocent's legislation as Salimbene was. In the *Carmen de Ottonis IV. destitutione,* ed. G. W. Leibniz, *Scriptores rerum Brunsvicensium* (Hannover, 1710), II: 525, the anonymous author as part of an attack on Innocent declared: "Qui decretorum non solum doctus [MS doctor!] es, immo auctor; non solum leges non destruis, immo auges." In context, these lines could be seen as exhortatory rather than descriptive, and they are typical of encomia bestowed on popes. There is no evidence from the rest of the poem that he has personal knowledge of Innocent.

28. Ibid., pp. 75–76.

29. Watt, *Theory of Papal Monarchy,* pp. 34–55 discusses Innocent's seven letters, and also see Maccarrone, *Chiesa e Stato,* who has examined the theological tradition with some care; Kempf, *Papsttum und Kaisertum,* pp. 181–230 has concentrated on the canonists.

30. And most difficult to interpret, see Tierney, *"Tria quippe distinguit,"* pp. 50–51.

31. PL CCXVII: 395. *Sermo Dominica "Laetare"* (Matt. 16:18 and plenitude of power); *Sermo in festo s. Silvestri,* col. 481 (Melchisedech and *regale sacerdotium*); *Sermo in festo d. Gregorii I papae,* col. 516–17 (Matt. 16:18 and *regale sacerdotium*); *Sermo in festo ss. Petri et Pauli,* col. 552–55 (Deut. 17:8 and Matt. 16:18); *Sermo II in consec. pont.,* col. 655–58 (Melchisedech, Matt. 16:18 and Jer. 1:10), *Sermo IV in consec. pont.,* col. 663–66 (Melchisedech), *De sacro altaris mysterio,* col. 778–79 (Matt. 16:18 and plenitude of power). Some of Innocent's most characteristic statements of papal power occur in his decretal letters which are in *Regestum Innocentii III papae super negotio Romani imperii,* ed. F. Kempf (Rome, 1947).

32. St. Bernard used Melchisedech to symbolize the pope's priestly office in *De consideratione (Sancti Bernardi Opera,* ed. J. Leclercq [Rome, 1963], III: 423), but Innocent was the first, so far as I know, to connect Melchisedech with the pope's royal powers. See Walter Ullmann, *Growth of Papal Government in the Middle Ages,* 2nd ed. (London, 1962), p. 444; Maccarrone, *Chiesa e Stato,* pp. 48–50; Buisson, "Exemples et Tradition," pp. 130–31. For further literature on the use of Melchisedech, see Michael Wilks, *The Problem of Sovereignty in the Later Middle Ages* (Cambridge, 1964), p. 258, n.2. As Watt observes, Innocent was the first pope to interject arguments drawn from the Old Testament into canonistic thought, *Theory of Papal Monarchy,* pp. 44–45, and Melchisedech is Innocent's most striking Old Testament figure.

33. Celestine III, Innocent's predecessor, had cited Jer. 1:10: see Yves M.–J. Congar, *"Ecce constitui te super gentes et regna* (Jer. 1:10) 'in Geschichte und Gegenwart,' " *Theologie in Geschichte und Gegenwart* (Munich, 1957), pp. 671–96 at pp. 681–82.

34. Even so, we cannot be sure that Innocent had a hand in drafting *Per venerabilem,* for stylistic arguments are obviously subjective. I think, though, that the decretal is probably Innocent's "own" product, and I will follow this assumption for the rest of the paper.

35. The text of *Per venerabilem* can be found in X 4.17.13, and in Innocent's registers, PL CCXIV: 1130–34.

36. Innocent IV, *Commentaria* (Frankfurt, 1570), fol. 481r. X 4.17.13 s.v. *habeat potestatem.* "Allegando loquitur," which might be translated as "he argued the count's case" (perhaps summarizing the arguments presented to the court by the count's advocates).

37. X 4.17.13: "Quod autem super hoc apostolica sedes plenam habeat potestatem, ex illo videtur, quod, diversis causis inspectis, cum quibusdam minus legitime genitis, non naturalibus tantum, sed adulterinis etiam dispensavit sic ad actus spirtuales illos legitimans ut possint in episcopis promoveri. Ex quo verisimilius creditur et probabilius reputatur, ut eos ad actus legitimare valeat saeculares, praesertim si praeter Romanos Pontifices inter homines superiorem alium non cognoscant, qui legitimandi habeat potestatem; quia cum maior in spirtualibus tam providentia quam auctoritas et idoneitas requiratur, quod in maiori conceditur licitum esse videtur et in minori." Watt, *Theory of Papal Monarchy,* p. 129, n. 49. The maxim is found in *Dig.* 50.27.110 and a similar rule was included among the rules of law in Boniface VIII's *Sext.* 5.13.53.

38. The canonists immediately saw that *ratio peccati* in *Novit* (X 2.1.13) not only was the fundamental argument in the decretal, but theoretically had no limitations, e.g. Johannes Teutonicus to *4 Comp.* 2.2.2 (X 5.40.26) s.v. *que ratione,* Padua, Bibl. Ant. MS N.35, fol. 257v: "Sed dici potest quod omnes cause indirecte spectant ad ecclesiam, ut supra eodem, Novit, lib. iii." The canonists saw no such argument in *Per venerabilem* based on the Roman law maxim. The canonical *locus classicus* for the maxim *In eo* was X 3.30.27. Yet no canonist that I know of cited *Per venerabilem* as an example of this maxim when he glossed this decretal until Hostiensis, who changed the interpretation of the decretal so as to make Innocent's use of the maxim valid.

39. X 4.17.13: "Per simile quoque id videtur posse probari, cum eo ipso, quod aliquis ad apicem episcopalis dignitatis attollitur, eximitur a patria potestate. Praeterea etiamsi simplex

episcopus scienter servum alterius in presbyterum ordinaret, licet ordinator satsifacere domino iuxta formam canonicam teneretur, ordinatus tamen iugum evaderet servitutis."

40. Innocent IV, *Commentaria,* fol. 481r: "Nam legitimatus ab uno principe, vel civitate, vel primate, non obtinebit ab intestato bona hereditaria in terra, quae non sit subdita legitimanti, quia sic auferuntur bona consanguineis defuncti, vel fisco qui debet succedere ab intestato." The principle which Innocent states here is that the pope may legitimize a person in the secular sphere as long as he does not prejudice another's rights.

41. Both Vincentius Hispanus and Johannes Teutonicus wrote: "Tamen per hoc non probatur quod papa habeat iurisdictionem in temporalibus, nam legitimare spectat ad voluntariam jurisdictionem, ut ff. de offit. procon. l.ii."—s.v. *potestatem, 3 Comp.* 4.12.2 (X 4.17.13), St. Gall MS 697, fol. 119v, Admont MS 22, fol. 224v. Innocent IV, *Commentaria,* fol. 481r: "Sed contra utramque opinionem videtur, quia non habet iurisdictionem contentiosam in temporalibus, supra de appell. Si duobus, sed dic licet non habeat iurisdictionem contentiosam, tamen voluntariam exercere potest, ff. de offit. procon. 1.2."

42. Watt, *Theory of Papal Monarchy,* pp. 108–17, discusses Hostiensis's gloss on *Per venerabilem.*

43. X 4.17.13: "Tu autem nosceris aliis subiacere, unde sine ipsorum forsan iniuria, nisi praestarent assensum nobis, in hoc subdere te non posses, nec eius auctoritatis exsistis, ut dispensandi super his habeas facultatem." Kempf thoroughly discusses the relationship of *Per venerabilem* to the letter with which Innocent legitimized Philip II's children, *Apostolica sedes.* See *Papsttum und Kaisertum,* pp. 256–58.

44. X 4.17.13: "Rationibus igitur inducti, regi gratiam fecimus requisti, causam tam ex veteri quam ex novo testamento trahentes, quod non solum in ecclesiae patrimonio, super quo plenam in temporalibus gerimus potestatem, verum etiam in aliis regionibus, certis causis inspectis, temporalem iurisdictionem casualiter exercemus."

45. Melchisedech occurs in Gen. 14:18. "At vero Melchisedech rex Salem, proferens panem et vinum, erat enim sacerdos Dei altissimi, benedixit ei, et ait: Benedictus Abram Deo excelso qui creavit caelum et terram; et benedictus Deus excelsus, quo protegente, hostes in manibus tuis sunt. Et dedit ei decimas ex omnibus." Melchisedech reappears in the Old and New Testaments as a symbol of priesthood: Ps. 109:4. "Tu es sacerdos in aeternum secundum ordinem Melchisedech." Heb. 5:6, 5:10, 7:11, 7:15, 7:17 also contain references to Melchisedech. Peter Comestor, *Historia scholastica,* PL CXCVIII: 1094, states: "Hunc Melchisedech aiunt Hebraei fuisse Sem filium Noe et vixisse usque ad Isaac, et omnes primogenitos, a Noe ad Aaron, sacerdotes fuisse."

46. E.g. Ordinary Gloss, PL CXIII: 120. "Quia autem ait: Tu es sacerdos in aeternum secundum ordinem Melchisedech, ministerium nostrum veri ordinis signatur, non per Aaron irrationalibus victimis immolandis, sed oblato pane et vino, idest, corpore Domini et sanguine consecrari."

47. See n. 32.

48. On the royalty of Christ in this period, see F. Quarta, "Regalità di Cristo e del Papa in Innocenzo III," *Angelicum* XIX (1942), 227–88; J. Leclercq, *L'idée de la royauté du Christ au moyen âge* (Paris, 1959). The royalty of the priesthood was first described in the New Testament at 1 Peter 2:9 as "regale sacerdotium," see G. Martini, *"Regale sacerdotium,"* *Archivio della Società Romana di Storia Patria* IV (1938), 1–166.

49. PL CCXV: 767. "Licet pontificalis auctoritas et imperialis potestas diversae sint dignitates, et officia regni et sacerdotii sint distincta, quia tamen Romanus Pontifex illius agit vices in terris qui est rex regum et dominus dominantium, sacerdos in aeternum secundum ordinem Melchisedech, non solum in spiritualibus habet summam, verum etiam in temporalibus magnam ab ipso Domino potestatem." See Maccarrone, *Chiesa e Stato,* p. 48. Innocent also graphically described the papal office as encompassing both royal and spiritual power—power which was prefigured by Melchisedech—in his sermon for the feast day of St. Silvester (PL CCXVII: 481): "Fuit ergo B. Silvester sacerdos, non solum magnus, sed maximus, pontificali et regali potestate sublimis. Illius quidem vicarius, qui est 'Rex regum, et Dominus dominantium,' (Apoc. 19) 'Sacerdos in aeternum, secundum ordinem Mel-

chisedech,' (Psalm 109) ut spiritualiter possit intelligi dictum ad ipsum et successores illius, quod ait beatus Petrus apostolus, primus et praecipuus praedecessor ipsorum: 'Vos estis genus electum, regale sacerdotium.' (1 Peter 2) Hos enim elegit Dominus, ut essent sacerdotes et reges. . . . Ex auctoritate pontificali constituit patriarchas, primates, metropolitanos et praesules; ex potestate vero regali, senatores, praefectos, judices et tabelliones instituit." Innocent did not claim that the pope could exercise temporal power everywhere without limitation, but that the pope exercised temporal power as a part of the papal office. Although the office of priest and king was normally separate, the papal office was an exception to this rule. James Powell has pointed out to me that Pope Honorius III carefully avoided Innocent's exaltation of the royal character of papal authority in his sermon for the same day. In striking contrast to Innocent, Honorius followed the form of Innocent's sermon and cited the same biblical texts, but emphasized spiritual and sacerdotal interpretations of the texts. See C. A. Horoy, *Opera omnia Honorii tertii*, 5 vols. (Paris, 1879–82), II: 94–106.

50. Maccarrone, Ullmann and Tillmann have noted that Innocent borrowed much of his phraseology from St. Bernard of Clairvaux. Can we see the origins of "certis causis inspectis" in a letter of Bernard? PL CLXXXII: 119: "Mihi propositum est nequaquam egredi de monasterio nisi certis ex causis."

51. PL CCXVII: 606: "Primo ad ostendendam duorum testamentorum concordiam, sicut enim veteri testamento unus fuit legislator . . . ita et in novo testamento unus fuit legis dator, videlicet Christus." See Beryl Smalley, *The Study of the Bible in the Middle Ages*, 2nd ed. (Notre Dame, 1964), pp. 214–63 and Henri de Lubac, *Exégèse médiévale: Les quatre Sens de l'Écriture* (Paris, 1959–64), I: 305–63, and II: 437–558.

52. "Ein Pamphlet der päpstlichen Kurie gegen Kaiser Friedrich II. von 1245/46 (Eger cui lenia)," *Deutsches Archiv* XXIII (1967), pp. 468–538. See also the recent article of C. Dolcini, "*Eger cui lenia* (1245/46): Innocenzo IV, Tolomeo da Lucca e Guglielmo d'Ockham," *Rivista di Storia della Chiesa in Italia* XXIX (1975), 127–48.

53. For a discussion of Matt. 16:18 in later thought, see Wilks, *Problem of Sovereignty*, pp. 530–7.

54. *Marsilius of Padua. The Defender of the Peace*, tr. A. Gewirth (New York, 1956), pp. 392–93. Although Melchisedech was not a cornerstone for later hierocratic thought, both St. Thomas Aquinas and St. Bonaventure connected the papal office with Melchisedech, see Maccarrone, *Vicarius Christi: Storia del Titolo papale* (Rome, 1962), pp. 135–40. Much later the imagery was incorporated into the conciliar canons of Trent and Vatican I.

55. PL CXIII: 469: "Sacerdotes ecclesie Dei instruit ut judicia ecclesiastica secundum potestatem sibi a Deo datam reverenter agant."

56. X 4.17.13: "Is vero super eos sacerdos sive iudex exsistit, cui Dominus inquit in Petro, 'Quodcumque ligaveris super terram, erit ligatum et in coelis, et quodcumque solveris super terram erit solutum et in coelis,' eius vicarius, qui est sacerdos in aeternum secundum ordinem Melchisedech, constitutus a Deo iudex vivorum et mortuorum." Innocent then described the three types of judgment: "Tria quippe distinguit iudicia: Primum inter sanguinem et sanguinem, per quod criminale intelligitur et civile; ultimum inter lepram et lepram, per quod ecclesiasticum et criminale notatur; medium inter causam et causam, quod ad utramque refertur, tam ecclesiasticum quam civile, in quibus cum aliquid fuerit difficile, vel ambiguum, ad iudicium est sedis apostolicae recurrendum."

57. In Anselm of Lucca, *Collectio canonum, una cum collectione minore*, ed. F. Thaner (Innsbruck, 1906–15), I: 75, under the rubric "Vt difficiliora iudicia ad sacerdotes deferantur," and in *Diversorum patrum sententie sive Collectio in LXXIV titulos digesta*, ed. J. Gilchrist, Monumenta iuris canonici, Series B: Vol. I (Vatican City, 1973), p. 19, under the title "De primatu Romane ecclesie," and the *Collection in Three Books*, Pistoia, Archivio capitolare, MS 135, fol. 8r under the title "De primatu Romane ecclesie (c. 1)." It is unlikely that Innocent used one of these collections.

58. PL CXIII: 470. "Christi qui est sacerdos in aeternum secundum ordinem Melchisedech, qui vicarios sibi substituit, quibus ait: Qui vos audit, me audit, qui vos spernit, me spernit."

59. On Moses, see Wilks, *Problem of Sovereignty*, pp. 539–41.

60. PL CXIII: 451. "Majora quaeque et difficilia discernere et judicare debet [sic] majores, parva et facilia minores." Peter the Chanter, *Verbum abbreviatum*, PL CCV: 86.

61. *Libri de iudiciorum ordine*, ed. F. C. Bergmann (Göttingen, 1842; r.p. Aalen, 1965), p. 136: "Et quidem causarum alia est criminalis, alia civilis, alia spiritualis, alia mixta."

62. Ibid.: "Si autem causa est civilis, puta de aliqua pecunia."

63. E.g. Johannes Teutonicus to 3 *Comp.* 4.12.2 (X 4.17.13) s.v. *civile.* Admont MS 22, fol. 225r. "Seculare." Tierney, *"Tria quippe distinguit,"* p. 54 n. 18 first pointed out the difficulty of "civile" in *Per venerabilem.*

64. X 4.17.13: "Paulus etiam, ut plenitudinem potestatis exponeret, ad Corinthios scribens ait: Nescitis, quoniam angelos iudicabitis, quanto magis saecularia?"

65. Pope Gregory VII used 1 Cor. 6:3 to justify his actions to Hermann of Metz, cf. Watt, *Theory of Papal Monarchy*, pp. 26, 38, 57–58.

66. Ordinary Gloss, PL CXIV: 528 s.v. *saecularia:* "Quia dixerat Apostolus eos posse de minimis judicare, determinat, qui ad huiusmodi negotia definienda sint constituendi, scilicet contemptibles qui sunt in ecclesia. Maiores enim spiritualibus intendere debent." Also Peter Lombard, PL CXCIX: 1576–77.

67. For the use of 1 Cor. 6:3 by later writers see Wilks, *Problem of Sovereignty*, p. 265, and the pope judging angels see Maccarrone, *Vicarius Christi*, pp. 266–67 et passim.

68. Maccarrone, *Vicarius Christi*, pp. 104–24 et passim.

69. Alfons Stickler, "Alanus Anglicus als Verteidiger des monarchischen Papsttums," *Salesianum* XXI (1959), pp. 346–406 at pp. 361–63.

70. Hostiensis, *Commentaria* (Venice, 1581), II: 39r, X 4.17.13 s.v. *quod non solum:* "Vt T. et Vin. dixerunt etiam postquam viderunt haec verba. Sed salva reverentia tantorum virorum, puto quod nimis (text: minus) perfunctorie transierunt, unde et super his verbis nihil, aut modicum glossaverunt ipsi vel alii, nescio si causa fuerit. Quia forsitan nimis duri erant in opinionibus suis, vel quia, sicut quidam sensuales dicunt, quando ad talia veniunt, de Deo loquitur, palea est plana sunt omnia, non tamen sunt multum curanda, attamen ad minus nimis presumptuosum est in tali casu maxime glossam facere contra textum, et recalcitrare tantae imperio potestatis, ut patet infra de excess. prelat. Tanta est clavis." I do not understand the text from "sicut quidam" to "plana sunt omnia," but have not been able to compare the text with any manuscript.

71. Ibid., s.v. *patrimonio:* "Illos solum de patrimonio suo legitimare protest, ut dictum est, secundum B. supra eodem i versic, finali. Ecce bona glossa quae dicit quod illos solum et textus dicit quod non illos solum."

72. On contemporary biblical exegetical techniques, see Lubac, *Exégèse médiévale*, II: 437–558, and Marjorie Reeves, *The Influence of Prophecy in the later Middle Ages: A Study in Joachimism* (Oxford, 1969).

73. For a list of texts in which Innocent III cited Jer. 1:10, see Congar, *"Ecce constitui te,"* pp. 680–81.

"Only the Truth Has Authority": The Problem of "Reception" in the Decretists and in Johannes de Turrecremata

BRIAN TIERNEY

William of Ockham, in the introduction to his *Dialogus,* suggested that his readers should consider not *who* expressed a particular opinion but *what* opinion was expressed ("non quis est alicuius sententiae auctor, sed quid dicitur attendentes.")[1] Ockham thought that theologians ought to decide disputed questions concerning the faith by right reason applied to Scripture. Christians could know that the truth of a doctrine was definitively established when it was accepted by the church without any dissent. (Ockham held that one single dissenter might maintain the true faith against all other members of the church.) Ulrich Bubenheimer has called this approach to truth and authority an "Ekklesiologie der Sachautorität"—an ecclesiology based on the internal authority of the fact itself rather than on the external authority of a defining institution.[2] Yves Congar, in a far-ranging article on reception of doctrine by the church expressed the same idea in the words, "Au fond, dans le domaine doctrinal, seule la vérité a autorité."[3]

Modern scholars have noted that this way of thinking occurs quite frequently in late medieval ecclesiology. The great canonist Panormitanus usually supported the conciliar position in the fifteenth-century disputes over the constitution of the church, but on one occasion he wrote that the opinion of a single private individual was to be preferred to that of either a pope or a council if the individual was "moved by better reasons from the Old or New Testament." Knut Nörr described this argument as a "foreign body" in Panormitanus's juridical thought. He discerned in it an attack on the whole institutional structure of the medieval church and an anticipation of Luther's ecclesiology.[4] Remigius Bäumer, on the other hand, has pointed out that Panormitanus's argument, slightly modified, enjoyed a certain popularity among the extreme papalists of the fifteenth century—for, if one single individual could be right and a whole council wrong, then that one single individual might well be the pope.[5]

The most interesting late-medieval variation of Panormitanus's argument was presented by the eminent theologian, Johannes de Turrecremata. Although he was a staunch papalist, Turrecremata conceded that the members of a council should normally be regarded as of greater authority than the pope in deciding a disputed question of faith. This was because the council could normally be assumed to possess a greater capacity for discerning the truth, a greater "reason." But Turrecremata also argued that in exceptional cases a single individual, the pope, might have greater reason on his side and that then the pope's opinion was to be accepted by the church. This seems like a pure "Ekklesiologie der Sachautorität." Remigius Bäumer found it "astonishing" that Turrecremata should have put forth such an argument and Ulrich Horst, in discussing the same point, also referred to Turrecremata's "erstaunlicher Weitherzigkeit."[6]

The position does indeed seem paradoxical. Turrecremata was a conservative defender of the visible institutions of the church. Ockham is usually considered a radical critic of them. Yet apparently Turrecremata argued, just like Ockham, that in receiving a given doctrine as true, the church ought to consider the content of the doctrine rather than the source of the definition. The paradox is partly resolved in Congar's article. Congar pointed out that reception based on the substantive content of a doctrine was a normal mode of establishing authority during the first thousand years of the church's history. Evidently then we are not dealing merely with a late-medieval aberration when we find a similar idea in either Ockham or Turrecremata. Congar suggested further, however, that this way of thinking fell into the background in the period after the papal reform movement of the eleventh century as the universal church came to be conceived of, not as a community of local churches, but as a single society subjected to a single monarchical authority. Other modern scholars (especially De Luca and Munier whose works are discussed below) have suggested that the earliest commentators on Gratian's *Decretum* turned away from an emphasis on substantive content in determining the validity of church law to an emphasis on the authority of the legislator. Our own purpose, in the following study, is to carry a little further Congar's discussion on truth and reception in the church by exploring the teachings of the medieval decretists in this area.[7] We wish to argue especially that the position of Turrecremata outlined above was no eccentricity in his thought but rather an intrinsic part of his whole system of ecclesiology, a system that gave great emphasis to the substantive content of a pronouncement and its reception by the church as decisive criteria for determining the validity of church law and church doctrine. Further we would maintain that, in this respect, Turrecremata did not depart from the central canonical tradition of the church as it had been expounded earlier by the decretist commentators of the twelfth and thirteenth centuries. We might quote as an introductory comment (and as a counterpart to the words of Ockham given above) some phrases from the thirteenth-century *Glossa ordinaria* to the *Decretum*. "We are to consider not who speaks but what is said as at D.19 c. *Secundum* . . . the truth is always to be preferred whoever expresses it . . . reason is equivalent to canon law."[8]

Stephan Kuttner has written finely on the tensions in the life of the church which are necessarily reflected in the church's law, and on the canonists' ways of resolving those tensions. "Only he who is blind to the mystery of the church could find that the bond of law and the bond of love are mutually exclusive." It is another tension that we have to consider, not one between law and love but between law and truth. This too arises out of the intrinsic nature of the church as the canonists perceived it, "a social body which is also the mystical body of Christ . . . a supernatural mystery which manifests itself in the structural forms of social life."[9] As lawyers, the canonists were concerned to define a structure of institutions whose laws and teachings could bind the faithful together into an ordered community. As Christians they knew that no law or teaching could bind the faithful if its content was repugnant to Christian truth. They were certain that the church as a whole could never err from the true faith. But, since the rulers of the church were human and prone to error, a possibility existed that a licit authority might promulgate a ruling that was unacceptable because of its inherent content. It was the canonists' constant awareness of this situation that led to their continuing concern over our problem of truth and reception. Not every truth of faith and morals needed to be defined authoritatively by the church; but, especially when disputes arose, some of them had to be so defined in order to maintain the integrity of the church as a community. A doctrine could thus be true but not authoritatively defined, as the author of the *Summa Induent sancti* observed in discussing the teachings of the church fathers, "Although the things they say are true, still they are not 'authentic' unless confirmed by the supreme pontiff." On the other hand, a pronouncement that was authentic in the sense of being promulgated by a duly constituted public authority (even a supreme pontiff) could not have enduring force if its content was inherently false. Such a statement could not be received; it would have to be repudiated. Thus one canonist wrote of Pope Anastasius II who, allegedly, was rejected by his clergy and condemned by his successor for having favored the Acacian heresy, "Here the pope defended Acacius and so was convicted of erring himself . . . I think nevertheless that at the time of Anastasius this decretal was 'authentic', but his successor presumed him a heretic . . . and judged his letter iniquitous." Another writer suggested that Anastasius' doctrine was rejected because it was not "received" by a council.[10]

For the canonists then, reception was an important criterion of the validity of law. Much of their discussion on this point is found in comments on D.15–D.20 of the *Decretum* where Gratian discussed the sources of canon law. The *Glossa ordinaria* accurately described Gratian's intention in a summarizing comment at D.15 *ante* c.1. "So far the Master has discussed natural law. Now he begins to discuss canon law . . . and he shows which works are received by the church and which are not." For the decretists the structure of law actually in force, the law that guided the life of the church, was precisely the law that the church had chosen to "receive." This was true even of the legislation of general councils, the highest "instance" of ecclesiastical authority known to the decretists. At D.15 c.2 Gratian presented a very influential text of Gregory I. "I receive and venerate four councils like the four gospels." Gregory gave two reasons why he received these particular councils (Nicaea, Ephesus I, Constantinople I, and Chalcedon). Firstly, they provided a firm foundation of faith and right norms of living for the church. Secondly, their decrees were established "by universal consent."[11] The decretists used similar criteria in evaluating other councils. They taught that a general council consisted of a pope "with all the bishops"[12] but they did not assert that an assembly could be known as a general council, whose definitions were permanently binding on the church, simply from the composition of its membership or from the formal mode of its convocation. The actual content of the council's legislation was also important. The decretists knew that an assembly which seemed to have the external characteristics of a true council might err in its pronouncements on the faith. The councils of Ephesus II and Rimini were known to have erred.[13] (These same two assemblies were often cited as examples of erring councils by the anti-conciliarists of the fifteenth century.) The legislation of such councils was not "received."

This was pointed out explicitly in another text included in D.15. After quoting the words of Gregory the Great, Gratian presented a letter attributed to Pope Gelasius which set out in detail the authorities received by the church. "After the writings of the Old and New Testaments which we regularly receive, the holy Roman church also does not forbid the following to be received." There followed a list of the first four general councils as given in the preceding chapter. Other councils celebrated by the holy fathers were to be received after these four. The argument continued: "And now there is set out below which books of the holy fathers are received in the Catholic church." After a long list of orthodox writings of the fathers the author continued, "For the rest, the Catholic and apostolic Roman church in no wise receives things written by heretics." The ensuing list of condemned writings began with the decrees of the Council of Rimini (which had approved a version of the Arian heresy in 359), and continued with numerous apocryphal works falsely attributed to apostles or church fathers.[14] Throughout the letter of "Gelasius" the essential criterion for determining which writings should be received by the church was their intrinsic orthodoxy—whether they proceeded from orthodox fathers or from heretics.

The problem of apocryphal writings was explored further in D.16 in connection with the so-called "canons of the apostles." One text declared that this collection possessed no canonical authority because it was composed "by heretics under the name of the apostles"; but another text held that the collection was authoritative since it was "received by many" and confirmed by a council. Other texts of this *Distinctio* repeatedly stressed the importance of reception in determining the validity of a disputed authority. Johannes Teutonicus observed that Gratian had presented a contradiction here but had not resolved it. The solution, Johannes suggested, was simple. "The canons put forth by true apostles are to be received, but not those put forth by pseudo-apostles."[15] But the author of the *Summa Animal est substantia* distin-

guished more carefully. Some writings were called apocryphal because the
author was unknown although the writings were certainly true. Such works
could properly be received by the church. Other writings were called
apocryphal because there was doubt concerning both their authorship and
their truth. Such writings were not received. Here again reception depended
on the intrinsic truth of the doctrine involved, not solely on the reputation of
the author.[16] The problem was complicated by the fact that different
chapters of D.16 mentioned different numbers of genuine "canons of the
apostles." There were fifty, sixty, or eighty-five genuine canons according to
c.3, c.2, and c.4 respectively. It could be argued that thirty-five of the
original eighty-five canons had fallen into disuse. Alternatively, by invoking
a process that might be called "progressive reception" a canonist could argue
that the church, faced with a mixture of genuine and apocryphal canons had
accepted first fifty, then sixty, then eighty-five of them as genuine.[17]

Similar problems arose when Gratian discussed the authority of papal decretals. The question was first mentioned in D.12, which was devoted primarily to the authority of licit customs, especially those approved by the
Roman See. The key text seems clear enough, "Quae a sancta Romana ecclesia et apostolica authoritate iussa sunt salutifere impleantur." But Huguccio discerned an ambiguity. The text might mean that commands which
were not "healthful" were not to be obeyed. (Huguccio's text was incorporated into Guido de Baysio's *Rosarium* and copied out almost word for
word in William of Ockham's *Breviloquium*.)[18] Gratian's principal treatment
of papal decretals came at D.19. Again the initial affirmations seem clear
enough. "We have shown that Leo and Gelasius commanded . . . that all
the decretals of our predecessors . . . are to be respectfully received and
held." "All the sanctions of the apostolic see are to be received as if confirmed
by the divine voice of Peter."[19] But then at D.19 c.6 a text of Augustine introduced a new theme. After observing that the letters of the apostolic see
were included among the canonical writings of the church, Augustine wrote,
"The enquirer should follow this method with canonical writings, namely
that he should prefer those that are received by all the churches to those that
some do not receive."[20] Among those that were not received by all the
churches the enquirer was to prefer those that were received by more numerous and more important ("graviores") churches. If one writing was
received by a greater number of churches, another by the more important
churches they were to be regarded as of equal authority. (On this Huguccio
commented tersely, "I understand this to be true if they are supported by
equal reason, otherwise not."[21]) Augustine's text introduced a considerable
complication into the argument. At first we are told that decretals must be
received by all the churches because of the intrinsic authority of the apostolic
see. Then we are told that the authority of the decretals is to be measured by
the extent to which the churches receive them.

Gratian compounded the difficulty by citing next the case of Anastasius
II, the pope who allegedly erred in faith in his letter to the heretic Acacius.

This letter, Gratian wrote, was issued "illicitly and not canonically" and so it was "repudiated" by the Roman church. The case of Anastasius gave rise to a great body of comment among the canonists concerning the problems of dealing with a heretical pope. The canonistic arguments on this point have been adequately discussed in modern works on medieval ecclesiology and we need not pursue them here.[22] It will suffice to quote Johannes Faventinus who closely paraphrased the words of Gratian himself and expressed the common opinion of the decretists, "Decretal letters . . . are to be observed devotedly unless they are found to differ from the precepts of the Gospel or the decrees of the holy fathers, like the letter of Anastasius."[23] Here again it was not only *who* said a thing but *what* he said that counted for the canonists. We shall next consider how this preoccupation influenced the decretists' treatment of certain problems (which would assume a major importance in fifteenth-century ecclesiology) concerning conflict of laws.

When the issues of "Sachautorität"—the authority of the truth itself—arose in fifteenth-century ecclesiology it was usually in connection with three problems, all of which were considered in detail by Johannes de Turrecremata. The problems can be posed thus: which authority was to be received (1) if a pope disagreed with all the fathers of a council? (2) if a church father disagreed with a pope or a council? (3) if two general councils disagreed with one another? We can best explain further the decretist background of Turrecremata's thought by considering some earlier treatments of these same questions.

The first question arose early in the *Decretum* at D.4 *post* c.3 which posed the general problem of reception of laws. Here Gratian wrote, "Laws are instituted when they are promulgated; they are confirmed when they are approved by the practice of those using them." And the *Glossa ordinaria* raised the further question whether a papal decree was to be accepted when all the bishops were opposed to it. Luigi de Luca devoted a lengthy article to the doctrines of reception elaborated by the decretists in commenting on Gratian's words.[24] He concluded that Gratian himself did not intend to propound a doctrine of popular sovereignty (as some later commentators suggested). Rather Gratian was adhering to an older way of thought, common among the church fathers, which saw law as a norm of conduct rather than as the command of a sovereign legislator and which judged the validity of law according to its objective content. De Luca did not, however, choose to investigate in any detail the persistence of this older idea in the numerous canonistic commentaries that he explored. Instead he concentrated on the canonists' treatment of legislation in its formal aspect, dealing with the problems of *consuetudo contra legem* and *approbatio utentium* primarily by dicussing the canonists' views on the respective législative authorities of the ruler and the people. Although De Luca no doubt did not intend this, his article could give the impression that, while Gratian still adhered to a patristic mode of thought which emphasized the objective content of law, his commentators were interested primarily in the formal aspects of legislative sovereignty. But this is not in fact the case. Gratian was interested in both the authority of the legislator and the substantive content of law. So were the twelfth-century decretists. So too were the fifteenth-century commentators on the *Decretum*.

It would be superfluous to explore once again in the present context all the well-known body of canonistic argumentation based on Gratian's assertion that a human law contrary to natural law was "vain and void."[25] But we may note that, just before introducing his doctrine of reception, Gratian set out at D.4 c.2 (a text of Pseudo-Isidore) the substantive qualities that a law had to possess in order to be valid (including the provision that the law had to be "secundum naturam"). The great majority of decretist commentators accordingly presented observations on the substantive content of valid law at D.4 c.2 and then turned to the formal criteria of validity in comments on D.4 *post* c.3, where they discussed the relative authorities of "princeps" and "populus." But the two areas could not be separated completely. Canonists who supported the authority of a *consuetudo contra legem* acknowledged that the *consuetudo* had to be "rationabilis" (following the definitions given by Gratian).[26] Occasionally, moreover, a concern for the substantive content of law was expressed precisely in connection with the problem of reception and the related problem of possible conflict between pope and bishops raised at D.4 *post* c.3.[27] De Luca, for instance, printed in rather fragmentary form some remarks of Huguccio on this dictum. But if more of the context of Huguccio's comment is restored a different area of interest becomes apparent. (We have added the italics in the following passage.)

> Certain canons cannot be abrogated by the pope as for instance those promulgated *concerning the faith and the general state of the church* . . . But cannot the clergy or people be compelled to carry out what the pope or prince wills since the pope has plenitude of power and all power is conferred on the prince? I believe that it can [be compelled] *if it wishes to deviate from reason or faith* . . . otherwise it ought not to be. Again, can the pope establish anything without or against the will of his cardinals . . .? He may do so *provided it is not contrary to reason or to the Old or New Testament.* But whatever is said, if they [i.e. pope or emperor] establish anything *that is just* it is valid and others are bound to obey.[28]

Evidently, in considering whether a law was to be received by the church, Huguccio was just as interested in the content of the law as in the authority of the legislator. (In the present discussion we have emphasized the views of Huguccio because they exercised a particular influence on the work of Turrecremata.)

The decretists also raised the problem of possible conflict between a pope and the members of a council in their intricate discussions on the problem of a heretical pope. They reached no agreement on the point. Some favored the pope, some the fathers of a council. Alanus suggested that the council fathers should be followed in matters of faith, the pope in all other matters.[29] But, again, the most relevant comment from our point of view was one of Huguccio's. Huguccio consistently maintained that, where a real doubt existed, the opinion of the pope was to be preferred; but he also made it clear that the issue could not be settled simply by weighing the authority of the pope against that of the council fathers. If the opinion of either was clearly iniquitous, then the opinion of the other was to be accepted.

> But see, a council is gathered together from the whole world; a doubt arises; the pope alone renders one decision, all the others another: which is to be preferred to the other? It is argued here that the pope is. But I distinguish and I say that if either contains iniquity it is to be rejected. But if neither contains iniquity and it is doubtful which contains the truth they may be considered equal and both held and one or the other can be chosen at will, for they are of equal authority, since on the one side is greater authority and on the other greater numbers as at D.19, *In canonicis* (c.6).[30]

Huguccio added that the pope was to be obeyed if he commanded that his decision be accepted in a matter of faith (provided of course that the decision did not contain "iniquity.") Much of his gloss was copied verbatim into Johannes de Turrecremata's commentary on the *Decretum*. Elsewhere Huguccio considered the relative authority of conciliar canons and papal decretals and wrote succinctly "If either has established anything contrary to reason the other derogates from it."[31] The idea that in case of conflict between pope and council the more "reasonable" view was to be preferred, which recurs in the fifteenth-century sources, had already been clearly expressed by the end of the twelfth century.

After discussing the authority of councils and of papal decretals, Gratian ended his review of the sources of canon law by considering the authority of the church fathers. Charles Munier discussed the whole canonistic hierarchy of laws in commenting on Gratian's treatment of this point,[32] and it will be convenient for us to consider here, in connection with Gratian's doctrine and Munier's treatment of it, the two further problems that arose in fifteenth-century ecclesiology—conflict between a church father and a pope or council, and conflict between two general councils.

Gratian began his discussion of the first problem by stating that anyone's words would seem to have greater authority the more they were supported by reason, "Quo enim quisque magis ratione nititur, eo maioris auctoritatis eius verba esse videntur." But, he continued, many church fathers such as Jerome and Augustine, "more filled with the grace of the Holy Spirit" showed more wisdom and adhered more to reason in expounding the Scriptures than some popes. It seemed therefore that the *dicta* of the fathers should be preferred to the decrees of such popes as canonical authorities. But then Gratian introduced a crucial distinction. "It is one thing to decide legal cases, another to expound the sacred Scriptures diligently. In settling legal affairs not only knowledge is required but also power." Peter, he continued, had received two keys from Christ, both a "key of knowledge" and a "key of power." This led Gratian to the conclusion that, "In expositions of sacred Scripture they [the church fathers] are to be preferred to the pontiffs; in deciding cases they deserve to be placed after them."[33]

The decretist discussion of Gratian's *dictum* led on to a clear distinction between the authority of private doctors, which was derived from their own expertise, and the authority of prelates with power to judge cases, which was derived from their holding public office in the church. A canonist of the Anglo-Norman school put the point crisply, "Peritissimi nisi habeant potestatem causas decidere non possunt."[34] This principle was generally accepted, but it raised further problems. The difficulty in the simple statement of the Anglo-Norman canonist was that figures like Jerome and Augustine were not just private doctors. They were teachers "filled with the Holy Spirit" whose *dicta* had been accepted as *auctoritates* by the whole church for many centuries. Hence the decretists soon realized that Gratian's rather simple solution—namely that the fathers were greater in "sacrarum scripturarum expositionibus," the popes in "causis diffiniendis"—was not entirely adequate. The two spheres could not be so neatly divided. Often they overlapped. Some sayings of the fathers were accepted as authoritative in canon law. Some judgments of the pope involved the interpretation of disputed texts of Scripture. The decretists often noted that if the pope, in his official capacity as pope, promulgated a decree interpreting some dubious point of faith where Scripture was ambiguous, his decision would normally be preferred in the church courts to a text of Jerome or Augustine.[35]

Charles Munier, in his book on the patristic sources of canon law, especially emphasized this point. Munier saw in Gratian's *dictum* a turning point in the history of canonistic doctrine on the sources of law. Until this time it had been widely assumed that all *auctoritates* received by the church were essentially equal to one another. The task for a commentator was to reconcile apparently divergent texts by deploying the well-known techniques of medieval scholastic argumentation. Gratian himself, Munier noted, adhered for the most part to this method. But in the dictum at D.20 *ante* c.1 he did plainly note that, in church courts, one type of source (papal decretals) took precedence over another type (church fathers). This inspired the decretists to attempt for the first time to arrange all the sources of law in an ordered hierarchy. And, Munier suggested, in doing so they subordinated the writings of the fathers to "properly legislative documents." Already within twenty years of the *Decretum's* appearance, Stephen of Tournai had produced an ordered list of authorities. "This is to be diligently observed in the decision of ecclesiastical cases, that evangelical precepts hold the first place and after them the words of the apostles, then the four councils mentioned above, then other councils, then decrees and decretal letters, and in the last place come the words of the holy fathers Ambrose, Augustine, Jerome and others."[36] Munier argued that, in producing such lists of authorities, the decretists decisively reoriented the treatment of legal sources "toward modern solutions." He was arguing, in effect, that the canonists moved away from the older way of thought, which paid attention primarily to the substantive content of *auctoritates* in seeking to reconcile them, toward a more modern, positivist approach which resolved conflicts of law by constructing a hierarchy of legislative authorities and assigning priority to the law promulgated by the higher authority. If this were true—or, rather, if this were the whole truth—our problem of "truth" and "reception" would have disappeared from canonistic thought.

Munier's approach resembles De Luca's. Each sees the *Decretum* as standing at a mid-point between patristic and modern conceptions of law. But each has chosen to pursue a particular strand of argumentation in isolation from the whole web of canonical jurisprudence into which the individual strands were woven. Hence, although each study is valuable in itself and valid within its limits, either of them, taken in isolation, could give a misleading impression of the development of canonistic ecclesiology from the twelfth century onward. As soon as we begin to examine the network of glosses surrounding Gratian's *dictum* at D.20 *ante* c.1 we find that, for the decretists, there was no simple rule that the validity of a law could be determined merely by referring to the legislative authority of the promulgator. (This is sometimes clear from the texts that Munier himself cites.) The decretists' hierarchies of sources provided only the vaguest of guidelines which proved to be full of anomalies and exceptions whenever difficult cases had to be considered. The anomalies and exceptions are important because, in discussing them, the decretists were led to reaffirm their underlying doctrine that, whatever the legislative source of a pronouncement, the ultimately decisive criteria for determining its validity were its substantive content (its conformity with divine truth) and its reception by the church. If we view the *Decretum* and the works of the decretists not simply as collections of ecclesiastical regulations but as sustained reflections on the nature of authority in the church—and the works of Gratian and his greater commentators deserve to be so considered—this principle will seem at least as important as the more positivist doctrines in their works which were emphasized by De Luca and Munier.

The anomalies that we have mentioned arose for the canonists when they discussed conflicts between different levels of authority in the hierarchy of laws (e.g. when a church father disagreed with a council) and also when they discussed conflicts within each level (e.g. when two general councils conflicted with one another). As for the first class of problems, we may note that the gospels, the apostles, and the councils were all accorded greater authority than the pope in Stephen's list and in other similar ones. Yet in fact the decretists commonly held that the pope could dispense against the gospels in matters of church discipline and sometimes argued that he was greater than the apostles since he succeeded to the office of Peter who was prince of the apostles. But then the decretists also remembered that Peter had erred in faith in the matter of "judaizing" and that Paul had had to rebuke him. They accordingly held that the pope was strictly bound by all the teachings of Scripture including those of "the Apostle" in matters of faith.[37] Similar problems arose in connection with general councils. All the lists of ordered authorities put the general councils before the popes. But the decretists all agreed that the popes could override the positive legislation of general councils either by dispensation or abrogation (except in very grave matters touching the general state of the church). It was just the opposite where matters of faith were concerned. If a pope promulgated a decretal which contradicted the faith already defined in an earlier council, his decretal was to be repudiated (as happened in the case of Anastasius).[38] Thus one cannot say simply that the pope was above or below Scripture, above or below a general council. The decision whether he was or was not depended in each case on the substantive content of a specific papal pronouncement.

Among the possible conflicts between different levels of the hierarchy of laws the case of a conflict between the authority of an individual church father and that of a pope or council has a special significance for our enquiry because it raised the precise point later discussed by Turrecremata—whether the view of a single individual could sometimes be accepted in preference to that of the established legislative organs of the church. Gratian himself noted one striking exception to the general principle that he had formulated in the *dictum* at D.20 *ante* c.1. At C.36 q.2 he produced a whole series of texts attributed to popes and councils which asserted that a rapist could not licitly enter into a marriage with his victim. Specifically, according to Gratian, a council of Meaux and a council of Aachen has forbidden such marriages. Against all these authorities Gratian cited only one contrary opinion, that of Jerome. Then he concluded that Jerome took precedence over all the other authorities since Jerome was "supported by the testimony of divine law."

The decretists often asserted that the Council of Meaux did in fact support Jerome's position, but this conclusion could be reached only by straining the words of the council and in any case it merely opposed one local council to another of equal authority.[39] The fact was that Jerome's view really did find support in Scripture and, moreover, it had been accepted in the common practice of the church. These considerations were enough to outweigh any contrary authority of popes or councils. One glossator wrote that when Jerome contradicted a council or a decretal letter three things were to be considered—equity, the cause of the law, and the custom of the place. If Jerome's view was more consonant with any of these it was to be accepted. In the particular case under discussion Jerome's view prevailed because it was in accordance with the custom of the church.[40] The *Summa Tractaturus magister* observed that the decision of the Council of Aachen opposing Jerome's view was rejected because it was "contrary to the authority of the Old Testament and the church," while Jerome's opinion was accepted because it was supported "by the witness of divine law" (even though his texts normally lacked legislative authority).[41] For Alanus, Jerome's view acquired canonical authority "because of the approbation of the church" (or because the Council of Meaux upheld the same position). He added that, if the force of an authority could be deduced simply from the order in which it was placed in a list of authorities, then Jerome's *dicta* would have to be preferred to papal decretals, for the writings of Jerome were listed before the decretals of the popes at D.15 c.2.[42] On the general principle that papal decretals were to be preferred to the *dicta* of the fathers "in causis diffiniendis," the author of the *Summa*

Animal est substantia observed briefly, "Unless [the fathers] say things more consonant with the Old and New Testaments."[43] But this simple reservation undermines the whole principle of a hierarchy of authorities based essentially on positive legislative power.[44] What really mattered in considering the value of any *auctoritas* was its conformity with scriptural truth. A lengthy gloss by Huguccio drew together all the threads of decretist argumentation on this point.

> *Preponuntur.* So that it is not permitted to supreme pontiffs to recede from [the fathers'] expositions . . . in such matters they are called to a part of the solicitude and not to a plenitude of power . . . and this is an argument that one greater in some thing can be less in another. . . . This is true generally that in the settling of cases the authority of a canon or of a pope is greater than the authority of Augustine and Jerome . . . unless the authority of Augustine . . . should be corroborated and supported by the authority of the Old or New Testament or by a canon or by the general custom of the church; for a council that was celebrated at Aachen declares that a rapist and the woman raped cannot be joined in matrimony . . . yet the authority of Jerome prevails, not of itself but because it is supported by the Old Testament and the Council of Meaux and by the general custom of the church. . . . For the same reason the authority of one father is preferred to that of another.[45]

Huguccio's view that a pope could not depart from the teachings of the fathers was incorporated into the *Rosarium* of Guido de Baysio composed about a century later and was repeated by Aegidius de Bellemera. Eventually it found a place in the ecclesiology of Johannes de Turrecremata. The argument about Jerome was also used by late-medieval writers, including Turrecremata, when they considered the possibility that the opinion of one individual might be preferred to that of a whole council. Huguccio had already made the important point that would be reiterated by fifteenth-century canonists and theologians. It was not the personal authority of Jerome that was important here but the intrinsic truth of the doctrine he stated and its reception by the church.

Let us turn now to the final type of conflict of laws that we need to consider, conflict between two general councils. In discussing Munier's hierarchy of laws we noted that disagreements could arise, not only between different levels of the hierarchy, but also within each level. This was noted already by Huguccio. In the passage just cited he mentioned not only differences between church fathers and councils but also differences among the fathers themselves. His argument continued, "Among the pontiffs one is preferred to another as Peter to Linus, Gelasius to Lucius; and likewise among the fathers Ambrose to Isidore, Augustine to Bede."[46] When conflicts arose between authorities of the same class it was necessary for the canonists to have recourse to such criteria as *scientia, veritas* and *ratio* in determining which should be received by the church.[47]

The most extreme example of such a conflict would arise if two general councils conflicted with one another. The decretists did not doubt that some general councils had to be regarded as more authoritative than others. Thus the author of the *Summa Elegantius* wrote "Among the universal councils eight are preeminent and of these four have superlative authority" and, again, when discussing the hierarchy of laws, "next come the four councils mentioned, after them the other universal councils."[48] The general rule laid down in the *Decretum* was that, in case of conflict between two councils, "the opinion of that council is to be preferred of which the authority is more ancient or more powerful" [antiquior aut potior].[49] But this was rather vague. Stephanus suggested "sapientia" and Rufinus "pietas" as the decisive criterion in weighing the authority of councils.[50] The *Summa Elegantius* commented, "Therefore, among the canons, neither the earlier prevails over the later nor the later over the earlier but the more authoritative and more useful for deciding cases prevails." The author decided, however, that this interpretation had "more words than sense" and continued, "The authority of that council is preferred which is more powerful because more ancient," with specific reference to the eight general councils.[51]

The problem remained of explaining why the "more ancient" councils should be considered "more powerful." There was a conflict here between the Roman law principle that later legislation superseded earlier and the actual words cited by Gratian (which were perhaps reinforced by the general medieval prejudice in favor of "good old law"). Alanus pointed out that canon law differed from civil because the former was based on immutable texts—the gospels, the precepts of the Apostle, and the four councils. He added that "potior" could be taken to mean "benignior" or it could refer to the greater authority of general councils as compared with local ones.[52] Huguccio developed similar arguments at greater length. In general, he wrote, a council of greater "pietas" prevailed. The word "antiquior" meant that if two councils were of equal "pietas," then the more ancient was preferred (unless the more recent one was widely received). Alternatively the word "antiquior" could refer specifically to the first four general councils, which possessed a special dignity and authority. But even they could be modified by later legislation except as regards articles of faith and "general statutes of the church." The early general councils possessed a special authority in matters of faith because such matters were discussed in the early church "more fully" and "more diligently" than in later times.[53]

Johannes Teutonicus also had no simple solution to this problem. He proposed that the "better" council should be preferred, not the more ancient one, and noted that the Council of Ancyra was more ancient than the Council of Nicea but that, nevertheless, Nicea was of greater authority.[54] Commenting specifically on the words "cuius aut antiquior aut potior existat auctoritas," Johannes asked, "Is not rather that opinion to be followed which is of greater 'pietas' . . . ? Because although a canon of the apostles may be more powerful because more ancient than other canons, nevertheless later ones are preferred to it." But this argument applied only when two particular, local councils were compared with one another, he noted. In the case of two general councils the later one was always to be preferred.[55] But

presumably Johannes must have had in mind here only acts of positive legislation.

The decretists' treatment of this whole question seems rather confused.
They do not seem to have analysed the most difficult problem, a conflict
between two general councils in a matter touching the faith or the general
state of the church. They did not always distinguish as clearly as one might
expect between disciplinary and doctrinal decrees, between councils approved by the pope and those not so approved, or even between the authority
of local and general councils. But this last ambiguity was perhaps not due to
mere oversight. The decretists possessed no officially approved list which distinguished all the general councils of the past from all other synods. (It may
be recalled that the author of the *Summa Elegantius* wrote of Gratian's eight
general councils as being "among the universal councils," though without
specifying any others.) We may note at any rate the frequent concern of the
decretists to establish a criterion based on the substantive content of legislation—its "pietas," "sapientia," "benignitas"—in weighing the authority of
two conflicting councils.

Evidently decretist theory on the sources of law was complex. As Congar
wrote, there was "a certain dialectic" involved. In receiving a law the ecclesiastical community had to weigh its objective content (as, for instance, in
accepting Jerome's opinion against that of popes and councils). But, as a
complementary principle, the validity of the objective content seemed established from the fact that a given enactment had been universally received.
Moreover certain sources of law, certain persons or institutions, possessed an
intrinsic right to have their pronouncements received—or at any rate
deferentially considered by the church—because of an authority inhering in
the source itself. The pope was the successor of Peter, bishops in council were
successors of the apostles, the church fathers were "filled with the grace of
the Holy Spirit." Yet still the words of such persons were valued, not simply
on account of some external principle of authority which they embodied, but
because of an underlying presumption that the content of their pronouncements would normally be in accord with divine truth. Popes were said to
legislate "pro catholica fide, pro sanis dogmatibus . . . et fidelium moribus." The four councils were especially venerated because they had so faithfully expounded the truths of Scripture. The writings of the church fathers,
according to Gratian, were informed with "ratio" and "scientia."[56] A final
corollary of all this was that, if the underlying presumption was invalidated,
if any pronouncement from any source failed to conform to the truths of
faith, it was not to be received by the church, however great the prestige of
the promulgating authority.

If we turn now to the later Middle Ages we shall see that this tension
between the authority of the legislator and the role of the church in receiving
or rejecting legislation on the basis of its substantive content persisted in an
extreme form in the ecclesiology of Johannes de Turrecremata.

Johannes de Turrecremata faced a difficult task when he undertook, in the mid-fifteenth century, to defend the unity and authority of the church and the sovereign power of the papacy within it.[57] The Council of Constance had restored unity to the church after a generation of schism. But the claim of Constance, formulated in the decree *Haec sancta,* that a general council was superior to a pope, gave rise to new problems once a universally acknowledged pontiff was elected. Extreme papalists revived old arguments going back to the mendicant disputes of the thirteenth century which asserted that bishops were mere vicars of the pope and that, accordingly, the pope and bishops assembled together in a council possessed no more authority than the pope alone. Extreme conciliarists asserted that sovereign authority inhered in the fathers of a council separated from the pope. All participants in the discussion were aware of Ockham's argument holding that neither pope nor council could adequately represent the church, that pope and council together might err, and that the true faith might survive in a few other Christians or even in one single person. Meanwhile, on different grounds, the Hussite movement was calling into question the authenticity of the whole established structure of church institutions.

Turrecremata was the first major theologian to deny the validity of *Haec sancta,* the crucial decree of the Council of Constance. But, as he moved from mere polemical writings to sustained reflections on the nature and structure of the church, he realized that merely to dispute the claims of Constance was not enough. To provide an adequate defense against them, it was necessary to rethink the whole ecclesiology underlying the conciliar doctrines. Turrecremata was discerning enough to see that this meant reappraising the whole structure of *auctoritates* assembled in Gratian's *Decretum.* All the polemicists in the conciliar disputes of the fifteenth century used selected excerpts from Gratian's work to support their various positions. Turrecremata was the only one who undertook a massive commentary on the whole of the *Decretum.* He was trained as a theologian rather than a canonist and, as he himself wrote, he found the task an arduous one, but he summoned up enough courage and persistence to carry it through to completion.

Turrecremata is usually regarded as an extreme papalist and the reputation is not undeserved. He certainly defended the supremacy of the Roman see staunchly against the attacks of contemporary conciliarists. And he also taught a personal and highly nuanced theory of papal infallibility. This did not, however, exclude the possibility that disputes might arise concerning particular papal decrees. In Turrecremata's theory, as in most theories of papal infallibility, not all teachings of the pope were considered to be defined infallibly. The problem could still arise, therefore, of deciding which particular pronouncements of a pope were to be received by the church.

The problem of reception did not arise for Turrecremata because of any doubts about the pope's legislative sovereignty. For him the pope was "prince of the laws." In the Roman pontiff there resided, "the totality and plenitude of ecclesiastical power." All other jurisdiction in the church was derived from him. Hence a pope was superior in jurisdiction to all the members of a council acting apart from the pope or against him. There could be no appeal from pope to council. A council could not judge "a true and undoubted pope."[58] A general council with the pope at its head was not greater in jurisdiction than the pope alone, just as a king with his subordinate officials was not greater in jurisdiction than the king alone, or God with his creatures was not greater in goodness than God alone.[59] In the order of juridical sovereignty, Turrecremata's doctrine was quite clear-cut. The pope was indeed sovereign. The point we wish to make is that Turrecremata's understanding of right order in the church was not bounded by the concept of juridical sovereignty. Like the early decretists he was deeply concerned with the substantive content of laws and, even more than them, with relating this concern to a very explicit and detailed theory of reception by the church.

In commenting on D.19, Turrecremata expanded Augustine's view that writings received by all the churches were to be accorded the highest authority with a series of quotations from Aristotle, "Things that all men assert cannot altogether lack truth as the Philosopher says." "A common saying is not altogether false as the Philosopher says." "What is said by the many and the wise is probably true as the Philosopher says." But he did not forget to add Huguccio's caveat on the words, "equalis auctoritatis": "I understand this to be true if they are supported by equal reason; otherwise it is not true."[60]

Also Turrecremata laid a firm foundation for his doctrine of reception by distinguishing carefully between the different ways in which the church could "receive" authorities. The question posed was whether all works of the fathers received by the church were necessarily approved by the church. It would seem, Turrecremata wrote, that this must be the case since the church itself was unerring. "The church cannot err since it is ruled and guided by the Holy Spirit, the teacher of truth. Therefore the works of the fathers that the church receives should be acknowledged without any suspicion of falsity." But Turrecremata then distinguished between three different types of reception. Some works, he wrote, were received by the church with an approbation that prohibited the contrary of their teachings to be held. The four councils, for instance, were received in this way. Others were received *ad usum lectionis*. Such were commentaries on Scripture, sermons, lives of saints and martyrs, sacred histories. These were to be treated with respect but it was not forbidden to dissent from their teachings on particular points. Finally some writings were received "through dispensation," that is to say the faithful were merely permitted to read them, as was the case with pagan authors like Plato, Aristotle, and Cicero. After further discussion Turrecremata concluded that teachings of the fathers were to be held for catholic truth only to the extent that they were approved by the church. "The works of the holy fathers do not receive authority from the authority of the authors, but from the approbation of the church because they are found consonant with canonical wisdom or reason."[61] Here the twin criteria of reception and objective truth were neatly bracketed together in one short sentence.

The concrete problem of reception of papal decretals by the church first arose for Turrecremata at D.4 c.3 where the *Glossa ordinaria* posed the question whether the decision of a pope ought to prevail if all the bishops of the church were opposed to it. Here Turrecremata showed little interest in the problems of popular sovereignty and *consuetudo contra legem* discussed in many of the canonistic quotations presented by De Luca. His discussion focussed almost entirely on the substantive content of a papal law. According to the text of Pseudo-Isidore quoted by Gratian at D.4 c.2, every law ought to be "honesta, iusta, possibilis, secundum naturam, secundum consuetudinem patriae . . . necessaria, utilis . . . nullo privato commodo sed pro communi utilitate civium conscripta." If a pope promulgated a law that conformed to these criteria, Turrecremata wrote, his decision was to be preferred to that of all others opposing it, since the pope, as vicar of Christ, possessed a superior authority which all were bound to obey. If, on the other hand, the pope promulgated a law which did not have the required qualities but rather their opposites, his law was not to be received. Turrecremata provided a far more detailed and systematic discussion of this question than any of the early decretists. If, for instance, a papal law was "inhonesta" because contrary to the Christian faith or "iniusta" because contrary to natural law, it was not to be received according to Turrecremata. It was the same if a law was not "possibilis." This could happen in two ways, either from the point of view of the legislator or from that of the subjects. From the point of view of the legislator it was impossible, for instance, for the pope to grant dispensations in things prohibited by divine law. From the point of view of the subjects it might be impossible for them to accept a law contrary to their customs and way of life. As an example Turrecremata mentioned that the oriental churches did not receive the law concerning celibacy of priests. If a papal law was harmful rather than useful (as for instance if the pope tried to depose all bishops) it was not to be received. If a law was promulgated for private convenience rather than public welfare (as for instance if the pope tried to name his own successor) it was not to be received. Finally, Turrecremata summed up his argument and reached the conclusion that the bishops might on occasion licitly contradict the pope, not because they possessed a greater authority than him but because of "the bad quality of the law itself."[62]

After this discussion Turrecremata raised tentatively for the first time the question whether in matters of faith a general council was greater than a pope. We can best follow his further discussions on truth and reception by considering in turn his treatment of the three possible conflicts of authorities that arose earlier, as we have seen, in the works of the decretists—conflict between a pope and the members of a council, conflict between a father of the church and a council, and, most difficult of all, conflict between two general councils. In his initial discussion of the first problem at D.4 c.3 Turrecremata suggested that the words of the *Glossa ordinaria*, "In matters of faith

. . . a council is greater than a pope," should be interpreted as meaning that the council was greater in "discretion of judgement" (though not in "power of jurisdiction") and that, accordingly, the judgment of all the bishops should be preferred to that of the pope in a doubtful matter of faith.[63] He returned to the question at D. 15 c.2, where Gregory I's text stating that the four councils were to be venerated "like the four gospels," was presented. Gregory did not mean, Turrecremata wrote, that the councils were equal in authority to the Gospels. The wisdom of God was preferred to any human authority. Rather Gregory referred to the content of the councils' teachings concerning the faith; they were revered because they conformed to evangelical truth. Accordingly, the pope was bound by them in matters pertaining to the faith and the general state of the church.[64] But, in his comment on the following chapter, Turrecremata's characteristic emphasis on the supreme authority of the pope appeared again. All laws derived their vigor and coercive force from the authority of the prince. But the pope received the principate over the whole church from God. Therefore the acts of a general council representing the community of the church received their authority from the approbation of the pope.[65] Just as the pope approved councils that were good and holy, so he rejected those that were evil and pernicious and subversive of the faith.

Turrecremata's comments so far seem to suggest contradictory answers to the question whether the pope or the fathers of a council were to be followed in case of conflict between them in a matter of faith. At C.9 q.3 c.17 he noted Huguccio's discussion of the point[66] and at D.19 c.8 presented his own solution. It was his comment here that some modern authors have found "astonishing"; yet Turrecremata's position was firmly grounded on earlier decretist thought, especially on Huguccio's (though Turrecremata's argument was probably derived immediately from the corresponding text of Panormitanus). Turrecremata first repeated his view that the words of the *Glossa ordinaria,* "A council is greater than a pope," could not be taken to refer to the pope's power of jurisdiction when "a true and undoubted pope" existed, for the pope possessed all power of rulership over the church. Then he continued:

> But regularly this is true [i.e. that a council is greater than a pope] concerning greatness of authority of discernment in judging (just as we say that 'the more one uses reason, the more authority his words seem to have') and this is presumed to be greater in the whole council than in one man. But I say 'regularly' because it may happen that even in a matter of faith the pope may be moved by better reasons and authorities than the council and then the definition of the pope should be supported. For a council can err like those of Rimini and Ephesus II and many others; also the council of which we read in 27 q.2 c. *placuit* and c. *tria* which determined that there could be no marriage between a rapist and his victim. Yet Jerome says the contrary, moved by better reasons and authorities of divine law, and his opinion is preferred to the determination of a whole council.[67]

Here again the issue could not be settled by any appeal to a formal power of jurisdiction. The decisive authority resided in the intrinsic truth of the doctrine maintained, even if the truth was maintained by one single person, and that person might be the pope or it might be a private doctor. Turrecremata concluded his argument by noting that, if a pope attempted to contradict a doctrine of faith already defined by a general council and approved by the apostolic see, the pope's opinion would not be followed but rather he would be presumed to err. Elsewhere Turrecremata held that if a pope was seen to err in faith his error was to be shown to him "from sacred Scripture or the determination of the universal church."[68] If he refused to recant he was to be considered as self-deposed from the papacy.

Turrecremata's attitude to the authority of church fathers is indicated by the reference to Jerome given above. When he discussed in detail the problem of a conflict between a church father and a pope or council, he distinguished carefully between "magisterial approval"—the expert opinion of a specialist in his own field, and "authoritative approval"—the decision of the one holding supreme public authority in the church. This distinction had been made in comments on Gratian's *dictum* at D.20 *ante* c.1 ever since the twelfth century. But, as we have seen, it did not automatically solve all outstanding problems. When Turrecremata came to comment on D.20, he relied heavily on the exposition of Huguccio. In the decision of cases, the popes were preferred to those expositors of Scripture who were "only expositors," and canons of councils were also preferred to the doctors of the church. But then came the crucial reservation. "This conclusion is regularly true, unless the decision of the doctor is confirmed and strengthened by the authority of the New or Old Testament, or by a canon, or by the general custom of the church." And he went on to quote the inevitable example of Jerome and the council of Aachen. Again, still following Huguccio and developing his thought, Turrecremata wrote that, in interpreting Scripture, the opinion to be preferred was the one "more consonant with reason." According to Gratian the fathers often "adhered more to reason" in their expositions. Hence it was not permitted even to supreme pontiffs to depart from certain opinions of the fathers, "namely those which concern the faith or the universal state of the church . . . or which are already received and approved by the universal church."[69] Once more we have the juxtaposition of objective truth and reception by the universal church as the ultimate criteria in determining the validity of canonical texts.

The final problem that we have to consider was the most difficult one for Turrecremata. If two general councils conflicted with one another which decision should the church accept? Here again Turrecremata provided a more adequate treatment of this problem than any of the early decretists while continuing the main lines of their thought. He carefully brought into play the relevant distinctions between general councils and local councils and between canons concerning the faith and those concerning church discipline. These distinctions produced straightforward solutions to many problems. Thus, a general council was always preferred to a local council in matters of faith. But, in matters of discipline the canon of a general council was not assumed to override the local legislation of provincial councils unless the canon expressed a specific intent to do so in a *clausula derogatoria*. When two provincial councils disagreed in a matter of faith the one to be preferred was the one supported "by the authority of sacred Scripture or of the holy fathers." If two local councils disagreed in a matter of church discipline the legislation of each was to be observed in its own district (provided it was not contrary to natural or divine law). If two local councils of the same province disagreed the later was preferred to the earlier one. If it was not clear which was prior in time the sentence "of greater piety" was preferred.[70]

When two general councils disagreed in a matter of positive law the later one took precedence over the earlier one. There remained a theoretical possibility that two general councils, legitimately summoned and confirmed by papal authority, might differ from one another on a question of faith. In spite of his devotion to the papacy Turrecremata accepted the common opinion of his day that an individual pope could fall into heresy. But, in the case that he had now envisaged, a whole council acting with the pope would have to be condemned as "not Catholic." Turrecremata was reluctant to admit that such a case could arise, but he did not neglect to provide a solution for it. Every effort should be made to harmonize the teachings of the two councils, he urged; but in the last resort, if their doctrines clearly conflicted, the later council was to be rejected, since the doctrine of the earlier one "had already been approved by the acceptance of the universal church."[71] Once again, even in this extreme case, reception by the church was the decisive criterion in deciding problems of conflicting authorities.

We began with a tension in the life of the church between "law" and "truth." It is a permanent and necessary tension. The church needs law to define its way of living as an ordered community. Law can on occasion conflict with truth. But the church must persist in the truth if it is to maintain its identity as a true church. When Stephan Kuttner wrote of a similar tension between "the bond of law" and the "bond of love" he explained that the canonists reconciled the apparent opposites in the ideal of canonical equity "which permeated their analytical thought and their solution of cases at every step."[72] Our tension between law and truth was resolved in the canonists' teaching on reception, which likewise permeated their thought whenever they had to deal with apparent dissonances in the area of ecclesiology. Here they looked for another kind of harmony. A word one often encounters in their discussions is *consona*. Always that authority was to be received by the church which was consonant with Scripture, consonant with truth.

There is one final point to be considered. The classical canonists—and, following them, Johannes de Turrecremata—held that in some circumstances the teaching of a single individual was to be preferred to that of any other authority in the church. Did the holding of this view really imply an attitude of persistent distrust toward the established institutions of the church, an anticipation of the ecclesiology of Luther? William of Ockham certainly used the canonists' arguments to defend his assertion that the whole institutional church of his own day had fallen into heresy. But this attitude was not typical of the mainstream of canonistic thought and it was entirely untypical of Johannes de Turrecremata. When a Huguccio or a Turrecremata wrote that the views of a single individual were to be preferred to those of any other ecclesiastical authority if the individual was supported by divine law, their underlying attitude was not one of skepticism toward the visible institutions of church government. Rather they were expressing a serene assurance that in actual fact, in the ongoing life of the church, the truth always would come to be accepted by the church as a whole (whatever its immediate source) and would eventually be proclaimed through the church's institutions. Their doctrine of reception was rooted in faith, not in doubt. Temporary distortions might occur, but the visible church, they thought, would always remain the vehicle of man's salvation precisely because it would always remain open to the reception of saving truth. Huguccio wrote, "The bark of Peter may be storm-tossed but never submerged."[73] Johannes de Turrecremata observed that the church had often erred but not in matters essential to man's salvation, not in ways that compromised her essential sanctity. "Not every error is damnable . . . in many things the church deceives and is deceived . . . and yet such error in no way derogates from the church's holiness."[74] The crisis of the sixteenth century came only when the actual conduct of ecclesiastical institutions gave rise to a widespread belief that the church was no longer holy, that it was no longer showing the way of salvation, that it could no longer be relied upon to receive the truth—whoever expressed it.

Cornell University

Notes

1. *Dialogus Magistri Guillermi de Ockham,* in M. Goldast, *Monarchia S. Romani Imperii* (Frankfurt, 1614), II: 398, "non quis est alicuius sententiae auctor sed quid dicitur attendentes."

2. U. Bubenheimer, *Consonantia theologiae et iurisprudentiae: Andreas Bodenstein von Karlstadt als Theologe und Iurist* (Th.D. dissertation, Tübingen, 1971), cited by S. Hendrix, "In Quest of the *Vera Ecclesia:* The Crises of Late Medieval Ecclesiology," *Viator* VII (1976), n. 64.

3. Y. Congar, "La 'Reception' comme Réalité ecclésiologique," *Revue des Sciences philiosophiques et théologiques* LVI (1972), 369–403, at p. 392.

4. K. Nörr, *Kirche und Konzil bei Nicolaus de Tudeschis (Panormitanus)* (Cologne-Graz, 1964), p. 133. See also H. Schuessler, "The Canonist 'Panormitanus' and the Problem of Scriptural Authority," *Concordia Theological Monthly* XXXVIII (1967), 234–41, and M. Watanabe, "Authority and Consent in Church Government: Panormitanus, Aeneas Sylvius, Cusanus," *Journal of the History of Ideas* XXXIII (1972), 217–36. Schuessler and Watanabe both mention Luther's references to Panormitanus. On this see especially C. T. Johns, *Luthers Konzilidee in ihrer historischen Bedingtheit und ihrem reformatorischen Neuansatz* (Berlin, 1966), pp. 28, 127, 130, 132–34.

5. R. Bäumer, *Nachwirkungen des konziliaren Gedankens in der Theologie und Kanonistik des frühen 16. Jahrhunderts* (Münster Westf., 1971), pp. 184–203.

6. Bäumer, *Nachwirkungen*, p. 190, "Erstaunlicherweise nimmt er Gedanken von Ockham und Nicholaus de Tudeschis auf, um sie für seine papalistischen Theorien zu verwerten." U. Horst, "Grenzen der päpstlichen Autorität. Konziliare Elemente in der Ekklesiologie des Johannes Torquemada," *Freiburger Zeitschrift für Philosophie und Theologie* XIX (1972), 361–88, at pp. 366, 378. As for Ockham's influence on Panormitanus and Turrecremata: Panormitanus, like Ockham, argued that councils could err since the true faith might survive in only one person as it had survived in Mary alone at the time of the Passion. Modern authors have often pointed out that the theme of Mary as sole guardian of the faith was no invention of Ockham. But Ockham, I think, was the first to use this old belief as an argument against the authority of general councils and so he did play a major role in its development as an ecclesiological argument. Turrecremata applied Ockham's argument to the members of a council separated from the pope but explicitly denied that it could apply to a general council united with the pope, *Summa de ecclesia* (Venice, 1561), III c.60. However, he was not quite consistent on this point. See below n. 70.

7. Congar was basically concerned to argue that the idea of "reception" has enduring validity in the life of the church but that its full meaning cannot be expressed in terms of juridical sovereignty (i.e. as an expression of popular sovereignty opposed to monarchical sovereignty). Reception, he suggests, is rather a recognition by the community of the truth proposed to it. This point, it seems to me, is true and can be demonstrated even from the "juridical" writings of the canonists themselves.

8. *Decretum Gratiani . . . una cum glossis* (Venice, 1550), *Gl. ord. ad* D.9 c.5 s.v. *Quantamlibet,* "Arg. quod non est considerandum quis dicat sed quod dicatur ut 19 dist. secundum (c.8) . . . quia veritas a quocumque prolata semper praeferenda est." s.v. *Probabiles,* "ratio aequivalet canoni." D.19 c.8 dealt with the case of the supposedly heretical pope Anastasius.

9. S. Kuttner, *Harmony from Dissonance* (Latrobe, Pa., 1960), pp. 41, 50.

10. *Summa Induent sancti ad* D.20 *ante* c.1, Douai MS 649, fol. 71ra, "Licet enim sunt vera que dicunt non tamen sunt autentica nisi a summo pontifice confirmata." *Summa Et est sciendum ad* D.19 c.8, Barcelona MS S. Cugat 55, fol. 70r, "Credo tamen tempore Anastasii hanc decretalem fuisse autenticam, eius vero successor presumpsit ille hereticus quia est fulmine percussus . . . quare et eius scripta iniqua iudicavit." *Summa Omnis qui iuste ad* D.19 *ante* c.9, Rouen MS 743, fol. 7ra, "Dici potest quod non erat receptum capitulum istud a concilio et ideo reprobatur." The texts are printed more fully in my "Pope and Council: Some New Decretist Texts," *Mediaeval Studies* XIX (1957), 197–218.

11. "Sicut sancti evangelii quatuor libros, sic quatuor concilia suscipere et venerari me fateor . . . quia in his velut in quadrato lapide sanctae fidei structura consurgit et cuiuslibet vitae atque actionis norma consistit . . . dum universale sunt consensu constituta."

12. *Gl. ord. ad.* D.17, *ante* c.1, "Universale est quod a papa vel eius legato cum omnibus episcopis statuitur."

13. Ibid., *ad* D.15 c.1 s.v. *Ephesina prima,* "Hoc dicit ad differentiam secundae quae fuit reprobata." For Rimini see the following note.

14. D.15 c.3, "Caeterum, quae ab haereticis sive schismaticis conscripta vel praedicata sunt, nullatenus recipit catholica et apostolica ecclesia Romana . . . In primis Ariminensem synodum."

15. See D.16 c.1, c.4 and *Gl. ord. ad* D.16 *ante* c.1 s.v. *Apostolorum,* "Solutio brevis est quia illi canones sunt recipiendi qui a veris apostolis sunt editi, sed illi non qui a pseudoapostolis sunt editi."

16. At D.16 c.1, Bamberg MS Can 42, fol. 103vb, "Et sciendum quod quandoque apocrifum dicitur illud cuius veritas certa est, auctor vero incertus . . . et tale apocrifum bene recipitur . . . quandoque dicitur apocrifum quando nec scitur auctor nec veritas et talis liber non recipitur."

17. See *Summa Parisiensis,* ed. T. P. McLaughlin (Toronto, 1952), p. 14, and Rufinus, *Summa Decretorum,* ed. H. Singer (Paderborn, 1902), p. 36, "Vel forte illa xxxv capitula olim

a quibusdam patribus apocripha habebantur, moderno autem tempore, cum ab omnibus recepta fuerint, pro auctoritate summa observantur."

18. See my "Ockham, the Conciliar Theory and the Canonists," *Journal of the History of Ideas* xv (1954), 40–50, at p. 45.

19. D.19 c.1, c.2.

20. "Tenebit igitur hunc modum in scripturis canonicis, ut eas quae ab omnibus recipiuntur ecclesiis praeponat eis quas quaedam non accipiunt."

21. *Summa ad* D.19 c.6, Admont MS 7, fol. 24, "*Equalis auctoritatis.* Hoc intelligo esse verum si equali ratione nitantur, aliter non."

22. See my *Foundations of the Conciliar Theory* (Cambridge, 1955), "Pope and Council" (above n. 10), H. Zimmermann, *Papstabsetzungen des Mittelalters* (Graz-Vienna-Cologne, 1968). On Anastasius' legendary reputation and on the confusions between him and other allegedly heretic popes in the Middle Ages, see H. Fuhrmann, "Die Fabel von Papst Leo und Bischof Hilarius," *Archiv für Kulturgeschichte* xliii (1962), 125–62.

23. Quoted in Guido de Baysio, *Rosarium Decretorum* (Strasbourg, 1473), *ad* D.19 *ante* c.1 (unpaginated).

24. L. de Luca, "L'Accettazione popolare della Legge canonica nel Pensiero di Graziano e dei suoi Interpreti," *Studia Gratiana* iii (1955), 193–276.

25. For texts and literature on this see R. Weigand, *Die Naturrechtslehre der Legisten und Decretisten von Irnerius bis Accursius und von Gratian bis Johannes Teutonicus* (Munich, 1967). For an excellent introduction to the cluster of canonical ideas surrounding the words "iustitia," "aequitas," "ratio" see E. Cortese, *La norma giuridica* (Milan, 1964). Another valuable discussion is that of L. Buisson, *Potestas und Caritas* (Cologne-Graz, 1958).

26. D.1 c.5, D.12 c.7. For a brief survey, with bibliography, see G. Le Bras, C. Lefebvre, and J. Rambaud, *L'Âge classique,* Histoire du Droit et des Institutions de l'Église en Occident vii (Paris, 1965), pp. 214–19, 533–57.

27. See the comments of the *Summa Reginensis* and of Ricardus Anglicus cited by De Luca, "Accettazione popolare," pp. 212, 235. The *Summa Parisiensis* required that the "general will" which could abrogate law by non-reception should be "prudens." *Summa ad* D.4 *post* c.3 s.v. *Mores,* "i.e. voluntas generalis omnium et sciens et prudens" (p. 5). The *Summa Animal est substantia* offered a particularly interesting argument. Since the legislator and the law itself intended to promote the common utility, a people did not really act against the will of the legislator when they abrogated an unacceptable law. *Summa ad* D.4 *post* c.3, Bamberg MS Can. 42, fol. 101ra, s.v. *Abrogare,* "Verum est dicunt quidam accedente consensu legis latoris tacito vel expresso . . . Set dico quod etiam sine consensu domini pape potest lex abrogari. Set consensus eius generalis et consensus etiam legis et ad hoc tendunt ut fiat communis populi utilitas. Unde si rate inspiciamus non sit hic contra voluntatem legis vel legis latoris scilicet quod aliqua lex abrogetur, cum lex velit fieri ad communem omnium utilitatem." This should be compared with the fifteenth-century view of Dominicus de Sancto Gemignano discussed by De Luca, "Accettazione popolare," p. 219. De Luca mentioned the text of the *Summa Animal est substantia* (p. 236) but was misled as to its significance by a faulty transcription.

28. *Summa ad* D.4 *post* c.3, Admont MS 7, fol. 6vb, "Set nonne clerus vel populus posset compelli ut impleret quod papa vel princeps vult cum papa habeat plenitudinem potestatis et omnis potestas sit in principe collata? Credo quod posset si a ratione vel fide [posset] vellet deviare . . . aliter non deberet. Item posset papa preter vel contra voluntatem suorum cardinalium aliquod statuere vel imperator preter vel contra voluntatem suorum baronum? Respondeo, non debeat si eorum consensum posset habere, alias posset dummodo non sit contrarium rationi vel veteri vel novo testamento. Set quidquid dicatur, si sic aliquid quod iustum est constituunt ratum erit et alii tenebuntur obedire." Cf. De Luca, "Accettazione popolare," p. 214, n. 38 (referring to Guido de Baysio's use of this passage), and p. 233, n. 74.

29. For the text of Alanus and other decretist comments see "Pope and Council," pp. 210–18.

30. *Summa ad* c.9 q.3 c.17, Admont MS 7, fol. 214vb, "Set ecce congregatum est concilium de toto orbe, oritur dubitatio, fertur una sententia a solo papa alia ab omnibus aliis. Que ergo cui est preponenda? Arg. hic quod sententia pape. Distinguo tamen et dico, si altera continet iniquitatem illi preiudicatur. Si vero neutra videtur continere iniquitatem et dubium est que veritatem contineat, pares debent esse et ambe teneri et hec vel illa pro voluntate potest eligi quia paris sunt auctoritatis dum hinc sit maior auctoritas, inde maior numerus, arg. di. xviiii In canonicis (c.6)." The most detailed presentation of Huguccio's views is provided by M. Fernández Ríos, "El Primado del Romano Pontifice nel Pensiamento de Huguccio de Pisa Decretista," *Compostellanum* VI (1961), 47–97; VII (1962), 97–149; VIII (1963), 65–99; XI (1966), 29–67.

31. *Summa ad* D.19 *ante* c.1, Admont MS 7, fol. 22ra, "et quidem si alterum illorum statuit contra rationem et ei derogatur per alterum."

32. C. Munier, *Les Sources patristiques du Droit de l'Église* (Mulhouse, 1957). See also S. Chodorow, *Christian Political Theory and Church Politics in the Mid-Twelfth Century* (Berkeley-Los Angeles, 1972), pp. 96–153.

33. D.20 *ante* c.1, ". . . absolutio vero vel condemnatio non scientiam tantum sed etiam potestatem praesidentium desideret; apparet quod divinarum tractores scripturarum et si scientia pontificibus praeemineant, tamen quia dignitatis eorum apicem non sunt adepti, in sacrarum quidem scripturarum expositionibus eis praeponuntur, in causis vero definiendis secundum post eos locum merentur." Gratian's text gave rise to a considerable body of canonistic commentary on the power of the keys. On this L. Hödl, *Die Geschichte der scholastischen Literatur und der Theologie der Schlüsselgewalt* (Münster-Westf., 1960).

34. Cambridge, Caius College MS 676, cited by John Watt, "The Early Medieval Canonists and the Formation of Conciliar Theory," *Irish Theological Quarterly* XXIV (1957), 13–31, at p. 28.

35. See B. Tierney, *Origins of Papal Infallibility* (Leiden, 1972), pp. 41–43.

36. J. F. von Schulte (ed.), *Die Summa des Stephanus Tornacensis über das Decretum Gratiani* (Giessen, 1891), p. 30. See Munier, *Sources,* pp. 190–91, 198–99.

37. These problems are explored in illuminating detail by S. Kuttner, "Pope Lucius III and the Bigamous Archbishop of Palermo," *Medieval Studies Presented to Aubrey Gwynn S.J.* (Dublin, 1961), pp. 409–53.

38. Tierney, "Pope and Council," pp. 210–12.

39. E.g. Rufinus *ad* C.36 q.2 *post* c.11, "Sed verbum Ieronimi et capitulo Meldensis concilii nititur et in veteris testamenti auctoritate fundatur," cited by Munier, *Sources* p. 203, n. 102. (Munier also quoted in part the texts of Alanus and Huguccio given below, but with some inaccuracies.) Rufinus' view was echoed by the author of the *Summa Omnis qui iuste,* "Set verbum ieronimi et canon meldensis concilii veteris testamenti autoritate fundatur" (Rouen MS 743, fol. 133ra). See also *Gl. ord. ad* D.20 c.1 s.v. *Illorum.*

40. Cited by Munier, *Sources,* p. 202, n. 96, p. 203, n. 106, *Gl. ad* D.20 c.1 s.v. *Illorum,* "Cum scripta Ieronimi inveniantur contraria consilio vel decretali epistolae, tria considerantur, aequitas, constitutionis causa, consuetudo loci, ut si Ieronimus magis consonat alteri istorum . . . standum sit dictis Ieronimi." "Nam quia ecclesiae est consuetudo, ut raptor post peractam paenitentiam raptam ducit, optinet Ieronimus." Munier quotes these glosses from Paris, Bibl. nat., MS lat. 3903, which I have not been able to see. He attributes them to Johannes Teutonicus but they do not occur in the *Glossa ordinaria*. Presumably they are derived from one of the other sets of glosses in MS 3903 described by Kuttner, *Repertorium der Kanonistik, (1140–1234),* Studi e Testi LXXI (Vatican City, 1937), pp. 39–40.

41. *Summa ad* D.20 c.1, Paris, Bibl. nat., MS lat. 15994, fol. 16ra, 86vb s.v. *Ieronimi,* "Contra tamen, auctoritas que est infra xxxvi Q. ult. Tria (c.8) prefertur constitucioni concilii ut causa eadem c. ult. Set illud ideo reprobatur quia contrarium est auctoritati veteris testamenti et ecclesie." *Ad* C.36 q.2 *post* c.11 s.v. *Hanc auctoritatem,* "Set hoc quia testi divine legis innititur, non quia Ieronimus legitur et sententia diffinienda."

42. *Summa ad* D.20 c.1, Paris, Bibl. nat., MS lat. 3909, fol 4ra, 53va s.v. *Conciliorum,* "Infra xxxvi Q.ii in fine [?] § ult. contra, ubi auctoritas ieronimi contra concilium aquisgranis

dicitur obtinere, set hoc est propter ecclesie approbacionem vel quia illud est contrarium con-cilio meldensi ut eadem, q. eadem, Si autem (c.10) licet Gratianus aliter senserit." *Ad* C.36 q.2 *post* c.11 s.v. *Nitatur,* "Nec est contra supra di. xx De libellis (a.c.1) ubi dicitur quod in questionibus iuris ad concilia et pape decreta debemus primo recurrere et tandem ad sanc-torum patrum dicta, quod ideo dicitur quia huiusmodi questiones sepius per decreta quam per sanctorum scripta soluuntur. Si enim vis fiat in ordine erunt ieronimi scripta decretalibus preferenda, arg. supra di. xv Sancta romana (c.3)."

43. *Summa ad* D.20 *ante* c.1, Bamberg MS can. 42, fol. 105ra s.v. *Merentur,* ". . . nisi ipsi dicant aliqua magis consona veteri vel novo testamento xxxvi q. ult. Placuit (c.11)."

44. Munier's argument on this point seems to rest on a presupposition that Scripture was regarded simply as a body of legislation essentially similar to, though higher than, canons of councils, decrees of popes etc. He emphasizes that patristic texts had juridical authority only when they were supported by Scripture or were generally accepted by the church, but fails to note that similar considerations were applied to the "properly legislative" texts also.

45. *Summa ad* D.20 *ante* c.1, Admont MS 7, fol. 24rb s.v. *Preponuntur,* "Adeo etiam quod summis pontificibus non licet recedere ab eorum expositionibus ut xxv q.i Sunt quidam (c.6) set preter eos. Sunt enim huiusmodi vocati in partem sollicitudinis non in plenitudinem potestatis ut ii q.vi Decreto (c. 11) et est arg. quod maior in aliquo potest esse minor in alio . . . Hoc verum est generaliter, scilicet quod in negotiis diffiniendis maior est auctoritas canonis sive apostolici quam auctoritas Augustini vel Ieronimi et huiusmodi nisi auctoritas Augustini vel huiusmodi corroberetur et iuvetur auctoritate veteris vel novi testamenti vel canone vel generali ecclesie consuetudine. Concilium enim quod fuit celebratum apud aquis-grani dicit quod raptor et rapta nullo modo possunt coniungi matrimonialiter ut xxxvi qu.ii Placuit (c.11). Ieronimus contradicit quod sic ut xxxvi q.ii Tria (c.8) et obtinet auctoritas Ie-ronimi non ex se sed quia nititur auctoritate veteris testamenti et meldensis concilii et generali consuetudine ecclesie . . . Hac autem causa auctoritas unius patrum preiudicet alteri."

46. Ibid., "Nam et inter apostolicos unus preponitur alteri ut Petrus Lino et Gelasius Lucio. Sic inter ipsos patres ut Ambrosius Isidoro, Augustinus Bede."

47. The problem often arose in discussions on D.20 *ante* c.1 when Gregory the Great's au-thority as a private doctor was compared to that of other church fathers. Gregory's authority was said to prevail when his words were "profundioris scientie" (Sicardus, Augsburg MS 1, fol. 80va; *Summa Antiquitate et tempore,* Göttingen MS iur. 159, fol. 25vb); "magis consona veritati" (*Summa Et est sciendum,* Barcelona MS S. Cugat 55, fol. 70v; *Summa Omnis qui iuste,* Rouen MS 743, fol. 7rb); "magis consona rationi" (Huguccio, Admont MS 7, fol. 24ra).

48. G. Fransen and S. Kuttner, eds. *Summa 'Elegantius in iure divino' seu Coloniensis,* Monu-menta iuris canonici, Series A: Corpus glossatorum I (New York, 1969), chapts. 51, 52, p. 15.

49. D.50 c.28, "quotiescumque in gestis conciliorum discors sententia invenitur, illius concilii magis teneatur sententia cuius aut antiquior aut potior extat auctoritas."

50. Stephanus, ed. Schulte, p. 71, "Cuius antiquior et sanctior. Ut haec duo concurrant; nec enim sufficit antiquiorem cum saepe priora trahantur ad posteriora. Vel antiquiorem dicit non tempore sed sapientia et auctoritate." Rufinus, ed. Singer, p. 122, "*Antiquior* tempore *et potior* maxime pietate . . . non sufficit ut sit antiquior."

51. Eds. Fransen and Kuttner, p. 40. "Verum quia hec interpretatio plus verborum quam sensus habet, potest non incongrue sic accipi ut eius concilii preferatur auctoritas que inde po-tior quod antiquior est, ut sic ad viii. universalia concilia referatur. Eorum enim conciliorum auctoritas potior est quorum auctores potiores." The *Summa Parisiensis,* ed. McLaughlin, p. 45, also referred to the early general councils in this context, "Dicimus ergo hoc intelli-gendum de illis octo universalibus synodis, vel de quatuor principalibus, quia si in aliquo sibi obvient, prior et quae potiores habuit patres praeiudicabit."

52. *Summa ad* D.50 c.28, Paris, Bibl. nat. MS lat. 3909, fol. 9vb, s.v. *Antiquior,* "Secus in canonibus quam in legibus . . . in canonicis enim scripturis quedam sunt que mutari non possunt ut evangelium et apostoli precepta et iiii concilia . . . de quibus potest hoc intelligi, vel intelligatur de provincialibus conciliis in quibus habet locum quod dicitur supra, di.xix,

In canonicis (c.6). *Potior* id est benignior et est arg. pro misericordia . . . vel potior id est maior sicut generale concilium maiorem habet auctoritatem provinciali."

53. *Summa ad* D.50 c.28, Admont MS 7, fol. 70ra, "*Antiquior* tempore et *pocior* presertim pietate ut hec duo concurrant . . . Sufficit autem si est pocior pietate vel dignitate . . . Set quid facit antiquitas cum idem sit, scilicet quod sententia modernorum conciliorum vel canonum prefertur si nitatur maiori pietati? Respondeo ad hoc. Potest valere quod si ambe sententie concurrunt et sint equalis pietatis et contradicant, sententia antiquioris concilii preferatur nisi sententia novi contra a pluribus observetur . . . Vel antiquior dignitate et auctoritate, ideo preponenda ut arg. di.xviiii, In canonicis (c.6). Priora trahuntur ad posteriora . . . nisi priora sunt summe dignitatis ut quatuor generalia concilia que vicem obtinent quatuor evangeliorum . . . Set et hec trahuntur in multis . . . Nota quod si papa ex certa scientia statuat contra statutum alicuius concilii vel pape vel augustini vel alterius prevalebit eius constitutio . . . exceptis articulis fidei et preceptis utriusque testamenti et ille que spectant ad generale statutum ecclesie, contra que papa statuere non potest . . . Set queras quare ille iiii^{or} vel octo generalia concilia sint maioris auctoritatis quam alia. Dico quia plenius ibi de fide tractatam est quam in aliis . . . et plenius in antiquis quam in modernis quia tunc pauci erant fideles et multi infideles . . . et ideo diligentior erat tunc inquisitio de talibus quam nunc."

54. *Gl. ord. ad* D.16 c.11 s.v. *Maiorem*, "Arg. quod non quia prior est tempore prior est iure sed melior praeferendus est." *Ad* D.16 c.4 s.v. *Praeponimus*, "licet Ancyrana synodus fuerit prior Nicaena, tamen propter maiorem auctoritatem Nicaena praeponitur."

55. *Gl. ord. ad* D.50 c.28 s.v. *Discors*, "Nonne ille sententia est potius sequenda quae maiorem continet pietatem? . . . Licet tamen canon apostolorum potior sit quia antiquior sit aliis canonibus, tamen praeiudicatur . . . Quod ergo dicitur hic intellige cum ambae constitutiones sunt particulares et locales et de illis loquitur 19 dist. In canonicis (c.6) . . . Sed si ambae sunt generales semper posterior praeiudicat." s.v. *Cuius aut antiquior*, "Si ambo sunt aequalis pietatis, 19 dist. In canonicis (c.6)."

56. D.19 c.1, D.15 c.2, D.20 *ante* c.1.

57. On Turrecremata see K. Binder, *Wesen und Eigenschaften der Kirche bei Kardinal Juan de Torquemada* (Innsbruck-Vienna-Munich, 1955). Binder, however, does not deal much with the problems we are investigating. P. Massi, *Magistero infallible del Papa nella Teologia di Giovanni da Torquemada* (Turin, 1957), is a simplistic treatment which emphasizes only the strongly papalist texts in Turrecremata. More balanced appraisals are provided by U. Horst,, "Grenzen," and P. de Vooght, *Les Pouvoirs du Concile et l'Autorité du Pape* (Paris, 1965), pp. 137–62. The fullest account of Turrecremata's ecclesiology is presented in Thomas Izbicki, *The Ecclesiology of Cardinal Johannes de Turrecremata* (Ph.D. dissertation, Cornell University, 1973).

58. These phrases are all taken from Turrecremata's *Summa de ecclesia*, III c.64, II c.83, III c.43, III c.50.

59. *Oratio synodalis de primatu*, ed. E. Candal (Rome, 1954), p. 86. In the following notes, because of the particular emphasis of this paper, we have illustrated Turrecremata's views from his commentary on the *Decretum*. Often the same views were expressed in virtually the same words in this work and in the *Summa de ecclesia*.

60. *In Gratiani Decretorum primam . . . commentaria* (Venice, 1578), D.19 c.6, p. 169, "et quae ab omnibus asseruntur non possunt omnino carere veritate ut dicit Philosophus primo rethorices et 7 ethicorum . . . sermo communis non est omnino falsus ut Philosophus dicit primo rethorices . . . ut dicit Philosophus primo topicorum, probabile verum est, quod a pluribus et sapientibus dicitur . . . *Aequalis authoritatis*. Hoc intelligo esse verum si aequali ratione nitantur, alias non est verum. Hu."

61. *Com. ad* D.15 c.3, p. 141, "opuscula sanctorum patrum habent authoritatem non ab ipsis authoritatibus, sed ab approbatione ecclesiae quae ideo approbatae sunt quia canonicae sapientiae aut rationi consonat reperta, secundum quod ait Augustinus in epistola ad Hieronymum et habetur in c. Ego solis (c.5) supra di. 9." At D.9 c.5 Turrecremata repeated the words of Johannes Teutonicus, "non est considerandum quis dicat sed quid dicatur." (p. 91).

62. *Com. ad* D.4 c.3, p. 62, "Respondeo dicendum quod si papa constituat leges aliquas habentes qualitates illas in superiori capitulo, Erit autem lex (c.2) . . . sententia papae praeferenda est omnium aliorum contradicentium sententiae . . . Si vero contingat quod lex posita a domino papa sive constitutio non habeat qualitates praedictas sed contrarias, recipienda non est, ut puta: Primo si non sit honesta utpote non conveniens religioni sive fidei Christianae . . . iudicio et sententiae episcoporum magis standum esset iuxta c. Anastasius (c.9) di. 19, et c. Si papa (c.6) di. 40. Item secundo, si lex aut constitutio papae esset iniusta, ut puta contra ius naturale, recipienda non esset . . . Tertio si constitutio papae non est possibilis et hoc sive respectu potestatis suae, quia excederet facultatem potestatis suae, ut puta si vellet dispensare in prohibitis lege divina . . . sive etiam sit impossibilis ex parte subditorum, ut si vellet constituere aliqua quae non convenirent moribus et consuetudini subditorum . . . de quo exemplum habemus in statuto de continentia non recepto ab episcopis orientalis ecclesiae . . . Quarto, si lex et constitutio papae non sit necessaria, id est expediens reipublicae . . . Quod enim contradicere possint huiusmodi subditi suo superiori, non ex maioritate autoritatis, sed ex ipsa mala qualitate legis."

63. *Com. ad.* D.4 c.3, p. 63, "Gl. illa dicens quod cum materia fidei ventilatur synodus maior sit quam papa loquitur de maioritate iudicii discretionis et non de maioritate potestatis iurisdictionis. . . . Et ideo ubi papa aliquid contra fidem instituere vellet, synodus ei contradicere posset et deberet, unde Paulus resistit in faciem Petri, ad Gal. 2, unde nobis videtur quod in dubiis quae circa fidem oriuntur, magis standum esset iudicio omnium episcoporum simul in synodo aggregatorum, quam iudicio solius papae, sed de hoc duce Deo, in alio loco plenius dicere intendimus."

64. *Com. ad* D.15 c.2, p. 136, "Sed denotare voluit (Gregorius) quia in hiis quae ex fide determinant conformia sunt doctrinae evangelicae quo ad veritatem. . . ." p. 137, ". . . non possit . . . immutare quae pertinent ad articulos fidei, ad generalem statum universalis ecclesiae."

65. *Com. ad* D.15 c.3, p. 139, "Patet leges non habent vigorem et virtutem coactivam nisi principis authoritate, sive ex eo quo totius communitatis principatus est collocatus. Sed Romanus pontifex est in quo Deus rex regum et dominus dominantium totius ecclesiae posuit principatum . . . Ergo ad ipsum spectabit approbatio gestorum per concilia universalia quae communitatem ecclesiasticam repraesentant."

66. *Com. ad* C.9 q.3 c.17, p. 369. Turrecremata quoted here from the gloss of Huguccio given above (n. 31).

67. *Com. ad* D.19 c.8, p. 176, "Quod vero consequenter dicit gl. quod tunc synodus est maior papa, videtur quod hoc non sit verum de maioritate potestatis iurisdictionis existente vero et indubitato papa . . . Sed bene regulariter verum est de maioritate authoritatis discretivi iudicii, secundum quod dicimus quod qui magis ratione utitur eo maioris authoritatis eius verba esse videntur ut in di. se.1 (D.20 *ante* c. 1), quae praesumitur maior est in toto concilio quam in uno homine. Dico autem regulariter, quia potest esse quod etiam in facto fidei papa moveretur melioribus rationibus et authoritatibus quam concilium unde tunc standum esset diffinitioni pape. Nam concilium errare potest, sicut Arimense, sicut Ephesinum secundum et plura alia, et concilium de quo in c. Placuit (c.11) 36 q.2 et c. Tria (c.8) quod disposuit ut inter raptam et raptorem non posset consistere matrimonium, et tamen Hieronymus dicit contrarium, motus melioribus rationibus et authoritatibus iuris divini, et dictum eius praefertur dispositioni totius concilii. . . . Bene tamen verum est quod ubi papa velit statuere in causa fidei contra statuta sacrorum conciliorum non esset standum papae, quia in hoc casu praesumeretur errare."

68. *Com. ad* D.17 *ante* c.1, p. 149, "ostendo per sacram scripturam aut per universalis ecclesiae determinationem errorem esse quod tenet."

69. *Com. ad* D.20 *ante* c.1, p. 177, "Si primo modo, scilicet in causis decidendis sit ista conclusio, pontifices praeeminent et praeferuntur sacrae scripturae expositoribus qui tantum sunt expositores . . . Canones conciliorum etiam praeferuntur doctoribus in decisione causarum . . . quae conclusio vera regulariter est, nisi decisio doctoris roboretur vel iuvetur autoritati novi vel veteris testamenti vel canone vel generali ecclesiae consuetudine. Concilium enim fuit apud Aquisgranum et dicit quod raptor et rapta nullo modo possunt coniungi matri-

monialiter . . . Hieronymus tamen dicit quod sic . . . et obtinet authoritas Hieronymi . . . In expositione sacrae scripturae praefertur qui rationi consona magis dixerit . . . unde a quibusdam dictis sanctorum doctorum sive expositionibus non licet etiam summis pontificibus discedere ut puta in his quae de fide sunt aut de universali statu ecclesiae . . . aut quae iam per ecclesiam universalem sunt recepta et approbata."

70. *Com. ad* D.50 c.28, pp. 417–18.

71. *Com. ad* D.50 c.28, p. 417, "Quod credimus standum esse sententiae antiquioris sive prioris concilii universalis, dum tamen fuerit authoritate Romani pontificis et approbatione fultum et roboratum . . . Aut ergo controversia vera non est, quod magis credendum est, aut aliquod illorum catholicum non esset, quod magis de posteriori praesumendum esset, cum antiquum iam totius ecclesiae acceptatione fuisset approbatum."

72. Kuttner, *Harmony from Dissonance,* p. 50.

73. *Summa ad* 9 q.3 c.17, Admont MS 7, fol. 214va, "Fluctuare potest petri navicula set non submergi."

74. *Summa de ecclesia,* III c.64, "non omnis error est damnabilis aut obvius sanctitati ecclesiae, ecclesia enim in multis fallit et fallitur . . . et nihilominus talis error non derogat sanctitati militantis ecclesiae."

Infallibility and the Erring Pope: Guido Terreni and Johannes de Turrecremata

THOMAS M. IZBICKI

Jean Gerson thought the tension between the church's spiritual mission and its institutional problems, particularly the Great Schism, resulted from confusion between divine and human elements in canon law. If both canonists and theologians became *ambidextri* and comprehended each other's disciplines, they would stop bickering and work together for the solution of those problems.[1] However, in the later Middle Ages both theology and canon law were highly technical subjects, and few were skilled in both disciplines. Thus interdisciplinary work was difficult and was rarely attempted. Only two noted theologians, Guido Terreni and Johannes de Turrecremata, became *ambidextri* and composed canonistic commentaries. Both men were defenders of orthodoxy, papal apologists and important figures in the development of the doctrine of papal infallibility. In this paper we shall study their views on infallibility and relate them to their exegesis of key texts from Gratian's *Decretum*.[2]

The *Decretum,* by its very nature, presented a challenge to papal apologists. It was a compilation of conflicting authorities whose meanings were to be reconciled. It included some texts which exalted the papacy and others which stressed the limits of papal power. Among the latter, as we shall see, were some which referred to the possibility of papal heresy or cited past instances of papal error. On these foundations the decretists built an ecclesiology which coupled exaltation of papal power with remedies for the abuse of that power. It is particularly notable that Huguccio of Pisa thought that a pope could lose his see not only for heresy but for any notorious crime. Johannes Teutonicus declared that, in matters of faith, including papal heresy, a council was superior to the pope. Critics of papal policy, from the time of Frederick II onward, appealed to the authority of the general council as a counterweight to the pretensions of the Roman see. Thus both Terreni and Turrecremata felt compelled to reinterpret the *Decretum*'s key texts in a manner more favorable to papal power. Moreover, they tried to reconcile canonistic references to papal heresy with their ideas of papal infallibility.[3]

Guido Terreni (d. 1342). a Catalan Carmelite friar, studied theology at Paris under Godfrey of Fontaines. In 1318 he became general of his order and then, under John XXII, bishop of Majorca (1321) and of Elne (1332). Pope

John employed Terreni—a prolific polemicist—on several theological commissions. One of these censured Pierre Olivi's commentary on the apocalypse.[4] Terreni and his colleagues seem to have been unaware that Olivi had created the Franciscan idea of papal infallibility. That theory acclaimed as irreformable past papal decisions on matters of faith. For the Franciscans, both spirituals and conventuals, a key irreformable pronouncement was *Exiit qui seminat* (*Sext*. 5.12.3), in which Nicholas III (1279) had affirmed the Franciscan belief that Christ and the apostles had owned nothing individually or in common. Any attempt by a reigning pope to revoke *Exiit* would prove him a heretic who, in accordance with Huguccio's doctrine, had fallen from his see through his loss of true faith. On this basis, after John XXII (1323) revoked key provisions of *Exiit*, Michael of Cesena and William of Ockham denounced the pope as a selfdeposed heretic.[5] Because the Michaelists contrasted the "heretic" John XXII with the infallible Nicholas III, they almost condemned as heretical the very idea of papal infallibility. However, condemnation was averted by such influential curialists as Guido Terreni. A constant defender of the pope, Terreni developed a coherent, propapal theory of infallibility intended to be a counterweight to the Michaelist doctrine.[6] At some time around 1330, Terreni formulated a *quaestio* on infallibility into which he poured all his thoughts on that subject. Terreni passed beyond tentative suggestions of Augustinus Triumphus and Herveus Natalis that the papal office was infallible, and that of Petrus de Palude that pope and cardinal together could not err in matters of faith. Terreni claimed that the pope's public pronouncements on matters of faith were made with the unfailing guidance of the Holy Spirit. Terreni's theory was the first clear adumbration of the doctrine of papal infallibility taught by the First Vatican Council (1870).[7] Among Terreni's later works was a commentary on the *Decretum* (ca. 1339) in which he corrected the opinions of the canonists on such subjects as papal heresy and papal infallibility. Terreni incorporated his *quaestio* into this larger work as part of his gloss on the canon *Haec est fides* (C.24 q.1 c.14).[8]

Johannes de Turrecremata (1938–1468) was faced with a greater crisis than the troubles of John XXII. He was born into the Great Schism, which had disrupted the cherished unity of Christendom. As a young Dominican friar, he attended the Council of Constance (1414–18), which settled the schism but inaugurated the conciliar crisis. These facts weighed heavily on Turrecremata's later career. After theological studies at Paris and tenure of office in his order, Turrecremata went to the Council of Basel (1431–47) as agent of both Castille and the Friars Preachers. At Basel he worked for reform and the defense of orthodoxy, as well as defending the papacy against conciliarist assaults. In 1439, at the Council of Florence, Eugenius IV rewarded Turrecremata for his services to the Roman see by making him a cardinal. Thereafter Turrecremata remained an influential member of the curia until his death in 1468.[9] Turrecremata was the most effective papal apologist of his time. His chief works were the *Summa de ecclesia* (1453), a comprehensive exposition of papalist ecclesiological doctrines, and a commentary on Gratian's *Decretum* (1464), intended to correct canonistic errors which had contributed to the formation of conciliar theory.[10]

Among the numerous authorities—Scripture, the fathers, theologians and jurists—cited by Turrecremata in his *Decretum* commentary was Guido Terreni, "Guido Carmelita" or "Guido Elnensis."[11] Therefore, it is well worth inquiring whether Turrecremata adopted and disseminated Terreni's doctrine of infallibility or whether he developed his own doctrine. This can best be determined by a study of their comments on key *Decretum* texts. First we shall explore their views on the problem of papal heresy as presented in the canons *Si papa* (D.40 c.6), *Secundum ecclesiae* (D.19 c.8), *Anastasius* (D.19 c.9) and *Nunc autem* (D.21 c.7). Any acknowledgment that a past pope had used his office to promulgate false doctrine or any admission that a present pope might do so could vitiate the very idea of papal infallibility. Next we shall examine Turrecremata's exegesis of *Haec est fides* to see whether he adopted the doctrine of infallibility which Terreni attached to that text.[12] Our inquiry will be limited to these points, leaving to other scholars and other studies full examination of the wider problem of the location of supreme authority in the church, whether in the Roman see or in a council representing the faithful. However, before proceeding, we should note the methods of commentary used by our two *ambidextri* and their general casts of mind. Terreni's comments were brief and pointed, backed by his knowledge of the fathers and some sense of history. They displayed Terreni's strong confidence in the papacy as the divinely guided chief agency of ecclesiastical government. Turrecremata's comments were more cautious and his methodology more exhaustive. Besides glossing each canon, Turrecremata posed and answered a series of scholastic questions inspired by key texts. Each opinion he expressed was buttressed with an immense weight of erudition.[13]

Perhaps the most important text for the problem of papal heresy was the canon *Si papa*. Allegedly the work of Saint Boniface, apostle to the Germans, *Si papa* was one of a series of canons which illustrated the example which prelates should set for the faithful. It denounced papal, or curial, negligence as damnable. However, a pope could not be punished unless he fell into heresy. Canonists, among them Huguccio and Johannes Teutonicus, exploited this breach in papal judicial immunity, interpreting any notorious crime as heresy.[14] Terreni approached this text gingerly. Unable to dismiss it, he limited its applicability to clear cases of doctrinal deviation. The pope, Terreni said, was superior to all human authorities, particularly the emperor. (This was a thrust at Louis of Bavaria.) The one exception was obdurate heresy, which made the pope subject to denunciation and resistance by inferiors. Terreni did not mention deposition. This suggests that he had in mind private errors of a reigning pope, like that of John XXII on the beatific vision.[15] Turrecremata, with his experience of the Great Schism, interpreted *Si papa* more broadly. The pope could lose his see automatically for obdurate adherence to false doctrine. This was essentially Huguccio's doctrine on the heretic pope. However, Turrecremata could not accept Huguccio's equation of scandalous conduct with doctrinal deviation. Instead, following Augustinus Triumphus, Turrecremata said that a pope living evilly could only lose his see if he defended his misconduct. Evil can not be described as good.[16] The pope could also fall from his see by endangering the whole church *("status ecclesiae")*. For example, the pope could not forbid anyone to accuse him of heresy. Turrecremata was obviously more fearful than was Terreni that the pope might become a danger to the church and thus lose his see.[17]

The difference between Terreni's and Turrecremata's ideas on this subject is equally apparent in their discussions of the best known case of papal heresy, that of Anastasius II (496–98). Anastasius's attempt to settle the Acacian Schism peacefully earned him open opposition in his lifetime and, after his death, a reputation as a heretic struck down by God. The *Decretum* contained the pope's epistle to Emperor Anastasius I, in which he accepted as valid ordinations performed by Acacius. Gratian thought this document, the canon *Secundum ecclesiae,* heretical. The canon *Anastasius* was an excerpt from the *Liber pontificalis* which gave a hostile account of the pope's career. Through most of the Middle Ages, this text was accepted as the best proof that past popes had erred. (The canonists only late became aware that a pope really had fallen into heresy. Honorius I [625–38] had been condemned as a Monothelite by the Third Council of Constantinople in 680).[18]

Only Guido Terreni, among commentators on the *Decretum,* tried to refute the whole charge against Anastasius II. Like others before him, Terreni argued that Gratian had wrongly interpreted *Secundum ecclesiae.* Anastasius could accept Acacius's ordinations as valid if the proper forms had been followed. Nor had any pope condemned Acacius's ordinations with his person and his errors.[19] Terreni's departure from tradition was an attack on the canon *Anastasius.* Terreni expressed his uncertainty whether the pope had favored Acacius at all, unless he had done so privately. This disposed of the possibility that Anastasius had publicly fallen into error.[20] Then Terreni said that he was surprised that no subsequent pope had condemned Anastasius or removed his name from the list of Roman pontiffs. Instead, Terreni said, an Anastasius II was revered in Rome as a saint. After making this unprecedented attack on an authoritative text, Terreni carefully concluded his gloss on *Anastasius* by referring the case to the unerring judgment of the Roman see.[21]

Turrecremata glossed *Secundum ecclesiae* and *Anastasius* as one text. He, like Terreni, respectfully disagreed with Gratian on the question of ordinations performed by a heretic. These ordinations were valid but illicit. Moreover, the knowing recipient of such an ordination lost all exercise of priestly powers until he was reconciled with the church.[22] Turrecremata parted company with Terreni on the question of Anastasius's guilt. The Dominican theologian accepted the authority of the *Liber pontificalis.* Anastasius had shown his heretical leanings by receiving into communion the deacon Photinus, an Acacian. This was tantamount to a declaration that

Photinus, and by implication Acacius, was orthodox. The heretic pope was abandoned by the Roman clergy and struck dead by God. There is little doubt that Turrecremata believed Anastasius guilty of misusing his office, not just of private error.[23] At the end of his gloss on *Secundum ecclesiae* and *Anastasius,* Turrecremata took issue with Terreni's historical arguments, from reverence for an authoritative text or from the need for caution in an age of crisis.[24]

The canon *Nunc autem* described another famous apocryphal case of papal error, that of Marcellinus (296–304). The Donatists had accused him of worshipping idols and surrendering the Scriptures to save his own life during Diocletian's persecution. When Pope Symmachus (498–514) was accused of heinous crimes before Theodoric the Ostrogoth, papal apologists gave a new twist to the story. Among the documents they forged to prove a pope immune from judgment by inferior powers were the supposed acts of a synod at Sinuessa. That assembly was described as a spontaneous meeting of bishops to hear the case of Marcellinus. The council was supposed to have declared itself unable to judge the pope and to have insisted that he judge himself. Marcellinus finally confessed his crime and, later, earned the crown of martyrdom. Although this fable was intended to prove the pope immune from judgment by lesser powers, Jean Gerson later used it as a proof that a council could hear charges against a Roman pontiff.[25]

Terreni treated the case of Marcellinus as one of moral failing, not of heresy. Thus he made no attempt, as he did in the case of Anastasius, to refute the charge. Terreni simply pointed out that a council, an inferior power, could not judge a pope.[26] Then Terreni summarized Huguccio's opinion that Marcellinus was not judged because he repented and became a martyr. The Council of Sinuessa was an example of the legitimate resistance to an erring pope mentioned by Terreni in his exegesis of *Si papa.*[27] Turrecremata's interpretation of *Nunc autem* was similar. Marcellinus had fallen into sin through cowardice, but not into heresy. He had not, in his heart, abandoned the true faith.[28] An actual lapse into heresy would have made Marcellinus, despite his judicial immunity, subject to a conciliar inquiry as to whether he was still pope. This was implicit in the canon *Si papa.*[29] Nor had Marcellinus made the mistake of defending his conduct, a course of action tantamount to heresy. Instead, Marcellinus had confessed his error.[30] The penitent pope had then earned the once shunned crown of martyrdom.[31]

The ideas of our two *ambidextri* on papal heresy can be summarized briefly. Guido Terreni did not wish to believe that a pope could err in his official pronouncements, though he might err as a private theologian. The damaging texts in the case of Anastasius II were subjected to thorough criticism to prove this point. Following this doctrine, Terreni felt obliged to provide remedies against private error by a reigning pope: resistance and excommunication. However, there was no need to detail procedures for removing a pope who had erred in his official capacity. Turrecremata, in contrast, was unable to reject the possibility of public papal error. Even in the face of Terreni's arguments, he believed Anastasius II guilty of heresy. Turrecremata's ecclesiology, influenced by traditional canonistic concepts and by his experience of the Great Schism, included machinery for dealing with a pope who abused his office by falling into heresy, disturbing the *status ecclesiae* or pertinaciously defending a sinful course of action. This contrast between two avowed papalists is illustrated by their exegesis of Gratian's *dictum* that the power of summoning a general council belonged to the apostolic see.[32] Terreni readily accepted this as the sole prerogative of the pope. The successors of Peter had, after all, the universal power of binding and loosing.[33] Although Turrecremata attributed this same power to the pope, he did so with two important qualifications. One was that a pope who refused to summon a general council necessary for the welfare of the church was suspect of heresy and could lose his see.[34] The second was that, in such a case, the power to call a council devolved on the cardinals, then on the princes, finally on other prelates. (This contention reflected the ecclesiological ideas made popular by the Great Schism as well as the convocation by the cardinals of the Council of Pisa [1409].) Turrecremata cited as proof the spontaneous gathering of bishops at Sinuessa to hear the case of Marcellinus. He also cited the canon *Si papa*.[35]

This contrast between Terreni's and Turrecremata's ideas on papal heresy colored their differing, though related, views on infallibility. Both attached their ideas on that subject to the canon *Haec est fides*. That canon, attributed to Jerome, expressed a willingness to be guided by the tenant of Peter's see in matters of faith. Anyone who refused to accept a profession of faith approved by the pope was a heretic. The text concluded with a description of the Roman church as ever immaculate, under the guidance of God and with the aid of Saint Peter.[36] Such a text might have been used early on to support a doctrine of papal infallibility. However, the canonists were inclined to interpret references to the unstained Roman church as applicable only to the universal church, not to the pope, pope and cardinals or the local Roman church. Conciliarists employed that same argument to prove a council, representing the church, superior to the pope.[37]

Terreni, as we have noted above,[38] made a point of attaching his *quaestio* on infallibility to *Haec est fides*. He was, in fact, drawing the conclusion which the canonists had not. Terreni's underlying supposition in the *quaestio* was an identification of unfailing faith with unerring judgment in doctrinal matters. Terreni's chief proof text for his doctrine of infallibility amply illustrates this point. This key citation is Luke 22:32, "I have prayed for you, Peter, that your faith may not fail. Strengthen your brothers." According to Terreni, Aquinas had interpreted this dictum as a promise that papal pronouncements on doctrinal questions would be unfailingly accurate.[39] Use of that text enabled Terreni to avoid reference to Luke 11:52, Christ's reference to the key of knowledge. Papalists avoided use of that metaphor because it was a favorite of the Michaelists and thus subject to hostile scrutiny by John XXII.[40] Terreni also cited Matt. 16:18, "And the gates of hell shall not prevail against it," as well as *Haec est fides* itself.[41]

Without infallibility, Terreni argued, the faithful would lack any sure guide able to keep them from error.[42] This gift belonged to the pope, identified with that ambiguous entity the Roman church, through the guidance of the Holy Spirit. Any assistance rendered by the cardinals or a general council was purely advisory. Terreni showed no sympathy for conciliarist ideas nor for the theory that the cardinals shared the papal plenitude of power.[43] The most significant of infallible decisions made by the popes, one without which the church would be sadly divided, was the determination of the canon of Scripture. Terreni cited as proof of this Augustine's dictum that he would not believe the Scriptures unless the church moved him to do so. This did not mean, as Georges Tavard has argued, that Scripture was the pope's creature. Rather, the Holy Spirit moved the pope to choose only the divinely inspired books and to compel the faithful to accept them as such.[44]

Confronting the problems of his day, Terreni denied that John XXII had revoked anything decreed by Nicholas III which pertained to dogma. Pope John had clarified the meaning of *Exiit* and changed the rules under which the Franciscans enjoyed goods donated for their support. This was legal under the Roman law maxim *par in parem non habet imperium.* Moreover, *Exiit* itself enjoined recourse to the Roman see for solution of any future problems of the Friars Minor.[45] Terreni expanded his argument to deny that God ever allowed any pope to err in his public pronouncements on matters of faith. As we have seen in his glosses on other texts, Terreni admitted the possibility of private error but not that of misuse of papal *magisterium.* On this basis, Terreni, unlike other papalists, did not have to outline procedures for the deposition of a pope who became a public heretic.[46] Terreni dismissed Peter's denial of Christ (Matt. 26:69–75) and the apostasy of Marcellinus as cases of moral failing. Peter had erred privately when he refused to eat with the gentiles, but he had accepted correction by Paul (Gal. 2:11). Terreni dismissed the case of Anastasius II as no obstacle. As we have seen above, he dealt with it effectively in his gloss on the canon *Anastasius.*[47] Terreni's answer to the possibility that a heretic pope might try to define false doctrine was that God would not allow him to do so. Divine Providence would bring about the pope's death or a change of heart.[48]

Turrecremata too was deeply concerned with the implications of *Haec est fides.* On the one hand, he was eager to provide an acceptable doctrine of papal infallibility. That would make the pope, not a general council, the sure guide of the faithful amid the theological perplexities caused by Lollards and Hussites.[49] On the other hand, as in his gloss on *Anastasius,* Turrecremata was eager to retain traditional safeguards against abuse of papal power. Thus Turrecremata's comments on *Haec est fides* display a dual tendency toward both acceptance of and rejection of Guido Terreni's doctrine of infallibility.[50]

Turrecremata openly identified infallibility with indefectibility. Since unfailing faith was assured by God, Peter and his successors, by virtue of their teaching office, could not err in matters of faith:

the pope, head of the Church, teacher and leader of the Christian people, can not err concerning matters of faith which must be held and believed. The apostle [the pope], by

virtue of his public office of teaching the Christian people, discerns or defines what must
be believed or held. The judgment of the apostolic see is indefectible, which is the same
thing.[51]

This gift was inherent in Luke 22:32, "I have prayed for you, Peter, that
your faith may not fail. Strengthen your brothers." It was also inherent in
Matt. 16:18 "And the gates of hell shall not prevail against it." These were
the same Scriptural citations employed by Terreni.[52] Turrecremata took for
granted the necessity of having a single, infallible tribunal to which all
doubts on matters of faith could be referred for unquestionable solution.
Otherwise, Turrecremata said, citing Bernard of Clairvaux, the faith would
be rendered devoid of value.[53]

If Turrecremata had followed Terreni's line of argument beyond this
point, he might have denied that the pope could err in official pronouncements on matters of faith. However, Turrecremata's doctrine of infallibility,
like those of Herveus Natalis and Augustinus Triumphus, was founded on
the office, not on the person, of the pope. It was the see, not its tenant,
which was guided by the Holy Spirit. Turrecremata did suggest that the
pope might be preserved from error.[54] However, visibly parting company
with Terreni, he referred to those who depended on God to prevent definition of heresy by a pope: Some say that "God would not permit (the pope) to
define heresy, or anything contrary to the faith; but would prevent him by
death, by resistance of other believers, by the instruction of others or by
internal inspiration, or by other means. . . ."[55] Turrecremata's final conclusion was entirely different from Terreni's. Moved by caution bred by the
Schism and by reverence for traditional ideas about papal heresy, Turrecremata went on to discuss the fall from his see of a pope who accepted officially
a doctrine previously defined as heretical. With Huguccio, he argued that a
heretic pope fell from his see because he lost the faith and thus ceased to be
pope. The heretic's erroneous pronouncements lacked any binding force,
since they were not those of a true pope:

> But we give another explanation . . . namely that if the Roman pontiff should fall into a
> condemned heresy, by the very fact that he falls from Peter's faith, he falls from Peter's
> chair and see, and consequently the judgment given by such a heretic would not be the
> judgment of the apostolic see. Thus his judgment must be said to have no authority or im-
> portance, since, when he should fall through heresy, "per consequens" he would be de-
> prived of the authority of judging.[56]

Some Catholic scholars, intent on reconciling Turrecremata's doctrines
with the decrees of the First Vatican Council, have tried to dismiss these
words as references to private error. Others have tried to equate the infallible
papal office with unerring pronouncements delivered *ex cathedra*.[57] Such
arguments ignore the fact that Turrecremata discussed, in the gloss cited
above, the attempt of a pope to give a "judgment" on a doctrinal question. A
pope could lose his see for misuse of his *magisterium*, which rendered his erroneous pronouncements null and void. This belief that a pope, despite
Providence, might become a public heretic vitiated much of Turrecremata's

argument for papal infallibility. The office might be divinely guided, but there was no certainty that this gift could be translated into unerring decisions.[58]

It is a known fact that Terreni's doctrine of infallibility had little impact on subsequent generations of Catholic theologians.[59] Our study of Turrecremata and Terreni gives some hint of a explanation. Turrecremata knew and cited Terreni's ideas. He gave them serious consideration. However, Turrecremata could never see his way clear to following them. Our two *ambidextri* gave similar interpretations of *Nunc autem* and *Secundum ecclesiae*. However, their exegesis of *Haec est fides* and *Si papa* differed on the question of the erring pope. Turrecremata outright refused to accept Terreni's interpretation of the canon *Anastasius*. The traditional interpretations of these canons were more relevant to the problems caused by the Great Schism than were Terreni's. Terreni's ideas were too novel and daring for a traditionalist like Turrecremata. Thus Terreni's doctrine of infallibility was not part of Turrecremata's legacy to subsequent generations of Catholic ecclesiologists. Instead Robert Bellarmine, Turrecremata's intellectual heir, passed on the Dominican theologian's cautious ideas on papal *magisterium* and papal heresy, with their faint tinge of conciliarism.[60] These same ideas were sufficiently flexible that, at the time of the First Vatican Council, Turrecremata's name could be invoked by both infallibilists and anti-infallibilists.[61]

Institute of Medieval Canon Law
University of California, Berkeley

Notes

1. L. B. Pascoe, *Jean Gerson: Principles of Church Reform* (Leiden, 1973), pp. 89–99; W. Ullmann, *Medieval Papalism* (London, 1949), pp. 1–37.

2. The canonist Zenzellinus de Cassanis, who glossed the constitutions of John XXII, was censured for meddling in matters theological; see B. Tierney, *The Origins of Papal Infallibility* (Leiden, 1972), pp. 194–96; P. Fournier, "Jesselin de Cassagnes, Canoniste," *Histoire littéraire de la France* (Paris, 1821), xxxv: 348–61 (hereafter HLF).

3. B. Tierney, *Foundations of the Conciliar Theory* (Cambridge, 1955), pp. 23–84, 250–54.

4. B. M. Xiberta, "De magistro Guidone Terreni priore Generali Ord. Carm. episcopo Maiorecensi et Elnensi," *Analecta ordinis Carmelitarum* v (1923–26), 113–206; Xiberta, "De doctrinis theologicis Guidonis Terreni," Ibid., 233–376; Xiberta, *De scriptoribus scholasticis saeculi XIV ex ordine Carmelitarum* (Louvain, 1931), pp. 137–41; P. Fournier, "Gui Terré [Guido Terreni] Théologien," HLF (Paris, 1827), xxxvi: 432–73.

5. M. Maccarrone, "Una Questione inedita dell'Olivi sull'Infallibilità del Papa," *Rivista di Storia della Chiesa in Italia* iii (1949), 309–43; Tierney, *Origins*, pp. 93–130, 171–237; R. Manselli, "Il Caso del Papa eretico nelle Correnti spirituali del Secolo XIV," *L'Infallibilità: L'Aspetto filosofico e teologico* (Rome, 1970), pp. 113–29. On Huguccio, see Tierney, *Foundations*, pp. 58–65.

6. Tierney, *Origins*, pp. 238–69; T. P. Turley, "Infallibilists in the Curia of Pope John XXII," *Journal of Medieval History* I (1975), pp. 71–101.

7. Guido Terreni, *Quaestio de magisterio infallibili Romani pontificis*, ed. B. M. Xiberta (Münster, 1926). J. Sikes, "John de Pouilli and Peter de la Palu," *English Historical Review*

XLIX (1934), 219—40; Turley, "Infallibilists," pp. 75—81; Xiberta, "De doctrinis," pp. 325—26; Tierney, *Origins,* pp. 131–70, 238–39, at 282, n.2: "The importance of Guido's work is that he built a whole structure of ecclesiology around the doctrine of papal infallibility."

    8. Guido Terreni, *Commentarium super Decretum Gratiani,* Vat. lat. MS. 1453, fols. 152rb–53vb. Fournier, "Gui Terré," pp. 464–68; J. Melsen, *Guido Terreni, Ord. Carm. (1260?–1342) Iurista* (Rome, 1939), pp. 8–10; Xiberta, "De magistro Guidone Terreni," pp. 176–84.

    9. S. Lederer, *Der spanische Cardinal Johann von Torquemada, sein Leben und seine Schriften* (Freiburg, 1879); K. Binder, *Wesen und Eigenschaften der Kirche bei Kardinal Juan de Torquemada O.P.* (Innsbruck, 1954); V. Beltran de Heredia, "Colección de Documentos inéditos para illustrar la Vida del Cardinal Juan de Torquemada O.P.," *Archivum Fratrum Praedicatorum* VII (1937), 210–45; Beltran de Heredia, "Noticias y Documentos para la Biographia de Cardenal Juan de Torquemada," Ibid. XXX (1960), 53–148.

    10. Johannes de Turrecremata, *Summa de Ecclesia* (Venice, 1561) (hereafter SE); J. de Turr., *Commentaria super Decreto,* 5 vols. (Venice, 1579) (hereafter *Comm.*). K. Binder, "Kardinal Juan de Torquemada Verfasser der *Nova Ordinatio Decreti Gratiani,*" *Archivum Fratrum Praedicatorum* XXII (1952), 268–93; T. M. Izbicki, "Johannes de Turrecremata, Two Questions on Law," *Tijdschrift voor Rechtsgeschiedenis* XLIII (1975), 91–94; A. Black, *Monarchy and Community* (Cambridge, 1970), pp. 53–84.

    11. For a citation to "Guido Carmelita," see *Comm. ad* C.19 q.1 *ante* c.1 (III: 153). For various versions of "Guido Elnensis," see ibid., *ad* D.19 c.8–9 (I: 176); ibid., *ad* D.22 c.1 (I: 208); ibid., *ad* D.66 c.2 (I:493).

    12. Tierney, *Origins,* pp. 31–57.

    13. Melsen, *Guido Terreni,* pp. 10–41; Izbicki, "Two Questions," passim.

    14. Tierney, *Foundations,* pp. 57–67, 251–52; J. M. Moynihan, *Papal Immunity and Liability in the Writings of the Medieval Canonists* (Rome, 1961), pp. 25–110; V. Martin, "Comment s'est formée la Doctrine de la Superiorité du Concile sur le Pape," *Revue des Sciences religieuse* XVII (1937), 112–43, 261–89, 404–27, at 124–30.

    15. Guido Terreni, *Comm. ad* D.40 c.6, fol. 31vb, "*Iudicandus.* Cum omnium sit superior omnes in hac vita imperatores iudicat, et a nemine [MS nomine] iudicatur quia iudicat superior de inferiori. *a fide devius.* Quia tunc inferior potest et debet superiorem increpare et ei resistere." There is also, at the end of this gloss, an ambiguous reference to condemnation of a pope. "Si papa pertinaciter et contumaciter ac pravam heresim tenet et deffendit, potest condempnari, id est, illud heresi. xxiiii. q. iii. *dixit apostolus* e supra di. xxi°. *nunc autem.*" Terreni also admitted that a heretic pope incurred automatic excommunication, see ibid., ad C.24 q.1 c.1, fol. 15lva. Tierney, *Origins,* pp. 177–237, 266; G. Mollat, *The Popes at Avignon* (New York, 1963), pp. 9–25.

    16. *Comm. ad* D. 40 c.6 (I: 352–53), "Papa extra casum haeresis non habet Iudicem superiorem in terris, a quo possit puniri pro culpa cuiuscunque alterius criminis. . . . Secundo potest responderi, ad illam glossam, ut quidam Theologici respondent, sicut Magister Augustinus de Anchona in summa sua de potestate ecclesiastica, quod papam esse incorrigibilem, potest intelligi dupliciter. Uno modo continuatione criminis, puta quia admonitus non destitit peccare peccato fornicatore ab aliquo alio accusatione digno, absque eo, quod crederet licite facere. Secundo modo, per ipsius criminis pertinacem defensionem, ut dicat, et defendat tale crimen, quod manifeste circumvolutim habet malitiam, non esse peccatum, glossa autem illa habet locum in secundo modo, tunc enim concordat glossa canonis Si quis pecuniam 97 di. Non autem habet locum, et in primo modo incorrigibilitatis." For Teutonicus's gloss on this text, see Tierney, *Foundations,* pp. 251–52.

    17. Ibid. (I: 353), "*a fide devius.* Tunc est cum a fide exorbitat pertinaciter, et a Petra fidei cadit, supra quam ecclesia fundata est Mat. 16, minor et inferior efficitur quocunque fideli tunc iudicari potest ab ecclesia, aut declarari condemnatus secundum illud Ioan. [3.b.]. Qui non credidit iam iudicatus est. Nec posset, Papa facere legem, ut de haeresi accusari non posset, quia sic tota periclitaretur ecclesia: et confunderetur generalis status ecclesiae, unde non credo, quod possit constituere aliquid in praeiudicium generalis status ecclesiae di. 15

sicut et 22 q.1 *sunt quidam* Hu." B. Tierney, "Pope and Council: Some New Decretists Texts," *Mediaeval Studies* XIX(1957), 197–218; G. Post, "Copyists' Errors and the Problem of Papal Dispensations *contra statutum generale Ecclesiae* or *contra statum generalem Ecclesiae* according to the Decretists and Decretalists ca. 1150–1234," *Studia Gratiana* IX (1966), 359–405; Y. Congar, "Status Ecclesiae," Ibid. XV (1972), 1–31.

18. J. J. I. von Döllinger, *Fables Respecting the Popes of the Middle Ages* (London, 1871), pp. 209–50; Moynihan, *Papal Immunity,* pp. 49, n. 23; Tierney, *Foundations,* pp. 38–39, 42–45. Turrecremata defended Honorius in SE II c.93, fol. 228r, for which defense he was later criticized by Döllinger, *Fables,* pp. 241–42.

19. Guido Terreni, *Comm. ad* D.19 c.8, fol. 15va, "Dicitur ergo salva reverencia gratiani rescriptum quod ad predicta anastasii est verum et conformat divinis et apostolicis decretis, scilicet, quod heretici servata forma licet in eorum dampnationem vera conferunt sacramenta. Nec obstat si felix papa tercius natione Romanus et zelaus [Gelasius] papa natione affer accatium excommunicaverunt hereticum quia per hoc—nisi sequitur quod dampnaverunt sacramenta per eum servata forma collata—non dixerunt ea nulla, immo de sacramentis per accatium collatis in condempnationis decretis suis nullam fecerunt penitus mentionem. Quare non est ad propositum conclusio Graciani."

20. Ibid., *ad* D.19 c.9, fol. 15va, "Hic papa si fuerit hereticus favens Accatio in errore nescio. Nisi quam Gracianus hic inducit possible est enim papam in fide errare prout est persona singularis."

21. Ibid., Terreni concluded his gloss with a reference to *Haec est fides* (C.24 q.1 c.14). Tierney, *Origins,* pp. 265–66.

22. *Comm. ad* D.19 c.8–9 (I: 174–75).

23. Ibid. (I: 176), "*Multi clerici.* Quia enim iste Anastasius publice communicaverat. Damnato haeretico Achaccio in errore Photini, qui Achacium sequeratur depravatus, et volens Achacium in suo errore defendere, merito ab eo clerus, et eius communione se separavit . . . iste Anastasius communicando Photino in errore iam damnato, et per consequens Achacio haereticus incidisset in haeresim iam damnatum eadem sententia fuit moderata cum illis quia eadem poena ferendi haereticus, et defensor eius . . . unde in hoc crimine potest Papa iudicari, ut di. 40. Si Papa, sine concilio. . . . Et ita voluit conducere, quod Achacius non fuisset haereticus, nec haeresim fuisse id pro se, quo damnatus erat. Et quia hoc publice faciebat, et illius haeresim publice praedicabat tanquam haereticus merito notatus est a clericis, et tandem a Deo percussus, quia ut dicitur dum assellaret, emisit intestina." In the same canon Turrecremata discussed at length the complex relationship of pope and council when they disagreed on a matter of faith, see U. Horst, "Grenzen der päpstlichen Autoritat: Konziliare Elemente in der Ekklesiologie des Johannes Torquemada," *Freiberger Zeitschrift für Philosophie und Theologie* XIX (1972), 361–88; P. de Vooght, "Esquisse d'une Enquête sur le Mot 'infaillibilité' durant la Période scholastique," *L'Infaillibilité de l'Église,* ed. O. Rousseau (Chevetogne, 1962), pp. 99–146, at 137.

24. *Comm. ad* D.19 c.8–9 (I: 176), " 'Quicquid tamen de hoc Anastasio dicatur, hoc credo, et teneo' inquit Dominus Guido Episcopus duensis [!], 'quod determinavit, et tenet sedes apostolica, et sancta Romana ecclesia, quam non credo in his, quae fidei sunt, et ad bonos mores pertinent, oberrare.' Ad id autem, quod dicitur, quod Romae colitur festum Anastasii, respondet, quod potest dici, quod ille secundus Anastasius, de quo hic dicitur, non fuit computatus in catalogo Apostolorum, quia fuit haereticus, unde Anastasius, qui postea fuit dictus est tercius, non est sanctus secundum Hug. etc." However, Turrecremata, like Terreni, defended the orthodoxy of John XXII's decrees on Franciscan poverty, see ibid., *ad* C.24 q.1 c.14 (I: 272).

25. Moynihan, *Papal Immunity,* 2–4; Tierney, *Foundations,* p. 57; Tierney, *Origins,* p. 152; Döllinger, *Fables,* pp. 79–85. The case of Marcellinus was also cited at Basel in the debate over the deposition of Eugenius IV (1439), see Aeneas Sylvius Piccolomini (Pius II), *De gestis concilii Basiliensis commentarium libri II,* ed. D. Hay and W. K. Smith (Oxford, 1967), pp. 36–37.

26. Guido Terreni, *Comm. ad* D.21 c.7, fol. 16vb, "Et inducitur hoc capitulum ad

probandum quod superior non debet ab inferioribus iudicari. Contra. Marcellinum enim papam de reatu suo noluit dare sententiam congregatum concilium quia superiorem eum cononscebant [!] ut concilium diceret."

27. Ibid., fol. 17ra, "Queritur hic quod cum marcellinus papa confessus esset se commisse crimen ydolatrie et heresis, quare concilium eum non deposuit? Respondet huguccio quod ideo quod paratus corrigi non erat inter hereticos computandus, xxxiii, q.i. iii^a. Dixit apostolus, nec marcellinus excusatus a culpa, quia coactus timore mortis hoc fecit que coactio non tollit voluntarium nec culpam quia ut dicit philosophus. iii° Ethicorum, ante debuit mori quam impi[i]ssimum ydolatrii crimen comittere. Sic enim movens martirri coronam."

28. *Comm. ad* D.21 c.7 (I: 202), "Non enim thurificavit idolis ex eo, quod crederet aliquid ibi esse divinum, vel quod esset licitum, unde non eligit thurificare, quasi credens verum, quod erat falsum, sed coactus volens mortem evitare, haec fecit tenens semper in corde suo veram fidem, unde licet peccaverit mortaliter, ut diximus in articulo praecedenti quia sanctius est mori, quam immolare idolis." Ibid. (I: 204), "Licet antequam de hoc haberetur veritas per eius confessionem diffamatus est de haeresi." Turrecremata used Bernard Gui's account of the life of Marcellinus, see ibid. (I: 203).

29. Ibid. (I: 202), "Cum Papa de heresi est taliter infamatus quod sine scandalo ecclesiae aut periculo fidei tolerari non posset universali ecclesia, et concilium universale habet [MS habent] potestatem inquirendi de ipso; et si ipsum deprehenderint hereticum manifeste procedendum est ulterius ad eius condemnationem . . . di. 40. Si papa: ergo etc."

30. Ibid. (I: 203), "Ego autem dico, quod non potuerunt, nec debuerunt eum condemnare, et hoc ideo, quia sponte, et humiliter confessus est errorem suum: tunc enim Papa damnari potest de haeresi, si pertinax fuerit, alias non." Ibid. (I: 204), "*ut dictum est.* Non est repertus pertinax, sed poenitens, et dolens de commissis."

31. Ibid.

32. D.17 *ante* c.1, "Auctoritas vero congregandorum conciliorum penes apostolicam sedem est."

33. Guido Terreni, *Comm. ad* D.17 *ante* c.1, fol. 13va, "Apud sedem apostolicam residet potestas generalia concilia congregandi. Et hoc rationaliter ut penes eum resideat potestas conciliorum que omnes et universaliter ligant apud quem est universalis potestas ligandi et solvendi que residet in successoribus petri. . . ."

34. *Comm. ad* D.17 *ante* c.1 (I: 149), "Si Papa requisitus per dominos cardinales, et alios catholicos maxime praelatos, et principes, et nollet congregare universale concilium, nec autoritatem praestare illud congregandi, tunc cum talis habendus veniret suspectus de heresi c. Error. di. 83, et per consequens dubius de papatu." See also S E III c.8, fol. 282r. On this point Turrecremata's doctrine was akin to that of the conciliarists; see Franciscus Zabarella, *De schismatibus authoritate imperatoris tollendis,* in S. Schard *De iurisdictione, authoritate et praeeminentia imperiali, ac potestate ecclesiastica* (Basel, 1566), pp. 688–711, at 690–95; J. B. Morrall, *Gerson and the Great Schism* (Manchester, 1960), pp. 76–93; F. Oakley, *The Political Thought of Pierre d'Ailly* (New Haven, 1964), pp. 160–61.

35. *Comm. ad* D.17 *ante* c.1 (I: 149).

36. C.24 q.1 c.14, "Hec est fides, Papa beatissime, quam in catholica ecclesia didicimus, quamque semper tenuimus; in qua si minus perite aut parum caute forte aliquid positum est, emendari cupimus a te, qui Petri et sedem tenes et fidem. Si autem hec nostra confessio apostolatus tui iudicio comprobatur, quicumque me culpare volverit, se inperitum, vel malivolum, vel etiam non catholicum, sed hereticum comprobabit. *Item.* Sancta Romana ecclesia, que semper immaculata permansit, Domino providente et B. apostolo Petro opem ferente in futuro manebit, sine ulla hereticorum insulatione atque firma et inmobilis omni tempore persistet."

37. Tierney, *Foundations,* pp. 36–46.

38. See above, n.8.

39. Guido Terreni, *Quaestio,* ed. Xiberta, p. 10, "Quia salvator ait Luc. xxii°. 'Symon, rogavi pro te, ut non deficiat fides tua. Tu autem, aliquando conversus, confirma fratres tuos.' Et istud dictum secundum beatum Thomam secunda secunde q.1^a. ar.x°. est intelligendum

de summo pontifice, ad quem spectat causas maiores et pertinencia ad fidem sentencialiter determinare, et ad ipsius auctoritatem qui preest toti ecclesie ut unitas fidei in omnibus fidelibus servetur; quod fieri non potest, nisi questio orta de fide determinaretur per eum qui toti ecclesie preest, cuius auctoritate sentencialiter determinata circa ea que sunt fidei sunt ab omnibus inconcusa fide tenenda." The Lucan text referred to the unfailing faith of the Roman church, according to Nicholas de Lyre, *Postilla litteralis super totam bibliam* (Lyons, 1545), v fol. 177vb. On Aquinas's conception of infallibility, see Y. M. Congar, "St. Thomas and the Infallibility of the Papal *Magisterium;* Sum. Theo. II^a–II^{ae}, q. 1.a. 10," *The Thomist* XXXVIII (1974), 81–106; U. Betti, "L'Assenza dell'Autorità di S. Tommasso nel Decreto Vaticano sull'Infallibilità pontificia," *Divinitas* VI (1962), 407–22.

40. Tierney, *Origins,* pp. 171–86, 240–44.

41. Guido Terreni, *Quaestio,* ed. Xiberta, pp. 21, 25.

42. Ibid., p. 15, "Quia ex quo auctoritas ecclesie non haberet certitudinem veritatis in sua determinacione, cum posset errare non videretur iustum quod obligaret fideles ad firmam et indubiam credulitatem ac certam de sua determinacione tenenda inconcussa fide."

43. Ibid., pp. 15–6, "Ergo eadem auctoritate summus et pontifex et ecclesia romana per Spiritum Sanctum directa absque errore docet et determinat veritatem in hiis que ad fidem pertinent, nec in hiis Spiritus Sanctus, qui docet omnem veritatem, permitteret summum pontificem aut ecclesiam errare. Quia ubi summus pontifex cum collegio dominorum cardinalium sive cum generali concilio congregantur in nomine Domini et pro fide eius, ibi est Christus, qui est veritas sine errore dicens 'non enim vos estis qui vobis.' Et quod papa in determinatione eorum que pertinent ad fidem dirigatur, potest accipi. . . ." Tierney, *Origins,* pp. 244–45; Tierney, *Foundations,* pp. 36–46, 179–98; M. Wilks, "The Idea of the Church as *Unus homo perfectus and its Bearing on the Medieval Theory of Sovereignty,"* in *Miscellanea historiae ecclesiasticae: Congrès de Stockholm. Aout. 1960.* Bibliothèque de la *Revue d'Histoire ecclésiastique* XXXVIII (Louvain, 1961), pp. 32–49; de Vooght, "Esquisse," pp. 112–23; G. Alberigo, *Cardinalato e Collegialità* (Florence, 1969).

44. Guido Terreni, *Quaestio* ed. Xiberta, pp. 17–18, "Et preterea constat quod auctioritate ecclesie libri canonis habent robur auctoritatis. Unde per ecclesiam libri biblie admissi sunt in auctoritatem et ex auctoritate ecclesie tenent fideles firmiter predictos libros continere infallibiliter veritatem. Nec constat aliter quod illis libris sit credendum firmiter nisi per ecclesie auctoritatem, quia ut Augustinus dicit in libro Contra epistolam fundamenti 'evangelio non crederem, nisi auctoritas ecclesie catholice me comoveret' . . . Igitur si ecclesia in electione scripture canonice, ut non erraret, creditur fuisse directa Spiritu Sancto, sic quod non liceret summo pontifici aliquid detrahere de libris canonicis aut contra eorum veritatem expressam determinare: sic credendum est quod non erret summus pontifex in determinacione fidei, apud quem residet auctoritas ecclesie catholice, sed in hiis regitur Spiritu Sancto." On the evil effects of error, see ibid., pp. 13–14, 20–22. On Augustine's dictum, see H. Holstein, "Traditio et Scriptura in patristica occidentali," *De Scriptura et Traditione,* ed. C. Balic (Rome, 1963), pp. 205–31, at 213; B. M. Xiberta, "Scriptura, traditio et magisterium iuxta antiquos auctores Ordinis Carmeliatarum," ibid., 253–73; G. Tavard, *Holy Writ or Holy Church?* (London, 1959), pp. 31–4; Tierney, *Origins,* pp. 251–59.

45. Guido Terreni, *Quaestio,* ed. Xiberta, pp. 22–24.

46. Ibid., pp. 30–31, "Non enim querimus, an papa possit esse in se hereticus, sed queritur, an papa determinando aliquid in ecclesia et obligando fideles ad fidem credendum possit errare, ut error eius non solum concernat personam papae, sed concernat omnes fideles et totam ecclesiam Christi. Quia error concernens personam potest inesse pape, non autem error concernens totam ecclesiam, que tenetur in fide determinacionem pape inconcussa fide sequi, quam Deus precaret a lapsu fidei et Christus rogavit, ne in ea deficeret fides vera." Tierney, *Foundations,* pp. 46–67; Tierney, *Origins,* pp. 131–70; Moynihan, *Papal Immunity,* pp. 43–135. Papalist admissions that a pope might err and lose his see occasionally trouble modern scholars; see Black, *Monarchy and Community,* pp. 135–38; M. Wilks, *The Problem of Sovereignty in the Later Middle Ages* (Cambridge, 1963), p. 500.

47. Guido Terreni, *Quaestio,* ed. Xiberta, pp. 29–31. Tierney, *Origins,* pp. 265–66.

48. Guido Terreni, *Quaestio.* ed. Xiberta, p. 26, "Ergo multo forcius, si esset papa haereticus, propter immutabilem veritatem Dei et fidei datam a Deo benediccionem toti ecclesie et populo christiano non permitteret Deus eum determinare heresim aut aliquit contra fidem; sed prohiberet eum Deus aut per mortem aut per aliorum fidelium resistenciam aut per aliorum instruccionem aut per internam inspiracionem aut aliis modis, secundum quos Deus ecclesie sancte et fidei veritati multipliciter providere potest."

49. SE II c. 107, fol. 248v; Johannes de Turrecremata, *Repetitiones super quibusdam propositionibus Augustini de Roma.* Mansi xxx: 979–1034, at 1019–20. F. Oakley, *Council Over Pope?* (New York, 1969), pp. 61–74; de Vooght, "Esquisse," pp. 122–27; R. C. Petry, "Unitive Reform Principles of the Late Medieval Conciliarists," *Church History* xxxi (1962), 164–81, at 168–69; H. Schuessler, "The Canonist 'Panormitanus' and the Problem of Scriptural Authority," *Concordia Theological Monthly* xxxviii (1967), 234–41; E. F. Jacob, "The Bohemians at the Council of Basel 1433," *Prague Essays,* ed. R. Seton-Watson (Oxford, 1949), pp. 81–123; P. Sigmund, *Nicholas of Cusa and Medieval Political Thought* (Cambridge, Mass., 1963), pp. 169–72.

50. Turrecremata's early views of infallibility changed from affirmation (Johannes de Turrecremata, *Propositio ad Dietam Maguntinam.* in P. Massi, *Il Magistero infallibile de Papa nella Theologia di Giovanni Torquemada* [Turin, 1957], Appendix IV) to avoidance of the question (J. de Turr., *Oratio synodalis de primatu.* ed. E. Candal [Rome, 1954], p. 55), before he settled on the doctrine taught in his exegesis of *Haec est fides.* Tierney, *Origins,* p. 271.

51. *Comm. ad* C.24 q.1 c.14 (III: 270–71), "Papa qui caput est ecclesie et magister et dux populi Christiani, non potest errare in his, que de fide tenenda et credenda; apostolus sui officio publice Christiano populo decerneret sive diffineret [que] esse credenda et tenenda, quod apostolice sedis iudicium in his que fidei sunt est indeffectibile, quod idem est." See also SE II c. 110, fol. 254v. Massi, *Il Magistero.* p. 78. Turrecremata thought the universal church unerring only in conjunction with the Roman pontiff; see Johannes de Turrecremata, *Oratio synodalis* ed. Candal, p. 54; *Comm. ad* C.24 q.1 c.9 (III: 268). De Vooght, "Esquisse," p. 137.

52. *Comm. ad* C.24 q.1 c.14 (III: 271). See also ibid., *ad* C.2 q.1 c.9 (III: 268); SE II c. 109, fol. 252r.

53. *Comm. ad* C.24 q.1 c.14 (III: 271), "Si apostolice sedis iudicium potest in his quae fidei sunt errare, sive quod nihil habebitur certum in his, quae apostolica sedes diffinivit de fide, et de condemnatione haereticorum, et de sacramentis, de canonizatione sanctorum, de interpretatione dubiorum, sed omnia essent ambigua, sed hoc est inconvenientissimum, quia fidem ecclesiae evacuat. Ait enim Bernardus fides non habet ambiguum ergo necesse est dicere, quod apostolicae sedis iudicium in his quae fidei sunt errare non possit." Turrecremata's doctrine on the selection of the canon of Scripture was substantially the same as Terreni's; see SE II c. 112, fol. 258r; *Comm. ad* C.25 q.1 c.6 (III: 316). Massi, *Il Magistero.* pp. 154–57.

54. *Comm. ad* C.24 q.1 c.14 (III: 271), "Assistentia spiritus sancti promissa a Christo non respicit personam pape, sed officium seu sedem. Et ideo cum opinari sit persone, iudicare vero sit officii, licet esset possibile papam mali opinari, errare tamen sententiando in iudicio de his quae sunt fidei non est possibile stante divina promissione." See also SE II c. 112, fol. 259v-60r. According to Turrecremata, the papal office was the truest form of that ambiguous entity the Roman church, see ibid., II c. 55, fol. 172v; ibid., II c. 64, fol. 187r; *Comm. ad* D.11 c. 3 (I: 106); ibid., *ad* D.22 c.2 (I: 211). W. Ullmann, *Principles of Government and Politics in the Middle Ages,* 2nd ed. (London, 1964), pp. 488–523.

55. *Comm. ad* C.24 q.1 c.14 (III: 271), "Rationem assignant quidem dicentes, quia deus non permitteret eum diffinire haeresim, aut aliquid contra fidem, sed prohibet eum aut per mortem, per aliam fidelium resistentiam, aut per aliorum instructionem, aut per internam inspirationem, aut per alios modos secundum quos Dei ecclesiae sanctae, et fidei unitati multipliciter providere potest."

56. Ibid., "Nos vero aliam rationem damus, quare neganda est illa minor, videlicet quia si Romanus pontifex incideret in haeresim damnatam, et ita effectus esset haereticus, ipso facto quo cadat a fide Petri, cadit a cathedra et sede Petri, et per consequens iudicium quod

faceret talis haereticus, non esset iudicium apostolicae sedis. Immo nec iudicium alicuius authoritatis esset dicendum, aut momenti; quia cum per haeresim cecidisset a praelatione, per consequens autoritate iudicandi privatus esset." See also SE II c.112, fol.260v. Turrecremata thought a council the only proper agent for an inquiry into a pope's orthodoxy, see *Comm. ad* D.17 *ante* c.1 q.3 (I: 149); ibid., *ad* D.21 c.7 q.3 (I: 202). Turrecremata also believed that councils could err and that the surest guide was the united judgment of pope and council, see SE III c.49, fol. 335r-v. Horst, "Konziliare Elemente," pp. 364–67; de Vooght, "Esquisse," p. 141.

57. Lederer, *Torquemada*, pp. 199–205, 239; Massi, *Il Magistero*, p. 101, 104; G. Thils, *L'Infaillebiliti pontificale* (Louvain, 1968), p. 53; J. Fenton, "The Theology of the General Council," *The General Council*, ed. W. J. McDonald (Washington, 1962), pp. 149–82, at 159–60.

58. Horst, "Konziliare Elemente," pp. 380–83.

59. Tierney, *Origins*, pp. 270–72.

60. J. B. Biciunas, *Doctrina ecclesiologica S. Roberti Bellarmini cum illa Iohannis Card. de Turrecremata comparata* (Rome, 1963).

61. Turrecremata was cited in favor of infallibility in Johannes de Turrecremata, *De inerrantia Romani pontificis (ex cura illius opere Summa de potestate papali)* (Turin, 1870); J. T. Chilardi, *De plenitudine potestatis Romani pontificis in ecclesia (opusculum ex operibus I. de Turrecremata)* (Turin, 1870). This line of argument was criticized in *De summi pontificis infallibilitate personali* (Naples, 1870), p. 8.

II
ORDERS AND OFFICES

Marginalia on a Tenth-Century Text on the Ecclesiastical Officers

ROGER E. REYNOLDS

In a study honoring Fr. Aubrey Gwynn, Professor Kuttner pinpointed a critical juncture in the history of the theology of sacred orders.[1] In the late eleventh century the subdeacon was firmly entrenched as one of the sacred orders because, like the deacon and presbyter above him, he was to be bound by the ancient law of celibacy.[2] Since the late eleventh century, controversy has continued to simmer over the exact status of the subdeacon in the ecclesiastical hierarchy. Is the subdiaconate a sacred, superior, and major order, or is it to be counted among the non-sacred, inferior, and minor orders? On 15 August 1972, Pope Paul VI in his *motu proprio* decree, *Ministeria quaedam,* finally put this old controversy to rest with the deletion of the subdiaconate from the ecclesiastical hierarchy.[3] The present study honoring Professor Kuttner deals with a text on orders written in the century preceding the eleventh, which placed the subdiaconate among the inferior orders.

The theological landscape of the tenth century has always been noted for its barrenness, and nowhere is this more conspicuous than in the theology of sacred orders. While liturgical scholars have emphasized the significance for the theology of orders of the introduction into Roman territories of the *Pontificale Romano-Germanicum* and its hierarchy of officers,[4] it is well known that original theological tracts and liturgical commentaries dealing with orders were rare in the tenth century and that what little was produced had but marginal consequences in later medieval discussions on the ecclesiastical hierarchy.[5] The paucity of tenth-century tracts dealing with the ecclesiastical hierarchy becomes especially pronounced if the output of the ninth and eleventh centuries is compared with that of the century between. During the ninth century there was the compilation and diffusion of the supplemented *Gregorian Sacramentary,*[6] the ordination rites of which wrought changes in the theology of orders felt in the church down to 1972. The origins and functions of the officers of the church were discussed extensively in the ninth century in such canonical and liturgical texts as the *Institutio canonicorum,*[7] the *Liber officialis* of Amalarius,[8] the *De institutione clericorum* of Raban Maurus,[9] and the Pseudo-Isidorian *Decretals,* all of which were to work their influence on the theology of orders for centuries.[10] On the other side of the tenth century there were numerous eleventh-century works in which aspects of the ecclesiastical hierarchy were treated: the canon law collections,[11] the *Micrologus*[12] and *De presbiteris*[13] of Bernold of Constance, and the *Sermo de excellentia sacrorum ordinum* attributed to Ivo of Chartres.[14] It is the purpose of this article to draw attention to the single most important tract on orders written in the tenth century, the Pseudo-Alcuinian *Liber de divinis officiis* (LDO), and to describe some of its diffusion and modification in the tenth century and beyond.

Among the *opera dubia* attributed to Alcuin there are two tracts containing sections dealing with the ecclesiastical hierarchy. In the ninth-century pedagogical tract, *Disputatio puerorum per interrogationes et responsiones,* cap. 9, there is a series of questions under the rubric "De gradibus totius ecclesiae dignitatis," in which the eight grades of doorkeeper, psalmist, lector, exorcist, acolyte, subdeacon, deacon, and presbyter are defined etymologically and their origins and duties enumerated.[15] The section on the ecclesiastical hierarchy from the *Disputatio puerorum* was to be included in numerous liturgical and theological tracts well into the thirteenth century.[16] The other tract attributed to Alcuin in which the ecclesiastical grades are described is the *Liber de divinis officiis,* thought to have been written sometime before the middle of the tenth century. In the LDO, as it is now printed in the *Patrologia Latina,* there are three chapters devoted to the ecclesiastical hierarchy.[17] In cap. 34, "De dignitate ecclesiastici ordinis," there is a discussion of the grades of doorkeeper, lector, exorcist, acolyte, subdeacon, deacon, presbyter, and bishop. The grades are eight in number because in the vision of Ezekiel there were eight steps in the ascent to the Temple, and they are shown to have been foreshadowed in the Old Testament, and some are said to derive also from the New Testament where the church is pictured as having received and improved upon the Old Testament hierarchy. Of the eight grades three are superior, the deacon, presbyter or *sacerdos,* and bishop, and the remainder by implication are inferior.[18] In cap. 35 of the LDO there is a very short discussion of the Old and New Testament origins of the tonsure, and it is followed by cap. 36, "De gradibus ecclesiasticis," which begins by defining the words *cleros* and *canon* and continues with an extensive treatment of the ecclesiastical grades. In cap. 34, the sequence of the lower grades was consonant with the Romano-Gallican sequence found commonly in ninth-century tracts on orders in which the exorcist was listed hierarchically superior to the lector and inferior to the acolyte,[19] but in cap. 36, a sequence of lower grades, rarely found in the Middle Ages,[20] is used in which the acolyte is described between the lector and exorcist. The verses for the grades in cap. 36 are made up of etymological definitions, dependent in part on Isidore's *Origines,* descriptions of each officer's duty in the church and occasionally his relationship to other grades in the hierarchy, and for the doorkeeper and lector a description of his ordination. Parts of the texts are reminiscent of the tracts of Amalarius and Raban Maurus, but they are clearly independent and show the compiler of the LDO to have been moderately creative in his descriptions of the ecclesiastical officers and in his mixing and modification of older texts. Despite this modicum of originality, the descriptions of the grades in the LDO were not to enjoy the degree of popularity in the Middle Ages which the better-known ninth-century tracts knew, and in fact, there are few remaining manuscripts of the LDO.[21] Nonetheless, portions of the descriptions of the grades in the LDO were occasionally repeated and modified in manuscripts of the tenth century and beyond.

Catalan Texts

The Ripoll Liber glossarum et etimologiarum.   Some of the earliest appearances of portions of cap. 36 of the LDO turn up in Catalan manuscripts. The famous *Liber glossarum et etimologiarum* of the monastery of Ripoll,[22] Barcelona, Archivo de la Corona de Aragon, MS 74, contains several sections dealing with orders.[23] In the etymological glosses substantial extracts from Isidore's *Origines,* 7.12, are repeated,[24] and in an independent section earlier in the manuscript there is a tract on orders beginning with a discussion of tonsure (not found in the LDO) and continuing with sections from cap. 36 of the LDO.[25] There are several interesting features of the text of cap. 36 as it is presented in the Ripoll manuscript which foreshadow later modifications of the text. Before the description of the word *canon,* there is a rubric with the question, "De canonico quare ita vocetur?" Later in the Middle Ages extracts from the LDO were commonly placed under interrogatory rubrics and were to be included as part of the *Liber Quare.* None of the texts from the LDO in the Ripoll manuscript is as complete as is the corresponding text printed in the *Patrologia Latina,* but the most noticeable omissions are the descriptions of the ordination rites for the doorkeeper and lector. There are also additions to the Ripoll text, the most prominent being in the description of the acolyte, where after it is said that he carries the candles when the gospel is read, the question is asked, "Et quid opus est tunc illam lucem temporalem inesse, cum dies sit, et satis videatur?" to which the response of the LDO is given, "Ut demonstretur quia de tenebris infidelitatis venimus ad lumen fidei."[26]

To reproduce here the text of the LDO in the Ripoll manuscript is unnecessary since it has been published from an almost identical form in the *Pontifical of Roda.*

Pontifical of Roda.   In this eleventh-century pontifical, Lleida, Archivo Capitular, MS 16,[27] the ordination rites, which are related to both the *Pontificale Romano-Germanicum* and the *Pontifical Romano-Hispánico* of Vic,[28] are preceded by the excerpt from cap. 36 of the LDO, whose verses were probably used as allocutions to each ordinand during his ordination. Like the identical text in the Ripoll manuscript, the sections from the LDO describing the *traditio instrumentorum* for the doorkeeper and lector have been omitted, probably because in the ordination rites themselves sections from the *Statuta ecclesiae antiqua* with the *traditio instrumentorum* are used.

Pyrenean Canonical Collection.   In the *Pontifical of Roda* the texts from the LDO are arranged with the grade of acolyte between the lector and exorcist, but in the ordination rite itself the grades are structured according to the Roman-Gallican sequence with the exorcist hierarchically below the acolyte and above the lector. Verses from cap. 36 of the LDO are rearranged according to this same Romano-Gallican sequence in another Catalan manuscript, this time in a late eleventh-century liturgico-canonical manuscript from Ripoll, Barcelona, Biblioteca Central de la Diputación Provincial, MS 944,[29] edited by Professor Martínez Díez.[30] At the conclusion of the canonical collection there is liturgical material which includes extracts from the LDO, cap. 36. In some respects these extracts resemble those of the earlier Ripoll and Roda texts, but in other respects they are different. Like the Ripoll and Roda excerpts, the descriptions of the ordination rites for the doorkeeper and lector from the LDO are omitted in the Pyrenean collection, probably because equivalent verses from the *Statuta ecclesiae antiqua* are used immediately after each verse from the LDO. Also each of the texts from the LDO is under an interrogatory rubric, e.g., "Quur clericus dicitur?" Moreover, the excerpted texts from the LDO have been altered or paraphrased,[31] and material not in the LDO has been added.[32] One of the more interesting additions is found in the verse for the exorcist. In the Ripoll and Roda manuscripts, exorcism was forbidden to all "nisi qui eundem gradum habet, aut presbiter aut diachonus aut subdiachonus aut exorcista,"[33] implying that the exorcist was indeed the grade below the subdiaconate. In the Pyrenean collection, however, where the exorcist is hierarchically below the acolyte, exorcism is forbidden to all "nisi superiores illo gradus habuerit." The major difference between the excerpts in the Ripoll and Roda and the Pyrenean collection lies in the number of grades described in terms of the LDO, cap. 36. In the earlier excerpts the grades from cleric through *pontifex* were described using the LDO, but in the Pyrenean collection it is only the tonsure, cleric, and seven grades from doorkeeper through presbyter which are so described.

Brescia Pontifical

It was earlier suggested that in the *Roda Pontifical* the extracts of the LDO functioned as a source for allocutions to ordinands. This suggestion is buttressed by a twelfth-century pontifical from Santa Giulia in Brescia, Bologna, Biblioteca Universitaria, MS lat. 794 (1556),[34] where extracts from the LDO are mixed with other materials, including the "Isidorian" *Epistula ad Leudefredum,* the *De officiis vii. graduum, Statuta ecclesiae antiqua,* and an Ivonian ordinal of Christ, to form allocutions given by the bishop to the seven grades from doorkeeper through presbyter: "Cum fuerint ante episcopum dicat eis episcopus. . . ." Like the Pyrenean collection, the extracts from the LDO are arranged in the Romano-Gallican sequence since the ordinations are performed in that sequence. And like the Catalan versions, the

Brescia text of the LDO is abbreviated. Among the materials prominently omitted are the descriptions of the ordination for the doorkeeper and lector and the definition of exorcism. An alteration in the verse for the exorcist confirms that the acolyte is superior to the exorcist, when exorcism is prohibited to all "nisi qui eundem gradum habet ut presbiter aut diaconus aut subdiaconus aut acolitus aut exorcista."[35]

Abstracted from the other texts in the ordination allocutions, the Brescia excerpt of the LDO reads:

> Hostiarius dicitur ab hostio ecclesie. Qui ita debet previdere . . . ut salva sint.

> Lector dicitur a legendo . . . in ecclesia.

> Exorcista grece latine dicitur adiurator. Illorum enim offitium est . . . nisi qui eundem gradum habet ut presbiter aut diaconus aut subdiaconus aut acolitus aut exorcista.

> Acolitus grece latine dicitur ceroferarius, id est cereum ferens. Illorum offitium est ut deportent cereos quando legendum est Evangelium. Sed quid est opus tunc temporalem lucem inesse cum dies sit et satis videatur? Ut demonstretur quia de tenebris infidelitatis venimus ad lumen fidei.

> Subdiaconus dicitur subminister eo quod subdiacono, id est subministro sit. Illius offitium est . . . quia de latere Domini processit sanguis et aqua.

> Diaconus grece latine minister dicitur quia ministrat ille presbitero. Ponit linteamen in altari, ponit calicem et panem . . . offitium competit consecrandi, ita diacono ministrandi.

> Presbiter grece latine dicitur senior non propter senectutem. . . . Quare? Quia sapientior illis fuit. Sacerdos grece latine dicitur sacrum dans, id est sanctum sacrifitium.[36]

The Romano-Gallican Sequence of Grades in LDO Excerpta

In the LDO, caps. 34 and 36, the lower grades are listed in different sequences: in the former the acolyte is hierarchically above the exorcist, and in the latter the acolyte is below the exorcist. This anomaly early caused several copyists of the LDO to arrange the grades in cap. 36 according to the Romano-Gallican sequence of cap. 34. In Paris, Bibl. nat., MS lat. 9421 (s. X), fols. 13r-14v, the text of cap. 36 lists the acolyte hierarchically superior to the exorcist, and it has been found in the Pyrenean collection and Brescia Pontifical that a similar alteration was made in eleventh- and twelfth-century excerpts of the LDO.

Vatican, MS Reg. lat. 234. One of the more remarkable instances of the alteration of cap. 36 to the Romano-Gallican sequence appears in this eleventh-century manuscript, where excerpts from the LDO are placed in a text described as an *Expositio Rabbani de celebratione misse et de ordinibus clericorum.*[37] The texts from the LDO are found in two separate sections of the manuscript, fols. 14v-15v and 16v-17r. In the earlier section an abbreviated text of cap. 36 is given with the exorcist listed hierarchically above the acolyte, and in the latter section the grades are presented in the Romano-Gallican sequence.

Text A (fols. 14v-15v)   Text B (fols. 16v-17r)

Cleros grece sors latine vel hereditas
Domini. Qui ergo ad clericatus . . . id
est sine capite religionis.

Canon grece regula latine eo quod
recto tramite . . . recte in sancta
ecclesia.

Ostiarius ab hostio ecclesiae dicitur   Hostiarii
quod ita debet . . . intra ecclesiam
sunt ut salva sint.   sunt in ecclesia quibus tradite
                                                 sunt claves . . . ac tuendae ecclesiae.

Lector dicitur a legendo . . . habeat   Lectores
in aecclesia.   quibus traditus est codex . . .
                                                 pronuntiando populo placeant.

Acolitus grece cerofarius latine, id
est cereum ferens. Illorum officium
est ut deportent cereos quando legitur
Evangelium in ecclesia. Et quid
necesse est ut lucem temporalem inter
esse cum dies sit et satis videatur?
Ut demonstretur quod de tenebris
infidelitatis venimus ad lucem fidei.

Exorcismus grece sermo adiurationis   Exorciste quibus data est potestas
sive increpationis dicitur latine, et   eiciendorum demonum non adiurationibus
inde exorcista adiurator. Illorum   Salomonis, sed invocationem Dei
officium est . . . nisi qui eundem offi-   omnipotentis et precibus sanctis.
cium habent aut presbiter aut diaconus
aut subdiaconus aut exorcista.

                                                 Acoliti qui nunc cerofarii dicuntur
                                                 qui cereos deferunt ante diaconem
                                                 quando legendum est Evangelium non
                                                 ad effugandas tenebras, presertin
                                                 cum sol in die rutilet sed ut
                                                 signum leticiae sit et ut sub
                                                 typo corporalis luminis lux illa
                                                 in memoria habeatur, de qua dicitur,
                                                 Erat lux vera et cetera.

Subdiaconus dicitur subminister eo   Subdiaconi qui grece ypodiaconi
quod subdiacono sit. Illius   dicuntur ut ipso nomine claret
officium est . . . processit sanguis   subdiaconibus constituti sunt
et aqua.   eisque officiis observiunt quae
                                                 circa altare aguntur. Tempore
                                                 enim sacrificii apparent in
                                                 conspectu pontificis vel presbiteri
                                                 parati ad nutum iubentis. Peracto
                                                 sacrificio mysteria . . . a diacono
                                                 colligenda vel deportanda
                                                 suscipiuntur.[38]

Text A (fols. 14v-15v)   Text B (fols. 16v-17v)

Diaconus grece hebraice levites latine   Diaconi id est ministri ab apostolis
assumptus . . . ita diacono ministrandi.   ordinati leguntur. Inter quos primus
                                               martyr Stephanus velut Sydus eximium
                                               rutilavit. Hi semper presto esse
                                               debent episcopo vel sacerdoti sacra
                                               mysteria celebranti. Ad ipsos
                                               pertinet ut oblata a populis super
                                               altare consecranda disponant et
                                               perfectis mysteriis, calicem
                                               sacrosancti sanguinis Domini
                                               fidelibus propinent.

Presbiter grece latine senior dicitur   Presbiteri id est seniores non
non propter senectutem . . . Quare?   tantum etatae quantum moribus et
Quia sapientior illis fuit.   sapientia. Hi potestatem habent
                                               catecizandi, baptizandi . . .
                                               concessum est officium predicandi.

Episcopus grece latine dicitur   Episcopis super hos, sicut loco et
superintendens vel superspeculator,   dignitate . . . quorum maioris gradus
id est supervidens quia ipse debet   excellentia crescat; sitque differentia
supervidere . . . dedi te domui Israel.   in vocabulis sicut precelsior locus
                                               honoris.[39]

Antistes quasi ante stans, idem ante
aram . . . dignitate et honore
superemineat.

Pontifex quasi pontem faciens. . . .
Pons autem est tabulatum super
aquas.[40]

If these two texts are compared with cap. 36 of the LDO as printed in the
Patrologia Latina, it is clear that Text A repeats most of the earlier sections of
the verses for each of the grades from the LDO and that Text B reproduces
the remainder of the text.[41] In Text B, however, there is new material introduced for several of the grades. For the exorcist and deacon Text A reproduces virtually the complete verse from the LDO, so in Text B new material has been added. The description of the exorcist contains a reference
probably to cap. 34 or the LDO and speaks of the invocations used by the
exorcist.[42] The text for the deacon is a rare combination of the New Testament origins of the diaconate and a catalogue of the deacon's duties reminiscent of the Isidorian *Epistula ad Leudefredum.*[43] For the subdiaconate
fragments similar to those from Isidore's *Origines*[44] and Amalarius' *Liber officialis*[45] are given first and are followed by the last portion of the text from
the LDO. Finally, the verse for the bishop in Text B, although taken from
the LDO, derives from the verse for the presbyter in the LDO.[46]

Paris, Bibl. nat., MS lat. 4286.   This twelfth-century manuscript
from St.-Martin of Tournai contains a variety of canonical pieces, including

the *Summa Haimonis.* [47] Following the canonical material is a text, clearly an allocution to ordinands, under the rubric "Sententiae dicendae super illos qui ordinandi sunt."[48] The grades from doorkeeper through bishop are arranged in the Romano-Gallican sequence, and each is described with a mixture of texts including the LDO, Isidore's *De ecclesiasticis officiis* and *Origines,* the *Statuta ecclesiae antiqua,* and *De officiis vii. graduum.*[49] These descriptions are followed by an Hiberno-Hispanic hierarchical ordinal of Christ similar to the one in the *Collectio Hibernensis* and a text on the vestments.[50] In the middle of this material on vestments there has been added under the rubric "De gradibus ecclesiasticis" the section on the *cleros* and *canon* from the LDO, cap. 36.[51]

To begin each description of the grades from doorkeeper through presbyter, material from the LDO is presented in an unusual way. A text for each grade almost identical to Text B of Vat. Reg. lat. 234, fols. 16v–17r, is given first, and this is followed by a text nearly identical to Text A of Reg. lat. 234, fols. 14v–15v. Only in the description of the presbyter has Text A been cut short with the words, ". . . et diuturnis temporibus et nocturnis intelligat ea quae cantat et legit."[52] To introduce the bishop, a text virtually identical to Text A of Reg. lat. 234 is given.

Bamberg, Staatsbibl., MS Msc. Liturg. 134 and Vienna, Öster-reichische Nationalbibl., 273.   In MS Vat., Reg. lat. 234 the texts on orders from the LDO were split into two sections, a longer description of the grades and their origins in Text A, and a somewhat shorter summary in Text B. A similar handling of the texts is found in an eleventh- or twelfth-century liturgical commentary which has at times been attributed to Frutolf of Michelsberg (1103). This commentary, which deserves an extensive study in the future, was briefly treated by Fr. Kennedy in 1938, who knew of only the eleventh- or twelfth-century manuscript, Bamberg 134 (Ed.V.13).[53] But there is another unfinished and fragmentary manuscript of the same text in Vienna 273 of almost the same date.[54]

The first book of the commentary is introduced by twelve chapters describing the ecclesiastical grades. Caps. 1-11 describe the cleric, tonsure, and then the grades from doorkeeper through bishop arranged in the Romano-Gallican sequence. Fr. Kennedy pointed out that very little of the material is original and that most of it is a patchwork of the LDO, the *Liber officialis* of Amalarius, perhaps the *De institutione clericorum* of Raban Maurus, and fragments from other authors. The compiler, who was a much more skillful mosaicist than Fr. Kennedy indicated, took fragments not only from cap. 36 of the LDO, but also from cap. 34, and combined them with other material to make up his commentary.[55]

In cap. 12 of the liturgical commentary, the compiler summarized his more extensive descriptions of the eight grades in caps 3–11 by repeating almost verbatim Text B from Reg. lat. 234. In only three verses do the texts differ substantially: for the subdiaconate Text B is cut short at the words "que circa altare aguntur"; for the diaconate the words from Text B are omitted, "id est ministri apostolis . . . sacra mysteria celebranti;" and for the episcopate the words at the conclusion of Text B, "maioris gradus excellentia crescat," are rounded off with the usual reading from cap. 36 of the LDO, "et minor ordo mensurae suae limitem recognoscat."

Summary Texts of the LDO

Virtually all of the texts of cap. 36 discussed thus far have been only moderately abbreviated. There are several versions which are, however, severely abbreviated or summaries, one being included in the fairly widely distributed *Liber Quare*.

Liber Quare.   The *Liber Quare* is a pedagogical tract which dates certainly to the late eleventh century and perhaps even back to Amalarius. In it liturgical and canonical texts are given in response to interrogatories. In several manuscripts of the *Liber Quare* a very short version of cap. 36 appears in which the acolyte is listed hierarchically inferior to the exorcist. Among these manuscripts is Vatican, Arch. S. Pet. H.11, fols. 320v–321r; Paris, Bibl. nat., lat. 2327, fol. 68r; and Cambridge, Pembroke College, 111, fols. 100v–101r.

Cleros grece latine dicitur sors vel hereditas Domini.

Canon grece latine regula. Inde canonicus, id est regularis.

Ostiarius ab ostio ecclesie dicitur.

Lector a legendo eo quod ministerium legendi habet in ecclesia.[56]

Acolitus grece latine ceroferarius, id est cereum ferens.

Exorcismus grece latine dicitur sermo adiurationis sive increpationis. Et inde exorcista, id est adiurator.

Subdiaconus subminister eo quod subdiacono sit, id est subministro.

Diaconus grece hebraice levites latine assumptus vel minister interpretatur, assumptus quia assumitur, id est elegitur ad servicium altaris, minister quia ministrat presbitero.

Presbiter grece latine dicitur senior non propter senectutem sed propter dignitatem.

Sacerdos grece latine sacrum dans populo vel sanctum sacrificium offerens Domino.

Episcopus grece latine dicitur superintendens. Episcopi supra scopos intendens.

Pontifex quasi pontem faciens eo quod pontem id est viam aliis verbo et vite exemplo prebere debet.

Pons enim tabulatum dicitur quod super aquas fit.[57]

Salisbury Cathedral 135.   This late eleventh- or early twelfth-century manuscript, which was at Salisbury between 1089 and 1125, begins with a liturgical treatise on the mass, vestments, creed, and so forth.[58] In the middle of the commentary on the mass there is a text describing the acolyte's duty.

Acoliti, id est illuminatores ecclesie tenent candelas usque ad Kyrrieleison et tunc deponunt quia oportet ut doctores ecclesie nullatenus populum de manibus relinquant antequam populas subiectus sciat dicere, Domine miserere mei. Pertinet enim Kyrrieleison ad divinam Patris excellentiam ut qui Filium suum pro nobis tradidit exuat nos a pena inferni. Christeleison celebratur ut Filius Ihesus Dominus noster una cum Patre det nobis vitam eternam.[59]

This is followed immediately by a summary text of cap. 36 of the LDO, striking because the text from the LDO on the acolyte is omitted.

Cleros grece latine sors vel hereditas Domini. Inde clerici dicti eo quod de sorte Domini et hereditate sint si regulariter vivunt. Si autem non vivunt regulariter non sunt clerici, Acefali, id est sine capite religionis.

Canon grece latine regula . . . recte in sancta ecclesia.

Ostiarius ab hostio ecclesie quod ita debeat providere et custodire ut ea que infra ecclesiam sunt salva sint.

Lector dicitur a legendo eo quod ministerium legendi habeat in ecclesiam Dei.

Exorcismus grece sermo adiurationis sive increpationis latine et inde exorcista adiurator. Illorum officium est . . . repellant demones ab eis.

Subdiaconus grece latine subminister eo quod subdiácono sit, id est subministro.

Diaconus grece levita hebraice asumptus latine vel minister. Assumptus quia assumitur, id est elegitur ad servitium altaris, minister quia ministrat presbitero.

Presbiter grece senior dicitur latine non propter etatem . . . ut intelligat ea que legit.

Sacerdos quasi sacrum dans, id est sanctum sacrificium offerens Deo.

Episcopus grece superintendens latine, id est supervidens quia ipse debet supervidere vitam subiectorum suorum qualiter credant qualiter Dei precepta custodiant. Speculatores animarum dedit Deus episcopos et presbiteros.

Antisites quasi antestans, id est eminens et superexcellens universum populum dignitate et honore.

Pontifex quasi pontem faciens. . . . Pons autem est tabulatum quia fit super aquas.[60]

From the number of examples of the LDO presented here—and there are undoubtedly more in the manuscripts—it would appear that the Pseudo-Alcuinian tract, at least in its chapters on orders, enjoyed a somewhat wider popularity in the tenth century and beyond than has often been attributed to it. Yet when one looks to the major late eleventh- and twelfth-century commentaries on orders by such masters as Ivo of Chartres, Hugh of St.-Victor, Gratian, and Peter Lombard, it is not the LDO but the pre-tenth-century texts of Isidore, Amalarius, Raban Maurus, the *Statuta ecclesiae antiqua,* and the *De officiis vii. graduum* which dominate as sources. Given the frequency of the texts on orders from the LDO in eleventh- and early twelfth-century manuscripts, it might be asked why they did not work their influence on the major commentaries on orders in the twelfth century and beyond. It may have been simply fortuitous, but there are probably other reasons. The first and perhaps most obvious is that the descriptions of the grades in caps. 34–36 of the LDO did not add very much to the pre-tenth-century texts, and hence twelfth-century authors went back to the originals. But there is another reason why the texts on orders in the LDO probably failed to exert more influence. In several of its propositions the LDO was out of step with the theology of orders developing in the late eleventh and twelfth century. In the eleventh century the *cursus* of lower orders was being established as door-keeper, lector, exorcist, and acolyte,[61] yet the LDO, cap. 36, placed the acolyte between the lector and exorcist. In several instances it has been seen how the LDO was altered to fit this Romano-Gallican sequence. Further, it was in the later eleventh and early twelfth century that some of the more prominent theologians, liturgists, and canonists were counting the orders at seven,[62] yet the LDO stated that there were eight. Finally, the LDO with its treatment of the subdiaconate as an inferior order was inconsonant with the notion—growing ever more popular in the late eleventh and early twelfth century—that the subdiaconate was among the superior, sacred, or major orders.

Carleton University
Ottawa, Canada

Notes

Research for this article has been supported in part by grants from the American Council of Learned Societies, American Philosophical Society, and Canada Council.

1. Stephan Kuttner, "Pope Lucius III and the Bigamous Archbishop of Palermo," in *Medieval Studies Presented to Aubrey Gwynn* (Dublin, 1961), p. 418.

2. On this question of celibacy for the sacred orders in the early Middle Ages, see A. M. Stickler, "La Continenza dei Diaconi specialmente nel primo Millennio della Chiesa," *Salesianum* XXVI (1964), 275–302; and Jean Gaudemet, "Gratien et le Célibat ecclésiastique," *Studia Gratiana* XIII (1967), 339–69.

3. "Ministeria in tota Ecclesia Latina servanda, hodiernis necessitatibus accommodata, duo sunt, Lectoris nempe et Acolythi. Partes, quae hucusque Subdiacono commissae erant, Lectori et Acolytho concreduntur, ac proinde in Ecclesia Latina ordo maior Subdiaconatus non amplius habetur. Nihil tamen obstat, quominus, ex Conferentiae Episcopalis iudicio, Acolythus alicubi etiam Subdiaconus vocari possit."

4. See Cyrille Vogel, *Introduction aux Sources de l'Histoire du Culte chrétien au Moyen âge* (Spoleto, 1966), pp. 187–203, and literature therein.

5. Adolph Franz, *Die Messe im deutschen Mittelalter: Beiträge zur Geschichte der Liturgie und des religiösen Volkslebens* (Freiburg, 1902), p. 407: "Nach der reichen Entwicklung der liturgischen Literatur in der Karolingerzeit nimmt sich das 10. Jahrhundert ärmlich aus. Die einzigen auf uns gekommenen Leistungen sind die Pseudo-Alkuinsche Schrift 'De divinis officiis' und eine für Schlzwecke bestimmte Messerkärung."

6. See Jean Deshusses, "Le Sacramentaire grégorien pré-hadrianique," *Revue Bénédictine* LXXX (1970), 213–37; his edition of *Le Sacramentaire grégorien: ses Principales formes d'après les plus anciens Manuscrits,* Spicilegium Friburgensis XVI (Fribourg/Suisse, 1971); and Klaus Gamber, "Der fränkische Anhang zum Gregorianum im Licht eines Fragments aus dem Anfang des 9. Jh.," *Sacris erudiri* XXI (1972–73), 267–89.

7. Cc. 1–9; MGH LL III, Concilia, II: 318–26.

8. 2.4–14; Joannus Michael Hanssens, ed., *Amalarii episcopi opera liturgica omnia,* ii: *Liber officialis* (Vatican City, 1948), pp. 209–36.

9. 1.2–12; PL cv: 297–305. On the manuscripts of this tract, see Raymond Kottje, "Hrabanus Maurus—'Praeceptor Germaniae'?" *Wissenschaft zwischen Forschung und Ausbildung,* Schriften der Philosophischen Fachbereiche der Universität Augsburg i, eds. Josef Becker and Rolf Bergmann (1975), p. 89; and "Hrabanus Maurus—'Praeceptor Germaniae'?" *Deutsches Archiv* (1975), 540–42.

10. On some of the sections on orders in the *Decretals,* see my "A Ninth-Century Treatise on the Origins, Office, and Ordination of the Bishop," *Revue Bénédictine* lxxxv (1975), 324–32.

11. Throughout the canon law collections of the eleventh century there are scattered texts on the ecclesiastical orders. On the various late patristic and early medieval texts as they appear in the collections, see my "Excerpta from the *Collectio Hibernensis* in Three Vatican Manuscripts," *Bulletin of Medieval Canon Law* n.s. v (1975), 1–9; "The Pseudo-Hieronymian *De septem ordinibus ecclesiae:* Notes on its Origins, Abridgments and Use in Early Medieval Canonical Collections," *Revue Bénédictine* lxxx (1970), 238–52; "The *De officiis vii graduum:* Its Origins and Early Medieval Development," *Mediaeval Studies* xxxiv (1972), 113–51; "The 'Isidorian' *Epistula ad Leudefredum:* Its Origins, Early Manuscript Tradition, and Editions," in *Visigothic Spain: New Approaches* (Oxford, forthcoming).

12. PL cli: 973–1022. On Bernold's authorship of this tract, see V. L. Kennedy, "For a New Edition of the *Micrologus* of Bernold of Constance," in *Mélanges en l'Honneur de Monseigneur Michel Andrieu* (Strasbourg, 1956), pp. 229–41.

13. MGH Lib. de lite II: 142–46.

14. On the authorship of this tract, which may have been written either in the late eleventh or early twelfth century, see my "Ivonian Opuscula on the Ecclesiastical Officers," *Studia Gratiana* 17 (1976), 311–22. Additional manuscripts of the *Sermo* are Cambridge, Corpus Christi College, 289, pp. 305–18; Erlangen 226, fols. 146r–52v; Hereford 0.6.XIII, fols. 178r–82r; London, Brit. Lib., Royal 6.B.VI, fols. 27r–30v; Minneapolis, Univ. Of Minnesota, lat. 1, fols. 11v–17v (attributed to Peter Lombard); Monte Cassino 325, pp. 124–34 (not seen); Oxford, Corpus Christi College, 137, fols. 28r–32r; Oxford, St. John's College, 158, fols. 104r–14r; Oxford, Magdalene College, 26, fols. 15r–22r; Rome, Bibl. Naz. Centr., Sessor. 172 (2082) (s.XV), fols. 142r–43v; Salisbury 164, fols. 7v–14r (mutilated), 71r–77v; and Siena, Bibl. com., F.II.13, fols. 44r–48v (not seen).

15. PL ci: 1131–34. Ninth-century manuscripts of this text with variant readings can be found in Vienna, Österreichische Nationalbibl., 458, a manuscript of the Salzburg master Baldo, and Vienna 966.

16. See, e.g., the *Dunstan Pontifical.* Paris, Bibl. nat., MS lat. 943; Edmund Martène, ed., *De antiquis ecclesiae ritibus libri tres . . .* (Venice, 1783) ii: 37; the *Lanalet Pontifical.* Rouen MS A.27(368), fol. 55v; G. H. Doble, ed., *Pontificale Lanaletense (Bibliothèque de la Ville de Rouen A.27. Cat. 368): A Pontifical formerly in use at St.-Germans, Cornwall.* Henry Bradshaw Society lxxiv (London, 1937), pp. 40f.; Munich, Staatsbibl., Clm. 5257 (s.XI), fols. 16v, 25r–v; Vic, Museo Episcopal, MS 39 (XXXV) (s.XI), fols, 135r–36r; Cambridge, Corpus Christi College, MS 44 (olim I.1) (s.XI), pp. 200–4; and Dublin, Trinity College, MS 218 (s.XIII), fol. 122r–v.

17. PL ci: 1173–1286, esp. 1231–36. For the editions of the LDO see A. Wilmart, "Expositio Missae," *Dictionnaire d'Archéologie chrétienne et de Liturgie* (hereafter DACL) (Paris, 1922), v. 1: 1027, n. 3. On the date of the LDO, see J. Joseph Ryan, "Pseudo-Alcuin's *Liber de divinis officiis* and the Liber *Dominus vobiscum* of St. Peter Damiani," *Mediaeval Studies* xiv (1952), 160. Cyrille Vogel and Reinhard Elze, eds., *Le Pontifical Romano-germanique du dixième Siècle* (Vatican City, 1963), ii: 1, place the tract before 910.

18. The acolyte is, however, directed to obey the superior grades. PL ci: 1232.

19. See my "The Portrait of the Ecclesiastical Officers in the *Raganaldus Sacramentary* and its Liturgico-Canonical Significance," *Speculum* xlvi (1971), 440.

20. See, e.g., Rather of Verona, *Praeloquium* 5.29; PL cxxvi: 313; the preface to the Monte Cassino ordinal of Christ of Monte Cassino, Bibl. dell'Abbazia, MS 217, p. 373, ed., André Wilmart, "Les Ordres du Christ," *Revue des Sciences religieuses* iii (1923), 314; and the ordinal of Christ in the twelfth- or thirteenth-century Psalter Commentary of Durham, N.C., Duke Univ., MS lat. 104, fol. 3v (a manuscript kindly brought to my attention by Mr. Paul Meyvaert).

21. See Vincent L. Kennedy, "The 'De officiis divinis' of *MS Bamberg Lit. 134,*" *Ephemerides liturgicae* lii (1938), 318, n. 23. I am very grateful to several members of the Pontifical Institute of Mediaeval Studies in Toronto for having searched—alas unsuccessfully—through Fr. Kennedy's notes for his references to the French and German manuscripts of the LDO. It is possible that at least some of these manuscripts are those listed by Wilmart, "Expositio Missae," col. 1027. At the Institut de Recherche et d'Histoire des Textes in Paris there are very few manuscripts of the LDO listed, and most of these contain only fragments of the text: Bordeaux 11; Freiburg-i-Br., Bibl. Univ., 147; Laon 471; Orléans 263 (219); Paris, Bibl. nat., lat. 6638; Vat., Borgh. lat. 204; Vat., Reg. lat. 234, 479, 1578; and Vat. lat. 3850. Also see Trier, Stadtbibl., 1736, cited in Franz, *Die Messe,* pp. 367–76, and Wilmart, "Expositio Missae," col. 1027; Bloomington, Univ. of Indiana, Poole 31, fol. 6v; and Phillipps 20749, fols. 33–35 (sold by Sotheby and Co., 30 November 1971, Lot 491).

22. See, e. g., Henri Focillon, *The Year 1000,* pb. ed. (New York, 1971), p. 92.

23. According to Ryan, "Pseudo-Alcuin's *Liber,*" p. 163, n. 21 (cf. PL ci: 1173, 1240), the author of the LDO refers to his home as *Gallia Braccata,* but this is not clear. If these words are, indeed, a reference to the author's home as *Gallia Braccata* (the old name for *Gallia Narbonensis*), then the early appearance of excerpta from the LDO in Catalan manuscripts may not be surprising.

24. Fol. 23r deals with the bishop; 30v with the lector; 33r with the acolyte; 33v with the *antistes;* 57v with the *cleros;* 67r–v with the episcopal grades, 68r with the *cleros;* 70v with the deacon, subdeacon, lector, acolyte, exorcist, and doorkeeper; and 72r with the presbyter and patriarch.

25. Fol. 12r–v.

26. Fol. 12r–v.

27. See Joan Bta. Altisent I Jové, "*Pontifical de Roda* (segle XI): Notes I Transcripció," *Analecta Sacra Tarraconensia* ii (1926), 533–35; the extensive bibliography on the manuscript in Alexandre Olivar, "Les Supervivències litúrgiques autoctònes a Catalunya en els Manuscrits dels Segles XI–XII," *II Congrés litúrgic de Montserrat iii: Secció d'Història* (Montserrat, 1967), 40; and most recently Miquel dels Sants Gros, "L'Ordre catalano-narbonès per a la Benedicció dels sants Olis," *Revista Catalana de Teologia* i (1976), 232. I have not, unfortunately, been able to use Josep Romà Barriga Planas, *El Sacramentari, Ritual i Pontifical de Roda. Cod. 16 de l'Arxiu de la Catedral de Lleida c. 1000* (Barcelona, 1975).

28. See Miguel S. Gros, "Las Órdenes sagradas del Pontifical *MS. 104 (CV) de la Bib. Cap. de Vic,*" *Hispania Sacra* xvii (1964), 104–16.

29. Fols. 175v–9r.

30. Gonzalo Martínez Díez, "Una Collección canónica pirenaica del Siglo XI," *Miscelánea Comillas* xxxviii (1962), 211–70, has edited the canonical collection. The Amalarian material in the manuscript has been cited by Hanssens, ed., *Amalarii opera,* iii: 481. According to Martínez Díez the manuscript is dated to the twelfth century because there is a letter of 1099 attributed to Urban II. In the manuscript the Urban text appears to be in a different hand than the remainder of the manuscript, and hence an eleventh-century date is preferred. On this important manuscript see Romà Barriga, "La Consagració episcopal en el *Pontifical de Roda* (Osca)," *Analecta Sacra Tarraconensia* xxxviii (1965), 6f.; Gonzalo Martínez Díez, "Dos Catálogos inéditos de la Biblioteca del Monasterio de Ripoll," *Hispania Sacra* xxii (1969), 333f.; and Bernard Lambert, *Bibliotheca hieronymiana manuscripta: La Tradition manuscrite des Oeuvres de Saint Jérôme* (Steenbrugge, 1970), iii.b nr. 911.

31. E.g., the text from the LDO for the acolyte is considerably altered: "Accolitus graece,

latine dicitur ceroferarius id est cereum ferens. Illorum enim offitium est ut deportent cereos ante evangelium. Nam illa temporalis lux ideo fertur ante evangelium ut ostendat ac leccione sacra nos de tenebris infidelitatis ad fidei lumen venisse."

32. E.g., the text for the tonsure has material added something like Isidore's *De ecclesiasticis officiis* 2.4 (PL LXXXIII: 779): "Tonsure habitus primum a nazoreis exortus est et in novo testamento a Priscilla et Aquila quos apostolus Paulus tonsuravit. Hi namque primi facti sunt clerici." To the text for the doorkeeper has been added: "Qui recte custos aecclesiae vocatur," reminiscent of the *Liber ordinum* 1.3.10, where the *custos sacrorum* is also called the *ianitor aditum et prepositus ostiariorum* (see *Le Liber ordinum en Usage dans l'Église wisiqothique et mozarabe d'Espagne du cinquième au onzième Siècle,* ed. Marius Férotin [Paris, 1904], col. 43). And to the text for the lector there are added the words: "Debet aetiam ea quae ex divina leccione intellexerit et verbo predicare."

33. Barcelona, Arch. de la Corona, MS 74, fol. 12v; and the *Pontifical de Roda,* p. 534.

34. Fols. xr–xxxr. On this manuscript see Réginald Grégoire, "Repertorium liturgicum Italicum," *Studi Medievali* IX (1968), 484.

35. Fol. xiiiv.

36. Fols. xr–xxxr. For reasons of economy the complete text of the LDO as it appears in the Brescia manuscript and others printed below has not been given, but the sections omitted are virtually identical with those in the edition printed in PL CI: 1231–36.

37. Fol. 31v. The earlier material listed in the index is Augustinian. As the manuscript now exists, only quires xxii–xxv remain.

38. In the manuscript the lower grades from doorkeeper through subdeacon have been gathered together in one paragraph, and the higher grades of deacon, presbyter, and bishop are treated individually.

39. Fols. 16v–17r.

40. Fols. 14v–15v.

41. PL CI: 1234–36.

42. Ibid., 1232.

43. Cf. PL LXXXIII: 895.

44. PL LXXXII: 292.

45. Hanssens, ed., *Amalarii opera,* II: 221.

46. PL CI: 1235.

47. Paul Fournier and Gabriel Le Bras, *Histoire des Collections canoniques en Occident* (Paris, 1932), II: 307.

48. Fols. 84v–94r.

49. See my "The *De officiis vii graduum*," pp. 149f.

50. 8.1; ed. Hermann Wasserschleben, *Die irische Kanonensammlung,* 2nd ed. (Leipzig, 1885), p. 26.

51. Fol. 91r. Immediately thereafter is a text on tonsure, which is not drawn from the LDO.

52. Cf. Paris, Bibl. nat., MS lat. 4286, fol. 88r; and Vat., MS Reg. lat. 234, fol. 15r.

53. Kennedy, "The 'De officiis divinis'," pp. 312–26.

54. The Vienna manuscript contains a miscellany of texts written in widely differing centuries. The liturgical commentary is the penultimate text bound into the manuscript. There are no initial letters before or any numbers assigned to each chapter. The text begins like the one in the Bamberg manuscript, but breaks off with the words ". . . serviant. Stolam collo super po . . ." in the section on vestments.

55. Material from cap. 34 of the LDO is found in bk. 1, c.3, 4, 7, 8, 9, 10, 12; and material from cap. 36 of the LDO is found in bk. 1, c.1, 4, 5, 6, 8, 9, 10, 11, 12.

56. In the Paris text there is an unusual "in monasterio" substituted for "in ecclesia."

57. Cambridge, Pembroke College, MS 111, fols, 100v–101r.

58. N. R. Ker, "Salisbury Cathedral Manuscripts and Patrick Young's Catalogue," *The Wiltshire Magazine,* No. 191, III (1949), 154, n. 1.

59. Cf. Amalarius, *Ordinis missae expositio* 1.2; *Eclogae: De ordine romano,* c.11; *Codex expositionis II,* cap. 11; Hanssens, ed., *Amalarii opera,* II: 300, 240; II: 272.

60. Fol. 6r.

61. See my "The *De officiis vii graduum,*" p. 145.

62. See, e.g., Peter Damiani, *Liber gratissimus,* c.15, MGH Lib. de lite I: 36; Ivo of Chartres, *Sermo II, PL* CLXII: 514; and Hugh of St.-Victor, *De sacramentis* 3.5, PL CLXXVI: 423.

The Structure of Holiness In Othloh's *Vita Bonifatii* and Ebo's *Vita Ottonis*

K. F. MORRISON

The interview between Christ and the Grand Inquisitor, which Dostoyevsky portrays in *The Brothers Karamazov,* may seem a strange point from which to begin a discussion of eleventh and twelfth century ideas. However, the encounter raises in sharp detail one matter that is central for us: namely, the pressures of institutional growth on the church's primitive ethos. The Grand Inquisitor's intricate argument that he had "corrected" Christ and allied with Satan so that Christ's ideals of peace and freedom could survive and be realized recalls many analogues to the mediaevalist's mind. One thinks of disputes that tormented Cluny and the Franciscan Order. All the issues involved in this ceaseless and, in some ways tragic, dialectic between ideals and experience center on one issue: their nucleus is holiness. Without resorting to the Inquisitor's cynicism, or to the insistence of some modern scholars that canonization has been yet another trophy of *Realpolitik,*[1] we can point to a number of changes in the way in which the visible church has thought about this subject. We are dealing with typology in process. It is well established that the early church considered the martyr as the epitome of holiness, and that, a little later, the type of the desert Father became dominant. In the Latin West, around the eighth century, people thought of bishops when they thought of holiness, and, beginning in the twelfth century, the religious gained a precedence that they have not lost until the present day. In an intricate and fascinating manner, each stage absorbed the traits of the earlier ones. The examples that will be studied combine the quest for martyrdom, the idealization of the ascetic life that is also the learned life, and the episcopal *magisterium.* The relative paucity of women and of diocesan clergy among those venerated as saints indicates persistent traits, both positive and negative, beneath this sequence of incremental change, which, of course, had its roots in the slow, collective experience of western Europe.

The structure of holiness that we are to consider had historical meaning because it had a place in the sequence of typologies just indicated: it held its dominance between the eighth and the twelfth centuries. This is our first ground-rule. We have a second: holiness was not yet defined by a tried and established juridical process. We are about to discuss St. Boniface and St. Otto of Bamberg. Apart from isolated and exceptional cases in the tenth and

eleventh centuries, the latter was one of the first whose credentials were reviewed by the papal court in a process bearing all the marks of canonization
as we know it. And yet, just as much as did Boniface and his biographer,
Otto belonged to the earlier age, when the juristic review was rough and im-
provised, and the recognition of holiness owed its integrity to Scripture and
the Fathers.

Any concept is made up of parts. Holiness is no exception to this rule.
Despite the fullness of Latin hagiographical literature, and despite the extraordinary care and lucidity with which that literature has been edited and
analyzed, there is still room for study of sanctity, as a concept, in terms of its
structure. A synthetic analysis would certainly require preliminary dissec-
tions of a large and representative sample of biographies. In this paper, I
mean to suggest a few directions indicated by two biographies written in
eleventh- and twelfth-century Germany.

Since they treat of missionaries, St. Boniface and St. Otto of Bamberg,
analogies with St. Paul were natural. The Apostle of the Gentiles also made a
direct contribution to the concept of sanctity as set forth by Othloh of St.
Emmeram and Ebo. His distinctions between appearance and reality—in
terms of the visible and the invisible, the flesh and the spirit, the animal and
the spiritual—drew a sharp line between man's outer existence and his inner
life; and, raised to the higher level of true and false knowledge, this distinction was fundamental to our authors' understanding of holiness. Theology
gives us the analytical categories needed to describe the structure of the concept: namely, the necessity, conditions, possibility, manner, and proofs of
holiness. These formed unconscious agenda for Othloh and Ebo, and they
gave hidden centers of gravity for unspoken assumptions. On each of the five
counts, they returned to the Pauline distinctions, with an emphasis on spirituality that was only to be expected in works intended to serve as apologetics
for monasteries against the encroachments of princes and worldly bishops.[2]

Othloh is known, on the one hand, as a monk whose peculiar visions supply titillating examples of abnormal psychology, and, on the other, as a
highly competent student of theology and classical learning. Both his
"psychopathologische Deutung" and his skill in divine and secular philosophy have been extensively treated by Helga Schauwecker in her recent
study.[3] His biography of St. Boniface, however, has never received a
thorough discussion, and we shall have to digress to locate it in his life and
oeuvre.

The reason for neglect is doubtless the very reason for the Vita's importance: namely, since Othloh was writing about a man who died three
hundred years before his own day, he could provide no eye-witness accounts,
but instead relied entirely on eighth-century materials. The brethren of
Fulda originally commissioned him to revise the biography of St. Boniface by
Willibald. The resulting work in fact combines elements from several narrative accounts contemporary with St. Boniface, and quantitatively, well over
half of Othloh's work consists of letters that passed between Boniface and the

popes of his day. As Hauck wrote, the biography by Othloh, "was originally intended to be nothing other than the stylistic improvement of an old, clumsy work. But here, too, the commission pressed the author further. . . . With their study [i.e., the study of letters to and from Boniface], he gained the insight . . . that the writing of history must as far as possible be grounded on primary sources. From this point of view, he not only smoothed out the form of the old biography, but he enlarged it with letters, and thereby created the first extant biography that rests essentially upon documentary material."[4] As we shall see, the use of sources was highly purposeful; it expressed convictions thoroughly rooted in Othloh's life, and in the intersection of his views with the experience of Fulda.

Othloh was born in the diocese of Freising (ca. 1010). After receiving an education, excellent for the day, at the monasteries of Tegernsee and Hersfeld, he entered the circle of Meinhard, bishop of Würzburg, and gained a fair reputation as a practitioner of the liberal arts. He made forays into monasteries for the purpose of studying books kept in their libraries. During one of those excursions, to St. Emmeram in Regensburg, he fell ill. On vowing to become a monk he miraculously recovered, and, in 1032, he entered the monastic life. For the next thirty years, Othloh was able to pursue his studies at St. Emmeram, and to develop skills in versifying, in rhetoric, in penmanship, and, not least, in polemics, of which he was extremely proud. Through much of that time, however, the monastery engaged Bishop Gebehard III of Regensburg (1036–60) in an intermittent conflict over property. New forms of the transfer and tenure of property were evolved to give the monastery a firmer grasp on its lands and emoluments; but Gebehard persisted in his "avarice." Over the years, Othloh came to see the struggle as a sign that the world was hastening toward its end, and as one of the reasons why men were afflicted with many disasters in his day, and why the rulers of the church should turn from their "immeasurable vanity" and seek ways in which God could be brought to cease his blows and show mercy to His people.[5] Gebehard's successor, Otto, found Othloh such a thorn in his side that the monk was forced to leave St. Emmeram and to seek asylum at Fulda, where he remained for four years. During that time, he composed several works, including the *Vita Bonifatii.* Subsequently, he returned to St. Emmeram, by way of Amorbach, and remained there until his death (ca. 1070).

Othloh discovered a familiar scenario in motion when he arrived at Fulda. The monks there were struggling with the archbishop of Mainz over the Thuringian tithes when Othloh came upon the scene. This conflict was a persistent one, and yet the monks had reason to hope that it might be resolved in their favor if an appeal were made *blande suaviterque.* The new archbishop, Siegfried (1060–84) was not only, as his predecessors had been, the successor of St. Boniface, who had founded Fulda and so esteemed it that he wished to be buried there rather than in Mainz, and whose relics still guarded the monastery. He had also been monk and abbot at Fulda. Siegfried had adapted all too well to the conventions of his see, gaining the support of the imperial court in his efforts to encroach upon the tithes rendered to Fulda and Hersfeld. He was so relentless and successful in this effort that, in 1065, Pope Alexander II joined forces with Fulda and, in 1068, forced him to return to the monastery holdings sufficient to restore its wealth to the level maintained when he had been abbot. Undaunted, the archbishop continued his efforts, and his persistence was rewarded by a synod held at Erfurt in 1073, which rejected the pleas of Fulda and Hersfeld and upheld Sieg-fried's.[6]

The matter bore the more heavily on Fulda because of its vulnerability to imperial intervention. At Christmastide 1052, as part of an agreement between Pope Leo IX and Henry III, Fulda, "and some other places and monastic communities which are said to have been given of old to St. Peter," were transferred from papal to imperial control.[7] During the regency of the Empress Agnes, and after Archbishop Anno of Cologne replaced her, the ominous possibilities of the transfer became obvious; for between early December 1056 and mid-December 1062 at least nine monastic properties were transferred by imperial authority to the control of bishops. This flagrant and repeated violation of traditional monastic privileges and liberties, and other arbitrary administration of proprietary ecclesiastical institutions of the Empire, forecast ruin for the monastic establishment or church whose representatives could not gain the favor of the regent. Abbot Egbert of Fulda saw the direction of things and, even in the pontificate of Leo IX, he sent records about St. Boniface to Rome as part of an effort to defend the prerogatives of his community,[8] an effort that gained, in 1057, a confirmation of privileges from Pope Victor II. Episcopal encroachments, sustained by the imperial regency, had advanced several stages by the time when Othloh arrived at Fulda, and Egbert had been succeeded as abbot by Widerad, a man in whom the brethren had little confidence.

A ceremonial dispute brought all these strands together. Convention gave the Abbot of Fulda the privilege of sitting beside the Archbishop of Mainz, the Metropolitan of Germany, in assemblies. Bishop Hezil of Hildesheim contested this privilege, and at Christmastide 1063 a street battle between his retainers and Widerad's brought the matter to a head before the imperial court. Although a panel of inquiry found Hezil's followers at fault, they went unpunished, whereas Widerad and his case were brushed aside. When news of the melee and subsequent indignities reached Fulda, the monks protested furiously against Widerad's feeble efforts. They sent emissaries to plead the case of Fulda before the imperial court. But their envoys received harsh judgments; Widerad was granted asylum at court and the power to end the monastic uprising in any way he chose. The initial question of protocol remained menacingly open.

The monks were "afire with the pain of the recent wound and with the memory of past wounds."[9] Since their formal legation had been spurned, they were in need of another means, more circuitous perhaps than direct recourse, by which to present their case to secular and ecclesiastical princes.

They had two ends in view: first, to gain a strong patron at the imperial court; and second, even if that dignitary were a bishop, to uphold the traditional monastic liberties from episcopal control. Siegfried of Mainz naturally came to mind. While the exact date of Othloh's *Vita Bonifatii* is not known, a date of 1063–64 is plausible in this historical context. Othloh mentions that the brethren had recalled Egbert's plan for a new biography of their patron, and that they would not let him decline the commission. This reversion to the plan of an effective abbot, the petulant insistence of the monks that Othloh describe the favors of Boniface toward Fulda, and the utter omission of any reference to Widerad indicate that the *Vita* may have been written in 1063–64, while the anger of the monks was hot, and Widerad had taken refuge among their enemies at court.

In his *Liber de tentatione,* Othloh wrote that biographies of saints should be read so that, by imitating holy exemplars, one could master the flesh and avoid the terrors of the Last Judgment.[10] In the *Vita Bonifatii,* he repeated his confidence in the didactic function of hagiography[11]; and his treatment of the documentary evidence put at his disposal by the monks indicates the particular lessons that he wished to teach. Othloh himself referred to his purposes in the prologue to Book 1. He wrote that he considered Boniface's correspondence of utmost importance, since the letters set forth most clearly the nature of Boniface's relations with the papacy; a description of his missionary activities and of his episcopal administration; an indication of the veneration which he received from Carolman and Pippin; and finally information as to his endowment of Fulda "with possessions and special tithes." The letters, therefore, were not simple glosses or ornaments; they comprised an integral part of Othloh's characterization, as well as of the historical facts deployed in that portrayal.[12]

It must be said at the outset that Othloh reproduced the texts of the Bonifatian letters accurately. He included thirty of them. With some exceptions, he arranged them in correct chronological order;[13] and, though he (or the copy that he consulted) suppressed some formulaic titles, statements, and datings,[14] the texts are exact and complete. The telling point is in the letters omitted. Some omissions are not important: for example, the two letters of Gregory II, and the three of Zacharias that exist in the *corpus* as we have it, but that do not appear in the *Vita Bonifatii.* They merely confirm, or repeat, information included in materials that Othloh did reproduce. Other omissions fall into a different category. Only three letters by Boniface himself were included, and one of them was, in effect, a synodal record. Othloh specifically excluded the Anglo-Saxon part of the Bonifatian correspondence, in order, he said, to avoid tiring the reader, "maxime cum nobis sufficiant nostra. Nostra autem dico, quae pro patribus nostris, Germanis scilicet, salvandis scripsit vel ab ullo scripta recepit."[15] This means, of course, that hagiographical importance of the letters, apart from their contents, lay in their origins and in their relevance to German ecclesiastical matters. Of the thirty letters which the *Vita* contains (including a spurious cession to Fulda attributed to Othloh), only two were issued by laymen: the edict that Carolman issued from the *Concilium Germanicum,* and the alleged grant of Pippin to Fulda. The three letters of Boniface have already been mentioned. It should also be observed that all of the three were addressed to the apostolic see, and that one of them is the *iuramentum* that Boniface submitted before his episcopal consecration. The remaining twenty-five letters were issued by the papal curia, seven of them under Gregory II, five under Gregory III, and thirteen under Zacharias. Sixteen of the letters were, or could have been thought to have been, received by Boniface; the remainder, not by him, were issued on his behalf to laymen, princes, and clergy. It is quite apparent that Othloh selected letters for inclusion so as to present, not Boniface in his own words and in the totality of his life, but Boniface in his functions as missionary and as the premier bishop of Germany, preaching and governing on the commission and under the direction of Rome, and with the filial support of secular princes. The inclusion of forged and genuine documents regarding Fulda served the purpose of his commission: namely, the demonstration of Fulda's extraordinary privileges that tied it, through Boniface, to the apostolic see.[16]

Omissions from other materials at Othloh's disposal also indicate his guiding motives. He alleged that one of his main purposes in consulting texts other than Willibald's life was to enlarge what Willibald had to say about miracles. Indeed, he did appropriate three miracles from the Mainz *Vita;* but he omitted a fourth miracle related in the same source (c. 12). Two of the appropriated miracles (the vision of St. Michael and the prophecy concerning Adelher's bequest) strongly underscore Boniface's role as defender and augmenter of monastic property. The third (the vision in which St. Boniface orders the removal of his body from Mainz to Fulda) was an essential part of the encomium to Fulda. The omitted miracle, a miraculous draught of fishes during the translation of Boniface's body, said something about sanctity, but nothing about Othloh's apologetic goals.

A second omission concerns the *Vita Sturmi,* a biography of Fulda's first abbot which Othloh quarried extensively. Othloh knew from that text that a bitter controversy divided Lull, Boniface's designated successor as bishop of Mainz, and Sturmi. Yet, writing within the walls of Sturmi's monastery, Othloh not only left out every trace of their dispute, but even took occasion to describe Lull (both in his own text and in the papal letters that he included) as a worthy and devoted disciple of Boniface. He underscored the closeness of their relationship by his description of the last interview between the two men, in which Boniface, as the master and friend, entrusted ecclesiastical and personal obligations to Lull.[17] This treatment of the bonds among Boniface, Lull, and Sturmi indicates an effort to revise the past according to the ideal relation that the monks of Fulda needed, and apparently wished to establish, with Siegfried, an effort indicated another way by the prominence given Mainz in the substance of the biography, both by its division into two books (the first treating of events before Boniface acceded to Mainz, the second of later events), and by the materials furnished to illustrate the subordination of Cologne to Mainz.

A third omission bears on Boniface's relationship with his contemporary popes. Othloh included two documents that indicated significant differences between Boniface's wishes, or actions, and Roman practice. Pope Zacharias denied Boniface the privilege of installing his own successor,[18] though Boniface did in fact consecrate Lull as bishop of Mainz under conditions that are unclear.[19] On another occasion, Zacharias declared himself astonished to hear that Boniface had ordered the rebaptism of those baptised by illiterate priests who garbled the sacramental formulae, and he admonished him to teach "as the holy fathers teach and preach."[20] Othloh followed Willibald, however, in leaving out all reference to Pope Stephen II, the last pope under whom Boniface served. From the Mainz *Vita,* he knew of the controversy that arose between Stephen and Boniface when the latter questioned the pope's right to consecrate a bishop in an archidiocese not his own without the consent of the bishop ordinary, a dispute that was inconsonant with Othloh's portrait since it could not be proven to have ended, as could the other two, in reconciliation.

Finally, a cluster of omissions illustrates Othloh's attitude toward the intervention of secular powers in ecclesiastical affairs, and indeed suggests how incompatible his monastic ideals were with the imperial church of his day. He avoided the word "patrocinium" in appropriating passages from the Mainz *Vita* and the Vita *Sturmi* which describe secular protection of the church. In this regard, it is also worth observing that Othloh omitted the Mainz author's description of an interview in which Pope Stephen "gave the power 'patrocinandi' " to Pippin; Boniface's reference in the *Vita Sturmi* to the royal defence of Fulda; Carloman's declaration, in the *Vita Sturmi,* that he transfered the site of Fulda "whole and entire" from his legal control; and the final provision in *ep.* 56, in which, without synodal approval, Carloman imposed penalties for pagan practices on the precedent of an act of Charles Martel. Othloh was intent on describing secular rulers as men who were devout sons of the church, disciples, rather than masters. Omissions such as those indicated suggest that, while Othloh acknowledged that secular princes could have a part in the elections of bishops, in the erection of episcopal sees, in the summoning of synods, and in the execution of synodal decrees, he rejected the view that rulers were privileged to act in affairs of religion on their own authority, or in a superior role. This attitude is also illustrated by an addition that Othloh made to his known sources. Carloman and Charlemagne appear as model princes, the latter obviously out of chronology. Among Boniface's contemporaries, Carloman took the palm for his personal devoutness and his support of the monasteries, even when he was beset by enemies on all sides. But Carloman had one further claim to distinction in Othloh's eyes, which he carefully inserted: "He chose the best part, which was not taken from him. For he relinquished kingdoms full of earthly power, and going to Monte Cassino, in which the strictest discipline of monastic life was then held, he was made a monk there."[21]

Othloh's selection and editing of materials tells a great deal about the deliberateness with which he constructed hagiographical models for emulation by his contemporary prelates and princes. But they also contribute fundamentally to an understanding of the concept of sanctity that informed his entire reconstitution of the past; for both his use of sources and his understanding turned on a fundamental distinction between appearance and reality, corresponding with the line that he drew, as Schauwecker has shown, between *divina* and *mundana philosophia.* That distinction, in turn, was central to many particulars, including the troubling fact that miracles had ceased at the tomb of St. Boniface.

Through Boniface's merits, many had obtained miraculous benefits for the interior man—in the remission of sins—and for the outer man—in the lifting of physical infirmities. The lapse of these benefits, Othloh said, was not due to God's inclemency or to any weakness in Boniface's intercessory powers before God, but rather to infidelity expressed in the negligence of divine service, in the incorrigible malice of the inhabitants of the land, in the ingratitude of those who, when miracles came to pass through the intercession of saints, neither rendered appropriate praise and thanks to God and His saints for them, nor even kept them in remembrance.[22] The distinction between the apparent world of the body and the authentic world of the spirit, that Othloh applied to a contemporary quandary, recurred in the documents that he incorporated into the *Vita*.

In one letter (*ep.* 82), Pope Zacharias admonished the German clergy with the words of Luke 12:4f., following them with a conflation of 2 Cor. 10:4f. and Eph. 6:10, distinguishing between body and soul, and carnal and spiritual weapons.[23] Boniface himself—who knew how wolves could masquerade in sheep's clothing[24]—confessed that, while he had been able spiritually to keep his vow to abstain from association with unworthy clerics, he had been unable physically to avoid them when he waited upon the Prince of the Franks.[25] For Othloh, the distinction pervaded every aspect of his story. It appears, rather conventionally, in passages that describe how Boniface, through studies, grew in virtues, and how this inner strength was externally manifested in priestly orders; how Boniface declined, first, an abbacy, to follow his vocation as missionary, and, second, an episcopacy, to obey his commission from Rome;[26] and how Boniface always sought *lucrum animarum* instead of *lucrum temporale*.[27] It appears most dramatically in the distinction between the apparent death of Boniface and his companions, and the corresponding victory of the pagans, and the real martyrdom, the *passio gloriosa,* of the "saints" attended by the spiritual and, not much later, the physical destruction of their slayers.[28]

In terms of Othloh's hagiographical purposes, the distinction was particularly cast as the higher antinomies of true and false. The specious piety of

Ananias and Saphira[29] was a scriptural analogue of the perjury which Boniface encountered, and for which he foretold a condign punishment;[30] of the effort of Aldebert to masquerade as an angel of the Lord in human form,[31] a hypocrisy that Boniface wished to end with perpetual imprisonment; and of the false story concocted by the people of Utrecht in an attempt to retain Boniface's body, which was unmasked by a miraculous pealing of the church bell.[32] Othloh understood Boniface's life and work chiefly in the light of this sort of pairing. On the one hand, there were the "fables and vain prodigies and signs," the false visions, and the fabricated relics of heretics.[33] On the other hand, there were the miracles, associated with Boniface, the visions authenticated by purgation, the relics bestowed by the apostolic see upon Boniface, those to which he had recourse in his last hour, and the primary and secondary relics of Boniface himself. On the one hand, there were heretics, false Christians, false priests, false bishops, false prophets, and pagans—pagans, not merely in Germany, but even in Rome, performing their detestable and pernicious rites in the shadows of the apostles' tombs.[34] On the other hand, there stood the orthodox: namely, the apostolic see and those (including especially Boniface) in communion with it and faithful to its order and doctrine. The former presumed to call themselves apostles, though they were members of Satan and precursors of Antichrist;[35] they called themselves holy.[36] But "apostolic holiness" remained among those who did not arrogate it to themselves,[37] though they granted the title "holiness" to others. It remained among the true imitators of Christ, who, following Him in carnal tribulation, carried His death in their bodies in such fashion that His life was also manifested in their bodies, and that they might be glorified by the catholic faith.[38]

The didacticism that informed Othloh's apologetic purpose intersected the exemplarism of theology. It was well and good to describe Carloman's generosity toward monasteries for the profit of those worthy to be edified by good examples and for the confusion of those who, contrary to their best knowledge, persisted in confessing God with their mouths while opening "the ears of their hearts" to love of worldly life.[39] Still, Carloman's benefactions were part of a wider exemplarism centering on Boniface. Just as Abraham is said to be the father of all those who believe in Christ because of the merit of his faith and obedience, merit to be imitated by all, Boniface can be called father of all the inhabitants of Germany in that he begot them through preaching, confirmed them by example and, in charity, laid down his life for them.[40] Those who failed to heed his example must forswear their evil ways lest death come, leaving no time for repentance.[41] Their wicked doings would weigh especially upon bishops who ignored the authority of his examples, which became a testimony of their damnation, as demonstrated by the Gospels and the prophet Ezekiel.[42] The immediate issue was monastic property; but soteriology was prior to that, and it was rooted in the theology of the apparent and the real, of the obvious and the hidden, of the outer and the inner man.

Naturally, the holiness that informed Othloh's exemplary model, Boniface, was also rooted in that theology of salvation. Thus far, we have examined the purposes for which Othloh wrote the *Vita,* and the selection and use of texts in the service of those ends. We have also indicated two kinds of theological tension that profoundly characterized Othloh's thought, and particularly his view of holiness: namely, the tension, first, between apparent and real, in its various Pauline formulations, and, second, between the ideal, or exemplar, and the actual. We have discussed (1) the way in which Othloh built up a characterization appropriate to the needs of the moment, and (2) dialectical aspects of his theology. It remains to suggest that both matters expressed an underlying structure of assumptions about holiness that can be described within the five categories that we mentioned earlier.

1. *Holiness is necessary.* From what has already been said, it is apparent that holiness is necessary to salvation. But, as a quality derived in men and original in God, holiness is also essential to the operations of grace and, hence, to providential history. The "venerable holiness" of Boniface derived from the "wonderful power" of God, as did the "holiness" of the gospel codex that Boniface raised against his slayer,[43] and it was part of the encounter with God that effected his vocation to the monastic life, his resolution to go as a missionary wherever grace directed, the conversion that through grace he achieved, and the assistance that, *divino nutu* or *divino affatu,* he received from ecclesiastical superiors or princes.[44] The papal letters, which Othloh allowed to carry much of his story, add some useful observations. God called Boniface to his missionary labors.[45] He assisted him, sent an angel before him to prepare his way, and strengthened his preaching by divine inspiration. As the kingdom of God approached and the world drew toward its end, divine mercy commanded that Boniface not only preach, but also preside over the entire province of the Gauls.[46] The eschatological and soteriological dimensions of necessity coincided in the third dimension of ecclesiology and, of course, in Boniface's role in the church. For unity, as a divine perfection, was also a note of the church, "one body," composed of many abounding in grace and striving to preserve unity of spirit in the bond of peace and charity, a unity manifested, in the Bonifatian letters, by faithful obedience to St. Peter and his see.[47] Othloh himself expressed this sense of unity in his anagogical application of Old Testament prophecies to his own day, and in his insistence that the foundation stones of the church were the earliest fathers, whose canons and definitions should continually govern ecclesiastical affairs and, who, as the canons themselves said, still lived in their establishments.[48]

2. *Holiness is conditional.* As Othloh developed his characterizations, holiness was conditional in two ways. In the first place, it presupposed the ability to distinguish between true and false. It rested, posteriorly, on knowledge as faith, and specifically on the "agnitio Christi," or the "agnitio

veritatis," or the "agnitio verae fidei."[49] Through his preaching, Boniface made people know the light of Christ,[50] and he was able to see the seeds of the divine word that he scattered in the hearts of the faithful germinate and bear fruit.[51] Pagans, heretics, and false Christians were defective, or entirely lacking in this recognitive capacity. In the second place, holiness was necessary, anteriorly, if men were to become cooperators with grace. The stages of Boniface's career are in fact benchmarks of a process by which a saint conveyed the faith handed down from Peter and Paul and the other apostles to the popes,[52] and the discipline transmitted from Gregory the Great to Augustine of Canterbury and thence to the Anglo-Saxons,[53] and by which he consequently moved from his initial vocation, through priesthood, prelacy, and martyrdom, to become for men a patron before God, and, through faithfulness, the father of the inhabitants of Germany, as Abraham was father of all believers in Christ.

3. *Holiness becomes possible.* Othloh recognizes that holiness derives from God through the grace of vocation, that it infuses a providential necessity into the lives of individual persons, the cosmos, and the church, and that it is conditional on faith and necessary for works. But how does it become possible? The examples of contemporary princes and prelates indicate that hearing the Word of God and knowing the prescripts of the canons is not enough in itself to procure holy actions, nor, perhaps, is even a holy life. Contemporary bishops and rulers see the better but approve and do the worse. Othloh used the example of Boniface to teach that holiness became possible through obedience to the Scriptures, to the canons, to St. Peter, to the Roman see endowed by God with the power of binding and loosing, and to the vicar of St. Peter.[54] For Othloh, Boniface exemplified the need to obey and to enforce canonical faith and order as it came from Rome. Following Willibald, he wrote that Gregory II, after consecrating Boniface, gave him "a book in which the most sacred laws of ecclesiastical institution, digests from assemblies of bishops, were contained." But then, departing from his source, Othloh stated that Gregory gave Boniface the book, "ordering that both the clergy and the other peoples to be subjected to his rule be instructed in such institutes."[55] Boniface's journies to Rome; his consecration and change of name by papal action; his resort to Rome for advice in greater and lesser aspects of ecclesiastical government; his adherence to "the tradition of the Roman Church";[56] his astonished disbelief of the possibility that Rome could judge against the canons[57]—all comprise one aspect of Othloh's portrait. Another is formed by Boniface's preaching, and especially by the disciplinary actions often associated with synodal judgment, through which he reformed an unwilling and corrupt clergy "according to the statutes of the sacred canons." As Pope Zacharias wrote to him, "according to the institutes of the canons, all have been bent to obey you."[58] Faith and order were parts of the same composition. Holiness was not possible outside the hierarchic church in communion with Rome—certainly not for the pagans, or for the

false Christians, false priests, and false bishops against whom Boniface called synods and gained sentences of deposition, excommunication, and imprisonment.

4. *Sanctity is divine love expressed in different modes.* Carloman, in his patronage of monasteries, and the companions slain with Boniface manifested holiness in particular modes. Othloh, to be sure, described Boniface most fully of all the *dramatis personae.* To him, as a scholar, Boniface's excellence in literary studies while a young man was of particular interest. It indicated, he thought, that Boniface was "full of divine power," for it led to a multiplication of virtues in him.[59] His preaching to the pagans, his correction of erring Christians, his construction of monasteries and churches, his endowment of them with possessions, his institution of good pastors in them and, finally, his martyrdom as an extension of his other testimonies to the divine word were all, in Othloh's presentation, episodic manifestations of the same holiness, as wisdom, of the same love of Christ through which Boniface became a missionary, the divine love through which the saint bore pain for the sake of Him who suffered for men, the charity that informed obedience and without which prophecy, tongues, understanding, faith, and works profited nothing.[60]

5. *Sanctity can be proven authentic.* Without this assumption, Othloh's hagiographical techniques would not have served his didactic purpose. He went to great lengths to provide demonstrations, objective in his own mind, of Boniface's sanctity. We see this effort in his use of texts, particularly of the Bonifatian letters, his descriptions of Boniface's dealings with princes and of his dependence upon Rome, his declared purpose of garnering miracles other than those narrated by Willibald, his comments on the general acknowledgment of Boniface's learning and worthiness of the heavenly sacrament, as leading to his priestly ordination,[61] his extensive reflection on the circumstances of Boniface's death and burial. Indeed, among the proofs still solicited in a canonization process are the writings of the *servus Dei,* the public recognition of his sanctity, testimonies of ecclesiastical superiors, miracles, the cause of witness (or martyrdom), the circumstances of death, and the conditions of the body (or relics). There was certainly every reason for Othloh to provide as many testimonials to Boniface's sanctity as he could, for he had to persuade his readers that miracles at St. Boniface's tomb had lapsed through the infidelity of recent times, and not because Fulda's intercessor before God had become as ineffective as her abbot before the imperial judges.

The dialectical binary structure that, for Othloh, defined holiness came to a resolution in the capacity of holiness for proof. Othloh did not understand Boniface in the complexity accessible through twentieth-century psychology, and it is doubtful whether he conceived of him as a unique personality. Certainly, the characterization lacks reference to physical appearance, temperament, motivation, or existential ambiguities. He did not feel moved to supply what his sources lacked. As testifier to divine truth, Boniface is less important than his testimony. He is circumscribed by determinants external to himself and, as we have said, these are necessary (divided into binary categories, such as saved and unredeemed, called and reprobate, transitory and eschaton, unity and separation), conditional (divided into categories of faithfulness and infidelity, knowledge, and ignorance), possible (divided into categories of obedience and disobience, reform and deformation, tradition and novelty), and modal (divided into love and estrangement from the life of God). The capacity of holiness for proof united these elements. For it posited that the ambiguity between apparent truth and real truth could be objectively resolved and that through the plain evidence of history authentic truth was taught by example.

Here, Othloh's thought discloses the hermeneutic tautology of any *a priori* pattern. In itself, the dialectic between apparent and real could not be resolved. As holiness could be manifested only by those capable of it, so its manifestations could be correctly read only by those already comprehended in unity, faithfulness, obedience, and love. Othloh appealed to the bar of history—from bishops and princes ill informed to bishops and princes better informed—although he fully recognized that disbelief might deafen "the ears of their hearts" and blind their inner eyes to exemplars of holiness. A monk, as *miles Christi,* had no need to be reminded of the warfare in the world between Christ and Satan, who transformed himself into the likeness of an angel of light, especially a monk acutely vexed, as was Othloh, by the Tempter in many visions. It was not astonishing that miracles lapsed at Boniface's tomb through the faithlessness of the day; for even Christ, in His own country, had been unable to do wonders through the disbelief of many.[62] The duty of the saints, united by imitation to Boniface and to Christ Himself, was to hold fast to their inner vision, to admonish, rebuke, testify to the hidden truth, and, if need be, endure the glorious passion.

Nearly 100 years after Othloh's *Vita Bonifatii* (that is, between 1151 and 1159), Ebo composed his life of Otto of Bamberg (1060/62–1139). While Ebo drew from a number of earlier writings—including at least some portions of Otto's correspondence, annalistic materials and a biography (the Prüfening *Vita*) written 1140–46—the substance of his account came from recollections of Otto's own companions, especially one named Ulrich of St. Egidius. Consequently, textual criticism of his deployment of materials is not so apt a means of detecting Ebo's frame of reference as it is in regard to Othloh's, and there is the additional difference that we do not have a *corpus* of writings by Ebo in which to locate his biography. Ebo's place in history depends on this one text. When all differences have been taken into account, close similarities do remain. Some of them are fortuitous. Otto and Ebo lived in the same region of Germany as Othloh, and both of them had been educated in the same curriculum as he, blending pre-Christian rhetoric and history with patristic theology. Before his conversion to the canonical life,

Otto, indeed, is said to have made a considerable fortune teaching the children of Polish magnates.[63] Both biographies were written on behalf of monasteries chosen by the subjects of the biographies as burial places. Both had a didactic, or apologetic purpose—namely, the defence of monastic possessions—which they characterized as a struggle of monastic spirituality against the worldliness of bishops and princes. Both examined the enigma of holiness in the setting of missionization and martyrdom.

For our purposes, the most important similarity is the appearance, in Ebo's account, of a concept of holiness much like the one set forth in the *Vita Bonifatii*. The dyad of inner and outer is, if anything, more pronounced in Ebo's work than it is in Othloh's. In particular, Ebo knew of crypto-Christians who lived in pagan territory for many years without benefit of Christian rites,[64] and disclosed their true commitment when Otto appeared among them. There were other examples. In Ebo's mind, spiritual richness and temporal wealth were related. One of Otto's principal characteristics was that he was prudent in economic matters. He became rich as a teacher; he served a niece of Henry IV "as another Joseph"; he demonstrated extraordinary managerial abilities as that emperor's master of works at Speier; and his stewardship at the imperial court led him once to decline election as bishop. After his accession, he had a keen eye for other men of practical acumen.[65] He smoothed his diplomatic negotiations with splendid gifts to ease the passage to love of heavenly goods by way of earthly;[66] and, in his zeal for building chapels, churches, and monasteries, he also looked to the future and took care lest the new establishments fall into want.[67] This knowledge of interior and exterior things, this conduct of the outer man that expressed the inner care of Otto's soul, had a counterpart in the monasteries that, under Otto, experienced wonderful increases of interior and exterior profit, and in the experience of those whose conversion was strengthened by seeing Otto's exceeding abundance of temporal and spiritual increase.[68]

Still, the correlation between inner and outer was not inevitable. It was desirable, but not necessary, that outward signs of spiritual dignity correspond with inner grace,[69] and that baptism, as an outer dedication, foreshadow the dedication of the heart.[70] Pagans made the mistake of identifying divine favor with sensual magnificence. They lavishly adorned their shrines with carvings and precious metals. How could they accept, as an emissary of the most high God, a man who came to them barefoot and in sackcloth? They sent him away with ridicule, teaching him the lesson that pagans were animals, entirely ignorant of spiritual gifts, and that they were not to be reckoned as men except in their external bearing.[71] St. Paul's distinction between the animal and the spiritual man (1 Cor. 2:10–16) lay behind this judgment, as his exposition of idolatry, the confusion of creature and Creator (Rom. 1), inspired Ebo's comments on the errors of native Pommeranian cults.[72] Ebo agreed that without knowledge of his creator, any man was a brute animal. Ignorant of the God who made them and coupled with senseless beasts of burden in the worship of something beyond sensory

erception, the pagans became, like animals, incapable of rational service of
he living God.[73] Pagans could not distinguish between appearance and
eality. They accepted opulence as an expression of invisible power, for, lack-
ng spiritual gifts, they also lacked the ambiguously hidden and disclosed
visdom of divine revelation and thus they were able to consider placing side
by side temples of Otto's God and theirs.[74] This view provides a telling
ontrast with Otto's conception of the sacred, for he shrank from "the foul-
esses of idolatry" as from pollution.[75] and commanded his new converts to
void the unconverted in all things, and especially to segregate their burial
places from those of the pagans.[76]

The pagans were not alone in defective understandings of hidden truth.
Otto, "the light of the Church" (3.26; p. 140) shone as the sun among other
bishops,[77] for the spirituality that he expressed in his preaching missions and
n his establishment and endowment of churches and monasteries was
ontradicted by their devotion to worldly concerns, such as the building of
astles, towns, and town walls.[78] Indeed, the connection between spiritual
nd temporal eminence that Ebo did accept ran into difficulties on this score.
ust as Othloh had to acknowledge that miracles ceased at Boniface's tomb,
ven though Boniface was still a powerful patron before God, Ebo had to ac-
nowledge that, through the misplaced values of recent bishops and
magnates, monastic temporalities had decayed, even though monastic dis-
ipline and virtues continued, even though Michelsburg was still adorned
with Otto's relics "as though with pearls" and sheltered by his heavenly
patronage.[79] Feeling he was writing "with the cooperating grace of the Holy
Spirit,"[80] Ebo was confident that the story was not yet over, and that a terri-
ble retribution was laid up in God's providence for Christians who ignored
he gospel as well as for pagans who rejected it and that a great glory was
tored there for the servants of God.[81] The cutting edge of the Last Judgment was part of the didactic exemplarism by which Ebo pointed out both
Otto's devout care of monasteries and the great company of spiritual sons
egotten there by him, sons who would attend Otto with their prayers in
his world and accompany him before the King of kings in the glory of the
esurrection.[82]

Confidence in retributive justice indicates that, behind Ebo's dyad of in-
er and outer, real and apparent, spiritual and animal, there was a wider con-
eptual structure resembling Othloh's concept of holiness. Let us take up
ach of our five points, in the same order as before.

1. *Necessity.* Expectation that scores would be settled at the Last Judgment posits necessity on the side of right, necessity expressed in different
vays through cosmology, soteriology, and eschatology. Here, as in Othloh's
Vita, the assumptions of unity and universality are included in that of
ecessity. The entire world is created, aging, and bound under sin.[83] Cosmic
enescence and human redemption were parts of the same movement, and the
providence informing the first was, for the second, the vocation by which
God predestined and called some to eternal life.[84] God had formed Otto in

the womb as His servant, as the light of the gentiles;[85] men entered the monastic life by way of vocation.[86] The necessity of vocation to individual conversion, and to works done by men through the spirit of adoption, had wide historical dimension; for it was eschatologically necessary that the gospel be preached in all the world for a witness to the gentiles before the end came.[87]

The sense of a guiding and unseen unity in history also shaped Ebo's understanding of the relation between the church's manifestation as a visible community and its authentic character as an invisible communion, in which the saints, through their relics, intercession, and canonical regulations were contemporaries in the eternal present of the body of Christ. They were united in time and out of time by charity, "the bond of perfection."[88] This interplay between apparent and real made vestments and sacraments more than signs; it made them symbols, filled with the power of the divine love that they represented.[89] It established identity between widely separated historical events, such as Otto's own *gloriosus transitus* and the martyrdom of St. Paul, whom Otto "strove to imitate before all others" giving them the same *dies natalis*.[90] It drew Christ into the ceremonials of the visible church, whether the dedication of a soul, as His temple, through baptism[91] or the dedication of a church. The latter was mimetic and mnemonic: a ceremony that must be observed with all devotion, in that it forecast the image and shadow of the heavenly dedication. Christ, the true pontiff, will have completed the temple that He built with the living and chosen stones from the beginning of the world to the end of time. Then, He will celebrate the longed-for and perfect solemnity to which the transitory acts of men direct the inmost desires of all the church's sons.[92]

2. *Conditionality.* The inner necessity of grace gave the preaching and the practices of saints an authenticity lacking to pagans and faithless Christians, despite outward show. But it was conditional in much the same ways as it was in Othloh's conception. It was conditional upon knowledge (or recognition), and it was a condition for works of holiness. Ebo adduced examples of converts who lapsed, and of pagans who obdurately rejected the yoke of Christian faith to which the entire Roman world had submitted, and who remained content to be abortive offspring, estranged from the church. For him these illustrated how slender the bonds of faith might be.[93] The "agnitio Christi" might come through human instrumentality, as it did through Otto's preaching,[94] but, ultimately it came through the infusion of divine grace, through spiritual adoption. Ebo frequently used the metaphor of illumination to describe that event. He was able to apply to Otto the word "lux gentium," an epithet originally applied to St. Paul.[95] But he knew that Christ was the "true light" and that God, "the Father of lights," had sent Otto to declare salvation to the ends of the earth so that the dark hearts of the gentiles might be irradiated with the light of faith.[96] The interplay between light and darkness recurs throughout Ebo's biography, when he refers to conversions as light scattering the shadows of idolatry or ignorance, to those

blinded by the devil so that they could not see the true light, and to the miraculous restoration of physical sight.[97]

This imagery was appropriate in view of Otto's devotion to St. John the Evangelist (as well as to St. Michael the Archangel);[98] it was also a convention in Christian rhetoric. In any case, it expressed the derived character of holiness, which did not inhere in the animal man and which, in fact, was opposed, not only by the devil's malevolence,[99] but also by what would now be called common sense: i.e., by the pagans' awareness that, if they abandoned their religion and took up that of "the German god,"[100] they would subvert their fatherland and their ancient laws.[101] It was this condition, working against odds, that made prayer, not merely an aspect of Otto's personal piety, but a dramatic element in Ebo's narrative.[102]

Holiness was conditional upon illumination, and necessary for the works holiness. The people of Stettin lapsed into apostasy when they became convinced that a plague could be lifted by sacrificing to their ancient gods.[103] Others wavered. But Otto, persisting in his faithfulness was no backslider. He achieved his building schemes. He reformed corrupt monasteries and infused new life into them. He converted the Pommeranians, precisely because he had responded in faith to God's election of him, and therefore was attended by divine grace, preceded by God's mercy, and inflamed by the fire of divine love.[104]

3. *Possibility*. When he thought about how holiness became possible, Ebo, like Othloh, thought in terms of a *magisterium spirituale* overseen by Rome.[105] Though the paradigm of one flock and one shepherd was deeply woven into the conventions of theology, the investiture conflict no doubt left its mark on Otto's understanding of church order, and hence on Ebo's account of his work. Ebo described Henry IV, Otto's greatest early patron, in a favorable light, but he also characterized Otto as attending scrupulously to canonical regulations and to the judgment of the apostolic see. For three years after the Emperor designated him as bishop, Otto delayed consecration, Ebo said, to prepare himself for the spiritual and temporal administration of his see. That there was a reason other than the need for study is indicated by Ebo's reference to the conflict between Henry IV and Ruothard of Mainz and by the shadow of simony that fell upon him because of his long and faithful labors in the royal court.[106] To clear his title, Otto went to Rome and abdicated, only to be recalled and consecrated by Paschal II, consecrated, the pope wrote, "as though by St. Peter's own hands."[107] When he undertook his missionary journeys, he secured papal sanctions and acted as a papal *missus,*[108] and he carefully observed the privileges of bishops through whose sees he travelled.[109] Certainly, the reform that he instituted in his own diocese was designed to elevate the level of spiritual devotion, and also to enforce on others the same obedience that marked his own sanctity.[110]

The emphasis on hierarchic order was part of the way in which Ebo understood the Christian ambiguity of freedom and bondage. Freedom from physical bondage formed part of Ebo's story.[111] It stood as a counterpart in the external world of Otto's work of conversion in the spiritual world. And yet, the spiritual freedom of converts was characterized exactly by submission to the yoke of Christ, to the yoke of the Christian faith,[112] expressed by careful adherence to the order and judgments of the visible Church.

Ebo was fascinated with Otto as a builder of churches and monasteries, and this attraction to the problem of form-giving also expressed itself in a fuller awareness of the possibility of holiness—that is, of holiness becoming—than we have found in Othloh's *Vita*. Consciousness of process, as the succession of organically related forms, was an important characteristic of twelfth-century German religious thought. It appears, not only in the historical works of Otto of Freising, but also in mystical perceptions, such as those of Anselm of Havelberg, and in apocalyptic visions, such as those of Gerhoch of Reichersberg. Otto, master of the works at Speier and builder of churches, is the counterpart of Christ, building through time His celestial church of living stones, and the sense of directed and progressive movement intrinsic in the analogue of architecture appears throughout Ebo's biography, both in his descriptions and in his metaphors. His description of the life and work of Otto as a *peregrinatio,* and not simply of his missionary journeys, is one instance, closely related to the metaphor of the way.[113] Ebo characterizes Otto as a good tree, flowering before it bears fruit,[114] as a fruitful olive tree;[115] and the metaphor of seed scattered abroad to produce a harvest often appears.[116] With their prayers, his spiritual sons surround him as beautiful flowers in God's sight.[117] These organic analogues—together with the additional one of Otto's fecund spiritual paternity—indicate several things about the way in which Ebo understood the becoming of holiness. They indicate that he considered it a dynamic process by which something that is not comes into being; that the means of becoming is subsumed in the goal; and that the process affirms its beginning as it moves towards its end. In other words, the metaphors of growth express a dynamic aspect of the same tautological conception that Ebo cast in another way as the mimetic pairing of heavenly temple and earthly church, and yet again as the light that Otto saw and by seeing, became.

4. *Manner.* As we have seen, charity was the bond of perfection that gave the church the necessity of its unity, and it was a condition for works of holiness. It was also the substance of this dynamic movement. For, as in Othloh's mind, so in Ebo's the ways in which holiness was articulated were all modes of divine love. Though this metaphorical reasoning had not yet been elaborated into a concept of progressive creation, Ebo concurred with Othloh in considering all the ways in which holiness became all modes of divine love moving toward an historical and eschatological end. Ebo understood Otto's apostolate—that is, his missionary labors as an extension of his episcopate,[118] endeavors undertaken, as was the office of preaching, solely for the love of Christ.[119] Entering his see as bishop-elect, he was inwardly aflame with divine love. As missionary, he strove to realize the breadth of the holy love that had been let into his heart by the Holy Spirit, and that was

with divine love. As missionary, he strove to realize the breadth of the holy love that had been let into his heart by the Holy Spirit, and that was expressed in one way by very detailed regulations on pagan practices to be avoided. He was moved by that love than which man has no greater when he stood ready to lay down his life for his flock; in his quest for martyrdom, "the most ardent lover of Christ thirsted to pour out his sweet life for Jesus, the most sweet."[120] More than Otto's own devotion was at issue; for, in his episcopal offices and in his apostolate, he was urged on by the power of Christ's own love; he was full of God who is love. Animated by this love, his very countenance revealed the light within him. His face shown with angelic brightness.[121]

5. *Proofs.* We have now come to the proofs of holiness. In a limited way, Ebo used two kinds of evidence that figured very prominently in Othloh's *Vita.* He incorporated eight letters from Otto's correspondence, only three of which were from Otto himself and, consequently, adduced writings of the *servus Dei* and the commendatory testimonies of his ecclesiastical superiors.[122] The burden of his evidence, however, fell into other categories. In the first place, he gave considerable emphasis to argument by analogy, perhaps with St. Peter[123] and St. Stephen, the protomartyr,[124] but particularly with St. Paul and with Christ. We have already indicated that the latter analogues were rooted in Ebo's mimetic conceptions of the spiritual world. In so far as analogues constituted proof, it was important for Ebo that Otto's missionary work replicated that of the apostle of the gentiles so closely that he too could be called the "light of the gentiles,"[125] received as though he were an angel of God,[126] and commemorated on the Feast of SS. Peter and Paul. The analogue with Christ was even more amply developed with regard to Christ as "true pontiff," as builder, and as the archetypal martyr who laid down His life for others. Ebo was ready to press similarities rather far, and not only by reference to Otto's entrance into his see with bare and blood-stained feet, or to the devout care for the sick and poor by which he offered up a sacrifice of toil and sweat.[127] Describing how Otto took leave from his followers when setting out on his second missionary journey, Ebo drew a specific parallel between Christ, the great high priest, taking leave of His friends before His Passion, and Otto, arrayed in full pontificals, going forth in search of martyrdom,[128] just as, later, when he was certain (though wrongly) that he would be killed by pagans at Stettin, he again went forth alone vested in full pontificals.[129] Ebo saw a second, even more striking parallel when Otto returned. He happened to re-enter Bamberg on Easter day. He was received as a "new apostle," returning as a victor after he had destroyed the gates of death among the barbarians. He entered his church, Ebo wrote, amidst a noble triumph, greeted by the antiphon, normally addressed to Christ, *Advenisti desiderabilis.* Alleluias resounded, and it seemed to everyone as though they had been receiving Christ risen from the dead.[130]

Of course, it was not enough that these analogues existed; they must also be generally recognized. To supply that requirement, Ebo included a long series of acknowledgments by others of Otto's holiness, ranging from Anselm of Speier's early perception of an extraordinary divine grace in his countenance,[131] through the testimonials that he received from popes, to the honors accorded him by Henry IV and other secular princes,[132] to the processions in which the people crowded upon him to kiss his hands, hallowed by almsgiving, his feet, consecrated by preaching the Gospel of peace, and his footsteps, a devotion foreshadowed in the unanimous acclamation of him as bishop.[133] Otto's holiness was apparent to all Christians.[134]

Finally, Ebo presented the evidence of Otto's works. The achievements of Otto's episcopate and apostolate were important as evidence, particularly in that he was able to bring them to fruition, since efficacy demonstrated the general rule that God perfected the works that He inspired.[135] Miracles carried authority that was equally convincing, and the concentration of miracles in the last book indicates the aura and the evidential base with which Ebo wished to authenticate his account of Otto's last years and death. Of all the miraculous events described by Ebo, only one was performed even indirectly by Otto himself.[136] The others were premonitory, or admonitory, revelatory, confirmative, or punitive.[137] They testified, without Otto's own agency, to the divine favor that he held, as also did miracles performed at his tomb.[138] In the evidence of works, Ebo certainly included Otto's efforts to achieve martyrdom.[139] Though that persistent effort failed, Otto yet died in a manner that, in itself and in the universal grief that it caused, composed a holy triumph of his glory.[140]

Materials bearing on the lives of saints intersect four areas of mental effort: history, rhetoric, liturgy, and iconography. In the present essay, we have examined the ground that those areas had in common and the language of metaphor and analogy that enabled hagiography to speak for them all. This unity existed because holiness, the thread running through the whole fabric of thought, had an absolute exemplary character, inseparable from the theology of salvation. Drawing on two monastic biographies of bishops, written in Fulda and in Bamberg nearly a century apart, we have been able to describe holiness as a concept made up of clearly identifiable parts. To be full of God was not to be full of *je ne sais quoi*. Theology, particularly the doctrine of substances, had not yet become sufficiently refined for either of our authors to discuss sanctity, as Thomas Aquinas did, in terms of the "connaturality" of the elect with God. The keystone of the structures that we have examined was the assumption that holiness was imparted to man by an act of grace that established mimetic likeness, or the capacity for such likeness, between him and God, and that that likeness consisted in knowledge or in faith as a kind of knowledge. It was also assumed that holiness had a social, or collective character. For visible church, as a vessel of holiness, possessed a spiritual magistracy, both by the continual presence of the Holy

Spirit, and by a tradition of faith handed down by Christ to the apostles, and by them to the bishops of Rome and to those in communion with, and obedience toward, the see of Peter.

We have examined ramifications of two fundamental distinctions. Those distinctions—between appearance and reality, and falsehood (or illusion) and truth—were sharpened by our authors' conviction that they were caught up in a war that was both temporal and spiritual between the forces of worldliness and those of righteousness. Under the category of necessity, we have described the symmetrical pairing of plurality and unity, of reprobate and called, the derived holiness of man and the original holiness of God. Under the heading of conditionality, infidelity was matched against faithfulness, and ignorance against knowledge. The category of possibility brought to light a pairing of disobedience (among false Christians as well as among pagans) and obedience toward the Roman see. When we considered the manifestations of holiness, we distinguished between acts which expressed estrangement from the life of God and those which were modes in which, through human agency, divine love articulated itself. Finally, in examining the proofs of holiness, we came to the tautological nature of our structure. For the evidence of grace could rightly be read only by those who had received grace; it was holy to the holy. And this returns us to the principle of ultimate unity running through degrees of likeness formed by knowledge of God.

The binary structure of thought through which these assumptions were articulated rested on even more fundamental principles. The philosophical components consisted of two kinds. Some of them were transcendent: for example, those of unity and universality, and spiritual virtues (such as wisdom). Some were immanent, as was the informing principle of divine love. There were also historical components derived from the Old Testament, as recast by the gospels and St. Paul, and among these can be mentioned creation, sin, election, fall, sacrifice, reconciliation, and judgment. As a system of binaries, the system achieved unity through its philosophical base of exemplarism. From this point of view, the dialectical tension between appearance and reality (or false and true as Othloh and Ebo understood it) mediated and resolved in a love that sanctified the profane, had come to our authors through often circuitous routes from the Latin and Greek fathers, Plotinus, St. Paul, and Plato. The symbolic universe within which they worked, as a conglomerate of disparate elements, permitted variant conceptions of the structure and functions of holiness even in their own day. Later in the procession of ideas, the incorporation of new philosophical elements opened profoundly new alternatives. Neoplatonic exemplarism shaded into St. Thomas's careful and brilliant reconciliation of opposites. And the historical modalities of divine love were recast in the doctrine of continual and progressive creation, so easily confused with pantheism, taught by Meister Eckhart and his followers.

University of Chicago

Notes

In writing this essay, I have drawn upon an earlier effort that I prepared as a master's candidate at Cornell, in 1957, and on seminar research done at the University of Chicago, in 1974. It is a particular happiness to acknowledge the dialogues in which I engaged as a student with Professor Theodor Mommsen and, as a teacher, with Miss Joan Luft, and MM. Michael La-Plante and Michael Ricks. The conceptualizations here set forth derive from a wider study, now in process, provisionally entitled, "I Am Thou: The Tradition of Mimesis and the Culture of Revolution."

1. On canonization as an aspect of ecclesiastical politics, see, for the twelfth century, M. Schwarz, "Heiligsprechungen im 12. Jahrhundert. Beweggründe ihrer Urheber," *Archiv für Kulturgeschichte* XXXIX (1957), 49ff, 53; and, in general, P. Delooz, *Sociologie et Canonisations* Collection scientifique de la Faculté de droit de l'Université de Liège, XXX (Liège, 1969), pp. 400 and *passim*, including his appendix on the monetary cost of the canonization process in the twentieth century. A series of articles on concepts of truth and falsity, especially as regarding relics, also has a considerable bearing on the content of this paper. See, especially, H. L. Mikoletzsky, "Sinn und Art der Heiligung im frühen Mittelalter," *MIöG* LVII (1949), 87 and *passim;* H. Fichtenau, "Zum Reliquienwesen im früheren Mittelalter," *MIöG* LX (1952), 63ff, 76; K. Shreiner, " 'Discrimen veri ac falsi.' Ansätze und Formen der Kritik in der Heiligen-und Reliquienverehrung des Mittelalters," *Archiv für Kulturgeschichte* XLVIII (1966), 5ff, and, by the same author, "Zum Wahrheitsverständnis im Heiligen-und Reliquienwesen des Mittelalters," *Saeculum* XVII (1966), 138f, 141, 145ff; and K. Guth, *Guibert von Nogent und die hochmittelalterliche Kritik an der Reliquienverehrung, Studien und Mitteilungen zur Geschichte des Benediktinerordens. Ergänzungsband* XXI, (Ottobeuron, 1970) x: 72ff, 95ff, 108ff. See also a discussion by K. Bosl, H. Fuhrmann, A. Nitschke, and H. Patze, "Die Fälschungen im Mittelalter. Überlegungen zum mittelalterlichen Wahrheitsbegriff," *HZ* CXCVII (1963), 529–601.

2. The magisterial work of Rudolf Otto rightly hovers before anyone who writes on the subject of holiness, but it will be apparent that a phenomenological approach to that subject, such as the one here attempted, leads to emphases and categories that Otto discounted. Two of R. Otto's points have a direct bearing on this essay: first, that the holy is an *a priori* category that does not originate in sensory experience (trans. J. W. Harvey, *The Idea of the Holy,* 2d ed. [London, 1950], p. 112) and, second, that man can not recognize the holy unless he is first like it in a way not open to all human beings (p. 160). Much of what R. Otto wrote concerning the sense of urgency, illumination, and ardent love pertains to the materials here discussed. And yet, his reliance on mystical categories produced in his reflections an almost exclusive emphasis on the authenticity of the experience of the holy for the person who has it. On the whole, he did not consider holiness as an attribute of communion, or community or, consequently, as a conception belonging to inherited collective wisdom. For Othloh and Ebo, and presumably also for their subjects and readers, the church was holy, because it was one, catholic, and apostolic, and holiness was described by and embedded in its doctrine. R. Otto's discussion of mystical aspects of the experience of the holy—the *mysteriosum, tremendum,* and *fascinosum*—of the erotic element, the aridity, the feelings of annihilation and guilt has little applicability to these biographies, and consequently, his central concept of the numinous is recognizable, in them, only by its adumbrations. Othloh and Ebo were much concerned, however, with the importance of holiness in the unfolding of human experience, and this posited assumptions regarding predestination and eschatology that, in the main, R. Otto left aside. They were also concerned with personal holiness in the context of the communion of saints, and, consequently, they thought in categories that R. Otto did not include at all in his frame of reference—for example, hierarchic order, orthodoxy of faith and practice, and the evidential base indicated by our fifth category. Finally, the dialectical binary structure of holiness, as set forth in these biographies, is present only by implication in R. Otto's discussion, pitched as it is at a high level of theoretical abstraction without reference to temporal variations, although it would need to figure in a specialist treatment of hagiography in the eleventh and twelfth centuries.

As expressions of a rhetorical tradition, saints' lives have structure in a literary sense. They have been arranged according to classifications proper to literary criticism, such as panegyrics, historical (or factual) accounts, romances, epics, and hagiographical cycles (cf. H. Delehaye, *Les Passions des Martyrs et les Genres littéraires* [Brussels, 1921]; R. Aigrain, *L'Hagiographie. Ses Sources, ses Méthodes, son histoire* [Paris, 1953]). In this connection, scholars have also studied the use of *topoi* and stereotypal outlines for different categories of saints (cf. R. S. Farrar's discussion of the lives of confessors and virgin martyrs in "Structure and Function in Representative Old English Saints' Lives," *Neophilologus*, LVII [1973], 83–93). Lately, Peter Brown has approached holiness as a matter of function within a particular social structure (especially, "The Rise and Function of the Holy Man in Late Antiquity," *Journal of Roman Studies* LXI [1971], 80–101). In the present essay, structure is meant, not in a literary or sociological sense, but in a conceptual one, and the effort is made to locate the idea of holiness in the larger symbolic universe of two authors.

3. *Otloh von St. Emmeram. Ein Beitrag zur Bildungs- und Frömmigkeitsgeschichte des 11. Jahrhunderts* (Munich, n.d.), esp. pp. 43f.

4. A. Hauck, *Kirchengeschichte Deutschlands* (Leipzig, 1920), III: 945f. See also J. Lechner, "Zu den falschen Exemptionsprivilegien für St. Emmeram (Regensburg)," *Neues Archiv* XXV (1900), 628; E. Dümmler, "Über den Mönch Otloh von St. Emmeram," *Sitzungsberichte der kgl. Preussischen Akademie der Wissenschaften zu Berlin* XLVIII.2 (1895), pp. 1095f. See also Schauwecker, *Otloh*, p. 43.

5. Cf. *De cursu spirituali*, in B. Pez, *Thesaurus anecdotorum novissimus* (Augsburg, 1721), III.2: 260. See Schauwecker, *Otloh*, pp. 11f.

6. Max Herrmann, *Siegfried I. Erzbischof von Mainz, 1060–1084* (Jena, 1889), pp. 16ff. G. Meyer von Knonau, *Jahrbücher des deutschen Reiches unter Henrich IV. und Henrich V.* (Leipzig, 1894), II: 188ff.

7. *Herimanni Augiensis chronicon*, MGH SS V: 132 (A.D. 1053).

8. Othloh, *Vita Bonifatii*, preface, ed. W. Levison, *Vita sancti Bonifatii*, MGH SS in usum schol. (Hannover-Leipzig, 1905), p. 111 (hereafter VB).

9. Lambert of Hersfeld, *Annales*, MGH SS V: 164 (A.D. 1063).

10. J. Mabillon, *Vetera analecta* (Paris, 1723), col. 114B. On the general objects of hagiography in this period, see B. de Gaiffier d'Hestroy, "L'Hagiographie et son Public au XIe Siècle," *Miscellanea historica in honorem Leonis Van der Essen* (Brussels, 1947), I: 135–66. This essay originally formed part of Fr. Gaiffier's *these* at the École des Chartes (1926), and he drew his materials primarily from Flanders and the Low Countries.

11. VB 1.39, 2.16; pp. 154, 202.

12. VB 1, prologue, 1.40, 1.44, 2.16; pp. 113, 154, 157f., 201f.

13. *Epp.* 21, 60, 61, 57, 58.

14. E.g., after the signatures in *ep.* 59, at the conclusion of *ep.* 28, and *epp.* 45, 60, 87, 88.

15. VB 1.44; p. 157.

16. Cf. VB 2.12, 2.13, 2.15; pp. 195ff., 201.

17. Cf. A. Göpfert, *Lullus der Nachfolger des Bonifatius im Mainzer Erzbistum* (Ph.D. dissertation, Leipzig, n.d.), pp. 16f.

18. *Ep.* 51, VB 2.2; p. 166.

19. Othloh presented no evidence that Zacharias's prohibition was reversed. In *epp.* 86 and 87, VB 2.12–13; pp. 194, 197, 199, Lull is still mentioned as a priest. Cf. Levison, VB, p. 45, n. 2.

20. *Ep.* 68, VB 2.3; p. 169.

21. VB 2.18; p. 204.

22. VB 2.32; pp. 215f.

23. VB 2.5; p. 179.

24. *Ep.* 59, VB 2.4; p. 171.

25. *Ep.* 86, VB 2.12; p. 194.

26. VB 1.3, p. 119. VB 1.6; pp. 121f. VB 1.10; p. 125.

27. *Ep.* 25, VB 1.20; p. 133. Cf. 1.30; p. 143.

28. VB 2.25, 28; pp. 209f., 212.

29. *Ep.* 16, VB 1.14; p. 128.

30. VB 2.20; p. 206.

31. *Ep.* 59, VB 2.4; p. 171.

32. VB 2.29; p. 213.

33. *Ep.* 59, VB 2.4; pp. 171, 173.

34. *Ep.* 50, VB 2.1; *ep.* 51, 2.2; pp. 162, 167.

35. *Ep.* 59, VB 2.4; pp. 172f., 176.

36. *Ep.* 57, VB 2.10; p. 192.

37. Cf. *ep.* 59, VB 2.4; p. 171.

38. *Ep.* 77, VB 2.8; *ep.* 80, 2.9; pp. 185, 188.

39. VB 2.16; p. 202.

40. VB 1.44; p. 158.

41. VB. 1.39; p. 154.

42. VB 1, prologue; p. 114.

43. VB 2.27; p. 211.

44. VB 1.1; pp. 117f., 2.22; p. 207. 2.23; p. 208. 1.6, 35; pp. 122, 148.

45. *Ep.* 51, VB 2.2; p. 168.

46. *Ep.* 60, VB 2.7; p. 181. *Ep.* 45, VB 1.34; p. 147 (Cf. 1.5; p. 121). *Ep.* 57, VB 2.10; p. 191. *Ep.* 21, VB 1.21; *ep.* 43, 1.31; pp. 134, 144. *Ep.* 58, VB 2.11; p. 193.

47. *Ep.* 82, VB 2.5; pp. 178f.

48. VB 1, prologue; p. 114.

49. *Epp.* 21, 28, VB 1.21, 27; pp. 134, 139.

50. *Ep.* 88, VB 2.14; p. 200.

51. VB 2.21; p. 206.

52. *Ep.* 80, VB 2.9; p. 186.

53. *Ep.* 50, VB 2.1; p. 162; *ep.* 80, 2.9; p. 186.

54. Cf. *ep.* 16, VB 1.14; p. 128.

55. VB 1.15; p. 129.

56. *Ep.* 45, VB 1.34; p. 147.

57. *Ep.* 50, VB 2.1; p. 163.

58. *Ep.* 88, VB 2.14; p. 200.

59. VB 1.1, 2; pp. 117ff.

60. VB 1.16; p. 122. VB 2.25; p. 210. *Ep.* 50, VB 2.1; p. 163.

61. VB 1.3; p. 119. See also the description of popular veneration of Boniface's corpse, 2.29–31; pp. 213ff.

62. Matt. 13:58. VB 2.32; p. 215. Professor Barbara Rosenwein recently completed a doctoral dissertation on hagiographical exemplarism at Cluny in the tenth century which provides interesting points of comparison: *Piety and Power: Cluniac Spirituality in the Time of St. Odo* (Ph.D. dissertation, University of Chicago, 1974).

63. Ebo, *Vita Ottonis,* 1.1, ed. J. Wikarjak, Monumenta Poloniae historica, n.s. VIII.2 (Warsaw, 1969), 10 (hereafter VO). On older scholarly studies see A. Hofmeister, *Das Leben des Bischofs Otto von Bamberg* (Leipzig, 1928), and bibliographical references in the *apparatus criticus* of Wikarjak's edition, parts of which were prepared by Casimir Liman. See also E. von Guttenberg, ed., *Das Bistum Bamberg,* Germania sacra II (Berlin, 1937), I.1: 115–38. J. Petersohn, "*Apostolus Pomeranorum.* Studien zur Geschichte und Bedeutung des Apostelepitethons Bischof Ottos I. von Bamberg," *Historische Jahrbuch* LXXXVI (1966), 257–94. Eberhard Demm, *Reformmönchtum und Slawenmission im 12. Jahrhundert. Wertsoziologisch-geistesgeschichtliche Untersuchungen zu den Viten Bischofs Ottos von Bamberg,* Historische Studien CCCCXIX (Hamburg, 1970). Demm did not use the Wikarjak edition. Consequently, his views on Ebo's use of sources vary from those here stated, particularly regarding the use of the Prüfening *Vita.* See ibid., pp. 15f.

64. Cf. VO 2.9, 3.6; pp. 70, 104f. Cf. 3.7; pp. 107f.

65. VO 1.3; p. 12. VO 1.4; pp. 13f. VO 1.19; 2.3; pp. 35ff., 58.
66. VO 2.4; p. 63.
67. Cf. VO 2.18; 3.26; pp. 89, 140f.
68. VO 1.9; pp. 21f. VO 1.4; p. 14. VO 1.19; p. 35. VO 3.17; p. 126.
69. E.g., the pallium, VO 1.12; p. 26.
70. VO 3.12; p. 112.
71. VO 2.1; p. 53.
72. E.g., VO 3.1; pp. 91ff.
73. VO 2.11; p. 72. Cf. 2.1; p. 53.
74. VO 3.1; p. 94.
75. VO 3.2, 5; pp. 96, 103. See Demm, *Reformmönchtum*, pp. 59f.
76. VO 2.12; pp. 73ff.
77. VO 1.20; 2.1; pp. 37, 49.
78. VO 1.16; 2.12; 3.24; pp. 30, 73, 137. Cf. on Boleslaus, 2.4; p. 62.
79. VO 3.27; p. 145.
80. VO 1, prologue; p. 4.
81. VO 3.15; p. 122. Cf. VO 2.8; pp. 67f.
82. VO 1.21; p. 42. Demm, *Reformmönchtum*, pp. 18f.
83. VO 2.1; p. 49.
84. VO 2.5; p. 64. Cf. Rom. 9:18–23. VO 3.3; pp. 97f. Cf. Rom. 10:15.
85. VO 2.16; p. 80.
86. VO 1.21; p. 41.
87. VO 2.1; pp. 91f. Cf. Matt. 24:14.
88. VO 2.3; 3.17; pp. 59, 83, and passim. Cf. Col. 3:14.
89. E.g., VO 1.18; 3.19; pp. 34, 128.
90. VO 3.27; p. 145.
91. VO 3.12; p. 112.
92. VO 1.22. Cf. reference to Otto's death, 3.25; pp. 46, 138.
93. VO 3.6; p. 106.
94. VO 2.12; 3.1; pp. 74, 93.
95. VO 2.16; p. 80. Cf. Acts 13:47.
96. VO 3.16; p. 124. Cf. 1.20; p. 37. Otto, in restoring discipline at Michelsburg, "velut aurora pulcherrima et lucifer matutinus ad discutiendas et illuminandas prisce conversationis caligines celitus effulsit."
97. VO 2.9; 3.23; pp. 71, 134. VO 3.16; p. 124. VO 3.21; p. 131.
98. VO 3.24; 3.26; pp. 137, 140. Otto established monasteries in honor of St. John at Michelsfeld and at Mullersdorf, 2.3; p. 58; 1.17; pp. 31f.
99. VO 2.14, 18; 3.16; pp. 78, 89, 124.
100. VO 3.1; p. 94. Cf. Demm, *Reformmönchtum*, p. 66.
101. VO 2.7, 11; pp. 67, 72.
102. E.g., VO 1.20; 2.11, 18; 3.2, 6, 15, 16, 19, 23, 26.
103. VO 3.1; p. 92.
104. VO 1.9, 18; 3.14; pp. 21, 33, 119f., and passim.
105. VO 1.20; p. 37.
106. VO 1.9; p. 22. VO 1.11; p. 24.
107. VO 1.14; p. 28. Cf. 1.11; p. 25.
108. VO 2.3, 4; 3.3; pp. 56, 63, 97.
109. VO 2.3; 3.3, 23; pp. 60, 99, 135.
110. Cf. VO 1.10; p. 23, where Otto applied St. Peter's words in Luke 22:33 to himself. Ulrich of St. Egidius uses the same passage of himself in his discussion with Otto, 2.3; p. 57.
111. VO 2.13; 3.2; pp. 77, 94ff. Cf. Acts 12:6ff. VO 3.12, 16; pp. 112ff., 125.
112. VO 3.1, 4, 16; 2.5, 18; 3.3, 6.
113. VO 2.2, 3, 12; 3.24; pp. 55, 56, 73, 137, and passim. Cf. Demm, *Reformmönchtum*, p. 52.

114. VO 1.2; p. 11.
115. VO 1.16; 3.26; pp. 30, 143. Cf. Ps. 51:10; Jer. 11:16.
116. E.g., VO 3.23; p. 135. Cf. the description of the new church at Kammin as a "novella plantacio," 2.5; p. 65.
117. VO 1.21; p. 42.
118. VO 2.12, 18; 3.1, 27; pp. 73, 86, 91, 145.
119. VO 3.9; p. 109f.
120. VO 1.9; p. 21. VO 2.12; p. 73. VO 3.13; p. 117. VO 3.23; p. 135.
121. VO 1.9; 2.3; pp. 21, 56. VO 1.17; p. 33. VO 2.3, 18; pp. 60, 89.
122. From Paschal II; VO 1.10, 12, 13, 14; from Otto: 1.15, 20; 2.12; from Wignand: 2.16.
123. VO 1.10; p. 23. Cf. Luke 22:33. Demm, *Reformmönchtum*, p. 88.
124. VO 2.3, 18; pp. 60, 89. Cf. Acts 6:15.
125. VO 2.16; p. 80. Cf. Acts 13:47. Petersohn, *"Apostolus Pomeranorum,"* pp. 268ff.
126. VO 1.16; 2.4, 18; 3.23; pp. 30, 63, 89, 133. Cf. Gal. 4:14.
127. VO 1.9; p. 21. VO 1.25; p. 139.
128. VO 2.3; p. 59. Cf. 3.16; p. 123, where Otto quotes Jesus' words before Pilate as in John 18:37.
129. VO 3.15; p. 121.
130. VO 2.18; pp. 88f. This view of Otto's return was very explicitly shared by several other contemporary authors. See Petersohn, *"Apostolus Pomeranorum,"* p. 258.
131. VO 1.5; p. 15.
132. VO 1.3–4, 6–7; 2.18; 3.13, 23, 24; pp. 12ff., 87, 115ff., 133ff.
133. VO 2.3, 4, 18; pp. 60, 62, 89. VO 1.8; p. 19.
134. VO 2.2; p. 55.
135. Cf. VO 2.15; p. 79.
136. VO 2.10; p. 71. Cf. 3.21; p. 131.
137. VO 3.19, 25; pp. 127f., 138. VO 1.19; 3.1, 12, 14; pp. 36, 94, 113f., 119f. VO 3.11, 17; pp. 111f., 126f. VO 3.16, 22; pp. 122f., 132f. VO 2.6; 3.1, 22; pp. 65f., 94, 133.
138. VO 3.27; p. 143.
139. VO 2.1, 3; 3.14, 15, 23; pp. 50, 56, 119, 121, 135.
140. VO 3.26; p. 142.

Cardinal Stephan of St. Grisogono: Some Remarks on Legates and Legatine Councils in the Eleventh Century

ROBERT SOMERVILLE

The use of legates by the eleventh- and twelfth-century "reforming" popes is well known. Such representation on behalf of the bishops of Rome was already at that time a venerable custom, whose origins must be sought in the patristic age. When Bruno of Toul became Pope Leo IX in 1049, the practice had evolved to the extent succinctly described by Auguste Dumas:

> The Roman church never ceased to act upon other churches through the dispatch of legates, who, when necessary, could be vested with full apostolic authority. There was constantly available to the church an adequate instrument to compel obedience. It only was necessary for the throne of St. Peter . . . to be occupied by energetic pontiffs determined to do their duty. Gregory VII and his successors will have no need to invent new institutions; they only must develop or transform those which exist already.[1]

The convocation of legatine councils was an obvious instrument through which the reformers' programs could be diffused throughout Christendom. A legate could, with apostolic authority, reiterate for a provincial audience decrees from papal synods, or promulgate other suitable regulations as the occasion required. He also could address himself to local ecclesiastical disputes. Hildebrand's treatment at Tours in 1054 of the eucharistic controversy surrounding Berengar is an example of such solicitude.[2] Both forms of conciliar activity would stress papal authority, and the second especially might demonstrate the effectiveness of that authority and the benefits to be gained through it. The legatine council was an arena for transforming papal theory into action.

In 1053 Pope Leo IX wrote to a group of bishops in North Africa that he did not wish for them to be ignorant of the fact that a "general council ought not to be celebrated without the approval of the Roman pontiff."[3] Such approbation could be given in various ways. The anonymous, mid-twelfth-century *Summa Parisiensis,* for example, designated papal or legatine presence as two means for constituting such an assembly.[4] These possibilities would not have been anachronistic in the second half of the eleventh century. The Pseudo-Isidorian forgers had inserted the following into a decretal ascribed to Pope Julius I:

> You published . . . [a] ruling which has no force, nor can it have, since this council was not conducted by orthodox bishops, nor were legates of the Roman church on hand although the canons prescribe that without its authority councils ought not to be held. No council is, or ever will be, approved, which is not fortified with that (i.e. Roman) authority.[5]

Pseudo-Isidore also transmitted an authentic letter of Pope Leo I, addressed to the great synod convened in 451 at Chalcedon.[6] The pontiff explained his own absence—"neither circumstance nor any custom" permitted attendance—[7] and then introduced his legates: "In these brothers . . . you should regard me as presiding over the synod."[8] Both of these texts made their way into important eleventh-century canonical books, the former being used by Anselm of Lucca,[9] the latter by Cardinal Deusdedit.[10] The attitudes reflected by Leo IX, "Julius," and Leo I, also found terse expression in the *Dictatus papae* of Gregory VII.[11] The sixteenth item of that series states that "no general council is possible without papal command," and the fourth entry asserts that a papal legate "takes precedence over all bishops in a council, even if he is of an inferior order. . . ."[12]

The impressions made on local officials by visiting legates in the eleventh and twelfth centuries would constitute, if sufficient information could be retrieved, a fascinating study. Even if the man were known personally in a region to which he was dispatched, the nimbus of authority surrounding such a commission must have exerted pressure on old relationships. It can only be wondered, for example, what observers at Reims thought of the seemingly bizarre appearance in their district of Cardinal-bishop Cono of Palestrina in 1117.[13] Cono was at the time a legate of Pope Paschal II, but traveled to Reims in disguise, since he had to journey through areas "which he knew were frequented by the emperor's spies." He chose the garb and identity of a writer ("scriptor"), and "until he entered Reims, the tools of this trade hung suspended from his shoulder, so that he would not be thought to be the bishop of Palestrina." Once secure in the city, however, he revealed himself, and convened a regional council in which he suspended certain prelates who had refused to participate.

In 1063 Pope Alexander II wrote thus to the archbishops of Reims, Sens, Tours, Bourges and Bordeaux:

> Since we are occupied with many ecclesiastical affairs and cannot come to you personally, we have taken care to send a man whose authority in the Roman church, after our own, is second to none, that is, Peter Damiani, the bishop of Ostia, who is our eyes, and the immobile foundation of the apostolic see. We have committed to him our complete authority.[14]

Peter was sent north primarily to deal with a struggle between Cluny and Bishop Drogo of Mâcon, and his activity in France included presiding over a synod at Chalon-sur-Saône.[15] One, if not *the* highlight of that assembly, was a public penitential submission before Peter by Drogo. How did observers in the council react to this humiliation, and what did they think of the ascetic and authoritative Italian in their midst? A monk at Cluny, writing of Peter's visit there before Chalon, described him as somewhat edgy, and "bruised all over from being bound with chains."[16] Even if corresponding vignettes from the council fathers are lost,[17] the investigator of the gathering at Chalon is fortunate in knowing who some of those particpants were. A privilege for the church of St. Stephan in Nevers was confirmed at the synod. The text survives, with subscriptions.[18] Thirteen French bishops are named among the witnesses. Not only would they have observed the episode involving Drogo, they also would have been privy to those matters which "were corrected with ecclesiastical censure," and to others, "stated with the vigor of canonical sanction."[19] When assessing the impact of papal reform in France during the early years of Alexander II's reign, it is useful to know which bishops received personal exposure to such material, from so magnificent an exponent of the Roman program.

Following a discussion of Hildebrand's legatine activity in France in the mid-1050s, Theodor Schieffer noted that "legates, behind whom stands the moral power of the 'Reformgedankens,' are becoming the authoritative (massgebenden) men in the French church."[20] The deposition of French simoniacal bishops by Hildebrand illustrates this, even if it is uncertain whom he deposed,[21] or what is to be made of stories about the inability of one recalcitrant simoniac to articulate, on command from the future Gregory VII, the name of the third person of the Trinity.[22] Clearly, when a contemporary of Hildebrand wrote that Pope Nicholas II "has sent me to this region, and, committing to me his powers, has enjoined that I should correct, in councils and through other labors with God's help, the things that I can in the French church," he has defined himself as the possessor of awesome power; he is a man capable of exercising the "authority of St. Peter and his vicar."[23]

These quotations are extracted from a letter written by Cardinal Stephan of St. Grisogono. The remainder of this study will be concerned with his legatine mission in the year 1060, to which that letter referred, and particularly with the synods convoked at Vienne and Tours. Nearly a decade ago, working as an assistant at the Institute of Medieval Canon Law then at Yale University, the author drafted an article on the legatine council at Beauvais in 1114, where Cardinal Cono of Palestrina presided.[24] It is appropriate that a thematic connection can be noted between that study—the author's initial publication in medieval conciliar history, prepared under the magisterial eye of Stephan Kuttner—and the present contribution. It is only proper that the legate whose activities frame the investigation at hand should be named *Stephanus*.

Various sources—assuming that they all refer to the same prelate—contribute information about Stephan and his activities in the service of the papacy.[25] Bonizo of Sutri identified him as a Burgundian, and called him "abbas et cardinalis."[26] If Stephan in fact were, as Bonizo stated, "ex Burgundionum genere," it could explain the assignment given by Nicholas II early in 1060, although he was not the only Burgundian cardinal in the reform circle at this period.[27] Stephan was abbot of the Roman monastery of

St. Andrea in clivo Scauri;[28] and Bonizo placed him in the early group of reformers who surrounded Leo IX.[29] His appointment to St. Grisogono was after 3 August 1057, for before consecration on that date as Pope Stephan IX, Frederick of Lorraine himself was cardinal-priest of that church.[30] Stephan had served, in 1058, as legate to Byzantium,[31] and also functioned in that same capacity for Germany in 1059–60.[32] He probably had contact at some point with Berengar of Tours,[33] was dispatched by Pope Alexander II again to France in 1067,[34] and the date of his death appears to have been 10 February 1069.[35] He thus gave two decades of service to the revived Roman church, and he surely belonged, to quote Klewitz, "zu den einflussreichsten Persönlichkeiten der Reformkurie."[36]

In the winter of 1060 Cardinal Stephan held councils at Vienne, beginning 31 January, at Tours, beginning 1 March, and perhaps also elsewhere.[37] A list of ten canons survives form the gathering at Tours. It was printed initially in 1648, by Luc D'Achéry, in notes to a *Vita* of Lanfranc contained in an edition of Lanfranc's *opera omnia*.[38] D'Achéry prefaced the text by stating that he was using a transcription ("antigraphum") of the decrees, written, in a hand which he deemed to be of the eleventh century, on a parchment page detached from a codex and which had suffered the ravages of cockroaches and worms ("rixante cum blattis et tineis"). Lest this material perish, d'Achéry decided to include it in the notes on Lanfranc's life, deeming possible a connection between Stephan's legation and the Berengarian dispute. These introductory comments are followed by the heading *Concilium Andegavense,* a misnomer engendered by a reference in the decrees' preamble to the *Basilica sancti Mauricii.* That could designate either Tours or Angers,[39] but since the text continues and states that the synod convened "at Tours, which is the *metropolis Galliae,*" d'Achéry's heading can be disregarded. The error might have been reenforced in his mind, however, by the provenance of this loose manuscript leaf. At the conclusion of the edition he wrote that the material derived "from the library of the monastery of St. Serge in Angers."[40]

This text, apparently snatched from certain doom, was reproduced in Labbé-Cossart's *Sacrosancta concilia* in 1671,[41] and thence made its way through the tomes of Hardouin and Coleti to Mansi.[42] The content of these canons has been summarized by Hefele-Leclercq, and by Theodor Schieffer,[43] and need not be repeated here. Schieffer has written that the decrees "set forth the principles of the reform with programmatic precision,"[44] although he continues, and observes that "the distribution of churches by laymen was not strictly forbidden, but even conditionally permitted,"[45] probably referring to c.4, which prohibits churches being received from laymen "quolibet modo," *without episcopal consent.* The relation of this text to the enigmatic decree from Nicholas II's Easter synod of 1059, which prescribed that clerics should, "nullo modo," receive churches "through" ("per") laymen, either freely or for a price,[46] requires future investigation. The assembly in 1060 at Tours was addressing the specific problems of the French church, as the preamble to the canons indicates, and some of the reformers' wishes may not have been practicable. But the concern reflected in the decrees about simony, clerical marriage, and, in general, the advancement of *puritas ecclesiae*, is predictable, and designates Stephan's legislation as an unambiguous component of the reform movement.

The synod which Stephan convened at Vienne, prior to Tours, has been documented by two texts. An incomplete set of canons has survived—the text breaks off after five words of the fourth decree—but what can be read repeats almost verbatim the Tours provisions. The only significant variation is in the introduction, which provides a different date and a place references to Vienne instead of to Tours. This text appeared in print first in 1714, in Jean Hardouin's *Acta conciliorum,* after discovery in a manuscript at the house of St. Aubin, Angers.[47] Three years later Martène and Durand printed the same material in the *Thesaurus novus,* apparently not from Hardouin, but directly from the manuscript.[48] The account passed into the work of Coleti and then Mansi.[49] Curiously, the latter editor claims, in a marginal note which must be lifted from Coleti, that he is following Martène and Durand, although the presentation given is that of Hardouin.

The modern investigator of these decrees is fortunate, for the manuscript used by Hardouin and Martène-Durand is identifiable. It was located easily, by using the index to the Angers volume of the *Catalogue général* of manuscripts in French provincial libraries.[50] Today it is MS 163 (155) in the Bibliothèque municipale at Angers. The book comes from St. Aubin, and contains the *Confessions* of St. Augustine. Added to the main work, at fols. 164r–66r, is a "copie incomplète des actes du concile de Vienne de 1060," which surely identifies the manuscript employed both by Hardouin and the editors of the *Thesaurus.*

The second source for Vienne relates information concerning one of the synod's *acta*. Within the rich collection of materials printed by J. Petit in 1677, as a supplement to his *Theodori . . . archiepiscopi Cantuariensis Poenitentiale,* a document is found, "Ex Chartulario de honoribus S. Juliano collatis in Comitatu Brivatensi," narrating the solicitude of Archbishop Leodegar of Vienne for the restoration in that city of the monastery of St. Ferréol-St. Julien.[51] After an unsuccessful attempt to associate this house permanently with St. Victor in Marseille, Leodegar resolved to transfer it to the canons of St. Martin in Brioude. The matter was raised in 1060 at the synod in Vienne, probably at the urging of Abbot Durand of St. Victor, and sustained discussion for two days. On the third day a judgment was given— Abbot Hugh of Cluny appears to have been influential in formulating it— which confirmed the donation to Brioude. The old privilege, which Durand of St. Victor "held in his hand"—perhaps he was waving it around as the verdict against him was pronounced—was taken by Cardinal Stephan and "torn to pieces, with everyone watching and approving."[52] The text printed by Petit concludes by noting that the names of the bishops who were on hand will follow. Unfortunately, the edition omits them with a series of dots. Whether they already were lacking in Petit's source is uncertain.

A portion of this account was paraphrased by Jean Mabillon in his *An-*

nales.[53] It was not, however, taken into the great conciliar works, and this would explain the episode's absence in Hefele-Leclercq. Petit's manuscript source, if it could be found, should be sought among the various texts designated by A. M. and M. Baudot, in their elaborate study of the great cartulary of St. Julien de Brioude.[54] It thus might be possible to rediscover the names of the participants at Vienne, and consequently to know which French bishops witnessed Cardinal Stephan's dramatic gesture against Abbot Durand.

The investigator of the synod at Vienne thus is confronted by two primary sources, both containing lacunae: not all of the canons have been available, and a list of the particpants has been excised, either in the middle ages, or in early modern times. It is now possible, however, to repair both gaps. The final item of MS 1386, in the Bibliothèque municipale at Troyes, is an early twelfth-century copy of the *Decretum* of Burchard of Worms.[55] Following Burchard, on fols. 298v–99r, is a text commencing thus: "Sancta sinodus [MS: Sanctam sinodum], que ex precepto domni nostri beatissimi summi pontificis et universalis pape Nicholai Vienne, que est metropolis Gallie, convenit." These lines, and their continuation, repeat the preface of the Vienne legislation edited by Hardouin and Martène-Durand, and identify the subsequent canons as products of the synod convened in that city early in 1060. The decrees are unnumbered, and variants notwithstanding, reproduce what was offered by the eighteenth-century editors, up to the point at which those versions end, that is, after the beginning of the fourth canon. But the Troyes rendition continues, and details a longer series of provisions which, in its entirety and again with variants aside, repeats the legislation which d'Achéry rescued from oblivion promulgated in Cardinal Stephan's council at Tours. This repetition is hardly surprising. Stephan went north armed with a definite program for the church in France,[56] and it is only sensible that he reiterated it in the assemblies where he presided.

A transcription of the canons from Troyes MS 1386 will not be given here. That endeavor can best be accomplished in an edition of the rulings from both Vienne and Tours; but it has been impossible, at present, to consult the Angers codex used by Hardouin and Martène-Durand, or to make a search for d'Achéry's fragment of the duplicate legislation from Tours. Furthermore, it has not been possible to look for additional manuscripts of this material, although the Troyes account of Vienne offers suggestions about where to search: the most striking factor in the text is a set of subscriptions following the canons, thus identifying participants who might have carried home copies of the legislation. This list of names also fills, at least in part, the lacuna at the end of Petit's *actum* concerning St. Ferréol-St. Julien. The subscriptions, written in two columns and followed by crosses, read thus:[57]

> Ego Stephanus sancte Romane ecclesie cardinalis sacerdos vocatus, vice domni pape Nicholai, sinodo presidens his constitutionibus a nobis canonice promulgatis subscripsi†

> Ego Leodegarius archiepiscopus Vien-
> nensis subscripsi† (Leodgar of Vienne)
>
> Ego Uncbertus Lugdunensis archiepis-
> copus titulatus fui† (Humbert of Lyons)[58]

Ego Poncius Valentine civitatis epis-
copus† (Pons of Valence)[59]

Ego Ugo sancte Crisopolitane ecclesie
archiepiscopus subscripsi† (Hugh of
Besançon)[60]

Ego Winemandus archiepiscopus Ebredun-
ensis subscripsi† (Winnaman of Em-
brun)[61]

Ego Agaddo indignus Edunensis ecclesie
episcopus subscripsi† (Agano of Autun)[62]

Ego Riabaldus archiepiscopus Arelaten-
sis subscripsi† (Rambaud of Arles)[63]

Ego Accardus Cabilonensis episcopus
subscripsi† (Achard of Chalon-sur-
Saône)[64]

Ego Petrus Diensis episcopus subscrip-
si† (Peter of Die)[65]

Ego Hugo Diniensis episcopus subscrip-
si† (Hugh of Digne)[66]

Ego Gothefredus Mariennensis dictus episcopus titulatus fui†[67]
(Geoffrey of St. Jean-de-Maurienne)

Not only does this list identify some of those who were at the synod, it also offers corrections and fills blanks in the available "listes des évêques" for Die, Digne, St. Jean-de-Maurienne, and Valence, as the notes referred to above indicate. It is impossible to draw any conclusions from the ordering of the names in the manuscript. The text is a copy of another, and scribal adjustments cannot be discounted. The position of Bishop Pons of Valence is particularly curious, since the archbishops of Embrum and Arles follow him in the first column. The absence of any abbots— Hugh of Cluny, for example, was present[68]—also is noteworthy. Whether or not the series reflects something about episcopal seniority, or about local customs at councils in this region, is unknown.[69] Cardinal Stephan heads the list, as would be expected, and Leodgar of Vienne is next, which also is not surprising. Surveying the names, however, and recalling that Stephan probably was a Burgundian, it can be wondered, in conclusion, how many of these bishops knew the cardinal personally, and apart from the formality of subscribing to the synodal decrees, what they thought of these "constitutions promulgated . . . canonically" by a legate, in whose presence was to be seen Pope Nicholas II himself.[70]

Columbia University

Notes

The following abbreviations will be used: de Montclos, *Lanfranc et Bérenger* = J. de Montclos, *Lanfranc et Bérenger. La Controverse eucharistique du XIᵉ Siècle,* Université catholique de Louvain, Spicilegium sacrum Lovaniense, Études et Documents XXXVII (Louvain, 1971); DHGE = *Dictionnaire d'Histoire et de Géographie ecclésiastiques,* in progress (Paris, 1912–); *Schieffer, Legaten* = T. Schieffer, *Die päpstlichen Legaten in Frankreich vom Vertrage Meersen (870) bis zum Schisma 1130,* Historische Studien CCLXII (Berlin, 1935). Bibliography will be limited throughout this paper, and no attempt will be made to provide either a comprehensive or a systematic treatment of legates. For an orientation in that regard see K. Ruess, *Die rechtliche Stellung der päpstlichen Legaten bis Bonifaz VIII.* Görres-Gesellschaft zur Pflege der Wissenschaften in katholischen Deutschland—Sektion für Rechts- und Sozialwissenschaft XIII (Paderborn, 1912), and F. Claeys-Bouvaert, *Dictionnaire de Droit canonique* (1957), VI: 371–77.

1. Émile Amann and Auguste Dumas, *L'Église au Pouvoir des Laïques (888–1057). Histoire de l'Église depuis les Origines jusqu'à nos Jours* VII (Paris, 1948), pp. 173–74.

2. See R. Somerville, "The Case Against Berengar of Tours—A New Text," *Studi Gregoriani* IX (1972), 56, and de Montclos, *Lafranc et Bérenger,* pp. 149–66. R. W. Southern, *The Making of the Middle Ages* (New Haven and London, 1963), pp. 145–51, writes in compelling terms regarding the importance of papal legates and legatine synods during the eleventh-century reform.

3. JL 4304: "Hoc autem nolo vos lateat, non debere praeter sententiam Romani pontificis universale concilium celebrari." See also JL 4305, and Horst Fuhrmann, "Das Ökumenische Konzil und seine historischen Grundlagen," *Geschichte in Wissenschaft und Unterricht* XII (1961), 681.

4. T. P. McLaughlin, C.S.B., *The Summa Parisiensis on the Decretum Gratiani* (Toronto, 1952), p. 17. See Fuhrmann, "Konzil," 686–87.

5. JK +196 (Paul Hinschius, *Decretales Pseudo-Isidorianae et Capitula Angilramni* [Leipzig, 1863], p. 471, c. xiii): "hanc regulam protulistis que nullas habet vires, nec habere poterit, quoniam nec ab orthodoxis episcopis hoc concilium actum est, nec Romanae aecclesiae legatio interfuit canonibus praecipientibus sine eius auctoritate concilia fieri non debere, nec ullum ratum est aut erit umquam concilium quod eius non fuerit fultum auctoritate."

6. JK 473 (Hinschius Decretales, p. 609).

7. Ibid.: "nec necessitas temporis nec ulla poterat consuetudo permittere."

8. Ibid.: "Tamen in his fratribus . . . me synodo vestra fraternitas aestimet praesidere. . . ."

9. Anselm of Lucca, *Collectio canonum,* ed. F. Thaner (Innsbruck, 1906), p. 97 (bk. 2, c. 47).

10. *Die Kanonessammlung des Kardinals Deusdedit,* ed. V. Wolf von Glanvell (Paderborn, 1905), p. 85 (bk. 1, c. 116 [95]). See the rubric for this decree in the *capitula* for book 1 (ibid. 7, l. 15): "Quod non sit consuetudo pape preesse universalibus sinodis nisi per legatos suos."

11. *Das Register Gregors VII.,* ed. E. Caspar, 2nd ed., MGH *Epp. sel* II (Berlin, 1955), II: 205.

12. (DP 16): "Quod nulla synodus absque precepto eius debet generalis vocari." (DP 4): "Quod legatus eius omnibus episcopis presit in concilio etiam inferioris gradus. . . ." For the meaning of "vocari" in DP 16, see Fuhrmann, "Konzil," 685, n. 45.

13. For what follows see the *Vita Theogeri abbatis S. Georgii et episcopi Mettensis,* MGH SS XII: 467: "Postquam ergo a Romano pontifice haec illi iniuncta legatio est, priusquam ad ea loca, quae a speculatoris imperatoris noverat obsideri, pertingeret, nomen sibi habitumque scriptoris induerat, et usquequo Remorum civitatem intraret, huius operis instrumenta ex humero eius suspensa pendebant, ut nihil minus quam Praenestinus episcopus putaretur. Sed ubi ad civitatem perventum est, ibi vero qualis sub scriptore lateret apparuit." See also Schieffer, *Legaten,* pp. 203–4.

14. JL 4516: "Quoniam igitur pluribus ecclesiarum negotiis occupati, ad vos ipsi venire non possumus. Talem vobis virum destinare curavimus, quo nimirum post nos major in Romana ecclesia auctoritas non habetur, Petrum videlicet Damianum Ostiensem episcopum, qui nimirum et noster est oculus, et apostolicae sedis immobile firmamentum. Huic itaque vicem nostram pleno jure commisimus. . . ."

15. See Schieffer, *Legaten,* pp. 66–72, H. E. J. Cowdrey, *The Cluniacs and the Gregorian Reform* (Oxford, 1970), pp. 47–49, and Mansi XIX: 1025–28.

16. *Bibliotheca Cluniacensis,* edd. M. Marrier & A. Duchesne (Paris, 1614), p. 461 (also in PL CXLV: 857–58): "Erat namque vir ille abstinentiae singularis usu, et ferreorum vinculorum nexu undique sic attritus." See Schieffer, *Legaten.* p. 68.

17. See the text printed by Cowdrey, *Cluniacs,* p. 48, n. 2, for hostility both toward Cluny and toward Roman support of the monastery.

18. *Gallia Christiana* (Paris, 1770), XII, Inst., p. 328.

19. Mansi XIX: 1027: "Is ergo apud Cabilonensem civitatem, synodum congregavit. Nonnulla . . . canonicae sanctioni vigore correxit; quae potuit, juxta ecclesiasticae disciplinae regulam servanda constituit." Cf. PL CXLV: 860, and MGH SS XXX: 1046.

20. Schieffer, *Legaten,* p. 57.

21. Ibid.

22. Ibid., p. 56, n. 5. See also A. Stacpoole, "Hugh of Cluny and the Hildebrandine Miracle Tradition," *Revue Bénédictine* LXXVI (1967), 356–59.

23. Mansi XIX: 928–30. See immediately below in the text. By the time of Pope Paschal II, when much of the so-called Gregorian reform program was under attack from various opponents, a letter to the pontiff from Liège provided a scornful appraisal of papal legates: see MGH Lib de Lite II: 459.

24. "The Council of Beauvais, 1114," *Traditio* XXIV (1968), 493–503.

25. See the summary in Hans-Walter Klewitz, "Die Entstehung des Kardinal kollegiums," *Zeitschrift der Savigny-Stiftung für Rechtsgeschichte,* Kan. Abt. XXV (1936) 162–63, and especially 163, n. 1. See also C. Erdmann and N. Fickermann, *Briefsammlungen der Zeit Heinrichs IV.,* MGH, Die Deutschen Geschichtsquellen des Mittelalters, 500–1500, Die Briefe der Deutschen Kaiserzeit V (Weimar, 1950), p. 167, no. 100, plus the accompanying notes, and pp. 157–58, and finally, see de Montclos, *Lanfranc et Bérenger,* passim.

26. Bonizo, *Liber ad amicum,* MGH Lib. de Lite I: 588.

27. Klewitz, "Entstehung," 163.

28. Ibid., 162, and 163, n. 1.

29. Bonizo, *Liber,* p. 588.

30. *Ante* JL 4371, and *ante* JL 4368 (where the page citation to the "Leonis Chron. Mon. Cas." is to MGH SS VII).

31. JL *4382. See Klewitz, "Entstehung," 163, n. 1.

32. Ibid. See also Otto Schumann, *Die päpstlichen Legaten in Deutschland zu Zeit Heinrichs IV. und Heinrichs V.* (Marburg, 1912), pp. 5–8.

33. de Montclos, *Lanfranc et Bérenger,* pp. 203, and 209–10.

34. Schieffer, *Legaten,* pp. 76–9.

35. Klewitz, "Entstehung," 164, n. 5.

36. Ibid., 162–63.

37. Schieffer, *Legaten,* pp. 62–4.

38. L. d'Achéry, *Beati Lanfranci Cantuariensis archiepiscopi . . . opera omnia* (Venice, 1745), pp. 18–19. The Paris, 1648 edition has been unavailable to the author. The text also occurs in PL CL: 64–65.

39. *Gallia Christiana* (Paris, 1856), XIV: 3 and 543.

40. See J. Vezin, *Les Scriptoria d'Angers au XIᵉ Siècle,* Bibliothèque de l'École des Hautes-Études, IVᵉ Section—Sciences historiques et philologiques CCCXXII (Paris, 1974), passim.

41. P. Labbe and G. Cossart, *Sacrosancta concilia* (Paris, 1671), IX: 1108–11.

42. J. Hardouin, *Acta conciliorum* (Paris 1714), VI.1: 1071–74; Coleti's work has not been available; Mansi XIX: 925–28.

43. C. J. Hefele and H. Leclercq, *Histoire des conciles* (Paris, 1911), IV.2: 1203–4, and Schieffer, *Legaten,* p. 63.

44. Ibid.

45. Ibid.

46. MGH LL IV, I: 547.

47. Hardouin, *Acta,* VI.1: 1073–76.

48. E. Martène and U. Durand, *Thesaurus novus anecdotorum* (Paris, 1717), IV: 93–94.

49. Coleti has not been seen; Mansi XIX: 925–26.

50. *Catalogue général des Manuscrits des Bibliothèques publiques de France* (Octavo) (Paris, 1898), XXXI: 243.

51. J. Petit, *Theodori . . . archiepiscopi Cantuariensis poenitentiale* (Paris, 1677), pp. 606–10. For St. Ferréol–St. Julien see L. H. Cottineau, *Répertoire topo-bibliographique des Abbayes et Prieurés* (Mâcon, 1939), II: 3368. The following synopsis is based on this text. See also Schieffer, *Legaten,* p. 62–63.

52. Petit, *Poenitentiale,* p. 607: "Privilegium sane, quod praedictus Abbas Durandus manu tenebat, a Cardinali susceptum, et particulatim disruptum est, omnibus videntibus atque laudantibus."

53. J. Mabillon, *Annales ordinis S. Benedicti* (Paris, 1707), IV: 679.

54. A. M. and M. Baudot, *Grand Cartulaire du Chapître Saint-Julien de Brioude*. Mémoires de l'Academie des Sciences, Belles-Lettres et Arts de Clermont-Ferrand XXV (Tome XCV of the Annales et Mémoires) (Clermont-Ferrand, 1935).

55. This information was very kindly put at the author's disposal by Prof. Gérard Fransen, Université catholique, Louvain. For this manuscript, see the *Catalogue général des Manuscrits des Bibliothèques publiques des Departements* (Quarto) (Paris, 1855), II: 575–76.

56. See his letter to Dol, which has been quoted above (p. 159): Mansi XIX: 929.

57. The author has regularized capitalization, and the various errors which occur in the spelling of "subscripsi." All proper nouns are reproduced as found in the manuscript.

58. J. Kleinclauz, *Histoire de Lyon* (Lyons, 1939), I: 213.

59. Despite its unreliability, the author has been forced to rely on P. B. Gams, *Series episcoporum ecclesiae catholicae*, 2nd ed. (Leipzig, 1931), p. 648, for Valence. This work gives the year 1056 as a terminal date for Pons's episcopate, which clearly is incorrect. The works edited by U. Chevalier, "Chronique inédite des Évêques de Valence et de Die," *Bulletin d'Histoire ecclésiastique et d'Archéologie religieuse des Diocèses de Valence Gap, Grenoble, et Viviers*, XI (1891; 2ᵉ partie), 61–86, and "Chronicon episcoporum Valentinensium," *Documents inédits relatifs au Dauphiné* (Grenoble, 1868), II, 5ᵉ Livraison, pp. 31–37, are not relevant.

60. DHGE VIII: 1154.

61. DHGE XV: 380.

62. DHGE V: 908.

63. DHGE IV: 242.

64. DHGE XII: 299.

65. DHGE XIV: 431, designates Peter as occupying this see in 1055.

66. DHGE XIV: 461, which notes evidence for a bishop Hugh in 1038 and 1040, but then provides no other precise information for the eleventh century.

67. As with Valence, see n. 59, here too the author has been forced to turn to Gams. Ibid., 803, gives no information applicable to the year 1060. A. Gros, *Histoire du Diocèse de Maurienne* (Chambéry, 1948), II: 131, has no knowledge of the occupant(s) of the see between about 1056 and about 1060. A man named Brochard "aurait siégé approximativement de 1060 à 1073." The designation "dictus episcopus" conceivably is equivalent to "electus"; but it should be noted that Cardinal Stephan's subscription contains the words "cardinalis sacerdos vocatus." What the difference was, if any, between "subscripsi" and "titulatus fui" (see also the subscription for Humbert of Lyons) is undetermined. It is possible, but perhaps rash, to see the latter as an indication that the appropriate subscription was actually written by the hand of someone other than the prelate named. See the various medieval usages of "titulare" given in J. F. Niermeyer, *Mediae Latinitatis lexicon minus* (Leiden, 1964), XI: 1029.

68. See above, p. 161.

69. See the discussion by C. N. L. Brooke, "Archbishop Lanfranc, the English Bishops, and the Council of London of 1075," *Studia Gratiana* XII (1967), 39–59, for seating customs in English councils at about this same time.

70. See above, and the subscription of Cardinal Stephan to the Vienne decrees.

The Archbishop and the Hedgehog

EDWARD M. PETERS

One of the bluntest and most famous pieces of advice that John of Salisbury ever gave to his master, Archbishop Thomas Becket, was that Becket forego the study of the law that he had undertaken during his exile at Pontigny, mitigate the exclusively juridical character of his dispute with Henry II, and base his defense and his cause instead upon his own spiritual stature:

> The laws and canons are useful to us, but . . . they excite curiosity rather than devotion. Do you not remember how it is written, "The priests and ministers of the lord shall mourn between the vestibule and the altar, saying, 'Have mercy, O Lord, and spare Thy people.' " [Joel 2:17]. . . . "For I have searched my spirit," said the prophet, "and lifted my hands to the Lord in the day of tribulation." (cf. Ps. 76:27) This teaches us that spiritual exercises and cleansing discourse avert the scourge and obtain the mercy of God. Whoever rises up from the study of the laws, or even of the canons, stricken with remorse? I say more: the exercises of the schools sometimes puff up knowledge, but they rarely, or never, inflame virtue. I would prefer that you meditate upon the Psalms, and turn your mind upon the moral books of St. Gregory, rather than philosophize in the manner of the scholastics. It would be profitable to discuss moral problems with some holy man by whose example you may be stirred up, rather than ponder and discuss the litigious minutiae of secular letters.[1]

John of Salisbury was not the only twelfth-century thinker who expressed concern over what he considered to be the deadly contrast between purity of devotion and secular and ecclesiastical learning on the part of prelates, nor did Becket wholly ignore his advice. Other sources, including some by John of Salisbury himself, picture Thomas's stay at Pontigny as a holy exile, and Thomas's martyrdom at Canterbury contributed more to his subsequent memory than did his study of the law. The cult that grew up around the dead archbishop after 1170 was that of a holy man, martyr, and thaumaturge, not that of a deceased scholar. It may be said that Becket rose up from the study of the laws and the canons with a contriter heart than most.

In another sense, John of Salisbury's advice was more than a little anachronistic by the 1160s. Under whatever circumstances it had begun, by 1166 the quarrel between Henry II and Thomas Becket was joined as an issue at law, and both sides of the dispute increasingly employed formal juridical arguments to defend their own cause and to attack each other. John of Salisbury, like St. Bernard and others before and after him, deplored the juridical character of prelatic activities and ecclesiastical disputes, having complained to Pope Adrian IV long before he wrote to Becket. St. Bernard had complained to his protege Pope Eugenius III in a similar vien:

> What leisure has thou left for prayer? What time remains over to thee for instructing the people, for edifying the Church, for meditating on the law? True, thy palace is made to resound daily with noisy discussions relating to law, but it is not the law of the Lord, but the law of Justinian.[2]

By the mid-twelfth century, however, the masters of the new sciences of law and theology were sweeping all before them, and neither the humane and pious classicism of John of Salisbury nor the mystical theology of St. Bernard long survived, in the legal arena at least, their most eloquent and passionate representatives.[3] To "ponder and discuss the litigious minutiae of secular letters" was a necessity, although perhaps not always a happy one, for most late twelfth-century prelates and popes. As Henry II knew well, it was also a necessity for late twelfth-century kings and their servants.

At the outset of the dispute between Henry II and the Archbishop of Canterbury, the differences between them did not appear framed in exclusively juridical terms. For several years Henry spoke, publicly, at least, of the vague ancient prestige of the crown, the good customs of the realm, and the congenial relations between earlier kings of England and Becket's ecclesiastical predecessors, who were more than once help up to the archbishop as saintly examples he would do well to follow. Becket's own episcopal colleagues, especially after the disaster at Clarendon, urged moderation, compromise, and charitable mediation. Between 1164 and 1170 most of them drew away from Becket precisely over these issues. The events of 1163 and 1164, however, one following hard and unexpectedly upon another, quickly stripped the dispute of all aspects except the juridical and the purely personal, at least for the two great protagonists. With the sudden appearance of a written text of the venerable ancient customs of the realm in the Constitutions of Clarendon in 1164, both Henry and Thomas lost considerable room to negotiate and maneuver.[4] The intransigence of the king and the archbishop between 1164 and 1170 is the result as much of the narrowness of the forum in which they conducted their dispute as of the personal characteristics of Henry and Thomas. Most contemporaries were appalled by what appeared to be the intransigence of the two sides, and few of Becket's colleagues were comfortable or helpful in the face of the written constitutions on the one hand, or the increasingly juridical demands of their archbishop on the other.

Even the heavy hands of earlier English kings did not fail to leave room for flexibility and negotiation in the relations between *regnum* and *sacerdotium*. Facing the explicit text of the Constitutions of Clarendon, however, Becket, first dismayed, then adamant, could take little less than a position as firmly based upon explicit law as was that of his opponent. This case illuminates, as do many others, Maitland's famous *dictum* that history does not proceed from the simple to the complex, but from the vague to the definite. The rich and idiosyncratic history of the relations between *regnum* and *sacerdotium* in

England, from Dunstan to Theobald of Canterbury, suddenly and unexpectedly became narrowed after 1164 to an issue of law, or, rather, to an issue of two laws. For not only the specifics of the written Constitutions of Clarendon, but also the incompatibility of two precocious and conflicting systems of law, brought suddenly and unexpectedly into opposition over one of the most fragile issues between them, hemmed in the king and the archbishop. Neither Alexander III nor the Compromise of Avranches satisfactorily solved the problem. It was, as John of Salisbury pointed out to Thomas, inviting and easy to go to law in 1164. Whether the law provided resolutions to such knotty disputes as that between Henry and Thomas, however, was not so clear. John of Salisbury, as secretary and, later, as a bishop himself, remained unconvinced.

Not only did the conflict narrow its terms after 1164, but it involved more and more participants. The papal court, the prelates and lords of northern France, the emperor, the anti-pope, and the English bishops were all drawn in. Of these, the English episcopacy was drawn in deepest. Lawyers and pastors, they proved no more at home in the polarized juridical world of *regnum* and *sacerdotium* than was John of Salisbury, and they are generally characterized by their silence or their temporizing. Even Gilbert Foliot, one of the ablest canonists among them, and no friend of Becket's, remained painfully aware of the forced division of his loyalties and the absence of any grounds for a reconciliation.[5] Henry's courtiers and knights, as courtiers and knights often were, were somewhat readier to pursue and condemn the archbishop. Both groups were caught up in the growing intensity of legal exchanges, however. Both were accused, attacked, threatened, coerced, and excommunicated. Having gone to law, no one involved in the quarrel could escape the law, and it is in the various exercises of the law on both sides of the dispute that some of the most interesting polemical literature of the late twelfth century is to be found.

An exchange of letters consisting of Becket's *Fraternitatis vestrae* written to the English higher clergy in 1166 and Gilbert Foliot's response, *Multiplicem nobis,* of the same year illustrates the narrowing of the dispute down to precise, intractable legal issues better than perhaps any other documents that survive.[6] Becket's letter abounds in specific citations of legal issues against the clergy and builds a formidable case in canon law against those prelates who had sided with Henry or appeared to be, at best, indifferent to the cause of their church and its archbishop. The same law that Becket cited so threateningly, however, lay open to others as well, and nobody as independent, learned, and genuinely distraught as the English bishops, could easily have let such accusations pass unanswered. Foliot's *Multiplicem nobis,* a work of greater legal rhetoric, if not of law, than Becket's letter, not only responded to the archbishop's charges in kind, but launched several new accusations at Thomas. The juridical formality and bitterness of both letters illustrate the validity of John of Salisbury's warning to Becket far better than John would have wished. Both Thomas and Gilbert drew increasingly upon the "laws and the canons" in attack and defense. Gone were the allegories, scriptural and classical references, and the whole apparatus of figurative expression that had permitted some earlier disputes great latitude in which to be settled. In their place are the *argumenta* and *canones* of a technical duel. More complex yet, these letters are not part of a formal legal case but rather constitute part of an increasingly popular genre of juridical epistolary invective very different from that of John of Salisbury and other twelfth-century writers.

Shortly after the exchange of Becket and Foliot, John of Salisbury wrote to Bartholomew of Exeter and characterized the archbishop and the king in these terms:

> Are not these two the princes of the people, of whom the one dispenses spiritualities and the other administers temporalities? Is not the law of dispensation and administration committed to their hands? These are the two cherubim whose wings overshadow the law and the propitiation, looking one towards the other, while both look toward the propitiation.[7]

The entire passage, with its elaborate references to *Hebrews* and *Exodus,* as well as the whole letter itself, echoes the style and logic of much of twelfth-century humanism, especially when its techniques were applied to the settlement of political or legal conflicts. It is very different in tone from Becket's letter, very different from *Multiplicem.* The rhetorical art of the schools now gave way to a new kind of rhetoric, one which echoed more routinely the exact language of the law. The idea of immanent justice, the complex exegetical references, and the simplified description of *regnum* and *sacerdotium* that John of Salisbury's letter to Bartholomew of Exeter so skillfully assembles and deploys belong to a different world from that of Becket's and Foliot's letters, a world that now substituted for the harmony of cherubim the clash of lawyers.

Becket's flight to Pontigny in 1164 and its treatment in the letters of Becket, Foliot, and others and in the *vitae* of Becket illustrates some of the consequences of the new legalism and casts some interesting light upon the various ways in which it was possible to treat a technical problem of canon law, the case of the fugitive prelate.

In the *Vita, Passio, et miracula S. Thomae Cantuariensis Archiepiscopi,* written around 1173 by William, a monk of Canterbury, the narrative of Becket's abrupt departure from the royal court at Northampton is interrupted by the following story:

> Behold the fugitive hedgehog, which a certain deacon saw in a vision. The king, with all of his archbishops, bishops, counts, nobles, priors, and abbots, was hunting in the forest at Wabridge, when a hedgehog suddenly ran out from among them, as if agitated by their commotion. The crowd, upon seeing him, began to grow excited, crying and shouting. The hedgehog, however, running ahead of the crowd, not in a straight path, but by darting and turning on its tracks, hastened toward the sea, bearing upon its back a book called the *Acts of the Apostles.* None of those who pursued it were without some stain of the body,

either blind or one-eyed, either lame or with nose or lips mutilated. When the hedgehog came to the sea it threw itself into it and did not emerge. Those who pursued it saw this and turned back. And behold, there arose a great and thick cloud which covered the face of the earth, and it was followed by a bloody rain.[8]

Beryl Smalley, in her fine recent study of Becket and the intellectuals of the controversy, has briefly discussed this passage, suggesting its singular appropriateness in catching Becket's character, that of "the wild, spiky archbishop."[9] But the anecdote is important in other ways as well. William of Canterbury was drawing upon a number of familiar traditions in recounting the deacon's vision. One of these, of course, was that of the *visio* itself at crucial points in the saint's life. Another was the vast body of zoological allegory in which the hedgehog, *ericius,* was included. The hedgehog's flight into desert places suggested both prudence and the flight of the holy man to Christ. The *Acts of the Apostles,* borne upon the hedgehog's spiky back as the hedgehog's food was said to be borne, suggests both general apostolic identification and perhaps, according to Smalley, Becket's identification specifically with St. Paul. Above all, the *visio ericii* belongs to that world of hagiographical rhetoric that was closely related to twelfth-century humanism and to the outlook of such writers as John of Salisbury.[10] It is picturesque, arresting, moral, and symbolic. It represents a world of discourse out of which it would be difficult to build anything resembling a legal case.

William has other things to say about Becket's flight as well. Just before he tells the story of the hedgehog, he cites the flights of Jacob from Esau, as well as those of St. Paul, David, and other biblical figures. He describes the archbishop's flight in commonplace rhetorical terms with further scriptural echoes. John of Salisbury also discusses the escape in similar terms in his own brief *vita* of Becket.[11] Herbert of Bosham also echoes William drawing parallels between Becket's flight and those of Jesus, St. Paul, Jacob, Moses, and Elias.[12] A number of writers cite the familiar text of Matt. 10:23: "When they persecute you in one town, take refuge in another." For the most part, Becket's biographers describe the flight from Northampton as an exile, set it firmly in a familiar scriptural context, and associate Becket with the timeless world of scriptural typology.

Becket himself, in many of his letters, adopts a similar tone. In 1165 he wrote to Pope Alexander III that he had been "driven out" of England; "crushed by the multitude of my foes, I have fled to your presence."[13] In the same year Alexander III wrote to Gilbert Foliot, describing Henry II as "having exiled from his dominions our venerable brother the archbishop of Canterbury."[14] In spite of Henry's and Gilbert's protestations that Becket's exile was purely voluntary, indeed, that Becket "has basely fled the country," Becket's letter *Fraternitatis vestrae,* written to the English bishops in 1166, sums up his own view of exile: "wherefore I chose to turn aside for a while, that I might dwell with greater benefit in the house of the Lord than in the tents of sinners, until their iniquity should be complete, the breasts of the wicked laid open, and the thoughts of their hearts be revealed."[15] Exile, persecution, *libertas ecclesiae,* the demands of conscience, the fear for his own salvation, all expressed in the figures of moral typology and in association with traditional scriptural references, these are the themes that Becket, his allies, and his biographers invoke when they mention the flight from Northampton in 1164.

Gilbert Foliot's letter *Multiplicem nobis,* the response to *Fraternitatis vestrae,* implicitly rejects these images of the absent archbishop and brings the topic of Becket's absence to another level, that of canonical culpability for having deserted his flock, a legal charge rather than a moral criticism. In his attacks on Becket, particularly in his denunciation of Thomas as a fugitive prelate, Gilbert creates a *libellus famosus,* making no references to scriptural common-places, none to St. Paul, Moses, or Elias, none to the moral grounds that Becket had used to explain his flight. Indignant, insulted, and threatened by canonical sanctions himself, Gilbert employed his skills as a canonist in several places in *Multiplicem,* nowhere more ably than in his attack upon Becket's absence from his see. Gilbert's charge against Thomas culminates a long rehearsal of Thomas's career, from the time when, as archdeacon of Canterbury and chancellor of the king, he was promoted to the see of Canterbury, to his flight and his attacks upon the king from his exile. Becket's forced election, the results of the *ira regis,* his earlier invasions of the *libertas ecclesaie* in his exactions for the siege of Toulouse, then Becket's lack of prudence in permitting the two swords to oppose one another, and finally Becket's failure to support the higher clergy against the king when they took a position Becket himself had commanded prepare for the sequel, the portrait of a prelate who broke and fled under slight pressure. Gilbert's version of Thomas's career as archbishop depicts Thomas as an opportunist, and an enemy of ecclesiastical liberty ("The sword of state was in your hand, shedding terror upon all whom you might view with an angry eye. It was the same sword which your own hand had plunged into the bosom of our holy mother church when you stripped her of so many thousand marks to pay the expenses of the expedition to Toulouse.") In short, Thomas, an imprudent and vacillating prelate, was a man who built his own power by illegitimately exploiting the temporal power at the expense of the spiritual, then alienating even the temporal power by his lack of judgment. When the consequences of his weakness and rashness were borne home to him, he collapsed and gave in to the king. In this light, Becket's whole ecclesiastical career becomes a clear indicator of his weakness and rashness, and when Gilbert treats the events of Clarendon and Northampton, he makes Thomas appear to have behaved in a manner perfectly consistent with his earlier actions. Gilbert's ominous roll call of the bishops who stood firm against the king at Clarendon concludes with the images of Thomas, "the leader of our chivalry . . . who turned his back, the captain of our camp who fled." Thomas, who proved "so easy to be turned," then violated the tranquillity of the prelates' "descent into Egypt" by breaking his promise to the king not to leave the kingdom without the king's consent, tried to flee, failed, went unpunished by the king, gave in to the king once more, again illegally, and finally, even after the king had given Becket his protection, "fled at night, in disguise . . . though no one was pursuing you . . . and now attempt to steer that vessel of the church, which you left without a pilot amid the waves . . . [from] a foreign land." "Obstinacy and perverseness" have led Becket to his flight. Gilbert's version of Becket's flight is very different from Becket's own, and it systematically undercuts the imagery of Becket and his supporters of the house of the Lord and the tents of sinners. The whole description of Becket's career as archbishop prepares for the archbishop's shameful flight, and that flight is dissected over a long passage that constitutes, in fact, the climax of the letter. In one sense, at least, *Multiplicem* is an indictment of the archbishop's whole career, but the episode of Becket's flight culminates that career. And the flight is shown as no exile, no pious attempt to save the archbishop's soul, but rather the result of weakness, obstinacy, pride, and perverseness. Becket is not a holy exile; he is a fugitive prelate.

Between 1164 and 1170 many English voices were raised suggesting that Becket either resign his see or be deposed. Some of these voices, such as that of the bishop of Lincoln, urged such a step as a matter of simple expediency. Others, however, suggested various grounds of incapacity or crime. Becket himself, of course, is said to have attempted to resign his see into the hands of Pope Alexander III, only to receive it back immediately.[16] In the late twelfth century, the problem of prelatic deposition or resignation took on a sharper character in the light of the development of the science of canon law, the consequences of the investiture conflicts, and the frequent clashes between temporal and spiritual authority. Although *Multiplicem* is not a formal legal document, it is possible to read it in the light of the canon law concerning prelatic deficiencies and to consider it specifically as Gilbert's case against Thomas, built step by step with canon law firmly in mind, and culminating in the charge of illegal flight which was recognized as one of the technical grounds for removing a bishop. *Multiplicem* may very well have been, as Christopher Brooke has called it, "a debater's answer" to Thomas's letter, but it was a debater's answer on legal grounds.[17] Although the entire letter cannot be analyzed here, it may be illuminating to consider the legal grounds for one, at least of Gilbert's charges, that Thomas was a fugitive bishop. For the figure of the bishop received much attention in the twelfth-century canon law, and episcopal flight was one of the knottiest problems that Gratian and other canonists faced.

The office of bishop in theology and law took shape between the second and the twelfth centuries under a number of very different kinds of influences. Scriptural and patristic literature, theological disputes, the assimilating of ecclesiastical theories of office to the ranks of the imperial Roman *cursus honorum,* and the social changes of early Germanic Europe each left its mark upon the idea and the institution of the episcopacy. Of the fathers, Augustine, Ambrose, and Gregory the Great left detailed descriptions of the duties and responsibilities of bishops, and early canon law and Roman law contributed an important juridical dimension to the episcopal office. Between the sixth and the ninth centuries the circumstances in which the episcopal office had been shaped gave way to the new world of episcopal insecurity, the appearance of monastic bishops, and the opportunities and dangers of a new European society that only in the eighth and ninth centuries began to restore to the episcopacy some of its earlier spiritual and temporal importance under the watchful eyes of the Carolingian kings. The *entrée en scène* of the Carolingian episcopacy has been the subject of a large literature, as has been the decline of episcopal prestige and power in the tenth century and its slow resurgence in the eleventh and twelfth centuries.[18] R. W. Southern has succinctly described some of the new circumstances in which episcopal power resumed and episcopal prestige increased during the eleventh and twelfth centuries.[19] Southern's principal thesis, that papal power transformed, but did not diminish episcopal functions, emphasizes the role of canon law in this process and the contrast between "the general uniformity . . . [in] the development of the episcopal office everywhere in Europe," and the particular social and political contexts in which each bishop exercised this office.[20]

The political and social context in which the archbishopric of Canterbury was governed between 1161 and 1170 shaped the roles of Henry and Thomas and provided the outlines for the conduct of Becket's episcopal colleagues, but the development of canon law also held up a uniform standard of episcopal conduct to which both sides could appeal. Gilbert Foliot's *Multiplicem*, particularly in its denunciation of Becket as a fugitive bishop, appealed explicitly to this uniform standard and, in the light of twelfth-century canon law, made a convincing case against Thomas.

By the time of Gratian's *Decretum*, a collection which Gilbert knew well, there had been amassed a great volume of old and new—and confused and conflicting—legal material concerning the nature of the episcopal office and episcopal conduct, and the treatment of this theme in Gratian and subsequent canonical collections is a fascinating and difficult study. In terms of the fugitive bishop alone, a large literature, from scripture to papal letters, none of it unequivocal, presented Gratian with one of the thorniest problems in his work. Gratian's general treatment of the episcopacy is, according to Gaudemet, quite original and versatile, consistent with the heightened attention given to the sacramental, legal, and theological character of the office from the Gregorian reformers to such twelfth-century ecclesiologists as St. Bernard, Hugh of St. Victor, Peter of Blois, and Gerald of Wales.[21]

Although the episcopal office is discussed in several places in the *Decretum*, C.7 raises particularly interesting questions concerning the character of the office of the bishop and the conduct of holders of that office. *Causa 7* presents the case of "a certain bishop, long beset by infirmity, [who] asked that another [bishop] be substituted for him. The pope conceded what he had asked. Afterwards, however, the bishop was cured and wished to take back his earlier request. Against him who had succeeded, he challenged that his throne still belonged to himself . . ."[22] Gratian's *quaestiones* ask, first, whether anyone may be made bishop in a church whose bishop is still living, and, second, whether a bishop may regain his throne after another has taken it at his own request. Gratian's texts and comments deal with a wide range of relevant topics, from illness, insanity, and other forms of incapacity to the various kinds of surrogates available to bishops. Advancing age, episcopal *ambicio,* translations, *necessitates temporis,* and other episcopal dangers are then taken up in order.

Gratian's conclusions, and those of the contemporary reformers, were based upon his desire to regularize the operation of the episcopal office, to enhance the sacerdotal singularity of the episcopacy, and to curtail the most common abuses that the extant literature cited. Hence, his argument is weighted heavily in favor of episcopal *stabilitas* within the diocese, and he considers very few exceptions to the rule that the bishop must remain in his church and with his flock as long as he is physically able. In addition to Matt. 10:23, Gratian cites John 10:12: the bishop who deserts his flock is a "mercenarius . . . non pastor," and behind Gilbert's use of the material in C.7 there lies yet the echo of another scriptural maxim: Prov. 28:1: "Fugit impius, nemine persequente."[23]

For Gratian, neither natural disasters nor persecution offer justification for a bishop's flight, except in a very few cases, and much of Gilbert's description of Thomas's flight is directed at denying these exceptions to the archbishop of Canterbury.

The interest of Gratian and others in episcopal stability echoes both the earlier literature on the episcopal office and the results of the reform movement of the tenth and eleventh centuries that had its roots in monasticism and, drawing heavily on the letter of St. Benedict's Rule, condemned monastic wanderings as vigorously as any other offence. One of the most striking aspects of the letters of St. Bernard, for example, is their reflection of Bernard's concern for fugitive monks, his considerable efforts to restore them safely to their monasteries, and the variety of approaches he employs in the different cases of those who must take them back, those who make it difficult for them to live in their monasteries, and those who try to tempt them into leaving. Monastic *stabilitas* too influenced the image of the bishop, particularly in an age when many, even most, bishops had been monks, and when many writers explored the parallels among the different *status vitae* of the twelfth-century church.[24]

Bishops differed from monks, according to Bernard, because they had to fulfill both "the service of nature and the service of grace." Although *stabilitas* was enjoined upon them, theirs was not to be the *stabilitas* of the cloister, but that of the *cathedra,* one which was of such a high ministry that to leave it, even to lead a more humble life, was generally forbidden. In 1140, Bernard wrote to Thurstan, archbishop of York, dissuading him from retiring to a monastery because of old age and an earlier vow.[25] As to the earlier vow to become a monk, Bernard argues that the bishop's ministry supersedes any such vow. In regard to Thurstan's age, Bernard answers that only grave sin or papal permission justify the abandonment of an episcopal ministry. Thurstan, Bernard writes, may "exhibit in a bishop the dress and holy life of a monk," but "you should stay where you are." As will be seen, canon law allowed somewhat greater latitude than St. Bernard did, but Bernard's letters constitute an important example of the range and attitudes of twelfth-century ecclesiology.

Monk and bishop both, although in different ways, were enjoined to *stabilitas,* and although flight might be forgiven, it must, with few exceptions, be followed by return and penance. Although Gratian explored the problem of the fugitive bishop more widely than did St. Bernard, his views were not fundamentally different. The theologian and the lawyer both shared the reform view of the distinctive character and responsibilities of both monastic and prelatic life. Such a view undoubtedly strengthened both roles generally and contributed, with other elements, to enhancing the prestige of monastic and mendicant orders and that of the secular clergy as well. Such emphasis upon the responsibilities of the prelate constitutes one of those new circumstances which Southern describes as a result of the growth of papal authority and administration and the spread of canon law.

The case of Thomas Becket, however, was a particular case with its own peculiarities. Not the least of these was the division of opinion concerning the archbishop himself, which surfaced long before the Council of Northampton and counted influential figures on both sides. A second element was the speed with which the relations between archbishop and king deteriorated, and a third was Thomas's isolation from the advice of his episcopal colleagues at the critical moments of 1163 and 1164. There was much, indeed, in Becket's style of being an archbishop that made him particularly vulnerable to attacks such as Gilbert's. Becket's case also possessed generic peculiarities. There have been periods in history when episcopal flight, or at least the occasions for episcopal flight, have been more numerous and pressing than at other times. Donatists drove out orthodox bishops in fourth-century Africa; invaders in the sixth and seventh, and again in the ninth and tenth centuries drove European bishops from many sees. Rivals and enemies could effectively oppress a bishop at any time. There were also varying occasions when flight was possible, just as there were periods when bishops could move about as freely—and for as long—as they wished, with no effective power to stop them. Becket lived in one of the last such periods before the Reformation of the sixteenth century. After 1200, there existed too many forces interested in episcopal conduct for flight itself to be very easy or likely. When thirteenth-century bishops fled, they usually fled to Rome.[26] Thus, the complex treatment that Gratian gave to the problem of the fugitive prelate and the use that Gilbert Foliot made of it in *Multiplicem* were not always as applicable as they were in the second half of the twelfth century, and rarely were they invoked to deal with a case as complex as that of Becket. It is precisely in the tension between the necessary generalities of the law and the complexity of Becket's own case that Gilbert's accusation and its juridical grounds are most interesting.

Not all of the texts that Gratian marshalls in C.7 q.1, of course, applied, even in a remote way, to the case of Becket. Most, in fact, of Gratian's concern is for the technicalities of replacing genuinely incapacitated bishops. After this, his concern is for those bishops, priests, and deacons who desert one church in order to move to a more attractive, richer, or more important one. Only at the end of q.1, in five *capitula* later designated *Pars* VIII and *Pars* IX, does Gratian face the question of a bishop's outright desertion of his see. The first text in this series, c.45 *(Hoc nequaquam),* is a text from the pseudo-Photian synod of 879 which forbids a bishop who has retired to the monastic life from resuming his prelatic rights later on. Gratian, in his *dictum* following c.45, points out that this rule pertains only to those prelates who have become monks for penitential purposes, not to those who have become monks in order to seek tranquillity. The latter are treated in c.46 *(Suggestum),* part of a decretal attributed to Pope Liberius in the collection of Pseudo-Isidore, which forbids prelates from deserting their sees because of the persecutions of the wicked. This point is emphasized in c.47 *(Sciscitaris),* part of a letter of Nicholas I which, in response to a bishop's request for permission to enter a monastery because of the depredations of the Norsemen, refuses such permission. The fourth text, c.48 *(Adversitas),* part of a letter from Gregory I to Reccared, describes tribulations as trials of the just, not divine punishments.

These four texts make a strong case against episcopal flight, even in the face of persecution. It is hardly a coincidence that the three most specific of them date from the late ninth century, when the office of bishop was a matter of particular concern to popes and Frankish clergy alike and when the pressures upon the episcopacy offered a number of cases of episcopal flight to the monastic life, not always, as Gratian was aware, for penitential purposes alone. It is also perhaps a sign of the range of ideas and concerns that are reflected in both the remarkable pontificates of John VIII and Nicholas I and in the collection of Pseudo-Isidore, a range that is considerably broader than studies that concentrate upon their importance for the theory of papal authority alone usually allow. There is one other text, however, of which Gratian makes use, not as a *capitulum,* but as a very long and complicated *dictum post* c.48, and that is St. Augustine's *Epistola* 228.[27] Augustine's letter is one of the most complete reviews ever written of the full complexity of a bishop's relation to his see and his status in the Christian community. Because it covers so wide a range of problems and offers little that is concisely excerptable, Gratian employs it as a framework for reviewing the entire *quaestio,* subdividing Augustine's analysis and his own into five categories, and he concludes the *quaestio* with c.49 *(Ibi adunati),* a somewhat general text from the *Dialogues* of Gregory I which, in extremely figurative terms, allows that there are times when a prelate may leave his flock and times when he may not. Gratian's own *dictum post* c.49 somewhat lamely makes the same point.

Canonist commentary on the texts discussed above, even if Gilbert Foliot did not know it, at least reflects twelfth-century legal opinion on the question. In his commentary on C.7, Rufinus takes the opportunity to enumerate the causes justifying the removal of a duly elected and consecrated bishop from his see: "Because of crime, illness, or age, levity of spirit, for administrative reasons, for necessity, or for humility."[28] The *Summa Parisiensis* (at c.46 [*Suggestum*]) states that it is clear that no bishop may become a monk, "causa fugiendi laboris," although "we do not deny that danger may be a cause for flight . . . and I say that you may not in any case turn to perpetual monasticism on account of hostility, so that when peace may again be given to the church you may return to the flock entrusted to your care."[29] Other canonistic commentary, while following Gratian's guarded approval of flight in certain specific cases, generally agrees that the cause of flight must be grave and that a bishop may not in any case become a monk permanently.

These texts and comments, particularly cc.46–48, formed the foundation for Gilbert's charge against Becket. Much of the criticism of *Multiplicem* is based upon the excessively tranquil picture that Gilbert draws of Henry II's attitudes towards Becket after Clarendon and Northampton, of Henry's promises of protection, and that of Becket's own promise not to leave the kingdom. Such a depiction of the king is attributable, I suggest, only to Gilbert's charge that Becket fled without opposition, without persecution by the wicked, without invasion of his see, without, in short, any of the circumstances that Gratian and the decretists consider extenuating circumstances against the otherwise firm rule that the bishop must not desert the flock that has been committed to his care. In such a depiction, the strictures of cc.46–48 are unequivocal, and they apply, in law and in Gilbert's epistolary juridical rhetoric, to Becket.

In a brief and unsuccessful interview with Pope Alexander III at Sens in 1164, Gilbert had once before attempted to charge Becket with illegal desertion of his see.[30] Then, Gilbert appears to have cited only the above-mentioned scriptural maxim, Prov. 28:1: "Fugit impius, nemine persequente." In a short, but ominous exchange, Alexander is said to have interrupted Gilbert, saying, "Spare, brother," Gilbert answered, "I will spare him, Holy Father," and the pope responded, "I did not tell you to spare him, brother, but to spare yourself." With that response, Alan of Tewksbury tells us, Gilbert fell silent and gave the floor to Hilary, of Chichester, who was also confounded, but in a much lighter way.[31] In *Multiplicem,* Gilbert did take care of himself. He drew up an indictment of Becket's whole career, an indictment that allowed Gilbert to rest his case on Gratian, not upon Proverbs, an indictment that the pope could not wave away because it was not uttered in his presence, nor was it a formal charge in a trial of Becket. The trial was held in an exchange of letters, and the judges were those letters' readers,

readers whose support might shift from Becket (or whose opposition might
be strengthened) if sufficiently solid legal grounds could be found to make a
case against him. *Multiplicem,* in fact, makes several cases against Becket,
some of them grounded in canon law, others not. It makes them within the
framework of a depiction of Gilbert's disinterest and Becket's character as a
rash and irresponsible prelate, and among them is the case that had failed
before Alexander III, strengthened and elaborated, the case of Becket as a fugitive bishop, the shepherd who had abandoned his flock, the pilot who
deserted his ship in troubled waters.

Gilbert goes further. Now, he says, the storm rages, the king has turned
his island into a fortress, and bishops who might legitimately take flight in
the face of real persecution and the king's wrath, cannot, and this, too, is
Becket's fault.[32] *Multiplicem,* then, may be considered a kind of *casus,* out of
which Gilbert can construct any number of cases against Thomas, in which
Gilbert's use of C.7 q.1 cc.46–48 is clear and skillful. Scripture, St.
Augustine's letter, three ninth-century texts, two excerpts from Gregory I,
and Gratian's use of these and his own commentary have provided Gilbert
with surer footing than Prov. 28. Gilbert in turn provides these texts and
their interpretation with a different setting from the usual ecclesiastical
court, a setting in epistolary rhetotic, out of the reach of Alexander's warn-
ings, and in a form that can sway the opinion of others, beside the pope, who
matter. *Multiplicem* may very well be considered Gilbert's answer to
Alexander's warning to watch out for himself. On its own terms, it is an
answer of considerable expertise.

It is not, however, an answer that shows Gilbert in an attractive light, nor
is the foregoing discussion likely to alter the picture of Gilbert that most histories of Becket preserve. In 1951, David Knowles, after gently criticizing
the extreme anti-Gilbert attitude of Raymonde Foreville, says harshly of Gilbert in *Multiplicem:*

> As a literary composition it must remain, with all its blemishes, a rhetorical masterpiece,
> but its cold and unrelenting hatred, which cannot pardon error or understand generosity,
> comes from the abundance of a heart in which humility and love had long ceased to
> harbour.[33]

Twenty years later, in his full-length biography of Becket, Knowles noted
the criticism that his earlier view had generated, but his revised view of Gilbert is scarcely less condemning than his earlier one:

> . . . a bitter, cold, and in some ways devious enemy of the archbishop, who uses ques-
> tionable arguments and procedural expedients to preserve his freedom of action. In the
> whole controversy the spirit of tolerance and the milk of human kindness are in short sup-
> ply on all sides, but nowhere is the deficit more evident than in the acts and words of
> Foliot.[34]

This paper has examined only one aspect of a single letter of Gilbert's and its
conclusions are unlikely to alter significantly such judgments as Knowles'.
At the most it may be said that whatever Gilbert's motives in writing *Mul-*

tiplicem, and however doubtful the portrait of Henry II in it may be, Gilbert's legal case at least hews closely to the letter of Gratian's *Decretum* and reflects a general twelfth-century canonistic attitude toward episcopal responsibilities. Indeed, in his insistence upon the church's need for peace with the king, even at the price of temporary concessions to the spirit of Clarendon, Gilbert appears to share the opinion of a large and diverse body of English churchmen.

Hard cases make bad law, and the supporters of different sides in hard cases have a particular responsibility toward the law, lest it be diminished or exploited in mean-spirited acrimony. In John of Salisbury's opinion, personal holiness was far safer ground than legal expertise, and for all the legal skill expressed in *Fraternitatis vestrae* and *Multiplicem,* both letters represent a diplomatic dead end in a case that was finally resolved on different grounds by different men. The exchange of charges contained in these letters, however, illustrates the considerable growth and spreading influence of the science of canon law between the late eleventh and late twelfth centuries. Neither the penances of Henry nor the popular appeal of the cult of the martyred archbishop slowed down its influence in England, and the regularization of ecclesiastical and temporal courts and the increasing familiarity of all levels of spiritual and temporal authority with canon law is one of the distinctive features of European history from the late twelfth century on.

Some parts of the law, however, were far more frequently exercised than others. Administrative responsibilities, new forms of social and political control, including control of mobility, and changing political circumstances closed in upon both bishops and kings after the late twelfth century, and both opportunities for flight and places of refuge became fewer. There are few well-known cases of the invoking of C.7 q.1 cc.46–48 after Becket, and the stability of the lower clergy, rather than that of the bishops, became the primary concern of the church.[35] In the fourteenth century and after, plague sometimes drove bishops from their sees, and the attractions of the courts of Rome and Avignon occasionally enticed visiting prelates to linger somewhat longer than was proper. Not until the reformation of the sixteenth century did episcopal flight again become a marked feature of church history, and then the circumstances were sufficiently distinctive so as to make C.7 virtually a dead letter. Not even the Reformation, however, changed the responsibilities of the prelate, and despite the notorious hostility expressed by the early reformers toward canon law, the structure of religious organizations later in the sixteenth and seventeenth centuries revised and transformed themes that had exercised the minds of canon lawyers from the ninth century to the thirteenth. On both sides of the division of the Reformation the responsibility of the priest, prelate, or minister to remain with and serve his flock, in time of plague, war, or social unrest, was recognized and written into law. Beza, Hooper, Latimer, the Council of Trent, and Pope Gregory XIII all addressed the problem of ministerial responsibility for the flock, and in this, as in many other instances, all agreed.[36]

Before the mid-twelfth century, the absence of a compact, universal source of canon law and the particular circumstances of European society generated a number of different attitudes toward the episcopal office, but not until Gratian's collection was the question of the fugitive bishop comprehensively addressed. The ninth-century sources do not cite Augustine's letter; Ivo of Chartres includes only one of the ninth-century sources in his *Decretum;* in Bede's account of Laurentius's proposed flight from England there is, of course, no mention of canon law. Nor was the charge brought against Anselm, nor against Theobald of Canterbury when he departed from England in 1148 for the Council of Reims.[37] In several important respects, as I have suggested above and will treat at greater length elsewhere, the thought of the compilers of Pseudo-Isidore anticipated many of the characteristic features of later ecclesiology, but that thought took time, a transformation of the organization and classification of knowledge, and a more precisely articulated church to achieve its full impact. Such circumstances were hardly possibly before the twelfth century.

Gilbert and Thomas, then, went to law at a moment when the law was particularly available, attractive, and appeared to offer solid grounds for both sides in the Becket case. That the ground was not as solid as it seemed and that their use of the law led to a juridical impasse was foreseen neither by them nor by John of Salisbury, for John's objections were on very different grounds. Of all the commentators, perhaps William of Canterbury best reflects, as Smalley suggested, both the significance and the consequences of Thomas's departure. He does so in a manner of which John of Salisbury would have approved, by the use of allegorical figures in the deacon's *visio,* the figures of the fleeing hedgehog and the rain of blood.

University of Pennsylvania

Notes

1. The letter is printed in J. C. Robertson, ed., *Materials for the History of Thomas Becket* (London, 1875–85), v: 161–65, at 163–64. Although John is here addressing a particular case, he speaks so generally and categorically that it seems justified to interpret his strictures as representing a broad view on his part. Hereafter, Robertson's work will be cited as MTB followed by volume and page numbers.

A much earlier version of part of this paper was presented to the Columbia Seminar on the History of Legal and Political Thought in 1971. I am grateful to the members of the Seminar for their interest and their comments. My friends and former colleagues Thomas G. Waldman and Robert Somerville have very kindly read and discussed this paper with me several times, and I am very grateful for their assistance.

2. PL CLXXXII: 727–808; *De Consideratione,* Lib. 4–5. See also S. Chodorow, *Christian Political Theory and Church Politics in the Mid-Twelfth Century* (Berkeley-Los Angeles, 1972), pp. 61–62 and Appendix II. For further references to John of Salisbury's interest in the problem, see Hans Liebeschütz, *Mediaeval Humanism in the Life and Writings of John of Salisbury* (London, 1950), pp. 1–19, 95–110.

3. See, e.g., M. D. Chenu, "The Masters of the Theological Science," in his *Nature, Man, and Society in the Twelfth Century,* trans. J. K. Taylor and L. K. Little (Chicago, 1968), pp. 270–309; and Stephan Kuttner, *Harmony from Dissonance* (Latrobe, Pa., 1960).

4. This point was made with particular emphasis by Z. N. Brooke, in his masterful study, *The English Church and the Papacy from the Conquest to the Reign of John* (Cambridge, 1931). It has been made several times since, with greater or lesser emphasis. The best modern approaches to Becket and his world are those of David Knowles, most recently Knowles's *Thomas Becket* (Stanford, 1971), with full bibliography. Among other useful studies, besides those cited below, I have profited from C. Brooke, "Thomas Becket," in his *Medieval Church and Society* (New York, 1972), pp. 121–38; W. L. Warren, *Henry II* (Berkeley and Los Angeles, 1973), pp. 399–558; and J. W. Alexander, "The Becket Controversy in Recent Historiography," *Journal of British Studies* IX (1970), 1–26.

5. See David Knowles, *The Episcopal Colleagues of Thomas Becket* (Cambridge, 1951), and Adrian Morey and C. N. L. Brooke, *Gilbert Foliot and His Letters* (Cambridge, 1965); Beryl Smalley, *The Becket Conflict and the Schools* (Oxford, 1973).

6. MTB v: 490–512; 521–44. Gilbert's letter should, however, be read in the superior edition of Adrian Morey and C. N. L. Brooke, *The Letters and Charters of Gilbert Foliot* (Oxford, 1967), pp. 229–43. Their comments are developed in *Gilbert Foliot and His Letters*, pp. 166–87.

7. MTB, v: 376–86 at 379–80.

8. MTB I: 39–42, at 41. See also below, n. 37.

9. Smalley, *The Becket Conflict and the Schools*, p. 109.

10. The literature on animal symbolism and iconography in the middle ages is enormous. In general, Francis Klingender, *Animals in Art and Thought to the End of the Middle Ages* (Cambridge, Mass., 1973), pp. 153–343, 384–94, and plates 222, 224 are particularly helpful. See also F. J. Carmody, ed., *Physiologus Latinus* (Paris, 1939); F. McCullough, *Medieval Latin and French Bestiaries* (Chapel Hill, 1962); George Druce, trans., *The Bestiary of Guillaume le Clerc* (Ashford, Kent, 1936); T. H. White, ed. and trans., *The Bestiary: A Book of Beasts* (New York, 1960), pp. 93–95, with further references. Isidore of Seville passed much of the antique tradition of Pliny to the medieval world. See *Isidori Hispalensis episcopi etymologiarum . . . libri* XX, ed. W. M. Lindsay (Oxford, 1914), pp. 12–13, in which the prudence of the *ericius* is its signal characteristic. Along with prudence and sagacity, however, the *ericius* also was associated with the devil and with gluttony among the seven deadly sins, although these latter associations appear to be characteristic of later medieval usage. See G. de Tervarent, *Attributs et Symboles de l'Art profane, 1450–1600* (Geneva, 1958), cols. 211–12.

The animal fables told by Eadmer in that portion of the *Vita Anselmi* dealing with Anselm's first exile from England are a curious parallel with the tale of William of Canterbury, although they are used in a different way. See below, n. 37.

11. MTB, II: 313.

12. MTB, III: 312–26. For John and Herbert of Bosham, see Smalley, *The Becket Conflict and the Schools*, pp. 59–108.

13. MTB, v: 138–41.

14. Ibid., p. 176. The usage is frequent throughout many letters of these years.

15. Ibid., p. 151, a casual reference in Henry II's letter to the bishops of England. The theme, however, is carried through a number of Henry's and Gilbert's letters of 1164 and 1165: e.g., in Henry's two letters to Louis VII, ibid., pp. 134–35 and the following letter, from certain "inimici Thomae" to Alexander III, ibid., pp. 136–38, which certainly sounds as though it had been written by someone familiar with the juridical polemic of the earlier twelfth century as well as with Gratian.

The text from *Fraternitatis vestrae* may be found ibid., p. 495.

16. References in Knowles, *Thomas Becket*, p. 106. For the bishop of Lincoln, see Morey and Brooke, *Gilbert Foliot and his Letters*, p. 181.

17. In Morey and Brooke, *Gilbert Foliot and His Letters*, pp. 169–70.

18. The history of the episcopal office has been treated in many studies. Particularly important concerning the relation between the requirements of the office and the human incumbent are Peter Brown, *Augustine of Hippo* (Berkeley-Los Angeles, 1969), pp. 138ff; F. van der Meer, *Augustine the Bishop* (London-New York, 1961); J. Gaudemet, *L'Église dans l'Empire*

romain (IVᵉ–Vᵉ Siècles), Histoire du Droit et des Institutions de l'Église en Occident III (Paris, 1958); Theodor Klauser, *Der Ursprung der bischöflichen Insignien und Ehrenrechte* (Krefeld, 1949); H. Hürten, "Gregor der Grosse und der mittelalterliche Episkopat," *Zietschrift für Kirchengeschichte* LXXIII (1963), 16–41, and J. Gaudemet, "Patristique et Pastorale: La Contribution de Grégoire le Grand au 'Miroir de l'Évêque' dans le *Décret* de Gratien," *Études d'Histoire du Droit canonique dédiées à Gabriel Le Bras* (Paris, 1965), I: 129f., all cover important points in regard to those aspects of the episcopal office before the thirteenth century that are the concern of this paper. Among the best studies of the ninth-century episcopacy is that of E. Delaruelle, "En relisant le *De institutione regia* de Jonas d'Orléans. L'Entrée en Scène de l'Épiscopat carolingien," *Mélanges d'Histoire du Moyen Âge dédiés à la Mémoire de Louis Halphen* (Paris, 1951), pp. 185–92. The best modern study of the role of canon law in shaping the twelfth-century episcopal office is Robert L. Benson, *The Bishop-Elect: A Study in Medieval Ecclesiastical Office* (Princeton, 1968).

19. *Western Society and the Church in the Middle Ages* (Baltimore, 1970), pp. 170–213.

20. Ibid., pp. 189–90.

21. Gaudemet, "Patristique et Pastorale," passim.

22. All references to Gratian's *Decretum* will be internal, except for that below in n. 27.

23. See below, n. 30.

24. See M.-D, Chenu, "Monks, Canons, and Laymen in Search of the Apostolic Life," in his *Nature, Man, and Society in the Twelfth Century,* pp. 202–38, with ample bibliography.

25. The most efficient guide through the material of Bernard's letters is the apparatus of the English translation: Bruno Scott James, trans., *The Letters of St. Bernard of Clairvaux* (London, 1953). The letter to Thurstan of York is no. 175, pp. 244–45. I am grateful to Thomas Waldman for this reference and for the following one. In Karl Pellens, *Die Texte des Normannischen Anonymous* (Wiesbaden, 1966), there are comments upon several aspects of episcopal flight, including flight to Rome. In the *Defensio Rothomagensis archiepiscopi,* J 4, the Anonymous cites Matt. 10:23 in defending the flight of the archbishop (Pellens, p. 40) of Rouen, and in J 28 (Pellens, p. 215) the Anonymous criticizes the requirement of the visit *ad limina apostolorum* on the grounds, among others, that such a papal command deprives the flock of its shepherd. On the general range of twelfth-century epistolary invective in ecclesiastical affairs generally, see the remarks in Morey-Brooke, *Gilbert Foliot and His Letters,* pp. 170f. I have by no means attempted to find every reference to the question of episcopal flight between 1050 and 1164, although during this period such a theme may have attracted many writers, as it did the Norman Anonymous, St. Bernard, and Gilbert Foliot. See also Giles Constable, *The Letters of Peter the Venerable,* 2 vols. (Cambridge, Mass., 1967).

26. See Richard Kay, "Martin IV and the Fugitive Bishop of Bayeux," *Speculum* XL (1965), 460–83. In contrast, see the mass flight of the Breton bishops before the fury of Peter of Dreux: Sidney Painter, *The Scourge of the Clergy* (Baltimore, 1937).

27. PL XXXIII: 1013–19. *The Correctores Romani* in the sixteenth century commented on Gratian's dependence upon this letter of Augustine's but their citation of the letter according to the old style of numbering Augustine's letters (no. 180), reprinted uncorrected by E. Friedberg *(Corpus Iuris Canonici . . . Pars Prior, Decretum Magistri Gratiani* [Leipzig, 1879], cols. 585–86), should be noted. In the modern style the letter is no. 228. Augustine's letter, written around 428 to Honoratus, Bishop of Thiave, responds to Honoratus's detailed, and perhaps obnoxiously persistent inquiries concerning a bishop's right to abandon his see in the midst of physical dangers. Augustine, exasperated because he claims to have answered this question in another letter, not now extant, responds in meticulous, even patronizing detail. Thus, Letter 228 constitutes the most thorough discussion in patristic literature concerning the episcopal right to flee. Each objection is taken up by Augustine in turn and disposed of, leaving only two permissible occasions for flight: when the flock itself is gone and there is no one for the prelate to care for, and when the prelate alone is persecuted, there being other ministers available to succor the flock. The first reason, of course, would not apply in Becket's case, and much of the thrust of *Multiplicem* undermines Becket's arguments for the second, had Becket explicitly referred to Augustine's letter, which he does not appear to have done.

28. Rufinus, *Summa Decretorum,* ed. H. Singer (Paderborn, 1902), p.286.

29. T. P. McLaughlin, ed., *The "Summa Parisiensis" on the "Decretum Gratiani"* (Toronto, 1952), at C.7 q.1 c.46 *(Suggestum).* The author of the *Summa Parisiensis* and Gratian allowed somewhat more leeway than had St. Augustine or St. Bernard.

30. Knowles, *Thomas Becket,* p. 105, relates the incident and gives the references to Alan to Tewksbury's account in MTB, II: 338.

31. MTB, II: 338.

32. Morey-Brooke, *Letters and Charters,* pp. 239–40.

33. Knowles, *Episcopal Colleagues,* pp. 180.

34. One important later use of these texts was their role in shaping the portrait of the *prelatus inutilis,* which in turn shaped the later image of the *rex inutilis.* I have discussed some of these changes in my *The Shadow King* (New Haven, 1970) pp. 116–69. One of the commonest charges against such figures, bishops and kings alike, is that of desertion of their office in time of danger. One root of such thought may have been Roman law, in which *fuga,* which originally meant the flight of a slave, became in later imperial constitutions *fuga munerum, fugere munus,* the evasion of public charges, particularly applied to the *curialis* class and enshrined in Justinian's *Code* (10.38.1: *curiales* who desert their "civitates" are "impii"). Gaines Post has cited later medieval glosses to this text and to *Digest* 49.15.19.4 (whoever deserts his own *patria* is to be numbered among its enemies); see his *Studies in Medieval Legal Thought* (Princeton, 1964), pp. 442–43. Among the many facets of *Multiplicem* may well be its evidence for depicting the image of a *prelatus inutilis* as such an image might be constructed in the 1160s by an assiduous canonist deeply enmeshed in the constitutional problems of a national church.

35. Knowles, *Thomas Becket,* p. 163.

36. The Council of Trent excused continued residence on the grounds of Christian charity, *force majeure,* obligatory obedience to a superior, and evident necessity. The *Codex Iuris Canonici,* c.338, 1–4 contains modern canon law on the subject, considerably expanded over Gratian's remarks in C.7 q.1. cc.45–49. For an example of Reformation echoing of these concerns, see Hooper's *Homily in Time of Pestilence of 1553,* in Bishop Hooper, *Works* (Cambridge, 1852), II: 174.

37. Ivo of Chartres, *Decretum,* 7.149 (PL CLXI: 581: Gratian, C.7 q.1 c.45 [*Hoc nequaquam*]). For Bede, see the *Historia Ecclesiastica gentis Anglorum,* 2.65 in C. Plummer, ed., *Venerabilis Bedae opera omnia* (Oxford, 1896), I: 92–93; cf. 2.20, I: 124–26. The many sources concerning the exile of St. Anselm in the last years of the eleventh century do not seem to indicate either English or papal concern for violating of canon law on Anselm's part, as violation of the commands of William II: e.g., Eadmer, *Historia novorum in Anglia,* ed., Martin Rule (London, 1884), pp. 110–11, 86–88, 98. See ibid., pp. 99–103, 160f., 174f. for various concerns of the English church during Anselm's second exile. In several other respects, however, the place of Anselm's exile as a model for Thomas Becket's is striking. Both disagreed with their kings over ecclesiastical liberties and ancient English royal customs; the exile of both is described in terms of animal fables; both expressed (Anselm, of course, more than Becket) a concern for their spiritual well-being threatened by *negotia secularia;* both offered or attempted to resign their offices to the pope. See also Eadmer, *The Life of St. Anselm,* ed. and trans. R. W. Southern (London, 1962). Anselm, in fact, is an interesting case of the prelate who desired to return to the monastery *causa humilitatis;* see the *Vita Anselmi,* ed. Southern, pp. 69–72, 80–81; *Historia novorum,* p. 103. For Theobald, see A. Saltman, *Theobald of Canterbury* (London, 1956), pp. 25f. M. Brett, *The English Church under Henry I* (Oxford, 1975) is the most recent study of the *regnum* and *sacerdotium* in England in the early twelfth century.

III
PROCEDURE

Dishonest Litigation in the Church Courts, 1140–98

STANLEY CHODOROW

This paper is concerned with the abuse of the papal judicial system by litigants who deceived or illegally manipulated the courts, called here dishonest litigants. Such litigants are always a problem for courts, but in the later twelfth century, they became a preoccupation of papal and lesser ecclesiastical judges. Bishops and others asked the pope what to do about such people—how to deal with them as they deserved while preserving the rights of honest litigants—and papal decretals often contain instructions on the problem.[1] The canonists were also concerned with such litigants, and they proposed that every papal letter, explicitly or implicitly, contain the qualification "si preces veritate nitantur."[2]

Two reasons can perhaps be suggested for the growth of this problem. First, the development of the ecclesiastical judicial hierarchy and of the law that governed the transfer of cases from one level of it to another made possible the use of the courts not only as centers of dispute resolution, but also as instruments of the litigants' will. Second, the permissive law of appeals allowed one or both parties to appeal to Rome at virtually any time. It was even possible for a person to appeal "in agro"—that is before he entered the case in court, while standing out in the field, just informed that a suit had been filed against him. Under such relaxed rules, it happened often that a party appealed to the pope without anyone, judge or opponent, knowing about it,[3] and usually, the pope acted solely on the *ex parte* statements of a single party. It was up to the appellant's opponent to chase him to Rome and to present his case to the pope before instructions were issued to judges delegate, and not surprisingly, the opposing party very often came too late and then sought letters to the judges based on his own case. Sometimes, the appellant succeeded in getting judgment before his opponent went for new letters on the basis of which a new, and contradictory, judgment was made. Papal letters are extant in which such cases are unravelled and committed yet a third time to judges delegate.[4] In each of these events, the litigants had, in effect, used the papal court as an instrument, since the pope had acted without considering the contradictory evidence or positions of the parties. A system that permitted such a wide latitude to parties and that regularly acted on *ex parte* presentations made it difficult to determine where the line between partiality and dishonesty lay.

Not only was there a fuzzy line between dishonesty and partiality (although it should be noted that the medieval canon law did not consider partiality to be quite so acceptable and honorable as does the adversary system of modern Anglo-American law), but what was considered an abuse of process was neither so harsh nor so broad in the Middle Ages as it is today. Many of the decretals to be studied here, undoubtedly more than is obvious from the language of most of the letters, may represent the progressive definition of permissible and impermissible court practice as the experience of handling cases accumulated in the church courts of the twelfth century. Several scholars have noted the problem of abuse. In the introduction to their calendar of Pope Innocent III's correspondence with England and Wales, the Cheneys remark that the pope often took precautions to prevent miscarriages of justice due to his being misled by petitioners or appellants. They point out also that even in Innocent's time the papal judiciary had not yet developed an adequate system to record its actions, and this weakness gave dishonest litigants an opportunity to deceive the pope.[5] In another place, Christopher Cheney noted a letter of Alexander III in which the pope said that he could not remember doing what he was now alleged to have done and that if he did it, it must have been because of overwork. In the same place, Cheney also referred to a complaint of Clement III that many abuses stemmed from overwork.[6]

In his lecture on writ procedure in twelfth-century England, R. C. Van Caenegem cast a glance at the papal judiciary to show that it, like the courts of contemporary English kings, had considerable difficulty with litigants eager to take advantage of its inability to maintain tight control over its business. He also noted the canonists' concern about such problems, but his examples of fraudulent behavior by litigants stem from the archival tradition analyzed by Walter Holtzmann in his *Papsturkunden in England,* and none of these letters, from the chanceries of Alexander III, Urban III, and Celestine III, had a subsequent canonical tradition.[7] They are therefore not likely to have been the basis for canonistic commentary on letters obtained through *subreptio* or *obreptio*. The source of concern must have been the ample supply of cases involving dishonest litigants to be found in the letters enregistered in the collections of the twelfth-century lawyers.[8]

The propensity of canonical suits to drag on and to have extremely complicated procedural histories gave room enough for abuses. The sorts of abuses that occurred in such cases have been illustrated by the discovery of an interlocutory document in the dispute between the chapter of Beauvais and the Cistercians of Chaalis in the diocese of Senlis over the forest of Charlieu (diocese of Mâcon).[9] Lohrmann, who discovered the text, estimates that the case lasted about ten years and was resolved not by a judgment, but by a settlement that favored the Cistercians. This result, confirmed by Alexander III in 1179,[10] ran counter to the collective judgment of the judges who had dealt with the case and rewarded the abbot of Chaalis for committing several offenses. The abbot had forced the issue by trespassing on the land in question; he had repeatedly failed to show up in court, waiting until the judges issued a peremptory summons before defending his position; he had repeatedly appealed to the holy see to avoid judgment; and he had arranged to buy the property for less than half its real value, with the assent of a few canons of the cathedral but without seeking approval of the whole chapter. Such a case indicates how policy, in this case pro-Cistercian policy, could affect the treatment of a case, and how reluctant Alexander was to restrict the right to appeal, lest an injustice be done.

This case concerning Charlieu serves as an entryway into the consideration of the main corpus of cases to be studied here. The abbot of Chaalis committed two kinds of actions that were recognized to be illegal or came to be so considered during the twelfth century: He used the right of appeal to delay judgment and ultimately to induce his opponents to settle the dispute in his favor, and he created the issue of the suit by trespassing on the land in question. Thus, he deceived the courts that dealt with the case, using their own procedural law to do so, and he manipulated those courts by creating the fact situation on which judgment would be given. In what follows, I will treat these two types of dishonest litigation—one perpetrated by deception, the other by manipulation—in turn.

As already mentioned, the law of appeals gave litigants, both honest and dishonest, a lot of room to maneuver. Gratian had collected the texts defining the right of appeal in *Causae* 2 (q.6) and 6 (q.4)[11] but he had not foreseen that prodigious use of the procedure would overwhelm the papal court in the pontificates of Alexander III and his successors, and he had not dealt with all the problems that could arise. Thus Alexander received many requests for instruction on appeals,[12] and in 1171 or 1172, he reviewed the law of appeals for Archbishop Henry of Reims in "Cum sacrosancta Romana ecclesia."[13] This letter became the basic statement of the law, but Alexander and his successors spent a good deal of their time blocking the avenues it left for dishonesty. A perusal of the title "De appellationibus" will show that much of this later legislation became part of the mainstream of canon law. But some of it did not. For example, a letter of Alexander,[14] which Bernard of Pavia included in his *Compilatio prima* but which Raymond deleted from the tradition, dealt with priests who appealed to Rome in order to avoid losing churches they held illegally. John of Wales included in his *Compilatio secunda* an undated letter of Celestine III, "Licet sit appellantibus," that covered several abuses of the right of appeal. Appeals ought not to be permitted, Celestine wrote, if the purpose was to avoid a judge, to suspend another's right (e.g., the right of a person ejected forcibly from his benefice to be reinstated prior to the hearing of a challenge to his possession), to delay judgment, or to prejudice a case. If the bishop suspects that an appeal from his court stems from any of these illicit purposes, Celestine continued, he has the right to restrict the term allowed for prosecuting the appeal to twenty days.[15] (The normal term was one year.) A letter of Clement III, "Licet appellationis remedium," written 1 January 1190, had gone still further.[16] It gave the episcopal judge the right to decide whether an appeal has just or malicious cause, and to prohibit an appeal if an evil purpose underlay it. Raymond rejected this letter just as he had "Licet sit appellantibus."

Clement's extreme restriction of the right of appeal becomes understandable in consideration of an encyclical he had written about ten months earlier than "Licet appellationis remedium," on 9 March 1189. In this piece, the pope set forth the most extensive and spectacular exposition of the problems created by the freedom granted to litigants by the law of appeals, and although it exists in only one copy, it, or the sorts of provisions it contains, may be the basis for a significant revision of Alexander's "Cum sacrosancta" that is apparently the work of Raymond.[17] Clement wrote:

> Since we are obligated by the office imposed on us to extend care to everyone, cases ought to be referred to the Roman see, interrupting the process of the case through appeal from any ecclesiastical judge if it happens that the right of anyone is endangered. Some very wicked petitioners, using the debt owed by our office for their advantage, do not cease to batter our ears with importunate clamoring on account of cases that are not their own, and nuncios do the same for controversies about which they are ignorant. Whence, indeed, it happens that we, when we ought to attend to greater affairs and to treat greater matters, are plagued continually by such cases (under the pretext of seeking justice which we want to deny to no one). Thus we neglect other cases which seem more important because we are occupied with these lesser matters more than is proper. Indeed, we cannot even give sufficient time to these lesser cases. Many also are unjustly vexed and, so that they should have peace, are forced to redeem themselves from the obtainers [of the letters], to whom the cases do not pertain, with money. And often it happens that those who are at peace with one another are forced to enter into a legal dispute by bearers of letters who were not commissioned to seek them, but who have obtained instructions. Sometimes, letters obtained for certain persons are given to their adversaries because he who received them had received a higher price for them. And because we are not able to have a memory of all things, cases committed to certain judges are committed immediately, on the petition of others, to others, and thus commission is frustrated by commission, and a note of levity is imputed to the Roman curia. Wanting therefore to remedy this evil by precautions which we can take, we command through apostolic writing that you have announced through all your dioceses on our behalf that from the resurrection of the Lord [i.e., 9 April 1189], no petition about any controversy will be received by us unless it bears the seal of an archbishop, bishop, abbot, prior, dean, or archdeacon, or of any person of note, and contains the name of the bearer, whether it is his own case or another's.[18]

Here, then, Clement made clear the degree to which the papal court was overwhelmed by appeals, the opportunity this situation provided for dishonest litigants, and the distressing frequency with which such persons took advantage of this opportunity. And he tried to revise procedure to prevent the rampant abuse of appeals. But the new arrangement was probably too complicated to work well in a world in which travel, communication, and the authentication of documents and signatures were difficult, and Clement exposed the measure of his distress about the situation by virtually abrogating the right of appeal in "Licet appellationis remedium."

The problem of the dishonest litigant could not be dealt with by adjusting the law of appeals, however, and most of the letters regarding fraudulent litigants attempt to deal with their illegal acts rather than with the judicial avenue through which the acts became effective. As noted above, the popes attempted to prevent deceiving litigants from achieving their ends by including in their letters a variety of clauses designed to reduce the possibility of injustice being done.[19] Much of this concern about *littere de iustitia* based on fraudulent statements actually came under the law regarding forgeries, because, as Peter Herde has shown,[20] the canonists considered letters obtained by fraud to be forgeries since they did not conform to the will of their author, even though they were formally authentic. Thus, the law against forgers was one of the principal tools used against dishonest litigants, and in fact, the provisions of this law directly contradicted the measures taken by Clement III in 1189 and 1190.

This contradiction is explicit in an unedited letter by Alexander III ("Si quis obiciat")[21] in which the pope ruled that when a question was raised about the authenticity of crucial documents, the appeal should be permitted even though the letters of delegation prohibited appeal. In addition, the term set for prosecuting the appeal could be longer than usual if the appellant showed that he needed the time to prove the allegation of forgery. But the popes did not often tamper with the basic provisions in one doctrinal area in order to resolve difficulties in another. They usually applied stopgap measures. Thus, in a letter to the bishop of Arras, Alexander treated the case of a certain priest whom the bishop had reproved for keeping a concubine.[22] The priest had appealed to the pope in order to escape punishment, but the letter's principal significance here is that the pope tried to prevent the fraudulent petitioner or forger from succeeding in his crime by setting up a standard of authenticity for any papal letters that might be issued in the case. He told the bishop to ignore any letter that did not contain the "seriem facti."[23]

Herde treated only Alexander's "Ex tenore litterarum" and a series of later letters from the chanceries of Lucius III, Urban III, and Celestine III.[24] To these, others could be added that covered much the same ground but that did not find entry into the mainstream of canonical literature.[25] It is no surprise that forgery and the obtaining of letters through fraudulent claims or representations were perennial problems, since the letter forms were standardized and well known and the increasing use of the courts in the pursuit of both economic and political business increased the opportunities and rewards of misbehavior. How lucrative and widespread the problem became is indicated by the famous letters of Innocent III, discussed by Herde because they contain important general instructions about how to detect forgeries and how to treat their makers, which reveal that soon after Innocent became pope an organized band of forgers was discovered in Rome.[26] The pope's agents clearly did not succeed in completely breaking up this organization because a few months later, the pope wrote to the clergy of Milan to explain that the authenticity of the seal on a papal letter could not be considered conclusive evidence of the letter's authenticity because forgers were introducing their products into the chancery "in-basket." Thus the chancery clerks themselves were placing authentic seals on forged documents.[27] Such practices speak for the skill and daring of the forgers, who faced severe penalties if apprehended,[28] and show that using the church's legal system for illegal ends had become a big business.

A few of the letters in the *corpus decretalium* for the period 1140–1198 recount enough of the facts in the cases to which they relate for us to see how fraudulently obtained letters might be used. H.-E. Lohmann edited a letter of Alexander from the *Collectio Wigorniensis* in which the pope dealt with an English cleric named Alan ("Meminimus iam pridem Alanum"; JL —).[29] Alan had claimed that he had been forcibly ejected from his church by William, and that after William died, the bishop and canons of Salisbury, considering the church to be a prebend of their chapter, had refused to reinstate him. Instead, they had granted the church to Richard, archdeacon of Lisieux. The original *littere de iustitia* had committed the case to the bishop of Worcester, but Alan wanted to avoid judgment by this judge because he knew the bishop would rule in his opponents' favor. They had shown that William had had that church as a result of a transaction between himself and Alan. (In addition, many had been prepared to testify that Alan was incontinent and had many other vices, but the bishop refused to admit their testimony.) The result was that Alan's son (!) went to Rome to obtain a new letter committing the case to other, unnamed, judges. This letter had been obtained fraudulently, and in "Meminimus," Alexander nullified it, ordered the bishop of Worcester to proceed with judgment of the case, and instructed him to assess Alan with the costs his opponents had incurred when forced to undertake a journey to Rome to defeat his fraud.

Robert of Colombelles (north of Caen, dept. Calvados) did not wait until he had lost, or was sure he would lose, in court before seeking new letters to new judges. Robert succeeded in getting two letters of commission before the case was heard. One of these was addressed to the archdeacon of Rouen and the other to his counterpart in Tours. In nullifying both letters, Pope Urban III explained to the bishop of Coutances that Robert had so arranged the affair that "if he was not able to win in the court of Rouen, he would not have to desist from injuring his adversary in the court of Tours."[30]

There was nothing particularly wrong with Robert of Colombelles's desire to assure himself a favorable court, but his action to accomplish this end was impermissible. Moreover, he pursued his goal in a way fraught with difficulties. It either required two trips to the papal court or created the danger that his case would be recognized when it reappeared on the docket.[31] Other litigants gained entry into a favorable court by other methods.

In Alexander's time, the problem of choosing the court in which a case would be heard was connected with that of *recusatio indicis,* the general problem of choosing judges delegate to ensure fair hearing of cases. It was Lucius III, as Linda Fowler shows, who introduced the distinction between *recusatio* and appeal, thereby establishing the basis for the development of doctrine on *recusatio*.[32] The distinction also became the foundation of doctrinal development on frauds connected with the choice of judges and courts, and Lucius's letters are the first ones to treat as illegal attempts by litigants who wanted to fix the choice of court to prejudice unfairly the case in their favor. The well-known letter of 1184–85, "Ad hec sumus,"[33] which pronounced letters not conforming to the will of the author to be forgeries, actually dealt with the claim of certain men to possess papal letters committing every case they might be involved in to certain judges delegate. Lucius noted that these men simply wanted to avoid the judgment of their ordinary judge and to ensure that the court in which their cases were heard would be favorable to them, and he quashed the letters as illicit forgeries either in fact or in effect.

A lesser-known letter of the same pope dealt with a case in which the petitioner, seeking possession of a church, arranged for the appointment of judges delegate whose court would be held eight days distant from the place in question.[34] The petitioner had won his judgment, but the diocesan had taken the side of the poor incumbent and had sent letters to Rome supporting his case. Variations of this case were treated in letters of Celestine III. In one case, a canon who had appealed to the holy see had succeeded in getting letters of commission to his fellow canons, who of course overrode the objections of their brother's adversary in proceeding to judgment.[35] In another case, the petitioner had arranged for a court far enough away from the place in litigation to prevent the attendance of his opponent's witnesses.[36]

The cases cited above indicate the purposes of the dishonest litigants, but do not reveal the pretexts on, or the ways in, which they obtained their papal letters. In those cases, disucssed last, in which the pope was induced to grant a petitioner a court far from the locus of the dispute in question, it seems fairly clear that the pope could be misled into doing so because he lacked knowledge of the geography of the petitioner's province. The Cheneys point out evidence of such ignorance in cases from their collection that involve no deception by the litigants.[37] A few of the extant twelfth-century decretals contain information on other ways of deception practiced by fraudulent litigants.

Heckel edited a letter of Eugenius III in which the pope told Archbishop Hubert of Milan that if he, the pope, had confirmed a person's right to property over which a suit was pending, his confirmation should be considered null and void.[38] Eugenius did not mention the fraud that must have accompanied the request for the confirmation, but Alexander III, dealing with a similar case, did. In a case involving a fraudulently obtained letter of confirmation, Alexander explained to Bishop Roger of Worcester that papal confirmations were not to be challenged in court unless it was certain that they had been obtained by fraud.[39] No cases falling under this rule are extant from the courts of other popes of the period 1140–1198, but a letter of Lucius III dealt with a variant of this case. In the first part of "Ad aures nostras,"[40] Lucius told Bishop Walter of Lincoln that the applications of certain wealthy clerics, who held rich benefices, for appointment to minor benefices should be rejected because these men had obtained the letters of appointment from the pope by sending deputies who had falsely represented their principals as men without titles or income.

Abusing the right of appeal and the right to seek an impartial forum, and taking advantage of the popes' willingness to protect through letters of confirmation those who held ecclesiastical property are actions that have a common thread. They are all perpetrated by deceiving judges in the papal judicial system. A second type of fraud committed by dishonest litigants relied not on deceiving judges but on manipulating the system by setting up fact situations that would produce the desired result in the courts. The cases in which a litigant obtained a papal confirmation of property in dispute might be construed as this type of fraud. Alexander's letter to Roger of Worcester required that lower courts in the church's judicial hierarchy honor papal confirmations;[41] so an episcopal court that based its judgment on a confirmation would be acting properly. It was, moreover, very difficult for an episcopal judge to determine whether a new confirmation had been obtained fraudulently because papal confirmations were sought and obtained from successive popes. Another device by which litigants tried to force a judge to act in their favor, this time by dismissing the case, was the interlocutory transaction.

Alexander set forth the principles for dealing with such cases in the second part of "Ex quorundam certa": no one could prejudice a case or dissolve a dispute by making a change in possession.[42] Another letter of Alexander, "Ex litteris vestris," gives a fairly clear picture of how the interlocutory transaction might be used by litigants.[43] In this case, a dispute over a church and a chapel belonging to it, one of the parties engaged a representative to defend his right. The representative, who was a layman, arranged to take possession of the benefice in question and then went to the papal court to seek a letter committing the case to judges delegate. The representative had to pose as a cleric to gain entry to the papal court. The intentions of the principal and his agent are not quite clear, but they apparently planned to take the case to the new judges, present evidence of the transaction through which the agent possessed the benefice, and ask for dismissal on the grounds that the suit named the wrong party. After the case was dismissed, the agent would reconvey the property to the principal, forcing his opponent to start the whole thing over again. Had the action been successful, the challenger of the principal's right would very likely have been discouraged from pursuing the matter. The opposing party was able, however, to bring the fraud to the pope's attention, and Alexander nullified the transaction and imposed a perpetual bar to litigation on the matter by the agent who had deceived him.

Alexander did not discuss the character of the transaction involved in "Ex litteris vestris," but it surely was in itself a questionable act. One of the transactors was a layman, and church was not a proper object for a transaction, although it was possible to transfer possession of one without simony and without depriving the diocesan of his right to control the *cura animarum* in his parishes.[44] While Alexander had no difficult declaring illegal transactions of the sort involved in "Ex quorundam certa" and "Ex litteris vestris," Lucius III hesitated before making the same declaration about another use of the interlocutory transaction. In the third part of "Quoniam ex plenitudine"[45] Lucius condemned a device that had come to his attention many times before but upon which he had been reluctant to pronounce. The device was very simple and looked innocent. Two clerics created a dispute over a benefice and then settled it through a transaction involving the payment of money. That the case emanated from England is probably significant because contemporary Englishmen had begun using the same device, the bogus law suit settled prior to judgment but under the authority of the court, to effect land transfers not permitted in law.[46] But while the royal judges accepted the practice, the pope could not do so, for the scheme was a form of simony. The case thus appears to expose a curious reversal of the usual direction of influence between the canon and secular law.

Alexander had already had to deal with a similar English practice in an undated letter addressed to the archbishop of Rouen and the abbot of Jumièges, "Audivimus in episcopatu tuo."[47] Here, the bogus suit resulted in a transaction that arranged for an annual pension from the income of the church to be paid after the present possessor died. The scheme apparently worked in the following way: in step one, "A" transferred the church to "B." In step two, "A" went to court on a claim to an annual pension from the church, and in step three, the dispute over this claim was settled by arranging for the *post mortem* payment of the pension. This scheme was perhaps less objectionable than the one Lucius later puzzled over—because the pension might never be paid if the grantor predeceased the grantee—but Alexander declared it illegal because it would deprive the church of control over benefices.[48]

Contracts for future payment of pensions were peculiarly suitable to the condition of the English church, and this fact is probably what elicited the strong reaction from Alexander in "Audiuimus in episcopatu tuo." England, as is well-known, had a greater number of married priests than any other province of the medieval church, and while successive popes and archbishops (from Lanfranc's time on) had been indulgent about permitting married men to retain their orders and their benefices, they had been adamant in prohibiting the sons of priests from succeeding to their father's benefices. Many of the decretals from the period 1140–1198 deal with cases in which priests whose fathers preceded them in their titles appealed to the popes for dispensation from the prohibition, and Raymond included a whole title on the subject in the *Liber extra*.[49] A scheme like the one described in "Audivimus in episcopatu tuo" would naturally be a much more serious problem in a province where the claim of the original party might be picked up by his son.

In fact, the widespread incidence of married priests in England had long been the source of dishonest schemes and pleadings. King Henry I had repeatedly promulgated the reform legislation against clerical marriage, and he had then demanded payment of stiff fines for the privilege of remaining in office while married.[50] This nice form of extortion has not enhanced Henry's reputation as a supporter of ecclesiastical reform, but condemnation of him should perhaps be muted by the revelation, from the decretals, that later in the century, clerics joined in the lucrative persecution of those caught in the net of the celibacy laws.

The victims of Alexander III's time were the sons of priests who had suffered under Henry I. The law permitted sons of priests to enter the priesthood but not to serve in the churches that had been served by their fathers. Some of these men attempted to circumvent this prohibition by deceiving the pope into giving them letters instructing their bishops to install them in the paternal churches,[51] but apparently, many had succeeded to their fathers' benefices without fraud.[52] In "Ex tua nobis," to the archbishop of York the pope dealt with a class of cases concerning the sons of priests. The letter noted that English clerics, who were the sons of priests and had received a papally-supported dispensation, sometimes had their rights of succession challenged by subsequent papal letters. The episcopal or archdeaconal courts often granted possession of the church in question to the challenger pending the appeal to Rome, which the incumbent had to undertake. Alexander wrote to the archbishop that papal letters received against sons of priests did not invalidate previous dispensations.[53]

The letter Clement III wrote in 1189, quoted in full earlier, was aimed at litigants like those mentioned in "Ex tua nobis," but these persons and dishonest sons of priests who created fictive disputes to effect their succession to their fathers' benefices[54] were certainly not the only types of appellants that Clement described as having burdened his court with suits that did not exist or with claims with which they had no connection. In "Ex parte Ade," Alexander had dealt with the case of a layman who had posed as a cleric in order to obtain letters ousting a priest from a church he coveted.[55] His ground for seeking the ouster was that the incumbent was the son of the previous *persona,* but this case has another significance, in comparison with those in which clerics went for redress to secular courts. Such clerics were acting like secular men, but no evidence suggests that they posed as laymen in order to take advantage of the lay courts. Thus, in an indirect way, "Ex parte Ade" indicates that the church courts refused to admit secular plaintiffs against clerics and that deception was the only way a lay plaintiff could gain entry to those courts.

In another letter, the second part of "Cum olim E.,"[56] Alexander described a case in which a fraudulent litigant succeeded in reviving for his own benefit a case already decided. The loser of the suit had died, but another cleric, posing as the original party, went to Rome to get letters reopening the case. The pope had caught up with the fraud when the original victor, dispossessed by the diocesan on the basis of the papal letter, appealed to Rome for redress. the pope not only nullified the letter obtained by the imposter, but also punished the bishop, indicating that he had been implicated in the deception.

These twelfth-century decretals concerning the treatment of dishonest litigants illustrate a point that Stephan Kuttner made over twenty years ago. In discussing Rudolph Sohm's distinction between the old catholic—i.e., sacramental—law and the legalism of post-Gratian law, Professor Kuttner pointed out that in the canons collected in the works of canonists down to and including Gratian, many areas of living canon law, such as procedure, monastic exemptions, and the law of tithes and church property, were virtually untreated and that an important feature of the twelfth-century rebirth of jurisprudence was the emergence of these areas into the light of the written law.[57] The decretals studied here show how that feature worked. Dishonest litigation was nothing new in the church of the later twelfth century, but the treatment of such cases had never been part of the written code of canon law. In the rapidly developing ecclesiastical judiciary of the post-Gratian period, these cases were referred to Rome and, with other areas of once customary and local law, became part of the systematic jurisprudence ultimately incorporated in the *Corpus iuris canonici* and its standard commentaries. This process produced not only an organization and unification of the law on dishonest litigation, but also some significant, although temporary, changes in the basic law of appeals.

Alexander III's letter "Si quis obiciat," which dealt with the problem of forgery, expanded the right of appeal to permit the courts and litigants to cope with the problem of false documents. It forms an important part of the historical background of Innocent III's great decretals on forgery, although Innocent implicitly rejected the indirect approach Alexander had taken devising instead methods for detecting forgeries.[58] The canonists had long before rejected "Si quis obiciat" by dropping it out of their collections of decretals. Clement III's "Cum ex imposito" and "Licet appellationis remedium" and Celestine III's "Licet sit appellantibus"[59] also reformed the law of appeals in order to prevent dishonest litigants from achieving their ends. As in the case of "Si quis obiciat," the canonists rejected these letters, apparently thinking that Alexander's basic decretal "Cum sacrosancta" gave lower judges enough latitude to deal with illicit appeals.[60]

Of the two types of dishonest litigation distinguished here—the deception of judges (including the use of false documents and letters) and the manipulation of the system through the creation of fact situations—the latter was never conceived as a unified problem. Nonetheless, the majority of letters concerned with manipulation were included in the *Decretals* of Gregory IX. Raymond used these texts not only because they contained significant doctrinal pronouncements, but also because they were *exempla* illustrating problems that had arisen in the administration of the area of law to which they pertained.[61]

In contrast, the cases dealing with deceptions did receive unified consideration during the twelfth century. Gregory VIII's encyclical of 1187, "Vel ex malicia," and Clement III's encyclical of 1189, "Cum ex imposito,"[62] made it clear to all that the occasional problems local judges had

had with litigants were not isolated, but constituted a single body of cases
that required unified action by the highest legal authority. The canonists, for
their part, had already comprehended the unity of the problem and had set
forth a single remedy for it—the inclusion in every papal letter, explicitly or
implicitly, of the qualification "si preces ueritate nitantur."[63] Moreover,
they did not undermine this unified approach by taking up *seriatim* the different types and methods of deception and fraud. It is no surprise that the
courts, faced with the cases one by one over many years and pontificates, took
longer to recognize and act upon this class of cases, but "Vel ex malicia" and
"Cum ex imposito" certainly mark the decisive step in that direction. By the
time Raymond set to work on the decretals, the unified approach had won
including Alexander III's "Ex parte venerabilis" in the title "De
rescriptis."[64]

The decretals studied here present a fine example of legal development in
the early part of the classical age of canon law. What Gratian had started, the
drawing of harmony from dissonance, to use Professor Kuttner's expression,
was continued by the popes as they unified and rationalized the areas of law
Gratian had only touched upon or had left entirely untreated. The law concerning dishonest litigation adds important detail to our understanding of
procedural law and practices, but it also illustrates the nature of the legal
revolution that took place on the basis of Gratian's work.

University of California, San Diego

Notes

1. See, for example, Alexander III, "Ex relatione," ed. H.–E. Lohmann, "Die Collectio
Wigorniensis,' *Zeitschrift der Savigny-Stiftung für Rechtsgeschichte*, Kan. Abt. xxii (1933), 118
(= *Wig.* 4.49), "nullis obstantibus litteris, si que sunt ab adversa parte super hoc impetrate."
Lohmann dated this letter, which is addressed to the bishop of Worcester and the abbot of
Evesham, 1159—81, but Holtzmann thought it must have been addressed to Bishop Roger of
Worcester (1164—79), since after Bishop Alufred died (27 March 1160) there was no successor
until Roger's consecration (23 August 1164) and after Roger's death (9 August 1179) there
was a year long vacancy until Baldwin was consecrated (10 August 1180). Alexander died on
30 August 1181. See also Lucius III, "Ex relatione R.," ed. H. Singer, *Neue Beiträge über die
Dekretalensammlungen* (Vienna, 1913), p. 253, "litteris nostris, si que fuerint harum tacito
tenore impetrate non preiudicantibus." This letter can only be dated to Lucius's pontifical
years. Besides these special phrases, the popes regularly used the phrase "si ita est, ut [the ap-
pellant] asserit," and its variants. See the comments of C. R. and M. G. Cheney, *The Letters of
Pope Innocent III* (Oxford, 1967), p. ix. See also the next note. For details about MSS and editions of the decretal collections, see W. Holtzmann, "Kanonistische Ergänzungen zur Italia
Pontificia," *Quellen und Forschungen aus italienischen Archiven und Bibliotheken* xxxvii (1957),
55—102, and xxxviii (1958), 67—175, at xxxvii (1957), 58—67.

2. The foundation for canonistic concern with letters obtained "falsa suggestione" was
Gratian's dictum at C.25 q.2 *p*.c.16, "Rescripta . . . expressam debent in se habere condi-
tionem: Si preces veritate nituntur. Mendax enim precator debet carere impetratis, et quibus

scripta diriguntur sunt puniendi; si precum mendacia vetuerint argui." This dictum was enlarged by Gratian's successors in the schools by the addition of a series of civil law citations from Justinian. Within this series, it was a rescript of the emperor Zeno ("Universa rescripta" [A.D. 477]; *Cod.* 1.23.7), from which the phrase "si preces veritate nitantur" derived, that became the basis for canonistic commentary. See, for example, *Summa Parisiensis,* ed. T. P. McLaughlin (Toronto, 1952), p. 232, *"universa.* Generaliter omnia rescripta sub tali conditione promulgari, si preces veritate nitantur." *Glossa Ordinaria, "precum,* id est, quod illa conditio sit apposita: ut preces, etc. hoc tamen non tenet: ut extra de rescrip. ex parte." The reference to the *Decretals* is to X 1.3.2, Alexander III "Ex parte venerabilis" (JL 14317), "in huiusmodi literis intelligenda est hec conditio, etiamsi non apponatur: 'si preces veritate nitantur'." This letter, addressed to Archbishop Richard of Canterbury (1174–84), was dated 1174–81 by Jaffé-Löwenfeld, but the copy in *Collectio Cantuariensis prima,* c.3, bears the date "Dat. Ferentini xvii kal. Augusti" (= 16 July 1175). See C. Duggan, *Twelfth-century Decretal Collections* (London, 1963), p. 162, who, however, does not correct the date of JL. The relationship between this letter and the canonistic commentary is somewhat problematical. None of the early decretists, Paucapalea, Rolandus, or Rufinus, mentions the conditional character of rescripts, nor does Stephan of Tournai's *Summa,* which relies on Paucapalea and Roland for its commentary on C.25 q.2. McLaughlin suggested an early date, ca. 1160, for the *Summa Parisiensis* on the grounds that it does not cite any letter of Alexander (McLaughlin, *Summa,* pp. xxxi–xxxiii); the traditional date had been set at ca. 1170 (see S. Kuttner, *Repertorium der Kanonistik* [Vatican City, 1937], p. 177). Now there may be a relationship between "Ex parte venerabilis" and the SP, but if so, that relationship is probably of the "common source" type; the civil law citations added to the *dictum* may underlie both texts. Nonetheless, it would be difficult to sustain McLaughlin's early date for the SP unless it were argued that its author was commenting on material inserted in the *Causa* almost immediately before, and not in the text Rufinus had used at the end of the 1150s. But that this new material did not influence Alexander's handling of the problem until 1175 is rather surprising if it had been accepted into the *Decretum* by ca. 1160. On the addition of Roman law texts from the *Corpus iuris civilis* to the *Decretum,* see A. Vetulani, "Gratien et le Droit romain," *Revue historique de Droit français et étranger* XXIV–XXV (1946–47), 11–48; Vetulani, "Encore un Mot sur le Droit romain dans le Décret de Gratien," *Apollinaris* XXI (1948), 129–34; S. Kuttner, "New Studies on the Roman Law in Gratian's Decretum," *Seminar* XI (1953), 12–50; Kuttner, "Additional Notes on the Roman Law in Gratian," ibid. XII (1954), 68–74; J. Rambaud-Buhot, "Le 'Corpus Juris Civilis' dans le Décret de Gratien d'après le Manuscrit lat. nouv. acq. 1761 de la Bibliothèque Nationale," *Bibliothèque de l'École des Chartes* CXI (1953), 54–64. Specifically on C.25 q.2, see Vetulani, "Encore un Mot," p. 132, and Kuttner, "New Studies," pp. 40–41.

The *Glossa Ordinaria* to the *Decretals* expands on the provisions of *Ex parte venerabilis:* "in rescriptis semper subintelligitur hec conditio, Si preces veritate nitantur: si ita est, etiam si non apponatur, ut hic in iuramentis, et aliis huiusmodi pactionibus subaudiuntur generales conditiones, ut puta, si Deus voluerit, . . . si res in eodem statu permanserit, et similia."

3. See Alexander III, "Cum sacrosancta Romana ecclesia" (JL 12020; X 2.28.7), "Si duobus—Romani Pontificis appellasse." This section of *Cum sacrosancta,* the whole of which is constituted by X. 2.28.5–7, is actually its fifth part. Throughout this article I will refer to the parts of decretals. These divisions are treated as separate, although they may not appear independently in either the *compilationes antique* or the *Decretals,* because they are separated somewhere within the canonical tradition. In this example, the segment "Si duobus—appellasse" occurs alone in *Collectio Regalis* 52.

4. See, for example, Alexander III, "Ad audientiam nostram", ed. Lohmann, "Collectio," pp. 142–43 (= *Wig.* 7.70); Alexander III, "Causam que inter," ed. Friedberg, *Quinque compilationes antiquae* (Leipzig, 1882), p. 15 (= *1 Comp.* 2.11.2); Clement III, "Cum sicut accepimus" (X 2.15.2). Alexander set forth general principles for handling such cases in the fourth part of "Quamvis simus multiplicitate", *inc.* "Ceterum si aliquis" (X 1.3.3 = JL 14156. Other parts of this letter were enregistered as JL 14152 and 14154 by Jaffé-Löwenfeld).

5. Cheney and Cheney, *Letters,* pp. ix–xi. See also C. R. Cheney, *The Study of the Medieval Papal Chancery* (Glasgow, 1965), with the literature cited there.

6. C. R. Cheney, *From Becket to Langton* (Manchester, 1956), p. 65, citing "Ex parte venerabilis" (see above note 2), "si taliter scripsimus, hoc ex nimia occupatione contigit," and Clement III, "Cum ex imposito," ed. Holtzmann, "Die Dekretalen Gregors VIII.," *Mitteilungen des Instituts für österreichische Geschichtsforschung* LVIII (1950), 122–23, "Et quia non possumus omnium habere memoriam, cause modo commisse quibusdam iudicibus ad aliorum statim petitionem aliis committuntur et ita commissio commissione frustrata Romane curie notam ingerit levitatis." Cheney also cites "Vel ex malicia litigancium" (JL 16056; ed. J. Ramackers, *Papsturkunden in Frankreich,* n.s. II [Normandy], Abhandlungen der Akademie der Wissenschaften in Göttingen, Phil.-Hist. Kl., 3rd ser., XXI [1937], pp. 383–84. Also ed. Friedberg, *Comp. ant.* pp. 24–25 [*1 Comp.* 2.20.47]). Cheney's whole lecture, "England and Rome," *Becket to Langton,* pp. 42–86 is relevant to the present subject. See especially his discussion of the complicated and drawn out Antsey case, which provides a closer look at the sort of cases cited in note 4 above (ibid., pp. 54–58). For a detailed recounting of another such case, see J. C. Moore, "Count Baldwin of Flanders, Philip Augustus, and the Papal Power," *Speculum* XXXVII (1962), 79–89. See also the same author's "Papal Justice in France Around the Time of Pope Innocent III," *Church History* XLI (1972), 295–306.

7. R. C. Van Caenegem, *The Birth of the Common Law* (Cambridge, 1973), p. 38, with notes 34–40. Van Caenegem cites Alexander III, "Cum monasterium sancti Eadmundi," ed. Holtzmann, *Papsturkunden in England,* vol. III, Abhandlungen der Akademie der Wissenschaften in Göttingen, Phil.-Hist. Kl., 3rd ser., XXIII (1952), pp. 363–64, no. 233; "Cum oblationes," ibid., vol. II, Abhandlungen, 3rd ser., XIV (1935), pp. 407–8, no.214; Urban III, "Significantibus vobis intelleximus," ibid., vol. I, Abhandlungen, 2nd ser., XXV (1930), p. 531, no.242; Celestine III, "Pervenit ad nos," ibid., III: 538–39, no.445; "Libellus querimonie," ibid., II: 477–78, no.283.

8. W. Holtzmann, "Über eine Ausgabe der päpstlichen Dekretalen des 12. Jahrhunderts," *Nachrichten der Akademie der Wissenschaften in Göttingen,* Phil.-Hist. Kl. (1945), pp. 15–36. See also S. Kuttner, "Notes on a Projected Corpus of Twelfth-century Decretal Letters," *Traditio* VI (1948), 345–51. Holtzmann published the first segment of his project in "Kanonistische Ergänzungen . . .," see note 1 above. This work was published separately (Tübingen, 1959) as well as in *Quellen und Forschungen.* I have been placed in a position to participate in the continuation of Holtzmann's work by the man to whom these articles are dedicated. Professor Kuttner is, with Professor Theodor Schieffer of Cologne, Holtzmann's literary executor.

9. D. Lohrmann, "Zur Vorgeschichte der Dekretale X 3.17.3: Der Prozess zwischen Beauvais und Chaalis," *Bulletin of Medieval Canon Law,* n.s. IV (1974), 1–7, document at 3–4.

10. Paris, Bibl. nat., MS lat. 11003, fol. 336, n. 1384; this confirmation will be published in *Papsturkunden in Frankreich* n.s., VII together with other letters relating to the case. See Lohrmann, "Collectio," nn. 7, 19.

11. In C.2 q.6, Gratian set forth the general principle "Causa vero viciata remedio appellationis sublevari poterit." He then cites nine Pseudo-Isidorian decretals, which he summarizes thus: ibid. *post* c.10 (c.2 is a *palea*), "Cum ergo Zepherinus dicat (c.8), ab omnibus esse appellandum, maxime tamen ab obpressis, et Marcellus scribat (c.6): 'Omnes episcopi, qui voluerint vel quibus necesse fuerit, appellare debent': patet, quod accusato (sive gravetur, sive non) appellationis vox non est deneganda." See also ibid. *post* c.14, "Patet ergo, quod nulli appellanti induciae sunt denegandae." But he continues in the same *dictum:* "Ceterum, si causa frustratoriae dilationis appellaverit, a iudice, ad quem provocatum fuerit, condempnabitur." The rest of the *questio* defines the number of times one can appeal, the points in the judicial processing of the case when appeal is permitted, the form the appeal must take, the prohibition of appeal from arbitrators chosen by consent of both parties, the time permitted for prosecuting an appeal, and other aspects of the appeal process. C.6 q.4 concerns the handling of a case about which a panel of judges has been unable to come to a unanimous

judgment. Having set forth the hierarchy of judges to whom such a case should be referred, Gratian says simply that even a unanimous judgment can be challenged through appeal to a higher court. See ibid. *post c.5*. On the law of appeals in general, see A. Padoa Schioppa, *Ricerche sull'Appello nel Diritto intermedio*, 2 vols. (Milan, 1967–70).

12. See, for example, Alexander III, "Quod te intelleximus" (Troyes, Bibl. de la Ville 103, fol. 2; to be edited by Chodorow in a forthcoming volume of unedited decretals, 1140–98). This letter deals first with the question whether a judge ought to defer to an appeal in a case committed to him "appellatione remota" and second with whether a judge ought to defer to an appeal by a person who has seized property and whose appeal is made to avoid adjudication of the consequent dispute over possession. Jaffé-Löwenfeld date the letter 1159–81, and no evidence permits a narrowing of these *termini*, but the letter's close relationship to "Cum sacrosancta" (see note 3 above and the next note below) suggests that it dates from before 1171–72, when "Cum sacrosancta" was issued, or shortly afterwards. "Cum sacrosancta" was received in the canonical tradition very soon after it appeared and covered the second question raised here. The first question was covered by Alexander III, "Ad aures nostras" (JL 13876; X 2.28.33), which defines the limits of the delegation "appellatione remota" in response to a question about appeals made on subsidiary points in a case committed "appellatione remota." The first 35 *capitula* of X 2.28 are responses of Alexander to questions about appeal. See also, Alexander III, "In eminenti specula" (JL 14350; *1 Comp.* 2.20.40) and "Cum olim E.," ed. Singer, *Neue Beiträge*, p. 280 (*Coll. Sangermanensis* 6.15.3). All these letters respond to a situation described by Rufinus before Alexander became pope: Rufinus, *Summa*, ed. H. Singer (Paderborn, 1902), p. 251, "Quoniam de appellatione multa diffuse confuseque in questione proposita memorantur . . ." commenting on C.2 q.6.

13. JL 12020; X 2.28.5–7. This letter appeared complete in twenty-eight collections and partially in another six. The systematic collections (see Holtzmann, "Kanon. Erg.," *QF* XXXVII [1957], 58–67) divide it up in the same way as the *Decretals*. The division is as follows: (a) Cum sacrosancta . . . Si frustratoria (*hic incipiunt Coll. regalis, Coll. Bridlingtonensis, Coll. Parisiensis prima;* X *incipit* Cum sit Romana. Fraternitati tue)—noscitur appellasse. (b) Si autem in agro—ad causam vocationes (*abbrev.* X). (c) Preterea si raptor—Apostolus excommunicavit. (d) Ad hec si in una causa—iudex suus ordinarius existat. (e) Item si duobus coram—pontificis appellasse (X *incipit* Si duobus). (f) Deinde quod in fine—tenere non credimus (X *incipit* Denique quod queris). The incipits and explicits indicated here stem from the earlier collections. In X. 2.28.5 = a,b,c; 2.28.6 = d; 2.28.7 = e,f. It is instructive to compare this decretal with C.2 q.6. Alexander treats the general right of appeal, the term for prosecuting an appeal, the consequences of failure to prosecute it, the points in a case when appeal is possible, informal appeals, appeals by manifest criminals, and appeals from secular to ecclesaistical courts. See also note 3 above.

14. "Ex crebris querimoniis" (JL 13814), ed. Friedberg, *Comp. ant.*, p. 22 (= *1 Comp.* 2.20.33). Jaffé-Löwenfeld dated this letter 1159–81. Robertson connected it with Thomas Becket and edited it under 1164: *Materials for the History of Thomas Becket* (London, 1875–85), v: 127, no.64. Holtzmann remarks in his notes that the content of the letter points to Richard not to Thomas as the addressee, and, since it is addressed "apostolice sedis legato" (in *Coll. Alcobacensis prima* 99, *Coll. Florianensis* 66, *Coll. Cusana* 87, *Coll. Fontanensis* 1.15), he dates it 1174–81.

15. JL 17648; *2 Comp.* 2.19.19. This letter was apparently considered too restrictive, and its main provisions were covered elsewhere. See, for example, Alexander III, "Super eo quod" (= part six of JL 13162; X 2.28.10); "Ad aures nostras" (JL 13876; X 2.28.33); and Clement III, "Cum in ecclesia" (JL 16579; X 2.28.38).

16. JL 17050; *2 Comp.* 2.19.12. Jaffé-Löwenfeld attributed this letter to Celestine III and dated it 1193. Holtzmann corrected the attribution and date in his study of the *Coll. Seguntina*, on which the correction is based. See Holtzmann, "La 'Collectio Seguntina' et les Décrétales de Clement III et de Celestin III," *Revue d'Histoire ecclésiastique* L (1955), 424, and "Kanon. Erg.," no. 103.

17. Raymond deleted part of the second part (see note 13 above) and inserted the rest in

part one. Thus, all the collections prior to the *Decretals* have at this point, part two of Holtz-mann's analysis, "Si autem in agro vel aliis locis ante ingressum cause fuerit appellatum, non solent huiusmodi dici appellationes sed ad causam vocationes." By deleting "Si autem in agro—fuerit appellatum," Raymond in effect revised the decretal in accord with the purpose if not the specific provisions of Clement's letter, for he removed from the law the informal avenue of appeal permitted by the original legislation. See also H. Schmitz, *Appellatio extraiudicialis* (Munich, 1970), pp. 75–77. Note that Mansi printed the letter (*Amplissima collectio conciliorum* XXI: 1079). Friedberg used this text to restore the one he published in X, and he referred to it as the original. Mansi was, however, reproducing the edition of Martène-Durand (*Veterum scriptorum . . . amplissima collectio* [Paris, 1724], II: 911) from the so-called letter collection of Reims; see now J. Ramackers, *Papsturkunden in Frankreich*, n.s., Vol. III (Artois), Abhandlungen der Akademie der Wissenschaften in Göttingen, Phil.-Hist. Kl., 3rd ser., XXIII (1940), pp. 17ff. This text is not an original, but it is complete. The letter is printed according to *Appendix concilii Lateranensis* 10.6 (= a,b,c; see note 13 above) in Mansi XXII: 313; this is a reprint of the edition of P. Crabbe (*Concilia omnia tam generalia quam particularia* [Cologne, 1551], II: 820ff.).

18. Ed. Holtzmann, "Die Dekretalen Gregors VIII." (see note 6 above).

19. See note 1 above.

20. P. Herde, "Römisches und kanonisches Recht bei der Verfolgung des Fälschungsdelikts im Mittelalter," *Traditio* XXI (1965), 291–362, especially 323–32.

21. *Coll. Cheltenhamensis* 17.23, "Si quis obiciat suggestione falsi et eam probare voluerit, si dicat probationes suas esse in transmarinis partibus et petat dilationem, danda est ei dilatio." The complete text of this letter will be edited by C. Duggan in the volume of *inedita* mentioned in note 12 above. See also Alexander III, "Consulvisti nos" (*incipit 1 Comp.* "In eminenti specula"), JL 14350; ed. Friedberg, *Comp. ant.,* pp. 23–24 (= *1 Comp.* 2.20.40), "Quod autem quesivisti (quesisti *Friedberg*), si aliquis appellaverit, quia delegatus iudex audire super falsi suggestione probationes recusat, an appellatio teneat, hoc tuam volumus discretionem tenere, quod in eo casu debet appellatio deferri." Lohmann ("Collectio," pp. 77–78), pointed out that Jaffé-Löwenfeld mistakenly included four separate decretals under JL 14350. "Relatum est auribus" (X 3.8.3) and "Proposuit nobis" (X 2.28.24) usually appear with "Consuluisti nos . . . In eminenti specula" (in *Coll. Wigorniensis*, they follow it), but there is no evidence that they were originally part of it. "Cum aliqua causa" does not correspond to any of the citations cited by Jaffé-Löwenfeld, and I have not been able to trace it. Lohmann remarks merely that its connection to JL 14350 appears to be based solely on a note of Friedberg to *Coll. Bambergensis* 42.34 (see Friedberg, *Die Canonessammlungen zwischen Gratian und Bernhard von Pavia* [Leipzig, 1897], p. 108).

22. "Super eo uero" (JL 13886; X 3.2.5). This letter is actually the second part of "Plene nobis innotuit." This first part of this letter (= JL 13748) is edited by Friedberg, *Comp. Ant.*, p. 38 (= *1 Comp.* 3.26.30). The letter occurs complete in eight early collections, which all bear the address "Atrebatensi episcopo."

23. "Super eo vero," X 3.2.5, "Porro si literas a nobis obtinuerit [the suspended priest], que facti seriem non contineant, nolumus literas illas sibi prodesse." Note that Raymond preserved only two sentences of this letter; see ed. Friedberg, *Corpus iuris canonici*, II: 455.

24. The former is JL 12253; X 2.28.4 and 2.20.20; the comment in Herde, "Römisches und kanonisches Recht," pp. 323–32. See Lucius III, "Improba pestis falsitatis" (JL 15207; ed. Friedberg, *Comp. ant.*, p. 100 [= *2 Comp.* 5.9.1]); "Ad hec sumus" (JL 15208; X 1.3.10); Urban III, "Ad audientiam nostram" (JL 15752; X 5.20.3); Celestine III, "Per falsarios" (JL —; ed. Friedberg, *Comp. ant.*, pp. 100–101 [= *2 Comp.* 5.9.3]).

25. Lucius III, "Dilectorum filiorum nostrorum" (JL 14769; ed. S. Löwenfeld, *Epistolae pontificum Romanorum ineditae* [Leipzig, 1885], p. 214, no.356 [= Martène's copy of *Coll. Abrincensis* 2.10.2 (see Singer, *Neue Beträge*, p. 364)]); "Ex litteris tue" (JL 15204; ed. [complete] Singer, *Neue Beiträge*, p. 286 [= *Coll. Sangermanensis* 7.11]. See also X 5.20.2 [incomplete: *incipit* "Super eo autem"]). Jaffé-Löwenfeld dated "Ex litteris tue" 1181–85, but the copy in *Coll. Wigorniensis* 7.82 bears "Datum Velletri," which narrows the date to 1182–3.

26. "Dura sepe mandata" (Potthast 202; X 5.20.4). See Herde, "Römisches und kannonisches Recht," pp. 334–35.

27. "Licet ad regimen" (Potthast 365; X 5.20.5).

28. See Herde, "Römisches und kanonisches Recht," pp. 329–34. In "Improba pestis falsitatis" (note 24 above), Lucius III set deposition and imprisonment as the penalty for clerical offenders and ordered laymen to be handed over to secular authority, which imposed mutilation and death on forgers. In "Ad audientiam nostram" (note 24 above), Urban III recommended branding and exile, the former penalty stemming from customary law and the latter from Roman law.

29. Ed. Lohmann, "Collectio," pp. 144–45. Lohmann dated the letter 1159–81, but since it undoubtedly was addressed to Roger of Worcester (see note 1 above), it can be dated according to his pontifical years, 1164–79.

30. "Sicut dilectus filius" (JL 15210; ed. Friedberg, *Comp. ant.,* p. 66 [= 2 Comp. 1.2.6]), "Rotbertus de Columbellis super ecclesia cuiusdam villae contra adversarium suum duplices litteras ad Rotomagensem archidiaconum et Turonensem iudices impetravit, ut si coram Rotomagensi optinere non valeat coram Turonensi iudice nocere adversario suo non desistat." Jaffé-Löwenfeld attributed this letter to Lucius III on the basis of *Coll. Gilberti* and *2 Comp.,* but *Coll. Rotomagensis* 17.3, which contains the most complete text, makes the attribution to Urban III, and Holtzmann accepted this attribution as correct.

31. It is possible that Robert presented the case on two separate and perhaps incompatible pleadings in order to give his case two alternative avenues to victory. As is well known, medieval law did not permit the pleading of incompatible defenses or plaints (e.g., "I am not guilty of trespass, but if I am, it is for just cause."), and Robert's action may have been designed to get around this prohibition. Unfortunately, Urban does not comment on the contents of the two letters of commission.

32. L. Fowler, "Recusatio iudicis in Civilian and Canonist Thought," *Studia Gratiana* xv (1972), pp. 719–85, especially 741–43. See Alexander III, Super eo vero" (JL 12293; X 2.28.12. This letter is part two of "Sicut Romana ecclesia" [JL 12293 + 13874]), which responds to the question whether the parties may refuse a judge in a case committed "appellatione remota." This question could not arise, of course, had a distinction been made between *appellatio* and *recusatio.* See also Lucius III, "Postremo fraternitati" (JL 14966; X 2.28.36. This letter is actually the third part of "Ad aures nostras" [JL 14965 + 14966; ed. Holtzmann and E. Kemp, *Papal Decretals Relating to the Diocese of Lincoln in the Twelfth Century* (Hereford, 1954), p. 52]).

33. JL 15208; X 1.3.10. One of the letters treated by Herde. See note 24 above.

34. "Constitutus in presentia" (JL —; ed. Singer, *Neue Beiträge,* p. 233 [*Coll. Sangermanensis* 5.4.22]), "Cum ecclesiam de N. per presentationem patroni et institutionem diocesiani episcopi canonice fuisset adeptus (the appellant) et eam aliquamdiu pacifice possedisset, H. clericus apostolicas litteras ad venerabilem fratrem nostrum Helyensem episcopum et dilectum filium nostrum abbatem de Croilande tacita veritate impetravit, quibus eum ad locum per octo dietas ab ecclesia ipsa remotum a delegatis fecit citari iudicibus." Dated 1184 because it mentions Bishop Bartholomew of Exeter (died 15 December 1184) and bears the date "Datum Verone" in the *Coll. Tanneri.*

35. "Conquestus est apostolatui" (JL —; ed. Holtzmann, "Die Dekretalensammlungen des 12. Jahrhunderts," *Festschrift zur Feier des 200jährigen Bestehens der Akademie der Wissenschaften in Göttingen,* Phil.-Hist. Kl. [1951], p. 124 [*Coll. Tanneri* 4.5.4 (in lower margin)]), "Cum ecclesiam de Wandesle canonice fuisset adeptus [the appellant] et eam diu pacifice possedisset, N. clericus, qui aliis redditibus ecclesiasticis proponitur habundare, eum super ipsa ecclesia traxit in causam per quasdam litteras a sede apostolica ad delegatos iudices impetratas, . . . qui eiusdem N. concanonici erant, remoti etiam plurimum et suspecti, et licet eos idem S. [the appellant] propter hec instantissime recusaret, ipsi nihilominus ad cognitionem cause contra iuris ordinem procedere presumpserunt." This letter cannot be accurately dated.

36. Celestine III, "Significauit nobis tua" (JL 17658; X 1.31.6. This letter is actually part one of a long and important decretal [JL 17658 + 17659 + 16631 +

17677 + 16619 + 17054 + 16553] of which the only complete copy is in *Coll. Seguntina* 110. See Holtzmann, "Kanon. Erg.," *QF* XXXVII (1957), pp. 97–101, where the whole letter is re-edited.

37. Cheney and Cheney, *Letters,* p. x. Of course, most of the erroneous names in decretals stem from the mistakes of copyists and not from the ignorance of the chancery clerks.

38. "De causa illa" (JL —; ed. R. von Heckel, "Die Dekretalensammlungen des Gilberts und Alanus nach den Weingartener Handschriften," *Zeitschrift der Savigny-Stiftung für Rechtsgeschichte* Kan. Abt. XXIX (1940), 261 [*Coll. Alani* 2.18.4 (Appendix 87)]), "De causa illa, unde nobis scripsisti, quod quedam ecclesia per instantiam petitoris fuit in nostro privilegio annotata, quando quidem controversia de ipsa movebatur . . . si cognoveris, quod petitor ille, cum privilegium impetravit, ipsam non possideret ecclesiam, auctoritatem privilegii nolumus in hoc ei posse proficere, sed causam ipsam libere dictante iustitia diffinias." Dated according to the pontifical years of Archbishop Hubert (1146–53); see Holtzmann, "Kanon. Erg.," no.84.

39. "De confirmationibus" (JL 11872; X 2.30.2. This is actually the second part of "Ex parte tua" [also JL 11872; first part = X 5.1.11]). See also "Causam que vertitur" (JL 14010; X 2.20.19). Jaffé-Löwenfeld date this letter 1159–81, but it probably dates 1174–75. This conclusion can be drawn from the relationship between this letter and two others, "Miramur plurimum" (JL 12666; ed. Friedberg, *Comp. ant.,* pp. 13–14 [*1 Comp.* 2.4.3]), and "Ex litteris vestris" (JL 14129; X 2.4.1), all of which deal with a dispute between the Benedictine monastery S. Michele di Martura and the dean and pastor of the collegiate church of S. Maria in the same town. See Holtzmann, "Kanon. Erg.," nos.28–30 (with the comment to these letters).

40. JL 14965; X 1.3.8. See note 32 above.

41. I.e., the second part of "Ex parte tua" (JL 11872; X 2.30.2). See note 39 above.

42. JL 14087; X 1.42.1.

43. JL 13159; X 1:36.6.

44. JL 14177; X 1.36.7. In "Meminimus iam pridem Alanum" (JL —; see note 29 above), it was reported that Alan's opponents pleaded a transaction between him and the man whose successor now held the church he sought. Alexander III did not comment on this transaction, which was the basis on which the first judges delegate had adjudged the church to the canons of Beauvais.

45. *Incipit* "Super eo quod." The first two parts of this letter correspond to JL 15164 (ed. Friedberg, *Comp. ant.,* p. 69 [*2 Comp.* 1.9.2]) and JL 16629 (X 1.9.5). It is transmitted complete only in *Coll. Cheltenhamensis* 19.22–25 and *Coll. Cottoniana* 6.20, on the basis of which the missattribution of part two to Clement III and of part three to Alexander III can be corrected.

46. No cases of this sort are extant from any other province of the church, and it seems likely none ever existed. On conveyances through the levying of fines, see F. Pollock and F. W. Maitland, *The History of English Law,* 2nd ed. (Cambridge, 1968), II: 94–102. See also S. Riesenfeld, "Individual and Family Rights in Land During the Formative Period of the Common Law," *Essays in Jurisprudence in Honor of Roscoe Pound* (Boston, 1962), pp. 439–62.

47. JL 14028: X 5.22.3. The pope makes clear the Englishness of the problem in his first sentence, "Audivimus in episcopatu tuo et in aliis episcopatibus Angliae."

48. X 5.22.3, "Audivimus . . . ut interdum, inter se [two clerics] collusione facta super beneficiis, quae possident, se sustineant ab aliis molestari, et postea, ut questioni cedatur, et iidem clerici beneficia quiete possideant, quasi nomine transactionis soluunt aliis de ipsis beneficiis annuam pensionem, ut post mortem eorum in beneficiis illis, super quibus est inter eosdem clericos collusio facta, ius sibi valeant vindicare . . . non differas appellatione remota perpetuo spoliare [such clerics], quia satis esset indignum et absonum, si fraus et dolus, quae in praeiudicium tui iuris . . . ."

49. X 1.17, "De filiis presbyterorum ordinandis vel non."

50. See A. L. Poole, *From Domesday Book to Magna Carta,* 2nd ed. (Oxford, 1955), p. 183

(citing *inter alia* Henry of Huntingdon, *Historia Anglorum,* ed. T. Arnold [London, 1879], p. 251).

51. See Alexander III, "Ex insinuatione prioris" (JL 13982; X 1.17.2, *incipit* "Ad presentiam nostram"), "Ad presentiam nostram accedens R. presbyter, tacito, quod esset filius sacerdotis, per fraudem literas impetravit a nobis, ut in ecclesia de Bilesbi, in qua pater eius ministravit, existeret capellanus." Jaffé-Löwenfeld dated this letter 1159–81, but Holtzmann and Kemp, who re-edited the letter (*Lincoln,* pp. 10–11, see note 32 above), corrected this to 1170–73. The earliest collections bear the address "G. Lincolniensi archidiacono"— Geoffrey Plantagenet, archdeacon of Lincoln 1170–73, elected bishop in 1173 but not consecrated. He resigned in 1182. For similar cases, see Alexander III, "Referente nobis dilecto" (JL —; ed. Friedberg, *Canonessammlungen,* p. 157 [*Coll. Brugensis* 37.1]), dated 1164–79 according to the pontifical years of Roger of Worcester, to whom it is undoubtedly addressed (see note 1 above).

52. See Lucius III, "Quoniam ex plenitudine" (JL 15164; ed. Friedberg, *Comp. ant.,* p. 69 [*2 Comp.* 1.9.2]; see note 45 above), "Personarum vero filios citra sacros ordines constitutarum, si tamen eorum merita suffragantur, parentibus suis succedere conniventibus oculis toleramus." Alexander III's "Ex tua nobis," cited below, implies the permission made explicit by Lucius; see the next note.

53. JL 13881; X 1.17.9, "Cum olim ad tuam consultationem super filiis sacerdotum tales a nobis literas recepisses, ut eos posses in ecclesiis, quas patres eorum nullo mediante possederant, sustinere, quos probatae vitae et sanae conversationis cognosceres, vel quos longo tempore illas tenuisse constaret: . . . si per priores literas nostras cum aliquibus clericis dispensasti, dispensationem tuam posteriorum literarum nostrarum intuitu nolumus irritari, sed eam servari praecipimus illibatam."

54. See note 51 above.

55. JL 13955: X 1.17.5 Jaffé-Löwenfeld dated this letter 1159–81, but the *Coll. Alcobacensis prima* names the abbot of Ford, who was one of the two addressees, as Baldwin, 1175–80.

56. *Incipit* "Cumque defuncto G." (JL —; ed. Singer, *Neue Beiträge,* p. 254 [*Coll. Sangermanensis* 6.1.22]), "Cumque defuncto G. ipsius prebende predictus E. possessionem haberet et aliquanto tempore tenuisset, accessit quidam clericus G. ad presentiam nostram et nulla facta mentione de ipsius cause progressu a nobis—cum supradictam prebendam spontanee abiurasset—litteras impetravit . . . Episcopum autem ipsum, qui post appellationem et confirmationem nostram eundem E. prebenda illa spoliare presumpsit, auctoritate conferendi beneficium appellatione postposita prives, donec per se vel per nuntium suum et per litteras suas de tanto excessu satisfacturus ad apostolicam sedem accedat. Preterea prenominatum G., si eundem E. super iam dicta prebenda molestare presumpserit, vinculo excommunicationis astringas, qua eum teneas usque ad condignam satisfactionem astrictum." I think the letter implicates the bishop in the fraud because failure to defer to an appeal nullified the judgment but did not, usually, result in a condemnation of the erring judge. The first part of "Cum olim E." was also edited by Singer from *Coll. Sangermanensis;* see ibid., p. 280 (*Coll. Sangermanensis* 6.15.3). The complete letter occurs in six early collections. It appears that the case is English, since the bishop of London and abbot of St. Albans are mentioned, in part one, as having been judges in the first suit. The bishop of Coventry is the erring bishop of the second part, although *Coll. Sangermanensis* 6.1.22 omits this identification. The letter cannot be accurately dated.

57. See S. Kuttner, "Some Considerations on the Role of Secular Law and Institutions in the History of Canon Law," *Scritti di Sociologia e Politica in Onore di Luigi Sturzo* (Bologna, 1953), II: 8–9, et passim.

58. See note 21 above.

59. See notes 14–18 above.

60. The first part of this letter permitted *iudices a quo* to set the term in which an appeal was to be prosecuted according to circumstances. See also Alexander III, "Ad aures nostras"

(JL 13876; X 2.28.33), "Cum incidentes quaestiones saepius praeiudiciales non immerito iudicentur, petitioni tuae [to include subsidiary questions under the prohibition of appeal in cases committed "appellatione remota"] in hac parte non duximus annuendum, sed, ne quae partium diutius frustratoriis iudiciis affligatur, appellanti ad prosecutionem appellationis terminus congruus praefigatur . . ."

61. When compared with his treatment of most texts, Raymond left in a considerable amount of factual detail in "Ex quorundam certa" (JL 14087; X 1.42.1), "Ex litteris vestris" (JL 13159; X 1.36.6), "Audivimus in episcopatu tuo" (JL 14028; X 5.22.3), and "Ex parte Ade" (JL 13955; X 2.20.7).

62. See notes 6 and 18 above.

63. See note 2 above.

64. X.1.3.2.

Reshaping a Decretal Chapter: *Tua nobis* and the Canonists

STEVEN HORWITZ

In his study of the beginnings of the French school of canon law Stephan Kuttner concluded that after a vigorous debut during the age of decretists (1141–90) French canonists "unwilling to comprehend the significance of the new papal law" grew dormant, while the Italian school produced commentaries around the *compilationes antiquae* in a continuous and fluid stream that enabled easy movement from the *Decretum* to *decretales*.[1] These observations are correct. As glossators, the French seem uninterested in the decretal collections. For more than forty years between the appearance of the *Compilatio prima* (1188–92) and until after the promulgation of the *Liber extra* (1234) the most interesting relics from the French are their versions of the *compilationes:* Gérard Fransen has delineated a group of manuscripts of the *Compilatio prima* that he terms "French" and in the past year Kenneth Pennington has uncovered a Gallic family of manuscripts for the *Compilatio tertia* (1209–10).[2]

Pennington has gone further. He demonstrates that among the French recensions there is an obvious bias for decretal texts culled from the *Compilatio Romana,* an earlier collection (1208) gathered by Bernard, archdeacon of Compostela, that the *Tertia* had been intended to supersede.[3] The *Romana,* accumulated by Bernard during a sojourn at Rome, drew both on older collections and on papal registers to provide a dossier of decretals for the first ten years of Innocent III's pontificate. Kuttner has calculated that approximately two-thirds of the 431 decretals edited by Bernard had been taken from earlier collections and, in most cases, had been compared critically with registered versions; the balance came directly from Bernard's examination of the registers.[4]

Bernard was dedicated to publishing a collection of decretals truly representative of Innocent's decisions, even annotating his collection with a small list of decretals he considered attributed falsely to that pope.[5] His collection entered the literature of the schools but, despite its scrupulous composition, was not favored at the Roman curia where certain decretals included by Bernard were judged insufficient to serve as model pronouncements.[6]

Within two years the *Compilatio Romana* was replaced by the more popular collection, the *Compilatio tertia,* produced by Peter of Benevento, papal notary. Where only Bernard's scholarship had guaranteed his material's authenticity, Peter of Benevento's work carried the approval of Pope Innocent III. In the bull with which Innocent prefaced the collection in dispatching it to the students and masters of Bologna it is announced that the decretals "compilatas fideliter et sub competentibus titulis collocatas . . . eisdem absque quolibet dubitationis scrupulo uti possitis, cum opus fuerit, tam in iudiciis quam in scholis."[7] For the first time a pope secured a collection's authenticity.

With such sponsorship the *Tertia*'s ascendance was assured; the *Romana*'s influence dwindled. Traces of the older collection persist in only stray citations.[8] Ironically, the now obsolete collection's greatest influence, though indirect, was exerted through the *Compilatio tertia.* Peter of Benevento honored the *Romana* by following many of its chapters, diverging from those usually by addition of passages suppressed by Bernard.[9]

There is then considerable irony when we turn to the French recensions of the *Tertia* and find that most often "French" means the reintroduction of material that Peter had suppressed from Bernard's version: of the twenty-four chapters (twenty-five if we include Bernard's epilogue) injected into the French manuscripts studied by Pennington, only three do not derive from the earlier compilation. Of the internal emendations uncovered, seven can be tied to Bernard, but none of the unidentified pieces can be traced to other collections.[10] Clearly many French canonists preferred the spurned Roman collection.

But why did the French tamper with the new papal collection? Innocent himself had witnessed its trustworthiness. Neither Fransen for the *Prima* nor Pennington for this collection, both concerned with discerning the existence and shape of these distinct manuscript traditions, had yet turned to the question. Pennington has suggested that much of the restoration and innovation was cosmetic or explanatory and that those responsible fell back on the *Compilatio Romana* as a source for new texts or for texts nearer to the registered originals.[11] Certainly this is true. But some texts did not stem from Bernard. And some did not clarify or explain. Rather they opened different issues, occasionally issues in conflict with views actively or passively offered in the primary Italian collections and glosses.

An example of just such a contentious restoration concerns the decretal *Tua nobis* sent by Innocent III in the second year of his pontificate to Albert Avogadro, bishop of Vercelli, who had sought papal aid in curbing the multifarious dodges employed by his subjects to evade tithe payments. The decretal had been recognized immediately by canonists as a significant papal opinion. The earliest Innocentian collection, Rainerius of Pomposa's *Collectio decretalium* (1201) which covers the first three years of his reign, included almost the entire text (11.2); the same edition was appended (c.16) to another early collection composed by Gilbertus Anglicus (1202–4); Alanus Anglicus included the text (3.15.4) in his collection (c.1206). From one or another of these *Tua nobis* passed with addition of material from the registers into first Bernard's and then Peter's collections (*Bern.* 3.24.2; *3 Comp.* 3.23.2). Johannes Teutonicus would later in his *Compilatio quarta* (1216) use part of the decretal (*4 Comp.* 3.9.4). Raymond of Peñafort eventually presented material from *Tua nobis* in his *Liber extra* (1234) (X 3.30.25–6). So persuasive did Bernard find *Tua nobis* that he made it do double duty. It appears under *De iudiciis,* the initial title of Book II, where an excerpt emphasizes the autonomy of clerks and *spiritualia* from lay legislation and privileges. Peter adopted this chapter as well (*Bern.* 2.1.1; *3 Comp.* 2.1.1).[12]

Bishop Albert had complained about persistent and widespread evasion of tithes by laymen: some customarily deducted expenses incurred in planting, cultivating and harvesting the crop before calculating the tithe; others ignored the parish churches, proper recipient for predial, i.e., agricultural, tithes, and diverted them to private chapels or to other clerks or to the poor or "in usus alios pro sua voluntate." Still others, repelled by their parish priests' unpriestly behavior, refused to support them with their tithes. Others displayed imperial privileges to claim exemption from rendering payment. Finally, others sought to extend control over previously held predial tithes, which they asserted were held *in feudum,* to agricultural *novalia,* i.e., crops from land not cultivated before and thus not included in any tithe concession.

In response Innocent underlines each Christian's spiritual obligation to offer tithes: "Verum si ad eum a quo bona cuncta procedunt assertores huiusmodi debitum respectum haberent, ius ecclesiasticum diminuere non contenderent, nec decimas quae tributa sunt egenum animarum, praesumerent detinere." Tithes are both a sign of divine universal dominion and the means by which the cultus, i.e., the clergy who serve God, can be sustained. Thus both lord and tenant, each from his share of the crop, must pay in full without subtraction for expense; those who detest the priest's sins owe the tithe to God, not to the priest, his agent, and cannot withhold it; no exemption can be based on an imperial privilege because no layman, not even an emperor, has power over *spiritualia.* Furthermore, despite any concession of *antiqua decimatio in feudum* no lay holder of tithes could extend this license to *novalia* since "in talibus non sit extendenda licentia, sed potius restringenda."

Innocent's firm stand against lay resistance to tithes was intended to protect the parishes' single most important regular income and a not insignificant source of diocesan revenue. These dodges threatened to disrupt tithe collection. But lay possession, especially infeudation, threatened not merely disruption but cessation of these resources. As will be shown, the *Compilatio tertia,* modelled on Bernard's edition of the *Romana,* deleted *Tua nobis*'s tolerant recognition of old tithing held in fief; some French manuscripts ignored the emendation and restored the passage.

Alienation of church income, of course, was an ancient abuse. Though deemed *spiritualia,* tithes were continually subverted to laymen's purposes.

Often tithes were acquired willy-nilly by the powerful, sometimes in connivance with churchmen, sometimes by simple usurpation. Occasionally, tithes together with the land to which they pertained, were distributed by grateful rulers in reward for military service. Tithes became the stuff of commerce. But regardless by whom or how they came to be held, tithes, until the late twelfth century, remained in the church's mind irreducibly unpossessable by laymen. Laymen, of course, saw the matter differently: tithes were personal property to be sold, exchanged, bequeathed, infeudated, used as collateral. In short, tithes were another battle in distinguishing the spiritual and temporal spheres.[13]

In successive reforms the medieval church sought to restore these *spiritualia* and to end further usurpation. Gratian, whose compendious *Decretum* (c. 1140) offers no room for lay tithe holders, conveys the church's position with a canon from Gregory VII's Lateran Council of 1080:

> Tithes, which canonic authority shows were conceded for pious purposes, we prohibit by apostolic authority to be possessed by laymen. Whether they be accepted from bishops or from kings or from whatsoever persons, unless they return them to the church, let them know that they commit the crime of sacrilege and incur danger of eternal damnation.[14]

After 150 years the situation seemed little changed. Bernard of Pavia, whose *Compilation prima* provided the structure for all later medieval canonical collections, gloomily concludes his comments on tithes in another work, the *Summa decretalium* (1191–98): "It should be noted that tithes cannot be possessed by laymen, though it is found otherwise almost everywhere."[15]

Still the church struggled. But the time came when both pope and canonists recognized the futility of total opposition to so ingrained an institution. The first signs of accommodation crop up in decretals such as *Tua nobis* in comments incidental to the letter's thrust. At about the same time canonists begin to hammer out a theory to rationalize the concession. A middle ground between the tolerance expressed in papal correspondence and its doctrinal formulation in learned commentaries is formed by the decretal collections themselves. Here by control of the fundamental stuff to debate—the words of popes and councils—the compilations determined what evidence of papal concessions circulated.[16] In this instance at least, the French revisions to Italian compilations reveal intellectual activity, a form of subtle commentary not to be equated with the prodigious output at Bologna but which hints at something more than dormancy.

We have seen how widely the letter circulated. But the casual note without rebuke on tithes held *in feudum* and their restriction to *antiqua* determined how *Tua nobis* would be handled in the compilations. In the collections of Rainerius, Gilbertus auctus and Alanus all significant elements are preserved, though some concluding comments (not outlined above) are absent. None of the early compilers considered substantive revision his prerogative. As noted, Bernard, followed by Peter, did cut the decretal critically: the letter appears under the title *De decimis* without Innocent's comments on imperial concessions and infeudated tithes. As is seen below, by dropping this portion of the response Bernard and Peter neatly bind Innocent's unrelieved disdain for the other evasions already refuted and these last two. For imperial concessions this elision is correct. In context the pope gives them no place. For infeudated tithes the emendation misrepresents Innocent's position. This is how the emended letter's critical passages appear in Bernard-Peter:

> Quidam insuper asserentes, se possessiones et omnia iura sua cum omni onere et districtu per imperialem concessionem adeptos, decimas sub huiusmodi generalitate detinere praesumunt. Occasione praeterea veteris decimationis, quam asserunt sibi concessam, aliqui decimas novalium non metuunt usurpare.

There follows Innocent's refutation of other dodges and then his comments on concessions and infeudation:

> Porro cum laicis nulla sit de spiritualibus concendendi attributa facultas, imperialis concessio, quantumcumque generaliter fiat, neminem potest a solutione decimarum eximere, quae divina constitutione debentur. Nec occasione decimationis antiquae, licet in feudum decimae sint concessae, sunt decimae novalium usurpandae, cum in talibus non sit extendenda licentia, sed potius restringenda.

Instead the text, marked with "Infra" to signify the gap, continues:

> Quoniam igitur pati nolumus, nec debemus ut ecclesiarum et clericorum iura presumptione qualibet miniantur, fraternitati tuae auctoritate presentium mandamus, quatenus omnes, qui ratione personarum aut etiam prediorum decimas ecclesiis et clericis tuae diocesis exhibere tenentur, ad eas cum integritate reddendas, appellatione remota, auctoritate apostolica compellas.

Bernard and Peter have retained the complaint in full but reported the judgment only in part with the result that all reasons appear denied and each *assertor* seems required to render tithes "ratione personarum aut etiam prediorum." In his narrative (which Bernard-Peter transmit) Innocent merely noted that some assert ("asserunt") an unspecified concession of *vetus decimatio*. But this seemed merely to equate their asserted right with the pretentions of others. In the full letter the other assertions are rejected. Only with Innocent's response is the possibility of infeudation of predial tithes conceded. Without that passage such claims appear equally specious. Bernard had vigorously edited the decretal both to preserve what was of value and to stifle what he perceived as harmful to the church. When Bernard and Peter pressed *Tua nobis* into service in *De iudiciis* they restored the passage on imperial concessions ("Porro si laicis . . . divina constitutione debentur") but avoided mention of *decimatio antiqua.*

Before we turn to *Tua nobis*'s treatment in French manuscripts and Italian glosses another *Tertia* decretal should be pointed out, since it deals with lay infeudation. *Cum apostolica,* addressed to the *magister scolarum* and a canon of the collegiate church of Saint-Oûtrille-du-Château in Bourges, dates from the first year of Innocent's reign.[17] The canons of Saint-Oûtrille challenged their bishop's sovereign right to bestow tithes donated by a layman on a church other than that from which the layman had acquired them. The canons insisted that the bishop must first get their approval. Without it he could not deprive a parish church of those tithes. Innocent supports the bishop's power by analogy to the required lone episcopal approval of any reception of churches and tithes "a manibus laicorum." Since the chapter had no function there, so the chapter should have no role in choice of a recipient. As Innocent drafted the decretal nothing is said about infeudation. But *Cum apostolica* has a fascinating textual tradition. Othmar Hageneder has shown that the decreatal first underwent revision in the papal register, where an unknown hand provided a fresh conclusion to the entry: "Hoc autem de his decimis intelligimus, que perpetuo sunt in feudum concesse."[18] The decretal is found in numerous collections before its appearance in the *Romana* and *Tertia*. In only one of the earlier works is the register addition included, in Rainerius's *Collectio,* but in all cases before the *Romana, Cum apostolica* appears in *De decimis.*

Now it would be better for the symmetry of the argument if Bernard or Peter had suppressed the allusion to infeudated tithes. They do not, and transmit it into the major commentaries and collections. But both collections diverge from Rainerius's and the other compilations by removing this decretal to the title *De his quae fiunt a prelato sine consensu capituli* (*Bern.* 3.13.1; *3 Comp.* 3.11.1). The focus is shifted from tithes to episcopal sovereignty. Further, the crucial addition provides for the cessation, not the institution or even the limitation of infeudated tithes. But above all, the allusion, even muted under a different title, demonstrates the great weakness of *all* medieval decretal collections when examined systematically: casual inclusion of contrary precedent. This difficulty goaded canonists to ingenious—and ingenuous—explications, prompted new collections to efface or counter such contradictions and eventually compelled Pope Gregory IX to commission a "final" compilation, the *Liber extra* to banish *contrarietas* from the decretal literature.[19] In balance then, *Cum apostolica* does not outweigh or seriously challenge Bernard's and Peter's object: to silence in *Tua nobis* Innocent's tolerance for limited lay possession and infeudation of tithes.

For this study thirty manuscripts of the *Compilatio tertia,* thirteen designated by Pennington as containing French interpolations and seventeen other manuscripts, were examined.[20] In four (or more correctly three, since MS Vat. lat. 2510 is a humanist copy of MS Vat. lat. 1378)—St. Omer MS 484, Graz MS 374, MSS Vat. lat. 1378 and 2510—the passage suppressed by Bernard-Peter resurfaces. In all three thirteenth-century manuscripts restoration occurs surprisingly in *De iudiciis* and only in MS Vat. lat. 1378 and its copy is a parallel change made under *De decimis.*

The French undoubtedly drew their fuller text from one of the pre-*Romana* compilations, likely that of Alanus, since all four of our manuscripts also include the single Alanus *capitulum* pointed out by Pennington. Did the restoration occur slowly as a marginal gloss migrated into the text or did the change occur in a single, conscious act? Pennington suggests in similar instances a slower infilatration.[21] In either case, the French, aware of a fuller text, revived that version in some *Tertia* manuscripts and exercised a critical independence from the official collection. We have found no Italian manuscript with this interpolation either in the text or added in the margin.

This is not to suggest that the Bolognese were uninterested in the problem. Rather we have no evidence that they revised their text. Among them, discussion of lay infeudation grew in the hot climate of debate over simony and the protection of ecclesiastical rights from lay infringement. The problem was explored also to determine whether tithes, specified as priestly income in the Old Testament and in church canons, could be extended to monks who were not priests. Though this last question has been examined meticulously by Giles Constable, there is no satisfactory modern study of the process that culminated in condoning lay tithe possession. How exactly the canonists travelled from Gratian's refusal to tolerate lay possession to thirteenth-century explanations that not only possession but infeudation (under certain conditions) was permissable, we do not know. Modern scholarship, however, places the mellowing of magisterial opinion in the late twelfth century and points to Huguccio, whose great *Summa* (after 1188) concludes the first age of canonistic commentary.[22]

Huguccio retains the traditional definition of tithes and oblations as "mere spirituale" which pertain only to "ecclesiasticis personis." But he parts from his colleagues when he abstracts from this *ius spirituale* a temporal element, i.e., the fruit or income derived from that right. This, he believes, can be possessed and even infeudated by laymen, since it is not a spiritual thing.[23]

But at least twenty years before Huguccio had proposed this distinction, a similar approach is implied in a French commentary, the *Summa Parisiensis:* "Item decimae semper ecclesiarum spiritualium sunt de numero, et secundum hoc quaeritur utrum simonia sit emere decimas, non dico fructus, sed ius decimationis."[24] This is not the occasion to trace the antecendents for Huguccio and the Paris master. Though there is disagreement as to whether the French *summa* should be dated c. 1160 or a decade later, in either case it antedates Huguccio.[25] The casual manner in which the Parisian *summa* tosses out the distinction—as if the author presumed the difference between *fructus* and *ius* would be on his reader's tongue—suggests its currency.

By the thirteenth century the possibility of lay possession of the *fructus decimarum* was common among the Bolognese as well. Once the taboo against such posssession had been ended, however, there remained the church's reluctance to see any more of its income alienated. And here is the purpose of Innocent's comments in *Tua nobis* on old and new tithes. If Innocent had conceded the infeudation of certain predial tithes, this was only incidental to the more pressing issue: resistance to tithes owed on agriculture and in particular usurpation of *novalia* by those who could demonstrate licit claim to *antiqua decimatio.* Accordingly the Bolognese masters, despite the silence of *Tua nobis* in the *Tertia,* comment on both aspects of the decretal.

Vicentius Hispanus, the only glossator whose surviving work spans the ages of the *compilationes antiquae* and the *Liber extra,* reveals his abiding interest in the *partes decisae,* the technical term for passages suppressed in canonical collections, when he wishes to make the point that possession of the fruit from predial tithes does not entitle the lay possessor to extend this privilege to *novalia:*

> Cum in talibus potius sit restringenda licentia quam amplianda prout dicitur in integra. Videtur tamen quod si cui concessa est vetus decimatio concedetur novalium. ar. infra c. prox. (*Ex parte tua; 3 Comp.* 3.23.3) sed hic loquitur cum laicis aliquibus privilegium huiusmodi concessum quod ut dixi restringendum est. Sed illud de privilegio religiosis indulto vel episcopis quod late interpretandum est; vel verius hic ab imperatore concessio facta fuit.[26]

Vincentius was sensitive to the authority of *Tua nobis,* though he did not hesitate to augment its papally authorized texts with pertinent deleted matter. Another master, Laurentius Hispanus, also utilized *Tua nobis* in an apparatus to the *Decretum,* the so-called *Glossa Palatina,* which assumed its definitive form c. 1215:

> quod [lay possession of tithes] fieri non debet ex i de decimis Prohibemus (*1 Comp.* 3.26.23). Unde nota quid bene fructus possunt dari laico ex causa. Sed ius decimale nequaquam nam aliud est ius aliud est ipsa res. Sicut dicit iurisperitus quod cum dicimus fructum victulum esse vacce non ius sed corpus demonstramus ff de evictionibus Vacce (*Dig.* 21.2.23). Possunt ergo dari decime i.e., res ipse in feodum. Sed tamen non transit ad heredes. ex i de decimis Ad hec (*1 Comp.* 3.26.27). Unde forte secundum quod proprie foedum acciperit non possunt dari. Accrescunt eis decimis novalium sed ecclesiis ex[tra] i[nnocentii] de decimis Tua nobis (*3 Comp.* 3.23.2).[27]

Acquaintance with a complete version of *Tua nobis* is also evident in the work of Tancred, the most influential glossator of the period, in his apparatus to the *Tertia* (1216–20). However, his citation to *Tua nobis,* unlike that of Vincentius, who distinguishes between the *Tertia* text and earlier versions, and unlike others which only refer to a *decretalis extravagans,* injects some ambiguity into the literature. Tancred counts five questions posed by Albert in *Tua nobis:* (1) expense deductions, (2) private disbursal of tithes, (3) refusal to support immoral clergy, (4) claims of exemption from payment based on imperial concessions, (5) lay usurpation of *novalia.* Methodically Tancred moves through them. At the juncture where Innocent responds to the last two, imperial concessions and lay usurpation, and where Peter had substituted "Infra" for Innocent's solution, Tancred observes: "Quarta non soluitur hic. Sed habes solutionem eius supra de iudiciis c.i lib. eodem (*Tua nobis; 3 Comp.* 2.1.1). Similiter quidam libri non habent solutionem quinte questionis."[28] Like Vincentius Tancred was aware of the full text and invokes a bit of it several lines later:

> Quoniam decimas sine peccato laici non possunt detinere ut xvi. q.i. c. ult. (*Quoniam quicquid;* c.68). Supra eodem titulo Prohibemus (*1 Comp.* 3.26.23) eodem Quam sit grave lib. ii. (*recte: Quamvis grave; 2 Comp.* 3.17.2) supra de his que fiunt ab episcopo sine consensu capituli c.i. lib. eodem (*Cum apostolica; 3 Comp.* 3.11.1). Et hec est causa quare non est extendenda licencia sed pocius restringenda quia odiosum est quod laicus percipiat

vel detineat decimas prediorum, supra de parochiis c.i. lib. ii (*Significavit nobis; 2 Comp.* 3.16 un.) T.[29]

This unacknowledged paraphrase of *Tua nobis* simply places Tancred among the many Bolognese masters who found the passage pertinent. But what did he mean by "quidam libri non habent solutionem quinte questionis"? One might presume that he alludes to the older collections used by the others. But might he mean other interpolated manuscripts of the *Compilatio tertia?* In fact, this is precisely what he does mean, since in an earlier work, his apparatus to the *Compilatio secunda* (1210–15; revised 1220) Tancred freely assigns the suppressed material to "Tua nobis in fi. lib. iii" while glossing the chapter *Quamvis grave* (*2 Comp.* 3.17.2):

> Et hoc ius non est ita spirituale ut primum ius. Immo est civile vel quasi et cadere potest in laicum etsi non in totum. Saltim quoad fructuum perceptionem, et secundum istud ius possideri possunt a laico in feudum concesse, ar. infra eodem Tua nobis in fi. lib. iii (*3 Comp.* 3.23.2) quod credo verum esse in decimis antiquitus concessis laicis. De novo autem nulle decime ei concedi possunt sicut nec alia feuda ut infra de feudis c.i. lib. iii (*Insinuatione presentium; 3 Comp.* 3.16.1) ar. hic ut supra eodem titulo Prohibemus (*1 Comp.* 3.26.23) supra de etate et qualitate Ex ratione lib. i. (*1 Comp.* 1.8.3) T.[30]

Can we believe that Tancred was familiar with an interpolated text or, even better, with an interpolated French manuscript? Or is this merely an error caused by excusable confusion between contents of an *extravagans* and *Tua nobis* in the *Tertia?* Given the thinness of our evidence, only a most hesitant hypothesis can be proposed that Tancred had seen "quidam libri" i.e. manuscripts of the *Compilatio tertia,* which contained the interpolation. There is no evidence for Italian manuscripts of this sort, and only scant examples of French texts. At best, the argument is inconclusive. What is clear, however, is that the greatest Bolognese master—and others undoubtedly— *thought* that *Tua nobis* in the *Tertia* conceded lay possession and specified its limitations. Equally important, other canonists made repeated use of a version of *Tua nobis* not transmitted in the common literature. Opinion reluctantly tolerated lay possession of the *fructus.* The French and the Bolognese insisted that their sources support this fact.

Some French canonists responded by restoring the silenced words. The Italians, on the other hand, do not seem to have tampered with the *Tertia* itself—or at least we have no manuscript to witness an interpolation to *Tua nobis.* Instead they supplemented the authoritative collection in their apparatuses with whatever was necessary, either advising the reader that the *Tertia* chapter had been edited injudiciously or noting that in another decretal not included in the collections an important opinion could be found. Tancred's comments fall into a third category, and, until either Italian *Tertia* manuscripts with interpolations appear or some solid proof of Tancred's acquaintance with "French" texts is developed, no conclusion is possible.

Among the French, of course, independent revision of *Tua nobis* had no consequence other than providing a few manuscripts reinforced with Innocent's concession and limitation. Among the Italians the result was substantial. Just as marginal comments in earlier manuscripts often migrate in later copies into the text itself, so in the decretal collections did the canonists' comments produce change.

These Italian references to *Tua nobis* come together in the work of Johannes Teutonicus. During an impressively fruitful three year period (1215–17) Johannes published his apparatus on the *Decretum* (1216–17), which became and remains the standard commentary, an apparatus for the canons of the Fourth Lateran Council (1216), the *Compilatio quarta* (1216), a collection that included the Lateran Council's canons complemented by decretals dispatched by Innocent since 1209, an apparatus to that collection, which for want of competition is also the authoritative gloss, and had begun his apparatus to the *Compilatio tertia,* not to be completed until 1220.[31]

Johannes had occasion to know his colleagues' interest in and confusion over *Tua nobis.* He lifted verbatim the *Glossa Palatina* section quoted above with its vague allusion to an *extravagans;* it is possible that he had knowledge of Tancred's *Tertia* gloss about *Tua nobis*'s diverse textual tradition and certainly had opportunity to read the same author's reference in the *Secunda* apparatus to a fuller version for the decretal. With this as background, Johannes installed the small section suppressed by Bernard and Peter in his new compilation under *De decimis* (4 *Comp.* 3.9.4). In his *Decretum* apparatus, Johannes can repair Laurentius's reference to read "extra iiii de decimis Tua nobis."

As a glossator Johannes has little to say about this tithes chapter, merely noting that it was part of the chapter *Tua nobis* which appears in the *Tertia,* and underlining the church's desire to restrain rather than enlarge such lay possession. In his *Tertia* apparatus, circulated about 1218, Johannes offers the standard decretalist advice about restraint and directs his reader, in most manuscripts, to the *Quarta* version of *Tua nobis.*[32] Henceforth the canonists have a firm locus for references to Innocent's comments on lay possession of old and new tithes.

If we ask from where Johannes took his text, the most likely candidates are the fuller, pre-*Romana* collections. There is slight possibility that he ventured into the papal registers since he labored in great haste.[33] Despite juggling the four other projects, he completed his collection within nine months after conclusion of the great council. Not surprisingly, Johannes depended heavily on earlier collections.

The ultimate destiny of *Tua nobis*'s voyages among the compilations comes in Raymond of Peñafort's *Liber extra,* commissioned by Pope Gregory IX to provide in one volume a harmonious and authoritative sourcebook for use in schools and courts. The decretal spans two chapters in the title *De decimis* (X 3.30.25–6). There is no doubt that Raymond used the *Tertia* for c.26, Innocent's catalogue of dodges; most likely, he took c.25 on lay infeudation and *novalia* from the *Quarta.* In both instances, however, he has made some adjustment.

In c.25 Raymond has gone one step further in restoring the text. He has appropriated, probably from *3 Comp.* 2.1.1. where Peter had consigned a segment of *Tua nobis,* the initial passage: "Porro cum laicis nulla sit de spiritualibus concedendi vel disponendi facultas" to provide a preface and the rationale for Innocent's comments on imperial concessions, lay infeudation and *novalia.* The second chapter is not expanded, but curtailed. Raymond deletes the narrative segment "Quidam insuper asserentes . . . non metuunt usurpare," which in the *Tertia* presentation had suggested that lay possession was impossible. In light of magisterial opinion that culminated in the *Quarta's* reinstatement of *Tua nobis,* such revision by Raymond was timely.

The *Compilatio tertia* enjoyed considerable appreciation among the canonists. It was *the* great decretal collection before the *Liber extra,* which it so deeply colors; it set a standard for authority with its papal promulgation. Yet its contents were not beyond criticism. *Tua nobis* poses a case in which not the decretal itself but its manipulation in the collection was challenged. Among both the French, who seem not to have developed a tradition of glosses to either the *Tertia* or any of the other compilations, and the Italians, who intensively commented on the decretals, the authority of the *Tertia* did not restrain interest in the use of material suppressed by that compilation. The French agressively restored the decretal; the Italians achieved the same end in their apparatuses, which in turn prompted reintegration of *Tua nobis* into the common academic literature. Not pope, not collection but the masters who served the one and created and commented on the other ultimately determined the content of this decretal chapter.

Institute of Medieval Canon Law
University of California, Berkeley

Notes

1. Stephan Kuttner, "Les Débuts de l'École canoniste française," *Studia et documenta historiae et juris* IV (1938), 202–4; Kuttner, *Repertorium der Kanonistik (1140–1234),* Studi e Testi LXXI (Vatican City, 1937), pp. 168-207, for the French school.

2. Gérard Fransen, "Les diverses Formes de la Compilatio prima," *Scrinium Lovaniense: Mélanges historiques Étienne Van Cauwenbergh, Recueil de Travaux d'Histoire et de Philologie* XXIV, 4th series (Louvain, 1961), pp. 235–53; "La Tradition manuscrite de la 'Compilatio prima,' " *Proceedings of the Second International Congress of Medieval Canon Law,* Monumenta iuris canonici Series C: Subsidia I (Vatican City, 1965), pp. 55–70, discussion p. 101. The French group reveals ten omissions and between twenty-one and twenty-four additions. Kenneth Pennington, "The French Recension of Compilatio tertia," *Bulletin of Medieval Canon Law,* n.s. V (1975), 53–71. For editions of the compilations see Emil Friedberg, *Quinque compilationes antiquae* (Leipzig, 1882), which must be used cautiously in tandem with his *Corpus iuris canonici* II (Leipzig, 1881). An alternative to Friedberg's cumbersome edition is that of Antonio Agustín, *Antiquae collectiones decretalium* (ed. princ. Lérida, 1576). For background on the compilations, Kuttner, *Repertorium,* pp. 322–44, 355–68.

3. Pennington, "French Recension," pp. 53–71. For the *Compilatio Romana*, see Kuttner, "Bernardus Compostellanus Antiquus: A Study in the Glossators of the Canon Law," *Traditio* I (1943), 277–78, 327–33. A summary edition with a fine introduction was published by Heinrich Singer, *Die Dekretalensammlung des Bernardus Compostellanus antiquus*, Wiener Sitzungsberichte CLXXI (Vienna, 1914). Also see, Friedrich Heyer, "Die Dekretalensammlungen aus dem 1. Jahrzehnt des 13. Jahrhunderts," *Zeitschrift der Savigny–Stiftung für Rechtsgeschichte*, Kan. Abt. IV (1934), 583–608.

4. Singer, *Dekretalensammlung*, pp. 17–29; Kuttner, "Bernardus," pp. 327–28; Rudolf von Heckel, "Die Dekretalensammlungen des Gilbertus und Alanus nach den Weingartener Handschriften," *Zeitschrift der Savigny-Stiftung für Rechtsgeschichte*, Kan. Abt. XXXIX (1940), 170–72.

5. Bernard lists five decretals he deems spurious: *Miramur non modicum, Ex litteris, De Prudentia, Queris, Super consultatione*, Singer, *Dekretalensammlung*, pp. 114–15. Christopher Cheney favorably gauges Bernard's accuracy in excluding these letters from the Innocentian corpus, "Three Decretal Collections before Compilatio IV: Pragensis, Palatina I, and Abricensis I," *Traditio* XV (1959), 480–83. For Singer's doubts on Bernard's criteria, see his preface, pp. 29–30.

6. "Tandem magister Bernardus Compostellanus archidiaconus, in curia Romana moram faciens aliquantam, de registris domini Innocentii Papae unam fecit decretalium compilationem, quam Bononiae studentes Romanam compilationem vocaverunt. Verum quia in ipsa compilatione quaedam reperiebantur decretales, quas Romana curia refutabat, sicut hodie quaedam sunt in secundis, quas curia non recepit, idcirco felicis recordationis Dominus Innocentius Papa III suas decretales usque ad annum xii. editas, per magistrum Petrum Beneventanum, notarium suum, in presenti opere compilatas, Bononiae studentibus destinavit." Tancred offers this in his historical preface to his apparatus on the *Compilatio tertia*, which has been printed by Ernest Laspeyres, *Bernardi Papiensis Faventini episcopi Summa decretalium* (Regensberg, 1860), pp. 356–57. For what Tancred means by "decretals which the Roman curia refuted" see Singer, *Dekretalensammlung*, pp. 29–32; Kuttner, "Bernardus," p. 331.

7. Friedberg, *Quinque compilationes*, p. 105.

8. For traces of the *Romana* in decretal glosses of Ambrosius, Albertus, Laurentius, Tancred and Vincentius, see Kuttner, "Bernardus," pp. 311–33.

9. Singer, *Dekretalensammlung*, pp. 27–28; Kuttner, "Bernardus," p. 331.

10. Pennington, "French Recension," pp. 53–59. Only item 15 can be traced to another collection, that of Alanus. Heckel found it in the appendix of his Fulda MS D.14 (c.55), and Kuttner places it as part of the mature redaction (1.9.3) found in Vercelli, Cathedral Chapter, MS LXXXIX. Heckel, "Gilbertus und Alanus," p. 319; Kuttner, "The Collection of Alanus: A Concordance of its Two Recensions," *Revista di Storia del Diritto* XXVI (1953), 37–53. The two other items (14, 24): 14 is known in no other source and 24 is found in only a single French manuscript, Paris, Bibl. nat., MS lat. 14611 and, according to Pennington, perhaps is not a true interpolation but only an appendix.

11. Pennington, "French Recension," pp. 63–64.

12. Potthast 898; edition, É. Baluze, in PL CCXIV: 802–4, (*Reg.* II: 242); Rainerius of Pomposa, ed. É. Baluze, PL CCXVI: 1174–1272; for Gilbert, Alanus and Johannes, see note 10. *Tua nobis* was at least the second papal consideration of abuse of tithes in Vercelli, since Pope Alexander III had addressed the decretal *Querela venerabilis* to the archbishop of Milan to restrain both laymen and clergy from usurpation of novial tithes. JL 14105; *1 Comp.* 3.26.1.

13. The standard monographs on tithes were published by Paul Viard, *Histoire de la Dîme ecclésiastique principalement en France jusqu'au Décret de Gratien* (Dijon, 1909), pp. 205–31 for lay possession; *Histoire de la Dîme ecclésiastique dans le Royaume de France aux xiie et xiiie Siècles*, (Paris, 1912), pp. 118–65; "La Dîme ecclésiastique dans le Royaume d'Arles et de Vienne aux xiie et xiiie Siècles," *Zeitschrift der Savigny-Stiftung für Rechtsgeschichte*, Kan. Abt. I (1911), 126–59, especially 145–59; also, Catherine Boyd, *Tithes and Parishes in Medieval Italy* (Ithaca, 1952), pp. 57–157; Giles Constable, *Monastic Tithes from their Origins to the Twelfth*

Century, (Cambridge, England, 1964), pp. 63–65; Giles Constable, "Resistance to Tithes in the Middle Ages," *Journal of Ecclesiastical History* XIII (1962), 184–85; P. Thomas, *Le Droit de Propriété au Moyen âge,* Bibliothèque de l'École des Hautes études: Sciences réligieuses XIX (Paris, 1906), pp. 25–27; 82–88; for Spain, Jesus San Martin, *El Diezmo ecclesiastico en España hasta el Siglo XII* (Palencia, 1940), pp. 135–44; Robert Burns, "A Medieval Income Tax: The Tithe in the Thirteenth-Century Kingdom of Valencia," *Speculum* XLI (1966), 438–52, and more recently in *The Crusader Kingdom of Valencia: Reconstruction on a Thirteenth-Century Frontier* (Cambridge, Mass. 1967) pp. 144–72. For the canonists the literature is slight, see Erwin Melichar, "Der Zehent als Kirchensteuer bei Gratian," *Studia Gratiana* II (1954), 104–7.

    14. *Decretum,* C. 16 q. 7 c. 1 *(Decimas).*

    15. Bernard of Pavia, *Summa decretalium,* 3.26.10, ed. Laspeyres, p. 107.

    16. Gérard Fransen, *Les Collections canoniques,* Typologie des Sources du Moyen âge occidental X (Turnhout, 1973), p. 50 draws our attention to the nuances of collections and recalls Gabriel LeBras's comment: " . . .tout un monde discordant de sentiments et d'idées, que les anciens érudits avient à peine entrevu, nous est révélé par les textes et encore mieux par le *choix,* le *groupement* des textes dans les collections." ("Notes pour servir à l'Histoire des Collections canoniques," *Revue d'Histoire de Droit Francais et étranger* XI, 4th series [1932], 158–60.) Charles Duggan, *Twelfth-Century Decretal Collections and Their Importance in English History,* University of London Historical Studies XII (London, 1963), underlines the selectivity of collections and warns us (p. 5) to distinguish "the general policies of the legislator [from] the local or specialist predilections of the compiler." The leverage exerted by collectors and collections in the late twelfth and early thirteenth centuries is set out by Knut Nörr, "Päpstliche Dekretalen und römisch-kanonischer Zivilprozess," *Studien zur europäischen Rechtsgeschichte* (Frankfurt am Main, 1972), pp. 54–56.

    17. Potthast 322. The letter, *Reg.* i: 313, is printed in the Baluze edition, PL CCXIV: 272–73, but should be consulted in *Die Register Innocenz' III.: 1. Pontifikatsjahr 1198/99,* eds. Othmar Hageneder and Anton Haidacher, Publikationen der Abteilung für historische Studien des Österreichischen Kulturinstituts in Rom I (Graz-Cologne, 1964), no. 313 (444–45). Its tradition in decretal collections: *Collectio Fuldensis* 3.20.6; *Gilbertus* 3.17.6; *Collectio Halensis* (Analysis: F. Heyer, "Dekretalensammlungen," p. 592); *Bern.* 3.13.1; 3 Comp. 3.11.1; X 3.10.7.

    18. The addition (which Baluze presumed to be part of the original text) was made sometime before Rainerius consulted the register (1201). However, the passage on infeudated tithes was not included in any other collection before Bernard's. For interpolations to the register, see Othmar Hagender, "Die äusseren Merkmale der Original-register Innocenz' III.," *Mitteilungen des Instituts für österreichische Geschichtsforschung* LXV (1957), 314–15.

    19. In the case of *Cum apostolica,* William of Rennes, author of the apparatus for Raymond of Peñafort's *Summa de casibus,* (before 1254) dismisses *Cum apostolica*'s authority on lay infeudation: "in illo capitulo recitatur factum, non constituitur ius." *Summa de casibus* (Rome, 1603), p. 128, s.v. *concessae.* The spirit of the *Liber extra* is expressed by Gregory in the bull of promulgation, *Rex pacificus:* "Sane diversas constitutiones et decretales epistolas predecessorum nostrorum, in diversa dispersas volumina, quarum aliquae propter nimiam similitudinem, et quaedam propter contrarietatem, nonnullae etiam propter sui prolixitatem, confusionem inducere videbantur, aliquae vero vagabantur extra volumina supradicta, quae tamquam incertae frequenter in iudiciis vacillabant, ad communem, et maxime studentium, utilitatem per dilectum fratrem Raymundum, capellanum et poenitentiarum nostrum, illas in unum volumen resecatis superfluis providimus redigendas, adiicientes constitutiones nostras et decretales epistolas, per quas nonnulla, quae in prioribus erant dubia, declarantur." Printed in Friedberg, *Corpus iuris canonici,* II: 1–4.

    20. No emendations were found in Pennington's MSS D, F, Lu, N, Pe, Pm, R, Ro, Vb. In MSS in which Pennington found no variation, none occurs around *Tua nobis.* I examined: Admont 22 and 55; Bamberg, Staatsbibl., Can. 19 and 20; Cordoba, Bibl. del Cabildo 10; Florence, Laur., S. Croce IV.sin.2; Graz, Univ., 106 and 138; Karlsruhe, Landesbibl., Aug. XL; Kassel iur. 11; Leipzig, Univ., 983; London, Brit. Libr., Royal 11 C.VII; Melk 333 and

518; Munich, Staatsbibl., lat. 3879; Padua, Bibl. Ant., N.35; Vat. lat. 1377.

21. Pennington, "French Recension," p. 63.

22. Boyd, *Tithes and Parishes,* p. 172; John Baldwin, *Masters, Merchants and Princes: The Social Views of Peter the Chanter and His Circle* (Princeton, 1970), I: 232. Bernard of Parma, author of the *Glossa ordinaria* to the *Liber extra* (several recensions between c. 1241–66) concedes the validity of *antiqua decimatio,* while rejecting new concessions or the older's extention to *novalia:* "Et ea fuit causa quare olim antiquis temporibus dabantur in feudum laicis, et etiam alia feuda, ut, videlicet defenderent ecclesias ab hereticis, et ab aliis oppressoribus. Postea cum causa cessavit, non fuerant concesse; immo expresse fuit prohibitum; quia sine peccato laici non possunt eas retinere supra de his que fiunt a prelato c. Cum apostolica (X 3.10.7) et infra eodem Prohibemus (X 3.30.19). Et decimas ab antiqua concessas adhuc possident laici et eorum successores; tamen si aliqua novalia consurgunt, in decimatione non accrescunt eis. infra eodem Tua nobis (X 3.30.25) propter rationem, que ibi redditur in fine. Bernardus." *Decretales Gregorii IX una cum glossa* (Venice, 1591), *Quamvis grave* (X 3.30.17) v. *concessit.* Raymond of Peñafort, whose attitudes were so pivotal to the shape of the *Liber extra* recognized the validity of a similar concession made to the knights of the reconquista and secured with papal privilege: ". . . si privilegium fuit concessum in perpetuum sibi, et suis successoribus ita quod fuit reale [et non personale] et propter hanc tam favorabilem causam, et a Sede Apostolica, possunt licite tenere, vel ad tempus, vel in perpetuum, iuxta formam in privilegio expressum." The bracketed words represent Raymond's addition to his *Summa de casibus* in its post-1234 redaction; the first version (c. 1224) is taken from Oxford Univ., Bodl. MS 146, fol. 162vb; the second version, which circulates in printed editions, was published c. 1235 (Rome, 1603), p. 129. For the changes and dating, see Kuttner, "Die Enstehungsgeschichte der Summa de casibus poenitentiae des hl. Raymund von Penyafort," *Zeitschrift der Savigny-Stiftung für Rechtsgeschichte.* Kan. Abt. XXXIX (1953), 410–34.

23. The older decretist position is elaborated by Rufinus (c. 1157–59): "Sciendum est enim quod ius ecclesiasticum aliud corporale, aliud spirituale. Corporale est quod potest competere etiam laicis, ut possessionum; spirituale est quod numquam potest competere nisi ecclesiasticis personis, ut: decimarum, oblationum. (C. 16 q.7 c.26 [*Pie mentis*]). *Summa decretorum,* ed. Heinrich Singer (Paderborn, 1902), p. 370. Huguccio retains Rufinus's passage, but had already demonstrated that aside from the purely spiritual, there was a related aspect that could be given, sold or possessed by a layman: "Ad hoc dicendum quod duplex est ius decimarum, scilicet, ius spirituale quod competit tantum ecclesie quod provenit intuitu ecclesiastici obsequii et hoc laicus habere non potest, sed nec clericus nisi nomine ecclesie. Ius decimarum dicitur ius percipiendi eas quia ratione feudi hoc ius feudatarium laici habere possunt": Admont MS 7, fol. 287rb. Huguccio repeats Rufinus's hard line on fol. 289va. For Huguccio, see Kuttner, *Repertorium,* pp. 155–60; for recent bibliography see Alfons Stickler's article, "Huguccio," in the *New Catholic Encyclopedia* (1967), VII: 200–201.

24. *The Summa Parisiensis on the Decretum Gratiani,* ed. Terence McLaughlin (Toronto, 1952), p. 79 (C.1 q.1).

25. McLaughlin proposed c. 1160. For a later dating used here, see Kuttner, *Repertorium,* p. 177.

26. Apparatus to *3 Comp.* 3.23.2 s.v. *usurpare,* Leipzig MS 983, fol. 148 rb. For Vincentius's appreciation of the *partes decisae* see Javier Ochoa Sanz, *Vincentius Hispanus: Canonista Boloñes del Siglo XIII,* Cuadernos del Instituto Juridico Español XIII (Rome, 1960), pp. 7–9. Vincentius had depended for this gloss on Laurentius Hispanus, Apparatus to *3 Comp.* 3.23.2 s.v. *metuunt,* Karlsruhe MS Aug. XL (no foliation). Tancred repeats the comment as well in his *Tertia* apparatus s.v. *non metuunt:* MS Vat. lat. 2509, fol. 228ra.

27. Vatican, MS. Reg. lat. 977, fol. 83vb, C.1 q.3 c.13 *(Pervenit)* s.v. *laicalibus.* For Laurentius as the author of the apparatus, see Alfons Stickler, "Il Decretista Laurentius Hispanus," *Studia Gratiana* IX (1966), 463–549.

28. Apparatus to *3 Comp.* 3.23.2 s.v. *Infra.* MS Vat. lat. 2509, fol. 228va.

29. Apparatus to *3 Comp.* 3.23.2 s.v. *reddendas.* MS Vat. lat. 2509, fol. 228vb.

30. Apparatus to *2 Comp.* 3.17.2 s.v. *concesserit,* Padua, Bibl. Ant., MS N.35 (first recen-

sion), fol. 103rb–va; the gloss is the same in the second recension, MS Vat. lat. 1377, fol. 124vab. For the two versions of the apparatus, see S. Kuttner, "La Reserve papale du Droit de Canonisation," *Revue Historique de Droit français et Etrange* XVII, 4th series (1938), 203, n.3; *Repertorium*, p. 327, 346; "Bernardus Compostellanus," p. 311, n.15.

31. For Johannes, S. Kuttner, "Johannes Teutonicus, das vierte Laterankonzil und die Compilatio quarta," *Miscellanea Giovanni Mercati*, Studi e Testi CXXV (Vatican City, 1946), pp. 608–34.

32. The pure Johannine apparatus to the *Decretum* is taken from Vatican, MS Pal. lat. 625, fol. 75va *(Pervenit)* s.v. *laicalibus;* For the *Quarta* apparatus, see Kuttner, "Johannes Teutonicus," pp. 627–28; Pennington, "The Manuscripts of Johannes Teutonicus's Apparatus to Compilatio Tertia: Considerations on the Stemma," *Bulletin of Medieval Canon Law*, n.s. IV (1974), 17–21. In one manuscript, Vatican, MS Ottob. lat. 1099, fol. 24rb the citation differs: whereas the main tradition commonly points only to the *Quarta* version of *Tua nobis*, here a double citation is made: "Cum in talibus restringenda sit licencia quam amplianda ut dicitur in extra iiii vel iii eodem titulo Tua." I have found one other contemporary writer who deals with the decretal's two parts in this style, Raymond of Peñafort. In his *Summa de casibus* (first recension) Oxford, Bodl. MS 146, fol. 162vb the same twin reference occurs. Whether Johannes or Raymond implied that in either collection there could be read "cum in talibus . . . amplianda" or, as is more likely, suggested that in the *Tertia* the problem was posed and in the *Quarta* was resolved, cannot be said.

33. Kuttner, "Johannes Teutonicus," pp. 619–23, 626–27; Cheney, "Three Decretal Collections," pp. 467–68.

IV
CHURCH AND SOCIETY

Oikonomia in Byzantine Canon Law

JOHN H. ERICKSON

It would be difficult for the historian of Byzantine church or state to avoid the subject of ecclesiastical *oikonomia*. In virtually all the great constitutional crises of the empire—in the moechian affair, for example, arising from the divorce and remarriage of Emperor Constantine VI, or the tetragamy affair, so called from the fourth marriage of Emperor Leo the Wise, or in a later period the divisions resulting from the various attempts at ecclesiastical reunion with the Roman church—the word *oikonomia* figures prominently in the primary sources. In the last few decades the term has entered the vocabulary of the secondary literature as well. Recognizing the inadequacy of explaining Byzantine church history simply in terms of caesaropapism and its opponents, many recent historians have favored a subtler analysis of the relationship of Byzantine church and state, distinguishing throughout the centuries between those "prelates and statesmen who, in times of crisis or necessity, were prepared to exercise a little tolerance or accept a certain amount of compromise in ecclesiastical affairs for reasons of state, so long as the fundamentals of the faith were not affected," and "those who refused to allow the right of the Emperor or the State to make even the smallest deviation from the strict principles of Orthodoxy"; between "those who would in certain cases apply the principle of *oikonomia* and those whose watchword was *akribeia*";[1] between the "moderates" and the "extremists," the "politiques" and the "zealots," the "economists" and the "rigorists."[2]

References to that "peculiarly Byzantine concept,"[3] that "famous principle" of *oikonomia* are numerous, as are convenient working definitions, according to which *oikonomia* is "the liberal policy of compromise in matters not concerning the fundamentals of the faith,"[4] or "elasticity in the interest of the Christian community," or "the relaxing of disciplinary canons—regarding the performance of the sacraments but *not* dogma—for the benefit, possibly political, of the community."[5] Yet, for all this interest in the "concept" or "principle" of *oikonomia* there has been little serious historical investigation of the word *oikonomia* itself, of its meanings and usages, technical or otherwise, in Byzantium, whether by professional historians or by specialists in Eastern canon law.[6] Instead, often from just a few isolated quotations, a monolithic "concept of *oikonomia*" is inferred (with ambiguities or imprecision in this concept ascribed to "the well-known freedom which characterizes the Orthodox Church"[7]). As a result of this illicit abstraction, the existence

225

and development of specific, well-defined uses of the term are ignored or obscured, while at the same time certain clearly nontechnical uses are distorted beyond recognition. (For example, with monotonous regularity the verb *oikonomein,* in contexts requiring nothing beyond the obvious "to administer or manage," is rendered as "to apply Economy.")[8] One begins to suspect that our "famous concept of *oikonomia,*" as a guide through the complexities of Byzantine church history, may be only slightly more reliable than the older, and now discredited caesaropapism.

Such considerations prompt the present survey of *oikonomia* in Byzantium. Its purpose is not to distinguish and trace a "principle" or "concept" of *oikonomia* but rather to examine a few key words, like *oikonomia* and *akribeia,* that occur frequently in Byzantine canonical texts and other literature dealing with church affairs, to see how these words are used in periods of relative calm as well as in moments of crisis. Two principle technical uses of *oikonomia* emerge, one closely connected with the administration of penance and concerned with the individual sinner, the other and broader use stressing the general well-being of the whole church. Closer investigation of these two uses, in turn, not only gives greater precision to our understanding of *oikonomia* in Byzantium but also sheds new light on several important episodes in Byzantine church history.

Of the meanings of *oikonomia,* the most obvious one is the most often ignored in discussions of the "concept of economy": management, arrangement, determination, in the strictly literal sense. In fact, emphasis at this point should be placed more on the verb *oikonomein* than on the substantive; for, as in pre-Christian usage, this is the form more often encountered, and the substantive itself, often found with an objective genetive, has a strongly verbal thrust: *oikonomia tinos,* the management, disposition, or "handling" of something.[9]

A few overtones add color to this basic meaning:

1. *Oikonomia* implies the idea of stewardship, of management on behalf of another, of a superior, ultimately of God. Hence prudent, responsible management is in order.

2. This human economy/management should imitate the divine economy. Of the nine columns in Lampe's *Patristic Greek Lexicon* devoted to *oikonomia, oikonomein, oikonomikos,* etc. roughly half of the citations have God as their subject: it is He who arranges all for the purpose of man's salvation and eternal well-being; and man, fashioned after the image and likeness of God, is called to imitate this divine activity.

This notion of *oikonomia* as theomimetic stewardship suggests the heavy theological content and highly positive connotations that the word had in Byzantium. This fact should not be lost sight of, nor has it been in recent studies of *oikonomia.*[10] Indeed, so great is emphasis on this point that a compensatory *monitum* is perhaps in order: the word can and does often retain a strictly neutral meaning. When, for example, the First Council of Constantinople (canon 2) enjoins "ton men Alexandreias episkopon ta en Aiguptō monon oikonomein, tous de tēs Anatolēs episkopous tēn Anatolēn

. . . diokein . . . kai tous tēs Asianēs dioikeiseōs ta kata tēn Asian monēn oikonomein," clearly "oikonomein" means "to administer or manage," a pure and simple synonym for "dioikein"; and although such management should be good, it certainly could be bad.

Technical usages of the word *oikonomia* in canonical literature reflect this essentially neutral meaning. The most obvious deals with administration of the actual material goods of a church or monastery by a professional steward (*oikonomos*). But close at hand is another usage: the fiscal administration of the *oikonomos* is paralleled by the pastoral care exercised by the *oikonomos tōn psuchōn,* pastoral care extending to all aspects of church life but centering on the administration of penance, on the cure of souls, on managing the terms of a penitent's reconciliation to the church. Hence the most precise and most often encountered use of *oikonomia* as a *terminus technicus* in Byzantine canon law: "the apportionment or disposition of a penance." For example, the form-letter for commissioning a spiritual father or confessor enjoins the recipient "to administer penance" [oikonomein tēn metanoian].[11] What this "administering" might involve can be seen in a typical canon from the canonical epistles of Basil the Great (c. 56):

> He who has committed willful murder, but has afterwards repented, shall not be a partaker of the sacraments for twenty years. The twenty years will be thus administered [*oikonomēthēsetai*] in his case: for four years he ought to 'mourn,' standing outside the doors of the house of prayer, and beseeching the faithful as they enter to make supplication in his behalf, and confessing his own lawlessness. And after four years he shall be received among the 'hearers'; and for five years he shall go out with them. For seven years he shall go out praying with those in 'prostration.' For four years he shall only stand with the faithful, but he shall not participate in the oblation. But, when those years have been accomplished, he shall share in the sacraments.[12]

Oikonomia thus understood obviously could be practiced in quite a wooden manner, with Basil's suggested arrangements followed to the letter. Hence, though the words *oikonomia* and *akribeia* often occur in the same context, no opposition between them need be involved. At least one Byzantine writer speaks of "economizing according to exactness."[13] But more frequent are texts suggesting that the prudent steward of souls will not rigidly keep to the prescribed terms of public penance, but will consider the circumstances of the case at hand. Of the patristic texts regularly cited as precedents for abandoning severity and for adopting "philanthropy" in assigning penances, a canon of Gregory of Nyssa (c. 5) may be quoted *pars pro toto:*

> For those who have proved the more zealous in their conversion and who show by their manner of life their return to the good, he who manages things profitably [*eksesti tō oikonomounti pros to sumpheron*] by means of ecclesiastical *oikonomia* can shorten the length of time required for a "hearer" and make him more quickly a "stander" and then shorten the length of time again, restoring him more quickly to communion . . . depending, again, on the state of the person being treated.[14]

In the many Byzantine texts that advocate this relaxation of penitential discipline, *oikonomia* often receives a qualifying adjective: *sumpathētikos* or *sunkatabatikos,* compassionate or condescending; and at times *oikonomia* without any qualification at all comes to mean this sympathetic modification of the terms of penance. Obviously much was left to the discretion of the confessor. But deposition awaited the one who "economized" simply out of human affection.[15] The sympathy, philanthropy and condescension to be demonstrated by the steward of the souls are not simply human affections but imitate Christ, and the resulting "economy" is not capricious or arbitrary but rather is based on an objective assessment of the plight of the sinner and how to remedy his situation. The steward of souls is obliged to consider whether the sin itself was committed knowingly or out of ignorance or stupidity, deliberately or out of fear and compulsion. He must take into account the total fabric of who and what the individual sinner is: his condition in life, his age, his marital status, etc. And, even more than these "prelapsarian" factors, he must assess the sinner's zeal for amendment of life, the sincerity of his repentance, and above all, whether he has given up his sin.[16]

This penitential meaning of *oikonomia* is not only well-attested in "everyday" canonical literature; it also is absolutely central in at least one major crisis of Byzantine church and state: the so-called tetragamy affair. The chronology of events surrounding Leo VI's fourth marriage, the personal vendettas involved, the underlying party strife, all have been scrutinized closely;[17] but *oikonomia,* though regarded as the central issue in dispute, simply has been taken for granted and hence left undefined or ill-defined (e.g., as "a decision of the church to make a special case of the marriage, so that it could be recognized and condoned").[18] Yet the episode cannot be reduced so simply to a squabble over the issuing of a marriage license. At the time, at least, it was understood as a case of sin and its remedy.

By wedding his dark-eyed Zoe, Leo had committed a grave offense. The canons of the eastern church, trying to uphold the ideal of perpetual monogamy, subjected second and third marriages to penances and condemned fourth marriages altogether, as "worse than fornication"[19] and demanding not only penance but also separation. As a result, Leo was excluded from the sacraments of the church and from all aspects of its life, including the solemn ritual of entering Hagia Sophia with the patriarch. Literally left standing at the doors of the church, Leo as a sinner begs the passing metropolitans to receive him, like the prodigal son. As a sinner he begs entrance to the church "as far as the railings," that is, to the official penitential station for "weepers," to begin to do penance for his sin.[20]

Difficulty arose not over "the principle of *oikonomia,*" for all the parties involved would accept the possibility of a speedy restoration for a repentant sinner, but rather over the legality of Leo's marriage. If Leo's marriage were permissible, *oikonomia* would be a fairly simple matter, his restoration to the church no problem. Hence the early efforts of Leo's supporters to prove that the fathers at least tolerated fourth marriages, permitted them by *sunchōresis* or *sunkatabasis (not* by *oikonomia).* On the other hand, if Leo's union is not a marriage but rather fornication, he obviously must separate from his partner before his return to the church can be "economized." Now that Zoe has delivered a son, Leo is told, she should be cast forth like Hagar; like a barge that has unloaded she should be sent to sea.[21] But Leo, whose only son's right to rule might be challenged were he to be considered illegitimate, refused to abandon his "marriage." Hence, a dilemma for the church: to economize without previous separation would imply toleration of the marriage, would imply that the church gives license to sin.

But not all insisted on recognizing these implications. For his part, Patriarch Nicholas Mystikos repeatedly insisted that if everyone else would accept Leo, he too would do so.[22] Entrusted with the task of maintaining the fragile religious peace established only a few years before between the Photian and Ignatian parties, he had to insist on unanimity. But unanimity eluded him. Under pressure, he resigns. It is left to his successor, Euthymius, to accept Leo as a penitent without demanding separation. But the conclusion that Leo's union with Zoe is a true marriage is assiduously avoided: Euthymius refuses to proclaim Zoe as Augusta, the priest who blessed the union is deposed, and the synod declares not only fourth, but even third marriages illegitimate.[23]

This convenient if hypocritical solution is easily rejected with righteous indignation when Nicholas Mystikos is restored to the patriarchate. In his letter to Pope Anastasius III, denouncing Rome's role in the affair, Nicholas eloquently sets forth the demands of penitential *oikonomia:*

> Is it in the power of Rome so to 'economize' that a lawbreaker goes unpunished, and with impure hands lays hold on what is holy? And to lead back into the divine precincts, whence they have been rightly expelled, those who have been driven forth for pollution, even though they have not put their pollution aside? This would be a mighty authority indeed of which you are possessed—an authority possessed not even by Him who "taketh away the sins of the world," let alone by any other, whether of His holy disciples or of the other teachers of the church! He indeed came to bear our sins, but, naturally, only when we have ceased to sin, not when we are cleaving to and performing without scruple those things which He "taketh away." I hear his injunction to the man He has healed: "Lo, thou art whole! Go and sin no more!" . . . Where have you discovered this unseemly *oikonomia*, which does not lighten the burden of sin, but makes it heavier? Which brings no salvation, but surrenders to destruction? . . . *Oikonomia* is a concession unto salvation, saving him who has sinned, stretching out the arm of help, and lifting up the fallen from his fall; not permitting him to lie where he has fallen nor rather pushing him toward a miserable pit. *Oikonomia* is an imitation of the divine mercy, a snatching out of the jaws of the beast that howls against us. . . . But he who still commits the sin is by no means snatched away: but only he who by the divine expedient of this *oikonomia* puts himself far off from his sin, and avoids its pursuit of him.[24]

Such is the meaning of *oikonomia* in the tetragamy affair. In this penitentially oriented understanding of the word, *oikonomia* clearly does not mean legalizing Leo's marriage, "making a special case of the marriage, so that it could be recognized and condoned." It is not a counterpart to the West's *dispensatio ad faciendum,* a temporary derogation from a law, a license (to put it crudely) to do something otherwise prohibited. It most assuredly does not imply "a little tolerance," "a certain amount of compromise in ecclesiastical affairs for reasons of state." Yet in Byzantium the word *oikonomia* was also used with another shade of meaning, one closer to that implied in the "concept of *oikonomia*" as understood by modern scholars. *Oikonomia* could be "an imitation of the divine mercy," "saving him who has sinned, stretching out the arm of help, and lifting up the fallen from his fall." But it could also imply accommodation, prudent adaption of means to an end, diplomacy and strategy, verging on dissimulation and the "pious lie."[25] Thus far we have seen the *oikonomos* as *iatros,* as physician, curing by means of appropriate medicines in appropriate doses the sin-sick souls that come to him. We now see the *oikonomos* as *kubernētēs,* as the pilot of a ship at sea, relaxing the tiller to avoid capsize, jettisoning what is less important to save the cargo, or steering between the scylla and charybdis of the day. *Oikonomia* in this sense of accommodation frequently occurs not only in secular but also in patristic literature, particularly in biblical exegesis, where the word is used to describe otherwise embarrassing incidents, like Paul's circumcision of Timothy. In addition, appeals to this *oikonomia*/accommodation were not absent from the world of ecclesiastical affairs, at least from the mid-fourth century on: in a church racked by theological controversies, some accommodation in dealing with the multitudes in some way tainted by schism or heresy increasingly became a matter of necessity.

It would be an arduous task to assemble all the instances in which *oikonomia* in the sense of accommodation is invoked in the course of the trinitarian and christological controversies.[26] The word is used often, in a wide variety of contexts, to justify an even wider variety of behavior, actions and policies. For example, Patriarch John VI of Constantinople, who had bowed his neck to the imperial will and signed a decree in favor of monothelitism, termed his action an *oikonomia;* had he not done so, hiding his own true feelings on the subject, a far greater evil would have ensued, for the emperor was threatening even to reject Chalcedon.[27] Or, Basil the Great had refrained from openly proclaiming the Holy Spirit as God; his *oikonomia* was defended by Athanasius, who observes, "to the weak he becomes weak to gain the weak."[28] Examples could easily be multiplied. But gradually *oikonomia*/accommodation receives if not technical precision then at least some delimitation. In canonical and related literature the term is most often employed in certain comparatively restricted contexts:

> 1. To justify remaining in (or entering into) commion with those who refuse to anathematize heretics, who keep the names of heretics in their diptychs, who have been in communion with heretics, etc.
>
> 2. To permit reception in their orders of clergy ordained by heretics or of clergy in some other way tainted by contact with heresy.[29]

In addition, the legitimate limits of *oikonomia* are more carefully defined.

The most noteworthy developments along these lines occur among the monophysites. Lacking the imperial church's facade of unity, they were plagued by factionalism. Violent disagreements arose not only over doctrine but also over church discipline, above all over how to deal with those compromised by contract with Chalcedon. Against the self-proclaimed champions of *akribeia,* who would ransack the archives of the churches to expunge the names of those long dead, and who would insist on rechrismation and reordination for repentant Chalcedonians, moderates like Severus of Antioch and Philoxenus of Mabbug explored the proper application and limits of *oikonomia.*

Most of this investigation was *ad hoc;* definition of *oikonomia* developed from case to case. But at least one attempt was made at a systematic presentation of *oikonomia.* Against a union patched up *kat'oikonomian* by two monophysite factions, Eulogius, Chalcedonian patriarch of Alexandria in the early seventh century, wrote a special treatise on the subject. The treatise, preserved to us only in résumé in Photius' *Bibliotheca,* is not without inconsistencies; but it does express what had come to be, and what would remain, the accepted understanding of *oikonomia* and its limits, for Chalcedonians and non-Chalcedonians alike:

1. By *oikonomia* a temporary concession can be made in matters of practice to avoid irremediably damaging the peace of the church.

2. By *oikonomia* differences of terminology can be tolerated indefinitely.

3. By *oikonomia* technical barriers to communion—an occasional heretic's name in the diptychs and other such vestiges of past error—can be ignored.

But in all three cases, present purity of doctrine in no wise may be compromised.[30]

Churchmen like Severus and Eulogius gradually gave *oikonomia*/accommodation greater precision by defining certain fixed limits that it had lacked earlier; and they did this in a typically eastern (or early medieval) way: by assembling apposite precedents, from scripture, church history and the writings of the fathers. Their method was faithfully followed in later centuries. Indeed, the history of *oikonomia* could easily be written as the history of certain key texts. For example, two letters of Cyril of Alexandria are transmitted almost exclusively in *florilegia* assembled to support specific applications of *oikonomia.* The letters, one addressed to a certain Maximus, deacon of Antioch, the other to Gennadius, a presbyter of Jerusalem,[31] urge the recipients to return to communion with their respective bishops even though the bishops continue to commemorate those accused of Nestorianism, on the grounds that this is in the best interest of the church as a whole. They are found first in a *florilegium* assembled by a group of moderate anti-Chalcedonians advocating union by *oikonomia* with the Chalcedonian imperial church on the basis of Emperor Zeno's *Henotikon.*[32] The letters occur next in the acts of the first session of II Nicaea, the Seventh Ecumenical Council. Facing the council is the problem of how to receive repentent iconoclast bishops: can they be restored in their orders, or have they, on account of their heresy, forfeited any claim to priesthood, making them eligible only for reception as laymen? And included among the texts advanced to support application of *oikonomia* are our two letters.[33] The letters next appear in the *Syntagma in Fourteen Titles,* the most important Byzantine canonical collection, in its so-called Tarasian Recension, assembled under Patriarch Tarasius shortly after II Nicaea to incorporate its canons.[34] Thus "canonized," the letters are alluded to in a number of later disputes and are included in integral form at least twice: in a *florilegium* dealing with union negotiations between Pope Urban II and Emperor Alexis Comnenus,[35] and in a treatise by John Chilas of Ephesus directed against the intransigence of the Arsenites.[36]

As this brief history of the two Cyril letters suggests, Byzantium's approach to *oikonomia* was conservative, to say the least. But it was by no means ossified. Within certain parameters development could and did occur. Rather as in the common law tradition, when a new case arose, precedents would be assembled and examined both as to their applicability and to their authority. Particularly noteworthy new cases might be used as precedents in later cases, or additional precedents from the past might be discovered, In either way, the prevailing understanding of *oikonomia* might subtly be modified.

One such modification was that, in canonical contexts at least, *oikonomia* lost many of its shadier connotations. *Oikonomia* as accommodation increasingly came to be interpreted in the light of *oikonomia* as penitential administration. Quite literally, the nautical imagery so often used to illustrate *oikonomia* as prudent accommodation to circumstances gives way to the medicinal imagery of penance. The shift, already underway with Severus and Eulogius, can be seen in II Nicaea's way of accepting the repentant iconoclast bishops in their orders, a "landmark decision" that sets the pattern for later cases involving *oikonomia.* Formerly application of *oikonomia* might be justified on the basis of enlightened self-interest, as in the two letters of Cyril. In II Nicaea, though the economy doubtless was of benefit to church and state, this is not adduced as justification for it. Formerly *oikonomia* might be invoked to justify "making a deal," putting together a bilateral agreement like that between the two monophysite factions opposed by Eulogius. Now there is not even a hint of "plea bargaining." The iconoclast bishops appear as penitents and throw themselves on the mercy of the court: "We have sinned in the sight of God, and in the sight of the whole church and of this holy synod; we fell through ignorance, and we have no argument in our defense."[37]

Along with this shift in tone comes the application of penitential criteria in judging whether *oikonomia* can be applied. *Oikonomia* for the repentant bishops, permitting not only their return to the church's communion but also retention of their episcopal dignity, is found in order on the grounds that they had acted in ignorance, trapped in a common error. On the other hand, those who acted in full knowledge, and especially those who initiated the heresy, may in no wise be received in their orders.[38] Whence a curious element in a number of later Byzantine cases involving *oikonomia:* the search for the heresiarch. A classic case is that of Eustratius of Nicaea, noted theologian and counsellor to Alexis Comnenus, who in the course of debate with Armenian monophysites had the misfortune to fall into the error of separating the human and divine natures in Christ to an exaggerated degree. The fact of his heresy was plain to all. The problem was his rehabilitation. Supporters, including the emperor, urged application of *oikonomia,* to restore the offender, repentant and with his treatises consigned to the flames, to episcopal rank, on the grounds that he had put forward his heretical teaching in ignorance and on the spur of the moment, without due reflection. His adversaries, on the other hand, dismissed the excuses of ignorance (How could a former professor at the patriarchal academy be ignorant of the doctrine of the hypostatic union?) and of improvisation (Was not Eustratius's teaching a deliberate restatement of that of his master, John Italus, who had been condemned as a heretic only a few years earlier?[39]). Therefore *oikonomia* is not in order; as II Nicaea had declared, "no head or fabricator of a heresy may be admitted to the priesthood."[40]

This pattern of argumentation occurs repeatedly in Byzantium. For example, fabricators of the so-called "anti-Photian dossier" try to prove that Photius, like Dioscorus or the leaders of iconoclasm, can never be restored to episcopal dignity, while his misguided followers, upon repentance, may be.[41] Similar is the case of certain Jacobites in the eleventh century: a measure of economy is in order for three suffragen bishops, who had been led astray by their patriarch but now repent. On the other hand, the patriarch himself, obdurate in his heresy, is deposed and condemned to exile; and should he ever repent, he may be received among the laity but never exercise the functions of priesthood.[42] An interesting variation is provided in the moechian affair. When the council of 809 demands acceptance of the rehabilitation by *oikonomia* of the priest who had blessed Constantine VI's adulterous marriage, Theodore of Studios concludes that a new heresy has been officially proclaimed: "But now a dogma against the Gospel, against the Forerunner and against the canons has been synodically promulgated through the reception of the joiner of adulterers . . ."[43] Indeed, so ingrained is this approach to *oikonomia,* so well-established are the rules governing debate on the subject, that the II Nicaea model often is employed even when circumstances might suggest a different, more flexible approach. For example, many of the peculiarities of Byzantine treatises concerning the Latins, particularly those of the twelfth century, depend on this very point: opponents of *oikonomia* towards the Latins try to prove that they are willful heretics, while supporters of *oikonomia* argue that they have not been formally condemned for starting a new heresy or upholding an old one, and that they act in ignorance in any case.[44]

The present examination of *oikonomia* in Byzantium is by no means exhaustive. Additional uses of the term could have been investigated; more cases, particularly from the empire's declining centuries, could have been examined and in greater depth. But even this brief survey suggests the need for greater caution and discrimination when the term is used in discussions of Byzantine history. Most assuredly *oikonomia* was important for the Byzantines. But for them it was not a vague principle of flexibility or compromise, opposed to an equally vague principle of strictness. The term of course could be used in a loose sense, as when the historian Gregoras defines it as "the policy of a prudent man to suffer a small loss for the sake of a greater advantage when under pressure of necessity."[45] But in certain contexts—in the realm of penitential discipline or in cases involving restoration of clergy in some way tainted by heresy—the word *oikonomia* could be used with technical precision, with arguments for and against its application arranged according to certain well-established patterns. Further, for the Byzantines *oikonomia* did not necessarily involve "a certain amount of compromise in ecclesiastical affairs for reason of state." In its principal technical uses *oikonomia* remained essentially the church's housekeeping, its prudent administration of the things committed to it by God, in which relations with the state were only tangentially involved. To be sure, conflicts over *oikonomia* did occur, and often the state as well as the church would be involved: complications might arise in the "management" of an imperial sinner, as in the tetragamy affair; or the imperial authority might have a vested interest in the rehabilitation of a particular heretic, as in the case of Eustratius of Nicaea. But these quarrels were not between a "principle of *oikonomia*" and a "principle of *akribeia*," but rather over whether specific applications of *oikonomia* were indeed *oikonomia* and not just sin or apostasy by another name.

St. Vladimir's Orthodox Theological Seminary
Crestwood, N.Y.

Notes

1. D. M. Nicol, "The Greeks and the Union of the Churches: The Preliminaries to the Second Council of Lyons, 1261–1274," *Medieval Studies presented to Aubrey Gwynn, S. J.,* ed. J. A. Watt *et al.* (Dublin, 1961), p. 464.

2. On these party labels and their link to the problem of *oikonomia* see among others Nicol, "Greeks and Union"; F. Dvornik, *The Photian Schism: History and Legend* (Cambridge, 1948), pp. 8, 24 and passim; P. Henry, *Theodore of Studios: Byzantine Churchman* (Ph.D. dissertation, Yale University, 1967), p. 15; cf. D. Geanakoplos, *Emperor Michael Palaeologus and the West* (Cambridge, Mass., 1959), p. 265, n. 28: "The problem of *oikonomia* involved two opposing points of view: the rigorist, which maintained that the church should be practically independent of the state, and the liberal, which insisted that when required by political necessity the church should subordinate itself to the needs of the state." More recently, H. Ahrweiler has attempted an even more comprehensive analysis of the fundamental principles of Byzantine political thought in terms of "ordre [taxis] et économie [oikonomia] et leurs rapports avec l'autorité temporelle et spirituelle": *L'Idéologie politique de l'Empire byzantin* (Paris, 1975), pp. 129–47.

3. D. Geanakoplos, *Byzantine East and Latin West* (New York, 1966), p. 74, n. 58.

4. Dvornik, *Photian Schism,* pp. 8, 45.

5. S. Runciman, *The Eastern Schism* (Oxford, 1955); noted by Geanakoplos, *Byzantine East,* p. 74, n. 58.

6. One exception is P. Raï, "L'Économie dans le Droit canonique byzantin des Origines jusqu'au XIe Siècle," *Istina* XVIII (1973), 260–326, whose presentation, however, is marred by the *a priori* assumption that *oikonomia* basically = *dispensatio,* an approach inherited from M. A. Stiegler's still fundamental *Dispensation, Dispensationswesen und Dispensationsrecht im Kirchenrecht geschichtlich dargestellt* (Mainz, 1901). On the other hand, the point of departure for the enormous modern Orthodox literature on *oikonomia* is the problem of application of "economy" in sacramental matters. Survey of positions: F. J. Thomson, "Economy," *Journal of Theological Studies,* n.s. XVI (1965), 368–420. Convenient bibliography: Y. Congar, "Propos en Vue d'une Thélogie de l''Économie' dans la Tradition latine," *Irenikon* XLV (1972), 155–206, at p. 179. More recent: P. Raï, "L'Économie chez les Orthodoxes depuis 1755," and K. Duchatelez, "Le Principe de l'Économie baptismale dans l'Antiquité chrétienne," both in *Istina* XVIII (1973), 260–358.

7. H. Alivizatos, *Hē oikonomia kata to kanonikon dikaion tēs Orthodoksou Ekklēsias* (Athens, 1949), p. 15. The work of Alivizatos has been often cited by Byzantinists dealing with *oikonomia: e.g.* Geanakoplos, *Byzantine East,* p. 74, n. 58; Henry, *Theodore,* pp. 98–99; and H.-G. Beck, *Kirche und theologische Literatur im byzantinischen Reich,* Handbuch der Altertumswissenschaft XII.2.1, (Munich, 1959), p. 77, n. 3. Concerning its place within modern Orthodox canonical literature on the subject, cf. Thomson, "Economy," p. 382.

8. E.g. in P. Dumont's French translation of I. Kotsonis's influential study, *Problèmes de l'Économie ecclésiastique* (Gembloux, 1971), passim.

9. H. Thurn, *Oikonomia von der frühbyzantinischen Zeit bis zum Bilderstreit* (Munich, 1961), p. 23.

10. E.g. K. Duchatelez, "La Notion d'Économie et ses Richesses théologiques," *Nouvelle Revue théologique* XCII (1970), 267–92.

11. J. Goar, *Euchologion sive Rituale graecorum* (Paris, 1647), p. 248.

12. R. Deferrari, ed. and trans., *St. Basil: The Letters,* (Cambridge, Mass., and London, 1962), III: 246–49.

13. Nicetas Stethatos, *Peri kanonōn,* ed. J. Darrouzès, *Nicétas Stéthatos: Opuscules et Lettres,* Sources Chrétiennes LXXXI (Paris, 1961), p. 468: "kata tēn tōn kanonōn oikonomoumen akribeian."

14. P.-P. Joannou, ed, *Discipline général antique,* Pont. Com. per la Redazione del Cod. Dir. Canon. Orientale: Fonti, fasc. IX (Grottaferrata, 1963), II: 219. Cited among others by Stethatos, *Peri kanonōn,* p. 468.

15. One such incident is recounted by Balsamon, PG CXXXVIII: 782.

16. See above all the various penitential works ascribed to "John the Faster," in J. Morin, *Commentarius historicus de disciplina in administratione sacramenti poenitentiae* (Paris, 1651), Appendix. The works in question have nothing to do with the sixth-century patriarch of that name but rather are monastic in origin, in line with the Studite tradition represented also by Theodore of Studios and Nicetas Stethatos. On the text: E. Herman, "Il più antico penitenziale greco," *Orientalia Christiana periodica* XIX (1953), 70–127.

17. This has been done above all by R. J. H. Jenkins, "Eight Letters of Arethas on the Fourth Marriage of Leo the Wise," *Hellenika* XIV (1956), 293–372; "Three Documents Concerning the 'Tetragamy'," *Dumbarton Oaks Papers* XVI (1962), 231–41; and more popularly in *Byzantium: The Imperial Centuries, AD 610–1071* (London, 1966), pp. 212–26.

18. Jenkins, *Imperial Centuries,* p. 218.

19. Deferrari, *St. Basil,* p. 260 (can. 80).

20. *Vita Euthymii* 12, 13, P. Karlin-Hayter, ed., *Byzantion* XXV–XXVII (1955–57), 81, 87–93.

21. L. G. Westerink, ed., *Arethae scripta minora,* no. 68, (Leipzig, 1968), pp. 67–68.

22. *Vita Euthymii* 13, Karlin-Hayter, p. 91.

23. V. Grumel, *Les Regestes des Actes du Patriàrcat de Constantinople,* (Chalcedon [Kadiköy], 1936), ii, nos. 625–629.

24. *Ep.* 32; R. J. H. Jenkins and L. G. Westerink, eds. and trans. *Nicholas I Patriarch of Constantinople: Letters,* Dumbarton Oaks Texts II (Washington, 1973), pp. 234–37; trans. slightly modified.

25. Cf. J. Reumann, *"Oikonomia* as 'Ethical Accommodation' in the Fathers, and its Pagan Backgrounds," *Studia Patristica* iii (1961), 370–79.

26. The beginnings of such a catalogue have been assembled by P. Raï, "L'Économie."

27. Grumel, *Regestes,* no. 322.

28. *Ep. ad Paladium,* PG xxvi: 1168D.

29. Here, it is important to observe, the central issue was not whether the clergy in question had "valid" orders. The sacramental acts of heretics (and for that matter of schismatics) regularly are described in the sources as *akuros* and *abebaios,* but these terms lacked the precision of modern western ideas of validity. Rather, the issue was whether those who have undergone (public) penance, obviously necessary for those repenting of heresy, can remain in, or enter into, the ranks of the clergy. Cf. L. Saltet, *Les Réordinations* (Paris, 1907), p. 70.

30. Cod. 227, ed. R. Henry (Paris, 1965), 111–14.

31. *Epp.* 56, 57, ed. Joannou, *Discipline,* ii: 284–287.

32. Analyzed by E. Schwartz, *Codex Vaticanus gr.1431: Eine anti-chalkedonische Sammlung aus der Zeit Kaiser Zenos,* Abhandlungen der Bayerischen Akademie der Wissenschaften, Philos.-philol. u. hist. Klasse, xxxii.6 (Munich, 1927).

33. Mansi XII: 1027.

34. Analyzed by V. N. Beneshevich, *Kanonicheski Sbornik XIV Titulov so vtoroi chetverti VII veka do 883 g.* (S. Petersburg, 1905), pp. 260–88.

35. London, British Library, MS Add. 34060; cf. W. Holtzmann, "Die Unionsverhandlungen zwischen Kaiser Alexios I. und Papst Urban II. im J. 1089," *Byzantinische Zeitschrift* xxvii (1928), 60–61.

36. J. Darrouzès, ed., *Documents inédits d'Ecclésiologie byzantine,* Archives de l'Orient Chrétien x (Paris, 1966), 248–404.

37. Mansi xii: 1018.

38. Ibid., 1030–31.

39. Thus, Nicetas Seides, Darrouzès, *Documents inédits,* pp. 306–7. Nicetas of Heraclea, *On the heresiarchs,* Ibid., pp. 304–5.

40. Ibid., pp. 278–79.

41. Mansi xvi: 433DE.

42. Grumel, *Regestes,* no. 839.

43. *Ep.* 1.53, PG xcix: 1105D; trans. by P. Henry, "The Moechian Controversy and the Constantinopolitan Synod of January A.D. 809," *Journal of Theological Studies,* n.s. xx (1969), 495–522, at p. 514. In my brief account of the council's acts, however, I have followed the interpretation of Grumel, *Regestes,* no. 378, rather than that of Prof. Henry. From Theodore (*Ep.* 1.48, PG xcix: 1077A) we learn that the council had anathematized "those not accepting the economies of the saints." This is taken to mean (pp. 516–17) anathema to those not accepting the economy of Tarasius, now among the saints, with regard to the marriage of Constantine VI. But unless Theodore's opponents were deliberately seeking trouble, they would hardly have brought up the dead and discredited emperor's adulterous union. More likely they tried to limit discussion to the problem of the restoration of Joseph of Kathara to exercise of the priesthood, claiming that this was in line with the economies of II Nicaea and with the patristic texts on economy cited there.

44. See especially the analyses of J. Darrouzès, "Les Documents byzantine du XIIe Siècle sur la Primauté romaine," *Revue des Études Byzantines* xxiii (1965), 42–88.

45. Cited by D. M. Nicol, "The Byzantine Reaction to the Second Council of Lyons, 1274," *Studies in Church History* vii, ed. G. J. Cuming and D. Baker (Cambridge, 1971), pp. 113–46.

Images of the Church in the Second Nicene Council and in the *Libri Carolini*

PATRICK HENRY

At the end of his history of the early church, Henry Chadwick remarks that after the era of the church fathers, ending traditionally with Gregory the Great in the West and John of Damascus in the East, "it is much more difficult to write the history of both Eastern and Western Christendom as if it were a single story."[1] We might add that the difficulty increases rapidly, and as early as the end of the eighth century there is already an ominous predisposition on either side to be displeased with the other. Simple misunderstanding is giving way to willful misrepresentation.

Clear evidence of tension is provided by the Western reaction to the Seventh Ecumenical Council (Nicaea II, A.D. 787). The Western reaction itself was not uniform; Pope Hadrian I was caught between his own qualified support of the council and the unqualified rejection of the council by his own most powerful supporter, Charlemagne. Despite the confusion in the West, however, it remains true that for an analysis of East/West ecclesiastical relations in the period when political schism became a practical reality, no enterprise is more important than the clarification of the connections between the *Acta Concilii Nicaeni II* (ACN) and the Frankish response to them, the *Libri Carolini* (LC), published some four or five years after the Council.[2]

It used to be thought that the relationship, at the textual level at least, was quite straightforward: the author of the *LC* was dependent on a garbled Latin translation of the ACN made at Pope Hadrian's request by someone who was certainly inept and probably prejudiced, and nearly a century later, in 873, Anastasius Bibliothecarius undertook to prepare for Pope John VIII a more accurate translation of the ACN. Particularly important was Anastasius's restoration of the full Latin text of Pope Hadrian's *synodica* addressed to Constantine VI and Irene, a letter which had been truncated in the Greek version read at the council.

Both in general and in particular this reconstruction has been called into question by Luitpold Wallach in a diplomatic study of the evidence. Wallach has placed the whole issue in the context of the customs of earlier councils and of papal *scrinium,* patriarchal library, and imperial chancellery, and has suggested that the history of textual tampering, mistranslation, and retranslation is more intricate than has been hitherto supposed. According to Wallach, Hadrian's *synodica* was read *in toto* at Nicaea in both Latin and

Greek, and, despite Anastasius's misleading remark, both versions were inserted in the official *acta;* it was during the Photian controversy in the second half of the ninth century that *both* the Latin original *and* the Greek translation were falsified in MSS of the ACN on deposit in Constantinople. Wallach's arguments are very interesting, though they leave some puzzling anomalies unexplained.[3]

It is not the purpose of this essay, however, to scrutinize the work of Wallach, or to enter the battle over the authorship of the LC.[4] Rather, I wish to assume both the undoubted importance of the ACN as an expression of Greek Christianity, and the contention of Ann Freeman that the LC are "a compendium or *Summa* of Carolingian thought,"[5] and go on from there to investigate some of the governing motifs of the two documents.

My method of approach here is more akin to literary criticism than to traditional historical criticism, and the literary criticism to which it is akin has affinities with the study of pictorial art.[6] Not inappropriately for an essay on an aspect of the Iconoclastic period, this way of looking at these texts was suggested to me by two pictures.

In the southwest vestibule of Hagia Sophia in Istanbul there is a famous mosaic which depicts the emperors Constantine I and Justinian I presenting their respective architectural offerings to Christ and the mother of God: Constantine, standing on the viewer's right, is holding the city of Constantinople; Justinian, on the left, is holding the church of the holy wisdom itself.[7] At a great distance in history, theology, and politics, as well as simply in miles, from Hagia Sophia, there hangs in the study of a Presbyterian minister in Minneapolis a modern linoleum-block print, titled "For He Had Great Possessions" (Matt. 19:22; Mark 10:22), which shows a priest who is so burdened with the elaborate church building he is carrying in his arms that he cannot even reach into his pocket for something to give to a beggar who has accosted him.[8] In both these instances an artist has made a point about his understanding of the nature of the church through a pictorial image of a church building in a man's hands: an ecclesiological statement is made eloquently, without words.

There are other sorts of images, too—words intended to suggest pictures, which themselves often call stories to mind. Poets have always known the rhetorical power of images, and modern psychology has investigated some of the mechanisms by which images penetrate beneath the surface of our analytical reason and move us in ways our intellect cannot always control.

For the historian, the following question arises: are there in the ACN and the LC, in both of which the proper place of *pictorial* images *in* the church is debated furiously, divergencies of *verbal* images *of* the church that help explain the acrimony of the debate, and, beyond the acrimony, the increasingly evident tendency to misunderstanding and eventual schism? Were East and West, apart from specific disputes over jurisdiction or theology, operating with incompatible governing images of the church? The conception of the church held by the mosaicist of Hagia Sophia cannot be brought into congruence with the conception of the church held by the modern linoleum-block artist. Do similarly incompatible conceptions confront one another in the ACN and the LC?

This indirect approach to ecclesiology is particularly suited to the iconoclastic period, for while there have been many eras of high passion in the history of the church, few have been so intense as the century and a quarter beginning with Emperor Leo III's original attack on icons in 729 to 730. Emotions heated up quickly, and remained at or near the boiling point for five generations. The Council of Nicaea treats the Iconoclastic Council of Hiereia of 754 with contempt, and the LC treat the arguments and decrees of Nicaea II with unrelieved derision. There is little attempt by any party, whether conciliar or individual, to see whether some other party might have a good point or two.[9]

If, however, passionate intensity has the unfortunate effect of blunting arguments, it has the merit of opening those persons subject to it to some of their own deepest feelings and attitudes. A psychiatrist knows he is getting somewhere when a patient gets angry. The fathers of Nicaea, and the author of the LC, were infuriated, and in their anger their real feelings and governing attitudes about the church came to the surface in the form of images. While putting their theological defenses up, they let their emotional defenses down.

There are in both texts, as one would expect, some traditional biblical images for the church: the body of Christ, the bride of Christ, the mother of Christians from whose breasts they derive nourishment, Jerusalem (and Zion), the sheepfold, the threshing-floor, the vineyard, the ark of the covenant.[10] The patristic associations of these and other word-pictures were rich and various—so various, in fact, that it would be difficult to extract any sharply defined portrait of the church from them. The governing images, which would themselves affect the particular interpretation of the traditional images, are to be sought elsewhere. The ACN and the LC reveal their fundamental attitudes in the way they talk about the church as a society, and in their manner of placing the church in history. The social and historical images are closely tied to one another, and there is some artificiality in separating them, but separation is necessary, at least provisionally, for purposes of analysis.

The governing social image for the church is that of the family. The Nicene Council was faced with the problem of tarnished family honor, and the search for a solution to that problem occupied much of the council's attention. In the year 754 a council of 338 bishops had met in Constantinople, had called itself the Seventh Ecumenical Council, and had unanimously anathematized anyone who undertook to portray Christ in a picture or who set up images of the saints.[11] By 787, iconoclasm had been government policy for more than fifty years, and for more than thirty years it had been the official policy of the church in nearly all the regions represented by the bishops now sitting at Nicaea. Theoretically one could say that any part of the church which accepted iconoclasm was schismatic and/or heretical, but in practical terms that would mean for most of the council fathers that they had never been in the church at all. The question was how to repudiate their parents without losing the inheritance—the inheritance of the apostolic tradition. And this was an intricate psychological dilemma as well as a canonical one: Hypatius, bishop of the host city of Nicaea, speaking for himself and several others, admitted that "we were not intimidated or forced, but we were born in this heresy of ours, and were educated and nurtured in it."[12]

How is it possible to repudiate the immediate past without raising the suspicion that other parts of the past, or perhaps the whole past, are likewise subject to radical criticism? At the time of Leo III's initial decree, Patriarch Germanus of Constantinople had noted the propagandistic capital that Jews and Muslims could make from the claim that the church had gone wrong in permitting images,[13] but the fathers at Nicaea in 787 had to deal with the analogous problem created by their own claim that much of the Christian world had been in error for many years by prohibiting images. It is for this reason that God himself is credited with the presence at the Council of Gregory, Bishop of Neocaesarea, who had been one of the leading figures at the Council of Hiereia in 754.

There were times when it appeared that monastic opposition to Gregory's being seated at Nicaea would succeed, and the ACN suggest a carefully articulated diplomacy on the part of Patriarch Tarasius to assure that the Bishop of Neocaesarea was finally admitted. It is clear why Tarasius was so intent on Gregory's presence: if the council's restoration of images were to be ratified by someone who had led the rebellion against images more than three decades previously, the sharp line between present and past would be blurred. The council's action could be seen as the return of the prodigal son rather than as the consigning of ancestors to eternal fire.

John the Logothete said: "It is a fitting thing [*arkei*] for your divinely gathered council, that Gregory of Neocaesarea, who was a leader [exarchos] of the earlier impious council, has been preserved [ephylachthē] to this very day, in order that he may denounce [katakrinai] his own heresy and teaching." John, priest and legate of the Eastern diocese: "We give thanks to God that men from that wickedly gathered council are left to refute and overturn the evil things they did and to make public their own shame."[14]

The link with Hiereia formed by Gregory of Neocaesarea was genuinely crucial, for as Tarasius admitted, it had been virtually impossible for anyone since 754 to avoid involvement in the heresy of iconoclasm. In the discussion about the credentials of Gregory and other bishops, various canonical passages of councils and fathers were brought up, and in response to one from St. Basil, Tarasius said it was necessary to bear in mind that Basil's contemporaries could easily have found orthodox bishops to ordain them, with the implication that in recent times long and impracticable journeys would have been required.[15] The return of Gregory to orthodoxy was, in effect, the return of the church to orthodoxy, and not simply the re-entry of a repentant heretic into the church which he had left. When the council is seen in this light, three declarations made during its Sixth Session appear as far more significant than the pious platitudes for which they might otherwise be taken.

The Sixth Session was the climax of the council; everything had led up to the reading of the *Horos* (Definition) of 754 and a point-by-point refutation of it. In introducing this lengthy document, the imperial secretary characterized the Definition of 754 as "entirely consonant with the impious thinking of God-detested heretics," and then went on to praise "a skillful and most effective refutation of it, which the Holy Spirit has furnished; for to triumph over it requires carefully chosen counterarguments, and it takes powerful analyses to rend it in pieces."[16] Councils from the time of the Council of Jerusalem in Acts 15 have credited their decisions to the Holy Spirit, and often there is a formulaic quality to such ascriptions; but at Nicaea II the Holy Spirit had to get the credit, since the church itself was in heresy: as the council would say in its summary letter to the emperor and empress, "the hierarchs had become heresiarchs."[17] When that happens, divine intervention is the only hope.

The Sixth Session was orchestrated so as to give dramatic expression to the restoration of family honor: it was Gregory of Neocaesarea himself who read the segments of the *Horos* of 754, to which the deacon Epiphanius then read the refutations. During the reading, at the conclusion of an account of the persecutions to which the supporters of icons had been subjected, thanks are given to God that "he has delivered his church from a long period of terrors; to him be glory, Amen."[18] So, God has delivered the church from persecution, and yet the church he has delivered is what was doing the persecuting, and at the conclusion of the refutation of the *Horos,* Epiphanius states: "We, who once were opponents [kategoroi] of orthodoxy and of the truth, have now become their advocates [sunegoroi]. Yet, for the rejection of ecclesiastical tradition, let us ask pardon for our sin."[19] Epiphanius is here speaking on behalf of the whole council, and it is noteworthy that he speaks of "us" repenting for sin, and does not say, "We have now received back into the church those who were opponents of orthodoxy and truth."

The LC, with undisguised and rather malevolent delight, recognize that this problem of family honor was central for the Fathers of Nicaea. Time and again the council is condemned for having anathematized their parents. We are divinely instructed to honor our parents, not to rebuke them. There is sinful presumption in judging the dead. And if the council considers their parents to have disgraced the church, the disgrace taints the children themselves. If they received birth, education, and consecration from the worst of all heretics (which is what they claim the iconoclasts were), then they can make no claims to any kind of legitimate authority. All that their ancestors did in the church is null and void.[20] No notice is taken of the council's prayer for forgiveness, no credit is given to Gregory of Neocaesarea as one of the "parents" who had condemned himself, and there is no hint that the Holy Spirit might have been at work at Nicaea. The LC suggest, in fact, that there is no way by which a church that has fallen into error can extricate itself. The LC agree with the ACN that there was error at Hiereia which needed to be corrected, but the LC's conviction that Nicaea II had promulgated even greater error masks their own inability to propose a way in which error might be legitimately overcome.

The image of the church as a family of many generations is made clearest in the following passage from the LC:

> We pray that the spirits of our parents will find rest in the bosom of Abraham; they wish the spirits of their parents to be damned along with Arius, Sabellius, Dioscorus, Nestorius, and Eutyches. We desire our parents to be included in the company of the blessed, while they desire theirs to be among the stubborn rabble of the heretics.[21]

Of momentous significance for the future is the sharp distinction here between "us" and "them." Not only does the author of the LC not consider himself to be in communion with the fathers of Nicaea II, but he also goes far beyond that, and implies that he and they are members of different ecclesiastical families. The attempt of the council to align itself with earlier patristic and apostolic authorities is abortive as far as the LC are concerned. It is the westerners who have the claim to the inheritance of the orthodox family; the easterners have acknowledged their parentage by repudiating it.

The logical structure of this argument precludes the possibility of the church's falling into error, for if it should fall into error, the only way it could get out is to disobey the divine command to honor father and mother. The unstated assumption is that God cannot permit the church to err, since the practical effect of his desire to have it return from error would run counter to one of his changeless decrees. A church whose family honor is besmirched is no church at all.

On first reading, the LC's periodic gloatings over the problem the fathers of Nicaea had with their parents appear to be little more than easy points scored in an artificial rhetorical game, but as the governing image of the family comes into sharper focus, it is clear that this form of argument is fundamental, and the divergence is seen to be symptomatic of deep seismic shifts taking place in ecclesiological attitudes, shifts that were already creating serious strain between East and West.

Common to both the ACN and the LC is the conviction that Christianity is not one thing yesterday, something else today, and yet another thing tomorrow. The attempt to bring theoretical changelessness and evident change into some coherent scheme gives to patristic and medieval ecclesiology a peculiar fascination, and the two texts under consideration display in their imagery for the church in history, as well as in the way they talk about the social reality of the church as a family, significant and decisive differences.

At one point in the ACN there is an allusion to the traditional Greek view of history—that things are running down, that these latter days are woefully deficient in comparison with the great days of the past—but it is an isolated instance, and does not adequately characterize the conciliar attitude.[22] There is in the LC a motif which might be thought to suggest a view of historical decline. The council argues on the basis of the biblical account of the construction and ornamentation of the tabernacle that images are legitimate in the church, and the LC respond with the contrast between Moses, a man chosen by God, and "some artisan or other" who has made the modern icon.[23] However, the LC boast that Charlemagne has lavishly decorated churches,[24] and the clear implication is that ornamentation is legitimate if done at the behest of those who have been chosen by God for positions of high honor. Charlemagne's penchant for having himself cast in the image of David is worth remembering;[25] if David has returned, history is not declining, but is repeating itself.

The governing historical image for the church in the LC might be characterized as a very liberal extension of the Vincentian Canon: the *ubique, semper,* and *ab omnibus* are not confined to the post-Incarnation era, but extend all the way back to creation.[26] The fact that Abel, Enoch, and Noah, as well as patriarchs, prophets, apostles, and monks could recognize God's power ("fortitudo") without icons to remind them of it becomes an argument against our using icons. The author goes on to ask whether the fathers of Nicaea think that the power of God is not adored in areas where the painter's art is not to be found.[27] This comes close to suggesting that the "natural religion" of which St. Paul speaks in Rom. 1 is not only necessary to Christianity, but is very near to being sufficient. The church is the company of all who have sought God with their minds, and the council has proposed a Christianity that is far too restrictive, one that will retroactively separate off from the church the majority of those who since the creation have belonged to it.

The council, following the lead of John of Damascus, considers that the post-Incarnation situation establishes the framework for determining what is Christian. The concern of the bishops and abbots at Nicaea was to believe and do what the apostles and fathers had believed and done, and for the purposes of our present investigation, it does not matter whether the use of icons was really ancient or not. The image of the church is reflected in the desire to be true to the norms that have been in force since the Incarnation.[28]

In thinking about the church in history, both the ACN and the LC of course have to come to terms with the Old Testament. Since the Old Testament is a very complex book, both sides have to thrust and then parry when using it.

The LC, which basically assume that the church is not affected by history, which collapse historical distinctions in the double oxymoron "new antiquity and ancient novelty" [nova antiquitas et antiqua novitas],[29] take comfort from the fact that God roundly condemns the making of images in Exod. 20, but are embarrassed by such material objects as the bronze serpent, the cherubim, and the various other ornaments which God commanded to be included in tabernacle and temple. The only way round this is to draw the contrast, which we have already seen, between the character of Moses and his workmen and that of contemporary painters. It takes a Moses or a David to do legitimately what Moses or David did.

The ACN could take comfort from the fact of temple ornaments, but had to be wary of putting too much store by such Old Testament precedent, since the main point was that the Old Testament was not normative, and hence the prohibition of Exod. 20 simply did not apply to the Christian dispensation. Caution was necessary, since if you appeal to the authority of Moses in matters of liturgical furnishings, you are *a fortiori* under obligation to follow him in matters of divine legislation. Moses and David are, so to speak, exhibits presented by the council for the defense of icons, but they are not part of the brief itself. They and their activities prefigure the reality of the church, but they do no more than prefigure, and it is always the privilege of those who interpret prefigurements to decide which aspects were designed to come to fruition and which are simply part of the narrative context.

The LC talk about prefigurements, but their governing image of the church in history undercuts any real significance in such talk, since the metaphysical conditions of past and present are the same. Effective prefigurement presupposes that when the new comes it will be really new; there will be a new situation, not simply more information.

Indeed, the sharpest contrast of all between the ACN and the LC may well be their different views of prefigurement. The LC consider carnal prefigurements to have spiritual fulfillments; and in relating temple to church, they say that whatever existed *literally* in the former exists *spiritually* in the latter.[30] The ACN, on the contrary, consider that until the Incarnation, true religion had to be "spiritual" in a quite restricted sense, since the error of idolatry was always a threat. But the reconstruction of the world by redemption exceeds the original formation; *all things* have been made new, so the relation of created man to the created world is fundamentally changed from what it was before.[31] With the sanctification of the flesh that resulted from the Incarnation of the Word of God, the danger of idolatry was averted.[32] Hence, in effect, the ACN are saying that what could exist only *spiritually* before can now exist *literally*. Prefigurement is turned inside out; or, to put it another away, the LC would say that the Christian penetrates through the literal shell of the prefigurement to its spiritual meaning, while the ACN would say that the Christian sees through the spiritual penumbra of the prefigurement to its literal significance.

There are two further contrasting historical images for the church which substantiate the broad differences suggested so far. The ACN continually call the church back to the company of the Fathers: it is they to whom we must listen, they with whom we must be in harmony. This is very different from a suggestion in the LC that we should go and sit at the feet of the Lord himself to learn what we should do: "Let us come to the Lord, let us sit with Mary at his feet, let us hear the word from his mouth, let us hear him speaking for himself."[33] The image of the church here is that of a single individual in direct contact with Jesus, who is himself portrayed as a teacher giving instruction to his pupil. The implication is that we do not really need the intermediary of the fathers and councils; we have the privilege of direct access to Christ himself *through his words*.[34] This might appear to run counter to the earlier suggestion that the LC accord no unique status to the Incarnation, but in fact it reinforces that suggestion, for it makes of the earthly career of Jesus a time like any other time, one to which we can go by reading about it. The character of history has not been changed by anything that has happened in history, so you can dip into one part of the past as easily as into any other part. If you want to know what is required of a follower of Christ, you simply go straight to the source.

The second contrasting image is one that appears at first glance to be similar in the two documents: it is the Garden of Eden as a model for the church. However, the uses made of the image are significantly different, and in fact bring us round full circle to the contrasting images of the church as family.

Men who have persuaded Christians that veneration of icons is idolatry are characterized by the ACN as the serpent who beguiled Eve in Eden.[35] This image has two important implications. First, iconoclasm is presented as the intrusion of an alien force seducing the church, and seducing it with an argument that has a certain plausibility (just as the serpent told Eve that the fruit of the tree was good to eat, and that God would not really be angry anyway). Second, the church is presented as having suffered a Fall as a result of this satanic machination. The church in the form of Eden is vulnerable, and just as man has been redeemed from the Fall by the work of Christ, so has the church now been redeemed from its Fall by the work of the Holy Spirit in the Council. Fallen mankind needed a divine intervention, so did a fallen church.

The LC, on the other hand, accuse the emperor and empress who summoned the council of having corrupted the church, just as Adam and Eve contaminated Eden. Mention of the serpent is subordinate, and we do not sense that the author is considering a power of evil apart from human sin that activates the sin itself.[36] This way of speaking about the church as Eden implies that once the Garden has been destroyed, it cannot be restored. But the church is Eden, and the church cannot be destroyed. Therefore, if you want to find the church now, you must look somewhere other than to those parts of it which have been destroyed by the arrogant, prideful behavior of the "new Adam" and "new Eve" responsible for the Nicene Council. They have not been able to destroy all of Eden.

There was, of course, a perfectly simple way to account for what was done at Nicaea II. Pope Hadrian put it in plain terms in his letter to Charlemagne: they have "returned to the orthodox faith of the holy Catholic and apostolic church," and had they not done so, the pope himself would have to answer for their loss at the Day of Judgment.[37] Earlier in the same letter the pope had countered Charlemagne's reprimand of the council for disrespect to parents by saying that men are worthy of praise who do not follow their parents in error, but instead return "to the true orthodox faith of the holy Catholic and apostolic church."[38] And Hadrian had said the same thing, with the significant addition of "Roman," to Constantine VI and Irene in his *synodica*: restore images "in order that you may be received into the arms of our holy, Catholic, apostolic, and blameless Roman church" [ut in hujus nostrae sanctae catholicae et apostolicae ac irreprehensibilis Romanae ecclesiae ulnis suscipiamini].[39]

That is not the way the council saw it. The Greek translation of this part of the *synodica* reads: "that you may embrace our holy, Catholic, and apostolic Roman church, which is without limit" [hina tautēn tēn hēmeteran hagian katholikēn kai apostolikēn Rōmaïkēn ekklēsian tēn akatalēpton enangkalisēsthe].[40] The fathers of the council welcomed Hadrian's intervention on the side of icons; bishops tried to outdo one another in expressions of appreciation for the *synodica*.[41] But what was welcomed even more was the *agreement* of Hadrian, Tarasius, and the eastern patriarchs. Tarasius himself credits the "breath of the almighty Lord" with being the instructor that has, by the reading of letters from both East and West, "brought us into agreement."[42] In his letter to Hadrian following the council, Tarasius recounts the reading of the *synodica* and says the pope served as "an eye directing the whole body into the path of right and truth"—but he concludes the letter with the most fervent praise of Constantine and Irene for having helped the church to recover unity.[43]

At the beginning of the council, Tarasius had said it was divine policy that children were not to die for their fathers' sins; each one dies for his own sin.[44] That, too, like Hadrian's "return to the arms of the Roman church," would have been an easy way to account for what the council was to do. But the church is too intricately tied to the past for such a neat distinction between generations to be made. The church in 787 cannot summarily cut itself loose from the church in 754, and hence the importance of Gregory of Neocaesarea. In writing to Hadrian, Tarasius is careful to make mention of this "repentance of the parents": "those who were still alive confessed the faith in written depositions."[45] Or, as one of the bishops at the council put it, in a different context, "Peter, prince [koruphaios] of the apostles, denied [Christ], but he repented, and was received back."[46]

The choice of Peter for the example here was, perhaps, not fortuitous. The point is that Christ himself received back the chief of the apostles. There is at least the implication that if Peter was not *irreprehensibilis,* then neither ought we to assume that his See is *irreprehensibilis.* There were many reasons why the fathers of Nicaea II did not want to adopt the Roman view of what they were doing; among those reasons were regional pride and jealousy of prerogatives. But this essay has attempted to show that the differing assessments of what the council was about were governed by fundamentally incompatible images of the church.

Indeed, we have come to a surprising conclusion. It is commonplace to say that one of the leading differences between eastern and western Christianity is that the former, the heir of Origen, lacks a historical sense, while the latter, the heir of Augustine, has one. Our analysis of the ACN and the LC would appear to call this distinction into question.

It is the fathers of Nicaea who effectively divide time into eras, while the LC see no fundamental difference between the age of Abel and the age of Charlemagne. Even more significant, however, is the fact that the ACN allow for real historical corruption *of the church.* The council had not only to deal directly with the recent history of the church in Byzantium, but also to take account, at least indirectly, of the Sixth Council's anathematization of Pope Honorius I for his Monothelite views.[47] The promise that the Holy Spirit will lead the church into the truth is no guarantee that the church cannot fall into error. The fathers of Nicaea are suggesting that on occasion (such as their own time) the Holy Spirit must intervene in history, and specifically *in the history of the church,* not simply on behalf of the church. The image of the Fall, typologically the beginning of history, can be applied to the church, which is thereby caught in the web of history, and only God can extricate it.

The LC, on the other hand, do not allow for real historical corruption of the church, and we see here the metaphysical groundwork for a belief in infallibility. The author of the LC would find it unthinkable that the church would ever have to repent of major doctrinal error as the fathers of Nicaea did. The promise of the Holy Spirit is the promise, in fact, that while the church may suffer many trials and tribulations, the church is not embedded in the web of history. The pope's dogmatic honor cannot be tarnished, and hence no true Christian will ever have to dishonor his parents by anathematizing them.

The practical situation in Byzantium, in Rome, and in the Frankish dominions made some of the LC's theorizing problematical, for the pope was more favorably disposed toward the Nicene Council than the LC were. But it has been the assumption of this essay that some deeply rooted attitudes were brought to the surface by anger over practical developments, and attitudes need not always be congruent with the facts.

In a way not so obvious—but more profound—the Seventh Ecumenical Council and the western reaction to it reveal the same emerging issue of infallibility that is presented by the Sixth Council in condemning the teaching of Pope Honorius. Among ecumenical stumbling-blocks today, few if any are as hard to get round as infallibility. One way of measuring and describing that stumbling-block is to set it against different images of the church as a family in history. And if it turns out that the easterners are more genuinely "historical" than the westerners, who can predict what further surprises might be in store?

Swarthmore College

APPENDIX
The Greek and Latin Versions of Hadrian's *Synodica*

As indicated in the introductory section of this essay, Luitpold Wallach has questioned the traditional explanation for the divergencies between the Greek and Latin versions of Hadrian's *synodica* in the *acta* of Nicaea II: "The Greek and Latin Versions of II Nicaea and the Synodica of Hadrian I (JE 2448): A Diplomatic Study," *Traditio* XXII (1966), 103–25. In my article, "Initial Eastern Assessments of the Seventh Oecumenical Council," *Journal of Theological Studies,* n.s. XXV (1974), 75–92, I repeated (pp. 79–81) the traditional explanation without taking Wallach's thesis into consideration. Wallach's challenge to the conventional view is strong, but I remain unpersuaded that the statement of Anastasius Bibliothecarius introducing the "restored" portion of the *synodica* at Mansi XII: 1073/74 "hardly refers to the election of Tarasius and the Seventh Ecumenical Council of 787" (Wallach, p. 111).

Wallach does not give adequate attention to the matters in the "suppressed" portion of Hadrian's letter besides the denunciation of Tarasius's rapid advancement to the patriarchate: the very stern rebuke of the use of the title "ecumenical" for the patriarch of Constantinople (XII: 1074AC), the demand for the return to Rome of jurisdiction over certain Italian ecclesiastical provinces (1073C–74A), and the fulsome praise of Charlemagne, with pointed reference to his generosity to the Roman see (1075C–76A). (The anomaly created by the reprimand of the rapid advancement in Hadrian's letter to Tarasius himself [JE 2449] is more apparent than real, since the words are relegated to a single participial clause [1078E], and actually serve to set off Hadrian's joy at the orthodoxy of Tarasius's faith. And Wallach's suggestion, that the mutilation of the much more extensive rebuke in the *synodica* would not have served a purpose at the council because "there was not any open quarrel at II Nicaea about the earlier uncanonical appointment in 784 by the Byzantine emperors of the layman Tarasius as patriarch of Constantinople" [p. 115], is something of a non sequitur, since the reading of that part of the *synodica* is just what would have been required to get a quarrel started.) It is *prima facie* unlikely that Irene would have permitted the reading of such statements in a council designed to moderate passions and restore unity.

If the supposedly suppressed passage was actually read, we have to account for the total lack of reference anywhere else in the council to the territorial question, and even more, we have to understand how bishops who indicated full assent to the letter proceeded without any compunction to address Tarasius as "ecumenical patriarch." This is a genuine anomaly, which begins (1078B) immediately after the reading of the *synodica,* and recurs often throughout the ACN. Wallach, p. 107, notes the first instance, but does not deal with the curiosity.

Wallach's strongest point (pp. 108–10) is the evidence that several decades after the council, Pope Nicholas I was instructing correspondents in Constantinople to consult their own copies of the ACN to see exactly what Hadrain had written on the subject of Tarasius's precipitate ordination. But, could it not have been that the copies of the *acta* sent to Rome in 787 simply had the full Latin text of the *synodica,* without a Greek translation, and without any indication that part of the letter had not been read? There is evidence in a letter of Theodore of Studios (*Epp.* I:38, PG XCIX: 1044C–45A) that Hadrian was unhappy with what his legates had done (for an extended discussion of this passage see Henry "Initial Eastern Assessments," pp. 76–83); perhaps they confessed to him that they had given in to imperial pressure to have that portion of the *synodica* omitted when the letter was read to the council. There must have been a great deal of political maneuvering prior to the council; the restoration of images was going to be a matter of extreme delicacy, as Tarasius and Irene found out when the first attempt to hold the council, in 786, was aborted by iconoclastic troops acting with the connivance of some of the bishops (Mansi XII: 990B–91D). Patriarch and empress could have made a persuasive case to the papal legates that the concluding section of the *synodica* would further damage the already frail chances for harmony.

There is no doubt that Wallach has raised serious issues in his specifically *diplomatic* study; my point is that the ecclesiastical situation in 787 was nearly as complicated as it would be in the Photian period, and it is likely that a lot went on behind the scenes earlier as well as later.

Notes

1. Henry Chadwick, *The Early Church* (Baltimore, 1967), p. 289.

2. ACN: Mansi XII: 951A–XIII: 486A. LC: MGH LL III, Concilia II Supplement. I have consulted the translation of the ACN by John Mendham, *The Seventh General Council the Second of Nicæa* (London, 1850), which also includes extensive extracts from the LC (of which Mendham is himself an impassioned partisan); however, all translations in this essay are my own.

3. See Appendix.

4. The dispute between Wallach and Ann Freeman has gone on for decades, and shows no signs of abating. Freeman, "Theodulf of Orléans and the *Libri Carolini,*" *Speculum* XXXII (1957), 663–705, argues for Theodulf's authorship on the basis of the convergence of literary, orthographic, and artistic evidence. In subsequent articles, "Further Studies in the *Libri Carolini,* I. Paleographical Problems in Vaticanus Latinus 7207; II. 'Patristic Exegesis, Mozarabic Antiphons, and the Vetus Latina,' " *Speculum* XL (1965), 203–89, and "Further Studies in the *Libri Carolini,* III. The Marginal Notes in Vaticanus Latinus 7207," *Speculum* XLVI (1971), 597–612, she has strengthened her case for the Mozarabic liturgical origin of anomalous scriptural citations in the *LC,* specifically in response to Wallach's insistence, "The Unknown Author of the *Libri Carolini:* Patristic Exegesis, Mozarabic Antiphons, and the Vetus Latina," in *Didascaliae: Studies in Honor of Anselm M. Albareda,* ed. Sesto Prete (New York, 1961), pp. 469–515, that the anomalies are to be accounted for as citations of patristic uses of the Old Latin. Wallach, "The *Libri Carolini* and Patristics, Latin and Greek: Prolego-

mena to a Critical Edition," in *The Classical Tradition: Literary and Historical Studies in Honor of Harry Caplan,* ed. Wallach (Ithaca, 1966), pp. 497–98, says he is now persuaded that Alcuin was author of the LC, and not simply editor, as he had previously thought, and in note 103 he promises a future publication on "Theodulf of Orléans' Alleged Authorship of the *Libri Carolini:* Fictions and Facts."

5. Freeman, "Theodulf," p. 665.

6. Professor Stephan Kuttner is partly responsible for my interest in a literary-critical approach to historical questions. The reading list he drew up for the Yale undergraduate course in church history in which I served as his graduate assistant for two years in the mid-1960s included Evelyn Waugh's novel, *Helena* (about the mother of Constantine the Great); and I recall his saying that if you could read only one book to get a sense of the Middle Ages, it should be Terence H. White's Arthurian romance, *The Once and Future King.*

7. Byzantine Institute of America, *Mosaics of Haghia Sophia at Istanbul* (Boston, 1950), plates 14–22.

8. The print, by Robert Hodgell, hangs in the study of the Rev. John R. Haas, Christ Presbyterian Church in Edina, Minneapolis, Minnesota.

9. The LC declare a plague on both eastern houses, but the action of Hiereia is gently reprimanded, while the action of Nicaea is sternly rebuked; see, e.g., LC 4.9, p. 189, l. 22, where abolition of images is called "levitas" and worshiping of images "culpa"; and 4.4, p. 179, l. 20, where the iconoclast error is classified as "inperitia."

10. Among instances of these images are the following: ACN Mansi xiii: 4b, 221d, 245d, 249d, 288a, 293a, 313e, 373e, 376ab; LC 1.24, p. 53, ll. 5–7; 3.17, p. 139, l. 32; 4.21, p. 214, l. 24–p. 215, l. 7.

11. These anathemas are in two of the chapters of the *Horos* of 754, quoted in ACN Mansi xiii: 344c, 345cd.

12. ACN Mansi xii: 1031d; cf. the statement of Bishop Leo of Rhodes at 1018de.

13. In his long letter (Venance Grumel, *Les Regestes des Actes du Patriarcat de Constantinople,* [Chalcedon (Kadiköy), 1936], ii, no. 330) to a fervent iconoclast, Bishop Thomas of Claudiopolis: ACN Mansi xiii: 124de.

14. Ibid., xii: 1118bc. For an account of the monastic opposition see Patrick Henry, "Initial Eastern Assessments of the Seventh Oecumenical Council," *Journal of Theological Studies,* n.s. xxv (1974), 83–84.

15. ACN Mansi xii: 1047a–50d.

16. Ibid., xiii: 204de.

17. Ibid., xiii: 401d (Grumel, *Regestes,* n. 358). In the same letter (401e) the rulers' action is credited to "the movement of the divine spirit dwelling in you" [hē aura tou theiou pneumatos].

18. ACN Mansi xiii: 329d.

19. Ibid., 364b: "kai huper tēs athēteseōs tōn ekklēsiastikōn paradoseōn aitēsōmetha sungnōmēn tou hamartēmatos."

20. Elements of this argument are scattered throughout the LC; there is a concentrated dose of it in 2.31, pp. 100–02. See also 4.6, pp. 184–86; 4.7, p. 187, ll. 23–25; and 4.13, p. 193, ll. 34–35, and p. 194, ll. 2–4.

21. LC 2.31, p. 101, ll. 25–29.

22. ACN Mansi xiii: 296a.

23. LC 1.19, p. 44, ll. 18–28.

24. Ibid., 4.3, p. 177, ll. 6–33.

25. See, e.g., Alcuin, *Ep.* 41 to Charlemagne (a.d. 794/795), MGH Epp. iv: 84, ll. 14–17: "Ita et David olim praecedentis populi rex a Deo electus et Deo dilectus et egregius psalmista Israeli victrici gladio undique gentes subiciens, legisque Dei eximius praedicator in populo extitit."

26. Vincent of Lérins, *Commonitorium* 2.3, PL l: 640.

27. LC 4.2, pp. 174–76, esp. p. 174, l. 37–p. 175, l. 10 (where it is noted that angels, as well as men, worship God without pictures); and 1.29, p. 59, ll. 19–37. Cf. 3.28, pp. 163–65; and 3.17, p. 140, ll. 7–23, where it is pointed out that "innumerabiles in caelesti

patria sunt legiones" who never had or worshiped images. This chapter (3.17) of the LC is based on the most egregious of all the misrepresentations of the ACN: Bishop Constantine of Constantia in Cyprus, who (Mansi XII: 1147B) makes a clear distinction between the degrees of worship offered to icons and to the Trinity, is quoted as having declared there is no distinction at all.

28. For a detailed account of this motif in the thinking of the iconodules, see Patrick Henry, "What was the Iconoclastic Controversy About?" *Church History* XLV (1976), 23–25.

29. LC 2.27, p. 88, l. 45.

30. Ibid., l. 19, p. 44, esp. ll. 33–36: "Cum videlicet tabulae et duo cherubim exemplaria fuerint futurorum, et cum Iudaei habuerint carnaliter res, quae typicis opertae figuris praefigurationes fuerint futurorum, nos habemus in veritate spiritaliter ea, quae illis exemplaribus sive praefigurationibus carnalibus praefigurabantur"; and 1.29, pp. 57–59, a long catalogue of material objects in the temple with their equivalent "spiritales virtutes" in the church.

31. ACN Mansi XIII: 284C–85B, concerning the timeliness of the Exod. 20 prohibition, given that the Israelites were just about to enter a land teeming with idol worshipers; 288B: "all Christians confess that Christ, *by his dwelling among us in the flesh,* has delivered us from the error of idols and all pagan worship"; 216A: "the Incarnate Word has delivered man from idolatry and remade him for immortality, and redemption is better than what there was before the Fall" [*kreitton tēs plaseōs ginetai hē anaplasis*].

32. This theme, reiterated often during the Council, is stated at the very beginning of the *Horos* of Nicaea II: Mansi XIII: 373E. In LC 1.20, p. 45, ll. 37–38, Tarasius is rebuked for diverting the minds of the people subject to him from spiritual things to carnal ones, from things invisible to things visible ("ab spiritalibus ad carnalia, ab invisibilibus ad visibilia"); there is a sense in which Tarasius could take this as commendation, for is not this kind of inversion a consequence of the Incarnation?

33. LC 2.28, p. 90, ll. 41–43: "Veniamus ad Dominum, sedeamus cum Maria ad pedes eius, audiamus verbum ex ore eius, audiamus eum in seipso, quem actenus in Apostolo loquentem audivimus." There is rhetorical convention here, to be sure, but the choice of this particular convention is significant.

34. Ibid., 2.30, pp. 92–100, is an extended praise of writing and books at the expense of painting and pictures: from Moses on Sinai to John on Patmos, God is always commanding people, even those who see visions, to write things down.

35. ACN Mansi XIII: 361CD. The iconoclasts in 754 had blamed Satan for insinuating idolatry into the church: 221CD.

36. LC 1.3, p. 14, l. 36 and p. 15, l. 3: "De eo, quod Constantinus et Haerena gesta vel scripta sua 'divalia' nuncupant. Priscae gentilitatis obsoletus error Christi adventu repulsus quoddam cernitur in his reliquisse vestigium, qui se fidei et religionis christianae iactant retinere fastigium, qui et intra ecclesiam novas et ineptas constitutiones audacter statuere affectant et se 'divos' suaque gesta 'divalia' gentiliter nuncupare non formidant. Unde fit, ut quod protoplasti perpetravere florigera in sede virosa serpentis promissione inlecti, hoc isti perpetrent in ecclesia antiqui hostis fraude decepti, cum videlicet et isti per inanis gloriae celsitudinem se 'divos' nominare non renuant et per avaritiae repacitatem, per quam vanae laudis culmen adire temptant, ecclesiae novum aliquod inferre contendant." The fact that the author of the LC is here taking the Greeks to task for misunderstood and misrepresented conventions of imperial style serves to enhance our suspicion that the image of Eden has been summoned up by anger, not by the requirements of the argument.

37. JE, 2483; MGH *Epp.* V: 56, l. 34– p. 57, l. 3.

38. Ibid., p. 40, l. 38– p. 41, l. 1. In the same section of the letter, p. 40, ll. 34–35, Hadrian expresses his annoyance at the way Charlemagne keeps harping on the theme of the Council's disrespect for parents.

39. ACN Mansi XII: 1071/72.

40. Ibid., 1071B. These are the final lines of the letter in the printed version of the Greek text.

41. Ibid., 1086A–1095A.

42. Ibid., XIII: 4A: "pnoē kuriou pantokratoros"; "sumphōnoi gegonamen." The "sumphōnia" is praised by several bishops at the end of the Third Session: ibid., XII: 1146C–51D.

43. ACN Mansi XIII: 459D (Grumel, *Regestes,* no. 359): "hōs ophthalmos to holon sōma pros tēn tēs eutheias kai alētheias tribon hypedeiknues"; praise of the emperor and empress: 462CD. The differences in conception of the *structure* of the church between East and West have been analyzed by Wilhelm de Vries, S. J., "Die Struktur der Kirche gemäss dem II. Konzil von Nicäa (787)," *Orientalia Christiana periodica* XXXIII (1967), 47–71: the easterners, by insisting on an ecumenical council, with all five patriarchs participating, demonstrated a view of authority counter to the papal assumption that the only thing necessary was a return of Byzantium to the faith and communion of the Roman see; and the council, despite its kind words about Hadrian, understood itself to have been summoned by imperial mandate. From this follows de Vries's conclusion, p. 71, that an eastern conception of an imperial church ("Reichskirche") confronted a western conception of a papal church ("Papstkirche"). I would suggest that the different images of the church outlined in the present essay provide the framework for the different conceptions of ecclesiastical structure analyzed by de Vries in his article.

44. ACN Mansi XII: 1042C.

45. Ibid., XIII: 462A.

46. Ibid., 61D.

47. In its own *Horos,* the Seventh Council reaffirms the position of the Council of Constantinople of 681, and lists Honorius among those driven out by that council: ibid., 377B. For a recent account of the Honorius question, see Patrick O'Connell, S.J., *The Ecclesiology of St. Nicephorus I (758–828).* Orientalia Christiana analecta CXCIV (Rome, 1972), pp. 73–75, and, in a more general framework, Jaroslav Pelikan, *The Spirit of Eastern Christendom (600–1700)* (Chicago, 1974), pp. 150–53. De Vries, "Die Struktur," pp. 48–49, notes the different implications for ecclesiology of the situations which gave rise to the Sixth and Seventh Ecumenical Councils.

The Structure of Medieval Society According to the *Dictatores* of the Twelfth Century

GILES CONSTABLE

One of the most serious responsibilities of professional letter-writers in the Middle Ages was to know the proper social standing of the senders and recipients of letters and to arrange their names accordingly in the salutation.[1] Already in the fourth century the author of the first known treatise on epistolary theory in Latin, C. Julius Victor, advised his readers to be neither jocular when writing to a superior, nor rude when writing to an equal, nor proud when writing to an inferior; and the anonymous writer of an isolated paragraph *De epistolis* found in an eighth-century manuscript from Monte Cassino urged that in the writing of letters, "Consideration should be given to who is writing to whom and about what." He then listed ten "accidents of persons" which should be considered: birth, sex, age, training, character ("ars"), office, behavior ("mores"), disposition, name, and dignity; and he added that "There is a great difference whether we are writing to a nobleman, or to an old man, or to a magistrate, or to a father, or to a friend, or to one for whom things are going well, or to a sad man, and such things as these."[2]

These particular works were probably not known well, if at all, in the eleventh and twelfth centuries, but they represented a tradition which was doubtless handed down as much in the practice as in the theory of letter-writing; and many of the *dictatores* who composed the manuals known as the *artes dictandi* or *dictaminis* therefore discussed the question of the structure of society. They were generally agreed that everyone could be classified as either high, middle, or low and that in salutations the names of higher persons (whether the sender or the recipient) must be put first and the names of equals either first or second, though humility and courtesy both suggested that the sender be named second. Lower persons were always named second. This teaching was probably more or less common knowledge in the twelfth century, and Heloise (who is not known to have read any formal work on *dictamen*) said in her second letter that, "It is indeed right and honest that someone who is writing to superiors or equals puts their names first, whereas when [they are writing] to inferiors, those who come first in the dignity of things should come first in the order of writing."[3] Many of the *dictatores*, however, went into greater detail in the matter of social rank and often differed in their descriptions of each class and its members, and they thus offer some insights into the contemporary view of the structure of society.

Alberic of Monte Cassino, who died about 1105, was "the first known exponent of the new art of letter-writing and the author of the earliest surviving treatise upon this art," according to C. H. Haskins.[4] He touched only briefly on the question of social status, however. In his *Breviarium de dictamine,* of which only excerpts have been published, he classified letters as "humilis," "mediocris," and "grandilocus" with reference to their style rather than to the rank of the sender or recipient;[5] but in the *Dictaminum radii* or *Flores rhetorici,* which may be a continuation of the *Breviarium* or perhaps, according to Lanham, the work of another author, emphasis is put on the need to consider the persons named in the salutation and to determine "whether he is exalted or humble, whether he is a friend or an enemy, and lastly what is his manner [modus] or fortune," emphasizing that the style of the letter must be suited to the condition and station of the sender and recipient.[6]

The rules for salutations were spelled out in greater detail by Adalbert Samaritanus of Bologna in his *Praecepta dictaminum,* of which the first version was finished by 1115. After explaining the law, as he called it, that the name of a greater person must precede that of a lesser and that the names of equals might be put either way "according to the wish of the writer," he said that "The salutation describes the person and the order by its varying nature, since we salute a superior in one way, an inferior in another, an equal in another. . . . As [there are] three orders of men, so there are three types of letters: exalted, middling, and feeble." A letter from a lesser person to a greater is called exalted because it ascends from an inferior to a superior and is marked by the three characteristics of flattery at the beginning, the reason for the flattery in the middle, and a request at the end. A letter from a greater person to a lesser is called feeble because it descends and is marked only by an order or request, with no flattery. A middling letter, between equals, is so called from its position between exalted and feeble. It neither ascends nor descends and is marked by the two characteristics of flattery (presumably at the beginning) and a request. Salutations therefore vary in accordance with this diversity of persons, and differing forms of address (of which Adalbert later gave examples) are used for clergy and laity; canons, monks, bishops, and abbots ("we praise one for his religion, another for his learning, another for both"); a father, mother, brother, sister, son, daughter, kinsman, and stranger; and a nobleman, a wise man, the holder of a princedom, and someone with no position.[7]

Two other *artes dictandi* composed in Northern Italy in the early twelfth century are the *Rationes dictandi* of Hugh of Bologna, which Haskins dated 1119–24,[8] and the *Aurea gemma* by Henry Francigena, who wrote soon after Hugh and was the first *dictator* to give his work one of the "poetico-allegorical" titles which later became popular and have proved an abundant source of confusion for scholars.[9] For Hugh, as for Adalbert, there were three orders of letters corresponding to the three orders of people: "Those to greater and elevated persons are called sublime; those to serfs or dependents, lowest; those to equals or comparable friends, middling."[10] Henry, however, went into greater detail than his predecessors on the nature of the orders: "Since there are innumerable people from lesser to greater, and since it would be beyond my powers to go through them all, I take comfort in brevity and confine everybody to three, giving them the names of greater, equal, lesser. Greater is called exalted; equal, middling; lesser, mean." He then listed the members of the three orders, putting at the top, among the exalted, the pope, emperor, kings, tetrarchs, archbishops, marquises, dukes, counts, bishops, abbots, abbesses, provosts, deans, "and other magnates"; in the middle, priests, soldiers, citizens, townsmen, moneyers, friends, "and others not raised to the highest honor nor depressed to the lowest"; and at the bottom, peasants, students, retainers, and serfs. In the salutation, the name of a greater man must come first, the name of a middling person either first or second, and the name of a mean person second.[11] Henry is the first known *dictator* to define the ranks and occupational groups in each order. The practice soon spread, however, though with differing definitions.

It appears in differing forms, for example, in two reworkings of the *Praecepta dictaminum* of Adalbert, who was the most influential of the early Bolognese *dictatores*. One of these, found in manuscripts at Leipzig and Oxford and entitled the *Aurea gemma,* was thought to be a version of the work by Henry Francigena until it was shown by Kantorowicz to be "an *ars dictandi* based upon Albert of Samaria but containing a few interlarded quotations taken from Henricus Francigena's work" and to have been written about 1130–43.[12] It did not enter into any details on the orders of persons, classifying them like Henry as exalted, middling, and mean (using the term "tenuis"). It then gave examples of suitably honorific terms to be used in salutations, stressing that they should correspond to the diversity of persons, and differed from Henry in ranking the pope as exalted but dukes and marquises only as middling.[13] The other version of Adalbert's work, found in two manuscripts at Copenhagen and Berlin, is dated to France in the mid-twelfth century by the accompanying letter-collection of Prior Peter of St. John at Sens.[14] This treatise is basically an independent work, though it drew on Adalbert and was also influenced by Henry Francigena or other sources. It defined the orders in the usual way as greater, equal, and lesser, saying that the names of greater persons must be put first and of equals either first or second. Then, following Adalbert, but reversing his distinctions, it said:

> As there are three orders of persons, so there are three principal types of letters: humble, middling, and exalted. A humble letter is one sent by a humble person, such as oxherds, cobblers, and pelterers and others who have no lower order beneath them. An exalted letter is one sent by an exalted person, as by a pope or emperor. An exalted person is one than who there is no higher dignity, as is the pope in ecclesiastical affairs [and] the emperor in secular affairs. A middling person is one who is between exalted and humble, such as tetrarchs, kings, marquises, counts, dukes, archbishops, captains, vavasors, vidames, and others who are between exalted and humble.[15]

Lists like this were doubtless useful as the forms of salutation became increasingly fixed as the century advanced—a tendency attributed by Schmale to the influence of the schools[16]—but the differences between them, reflecting, as it seems, the personal views of the *dictatores,* must also have been at times confusing.

Meanwhile in Italy another treatise, also entitled the *Rationes dictandi,* was produced in the region of Emilia or Romagna in the late 1130s.[17] Its author is unknown, but it influenced (and may, according to Savorelli, even have been the first version of) the important *Introductiones prosaici dictaminis* by Bernard of Bologna, of which the first redaction was written in Romagna in 1144–5 and the second, probably revised by the author, in 1145–52 and of which various later versions were produced north of the Alps, which have contributed to the confusion between this Bolognese Master Bernard and the French *dictatores* Bernard Sylvestris, who taught at Tours in the middle of the twelfth century, and the Master Bernard who taught *dictamen* at Meung in the 1180s.[18] The section on the salutation in the anonymous *Rationes dictandi* began with the statement that "A salutation is a prayer for welfare indicating a feeling not disagreeing with the position of the persons." After describing various types of salutations and their embellishments, such as titles and offices, it said, in partial disagreement with other treatises, that "The names of the recipients should always precede the names of the senders . . . except when a greater [person] writes to a lesser, in which case the name of the sender is put first, so that his dignity may be shown by the position of the names." Later it went on, after discussing the use of the dative and accusative cases, with a standard division of all people into excellent, middle, and lowly and defined the excellent as those without a superior, like the pope and the emperor.[19]

Bernard of Bologna defined the salutation in the same way as the anonymous *Rationes dictandi,* adding that "A prudent *dictator,* therefore, in order to furnish a suitable salutation to each letter, must know in advance the persons of the sender and the recipient." He went on at once to divide all people into outstanding, middling, and lowly and then described these groups in an original fashion, which agreed with Adalbert in distinguishing clergy from laity (a distinction not made by Henry Francigena or in the Copenhagen-Berlin version of Adalbert) and showed an exceptional sensitivity to the differentiating factors of power, office, dignity, birth, and nobility.

> Persons are called outstanding to whom no one is superior either in birth or in dignity, such as the pope and the emperor of the Romans. We consider lowly, however, those than who no one lower can be found in birth or dignity, such as 'servi empticii' and lowly retainers. Those to whom there are some superior [and] some inferior in birth, power, and dignity are rightly called middling. There is a great mass of these men in the middle, some equal, some unequal. Among both the clergy and the laity, we call equal those who are comparable in office, dignity, and power, like (among clerics) bishops between themselves, archbishops, archdeacons, deans, parish priests, abbots, priors, priests, deacons, clerics, and some holding other offices, and (among laymen) kings, dukes, marquises, counts, lords, consuls, vidames, and men with other dignities or offices. But we also have examples of unequal persons. Although laymen may always excel in power or nobility, they are called inferior to the clergy out of reverence for the ecclesiastical dignity, and if magnates write even to priests, they should therefore do so as to greater persons. A

father, grandfather, or greatgrandfather is always greater than a son or grandson, even if greater power or dignity is on the other side, and a bishop should therefore write to his father, grandfather, or greatgrandfather as to a greater person. They, however, should not write to a bishop as to a lesser person.[20]

Here for the first time a sort of hierarchy of distinctions was adumbrated, differentiated primarily by dignity and office but also, to a lesser extent, by family relationships, status, and birth. "According to the skill of the *dictator,*" Bernard said later, "the diversity of persons in every order and manner penetrates the diversity of salutations."[21]

The work of Bernard of Bologna had a wide influence both in Italy and north of the Alps, where it can be seen in two anonymous treatises in Vienna manuscripts 246 and 896, of which the former is from France and was dated in the 1150s (or possibly 1153–91) by Savorelli and in the early thirteenth century by Haskins, and the latter according to Zöllner is from Burgundy in the late 1190s.[22] The treatise in Vienna 246 followed Bernard of Bologna almost verbatim in defining a salutation and saying that a *dictator* must know in advance the persons of the sender and recipient but continued somewhat differently, in wording if not in sense, to say that "The quality of people should be observed in the salutation, which should vary according to their differing status," and immediately to distinguish the clergy from the laity. The clergy were then divided into three ranks: superior or outstanding, such as apostolic men, patriarchs, and the pope; inferior or lowly, such as simple clerics, deacons, levites, parochial clergy, priests, and others "who have no dignity in the church"; and middling or middle, such as archpriests, archdeacons, provosts, deans, priors, abbots, archbishops, and bishops, adding that "Archbishops and bishops, however, may be counted among the superior persons." The same division was made among the laity: only the emperor was superior; *servi emptitii,* retainers, cobblers, pelterers, smiths, shepherds, and the like were inferior; and between them were the middling persons, such as the prefects of a town, tribunes, marquises, dukes, counts, viscounts, and kings, again adding that "Kings are said by some to be among the superiors." The author then distinguished, like Bernard, between those who are equal in birth, office, power, or dignity, such as archbishops or kings among themselves, and those who are unequal, such as archbishops and bishops or kings and counts, repeating that "The salutation should vary according to these varying statuses." After a conventional statement that the name of the superior person should come first, it again followed Bernard almost verbatim on the precedence of the clergy over laymen and fathers over sons. Among equals, however, as when a bishop writes to a bishop or a count to a count, the sender's name should come second out of reverence and humility. After a brief and inconclusive discussion of the differentiating factors of birth, office, power, and dignity, stressing that all of these must be taken into consideration in writing a salutation, this section concluded with a description of the various types of salutation, like that in the anonymous *Rationes dictandi,* and of their grammatical construction.[23]

The treatment in the *ars dictandi* in Vienna 896, though shorter, also followed the sense of Bernard of Bologna, but not always his wording. It inserted into his definition of a salutation, for instance, the term "brief," adding that, "Prolixity is a vice in a salutation, which ought to be brief and succinct." After saying, as in Vienna 246, that, "The salutation of persons should vary according to their differing status," and dividing people into clergy and laity and into superior, inferior, and middle, it defined the superior clergy as the pope, archbishops, and bishops; the inferior clergy as simple canons, parochial clergy, priests, and poor clerics; and the middling clergy as deans, provosts, archdeacons, subdeacons, parish priests, precentors, succentors, "and others having some dignity in the holy church." Among the laity, emperors and kings are superior; commoners and peasants, inferior; and counts, viscounts, marquises, and castellans, middling. And it concluded, before giving the rules of priority and examples, as in Vienna 246, by repeating that the salutation must vary according to all these status. A very similar listing to this is found in a late twelfth or early thirteenth-century *Summa grammaticalis,* probably from Languedoc, by Master William,[24] who added patriarchs and primates to the upper clergy and townsmen to the inferior laity and who in the middling groups added abbots, dukes, and seneschals but omitted subdeacons, parish priests, and marquises. He went on, however, in an interesting way to distinguish three grades within each order, calling the pope highest, archbishops and primates higher, and bishops high; archdeacons low, priests lower, and simple clerics lowest; and the emperor highest, great kings higher, and kings and kinglets high; "and likewise for the middle and lower [persons] who are distinguished into three grades."[25] He thus really substituted a nine- for a three-stage hierarchy among both the clergy and the laity, making a total of eighteen categories, but he did not spell them all out.[26]

In the Italian *artes* of the second half of the twelfth century, it was less usual to list the members of the various orders. Albert of San Martino, a canon of Asti, whose *Flores dictandi* was dated about 1150 by Haskins, called the three types of letters, corresponding to the orders of people, weighty, middling, and light, explaining that weighty letters were to elevated people or about major concerns, middle letters to those of lower but not the lowest status, as between equals and friends of comparable rank, and weak letters to dependents. After explaining that the salutations should correspond to these orders, he added that suitable adjectives should be used, "by which we can express the variety of persons. For we speak in different ways to a pope, king, bishop, abbot, monk, vigorous soldier, companion or dear friend."[27] Paul of Camaldoli was another *dictator* working in the north of Italy probably in the last third of the twelfth century. He classified the three orders as the exalted who had no superior, like the pope and emperor, the mean who had no inferior, and the middling who came between. "A true consideration of things teaches us to write in a different way to different persons, depending on their greatness," he said, and added after commenting on the order of names in the salutation:

A good *dictator* should know in advance the order of persons so that he may better fit the manner of speaking to their greatness and quality. For to exalted persons and in great causes the splendor of the words and greatness of the deed should be displayed in a manner fitting the material. To middling people, however, suitable things can be said temperately, whereas a weak person should have fewer words the lower he is and use no long sentences, provided that his brevity or that of his interlocutor generates no obscurity and is not deprived of vigor in joining words to matter. By keeping these qualities well, we shall legitmately fulfill the triple manner of speaking which many call humble, middling, and grandiloquent.[28]

These distinctions were carried further by Master Geoffrey, whose *Summa de arte dictandi* was written at Bologna in 1188–90: "Since every salutation derives from a person, we should see, first, what the person is in this situation, second, what is the diversity of persons, third, to whom a salutation is owed and to whom not, fourth, who should precede whom in the salutation, fifth and last, the diversity created by diverse people in diverse themes." Having established that only rational creatures (that is, sane adults) send and receive letters, Paul examined their diversity, separating enemies from nonenemies and dividing nonenemies into the usual ranks of exalted, middling, and humble, and then gave his examples.[29]

By the turn of the century the formal rules for salutations were therefore established and *dictatores* like Thomas of Capua and Guido Faba concentrated on more difficult questions. Thomas, as a papal notary under Innocent III and later cardinal-priest of Santa Sabina, was among the most prominent *dictatores* of his day. In the section on salutations in his *Ars dictaminis,* written in the first decade of the thirteenth century, he not only gave the standard instructions concerning the precedence of greater persons and of the recipient among equals (though adding that either name might be put first in a letter from a middling person to a somewhat lesser one) but also discussed the nature of a salutation, which he said implied a measure both of good-will and of equality and should not therefore be used either for enemies and excommunicates nor for great lords, to whom reverence rather than good-will was owed. "For to salute and to bless flows from the authority of the greater, not from the presumption of the lesser. We salute our equals, however, or those a little greater, without fear of offense."[30] He then studied the grammatical structure and wording of salutations, pointing out among other things that "Dei gratia" might be used by a magnate of himself except when addressing the pope or king but not by middling or lowly people, since "it suggests either great dignity or magnificence."[31] Thomas's contemporary Guido Faba likewise studied the finer points of salutations in his *Summa dictaminis,* although he also stated "the general doctrine of all salutations" with regard to putting first the name of a greater person "in both the ecclesiastical and the secular orders" and the name of the recipient in a letter between equals, adding later that in a letter from a middling to a lesser person, the *dictator* might put either name first. Like Master William in Languedoc, he drew distinctions within the orders, differentiating, for example, from the point of view of a bishop, between the most greater (the pope or emperor, to whom no salutation was customarily given), the middle greater (such as a metropolitan), the middle lesser (such as a canon or episcopal cleric), and the much lesser, or base person (such as a minor canon, syndic or cleric of a small place, or an almost illiterate person).[32]

A final witness from north of the Alps is Peter of Blois, whose unpublished *Libellus de arte dictandi rhetorice,* written probably in France in the 1180s, has suffered some unmerited abuse at the hands of scholars,[33] since at least on the matter of salutations it is not without originality and interest. For after saying that "The varieties of salutations are distinguished according to the diversities of persons," Peter listed five, not three, ranks: highest, exalted, middling, private, and lowly:

> The highest are those to whom no one is superior in dignity, like the lord pope and the Roman emperor. The exalted [are] such as patriarchs, archbishops, kings, bishops, dukes, counts, palatines, marquises. The middling are such as deans, archdeacons, abbots, provosts, sacristans, treasurers, castellans, reeves, consuls who are called peers in some towns. The private [persons] are those who administer no dignity, such as soldiers and clerics. The lowly are such as peasants and everyone occupied with civilian works, like cobblers and others.

Some of the exalted and middling persons are equal in office and dignity, such as bishops or archdeacons among themselves; but (and here Peter followed Bernard of Bologna almost verbatim) the clergy are superior to the laity and fathers to their sons, though Peter added to the relations cited by Bernard the paternal uncle, mother, grandmother, and maternal aunt. He ended this section with another passage adapted from Bernard, saying that, "When the studious *dictator,* knowing this variety of persons, comes to writing, he should first consider whether an equal is writing to an equal or a superior to an inferior or to an equal."[34]

In conclusion, three points may be made, one about the works of the *dictatores* and two about their view of society. With regard to the *artes dictandi* consulted for this article, in spite of many general similarities and dependencies, no two were the same in their discussions of salutations. The accusation of monotony and repetitiveness often brought against this type of work is not therefore fully justified. A complete comparison will be possible only when satisfactory critical editions of all the *artes* have been produced,[35] but the evidence here suggests that their authors and revisers contributed a more personal touch than is sometimes said and that even small differences between them are of interest.

With regard to the structure of society, almost all the *dictatores* agreed on the division into upper, middle, and lower orders. The upper order was called "sublimis," "maior," "summus," "altior," "superior," "supremus," "gravis," "excellens," or "eximius." The middle order was called "mediocris" or "medie," for which "par" or "equalis" was occasionally given as an alternative. The lower order was referred to as "exilis," "tenuis," "minor," "humilis," "inferior," "infimus," or "extenuatus."[36] Peter of Blois was alone in positing five orders, and Master William, and to some extent Guido Faba, in seeking sub-categories within the orders. Aside from those who separated the clergy from the laity,[37] there was no trace of the customary medieval divisions either into clerics, monks, and laymen or into prayers, fighters, and workers. Even Peter of Blois, who followed Bernard of Bologna in asserting the superiority of the clergy, mixed bishops and counts, abbots and castellans, and clerics and soldiers in his lists. What mattered to the *dictatores* was not profession in the technical sense of the word but dignity, power, and office, and to a lesser extent, as Bernard of Bologna shows most clearly among the authors considered here, birth and nobility. Thus for Peter of Blois the principal characteristic of his one but lowest class, the private persons, was that they held no dignity. Wealth and poverty, apart from a couple of references to "pauperes clerici" in the lowest rank, hardly came into the matter at all. The terms used for the lower order all imply weakness and inferiority rather than poverty, and those for the upper order, greatness and superiority rather than wealth.

The main difference among the *dictatores* was with regard to the membership in the various orders. For some, the pope and the emperor alone, since they had no earthly superior, belonged to the upper order, whereas for others it included at least kings, patriarchs, primates, archbishops, and bishops; and Henry Francigena, who was the most liberal in this respect, added marquises, dukes, counts, abbots, abbesses, provosts, and deans. At the other end of the social spectrum, the lower order included manual laborers and sometimes, more generally, commoners, townsmen, and retainers. "Milites," whom Henry Francigena with his usual generosity classified as "mediocres," were put in the lowest order by Ludolf of Hildesheim and in the one but lowest, the private persons, by Peter of Blois, together with the clerics.[38] Others put clerics, parochial clergy, canons, and even deacons and priests into the lowest class. Students, scholars, and, for Ludolf, even masters were also in the lowest class, presumably because they held no office or dignity.

Most interesting of all is the middle class. For Henry Francigena this was a comparatively humble rank, including priests, soldiers, citizens, townsmen, moneyers, and friends, but for most of the *dictatores* it was much more exalted. Some, indeed, included in it everyone below the pope and emperor and above the lowest class, including tetrarchs, kings, archbishops, and dukes; and Bernard of Bologna, who was the most all-inclusive in this respect, put all the clergy from archbishop to simple clerics and the laity from king to vidame among the "mediocres," though his followers as a rule pared his list at both ends, including the higher ranks in the upper class and the humbler ones in the lower. The treatise in Vienna manuscript 246 included prefects of towns and tribunes in the middle class, and Peter of Blois mentioned prefects and "consuls who in some towns are called peers," but Ludolf, reflecting perhaps the more traditional society in Germany, put the lords of towns but not urban officials in the middle class and relegated merchants to the lower order.

The Middle Ages had long known a middle class in a legal sense. "Mediocres" and "mediani" appear in the Burgundian and Alamannian codes and are found for many centuries in the legal sources from certain regions.[39] The term was also sometimes used in a more general sense to imply a status between noble and ignoble or between rich and poor—usually closer to the noble and rich than to the ignoble and poor end of this spectrum.[40] The twelfth century *dictatores* were the first, however, to develop a reasonably clear concept of a middle class of society. It reached higher than any modern idea of the middle class and included ranks which by later standards would have been counted as aristocracy. It had little to do with birth or wealth as such, and nothing with urban or economic development. Townsmen and merchants, when mentioned at all, were put in the lower order. It reflected, on the contrary, a characteristically medieval concern for the importance of office and established positions in society, and a corresponding disdain for dependents and even for independent people without formal dignities. As such, it represents, in spite of its confusions and inconsistencies, an interesting and original contribution to western social thought.

Harvard University

Notes

No effort will be made in this article to cover more than a selection of the twelfth century *artes dictandi*, many of which exist only in manuscript or in unsatisfactory editions. For a recent bibliography, covering both primary and secondary works, see James J. Murphy, *Medieval Rhetoric: A Select Bibliography*, Toronto Medieval Bibliographies III (Toronto, 1971), 55–70. The Latin will be cited in the notes only for unpublished texts. I am deeply indebted to Professor Richard H. Rouse, Sister Benedicta Ward, and the late Dr. Ethel C. Higonnet for their help with manuscripts from, respectively, Paris, Oxford, and Cambridge.

1. On the epistolary salutation, see Paul Krüger, *Bedeutung und Entwicklung der Salutatio in den mittelalterlichen Briefstellern bis zum 14. Jahrhundert* (Greifswald, 1912), who concentrated on the period from the eleventh to the fourteenth century and referred to the development of the salutation as "ein Spiegelbild der Kultur des Mittelalters" (p. 52), and especially Carol D. Lanham, *Salutatio Formulas in Latin Letters to 1200: Syntax, Style, and Theory*, Münchener Beiträge zur Mediävistik und Renaissance-Forschung XXII (Munich, 1975).

2. Karl von Halm, *Rhetores latini minores* (Leipzig, 1863), p. 448 and p. 589, citing Paris, Bibl. nat., MS lat. 7530; cf. Lanham, *Salutatio Formulas*, pp. 89–90, who attributed to C. Julius Victor the introduction into epistolary theory of the three ranks of superior, equal, and inferior.

3. Abelard, *Historia calamitatum*, ed. J. Monfrin, Bibliothèque des Textes philosophiques (Paris, 1959), p. 118.

4. C. H. Haskins, "Albericus Casinensis," *Casinensia* (Monte Cassino, 1929), I: 116; cf. James J. Murphy, "Alberic of Monte Cassino: Father of the Medieval *Ars dictaminis*," *American Benedictine Review* XXII (1971), 129–46, esp. 138–46 on Alberic, whom he called "a pivotal figure in the history of medieval rhetoric"; Aldo Scaglione, *Ars grammatica*, Janua linguarum: Series minor LXXVII (The Hague-Paris, 1970), 131–39; and Herbert Bloch, "Monte Cassino's Teachers and Library in the High Middle Ages," *La Scuola nell'Occidente latino dell'alto Medioevo*, Settimane di Studio del Centro italiano di Studi sull'alto Medioevo XIX (Spoleto, 1972), 587–99, who called him "the first representative of the *ars dictaminis*" (p. 593) and referred to other secondary literature.

5. Ludwig Rockinger, *Briefsteller und Formelbücher des eilften bis vierzehnten Jahrhunderts* Quellen und Erörterungen zur bayerischen und deutschen Geschichte IX (Munich, 1863), I: 30. This edition is incomplete and unsatisfactory, and a new one, according to Bloch, in *La Scuola,* p. 590, n. 82, is in preparation by P.-Chr. Groll.

6. Alberic of Monte Cassino, *Flores rhetorici,* ch. 5, ed. D. M. Inguanez and H. M. Willard, Miscellanea Cassinese XIV (Monte Cassino, 1938), 35; cf. on this work Bloch, in *La Scuola,* pp. 591–92 (and p. 589 on the title, on which see also Murphy, *Rhetoric,* p. 60) and Lanham, *Salutatio Formulas,* pp. 94–97, who stressed the difference between the *Breviarium* and the *Flores* and implicitly questioned their single authorship.

7. Adalbert Samaritanus, *Praecepta dictaminum,* chaps. 1–3, ed. Franz-Josef Schmale, MGH III: 33–35, cf. 12 on the date and 7 on Adalbert's name, on which see also Ernst Kantorowicz, "Anonymi 'Aurea gemma'," (1943), reprinted in his *Selected Studies* (Locust Valley, N.Y., 1965), p. 249, n. 17. On Adalbert, see also C. H. Haskins, *Studies in Mediaeval Culture* (Oxford, 1929), pp. 173–77; Max Manitius, *Geschichte der lateinischen Literatur des Mittelalters* (hereafter, *Lat. Lit.*) Handbuch der Altertumswissenschaft IX, 3 vols. (Munich, 1911–31), III: 305–6; Franz-Josef Schmale, "Die Bologneser Schule der Ars dictandi," *Deutsches Archiv* XIII. 1 (1957), 16–34; and Lanham, *Salutatio Formulas,* pp. 97–99.

8. Haskins, *Culture,* p. 180; cf. also Manitius, *Lat. Lit.,* III: 309; Kantorowicz, *Studies,* p. 248; Scaglione, *Ars,* p. 139 (proposing a date of after 1140 in North Italy); and Lanham, *Salutatio Formulas,* pp. 99–100.

9. Kantorowicz, *Studies,* p. 256, also 248, calling Henry "a master of *dictamen* not too well known who, however, taught in Pavia after 1120, whose name suggests French, perhaps Provençal, origin and who depends on Bologna, especially on Hugh of Bologna," and 262–63, with examples of his borrowing from Hugh; Haskins, *Culture,* pp. 178–80 and 190, who dated the *Aurea gemma* to Pavia ca. 1119–24 and said that "Henry's French origin, as seen in his name, cannot be taken as showing any French influence upon the doctrine of his Pavian treatise." Cf. also Manitius, *Lat. lit.,* III: 307; N. Denholm-Young, "The Cursus in England" (1934), reprinted in his *Collected Papers on Mediaeval Subjects* (Oxford, 1946), p. 50; Botho Odebrecht, "Die Briefmuster des Henricus Francigena," *Archiv für Urkundenforschung* XIV (1936), 230–61, who is concerned less with the treatise on *dictamen* than with the letter-collection, which he dated to Pavia in 1121–4, but who also mentioned Henry's use of Hugh of Bologna (pp. 234–35); and Lanham, *Salutatio Formulas,* pp. 101–5.

10. Rockinger, *Briefsteller,* I: 55.

11. Paris, Bibl. nat., MS n.a.1. 610, fol. 29r–v: "Set cum persone a minori usque ad maiorem, sunt innumerabiles, et cum per omnes de viribus nostris diffidentes ire nullatenus valeamus, in tres brevitate gaudentes omnes personas restringamus. Hec inponentes eis nomina Maiorem, equalem, Minorem. Maior, sublimis appellatur. Equalis, Mediocris. Minor, tenuis." The translations of some of the occupational groups are doubtful. Here and below, "miles" is translated "soldier," not "knight," because it clearly refers to a relatively low social rank. "Rusticus" is translated "peasant"; "discipulus," "student"; "cliens," "retainer"; "servus," "serf." In later lists, "plebei" is translated "commoners"; "subiecti," "dependents"; "burgenses," "townsmen"; "ecclesiasticus," "the clergy" or occasionally "cleric"; "clericus," "cleric"; "plebanus," "parish priest"; and "parrochialis," "a member of the parish clergy" or the equivalent.

12. Kantorowicz, *Studies,* pp. 251 and 261. Already in an earlier article on "Petrus de Vinea in England," published in 1937 and reprinted in *Studies,* p. 216, n. 17, he denied the attribution of this treatise to Henry *Francigena,* as had Odebrecht, "Briefmuster," p. 233. Cf. Schmale, "Bologneser Schule," p. 29, on this and other treatises of the "*Aurea gemma* group" which depend on Adalbert.

13. Oxford, Bodl. Lib., MS Laud Misc. 569, fols. 184r–185r. The text seems to lack some rubrications and reads, "[ma]rchiores [sic] duces et alie mediocres persone" (fol. 184v). The manuscript was dated to the thirteenth century by Haskins, *Culture,* p. 178 (and 182, saying that it was made for the use of the Cistercians), but to the twelfth century by Odebrecht, "Briefmuster," p. 233, and Kantorowicz, *Studies,* p. 216, n. 17.

14. See the discussion and brief excerpts in my article, "The Letter from Peter of St John to Hato of Troyes," *Petrus Venerabilis, 1156–1956,* ed. Giles Constable and James Kritzeck, Studia Anselmiana XL (Rome 1956), 38–52, and in my edition of *The Letters of Peter the Venerable,* Harvard Historical Studies LXXVIII (Cambridge, Mass., 1967), II: 36, with references to the two articles by C. H. Haskins, "An Early Bolognese Formulary," *Mélanges d'Histoire offerts à Henri Pirenne* (Brussels-Paris, 1926), I: 201–10, and Walther Holtzmann, "Eine oberitalienische *Ars dictandi* und die Briefsammlung des Priors Peter von St. Jean in Sens," *Neues Archiv* XLVI (1925–26), 34–52; see also Schmale, "Bologneser Schule," pp. 19–21.

15. Copenhagen, Kongelige Bibl., MS Gl. kgl. S.3543, fol. 19v: "Ut sunt tres ordines personarum, sic sunt tres principales species epistolarum, humilis, mediocris, et sublimis. Humilis epistola est que ab humili persona mittitur, ut sunt bubulci, cerdones, et pelliparii, et ceterae que non habent sub se inferiorem ordinem. Sublimis epistola est, que mittitur a sublimi persona. Ut ab apostolico vel imperatore. Sublimis persona est qua nulla dignitas est superior. Ut est apostolicus in ecclesiasticis, imperator in secularibus. Mediocris est que media est inter sublimem et humilem. Ut sunt tetrarchae, reges, marchiones, comites, duces, archiepiscopi, capitanei, vavasores, vicedomini, et ceterae personae que sunt mediae inter sublimem et humilem." Among the more important variants from Berlin, Staatsbibl., MS Phillipps 1732, fol. 57v are the addition of "subulci" ("swineherds") after "bubulci," the substitution of "dignitate ingenem suo superatur, ut" for "dignitas est superior. Ut est" and of "consules" for "comites," and the omission of "vavasores."

16. Schmale, "Bologneser Schule," p. 27, n. 34.

17. There is a considerable but scattered literature on this work, of which part I was published by Rockinger, *Briefsteller,* I: 9–28, as by Alberic of Monte Cassino and translated in *Three Medieval Rhetorical Arts,* ed. James J. Murphy (Berkeley-Los Angeles-London, 1971), pp. 5–25. See C. H. Haskins, "An Italian Master Bernard," *Eassys in History Presented to Reginald Lane Poole,* ed. H. W. C. Davis (Oxford, 1927), pp. 214–15, and *Culture,* pp. 181–82, and *Casinensia,* I: 117; also Mirella Brini Savorelli, "Il 'Dictamen' di Bernardo Silvestre," *Rivista critica di Storia della Filosofia* XX (1965), 191–92; Bloch, in *La Scuola,* p. 588 and n. 76, citing the evidence that it should be dated after 1137; and Lanham, *Salutatio Formulas,* pp. 105–7.

18. On Bernard Silvestris, see Savorelli, "'Dictamen'," pp. 182, 230, with full references to earlier literature, and on Bernhard of Meung, Walter Zöllner, "Eine neue Bearbeitung der 'Flores dictaminum' des Bernhard von Meung," *Wissenschaftliche Zeitschrift der Martin-Luther-Universität Halle-Wittenberg: Gesellschafts- und Sprachwissenschaftliche Reihe* XIII (1964), 335–42, with references to previous literature in n. 1 on p. 342, including Franz-Josef Schmale, "Der Briefsteller Bernhards von Meung," *Mitteilungen des Instituts für österreichische Geschichtsforschung* LXVI (1958), 1–28.

19. Rockinger, *Briefsteller,* I: 10–12.

20. Graz, Universitätsbibl., MS 1515, fols. 53v–54v: "Ut ergo providus dictator cuique epistole congruam salutationem adhibeat, semper necesse ei est, mittentis et recipientis prenosse personas. . . . [E]ximie persone dicuntur, quibus vel genere vel dignitate nulla superior reperitur, utpote apostolici, et Romanorum imperatoris. Infimas autem eas arbitramur personas, quibus genere vel dignitate nulla valet inferior reperiri, ut serui empticii, infimique clientes. Mediocres iure appellantur, quibus genere, potentia, dignitate, quedam superiores, quedam inferiores inveniuntur. Harum magna copia est. Quarum videlicet mediocrum, alie sunt pares, alie sunt dispares. Pares illas vocamus, tam in ecclesiasticis quam in secularibus, que offitio sive dignitate, aut potentia, sibi invicem parificantur. In ecclesiasticis ut episcopi inter se, archiepiscopi, archidiaconi, decani, plebani, abbates, priores, sacerdotes, levite, clerici, et quidam aliorum officiorum. In secularibus vero, ut reges, duces, marchiones, comites, proceres, consules, vicedomini, et aliarum dignitatum, sive officiorum viri. Disparium autem personarum, non indigemus exemplis. Seculares tamen persone, licet semper excellant potentia, vel nobilitate, ob reverentiam ecclesiastice dignitatis inferiores ecclesiasticis designantur. Ideoque si magnates scribunt etiam sacerdotibus tamen ut maioribus id

facere consuerint. Pater etiam avus, vel proavus, maiores semper filio, vel nepote inveniuntur, quamvis maior potentia, sive dignitas opponatur. Unde etiam fit ut episcopus patri, vel avo, aut proavo, tanquam maioribus scribat, sed ab eis episcopo non tanquam minori scribendum est." The term "servi empticii" found both here and in the treatise in Vienna MS 246 (see n. 22 below) is not in the standard dictionaries of medieval Latin or handbooks of medieval institutions, but it seems to refer to a serf who has been or can be purchased: cf. *Cartulaire de l'Abbaye de Saint-Père de Chartres,* ed. B. Guérard (Paris, 1840), II: 310, no. 59, for a reference in a document of 1117 to two arpents of land "unum empticium, alterum de patrimonio."

21. Graz, Universitätsbibl., MS 1515, fol. 58r: "Diversitas quidem personarum in omni ordine, et manerie, diversitatem insinuat salutationum iuxta dictantis periciam." The second redaction of Bernard's treatise is found in Mantua MS A.II.1, fols. 73–122, which I have not seen but which is described by Hermann Kalbfuss, "Eine bologneser Ars dictandi des XII. Jahrhunderts," *Quellen und Forschungen aus italienischen Archiven und Bibliotheken,* XVI.2 (1914), 1–35, who summarized the relevant sections as follows: "Die Definition der *Epistola* und ihre Zergliederung leiten dann zu dem wichtigen Kapitel der *Salutatio* über. Mit echt mittelalterlicher Freude an ständischer Gliederung wird es eröffnet durch eine allgemeine Einteilung der Menschheit in drei Klassen: zu unterst *serui emptitii, serui glebe* und ihresgleichen, als zweite Stufe Herzoge, Markgrafen, Grafen, Pfalzgrafen, Patriarchen, Primaten, Erzbischöfe, Bischöfe, Pröpste, Archidiakone, Pfarrer und Äbte, kurz alle, die zugleich Untergebene haben und ein Oberhaupt anerkennen; zu höchst auf dieser Stufenleiter stehen Papst und Kaiser." This suggests that the lists in the two versions, though corresponding roughly, differed in organization and in the precise listing of ranks.

22. On Vienna MS 246, see Savorelli, " 'Dictamen'," p. 192, basing the date on references to Count Theobald of Blois and apparently disregarding the reasons for a later date suggested by Haskins, "Italian Master," pp. 219–20, who said that, "In treatment, as well as in time and place, we have travelled far from the Italian Bernard," and in *Culture,* pp. 182–83, calling it "a greatly modified version made in France in the time of Innocent III." On Vienna MS 896, see W. Zöllner, "Eine neue Bearbeitung der 'Flores dictaminum' des Bernhard von Meung," *Wissenschaftliche Zeitschrift der Martin-Luther-Universität Halle-Wittenberg* XIII (1964), 336. It is impossible to enter here into the question of the traditions influencing these works, in which Savorelli and Zöllner (as the titles of their articles suggest) find respectively the influences of Bernard Sylvestris and Bernard of Meung. The sections on salutations in both show clearly their debt to Bernard of Bologna.

23. Savorelli, " 'Dictamen'," pp. 204–7. The presence of both "diaconi" and "levite" among the lower clergy should be noted, since the terms are usually regarded as synonyms. On the "servi emptitii," see n. 21 above.

24. Charles Samaran, "Une *Summa grammaticalis* du XIIIe siècle avec glosses provençales," *Archivum Latinitatis medii aevi (Bulletin Du Cange)* XXXI (1961), 157–224, from Paris, Bibl. nat., MS lat. 16671, which Samaran apparently dated palaeographically in the second half of the twelfth century while dating the treatise, on the grounds of style, in the first half of the thirteenth (p. 163).

25. Ibid., p. 215. This summary covers a few verbal differences and differences in word order. The comma between "parrochiales, presbyterii" in the edition of the Vienna treatise, for instance (which is accordingly translated here as "parish clergy, priests") is omitted in the edition of Master William, which may account for his omission of the "plebani" among the middle clergy.

26. Another similar but simpler ranking to that in Vienna 896 and Master William is that in the *Ars dictandi Aurelianensis* published by Rockinger, *Briefsteller,* I: 103–14, and attributed to Ralph of Tours, at the end of the twelfth century, by C. H. Haskins, *Culture,* p. 6, n. 2 (and p. 190). Cf. also Manitius, *Lat. lit.,* III:310, who said that it came from Orléans or St. Lifard soon after 1180 and that the letter-collection of Ralph of Tours was added in the thirteenth century. Here the clergy were classified as higher (pope, cardinals, archbishops, bishops), middle (deans, subdeans), and inferior (clerics, scholars) and the laity likewise as higher (emperors, kings), middle (counts, viscounts ["semicomites"], castellans) and inferior

(commoners): Rockinger, *Briefsteller*. I: 104. In the later *Summa dictaminum* of Ludolf of Hildesheim, who was active from 1221–60, the clergy were classified as highest (pope, cardinals, archbishops, bishops), middle (abbots, provosts, deans), and lowly (simple canons, simple priests, masters, students) and the laity as highest (emperors, kings, palatines, dukes, marquises), middle (counts, barons, "those holding the lordships of towns") and lowly (soldiers, townsmen, merchants): ibid., pp 360–61; cf. Wilhelm Wattenbach, *Deutschlands Geschichtsquellen im Mittelalter*. 6th ed. (Berlin, 1893), II: 361.

27. Paris, Bibl. nat., MS n.a.l. 610, fols. 4v–5r: "Adiectiva preterea personis competencia, in ipsis salutacionibus debemus addere, quibus varietatem personarum valeamus exprimere. Aliter enim papae, aliter regi, loquimur, aliter episcopo, aliter abbati, aliter monacho, aliter militi strenuissimo, aliter socio vel amico karissimo." Cf. Haskins, *Culture*. p. 184. A classification of letters into "gravis," "mediocris," and "attenuatus," like that of Albert but without the corresponding social classes, is found in London, British Library, MS Add. 21173, fol. 67v, in an anonymous treatise dated ca. 1138–52 by Haskins, *Culture*. p. 184.

28. Paris, Bibl. nat., MS lat. 7517, fol. 55v: "Diversis itaque personis, secundum quantitatem eorum diverso modo scribere vera consideratio rerum nos edocet. . . . Bonus itaque dictator designatum prevideat ordinem personarum, ut secundum quantitates et qualitates earum modum loquendi convenientius informet. Sublimibus namque personis et in magnis causis, secundum meterie congruentiam splendor verborum factorumque magnificentia exiberi debet. Mediocriobus [*sic*] vero personis oportuna temperate dici potuerunt. Tenuis autem persona quantomagis infima est tanto minus verbis affluit, et magnarum sententiarum lege privatus, sic tamen ut brevitas eius vel ad illum loquentis nullam generet obscuritatem et verborum iunctura vigorem materie non deserat. Has quidem proprietates si bene custodierimus illud trimodum loquendi genus quod a plerisque dicitur humile, medium, grandi loquum sine dubio legitime complebimus." The three categories of letter in the final sentence correspond to those mentioned by Alberic of Monte Cassino in his *Breviarium de dictamine*. cited above. On this manuscript, see Charles Thurot, "Notices et extraits de divers manuscrits latins pour servir à l'Histoire des Doctrines grammaticales au Moyen Âge," *Notices et Extraits des Manuscrits de la Bibliothèque impériale* XXII.2 (1868), 24–25, and, on Paul of Camaldoli, Haskins, *Culture*. p. 188, dating him in Italy in the generation after 1160, and Bloch, in *La Scuola*. pp. 586–87, n. 71a, with references to other secondary works.

29. Vincenzo Licitra, "La *Summa de arte dictandi* di Maestro Goffredo," *Studi medievali*. VII, 3rd series (1966), 886–87; cf. 867–76 on the date and place of composition, stressing that Geoffrey was a guest at Bologna at the time of writing and not a native of the city.

30. *Die Ars dictandi des Thomas von Capua*. ed. Emmy Heller, Sitzungsberichte der Heidelberger Akademie der Wissenschaften: Philosophisch-historische Klasse, 1928–9, Abh. IV (Heidelberg, 1929), p. 17 (chaps. 5–6); cf. pp. 49–53 on the date, and also Kantorowicz, *Studies*. p. 195.

31. Thomas of Capua, *Ars dictandi*. c. 10, ed. Heller, p. 21.

32. Guido Faba, *Summa dictaminis*. II: 8, ed. A. Gaudenzi, *Il Propugnatore* XXIII. 1 (n.s. III), (1890), 299; cf. Haskins, *Culture*, p. 6, n. 2; Thomas of Capua, *Ars dictandi*, ed. Heller, pp. 48–49; Denholm-Young, *Papers*, pp. 48–50; and Kantorowicz, *Studies*, pp. 196–97, dating him from before 1190 to ca. 1245, and 255. Faba's *Doctrina ad inveniendas, incipiendas et formandas, materias* is printed in Rockinger, *Briefsteller*, I: 185–96, but has nothing on salutations except an injunction to divide the world three ways and to observe the three classes of "maiores," "equales," and "minores," and to address each accordingly (p. 186).

33. Cf. Ch.-V. Langlois, "Formulaires de Lettres du XIIe, du XIIIe et du XIVe Siècle [IV]," *Notices et Extraits des Manuscrits de la Bibliothèque nationale, XXXIV.2 (1893), 9–15, publishing sections and saying that its originality rested solely "dans un arrangement nouveau de matières banales" (p. 11), and R. W. Southern, "Peter of Blois: A Twelfth Century Humanist?" *Medieval Humanism and Other Studies* (Oxford, 1970), p. 115: "While the letters [of Peter of Blois] went on to fame and fortune, the treatise to which they formed a body of illustrations was forgotten. Rightly so. Peter's treatise, like all the others of the same kind, de-

served to be forgotten." It has nevertheless attracted some attention owing to the celebrity of its author and to his reference in the introduction to "the avid followers of Master Bernard and of [the *dictatores* of] Tours." This Bernard has been identified both as Bernard Sylvestris and as Bernard of Meung (on whom see n. 18 above): Langlois, "Formulaires," pp 10–11; Émile Lesne, *Histoire de la propriété ecclésiastique en France*, v: *Les Écoles de la Fin du VIIIe Siècle à la Fin du XIIe*, Mémoires et Travaux publiés par des Professeurs des Facultés catholiques de Lille ʟ (Lille, 1940), 190–91; Savorelli, " 'Dictamen'," p. 191. The evidence on salutations presented here suggests that Peter used the work of Bernard of Bologna. Cf. also Manitius, *Lat. lit.*, ɪɪɪ: 296–97; Denholm-Young, *Papers*, p. 50; and Kantorowicz, *Studies*, p. 217.

34. Cambridge, Univ. Lib., MS Dd.IX.38, fol. 116r: "Summe sunt quibus dignitate nulla superior reperitur ut dominus papa et imperator Romanus. Sublimes ut patriarche, archiepiscopi, reges, episcopi, duces, comites, palatini marchiones. Mediocres sunt, ut decani, archidiaconi, abbates, prepositi, primicerii, thesaurarii, castellani, prefecti, consules qui in quibusdam civitatibus pares dicuntur. Private sunt que nullam administrant dignitatem ut milites et clerici. Infime sunt ut rustici et omnes opera civilia frequentantes, ut cerdones et huiusmodi. . . . Hac personarum varietate cognita cum studiosus dictator accesserit ad scribendum, primum sibi intuendum est si par pari, aut superior inferiori aut equo scribat."

35. Work is at present proceeding in a somewhat piecemeal fashion in spite of the projected *Corpus dictatorum Italicum*, on which see Helene Wieruszowski, *Politics and Culture in Medieval Spain and Italy*, Storia e Letteratura: Raccolta di studi e testi ᴄxxɪ (Rome, 1971), 641–42.

36. I have tried to translate these consistently as "exalted" ("sublimis"), "greater" ("maior"), "highest" ("summus"), "higher" ("altior"), "superior" ("superior"), "supreme" ("supremus"), "weighty" ("gravis"), "excellent" ("excellens"), and "outstanding" ("eximius") for the upper rank and "feeble" ("exilis"), "mean" ("tenuis"), "lesser" ("minor"), "humble" ("humilis"), "inferior" ("inferior"), "lowly" ("infimus"), and "light" ("extenuatus").

37. Most of these seem to have been of the Bolognese school, stemming from Adalbert Samaritanus and Bernard of Bologna.

38. In the treatise in Vienna MS 246 the "milites," while not formally put with the "infimi," were clearly ranked with the "plebei" in contrast to the counts, dukes, marquises, and barons: see Savorelli, " 'Dictamen'," p. 218.

39. See Edgar H. McNeal, *Minores and Mediocres in the Germanic Tribal Laws* (Columbus, 1905), who said that the term referred to a class of landlords usually holding grants of land from the king (p. 124), and Eberhard Otto, *Adel und Freiheit im deutschen Staat des frühen Mittelalters*, Neue deutsche Forschungen: Abteilung mittelalterliche Geschichte ɪɪ (Berlin, 1937), 151–55.

40. I plan to gather into an article these various references to "mediocres" in charters, chronicles, and biographies.

V
LOCAL CHURCHES

The Blickling Homilies: A Reflection of Popular Anglo-Saxon Belief

ROBIN ANN ARONSTAM

The eighteen Old English homilies in the so-called Blickling collection—named for Blickling Hall in Norfolk where the unique manuscript was preserved from the eighteenth through the early twentieth centuries—have a particular importance in the history of medieval literature. They are among the earliest and most primitive of the compilations of material for preaching which became common in late tenth- and early eleventh-century England, whose best-known authors were Abbot Aelfric of Eynsham and Archbishop Wulfstan.[1] The composer of these homilies is, however, unknown, and perhaps for that reason they have survived precariously, in a manuscript of unknown provenance which now forms part of the Scheide Library in Princeton, New Jersey.[2]

These texts have not received detailed attention from contemporary scholars, but are mentioned only fleetingly in general works on Old English literature and homilies.[3] A number of reasons could be advanced for this undeserved neglect. Students of literature often have been attracted to a work as much by the personality of the author as by the quality of his composition. The anonymity of the Blickling collection removes this attraction, and the relative inaccessibility of the manuscript, which remained in private hands until its recent deposit at Princeton, also has contributed to the neglect of this material.[4] Furthermore, M. R. Godden has suggested that the oversight also may stem from their relative lack of sophistication and dependence on conventional themes like "exhortation to repentence," when they are compared with the work of Aelfric or Wulfstan.[5]

The lack of attention devoted to these texts cannot stem, to any great extent, from scholars' ignorance of their existence, since R. Morris, between 1874 and 1880, provided for the Early English Text Society an edition and translation of the homilies.[6] It is especially useful in that it contains a complete glossary of the homilist's vocabulary. Morris did not, however, recognize the extent to which the pages of the manuscript had become disarranged in the course of successive bindings.[7] A new critical edition now underway will correct this oversight and will present the homilies in their original sequence.[8] In the meantime, recourse may be had to Professor Raymond Willard's reproduction of the manuscript in the tenth volume of Early

English Manuscripts in Facsimile.[9] Together with the convenient and well-indexed Morris edition, this forms a reasonable working text. Professor Willard's introduction provides extensive information on the arrangement of the book, but N. R. Ker's description in his *Catalogue of Manuscripts Containing Anglo-Saxon,* although using the older foliation, remains definitive.[10]

In the past forty years, scholars have come to realize the significance of trade, travel and the transmission of ideas between Anglo-Saxon England and the continent.[11] Much of the cultural and legal development of the late Anglo-Saxon period was predicated on the use of continental models, and the religious revival of the tenth century derived much of its inspiration from continental sources.[12] It is not surprising, therefore, that the Blickling homilies are based on continental texts; indeed, several of the homilies are little more than translations of Latin material from the continent.[13] Does it make sense, then, to assume that the Blickling collection reflects concerns or attitudes which were current in England? It is important to bear in mind the principle of selectivity. We know from a glance at the sources used that the author had at his disposal a wide range of patristic exemplars as well as Germanic texts.[14] He would have chosen for translation or paraphrase only those which he felt would be most applicable to the needs and interests of his audience. The Blickling homilies can be accepted, therefore, as materials which reflect English concerns of the late tenth or early eleventh century. The Old English vocabulary chosen to paraphrase a Latin statement can also be revealing, since translation is always interpretation.[15] Both in content and expression, the homilies can be seen as a mirror of Anglo-Saxon interests, which might or might not coincide with those current on the continent.

Homilies which, like the Blickling series, actually were intended to be preached (as opposed to literary tracts cast in homily form) are extraordinary in that they are virtually the only surviving form of early medieval writing which was directed to a general audience composed principally of laymen.[16] Although the compiler of the Blickling homilies was an educated man, certainly a cleric and very likely a monk, he was addressing what he considered to be the most urgent needs of lay people. It has long been recognized that tenth- and eleventh-century England produced first-rate theologians and lawyers, but only a study of homiletical literature can reveal how theology and the law of the church were presented to the faithful.[17] One will not find here the highest intellectual achievement of the Anglo-Saxon church, but rather the elements of popular belief—the folk religion of Christianity (corrected, it is true, by a theologian). The compiler's purpose could be termed evangelical. He wanted to present a version of the Christian message which would stimulate his hearers to a better life. The emphasis in not theological but moral. Through fear and inspiration, the hearer is urged to fashion his life in a manner deemed to be more acceptable to God. This collection, like most homiliaries, is arranged according to the calendar of the church, and the sermons are designed for the Annunciation and the Assumption, Lent, the Passion and Easter seasons, Rogationtide, Pentecost and the feasts of St.

John the Baptist, SS. Peter and Paul, St. Michael, St. Martin, and St. Andrew.

In spite of the fact that homiletical and canonical texts are often found together in Anglo-Saxon manuscripts, there are fundamental differences in the type and treatment of the material which they include.[18] A survey of these differences will clarify the homilist's intention. Preaching and the administration of justice both pertained to the clerical office, and especially (though certainly not exclusively) to that of the bishop, but they had differing ends. The preacher intended to persuade his audience to stronger faith and to a more moral life in a pastoral situation; the bishop as judge was concerned with enforcing aberrant patterns of public behavior.[19] Canon law can, at times, because of its restrictive character, serve as a hortatory device. The homilist, aware of this effect of the law, mentioned the judge's duty to lead the community to conscientious divine service.[20] The cultivation of Christian morality is rarely, however, more than a secondary purpose of law, which cannot achieve more than a set of minimal standards; through sermons the hearer confronts the highest moral ideals. The rationale for the work of both homilist and canonist was theological, but they applied their theology in different ways. A comparison of the Blickling homilies with a roughly contemporary canon law collection, the *Excerptiones Egberti,* is instructive.[21] The latter collection was very probably the operative norm for the execution of canon law in early eleventh-century England.[22] The *Excerptiones* prescribe the models for organization of the life of the institutional church, for clerical deportment, and for right administration of the sacraments, but they offer little which relates directly to the conduct or faith of the laity.[23] The great exception to this generalization is, of course, matrimony; the *Excerptiones* set out a version of the law of marriage in some detail.[24] Otherwise, however, the layman becomes of interest only if he violates the moral or legal code of society—if he becomes a thief, a sorcerer, or murderer or a fugitive.[25] The homilies, as will be suggested, can sometimes reveal more about the layman who was not alienated from his church or society, although the layman remained the audience, and not the topic, of the sermons. In the homilies we see the Christian, at least potentially, at peace with the church.[26]

The remainder of this paper will examine the most important themes in the Blickling collection, in an effort to discover some of the preoccupations of popular devotion in one of the earliest and most theologically primitive of the homilies. The central subjects which emerge are judgment, penance and faith; Christology; Mariology; moral imperatives; and hagiography.

The Anglo-Saxon world view, like its continental counterparts, was one of a cosmic struggle between the demonic and the divine. Christ and the devil are spiritual alternatives; if a man is not devoted to one, he must embrace the other.[27] Of the eventual victory of Christ there is no doubt, but the consciousness of the possibility of individual, eternal damnation forms the pervasive background of the homilies. There are two types of devils represented: Satan himself, the antitype of Christ, and his host of minor devils who are, in fact, translations of the animist spirits of Germanic paganism.[28] This is perhaps clearest in the author's version of the Christian legend in which Peter, Paul, and Simon Magus present the competing claims to divinity of Christ and of Simon himself.[29] Simon is a fraud who tries to deceive Nero, offering a sheep's head instead of his own to prove his death (and subsequent resurrection), but he controls, nevertheless, a considerable stable of fiends who, though they cannot rival the power or authority of the apostles, can produce permutations in the natural order.

It is the duty of Christians to oppose and thwart such demons, or to suffer in hell with them.[30] Prayers of the saints and of the faithful are effective in freeing souls which might otherwise be lost, and Christians have this power since, just as Satan is the antitype of Christ, the minor devils are the antitype of the Spirit.[31] Christians living in the Spirit can, therefore, overcome the demonic. Satan's work is not executed only by supernatural agents. Corrupted human beings are members of Satan ("deofles leomo"), just as the righteous are members of Christ.[32]

Anticipation of the *eschaton,* when the confusion of good and evil will finally be resolved and when Christ and Satan will claim their own, is the single most powerful theme in the homilies. It is the principal notion in two of the sermons, and occurs in many others.[33] The Anglo-Saxons shared with most medieval Christians a strong sense of living at the end of time. As the homilist says, all the prophesied signs which were to precede this world's end have been accomplished, except the coming of the Antichrist.[34] The disasters which are to presage Doomsday—wars, plagues, disease, inexplicable death—are reminiscent of those against which Gregory I had warned Aethelbert of Kent, four centuries earlier.[35] Although tales of the Last Judgment are intended to provoke conversion of life through fear, the fundamental message is one of joyous anticipation.[36] The Christian who has prepared himself will, after all, become the companion of the angels in bliss. Greater stress is placed on the terrors of damnation than on the delights of salvation, but the latter are not neglected. Righteous men will inherit the devil's forfeited seat in heaven, and enjoy the vision of God.[37]

With the realization of the facts about the divine plan, the individual Christian is called to a recognition of his sins and to penance and the remedies of the penitentials.[38] In the homily on the soul's need, repentence is presented as the first requisite for salvation, before almsgiving, fasting, or any other good deeds.[39] The implication is that no positive human act can achieve salvation; it is promised rather to those who with meek heart believe in God in a vague and unspecified way.[40] This is certainly no invitation to licentiousness, for good deeds are the responsibility of all. There is a heavy emphasis of the connection between morality and salvation which might seem to indicate a Pelagian orientation, but the homilist is careful to call attention to the concomitant necessity for faith. The summons to penance is in itself an acknowledgement of man's need for grace. The stress on morality probably reflects not conscious theological aberration but the desire to foster right-living among those listening. This pastoral intention, however, parallels that of Pelagius himself, who "was anxious to show . . . it was not a question of dogma, but a practical question."[41] The homilist's belief comes closest to that of the fifth- and sixth-century theologians John Cassian, Vincent of Lérins and Faustus of Riez. These have been called both "Semi-Pelagian" and "Semi-Augustinian" since they rejected the Augustinian doctrines of predestination and of total human depravity after the Fall, preferring to assert the possibility, in come cases, of the cooperation of the human will with divine grace. They did not dispute the necessity of gracious action, but broadened the possibility for human response to God's universal call to salvation.[42] Any approach to the problem of sin and grace which, like the homilist's, calls for the exercise of human responsibility, and relates this responsible action to the believer's hope for salvation, may be seen as a reflection, albeit unconscious, of this early reaction against extreme Augustinianism.

A general reluctance on the part of the faithful to undertake the rigors of penance, or to confess the full sum of their sins, is admitted by the homilist.[43] F. Barlow had noted that sacramental penance was reserved in the late Anglo-Saxon period for the scrupulous; for the most part only public sins were corrected, not in private confession but before an ecclesiastical court.[44] Reluctance to undertake voluntarily needed penance is also the best motivation for what M. R. Godden had identified as a common motif in Anglo-Saxon preaching: "it is better to be shamed for one's sins before man [the confessor] in this life than to be shamed before God and before all angels and before all men and before all devils at the Last Judgment."[45] While this particular theme is not explicit in the Blickling homilies, the homilist does warn against hiding one's sins from the confessor. Priests for their part are not to accept a superficial confession, but are instructed to probe for what the sinner does not wish to tell. Here is a double injunction: the guilty must be motivated to seek out a priest, while the latter are to administer penances according to the prescriptions of the accepted penitentials ("scrift-béc"), which set out for souls the proper medicine that a merciful God provides.[46] It is here, in penitential discipline, that theology, homiletics, and canon law intersect. It is significant that in the Anglo-Saxon commonplace books theological tracts on penance coexist with the *Excerptiones Egberti,* with homilies, and with penitential material.[47]

The institutionalization of penance in the Lenten season is treated at some length. This period of abstinence and purification was interpreted as a gift of time to God, which supplements the economic offering. Days, like property, are tithed; the forty days of Lent, minus Sundays, equal one-tenth of the year, which is to be completely devoted to God.[48] The attitude toward almsgiving reflects the contemporary practice of substituting gifts to the poor for more demanding penitential activity.[49] Those who receive alms are instructed to be properly grateful to their benefactors; it was more commonly the case that the poor considered that they did their patrons a service by providing them with an opportunity to earn divine forgiveness.[50] While alms-giving is praiseworthy, and indeed a necessary component of good works, it is in itself insufficient for achieving salvation.[51] It is evident that almsgiving had come to be employed as a major penance, replacing the stricter demands of the penitentials.

Beyond the specific responsibilities of almsgiving and tithing, other instructions for Christian conduct are offered. The right use of property was certainly an important duty, as was aiding the poor.[52] Special injunctions are given to judges and to other secular authorities, whose positions give them a measure of responsibility for their inferiors.[53] Parents have a particular duty to provide a healthy discipline for their children.[54]

The Christology of the Blickling homilies is simple and orthodox. Al-though the soteriological mechanism is not clearly defined, Christ is seen as man's means to salvation, present in the world through baptism, faith and preeminently through the sacrament of the altar.[55] There is nothing like a fully worked out sacramental theology in the homilies. The Eucharist is presented as a duty which can at times impart miraculous cures for illness to a communicant, but there is no attempt to explain the efficacy of the sacra-ment, as Aelfric was later to do.[56] Christ provided in his life the most perfect model for human conduct, and is acknowledged as creator of the world.[57] Except in the Easter sermon, however, he is more often the background than the subject of the homilies, and the Easter sermon, though starting with the Passion and Resurrection, is almost totally eschatological, looking forward to the Second Coming and Doomsday.[58] The final lesson of Easter, therefore, returns to the familiar theme or repentence and the effort to become worthy of divine mercy.[59] The soteriological function of Christ is subordinated to the exemplary, not because the latter is more important, but because it re-quires a more definite human response.

The old dichotomy between Eve, whose weakness caused the fall of man, and Mary, the new Eve, whose son's death obviated the consequences of the Fall, is an idea which received an optimistic alteration in the homilist's ac-count. The remedy of penitence was not forbidden by God to Adam and Eve, but Adam, less guilty than his wife, won salvation through his prayers alone.[60] Eve received forgiveness only for the sake of her daughter Mary, through whom Eve can claim kinship with Christ.[61] In this account, however, there is none of the bitterness toward Eve, or toward women in general, which sometimes characterized medieval representations of the Fall.[62] Excepting Mary, women were not considered significant except in their roles as mothers. The homilist cautions his hearers against condemning Elizabeth, even though she was barren until late in life.[63]

Devotion to Mary was popular in Anglo-Saxon England, as the two ho-milies on the Annunciation and on the Assumption suggest. These are the more interesting because they do not convey great doctrinal truths or even set models for human behavior. They are rather works of loving contemplation, retelling legends which indicate the deep feeling for the "holy virgin."[64] The saints' lives—stories about John the Baptist, Peter and Paul, Andrew, and Martin—partake of this devotional quality, but also serve as exemplars of human virtue. John's asceticism is a lesson and a rebuke to gluttons, lovers of luxury and gossip.[65] Paul's deference to Peter is interpreted as a model of Christian humility.[66] Martin is the only monk who appears in the homilies; his fidelity to this vocation is praised,[67] but it is the public rather than the monastic aspect of Martin's life that the homilist finds significant—his gifts to the poor, and especially his miracles. Hunger for the miraculous, imparting the conviction of divine presence and omnipotence, is amply satisfied by the homilist.[68] The lack of attention to peculiarly monastic ideals would be remarkable, given the fact that religious reform in tenth and early eleventh century England was begun and executed by monastic communities,[69] if the homilies' audience were to include many religious. Since their public was composed of laymen, however, the homilies concentrated on those portions of Martin's life most suitable for emulation by the laity.

These are the most obvious elements of Christian faith and life as they appear in the Blickling homilies. They are theologically primitive, oriented more toward conversion than education, yet they bring us closer than most other surviving texts to the concerns of ordinary Christians in the late Anglo-Saxon period. The portrait of the church which might be deduced from the homilies alone would be incomplete, even inaccurate. No appreciation of the complexity of religious life could be derived from these texts, which focus on lay devotion. The monastic revival which was the spur to church-wide reform could not even be guessed from a reading of the homilies. To learn about the institutional structure, and the ecclesiology, of the Anglo-Saxon church, we must have recourse to canonical and theological texts, like the *Excerptiones Egberti* or Archbishop Wulfstan's *Institutes of Polity.*[70] But, conversely, our concept of the Anglo-Saxon church would be only two-dimensional and flat without the depth provided by insights into the popular mind, and it is this that the early homiliaries offer. The Blickling collection suggests not only the basic doctrines of primitive English Christianity, but also the ways in which these doctrines may have altered the conduct and lives of the believers.

St. Joseph's College
Philadelphia

Notes

1. Aelfric's homilies were printed by B. Thorpe, *Sermones catholici or Homilies of Aelfric,* 2 vols., Homilies of the Anglo-Saxon Church 1 (London, 1844–46); cf. N. Eliason and P. Clemoes, *Aelfric's First Series of Catholic Homilies: British Museum Royal 7 C.XII, fols. 4–218,* Early English Manuscripts in Facsimile XIII (Copenhagen, 1966). Thorpe's collection is supplemented by J. C. Pope, *Homilies of Aelfric,* Early English Text Society CCLIX–LX (Oxford, 1967–68). D. Bethurum has edited the *Homilies of Wulfstan* (Oxford, 1957).

2. W. H. Bond and C. U. Faye, *Supplement to the Census of Medieval and Renaissance Manuscripts in the United States and Canada* (New York, 1962), p. 315. N. R. Ker, *Catalogue of Manuscripts Containing Anglo-Saxon* (Oxford, 1957), p. 451, dates the manuscript late tenth or early eleventh century. He notes, p. 455, that it was held at Lincoln from the turn of the fourteenth until the early seventeenth century, but its earlier history is not known.

3. E.g. K. Sisam, *Studies in the History of Old English Literature* (Oxford, 1953) and the excellent introduction to Pope's *Homilies*. M. Deansley discussed the homilies briefly in *Sidelights on the Anglo-Saxon Church* (London, 1962), pp. 39–40. Only brief reference is made to the Blickling collection in G. R. Owst, *Literature and Pulpit in Medieval England*, 2nd edition (New York, 1961), where the concentration on the Last Judgment is noted, p. 516.

4. R. Willard, *The Blickling Homilies*, Early English Manuscripts in Facsimile x (Copenhagen, 1960), provides a history of the manuscript's owners down to 1960, pp. 15–17; it was later moved to Princeton (see n. 2).

5. "An Old English Penitential Motif," *Anglo-Saxon England* II (1973), 221.

6. R. Morris, *The Blickling Homilies*, Early English Text Society LVIII (Oxford, 1874), LXII (Oxford, 1876), LXXIII (Oxford, 1880); reprinted in one vol. (Oxford, 1967).

7. Ker, *Catalogue*, p. 454; Willard, *Blickling Homilies*, pp. 21–25.

8. Professor Rowland L. Collins of the University of Rochester has undertaken this important work.

9. See above n. 4. To facilitate photography of the codex for the facsimile edition, it was unbound. In rebinding, the folios were put in proper order and the entire manuscript was refoliated. (A concordance of old and new folio numbers has been provided in the introduction to the facsimile.)

10. Pp. 451–55.

11. First noted, for an earlier period, by W. Levison, *England and the Continent in the Eighth Century* (Oxford, 1946), this interdependence is also noted by R. R. Darlington, "Ecclesiastical Reform in the Late Old English Period," *English Historical Review* LI (1936), 385–428, and by F. Barlow, *The English Church 1000–1066* (Oxford, 1963).

12. For the revival in general, see Darlington, "Ecclesiastical Reform," passim.

13. For a list of the homilies with their sources, and references to appropriate source studies, see Ker, *Catalogue*, pp. 453–54.

14. Ker's summary (ibid.) includes works of Augustine, Gregory I and Pseudo-Gregory as well as hagiographical material.

15. The linguist will be particularly interested in N. O. Halvorsen, *Doctrinal Terms in Aelfric's Homilies*, U. of Iowa Humanistic Studies V.1 (Iowa City, 1932), which explores the way in which the English language was used to express theological concepts.

16. "Men tha leofstan," the formal address in these and most other Anglo-Saxon homilies, is best translated "Dearest people"—a phrase which indicates a general audience; Morris, *Blickling Homilies*, p. 340.

17. This is most amply demonstrated in Barlow's chapter (in *English Church*) on the personnel of the English church, especially pp. 62–95.

18. For the commonplace books, in which the juxtaposition on canonical and homiletical texts is most evident, see D. Bethurum, "Archbishop Wulfstan's Commonplace Book," *Publications of the Modern Language Association* LVII (1942), 912–29.

19. For the administration of ecclesiastical justice in late Anglo-Saxon England see Barlow, *English Church*, pp. 146–53, and R. Aronstam, *The Latin Canonical Tradition in Late Anglo-Saxon England: The Excerptiones Egberti* (Ph.D. dissertation, Columbia University, 1974), pp. 131–39.

20. Morris, *Blickling Homilies*, pp. 62–63.

21. Aronstam provides a critical edition of the *Excerptiones*, pp. 55–129.

22. Ibid., pp. 146–49.

23. Ibid., pp. 162–99.

24. Ibid., pp. 208–11.

25. Ibid., pp. 199–202; 205–8.

26. The wide penitential literature which was current in late Anglo-Saxon times does something to bridge the gap between the *Excerptiones* and the homilies, since it deals with a wider range of problems within the lay order, which were often pastorally rather than judicially disposed, but they also are concerned with deviations (however common) from acceptable moral behavior. A number of penitentials was in circulation, most notably (though by no means exclusively) those of Theodore, Pseudo-Theodore and Egbert. The penitentials of Theodore and Egbert are printed in A. Haddan and W. Stubbs, *Councils and Ecclesiastical Documents* . . . (Oxford, 1871), III: 173–204, and 413–31. For Pseudo-Theodore, see F. W. H. Wasserschleben, *Die Büssordnungen der abendländischen Kirche* (Halle, 1851), pp. 566–622.

27. Morris, *Blickling Homilies,* pp. 74–77.

28. D. P. Kirby, *The Making of England* (London, 1967), p. 39. The survival of pagan beliefs and rituals even into the late Anglo-Saxon period can be documented from canonical and legal sources; e.g. Aronstam, *Excerptiones,* pp. 200–1 and A. J. Robertson, *Laws of the Kings of England from Edmund to Henry I* (Cambridge, 1925), pp. 6–7 (I Edward 6), pp. 92–93 (VI Aethelred 7), pp. 176–77 (II Canute 5.1).

29. Morris, *Blickling Homilies,* pp. 170 ff. The version of the passions of SS. Peter and Paul is the translation of a Latin *passio;* Ker, *Catalogue,* p. 453.

30. Ibid., pp. 56–57.

31. Ibid., pp. 46–47. Ibid., pp. 134–35.

32. Ibid., pp. 32–33.

33. *On Last Judgment* and *On Holy Thursday.*

34. Morris, *Blickling Homilies,* pp. 116–17.

35. Ibid., pp. 108–11; and Bede, *History of the English Church and People,* ed. B. Colgrave and R. A. B. Mynors (Oxford, 1969), pp. 112–15.

36. Morris, *Blickling Homilies,* pp. 110–11; cf. the description of hell, pp. 60–61.

37. Ibid., pp. 120–21.

38. See below, n. 44.

39. Ibid., pp. 100–101.

40. Ibid., pp. 46–47; cf. Peter to the impious ruler on the necessity of belief, ibid., pp. 150–51.

41. A. Harnack, *Outlines of the History of Dogma,* trans. E. K. Mitchell (Starr King Press, 1957), p. 365; cf. J. Pelikan, *The Emergence of the Catholic Tradition* (Chicago, 1971), p. 313.

42. Ibid., pp. 319–31.

43. Morris, *Blickling Homilies,* pp. 42–43.

44. Barlow, *English Church,* p. 273.

45. Godden, "Penitential Motif," p. 222.

46. Morris, *Blickling Homilies,* pp. 42–43, 96–97. For the penitentials, see P. Fournier and G. LeBras, *Histoire des Collections canoniques en Occident* I (Paris, 1931), 347–62, and Barlow, *English Church,* pp. 262ff. See also above, n. 26.

47. These texts are printed by B. Fehr, *Die Hirtenbriefe Aelfrics in altenglischer und lateinischer Fassung,* Bibliothek der angelsächsischen Prosa IX (Hamburg, 1914), pp. 240–49.

48. Ibid., pp. 34–35.

49. Barlow, *English Church,* p. 273.

50. Ibid., pp. 42–43.

51. Ibid., pp. 36–37. In fact, the most common penitential discipline in late Anglo-Saxon England was fasting: Ibid., p. 263.

52. Morris, *Blickling Homilies,* pp. 108–9.

53. Ibid., pp. 62–63, and 108–9.

54. Ibid., pp. 108–9.

55. Ibid., pp. 74–77.

56. Thorpe, *Sermones catholici,* II: 262–83.

57. Morris, *Blickling Homilies,* pp. 74–75, 134–35.

58. Ibid., pp. 82–97.

59. Ibid., pp. 94–97.

60. For Eve's guilt, see ibid., pp. 4–5.
61. Ibid., pp. 88–89.
62. E. Auerbach, *Mimesis* (Princeton, 1953), pp. 143–73.
63. Morris, *Blickling Homilies.* pp. 162–63.
64. Ibid., pp. 136–37.
65. Ibid., pp. 166–69.
66. Ibid., pp. 138–41.
67. Ibid., pp. 218–19.
68. Cf. A. Mirgeler, *Mutations of Western Christianity* (Notre Dame, 1968), pp. 44–65.
69. Darlington, "Ecclesiastical Reform."
70. *Die "Institutes of Polity. Civil and Ecclesiastical."* ed. K. Jost, Schweizer anglistischen Arbeiten XLVII (Bern, 1959).

Ramon de Caldes (c. 1135–c. 1200): Dean of Barcelona and King's Minister

THOMAS N. BISSON

The man who compiled the *Liber feudorum maior* in the last decade of the twelfth century is not unknown to history. His proud and graceful prologue dedicated to King Alphonse II (I in Catalonia) surely stamps him as a person of character and culture, and it is accompanied in the manuscript by a famous miniature showing him seated beside the king in the act of selecting the parchments that were to be transcribed in the cartulary. The production of the *Liber feudorum* was a lustrous event in the administrative history of the Crown of Aragon, an undertaking for which Ramon de Caldes, dean of the cathedral church of Barcelona, has always shared the credit with the king who commissioned it.[1]

Nevertheless, surprisingly little else is generally known about him. Only the most elementary facts of his ecclesiastical career have been culled from the great cartulary of the see of Barcelona, or more exactly, from the summary analyses of its contents published in 1914–15. There it appears that Ramon de Caldes became associated with the cathedral community of Barcelona about 1155, was dean of the chapter from 1161 or 1162, and died in 1199 or soon thereafter.[2] He was thus contemporary with Alphonse I (reigned 1162–96); the work for which he is well known came late in their careers; so that it would seem worth asking what had happened in the years before the *Liber feudorum* was compiled to draw Ramon into the king's confidence. This question seems not to have been asked by historians, or at any rate, it has not been answered. Yet it proves to be the critical question for enlarging our comprehension of Ramon de Caldes, for it naturally draws our attention to the royal archives, where the key to his career—a rather considerable career in administrative history—is certainly to be found.

Ramon's homeland was the Vallès Oriental, a fertile rolling valley some twenty kilometers north of Barcelona. He must have been brought up at Caldes de Montbui, for his parents had their estates there, and his proper name was invariably *Raimundus de Calidis*. An ancient thermal station, Caldes had become a prosperous market town in the twelfth century.[3] It was also an important administrative center, for the count of Barcelona had some twenty-five manses there, together with important economic and judicial rights, when his domain was surveyed in 1151. A comital *batlle* ("baiulus"), or bailiff, held a major share of these rights in fief, and his presence, in the name of Ramon Berenguer IV, the conqueror of Tortosa and Lleida, would have been an appreciable factor in the communal life of Caldes during Ramon's youth.[4] And it seems as certain as such things can be, in the absence of explicit testimony, that this experience made its mark on Ramon, for the bailiff of Caldes at that time was none other than his own father. Of this man, named Porcell—"Porcellus, baiulus comitis," as he was often recorded—we know two facts which help us to characterize the family's fortune. First, he (and his wife) purchased the honor, consisting of houses, lands and orchards adjoining the market of Caldes, which was subsequently to be his son Ramon's inheritance.[5] Besides his allods and feudal holdings Porcell evidently had liquid assets. Secondly, Porcell was an ambitious man. His encroachment on a neighbor's field, although he tried to justify it in the name of the count, was condemned by a panel of "good men" in 1149.[6] It seems likely that Porcell's wealth was of recent acquisition, much of it perhaps derived from the proceeds of his office. Ramon's mother, named Maiencia, is more obscure. Hers may have been the religious influence, for it was she, not Porcell, who consented to the major benefaction of property at Caldes which attended Ramon's acceptance in the chapter of Barcelona in 1156.[7] Ramon had at least two brothers: Porcell, sometimes called "Porcelletus," probably to avoid confusion with the father, and later to be known as "Porcellus de Calidis"; and Bernat.[8] Both men were to distinguish themselves, and Bernat pursued a career closely parallel to Ramon's.

Of the known brothers, only Porcell remained independent of the church, so it may be that he was the eldest.[9] The date of Ramon's birth can only be conjectured from the earliest records of his association with the canons of Santa Creu and Santa Eulària of Barcelona in 1155–56. He must at that time have been nearly twenty. He is first recorded on 22 May 1155, as signatory to a major charter of ecclesiastical endowment by the bishop of Barcelona, which was promulgated in the presence of the cardinal-legate Jacintus and the archbishop of Tarragona.[10] He was not yet then a canon, his formal profession, accompanied by the donation already mentioned, coming only a year later.[11] Even then he probably remained a layman. His unqualified subscription "Raimundus de Calidis" persists down to the summer of 1161, only a year before his first extant signature as "Raimundus levita atque decanus," the title he was to retain for the rest of his life.[12] Conceivably he assumed the clerical estate, if he ever did, only at the time of his promotion to the deanship.[13]

Certainly Ramon de Caldes never advanced beyond the minor orders. Since there is no evidence that he interested himself in pastoral affairs, it seems clear that his administrative talent together with his family's generosity and influence accounted for his early promotion.[14] The only thing certainly known about his activity as a young canon is that he learned the notary's art. Already in 1159 he wrote a very correct instrument defining a major privilege in Roussillon for Ramon Berenguer IV.[15] Having probably received his first instruction from the clerks associated with his father's administrative work at Caldes, he gained valuable experience in the company of expert scribes in the chapter of Barcelona. But there was no lack of notaries in the episcopal and comital services, and Ramon seems never to have devoted himself routinely to writing charters.[16]

Accordingly, the main tendency of Ramon de Caldes's career was hardly fortuitous. He was born to the princely service; or, more exactly, his generation was, for his brothers, too, served the count-kings and the see of Barcelona. Their preferment must, at first, have owed as much to their fidelity as to their talents. But we must understand that theirs was no provincial family. In the middle of the twelfth century, the Vallès Oriental was still a central domain of the counts, astride the main routes to their ancestral counties of Vic, Girona, and Cerdanya, and better supplied than Barcelona. In addition to his manses at Caldes de Montbui, Ramon Berenguer had extensive holdings, together with a palace then ceded to the queen, at Sant Pere de Vilamajor, where, in a record of 1157, Porcell de Caldes can be glimpsed on comital business.[17] The relative economic importance of this region was to decline during the reign of Alphonse I, who had the wealth of New Catalonia—a "great western" frontier—to exploit.[18] But the horizons of the Caldes family expanded apace with the king's. Bernat, who was a royal notary from at least 1167 and had joined his brother as canon of Barcelona in 1171, acquired a canonry at Lleida at about the same time;[19] and in the course of the next decade Bernat and Ramon both acquired houses at Lleida.[20] Only Porcell de Caldes remained in his homeland, where he evidently raised a family.[21] His son Arnal followed his uncles' path into the chapter of Barcelona, where he was to be dean, in his turn, in the early thirteenth century; his initial endowment consisted of his uncles' houses at Lleida.[22]

Ramon de Caldes was faithful to his responsibility in the chapter. For more than a decade after his promotion he is visible only as signatory to episcopal and capitular documents.[23] Many of these had to do with fiscal rights and endowments, which may suggest that his specialty in that work developed during these years. And there is one solid indication to that effect. In December 1177 Ramon and Bernat de Caldes acted together as *prepositi* for October, that is, as superintendents of capitular supply according to the monthly division of responsibility then being organized in the cathedral churches of Catalonia.[24] This is one of the earliest allusions to this institution in the chapter of Barcelona; and since such work fell plainly under decanal supervision, it looks as if Ramon was a founder of the *prepositurae* at Barcelona.[25] On the other hand, the silence of royal documents should not cause us to imagine that Ramon's interest in the royal government was interrupted. Very little evidence of local administration in Catalonia has survived from the early years of Alphonse I; we do not even know with certainty who succeeded Porcell the elder as bailiff of Caldes. Down into the 1170s one Bertran de Castelet, who had supervised the comital domains under Ramon Berenguer IV, remained influential in royal finance, although not with conspicuous success, for the young king contracted heavy debts at this time.[26] Only in the later 1170s do we begin to find traces of an orderly recording of the king's feudal and fiscal rights, and it can hardly be accidental that Ramon de Caldes reappears in these documents in a perceptibly influential role.

The evidence falls into two categories. Some of it shows Ramon, "levita atque decanus," subscribing to major administrative enactments relating to the royal domains. The earliest of these records date from 1178–79. On 18 December 1178 Ramon attested the king's purchase of Castellgalí for 250 *morabetins*, one of the largest expenditures of its kind known for the entire reign.[27] The castle in question dominated the pass from the lower Llobregat valley into the Bages region, where royal authority was to increase dramatically in the next two decades. A few days later Ramon signed a privilege for Santes Creus by which the king ceded the service, house and obligations of a man in each of four towns: Lleida, Tortosa, Besalú and Hix.[28] The monks needed servants not only in the burgeoning frontier cities, but also in the uplands of old Catalonia, where their sheep grazed in summer; and among the signatories to this privilege only Ramon de Caldes is likely to have known just what rights the king had to confer in the four places specified. Then at Tàrrega, on 1 January 1179, Ramon was listed first among the signatories to a charter securing the engagement of the men of the remote castle of Mur to provide the king with thirty measures of good wheat and thirty of barley—a major supply for a frontier stronghold—in return for the royal protection; among others, the bailiff of Tàrrega attended, and there can be no doubt that the problem of redefining domain rights collectively had been discussed there.[29]

From this time on, Ramon de Caldes often figured in conventions and settlements relating to castles and domain rights. It was in work of this sort that he became familiar with the royal archive, which is first mentioned as such in 1180, and of which his selection was to form the *Liber feudorum maior*.[30] Nevertheless, his role in the great cases—those issues of title to castles which were then urgently demonstrating the need of such a compilation—must not be exaggerated. Some important cases were resolved without his recorded intervention in the 1180s, nor did he regularly serve as judge or assessor in issues of right.[31] More typical of his secular work in this period are the king's strictly fiscal transactions: for example, his purchase of milling rights together with a manse at Terrassa in 1189, and his commendation of mills at Sant Feliu de Llobregat in 1190.[32] Even in charters relating to great tenures, the nature of Ramon's involvement may be inferred from detailed fiscal stipulations, such as the reservation of a manse and its services to the king in the enfeoffment of Pierola castle in 1190.[33]

Our impression of Ramon's administrative qualifications, as derived from the royal charters, is overwhelmingly confirmed by a different category of evidence: the financial accounts rendered by bailiffs of the royal domains in Catalonia.[34] Beginning about 1178, Ramon de Caldes frequently served as auditor for the bailiffs. He received their statements of receipts from rents, impositions, agrarian dues and fines, of payments on their farms, and of expenses; verified these statements by reference to inventories of the king's domains; and recorded the estates of account as these were acknowledged in periodic sessions of account ("computa").[35] Ramon was not alone in this responsibility: the king himself sometimes participated, as did other officials, including certain bailiffs. But from about 1186 the dean seems to have been in charge of the accounting, if not, indeed, of the entire domain administration. Between 7 May 1186 and 27 April 1194 he appears (in extant texts) no less than 33 times as recipient of the accounts, usually accompanied by the king's scribe, Guillem de Bassia. In 1191 Ramon and Guillem were *procuratores domini regis in Catalonia* for the purpose of recovering debts to the king from the estate of a deceased bailiff.[36] During these years of Ramon's incessant fiscal service, the written accounts of the bailiwick ("summe computorum") assumed a regular form of impressive lucidity.

It is in this financial work that we perceive Ramon de Caldes most clearly. Here he not only subscribes, he acts, and something even of his manner of action comes through. We see him judging whether certain expenses claimed by the bailiff of Barcelona should be allowed or not.[37] We see him disturbed by the rumor that the bailiff of Cervera and Tàrrega has falsified his favorably balanced account, and imposing an equitable adjustment to remove "bad suspicion."[38] We hear of his receiving silver money from bailiffs to whom the king had advanced the equivalent in gold during travels in Aragon.[39] We can almost reiterate his firm questions to the bailiff of Vich, who was obliged to insist that he had received nothing from pleas and sales in 1188–89.[40] Above all, we sense a certain modesty or discretion in his proceeding: although the dean's name always precedes these of his fellow assessors, he never appears to act arbitrarily. When his associate is absent, the record carefully notes the "presence" of some other royal dignitary, and there is also mention of local panels of inquiry appointed to determine the truth in points at issue between the king and his bailiffs.[41]

Ramon de Caldes was certainly not the creator of this procedure of account. He must often have thought of his father as the bailiffs came before him, for the inventories of comital domains and isolated accounts surviving from the 1150s and 60s reveal a fiscal structure already substantially like that of the 1180s.[42] Moreover, there was some continuity of personnel and office from the time of Ramon Berenguer IV. Just as Ramon seems to have taken over Bertran de Castellet's function, so his associate, the royal scribe Guillem de Bassia, succeeded the scribe Domenech, who continued active in accounting until about 1182.[43] Accounting remained closely tied to the chancery work; a *computum* of 1180 was recorded in the presence of no less than five royal scribes: Domenech, Ponç de Osor, Guillem de Bassia, and the brothers Caldes.[44] Ramon may have written accounts or fiscal memoranda himself, for he retained a practiced hand into the 1180s, but none of the extant manuscript *computa* can surely be traced to his pen.[45]

What Ramon de Caldes contributed to the Catalan fiscal administration was a sense of bureaucratic order. Under his direction the written accounts became a distinct and efficient species of charter.[46] Moreover, so many more of the king's copies survive from his time (1178–94), and their numbers and regularity decline so perceptibly thereafter, that it looks as if he and Guillem de Bassia took some unusual interest in preserving them.[47] This presumption is strengthened by our certain knowledge of Ramon's familiarity with the royal archives. Although not explicitly so called in our documentation until 1207,[48] the accounts ("compoti") were already an office with its own records in the 1180s; and the dean was quite conceivably the organizer of the fiscal archive just as he was that of the general treasury of charters from which the *Liber feudorum maior* was compiled.

Our grasp of Ramon's administrative achievement would be strengthened if we knew more about the balance of the royal accounts in the 1180s and '90s. But the system, at its best, did not allow for central budgeting or balancing, nor can we fully reconstruct the king's account from records of his receipts, purchases and debts. One significant fact does appear, however: it is that the records of massive debts on the count-king's part, which are all too frequent in the 1150s, '60s and '70s, thin out in the 1180s, and practically disappear in the years of Ramon's fiscal supervision.[49] The disruptive practice of pledging entire bailiwicks to great creditors seems to have been reversed in the years 1186–94, when most of the known debts were for modest sums advanced by the bailiffs themselves.[50] Even for pledged bailiwicks, Ramon de Caldes received accounts, such as those for Ascó and Tortosa (1189), then in the hands of the Templars.[51] It is true that the relative solvency attained by King Alphonse in this period soon collapsed, for reasons that have not yet been made clear; but the circumstances suggest that Ramon de Caldes had been a sound administrator of the royal finances.

Such was the man to whom the king entrusted the vast work—"ordained in two volumes," as Ramon explained, "because, owing to its excessive ponderosity, it could not be compiled in one"—which was later to be known as the *Liber feudorum maior,* one of the first great registers of a European monarchy.[52] The work must have been all or nearly done by the early months of 1196, for it was presented complete to the king, who died on 25 April of that year; and much of it, at least, must have been done after August 1194, when Ramon subscribed to the record of a major feudal settlement that was included in the register.[53] The fact that Ramon's last extant account dates from April 1194 gives added reason to think that he devoted full attention to the compilation during the months thereafter.[54]

Although the dean referred to a specific verbal command by the king, it is difficult to believe that the work had not been long contemplated. Perhaps the precipitating event was the conclusion of a war with Ponç de Cabrera in charters of August 1194 which were almost the latest instruments included.[55] The settlement was reached in a great court ("plena curia") held at Poblet, in the company of most of the prelates and major barons of Catalonia. Ramon attended, too, and it is tempting to imagine that he received the command then and there. The king's power over infeudated castles had been the major problem not only of the war just ended but also, in a way, of the reign as a whole. It was explicitly to ease the resolution of such issues that the king had ordered the compilation, Ramon observed, with only a passing hint at a less juristic motive in his reference to the "eternal memory of great things."[56]

The *Liber feudorum* was, in obvious ways, a very different kind of enterprise from the financial work that had lately occupied its compiler. Yet it was organized territorially, just as was, undoubtedly, the registral inventory of the direct domain over which Ramon de Caldes must often have pored, and like that register it at first bore the title *Liber domini regis*.[57] Was this older register—possibly the first of the great series of paper registers of the Crown of Aragon, but lost at an early date—also the work of Ramon de Caldes? If so, and it is not unlikely, then his achievement in creative administration was even greater than has generally been recognized.

The dean had remained active in his chapter and had continued to reside in Barcelona during these later years.[58] Although he sometimes travelled out to the bailiwicks of New Catalonia, which he and his brother had helped to organize, and to Poblet, he does not seem to have accompanied the king on his distant travels.[59] But his capitular work can only be described as routine. His fiscal expertise remains perceptible in the documents he subscribed, as does his loyalty to the canons and his relatives.[60] Although little is known of his estate, for his will seems not to have survived, he was certainly a man of means. In 1190 he purchased for 750 sous the major part of a vineyard near Barcelona, which he then donated to the chapter in augmentation of his nephew's endowment;[61] and his bounty likewise supported another nephew, Berenguer.[62] Ramon seems to have retired from the king's service in 1196, for there is no evidence that he served the new ruler, Peter I (1196–1213). The dean's old colleague Guillem de Bassia, having bequeathed a fine robe to Ramon, had died in November 1195.[63] During 1196–97 Ramon continued busy in the chapter, sometimes in association with Arnau de Caldes (whose interests were to be more strictly ecclesiastical than his uncle's).[64] Ramon must have been in failing health by 1198, when his familiar subscription disappears from extant documents.[65] Of his death, which probably occurred in the late summer or early fall of 1199,[66] we know nothing.

There is something imposing about the tall, canonically garbed figure, subtly larger, subtly more central, than the king seated to his right, who faces us in the great miniature which adjoins Ramon de Caldes's prologue to the *Liber feudorum maior.* The appearance befits the man we know from his work. In a land where church and state had not parted ways, he had made his career in his bishop's see and his reputation in the king's service. Practical, faithful, judicious, his private life apparently untouched by scandal or crisis, he was a respectable, and respected, man. Had he some sense of achievement at the end of his life? Perhaps he indulged himself a passing thought of his career as a whole when, with correctly restrained pride, he wrote of the laborious completion of his enormous cartulary.[67]

The royal service, which he had known from childhood, was his real vocation. He was not so much a political adviser as an administrative expert. "Politics" was for the baronial class in Catalonia, and Ramon de Caldes knew his station. He was a jurist only in the least technical sense: knowing the value of evidence obtained by prudent inquiry, he judged accordingly as the king's chief accountant. His early efforts were devoted to his capitular administration, which he probably helped to reorganize. He reformed the royal fiscal service—this was his major accomplishment—and he seems to have had some responsibility for the dawning practice of fiscal enregistration in Catalonia. He was the first great archivist of the Crown of Aragon.

Devoted to his homelands, which attained the territorial limits of historic Catalonia just during his lifetime, Ramon de Caldes never aspired to international recognition. He can hardly have been tempted to compare himself with St. Thomas Becket, whose cult he saw spreading in Catalonia (where the murder of archbishops was then likewise an appalling reality).[68] His culture, like that of his chapter, was a trifle provincial and very traditional. Perhaps Ramon came to realize this, for as a professional scribe he cannot have failed to notice the influx of Romanist formulas during his last years,[69] when, moreover, Arnau de Caldes, with his uncle's evident approval, undertook seriously to study the Roman law.[70] Ramon's had been an older way. He was one of those devoted secular clerks, more often obscure than otherwise, upon whom rulers of his age everywhere relied to build their authority. He was a founder of royal government in Catalonia.

University of California, Berkeley

Notes

1. See Archivo de la Corona de Aragón (hereafter ACA), Cancillería, Registro 1; also Reg. 4; ed. Francisco Miquell Rosell, *Liber Feudorum Maior. Cartulario real que se conserva en el Archivo de la Corona de Aragón,* 2 vols. (Barcelona, 1945–47; hereafter LFM), I: vii–viii, 1–2, and plate 1; also Josep Gudiol i Cunhill, *La Miniatura catalana* (Barcelona, 1955), pp. 139–40, who refers to Eduardo González Hurtebise, in *Suplemento al Boletin de Archivos, Bibliotecas y Museos* (1919), p. 474, which I have been unable to see. There are recent sketches of Ramon de Caldes's career in *Diccionari biogràfic.* 4 vols. (Barcelona, 1966–70), I: 394; and (by A. M. Mundó) *Gran Enciclopèdia catalana,* 8 vols. to date (Barcelona, 1970–75), IV: 137.

2. Arxiu Capitular de Barcelona (hereafter ACB), *Libri antiquitatum* (hereafter LA), as registered by Joseph Mas, *Notes històriques del Bisbat de Barcelona*. 13 vols. (Barcelona, 1906–21), XI (part of series entitled Rúbrica dels *Libri Antiquitatum* de la Sèu de Barcelona): nos. 1730, 1742, 1850; XII. nos. 2312 and following; cf. the sketches cited in n. 1.

3. On Caldes (de Montbui; not to be confused with Caldes de Malavella, likewise an old thermal place and comital center), see *Enciclopèdia catalana*. IV: 139–40; or *Diccionari nomenclàtor de Pobles i Poblats de Catalunya*. 2nd ed. (Barcelona, 1964), p. 75; and Enric Moreu-Rey, *La Rodalia de Caldes Montbui. Repertori històric de Noms de Lloch i de Noms de Persona* (Barcelona, 1962), esp. pp. 50–51; Moreu-Rey, *Caldes de Montbui, Capital degana del Vallès* (Barcelona, 1964). The "mensura de Calidis" is mentioned, e.g., in ACA, Gran Priorato de Cataluña, 1ª, Arm. 1 (Barcelona), no. 167.

4. ACA, Cancillería, pergaminos of Ramon Berenguer IV, 233 (no. 1.B in a forthcoming edition cited below, note 34).

5. ACB, LA, III: fol. 75rv, no. 201 (Mas, XI no. 1742). The honor, which came to be called "de sancta Susanna," was considerably developed during Ramon's lifetime; it passed to his nephew Porcell de Caldes after the canon's death (ACB, perg. Diversorum B.280 [7.VI.1202]). That Ramon's father was identical with Porcell the bailiff is proven by comparison of the property described in LA, III: no. 201 with that described in text cited in next note.

6. ACA, perg. Ramon Berenguer IV, 218.

7. ACB, LA, III: fol. 75rv, no. 201 (Mas, XI: no. 1742). Porcell the elder was probably still living then (see below, note 21).

8. Both are mentioned as Ramon's brothers in LA, III: no. 201, although the copyist evidently altered the order of *signa* to the lost original.

9. He presumably inherited the allodial land, but I have found no evidence on that. For the documentation, see n. 21.

10. ACB, I: fol. 122, no. 307 (Mas, XI: no. 1730); ed. Sebastián Puig y Puig, *Episcopologio de la Sede barcinonense* (Barcelona, 1929), Apéndices, p. 422, no. 78.

11. ACB, LA, III: no. 201 (Mas, XI: no. 1742).

12. Documents registered by Mas, XI: nos. 1767, 1772, 1828, 1831, 1835, 1850; also nos. 1863, 1913, 1948, etc.

13. Dr. Eduard Junyent argues, on the basis of his thorough knowledge of the archives of Vich, that the designation "levita" invariably attached to lay administrators of clerical communities.

14. Caldes de Montbui was a parish of Barcelona, and there is other evidence, too, of episcopal interests there (e.g., ACB, perg. Diversorum B.13726[11.XI.1149]).

15. LFM, II: no. 804.

16. E.g., Ponç de Osor and Pere de Corró. In his mature years, however, he always insisted on writing his own subscription in distinctive capital lettering, followed by a *signum* derived from the old SS (or *subscripsit*), e.g., ACA, perg. Alfonso I, 256, 301, 315.

17. ACA, perg. Ramon Berenguer IV, 233 (no. 96A in edition cited below, note 34); perg. Ramon Berenguer IV, sin fecha 16. For the background, see Anscari M. Mundó, "Domains and Rights of Sant Pere de Vilamajor (Catalonia): A Polyptych of c.950 and c.1060," *Speculum* XLIX (1974), 238–57.

18. The qualification is important, for the Templars of Palau solità, some five kilometers south of Caldes, were to become the chief institutional creditors of the kings in the later twelfth century, a relationship undoubtedly fostered by the Caldes family; see provisionally T. N. Bisson, "Credit, Prices and Agrarian Production in Catalonia: a Templar Account (1180–1188)," *Order and Innovation in the Middle Ages: Essays in Honor of Joseph R. Strayer*. ed. W. C. Jordan, Bruce McNab and T. F. Ruiz (Princeton, 1976), ch. 7. See generally José Maria Font Rius, *Cartas de Población y Franquicia de Cataluña*. I: pts. 1 and 2 (Madrid-Barcelona, 1969).

19. For Bernat's early charters, see, e.g., LFM, II: nos. 794, 681, 682; I: no. 484; cf. Archivo Histórico Nacional (Madrid), Clero (Poblet), carpeta 2006, no. 13 (written by B. de C., *scriba regis*. possibly before 1167); his later charters as *scriba regis* are too numerous to cite. For

the canonries, see ACB, LA, III: fol. 75v, no. 202 (Mas, XI: no. 1948); perg. Diversorum C, capsa 6.227 [30.IV.1173]; Arxiu Capitular de Lleida, *Llibre vert*, fols. 33v–34r. On 17 April 1185 Bernat sponsored the entry of his nephew Guillem de Caldes (son of Porcell the younger?) to the chapter of Lleida, endowing him with *operatoria* in Almacelles (AC Lleida, *Llibre vert*, fol. 34r).

20. ACB, perg. Diversorum B.672 (1.IV.1182); or LA, I: fol 179, no. 475 (Mas, XI: no. 2101); ACA, Gran Priorato de Cataluña, Cartulary of Gardeny, fols. 87v–88r.

21. He is the most problematical member of the family. If his father had died by 1156 (as Moreu-Rey, *Rodalia de Caldes*, p. 170, assumes), then he succeeded his father as bailiff (ACA, perg. Ramon Berenguer IV, 326; and cf. the dubious text printed by Moreu-Rey, pp. 100–101). I think it more likely that the son continued to be known as "Porcellet[us]" and as "Porcellus" (or "Purcellus," or "Porcelletus") "de Calidis" after 1156 because his father survived for some time: ACA, perg. Ramon Berenguer IV, sin fecha 16; perg. Alfonso I, 43, 127, 141; *Cartulario de "Sant Cugat" del Vallés*, ed. José Rius Serra, 3 vols. (Barcelona, 1945–47), III: no. 1079; Biblioteca de Catalunya, pergamins Miret i Sans, 2169; Mas, XI: nos. 1742, 1838, 1920, 2049, 2074, 2093, 2098; XII: nos. 2714, 2722. The "Porcellus" (unqualified) who was active in the Vallès Oriental, although perhaps indistinguishable from the father in 1158 (ACA, perg. Ramon Berenguer IV, 322) can surely be identified with the younger Porcell in later years (perg. Alfonso I; 77 [Moreu-Rey, *Rodalia de Caldes*, Ap., no. 25], 300, 531); he may have travelled with the king as a young man (LFM, II: nos. 870, 898, 899). He had probably died by 1202 when his late brother's endowment was returned to the family by the chapter (ACB, perg. Diversorum B.780 [7.VI.1202]); the "Porcellus de Calidis" who benefitted from that cession, if indeed Porcell III, was the brother of Arnau de Caldes, canon of Barcelona, and of Guillem de Caldes, canon of Lleida (above, note 19, and Moreu-Rey, *Rodalia de Caldes*, Ap. no. 29).

22. ACB, LA, I: fols. 180v–181r, no. 479 (Mas, XI: no. 2098); fol. 89, no. 210 (Mas, XII: no. 2216); perg. Diversorum C, capsa 7.388, 389 (4.V.1198), Diversorum B.774 (13.III.1212); LA, I: fol. 398, no. 1119 (Mas, XII: no. 2518); Moreu-Rey, *Rodalia de Caldes*, Ap., no. 29.

23. ACB, LA, texts registered by Mas, XI: nos. 1860, 1882, 1883, 1894, 1900, 1913, 1948, 1980, 1986, 2006, 2021, 2023, 2034, 2069.

24. ACB, LA, IV: fol. 163, no. 382 (Mas, XI: no. 2034).

25. The origins of this institution are in need of study. They are probably connected with the effort to fix agrarian dues on the kalends rather than on feast-days; thus we find Ramon and Bernat de Caldes, *prepositi* of October in 1177, acting together again in 1180 (or 1181) in an episcopal concession of land for which the render was due on 1 October (ACB, perg. Diversorum B.654 [16.III.1180]; Mas, XI: no. 2069). See also perg. Diversorum A.2397 (21.III.1177); Mas, XI: no. 2018; LA, I: fols. 353–54, nos. 1012, 1013 (Mas, XI: nos. 2028, 2029). The *prepositurae mensium* were certainly present in the 1180s (LA, III: fol. 121, no. 313, I: fol. 98, no. 235; Mas, XII: nos. 2121, 2138).

26. ACA, perg. Ramon Berenguer IV, 233, 347, apéndice 9, sin fecha 16; perg. Alfonso I, 200. For evidence of debts, perg. Alfonso I, 126, 140, 171.

27. ACA, perg. Alfonso I, 256 (LFM, I: no. 199).

28. *El "Llibre Blanch" de Santas Creus (Cartulario del Siglo XII)*, ed. Federico Udina Martorell (Barcelona, 1947), no. 211. See also Manuel Riu, *Formación de las Zonas de Pastos veraniegos del Monasterio de Santes Creus en el Pirineo, durante el Siglo XII* (Santes Creus, 1962).

29. LFM, I: no. 168.

30. Ibid., no. 225; *Archivo de la Corona de Aragón. Guia abreviada* (Barcelona, 1958), p. 8.

31. LFM, I: nos. 225, 400; II: no. 621; ACA, perg. Alfonso I, 352, a settlement in the Berguedà (28 October 1183), which did not involve the king, is more nearly akin to the accounting discussed below; it is one of the few surviving documents written in Ramon de Caldes's own hand.

32. LFM, I: no. 376; ACA, perg. Alfonso I, 560.

33. LFM, I: no. 348; cf. no. 266.

34. This neglected documentation is edited and studied in my "Fiscal Accounts of Catalonia under the Early Count-Kings (1151–1213)," forthcoming. There is a pioneering sketch by Antonia M. Aragó Cabañas, "La Institución 'baiulus regis' en Cataluña, en la Época de Alfonso el Casto," *VII Congreso de Historia de la Corona de Aragón*. 3 vols. (Barcelona, 1962), III: 137–42.

35. ACA, perg. Alfonso I, 253, 292, 310, 315, 414, 418, 435, 442, 443, 476, 478 *dupl.*, 485, 521, 519, 526–528, 537, 543; perg. Pedro I, 48, 8; perg. Alfonso I, 550, 568, 579–581, 588, 592, 603, 652, 662, 674, 672, 678.

36. ACA, perg. Alfonso I, 579.

37. ACA, perg. Alfonso I, 435.

38. ACA, perg. Alfonso I, 448.

39. ACA, perg. Alfonso I, 526.

40. ACA, perg. Alfonso I, 527: "Interrogatus de placitis et de tercio si inde habuerit aliquid, affirmavit nichil inde in dicto anno habuisse."

41. E.g., ACA, perg. Alfonso I, 526, 527, 579, 588.

42. ACA, perg. Ramon Berengùer IV, 233, 347.

43. ACA, perg. Ramon Berenguer IV, 347; perg. Alfonso I, 253, 310; Joaquim Miret y Sans, "Pro sermone plebeico," *Boletín de la Real Academia de Buenas Letras de Barcelona* XIII (1913), 114–15.

44. ACA, perg. Alfonso I, 310.

45. Cf. perg. Alfonso I, 352, which he certainly wrote, with, e.g., no. 526, or with Alfonse I, extrainventario 2612.

46. This point is developed, together with others in this paragraph and the next, in the introduction to "Fiscal Accounts of Catalonia."

47. There are some forty-three accounts for the years 1178–94, as compared with eleven for the period 1196–1213.

48. ACA, perg. Pedro I, 246.

49. This assertion is based on an analysis of texts too numerous to cite here. Cf., however, ACA, perg. Ramon Berenguer IV, Apéndice 9; perg. Alfonso I, 58 and extrainv. 3627; with perg. Alfonso I, 389, 435, 519.

50. E.g., perg. Pedro I, 8; perg. Alfonso I, 568.

51. Perg. Alfonso I, 519.

52. LFM, I: 1 (quotation in note 71).

53. Ibid., 1–2, and no. 413.

54. ACA, perg. Alfonso I, 678.

55. LFM, I: nos. 412–414.

56. Ibid., 1: "Viva expressistis voce, vos habere votum et desiderium ut omnia instrumenta propria et inter vos vestrosque antecessores ac homines vestros confecta, et in ordinatione confussa, sub uno redigerentur volumine, tum propter subiectorum scilicet utilitatem, ut, his instrumentis ad memoriam revocatis, unusquisque ius suum sortiatur, tum propter eternam magnarum rerum memoriam, ne inter vos et homines vestros, forte oblivionis occasione, aliqua questio vel discordia posset oriri."

57. Ibid.; for the lost *Liber domini regis*. mentioned in at least twenty-three accounts, see, e.g., ACA, perg. Pedro I, 8; Alfonso I, 485. There is also mention of the "quaterniones" kept by the bailiffs for their purposes. That Ramon de Caldes was familiar with paper registers is rendered the more likely by the circumstance that his associate Guillem de Bassia wrote his will (June 1195) "in quodam libro de paperio," ACB, LA, II: fols. 434–44v, no. 121 (Mas, XII: no. 2276).

58. His house in Barcelona was the site of at least one accounting session, ACA, perg. Alfonso I, 519.

59. ACA, perg. Alfonso I, 568; LFM, I: no. 266; Udina, "*Llibre Blanch" de Santas Creus*, no. 372; *Cartulari de Poblet*—, ed. Joan Pons i Marquès (Barcelona, 1938), no. 298. I have not traced him farther east than Perpignan (LFM, II: no. 792), the most remote bailiwick of Old Catalonia.

60. ACB, LA, as registered by Mas, XII: nos. 2170, 2174, 2194, 2211, 2216, 2218, 2227, 2234, 2261, 2268, 2269, 2273, 2275, 2277.

61. ACB, LA, I: fol. 89v, no. 212 (Mas, XII: no. 2211); fol. 89r, no. 210 (Mas, XII: no. 2216). The property was at *Albedon*, which I have been unable to locate, but which was certainly a domain of the bishop and chapter of Barcelona (cf. perg. Diversorum A.2292a, b [15.III.1158]; Mas, XI: no. 1777; Udina, *"Llibre Blanch" de Santas Creus*, nos. 166, 318).

62. ACB, LA, I: fol. 89, no. 211 (Mas, XII: no. 2277). Was Berenguer Arnau's brother? He was active in affairs of his bishop and chapter after his uncle's death, Biblioteca de Catalunya, perg. Miret i Sans, 2927; Mas, XII: nos. 2353, 2355, 2367, 2377, 2391, etc.

63. ACB, LA, II: fols. 43r–44v, no. 121 (Mas, XII: no. 2276).

64. Mas, XII: nos. 2269, 2273, 2275, 2277, 2278, 2296.

65. His last registered subscription is ibid., no. 2312 (29 July 1199).

66. The *terminus ad quem* is July 1202, when the late dean's endowment at Caldes was reassigned (ACB, perg. Diversorum B.780 [6.VII.1202]); but his successor as *decanus* is already mentioned on 6 November 1199 (Mas, XII: no. 2316).

67. LFM, I: 1–2: "Inde est quod michi vestra dignata est mandare et iniungere magnitudo, ut hoc opus, licet viribus meis impar, inciperem, inceptum complerem, et ad optatum deducerem effectum . . . opus incepi, inceptum ordinavi, ordinatum per duo volumina, que in uno pro nimia ponderositate redegi non poterat, divisi, divisum per claros titulos distinxi, distinctum fine felici consumavi. Nec ad iactantiam loquor, sed ad maioris veritatis evidentiam. . . ."

68. On the murders in Catalonia, see Puig y Puig, *Episcopologio*, pp. 166, 172; Miquel Coll i Alentorn, *La Llegenda de Guillem Ramon de Montcada* (Barcelona, 1958). Ramon de Caldes attended the endowment of an altar dedicated to St. Thomas of Canterbury in the cathedral of Barcelona on 29 December 1186 (ACB, LA, I: fol. 350, no. 999; Max, XII: no. 2174); he would surely have known of the cult at Terrassa, where a fresco depicting the martyrdom of Thomas, and dating from these years, can still be seen.

69. E.g., ACA, perg. Pedro I, 16.

70. ACB, LA, I: fol. 74rv, no. 167 (Mas, XII: no. 2261); Ramon witnessed his nephew's recognition (June 1196) that he held for life his cathedral church's collection of *Code, Digest, Novels* and *Institutes*. None of these codices survive in the modern capitular collections of Barcelona; nor do we know of canonist mss. of Barcelona antedating the thirteenth century. Arnau's acknowledgement of "omnes libros legum qui sunt et pertinent predicte ecclesie" probably refers only to the *Corpus Iuris Civilis*. Cf. *Scrinium* VII (1952), pp. 10–11; Puig y Puig, *Episcopologio*, p. 174.

Localism and Longevity: The Example of the Chapter of Rieti in the Thirteenth and Fourteenth Centuries

ROBERT BRENTANO

In an effective set of passages within an effective book, Professor Geoffrey Barraclough proclaimed a now famous victory, the "victory of the papacy, a victory—if not a final victory—over localism and particularism, a victory within the church and within the spiritual realm." Professor Barraclough wrote that not only the papacy's "power but also its jurisdiction and its sphere of influence at the end of the period in question [1303], knew no bounds."[1] The attentive reader of Professor Barraclough's whole *Papal Provisions* must be aware of many at least implied qualifications to these generalizations; but a reader who accepted the generalizations unquestioningly and who was, surely like most readers, less sophisticated than Professor Barraclough himself, might believe that by the end of the thirteenth century the clogged, repelling provincialism of local churches had been cleared away. He could believe that local churches were free and open to receive unreservedly into their papally controlled selves papal law and papal administrative act. He could certainly be expected to think that those old controlling nests of "localism and particularism," cathedral chapters, had been cleaned and aired and made functioning, provided parts of the universal church.

It is difficult to believe that these attitudes would have been shared (except perhaps in aged Joinville-like moments of lament over the lost days of youth) by Don Bartolomeo di Oddone Alfani, canon of Rieti, in the year 1318. In that year, on 20 December, in the sacristy of Rieti's San Domenico, although still healthy, Don Bartolomeo made his will and included in it twenty-five florins for the fabric of the church of Rieti, his church. He could then look back to at least sixty-nine years of having been a canon there, in the cathedral church close to his own locally powerful family's palazzo, called, in his youth, in 1252, the palazzo "filiorum Alfanorum."[2]

One could reasonably argue that Bartolomeo Alfani is a single case, that only a minority of canons can have been so markedly local, that few can have become canons so young or lived so long. It is true that Bartolomeo is probably unique in specifically carrying the ideas and values of the Reatine church of 1249 to the church of 1318. But even his single existence questions the idea of total revolution. Furthermore, he tempts the historian to look to see what characteristics of other specific canons might suggest a composite body resistant to violent change. More specifically Bartolomeo encourages one to look for further evidences of localness and longevity in his chapter.

Even if it could be proved, of course, that the chapter of Rieti had completely resisted serious change in the later thirteenth century nothing would be proved of any other place. Local histories can, rather glossily, be considered soundings which establish or deny the generalizations of general history. But, looked at more purely, they must always seem specific and particular, objects to be used, if at all, additively or for comparison. Local history almost must be tartly nominalistic. The historian of the chapter of Rieti may feel compelled to step across diocesan boundaries to use or point out limited but helpful similarities in the neighboring dioceses of Narni and Sabina, but in some real and important ways a church like Rieti's can only talk about Rieti.

Rieti is a city about eighty-five kilometers northeast of Rome on the Via Salaria.[3] In the thirteenth century the extension of its walls indicates that it was a growing city, growing, its size suggests, from about 2,000 to about 3,500 people. Rieti is the capital of the land of the Sabines, but it and its diocese lie and lay on and across many borders, those between Lazio, Umbria, and Abruzzo, the old border between the Regno and the papal states, the boundaries between the urban west and the hamleted east and between Fernand Braudel's mountainous and his Mediterranean olive-growing cultures.[4] Superficially at least the diocese of which Rieti was the ancient episcopal see changed considerably during the thirteenth century. Its size and shape were changed by the creation of the new diocese of L'Aquila in the middle of the century. The regular religious in the diocese changed. Although the Benedictines of San Salvatore Maggiore to the south maintained their potency, at least intermittently, in spite of wars, their brother Benedictines to the northeast at San Quirico lost their monastery to Premonstratensians when, early in the century, their decayed state was called to papal attention by their murdering their abbot.[5] The Cistercians of San Matteo by Rieti, afflicted, as were Cistercians elsewhere, by their settlement in a low marshy place, survived their move to San Pastore in the hills.

The most significant change, in terms of formal religion, however, was the arrival, in this famously Franciscan place, of the friars. Franciscans, Dominicans, and Augustinians came to Rieti, and Franciscans to the sacred hermitage places in the hills. Franciscan and Dominican nuns came to the diocese, among them the Claresses in the house at Borgo San Pietro in the Cicolano, built by, and then around the cult of, the uncanonized saint, Filippa Mareri, of the Cicolano-ruling family of the Mareri.[6] One should not, of course, form too quick a picture of neatly organized convents crisply sitting in the Reatine countryside. It was even possible to argue that places which claimed to be monastic establishments were not monastic. In a document from 1338 it is protested that a woman cannot be, as she has claimed, "habatissa" of the convent of Volta in Rocca Sinibaldi near Rieti, because it is not a convent, since it is without an approved rule and is not part of an approved order, and because at it there are not nuns to make up a chapter.[7]

Nevertheless, the changing of religious orders within the diocese during the thirteenth century is clearly important in many ways. One of those ways is closely connected with the problem of localism. There is a distinct and observable difference between the places of origin of the religious in the houses of the old orders and those in the houses of the new male orders. The monks from the neighboring Benedictine monastery of Farfa, actually within the borders of Rieti's neighbor diocese of Sabina, assembled in 1279, make a good example of a house of one of the old orders. Almost all of the thirteen monks listed come from towns or villages very close to the monastery: four, including the prior, are in fact from closely neighboring Fara in Sabina; one is from Toffia; two are from Rocca Sinibaldi; one is from Scandriglia. One comes from the slightly greater distance of Cerchiara, and two from Rieti itself; but it is a very close little village group.[8]

In 1342 the group of Cistercians at San Pastore near Rieti was even closer. Although the major cellarer was from Narni, every other identified monk and *conversus* was from the very immediate area. Two of the seven monks and two of the eleven *conversi*, for example, came from the immediately neighboring village of Greccio (of Franciscan fame)—and one of these *conversi*, Brother Francesco of Greccio, in his name, suggests the strength of the natural pull of local neighborhood over that of other attractions to religious order. Among the San Pastore Cistercians, origins in villages like Contigliano, Rocca Alatri, and Monte San Giovanni are very noticeable. One of the monks and five of the *conversi* are identified as being from Rieti itself.[9]

For contrast with the Benedictines and Cistercians, one can turn to the Dominicans of Rieti. In 1315 one finds among them more friars from Spoleto (three) than from Rieti (two), and friars from Orvieto, Cortona, Arezzo, and Rome. In 1319 one also finds friars from Viterbo and Veroli. At no point do the friars from the diocese clearly outnumber those from outside the diocese.[10] This pattern very definitely does not occur later, when it can be checked, among the Claresses in Santa Filippa's convent at Borgo San Pietro. They are, as everything one knows about their house and order would suggest, very local, the nuns came from their part of the Salto valley (as they do to this day), although from both the papal and the Sicilian-Neapolitan sides of the valley.[11]

Obviously the friars did not bring the first foreign religious to the diocese of Rieti. In spite of the diocese's provincial rusticity, its see was an intermittent papal capital. At the beginning as well as at the end of the thirteenth century the whole motley crowd of the papal curia moved through Rieti. Still the difference between the old and new types of religious is striking. In quite obvious ways, but not always, the friars were clearly the enemies of localness, as, in a familiar story, Saint Francis himself tried to explain to the knights in the piazza of Perugia.[12] The friars would seem the heralds or the companions of the provided bishops and canons who with their provisions would break the little walled areas of the old provincial church.

At Rieti, to a certain extent and at first, the thirteenth-century bishops seem to support this pattern. Certainly at the beginning of the century, Reatine bishops seem, insofar as they are visible, to have been members of the minor military aristocracy of central Italy, and their pontificates are said, by later contemporaries, to have been affected by their families' involvements in local wars.[13] In 1249 a saintly Aretine Franciscan was elected by the chapter and pressed by Innocent IV to accept the see. Upon his resignation he was succeeded by a providee from Innocent's curia, and then by a series of providees and translatees. Although the provided "style," "dei et apostolice sedis gratia," does not come to be used regularly by Rieti bishops until the pontificate of Bishop Giovanni Muto de Papazurri (1302–36), provision came a half-century earlier. The pattern would seem to be local electees until 1249, then providees from outside.[14] This impression of pattern would seem at first to be confirmed by the sort of men who became bishops of Rieti in the late thirteenth and early fourteenth century: the inquisitor Angelo, the ecclesiastical politician Pietro of Veroli (moving through a number of sees on the way to Aquileia), and a cluster of men translated from places like Tivoli, Sora, Ancona, Nepi, and Imola.

In fact much of the foreignness of these foreign bishops disappears as one looks at them more closely. The inquisitor, for example, was in fact Angelo da Rieti. One of the two providees from Sora had gone to Sora from a canonry at Rieti. The Cistercian Nicholas's connections with the local house of San Pastore seem suspiciously close. Even the very foreign sounding translatee from Imola, and before Imola from Olena, had been a canon of the Lateran and was from the not, after all, very distant Roman family of the Papazurri.

Most of these particular bishops, as their numbers suggest, did not rule long at Rieti. The one bishop who did rule very long, Giovanni Papazurri, seems to have spent the last third of his pontificate in a sort of exile from Rieti. The caution that one must still use in talking about this period of exile in the 1320s and 1330s is in itself revealing. It is particularly revealing because the movement and activity of the bishop are so obscure during a period for which there exists a full and excellent cartulary of the church of Rieti. The cartulary was written by Matheus Barnabei, or Matteo di Barnabeo, citizen of Rieti, and notary by imperial authority, who seems generally to have identified himself as "nunc notarius dictorum dominorum episcopi et capituli" (now notary of the lords bishop and chapter of Rieti) from 1315 until 1319 when he adopted "nunc notarius dicte ecclesie" (now notary of the church of Rieti).[15] The cartulary, which covers the period from February 1315 to January 1348, is made up of twenty-four twelve-folio gatherings of parchment. The significance of the difficulty of tracing the bishops' activity in this large and initially very clearly written cartulary is that it underlines either the mutual involvement of bishop and chapter in the affairs of the church or the ability of the church as a community to proceed with its ordinary business under the direction of vicar and canons without much noticeable, specific interference by the bishop. This suggested mingling of interests recalls the retarded separation, at Rieti, of episcopal and capitular properties and incomes. It is made tangible in the description of a common episcopal-capitular seal in 1287.[16] Together bishop and chapter composed the church of Rieti, and on occasion a bishop of Rieti could call the members of his chapter his co-canons.[17]

It was not the bishop, or not the bishop alone, but rather the bishop with his chapter—of twenty canons in the thirteenth century and twenty-one in the fourteenth—who had stood for the Reatine local quality of the church of Rieti in the early thirteenth century. Whether or not the bishops of Rieti seem, after more serious examination, to have remained essentially local in spite of the obvious and apparent change in their type after they became provided bishops, the Reatine quality of the church of Rieti could have been riddled by the papal provision of alien canons late in the thirteenth century or preserved by the continued presence of a significant number of Reatines.

In a series of dramatic scenes from the year 1334 one is made aware of the probable Reatine representativeness of the chapter and its adherents.[18] The scenes are progressive events in the trial of Paolo Zoppo, a hermit who wore the dress of a spiritual and who had lived in the hermitage of San Leopardo at Rieti. Paolo was accused of gross sexual behavior which was a physical expression of heretical belief. He was tried before the Franciscan Simone di Filippo da Spoleto, inquisitor for the Roman province. The intricate story of complicated events repeatedly suggests the tension between local sentiment, particularly represented by defenders of the heretic and his accomplices or those to whom they appealed (and the names Alfani and Secinari are both involved) on the one hand, and the reforming nonlocal Franciscan inquisitor on the other. The inquisitor properly involved in his process local learned and informed opinion through his selection of local counselors including the episcopal vicar and representatives of the church and chapter. Within this group there seems to have been support for the patriotic position against torturing the heretic, that he ought not to be tortured "propter famam conservandam personarum Reatinorum et propter honorem civitatis." It is easy to imagine, in these circumstances, in a place long apparently without a resident bishop, in a place where the dominant religious orders had among their ranks an abundance of nonlocal friars, during that nervous and uncertain period in central Italian politics, that the chapter was a bulwark of local sentiment and strength. This imagining would be made easier if the local chapter were the natural home of long and local memories.

With this in mind one can return to the matter of longevity in the chapter of Rieti. In general a canon's longevity must be measured by his appearance in enumerations of members of the chapter or in witness lists, unless some chance document or occasional registration preserves record of his selection, provision, institution, or installation, or another some record of his death. This limitation means that one can usually only say that a canon was a canon for at least a certain length of time. Another, but, at least in the case of Rieti, less severe problem arises from the fact that it is sometimes difficult to be sure that the same repeated name in lists represents a single person.

The latter problem can be exposed immediately in the case of Jacobus Sarracenus, Jacopo(?) Sarraceno. Jacobus appears probably as the senior canon, as his position in the list would indicate, on 20 June 1280. He holds the same position in a list from 1261. It is thus startling but pleasing to find him (Jacobbus Sarracenus) in a short list of canon witnesses, which also includes Teballus Sarracenus, who is familiar as Saint Francis's Reatine host, on 10 July 1220. The very distant churches of Honorius III and Nicholas III seem brought together in the long career of this member of a patrician family long connected with the church of Rieti. (In 1152, for example, Rainaldus Sarracenus had given his whole inheritance to the church, or to its Virgin saint, through the hands of Bishop Dodone.) The reader's credulity is strained to breaking, however, when he finds Jacobbus Sarracenus listed as a canon in 1181. There must have been at least two of them. An examination of successive lists makes it seem probable that the 1280 Jacobus Sarracenus became a canon in or slightly before 1238. Disappointingly for the searcher for longevity the 1280 Jacobus seems to have been a canon for only forty-two years.[19] Nevertheless even this probable career connects the pontificates of Gregory IX and Nicholas III. The importance of this connection is amplified as one realizes that for more than thirty years the later, probable Jacobus and Bartolomeo Alfani were co-canons, generally resident, and that Jacobus's additional memories, imparted in countless meetings of the chapter, could be carried with his own by Bartolomeo into the pontificate of John XXII. These long strands of the memories of local resident canons can be seen being woven together to form a pretty stout cord. These particular strands can be pulled backward when it is seen that a number of Jacobus's co-canons in 1238 had been canons at least since 1230: Sinibaldus Mareri, Berardus Moysi, Jacobus de Ponte, Berardus Rainaldi Sinibaldi Dodonis, the priest Raynaldus, and almost surely Oddone Alfani, Matheus Laurentii, and Berardo Pasinelli. Two more of Jacobus's 1238 co-canons, Rainaldus Fatuclus and Rainaldus Beraldi, had been canons at least since 1233.[20] One, Berardus Salectus, had been a canon since 1220; and when another, Bernardus Salonis, testifies, in 1246, that he has been a canon for twenty-four years and more, in spite of one's natural doubt about exact numbers of years in testimony establishing long term custom, and in spite of the fact that Berardus will still be a canon in February 1261, one tends to believe him.[21] Moreover, at least six of the canons of 1233 were still canons in 1253. At least five of the canons of 1253 were still canons in 1280. These were generally resident canons who met, talked, prayed, witnessed, made property adjustments, and engaged in litigation together. Their very existence argues against sudden break and argues for continuity of procedure, interest, and values.

Within this braided cord of woven lives, the strands of individually long-lived canons continue to catch one's eye. Beside Bartolomeo Alfani's almost seventy years, one can put the fifty-nine years of Bartolomeo Bontempi, canon at least from 1261 to 1320. Another canon lived as canon thirty-five years, another thirty-three, another thirty, two more twenty-eight, another twenty-seven, two more twenty-six, another twenty-five, another twenty-three, and at least three more twenty years. Although few of these canons may have been priests, one can adjust to them the familiar line: "Se vuoi star bene sempre, fatti prete." The longevity of these canons, moreover, ties together the whole length of time from 1220 to 1347. There is within that period no significant general break.

The break in 1348 seems severe. In a number of ways the church the historian finds in 1349 seems very different from the church he left in 1347. But a great deal of that difference may be due to the death of the record-keeping notary, Matheus Barnabei. He and his successors kept records differently; they did not try to show their reader the same things. There was, in any case, some little continuity in the chapter. Liberato, who was a canon by 1347, could tell his colleagues of the customs of the preplague chapter as late as the 1390s, by which time new continuities had been established.

The importance of Matheus Barnabei to the historian's perception of the chapter of Rieti reminds one of the overwhelming importance to the chapter of its chief notary and scribe, the man who performed for it the functions of a quasi-chancellor and permanent secretary. The importance of this sort of figure can probably not be stressed too strongly. Just as readers of notarized medieval wills must continually suspect that they are reading in some part the mind of the notary rather than that of the testator, so must readers of capitular documents sometimes suspect that the action they are observing was not only preserved for them by its notary but also given its initial coherent form by him, particularly if that notary had already established himself as the long accustomed recorder of his institution's acts.

At Rieti the episcopal-capitular chancery, insofar as that perhaps too neatly institutional phrase is applicable, was composed of a changing group of scribes and notaries. The surviving Reatine evidence does not force one to believe that any one of these men was ever the sole scribe of the church or that any of them was employed only by the church, in spite of the fact that over long periods of time one man, like Matheus Barnabei, played a visible and singularly important role. The reader will recall that Matheus described himself successively as "notary of the lords bishop and chapter" and "notary of the church." His description of himself as being employed by both the capitular and episcopal officers in the church is important and should be noticed. Like the retarded separation of episcopal and capitular incomes at Rieti this description reveals a significant lack of separation, a significant clinging to an old concept of community, and also it identifies a significant agent in maintaining that community—the notary himself. It is difficult to imagine an officer whose long tenure in office would more readily guarantee continuity in the local church's business than would that of the church's notary. That longevity in office was sometimes achieved has been demonstrated in the career of Matheus Barnabei himself; his cartulary for the church, it will be recalled, stretches from 1315 to 1348.

Impressive as Matheus's working longevity is, he was surpassed in length of service by his predecessor, Johannes Petri or Giovanni di Pietro.[22] In an act of Bishop Nicholas of Rieti, from 1294, Giovanni is given, in the genitive, a full name and title: "Johannis Petri Johannis Tedemarii, notarii, familiaris, et prebendarii layci nostri capituli et ecclesie Reatin'." The business of Bishop Nicholas's act was to confirm grants which the chapter had made to Giovanni during the episcopal vacancy of the preceding year. In 1293 the chapter had ordered that as a reward for his continued service to chapter and church Giovanni be admitted, as familiar and lay prebendary, to his portion of the daily distribution of commons and that he be granted as his prebendal benefice eight *giunte* of land (at a time when 30 *giunte* seems to have been the standard nucleus of a canon's prebend). By 1265 this Giovanni di Pietro had already been recognized as an official titled employee of the church of Rieti. In that year, in a document he wrote for Bishop Gotifredus, he called himself "Johannes Petri dei gratia Romane ecclesie et Reatine civitatis et dicti episcopi notarius." Even before 1265 he had been active in church business: he acted as notary for the chapter on 13 June 1263; he was a witness, in the choir, on 4 February 1261. He was to remain active until at least 3 May 1314 when he wrote in his protocols the draft of a document (which he himself did not extend) in which he described himself as "dictorum dominorum episcopi et capituli scriba." He thus spent more than 53 years as a professional scribe involved in capitular and episcopal business—a long time. He was surely dead by 23 September 1314 when Symon Bonjohannis extended and redated the May document from "protocollis quondam notarii Johannis Petri de Reate."[23]

Giovanni was probably a native Reatine. As an adult he identified himself as a citizen of Rieti. He seems always to have been a layman. His father's name was Petrus Johannis, of which his own name was a characteristic inversion; central Italian boys seem frequently to have been named for their grandfathers so that a pattern of two alternating names is formed in a single line of geneology. Almost surely Giovanni's paternal grandfather's name was also Giovanni (Johannes). The Tedemarii or Teodemarii may have been and probably was fixed as a patronymic surname by Giovanni Petri's generation; his own name, at least once, includes the "Teodemarii" without the preceding "Johannis." Giovanni may have been related to a Thomas Tedemarii recorded selling a property in the borgo (for seven *lire*) in 1217 or to the Bartholomeus Tedemarii listed as a neighbor in a transaction in the Porta Carceraria quarter of Rieti in 1226; but both of these possible relatives may just have had fathers named Tedemarius. By 1294 Giovanni himself held property in the Porta Cintia quarter near San Domenico and was acquiring more; in January of that year he promised 33⅓ florins for a third of a house next to some of his own property there. In 1293 and 1294 he was granted, installed, and confirmed in his prebend of eight *giunte* located in a dependency of Collebaccaro.[24]

In his will Giovanni made the greater church of Rieti his universal heir, and specified that the value of his inheritance should be spent for the fabric of the church, after the death of his wife Verardescha, who was to have the use of his properties for her lifetime. By 21 August 1318 Giovanni's properties, lands, vineyards, and a house in districts pertaining to Rieti, had been sold, after a public proclamation announcing the sale, to Jacobus de Sancto Liverato (Liberato), a prebendary of the church, acting for Bishop Giovanni Papazurri, for a price of 100 florins, in a transaction supervised by one of Giovanni's executors, Thomas Capitaneus, prebendary and chamberlain of the church. With the purchased properties the bishop endowed his chapel "sub vocabulo Beati Salvatoris" in the cathedral church. Giovanni's 100 florins were to be spent to help defray the expenses of the new tribune of the church then under construction.[25]

Nothing is more obvious in the documentary remains of the church of Rieti from the years between the 1260s and the 1310s than the work, hand, and notarial sign of Giovanni di Pietro, citizen of Rieti. Fittingly his substance was, in the end, built into the fabric of the cathedral church which he had served. He was a symbol and agent of long-lived localism there.

Giovanni brings to our attention the prebendaries or Rieti. They are increasingly apparent in the early years of the fourteenth century. In the later part of the century, in the account books which become regular after Matheus Barnabei's death, lists of prebendaries complement lists of canons. In Giovanni's own time his executor and fellow prebendary Thomas Capitaneus, underlines, as does Giovanni himself, the localness of the ecclesiastical establishment at the greater church of Rieti, prebendaries as well as canons.

Avoiding for the moment the problem of change and the special problem of providees, one can certainly say that the great majority of the canons, as far as one can tell, were local. They were, again insofar as they can be identified, and excepting a few special clerks, members of the local upper classes, with those classes interpreted unrigorously as the usual middle-Italian mélange of urban patriciate and country lords, although there is nothing at all to suggest any institutional restriction of the chapter to people of relatively elevated birth. The identifiable canons were from families like the Mareri, the Pasinelli, the Alfani, the Sarraceno, the Secinari, the lords of Labro. These identifiable families make a decent little spectrum: the lords of Labro (and their connections, the lords of Morro) to the north, toward Umbria, near Terni, in papal territory remembering a ducal past, feudal-seignorial; the Mareri in the south, in Cicolano, the Regno, not very old as an identifiable ruling family, ruling their villages heavily, very Neapolitan-Sicilian feudal, "propelling" a sister to sainthood; the Alfani, an urban patrician family, capable of protecting religious exotics, and on its way to a sort of local despotism; the Sarraceno, an urban patrician family harboring memories of Francis.[26] The Secinari, the lords of Secinaro, are revealed with locally unusual clarity because of the fortunate survival of the will of a member of the family, Johannes or Giovanni, son of the late lord Pandulphus de Sicenario, from 1311.[27]

Johannes, acting "in domo . . . filiorum domini Pandulphi," made his brothers his heirs, seven of them, and left bequests to three sisters, two of whom were nuns in local convents. Giovanni's bequests were divided into two clusters: one centered in Rieti, where Giovanni lay, he feared, dying; the other centered in Secinaro near Sulmona, the town from which his family took its name and where he himself had tenants still. Among Giovanni's brothers was Berardo, possibly the Berardo who would become a canon of Rieti, to whom Giovanni left a contingential legacy to help him with the expenses of building his chapel at San Clerico in Secinaro. The country and the city of this canonical family are clearly visible; the country, which their name would have suggested, is distant, in another diocese and even in another country, but it is normal in its rural supporting nature, and it will remain in accounts of the chapter of Rieti long into the future. The neighborhood which Secinari holdings and interests define is not geographically an immediately obvious one, but it is not culturally irrational. The localness of the Secinari family as it appears in the cathedral chapter is thus somewhat complex, but it is firm, and marked still by the palazzo Secinari in the center of Rieti.

One might well ask if these canonical patrician families represented a particularly black, clerical segment within the local patriciate, a specific group of families whose power and wealth were buttressed by adherence to the local ecclesiastical establishment. A definite answer would not, at present, be possible. The division of Rieti into "Guelf" and "Ghibelline" in the fourteenth century could indicate, for that later period, such a black-white separation. But nothing in the thirteenth century seems to suggest it. A dispute between the chapter and detainers of chapter holdings, with which, in 1251, Bishop Thomas tried to deal, for example, argues that the chapter and its opponents came from exactly the same cluster of families, and even the very same families, whose branches or members were temporarily motivated by different and opposing proprietary and monetary interests. In 1251 the detainers of chapter holdings in Collebaccaro included three Capitanei brothers, four Sassone, two Alfani, and three Carsidonii. Apparently the same families who sought and obtained cathedral stalls and prebends for their members were sometimes overcome by their greed and seized capitular land and rights directly for themselves. One sees, at least in 1251, diversification of style and movement, a division among individual members of families, not a division among familial groups within that local patriciate who furnished its members to the chapter.[28]

Into this toughly long-lived and local chapter of Rieti, defined by its long-lived and local scribes and notaries, the thirteenth- and fourteenth-century popes intruded their providees. What effect, one must ask, did this provision have upon the consistency of the chapter? Were alien, disruptive, locally disloyal or incoherent elements intruded with the provided canons?

One may start to answer by looking at a specific papal intrusion of a canon which the chapter was forcefully resisting in 1252. The papal providee was Jacobus or Jacopo Pasinelli. At a first and very narrow glance this might seem an example of a papal attempt to break, for whatever motives, the localness of the chapter, an attempt, through the force of papal letters, to place a foreigner in the chapter. But this man, Jacopo, was in fact from the local family of Pasinelli and already a canon of the local collegiate church of Sant'Eleuterio. A Pasinelli, Senebaldo, had been a canon of Rieti as early as 1181. In the 1230s Berardo Pasinelli had been a canon. Jacopo himself, after Bishop Thomas, as arbiter between him and the chapter, had ordered his installation and proved an active, resident, long-lived canon, still present as late as 1280. Within his first year, 1253, Jacopo was already acting as a chapter official in important business with his fellow and senior Angelo Mathei (Angelo Angeli Mathei) who had been a canon since at least 1238; ten years later the same pair was again engaged for a particularly difficult transaction. Neither before nor after Jacopo's provision does there seem anything faintly strange or foreign about him except the mode of his selection. This point is underlined in an official description of a later Pasinelli providee, a canon expectant whose commons the chapter had been witholding in 1290. He is called, in the genitive, "Oddonis nati nobilis viri Phylippi de Pasinellis de Reate militis."[29]

The quality of the Pasinelli providees is exactly what one would have been led to expect by the provisions observable in recently published documents from the capitular archives at Narni, Rieti's neighbor. A short and perhaps heavily abbreviated history of Narni provision in the thirteenth century is incidentally recorded in the *consilium* requested of, and in 1277 provided by, the legist Master Clericus of Pisa in the dispute between the bishop and chapter of Narni over the bishop's role, if any, in the reception and institution of canons. The provided canons include the relatively fully identified (in the accusative) "Bernardum clericum natum condam Angeli militis Narn[iensis] [*sic*]" and "Massaronum clericum natum nobil[is] viri Radi civis Narn[iensis] [*sic*]." In other cases Narni origins are implied or stated as in the case of "Jacobum natum Nicolai Martini de Narn[ia]." The Narni localness of the church of Narni is further revealed in the strong communal resistance to Alexander IV's provision of his relative, the Dominican Orlando, to the bishopric in 1260; the communal government refused to accept Orlando and insisted upon recognizing the bishop elected by the chapter, the Narni canon, Rainaldo de Miranda. Narni was forced to accept, as Rieti did accept, provided bishops, but in both cases their canons seem, when identifiable, preponderantly local.[30]

In October 1252 the chapter of Rieti was resisting the provision both of the papal *scriptor*, Nicholas, and of Andreas Pernatarum (Impernatoris), canon of Sant'Eleuterio. In the same month Bishop Thomas, the mutually accepted arbiter in both cases, ordered the chapter, in separate decisions, to receive and induct both providees. Nicholas the *scriptor*, who might seem an alien if valuable intruder, was actually present in Rieti as late as 1278, and he seems, out of Rieti, to have been called Nicholas Reatinus. Andreas was clearly connected with Rieti before his provision; and Impernatorio was a Rieti name. Andreas was present in Rieti in the 1260s. In 1276 Pope John XXI provided Ventura Raynaldi or Raynerii, a chaplain to Giacomo Savelli, cardinal deacon of Santa Maria in Cosmedin, to a canonry at Rieti or to the expectancy of a canonry. By 1278, at least, Ventura was an accepted canon. He, too, established himself in Rieti and was a resident canon there as late as 1315.[31]

This seems the normal pattern of provision. Popes regularly provided men who already had or came to have strong Reatine interests and connections. Alexander IV, an early provider, seems to have been an exception, and to have attempted to provide family and neighbors to the chapter of Rieti as he did to the episcopal see of Narni. In 1256 he provided the clerk Benencasa di Nicola, the son of a citizen of Anagni, and in 1259 he provided his own relative, the clerk Tomasso di Giacomo de Pesclo (in a letter written from Anagni). Neither provision seems to have been successful, although Roman canons resident are rather more noticeable in the fourteenth century. But even in the flamboyant display of provision and pluralism in the register of the "foreign" pope, John XXII, a prominent performer, Berardo Mathei Infantis, among many other things a canon of Rieti, was a Reatine. The obviousness of the mechanism for representing the absent canon Francesco Papazurri (during the episcopate of Giovanni Papazurri) underlines its unusualness.[32]

If the popes chose to provide clerks with Reatine interests and intentions how did they choose which of them to provide? Some answers suggest themselves. Ventura was the chaplain of a cardinal, Giacomo Savelli. Oddone Pasinelli was the chaplain of Matteo Rosso Orsini, cardinal deacon of Santa Maria in Porticu. Nicholas the *scriptor* was or became the chaplain of Hugh of St. Cher, then cardinal priest of Santa Sabina. The canon Berardo da Poggio Bustone, active in Rieti at least from 1261 to 1280, was in 1263 a chaplain of Ottobuono Fieschi, cardinal deacon of Sant'Adriano, and Berardo was in Lyons with Cardinal Ottobuono in 1274. Leonardo Arcangeli, a canon present in Rieti as early as 1253 and as late as 1263, had been a canon of Rieti and chaplain to Ottone da Tonengo, then cardinal bishop of Porto, in 1246.[33] Certainly one sort of connection which is noticeable among successful providees is a connection with Roman cardinals, particularly as their chaplains. But it is quite possible that this connection seems more important than it should, and it is quite obvious that it is more apparent than it would earlier have been, because of the recent publication of Agostino Paravicini Bagliani's important book, *Cardinali di Curia e 'familæ' cardinalizie dal 1227 al 1254*. The scattering of Rieti canons' names through the registers of thirteenth- and early fourteenth-century popes suggests the efficacy of a variety of curial connections. It is worth remembering that Bartolomeo Bontempi, canon of Rieti at least from 1261 to 1320, was already, in 1254, being called our "familiaris" by Pope Innocent IV, and receiving, or owed, income from very distant places, like Majorca and Leon.[34]

On 2 August 1289 Bishop Andreas, who had previously been a canon of his church, and three canons, acting as vice-gerents and commissaries for the whole body of canons, received as their brother canon, Bartolomeo domini Raynalli de Rocca. Long before, in 1259, Pope Alexander IV, "at the instance of Marcus our *ostiarius*" had ordered the provost and chapter of the collegiate church of Santa Cecilia, Rieti, to receive as a canon Bartolomeo Raynaldi de Rocca, then described as a Reatine *scolaris,* "postquam fuerit clericali caractere insignitus." In 1319, after years of residence as a canon of the cathedral church, Bartolomeo received from the abbot of Citeaux, at the request of the abbot of San Pastore, Rieti, participation in the spiritual benefits of the Cistercian order. In 1308 Cardinal Giacomo Colonna writing from the palazzo of San Lorenzo in Lucina in Rome received Bartolomeo as his chaplain and welcomed him into his *consortium* of chaplains.[35] In granting this, Bartolomeo's request, Giacomo said, he responded to the continued devotion of Bartolomeo's brother and relatives to his house, the house of Colonna. Bartolomeo and Giacomo not only expose the Reatine canon becoming chaplain rather than the chaplain canon, but also they raise the daunting question: were cardinal's chaplains preferred because their patrons were cardinals or because their patrons were, when they were, Savelli, Orsini, or Colonna?

It is a question without a direct answer. But there are observable conditions which would affect such an answer were it possible to give one. For one thing, toward the end of the thirteenth century there are indications that the power of the local patriciate was becoming more dependent upon that patriciate's connection with the powerful curial families of Rome and the *campagna* (Colonna, Orsini, Savelli), as well perhaps as with the Neapolitan court. The pattern of power in central Italy distracted by the concluding phases of the papal struggle with the Hohenstaufen seems to be finding a new coherence around 1300. But although in 1285, for example, Colonna power was institutionally present in the city of Rieti through the captaincy of Giovanni Colonna, no bishop or canon of the period seems himself to have been a member of a Roman family of the first order; the series of Colonna bishops would not begin until 1477.[36] There had been a canon named Ponte in the 1230s who quite possibly was a Roman Ponte. There would be a Sant'Eustachio, quite surely a Roman Sant'Eustachio, canon by 1349; and he would have among his twenty colleagues two other identified Romans, in a chapter of relatively rather noticeable open geographic background, including a canon from Terni and one from Leonessa, for example, as well as an Alfani, a Secenari, and two Labrese.[37] The Roman intrusion of the early fourteenth-century is Papazurri. Curial families affected the late thirteenth and early fourteenth-century chapter through patronage generally of specific Reatines, or men from the district, like Bartolomeo di Don Rainaldo de Rocca, rather than through the intrusion of their own members.

This Roman patronage opens the way to answering the question of whether or not provision changed the sort of canons installed in the choir of Rieti, whether or not the chapter of Rieti was changed by the era of provision. The answer is both yes and no. Essentially the same families and types of families from essentially the same places, insofar as these things can be observed, found canonical stalls for their sons and brothers. They did this, however, through a different mechanism and with different connections. The clerical sons and brothers, moreover, seem to have had different educations; in particular, more of them seem to have had experience at the papal curia. There may have been fewer priest canons at the end than at the beginning or the thirteenth century; fewer priests identify themselves. But some of the functions of the identified priests may have been taken over by emerging prebendaries; and also priesthood may have seemed less of a distinction. The Reatine canons of 1300 and their families were part of their world, not the world of their own ancestors in 1220 or 1230. Theirs was, in a way, the more sophisticated world of Orsini, Colonna, and a more obviously impinging and attracting papal curia. One could say, and reasonably, that the function of papal provision at Rieti had been to facilitate the maintenance of capitular power by the local Reatine patriciate in a vastly changed church within a vastly changed universe. In this sense papal provision was a conservative force at Rieti.

But this seems a rather casuistic sort of conservatism when it is seen against the bluntly realistic conservatism of personal longevity. Was the chapter of 1315 different from the chapter of 1250? Bartolomeo Alfani could tell us. His steadiness in office, and that of his colleagues, both shows and in some part explains real resistance to change. The chapter of Rieti was literally Reatine; it represented Rieti and knew its job, early in the thirteenth century when, in 1205, it made a gift in land to the local Cistercians so that God would preserve the people of Rieti, and in the second quarter of the fourteenth century when representatives of the chapter worried over Reatine honor during the trial of Paolo Zoppa. The canons' and their prebendaries' substance remained in the church after their deaths, a symbol and extension of the longevity of their adherence to their place: Giovanni di Pietro in the tribune; Corrado di Don Riccardo de Morro, who left the income from a specific *clusa* for the wine, the hosts and incense of the masses to be celebrated in the church *continuis temporibus,* and who insured the future celebration in the church of the anniversaries of his father, his mother and himself on 11 March, 22 July, and 10 August; and Bartolomeo Alfani, himself, whose psalter, remembered still as being made for him, was preserved in the cathedral sacristy, with other books, in 1353.[38]

Innocent IV's relations with the church of Rieti summarize, in their heightened detail, the sturdy and resistant Reatine quality of the chapter. Innocent IV's first missionary to Rieti was the Franciscan Rainaldo of Arezzo, whom he did not provide but whom he at first declined to absolve from his election by the chapter, whose members had known him as Franciscan lector to the Franciscans at Rieti. Rainaldo went back to Rieti and tried to reform the cathedral clergy with some individual successes, at least that of the young patrician canon with lay ways, who may have been Bartolomeo Alfani, and whose relatives "qui erant nobiles, divites et potentes," approved Rainaldo's disciplining of him. But, in general, in spite of Rainaldo's synodal canons of reform aimed specifically at wild capitular abuse, he was unsuccessful; he left his clergy "videns quod ad viam honestatis et rectitudinis redire nolebant." More than a decade later, a letter of Urban IV could recognize and again oppose Reatinity in nullifying the appointment of a group of canons, whom it called illiterates and boys, cousins and nephews of the older canons themselves.[39]

The second incident in which Innocent IV imposed himself on Rieti involves the canon Palmerius or Palmerio Leonardi, who in 1251 was a clerk of the papal camera, and by 1252 was a canon of Rieti, and in 1261 was a condemned heretic. Palmerio Leonardi sounds as cosmopolitan as any Reatine canon is likely to sound. But like many other canons, he reveals, on close inspection, intricate Reatine connections. In 1251, in his house in Rieti, he is seen acquiring family property. In January 1261, before his condemnation, he is seen ceding his property, while reserving its use for his lifetime, to his son, Giovanni, born of Rainallucia, an unmarried woman at Giovanni's conception, who had later married a man named Giovanni Calantre. In November 1261, after Palmerio had been condemned and his properties confiscated, at the plea of his son (Johannes Magistri Palmerii Leonardi), the podestà of Rieti, acting in a Rieti palazzo then used as a court, returned wrongly confiscated tenements to Palmerio's son.[40] The house, in which the heretical acts and receptions which caused this trouble were said to have taken place, was in the Porta Cintia, before the Duomo, in the center of Rieti. During the pontificate of Innocent IV, foreign reformers are repulsed, and exotic seeming intruders expose themselves as Reatine.

Surrounded by the drifting Franciscans and Dominicans, the twenty or twenty-one canons of the great church of Rieti, most of them local men, most of them (and sometimes all of them) resident, prayed and did business in their church and in the *palazzo* next door. They collected their local rents, including baskets of those *gamberi,* which pressed their Reatinity on Saint Francis by arriving with the fish he had wanted, and perhaps miraculously got, from the canons' freshwater see.[41] The canons' seal held an image of the Virgin, and their church was rededicated to her by Pope Nicholas IV when he was in Rieti in 1289.[42] Individually long-lived and institutionally permanent, the canons as chapter, with their rents and their cult, gave Rieti something firm, solid, and Reatine in a time and place of general indistinctness and insolidity.

What does this local institution, the heart of the Reatine church, with its long-lived canons, have to tell historians of canon law? Two things at least: the church to which the *Sext* was issued, as well as that to which the *Decretals* were, was composed of segments, some of which—this one at least—were tenaciously local in their attachments, and so, presumably, in their interpretations. Those local churches which were at all like Rieti (and at least there was Narni) offered a restricting social, external reality which mirrored the "argument in favor of limited monarchy which we find in the writings of almost all of the thirteenth-century canonists," or was mirrored by it.[43]

Finally, one might, dangerously, parody Professor Barraclough's proclamation of victory. The chapter of Rieti in the thirteenth and early fourteenth centuries seems to have won a victory, a victory perhaps even over the papacy, a victory—if not a final victory—for localism and particularism, a victory within the church and within, in a way, the spiritual realm.

University of California, Berkeley

Notes

I should like to thank Monsignor Emidio de Sanctis for generously permitting me to use Archivio capitolare at Rieti. Many of the ideas and much of the information presented here were first aired in two talks: "The Church and Society in Central Italy in the Thirteenth Century," presented at a meeting of the Mediaeval Academy of America in Kalamazoo in the spring of 1974; and "Sin in a Small Italian City: Fourteenth-Century Rieti," presented at the Tulane University Medieval Symposium for 1975, "Sin in the Middle Ages." I have benefited from comments and questions offered and asked on both occasions. All of the material presented here derives from my work for my forthcoming book on Rieti in the thirteenth and fourteenth centuries. It is still very much work in progress, uncertain and unfinished. I hope that Professor Stephan Kuttner's being so clearly a working historian will help a little to excuse this condition.

1. Geoffrey Barraclough, *Papal Provisions* (Oxford, 1935), p. 2.

2. Rieti, Archivio captiolare, 4.N.3 "6", 2.D.10, 3.D.10, 4.K.3, 2.B.2, 4.F.4, 3.D.2. Rieti, Archivio di stato, Comunale, 6. Possibly Bartolomeo's absence from lists in the 1250s indicates that he was temporarily removed from the chapter by Bishop Thomas or that for some other reason he was absent from the chapter. It seems to me very likely that he was the young canon of whom his colleagues complained to Bishop Rainaldo in a passage in Salimbene; they spoke "de quodam concanonico suo iuvene et lascivo, qui magis laycus quam clericus videbatur." Rainaldo corrected him with a pull of his long hair and a slap; and he called "parentes ipsius et propinquos, qui erant nobiles, divites et potentes," and told them that their son must choose one life or the other. The relatives replied: "Placet nobis quod clericus sit. . . ."—which says something about who chose the canonical life for young canons: Salimbene de Adam, *Cronica,* ed. Giuseppe Scalia. Scrittori d'Italia CCXXXII–CCXXXIII (Bari, 1966), p. 475.

3. For the history and geography of Rieti see: Michele Michaeli, *Memorie storiche della Città di Rieti* (Rieti, 1897–99); Francesco Palmegiani, *Rieti e la Regione Sabina* (Rome, 1932); Pierre Toubert, *Les Structures du Latium médiéval* (Rome, 1973); Daniel Waley, *The Papal State in the Thirteenth Century* (London, 1961).

4. Fernand Braudel, *The Mediterranean and the Mediterranean World in the Age of Philip II,* vol. I (London, 1972).

5. For San Quirico see Christopher R. Cheney, "Gervase, Abbot of Prémontré: a Medieval Letter-Writter," *Bulletin of the John Rylands Library* XXXIII (1950–51), 25–56; Charles Louis Hugo, *Sacrae antiquitatis monumenta* (Étival, 1725), I: 29–30 (for which reference I am indebted to Professor Cheney).

6. Aniceto Chiappini, *Santa Filippa Mareri e il suo Monastero di Borgo S. Pietro de Molito nel Cicolano* (Perugia, 1922), also in *Miscellanea Francescana* xxii (1921), 65–119.

7. Rieti, Archivio capitolare, 2.D.1.

8. Rome, Archivio de stato, S. Francesco di S. Vittoria in Materano, sec. 13.1. In these lists, particularly perhaps of friars, place names normally quite surely do mean places of origin, or places with which the individual is connected in his companions' minds.

9. Rieti, Archivio capitolare, 6.E.3.

10. Rieti, Archivio capitolare, 4.H.4, 6.B.1; and see also 5.E.1.

11. Borgo San Pietro, Archivio di Santa Filippa Mareri, "1381."

12. Rosalind B. Brooke, ed. *Scripta Leonis, Rufini et Angeli sociorum S. Francisci* (Oxford, 1970), pp. 150–51.

13. Rieti, Archivio capitolare, 4.P.1.

14. Rieti, Archivio capitolare, 2.B.2, 6.G.11, 4.G.8, 3.C.4, 4.F.4, 4.K.13, 4.G.7, 4.Q.3. Rieti, Archivio capitolare, Liber Instrumentorum, 1315–47 (actually 1348), or Liber Mathei Barnabei. Bishop Giovanni's episcopate has been poorly and indecisively dated in the past. The Liber Mathei Barnabei makes it certain that he died between 4 February and 12 June 1336 and that he was still bishop of Rieti in 1336. Michele Michaeli divided Giovanni in two and let the second Giovanni live until 1339: *Memorie*. iv: 225; Conrad Eubel corrected a similar division in his predecessor Pius B. Gams, but he did not record the restored Giovanni's correct death date: *Hierarchia catholica medii aevi* (Münster, 1913), i: 416.

15. Rieti, Archivio capitolare, 4.Q.10, 4.K.13, 3.B.5, 4.G.8, 3.B.7, and the Liber Mathei Barnabei, the cartulary.

16. Rieti, Archivio capitolare, 3.B.1, fol. 2v. Separate seals of both bishop and chapter survive from the thirteenth century. The first, of which I am aware, is that of Bishop Rainaldus/Rainaldo on the capitular statutes which he issued in 1250: 2.B.1 (a document, unfortunately, missing from the archives in 1974 and 1975). The seal, a pointed oval in white wax, bears a standing bishop surrounded by a legend of which "EATINI EPI RAINAL" remains. The first surviving capitular seal, of which I am aware, survives on a document from 1280 in which twelve canons make two co-canons their proctors: 3.C.3. The pointed oval seal in pinkish white wax bears the legend "SIGILLUM CAPITULI REATINI," within which a seated Virgin in gothic draperies holds a Child on her left arm and a lily or liliated scepter in her right hand. The style of the image and, particularly, the lettering suggests that the matrix cannot have been very old in 1280. For the retarded separation of Rieti incomes and finances: Robert Brentano, "Innocent IV and the Chapter of Rieti," *Studia Gratiana* xiii (1967), 383–410.

17. For example: Rieti, Archivio capitolare, 4.G.3, 4.Q.4.

18. Vat. Lat. 4026, particularly fol. 16v; Luigi Fumi, "Eretici e Ribelli nell'Umbria dal 1320 al 1330 studiati su Documenti inediti dell' Archivio Segreto Vaticano," *Bollettino della r. Deputazione di Storia patria per l'Umbria* iii (1897), 257–85, 429–89; iv (1898), 221–301, 437–86; v (1899), 1–46, 205–425—particularly v: 349–409, especially p. 368.

19. Rieti, Archivio capitolare, 3.C.3, 3.B.6 (1), 6.G.7, 4.L.10, 4.Q.2, 4.N.2 "2", 4.D.1. Brooke, *Scripta Leonis*. pp. 130–31: The "communal" life of Rieti canons perhaps suggests that *camera* should be translated more literally.

20. Rieti, Archivio capitolare, 4.D.1, 4.G.3, 6.G.7, 4.O.5.

21. Rieti, Archivio capitolare, 4.O.5 "5", 2.D.10; for other Berardus Salonis references: 4.G.3, 4.D.1, 4.D.4, 4.Q.3, 2.D.3, 2.D.5, 2.D.10.

22. In the difficult matter of the translation of names, I am, as the text makes apparent, at present undecided, at least for Rieti.

23. Rieti, Archivio capitolare, 4.G.4, 4.A.3, 3.D.10, 2.D.10, 4.F.4, 4.Q.3, 4.N.3, 6.G.11, 3.C.4, 4.G.8. When I was less familiar with Giovanni's work I mistakenly wrote that he died in 1306, because an important document of which he wrote the draft (6.G.11) on 6 May 1306 was redacted by another notary in 1318: *Two Churches* (Princeton, 1968), p. 295, and n. 14.

24. Rieti, Archivio capitolare, 9.F.5, 2.C.4; Archivio di stato, fondo Domenicano (San

Domenico), 7 (old 92). For some other helpful Giovanni documents, see Archivio capitolare, 7.F.4, 3.D.10, 7.F.3, 2.E.6, 7.F.5, 2.B.2, 3.C.3; Archivio di stato, fondo Domenicano (San Domenico), 5 (old 2).

25. Rieti, Archivio capitolare, *Liber Mathei Barnabei,* pp. 129–30. (The manuscript is paginated.)

26. It is not always possible, at least for me, to be sure whether individual men are members of important aristocratic families or merely men from the towns which have given the families their names; normally circumstances and positions help in this decision, and sometimes specific documents are helpful as, in the case of the lords of Labro and Morro, are: Rieti, Archivio capitolare, 1.D.2, 1.E.2. The Mareri are unusually visible both because of their saint and convent and because of the preservation of "statutes" for Mareri communities in the Cicolano: Archivio segreto vaticano, A.A.Arm.1–18.3660; Pietro Sella, "Statuti del Cicolano," *Atti e Memorie di Convegno storico Abruzzese-Molisano (1931)* (Casalbordino, 1940), III: 863–99; cf. *Catalogus Baronum,* ed. Evelyn Jamison, Istituto storico italiano per il Medio Evo, Fonti per la Storia d'Italia CI (Rome, 1972). For a Mareri connection, see *Les Registres d'Innocent IV,* ed. Étienne Berger, 4. vols., Bibliothèque des Écoles françaises d'Athènes et de Rome, 2e série (Paris, 1884–1921), II: 96, no. 4603.

27. Rieti, Archivio capitolare, 4.N.3 "3". See also 3.A.1 (1484).

28. Rieti, Archivio capitolare, 2.D.8; see also 2.D.7, from 1261. I suppose that it is possible that the del Giudice, Sarraceno, Arcangeli and their allies formed one faction in the chapter and were particularly active and strongly opposed to the lay Alfani, Carsidonii, and others; but I see no evidence to that effect. On the other hand, one cannot ignore local Hohenstaufen attachments still apparent among, for example, the Mareri and Labro in Manfred's time: 1.E.3.

29. Rieti, Archivio capitolare, 2.D.3, 4.Q.2, 4.D.1, 4.G.3, 3.C.3, 3.D.2, 4.D.1, 3.D.10, 7.B.4.

30. Wolfgang Hagemann, "Kaiser- und Papsturkunden im Archivio capitolare von Narni," *Quellen und Forschungen aus italienischen Archiven und Bibliotheken* LI (1971), 250–304, particularly 299–304, 296, 302–3, 298, 293–95. The opposition to Alexander's Dominican relative, Orlando, may have included anti-anti-heretical elements, like the opposition to the Franciscan inquisitor who later attacked Paolo Zoppa in Rieti.

31. Rieti, Archivio capitolare, 2.D.3, 2.D.4, 2.C.1, 3.D.2, 7.E.2, 4.D.5, 3.B.6, 7.E.8, 2.B.2, 4.F.4, 4.A.5, 4.O.5; *Liber Mathei Barnabei,* p. 14. Agostino Paravicini Bagliani, *Cardinali di Curia e 'familiae' cardinalize dal 1227 al 1254,* Italia Sacra: Studi e documenti di storia ecclesiastica XVIII–XIX (Padua, 1972), p. 268 for Nicolaus Reatinus. Compare 4.G.6.

32. Rieti, Archivio capitolare, 7.E.4, 7.E.5; for Francesco, e.g., 4.F.4.

33. Paravicini, *Cardinali,* pp. 268, 369, 94. For Leonardo Arcangeli, see *Les Registres d'Innocent IV,* ed. Berger, I: 34, no. 2108 (Leonardo's provision); *Les Registres d'Urbain IV,* ed. Leon Dorez and Jean Guiraud, 2 vols, Bibliothèque des Écoles françaises d'Athènes et de Rome (Paris, 1892–1929), I: 360 (in 1264), no. 754.

34. Rieti, Archivio capitolare, 10.A.4; it is also worth remembering that in Leon the canon Bartolomeo Bontempi can hardly have been considered a native. See also 4.N.3.

35. Rieti, Archivio capitolare, 7.F.3, 6.C.1, 7.C.6, 7.A.4.

36. Rieti, Archivio capitolare, 1.E.2 for Giovanni Colonna.

37. Rieti, Archivio capitolare, 4.D.1, 4.G.3; Liber 4, fols. 25–37v.

38. Rieti, Archivio capitolare, Liber 4, fols. 19v, 47v.

39. Salimbene, *Cronica,* p. 475. Rieti, Archivio capitolare, 2.B.1, 4.F.3.

40. Rieti, Archivio capitolare, 3.D.10, 2.D.2.

41. Brooke, *Scripta Leonis,* pp. 140–41, Rieti, archivio capitolare, 4.O.1, 4.P.5, 8.A.2.

42. Rieti, Archivio capitolare, 5.B.7.

43. The quotation is from Kenneth Pennington, "The Canonists and Pluralism in the Thirteenth Century," *Speculum* LI (1976), 48.

Utilia Metensia: Local Benefices for the Papal *Curia,* 1212–c. 1370

CHARLES McCURRY

Papal provisions were a basic means of financing the administrative activity of the papacy in the thirteenth and fourteenth centuries. By assigning benefices in distant churches to family, followers, clients, and allies, the popes redistributed the income of a substantial part of the ecclesiastical endowments of Europe. Scholars have written extensively on the administration of and contemporary reactions to provisions, but little has been done in a systematic way to estimate the impact of papal needs on a single church.[1]

Provisions were made to support the staff of the *curia,* to satisfy the powerful, and simply to increase revenues. They regulated access to ecclesiastical benefices, channeled the process through the curia, and exacted fees. The cost of the papal bureaucracy itself can be estimated by studying one of these three aspects: the extend to which a local church was required to give prebends to distant curial officials. They way in which prebends were granted can also throw some light on changes in the central administration itself. The assignment of local revenues to support papal administration was, moreover, a great innovation; the powerful had long been accustomed to their perquisites, though in smaller regions; recruitment funneled through the papal court still allowed qualified local clerics to gain prebends. As they had under a system of election, sons of prominent families and the talented still had access to benefices, though the assignment of prebends to curialists left fewer for others. Once they had won provision to the cathedral of Metz, the staff of the papal court were generally more successful in actually gaining possession of a prebend than were the general run of providees. The accounts of the papal collector from 1345 to 1355 include a rubric, *Inutilia Metensia* for provisions which had not worked and therefore represented no taxable acquisition of a benefice. Only three curial officials were named under that rubric, and two of them in fact returned to the fray and emerged successful.[2]

The cathedral chapter was the object of most provisions to the diocese of Metz. Because of the substantial surviving archives, it is also the church in which the extent and effectiveness of papal provisions can best be judged. The chapter's considerable income supported fifty-eight canons, whose two principal dignitaries (the *primicerius* and the dean) held double prebends. A good example of a fairly large, prosperous chapter in the Empire, whose members were not required to be noble, Metz was not protected from papal interest by an effective sovereign jealous enough of his rights to obstruct provisions.

Disputed episcopal elections in the middle of the thirteenth century made Metz even more visible to curial notice. Only two curial officials, however, became bishops of Metz, and both were apparently elected by the chapter. Guillaume de Trainel, canon of Verdun and Sens and papal chaplain, was provided to the next vacant prebend and office ("personatus") in the cathedral of Metz in 1263.[3] Meanwhile, a disputed election had been in litigation since 1261; Guillaume was successfully urged upon the chapter by his uncle, the count of Bar. His successor in 1270, when the papal see was vacant, was again a curial official, *magister* Laurentius. Elected canon of Trier in 1249 and *officialis* by 1253, he had become Chaplain of cardinal Pietro Capocci by 1258, when he was provided a second time to Metz;[4] a general constitution (*Execrabilis*) issued by Alexander IV had had the effect of cancelling his earlier provision by Innocent IV. By 1263 he had become a papal notary and was active as a papal agent in the province of Trier in the spring and summer of 1264. In 1265, he was back in Italy collecting papal revenues, but returned to Trier in November 1266.[5] A chronicle of the late fourteenth century described him as papal protonotary and administrator of Trier at some unspecified time.[6] He was elected in 1270 and spent a troubled nine years as bishop before his death in Italy in 1279.[7]

The bishops of Metz continued to be elected by the chapter until the death of Renaud de Bar in 1316. A disputed election and protracted litigation resulted in the provision of Henri de Vienne, the first of an unbroken line of papal providees. None of these providees, however, had a curial background. The episcopal prize was one suited to members or servants of great families— the five bishops from 1319 to 1383 included two members of the house of Vienne, two from the house of Poitiers, and a candidate of Emperor Charles IV; the following century was no different. Curial officials rewarded by the pope received a variety of prebends and offices instead of episcopal dignities. Such prizes were lucrative but not such a scarce resource in papal diplomacy.

Innocent III made the first surviving provisions to Metz in 1212 in favor of a certain P., nephew of Henri de Marcy, cardinal bishop of Albano, who had died in 1189. Papal intervention in this case was also a corrective. Innocent had already ordered the three delegates to fill eight vacant prebends, one of which was now to be given to P., regardless of the chapter's reported sale of the revenues of all eight prebends for a term of four years.[8] Although P. was not described as a member of the *curia*, it can be assumed that provision for a nephew was one of the perquisites of high curial office, apparently even posthumously, and that a local church thereby defrayed an expense of papal government.

A *magister* Octo, papal *scriptor*, was provided to Metz by Honorius III in 1216, the first papal official so provided.[9] Two cardinals succeeded in mid-century in obtaining Metz prebends for several of their staff. Cardinal Pietro

Capocci was papal legate in Germany in 1254 and 1255; two papal chaplains who accompanied him, M. Huguitio de Cingulo and M. Laurentius, were canons of Metz. Two of the cardinal's own chaplains became canons of Metz subsequently: his nephew, Oddo, chaplain and *camerarius*, and Conrad de Lichtenberg, member of a great Alsatian noble family, who became bishop of Strasbourg in 1273. M. Riccardus de Poifis (not the author of the formulary), who had been in Capocci's service in 1257, is mentioned as canon of Metz in 1264, when he was chaplain of Cardinal Jordanus Piruntus de Comitibus. Cardinal Guillaume de Braie, former dean of Laon, in 1264 acquired provisions to Metz for his nephew Henricus and for Guillelmus Nicolai de Trecis, his chaplain, who in other letters of the same year is mentioned as his notary and scriptor. The only other cardinal's chaplain provided to Metz in this period was Roger de Vandières, who served Cardinal Hugues de Saint-Cher and in 1257, already canon of the cathedral, was provided dean of S. Sauveur by Alexander IV, repeating a provision of Innocent IV. He too was a local man, bequeathing to S. Sauveur in 1272 a rent constituted on his property in Arnaville, a village on the Moselle between Vandières and Metz.[10]

Besides these clerics who owed their provisions to a cardinal's favor, only one other cardinal's chaplain was provided to Metz before the pontificate of Clement V; whether that forty-year scarcity of provisions—or their registration—to Metz for cardinals' chaplains was coincidence or not cannot be decided until further local studies have been done. The one chaplain was Johannes *dictus* Avemaria, mentioned as canon of Metz in 1291 and chaplain of Cardinal Benedetto Caetani. Even though Johannes was probably not French, he nevertheless appears to have retired to Metz, where he made a bequest for his anniversary in 1311.[11] It seems likely that his curial career was linked too closely to the distasteful memory of his master, who became Boniface VIII, to continue in the *curia* beyond the death of Boniface.

The distinction between papal chaplains and cardinals' chaplains is an uncertain one in several of the cases which have been and will be discussed. Given that qualification, it can be noted that fourteen curialists, in addition to the clerics discussed above, held prebends in Metz in the thirteenth century. Seven Italians are mentioned near the end of the century. The other seven, however, were natives of Lorraine who had joined the papal service. In background and reward they were similar to their local colleagues in the chapter. The carrer which they had chosen was their only point of difference. In fact, one is reluctant to conclude that they all gained their prebends by provision as a reward for curial service. The two relatives of the duke of Lorraine in particular might well have acquired prebends quite independently of their curial service. Henri de Fénétranges had become a papal chaplain and a canon of Metz, both before 1248; cantor of Verdun, he was provided dean of Metz in 1254 and six years later became archbishop of Trier. Philippe de Florange, cousin of the duke of Lorraine, was mentioned as a canon of Metz in 1248 and as a papal chaplain in 1255. He was one of two candidates in the disputed Metz episcopal election of 1261 and lost the resulting lawsuit even though he survived his opponent: he was obliged to resign his claim, and a third party was elected. Philippe remained canon and became treasurer, a post which he still held in 1297.[12]

Five other less distinguished clerics from Lorraine became papal chaplains and had prebends in Metz. Simon de Châtel, canon of Metz in 1253 when Innocent IV named him executor of a provision, was addressed as papal chaplain by Honorius IV in 1264 when he was confirmed in a chaplaincy granted by Philippe de Floranges. M. Laurentius acted as his proctor in the *curia*. He had been dean of the chapter at least since the previous year, and presumably since Henri de Fénétrange's election to Trier in 1260. Otherwise unidentified, a certain Julianus, archdeacon of Metz and papal chaplain, received a provision to Toul in 1257; he died in Rome in 1264, still archdeacon of Metz, where he had succeeded in obtaining a provision for his nephew. Stephanus de Eugneyo was described in 1264 as "familiaris apostolicus" when he was provided to Metz; he was already dean of Toul and canon of Verdun. M. Simon de Marville was mentioned as papal chaplain and treasurer of Metz in 1303 and continued to flourish under Clement V, who in 1306 reserved for him any office in the chapter of Liège, where he already had a prebend. In the same year, addressed as papal chaplain, he was provided to Verdun in consideration of Cardinal Petrus Roderici; Simon was his *auditor* and chaplain. Henri de Motas belonged to a bourgeois family and does not appear in the papal registers; nevertheless he was styled canon of Metz and papal subdeacon in a capitular act of 1297.[13] Gerardus, papal subdeacon, son of P., lord of "Granzano" (unidentified), like Roger de Vandières, had first been provided by Innocent IV but had to be provided again in 1259 by Alexander IV because the original provision had been cancelled by the same papal constitution. The addressee of his provision—perhaps a clue to his origin—was the prior of Romainmôtier (diocese of Lausanne).

The considerable number of Lorrainers in the *curia* had at least one inspiring example of success which may have made a curial career seem more promising. M. Pierre de Bar (never a canon of Metz) was a member of the family of the counts of Bar and cardinal priest of San Marcello from 1244 to 1253. His own household, however, included no one who held a Metz prebend; the reason may have been that the family of the bishop of Metz, Jacques de Lorraine, was Bar's great rival.[14]

The seven curialist Italian canons of Metz were of the grander sort. The first was a notary, Jacobus de Capua, active during the pontificate of Clement IV who is addressed as canon of Metz in an undated letter of an unnamed pope in the formulary book of Marinus of Eboli. The pope's predecessor had provided Jacobus to Metz, but the chapter had responded by refusing to pay him the revenues of his prebend unless he were in residence for the first year. The pope commanded that all revenues except daily distributions be paid to Jacobus.[15] Alero Ricciardi, canon of Metz from an unknown date until he was named bishop of Torcello in 1290, was active in central Europe in 1285 as collector of the tithe ordered by the Council of Lyons.[16] M. Nicolaus de Trebis was mentioned as papal *camerarius* in 1289, as *auditor causarum* in 1291, and as *primicerius* of the cathedral of Metz in 1291 and 1294. Johannes de Pappazurris, papal chaplain and canon of Metz in 1291, became bishop of Olenus in 1297, bishop of Imola in 1300, and bishop of Rieti in 1302. Randolfo Savelli, brother of Honorius IV and papal chaplain, was mentioned as a canon of Metz in 1291 when he was granted an expectation of an office in Salisbury and given a dispensation to hold it along with his seventeen other benefices.[17] Jacopo Savelli was *primicerius* of Metz from an unknown date until his resignation in 1301.* (On usage of * see n. 3) Nicolaus de Pappazurris was mentioned in 1302 and 1316 as canon of Metz and provost of the collegiate church of Notre-Dame-la-Ronde; he died at the *curia* in 1317.* That all received papal provisions is only an assumption. Prelates and rulers elsewhere had given benefices to members of the *curia* in order to win or reward friends at court, but no such cases are known in Lorraine.[18]

The pace of curial provisions clearly was not a constant one in the thirteenth century, nor was it to be in the fourteenth. While imperfect documentation and the question of registration may be a source of exaggeration, it is still noteworthy that after the first curial provisions in 1212 and 1216, only four thirteenth-century popes provided Metz with members of the *curia* who came from outside Lorraine: Alexander IV, five; Urban IV, two (Jacobus de Capua may be a third); Nicholas IV, five; and Boniface VIII, two. Of the seven members of the *curia* from Lorraine, apparently three became canons during the pontificate of Innocent IV, as archdeacon Julian, first mentioned as canon in 1257, also may have. Honorius IV provided one, and two appear first under Boniface VIII.

The same intermittent pattern is evident in fourteenth-century provisions. Of forty-one members of the curia provided to Metz, only two were provided by Clement V, none was provided by Benedict XI; and three were provided by Benedict XII. Sixteen were provided by John XXII, Clement VI provided five, Innocent VI, nine, and Urban V (so far as Sauerland's extracts indicate), four.

Cardinals were not provided to Metz prebends until the fourteenth century. Bernard de Jarre, a nephew of Clement V, was the first, in 1310.* Six other cardinals received prebends there in the following sixty years, but their chaplains were only rarely recipients of identical largesse. In contrast to the association of five Metz-provided clerics who served Pietro Capocci, the households of only two fourteenth-century cardinals included as many as three providees to Metz. Two providees in one household were not uncommon, but a single providee to Metz was the most frequent number. Provisions for cardinals' households were likely a matter of curial routine, no longer the object of an enterprising provider like Capocci.

The cardinals provided to Metz represent the general range of the college;

they were given Metz prebends presumably as their merits moved the pope to grant them further preferment and with no specific reference to the region. In the cases of Bernard de Jarre and Gilles Aycelin de Montaigut, both papal nephews, Metz prebends were among the emoluments which accompanied their elevation to cardinal. Hugues de Saint-Martial became cardinal in 1361, was provided to Metz in 1363, and may have set a record for curial longevity in a Metz prebend, living until 1403. Guillaume Bragose, cardinal in 1361, was provided archdeacon of Metz in 1365. Annibaldo Gaetani, cardinal from 1327 to 1350, acquired a deceased chaplain's prebend in 1331.[19] Gui de Boulogne, cardinal from 1342 to 1373, obtained a Metz prebend at an unknown date and resigned it in 1349 when he undertook a legation to Hungary. Bernard de la Tour, however, was provided archdeacon of Saarbourg in 1325, seventeen years before he became a cardinal.[20] His uncle was Pierre Roger, the future Clement VI, who in 1327 was still abbot of Fécamp.

Chaplains of only two of these cardinals received prebends in the cathedral of Metz. Annibaldo Gaetani's nephew of the same name appears as canon of Metz in 1348,[21] and Hugo de Montejustino, one of the cardinal's French chaplains, was provided to Metz in 1326 and held the prebend only five years until his death, when Cardinal Annibaldo was provided to it.

A career in the *curia* was still one means for a local cleric of distinguished family to gain an important ecclesiastical office in Lorraine. Such clerics came in the fourteenth century, however, not from great as well as lesser noble families, as in the thirteenth century, but from families of the second rank, notably bourgeois families. The great nobility in fourteenth-century Lorraine seems generally to have neglected the pursuit of high ecclesiastical office. Only one member of the houses of Bar or Lorraine held the bishopric of Metz, Toul, or Verdun from the mid-fourteenth century to the end of the fifteenth.[22] In contrast to Henri de Fénétranges and Philippe de Floranges, local clerics in the curia were such as Foulque Bertrand, provided to Metz in 1317* at the request of Cardinal Francesco Caetani. Foulque was a banker's son and eventually became *primicerius,* the second bourgeois cleric to become principal dignitary of the cathedral. He continued to serve the *curia,* acting as subcollector for the diocese of Metz in 1340.* M. Albericus, chaplain and *auditor causarum,* who was provided to Metz in 1316, was named archdeacon in 1321 and soon thereafter retired to Metz; his family name is not known. His successor was Baudouin Le Gronnais, of a family of important Metz bankers; he was chaplain of Pierre des Prés and continued on the cardinal's staff, dying in Avignon in 1357. Usually, one can only presume local resentment of providees, but for Baudouin there is explicit evidence. Resident in Metz for the initial required period after his nomination, he evidently was assaulted in the cathedral by Canon Philippe Griffonel, a relative.[23] The most successful bourgeois canon, Jean de Heu, was a versatile man who first made a career in the service of John of Bohemia and was rewarded with several prebends. While *primicerius* of Metz, he acted as collector of papal revenues at first for Metz in 1355 and finally for the whole province in 1363, when he was provided bishop of Toul. No strictly curialist canon of Metz of local origin did so well.

The only curialist canon of Metz who came from the important local nobility in the fourteenth century was Johann von Saarwerden, cousin of Count Johann von Saarwerden. Papal chaplain in 1330 when another relative, Bishop Adémar de Monteil, supplicated the pope for an office and prebends in Metz for him, he accumulated a considerable number of benefices but never rose to episcopal office. Other sons of the local nobility who served in Avignon came away with comfortable rewards but none made a dazzling career. Hugues de Mirabel (Meilberg) came of a family which furnished three other canons between 1290 and 1350. He became canon before 1335 and then *circator;* he died in 1358, when a papal letter described him as papal chaplain.[24]

Four others came from Lorraine to make a career in Avignon. Jean de Molans had been a papal chaplain and was *scholasticus* of Toul by 1312, when he was an unsuccessful candidate in an episcopal election. Provision as dean of Toul (with an obligation of residence) seems to have been his consolation prize, and by 1316 he had become *primicerius* of Metz in addition.[25] M. Nicole de Francheville was provided *scholasticus* of Metz in 1354, had to enter into litigation, but in 1361 died canon of Metz—and chaplain of Elias Talleyrand, cardinal bishop of Albano. Gérard de Francheville the younger, *scriptor* in the *curia,* was provided in 1359, apparently without success, and again in 1361. He seems to have retired to Metz fairly promptly, for he appears in local sources in 1368 and was still active in 1385 in Metz. Jean de Bischdorf, chaplain of Cardinal Pierre des Prés, in 1353 was already a canon of Metz and curé of S. Livier in the city when he was provided to a chapel near the city.*

The other fourteenth-century curialists not of local origin present a significant contrast to those of the thirteenth century. A large proportion of earlier providees belonged to important families, but those of the fourteenth century, even counting the six cardinals, were of much more modest—and academic origins. The vastly expanded personnel of the fourteenth-century *curia* simply could not have been recruited from the same families (or even an equivalent number of great French families) who had served the papacy for centuries in Rome. The enormous expansion of the *curia* meant that opportunities both for new dynasties and for a much wider range of society became available, even disregarding the change from a largely Italian to an almost exclusively French *curia.*

There was of course a transition. The provisions granted by John XXII were numerous enough to include the old order as well as the new. Cardinal Annibaldo Caetani in 1331 was provided to the prebend left vacant by the death of Hugo de Montejustino, a Cahorsin and his chaplain.[26] The cardinal's nephew apparently was also provided to Metz. Standing behind both Caetani was Giacomo (Jacobus) Caetani de Stephanesci, cardinal from 1295 to 1344, and uncle of both the elder Annibaldo and of Nicolo (Caetani) de

Ceccano, who was provided to Metz in 1316* and by 1328 was *primicerius*.* When he died in 1337, this prebend was provided to one of the cardinal's French chaplains, Egidius de Ulcheyocastro (Oulchey-le-Chateau).* Chaplains of two other cardinals from Roman times were also provided to Metz: Felicianus de Assisio in 1316, chaplain and physician of Cardinal Jacopo (Jacobus) Colonna; and Johannes de Unzola of Bologna, doctor of laws and chaplain of Napoleone Orsini, cardinal from 1288 until his death in 1342. The old cardinal was likely responsible as well for the provision at some time before April 1336 of Teobaldo Orsini, who became archbishop of Palermo at the age of twenty-seven, retaining his Metz prebend.

Avignon cardinals were nearly all French, and so were their chaplains who were provided to Metz. Besides the cardinals and their relatives and the local clerics, there were another thirteen providees who belonged to the households of various cardinals rather than to the papal *curia* itself. Cardinal Pierre des Prés was served at various times during his forty-one years as cardinal (1320–61, vice-chancellor 1325–61) by three chaplains who had Metz prebends. The first was Petrus de Vaureillis, described in 1327 as his *familiaris* and procurator; he was provided in 1323 and exchanged the prebend and office of *camerarius* in 1326 for a parish church in the diocese of Geneva, presumably nearer his homeland. The cardinal's other two chaplains with Metz prebends were Baudouin Le Gronnais and Jean de Bischdorf, discussed above.

The other cardinal who had three chaplains with Metz prebends was Nicolas de Besse, who did not favor locals; nephew of Clement VI, a Limousin, he preferred at least one Limousin, Guillelmus de Neyraco. Upon the latter's death in 1356, the prebend was provided to Guillelmus de Blezis (Blois), who had two other benefices in Lorraine.* Another chaplain, M. Bernardus Melioris, was provided to Metz at the same time that the cardinal was promoted.[27] When M. Bernardus resigned in 1363, Nicolas was unable to retain the prebend in his household; it was given to the newly created Cardinal Gilles Aycelin de Montaigut.

Metz prebends in six of the eight remaining cases seem simply to have been part of the benefice pool upon which cardinals might draw to support their chaplains, and in one case a relative.[28] Johannes de Vayrolis, nephew of an unnamed cardinal, was provided archdeacon of Metz in 1357; already canon of Cahors and Carpentras and secular prior of Corcolèze (diocese of Carpentras), he had become *auditor causarum* in the *curia* by 1381, when he was provided to a parish church in the diocese of Cologne.[29] The other two cases were an exchange involving two presumably related clerics. Galhardus de la Casa, clerk of the camera and archdeacon of Saarbourg while still a student, in 1317 traded his archdeaconry to M. Guillelmus de la Casa for the parish church of Lauzon in the diocese of Bordeaux. Guillelmus appeared in 1329 as familiaris of Cardinal Arnaud de Via. Such a transaction not only illustrates the curialist's freedom to shuffle his portfolio, it also serves as a reminder that the distinction between chaplains of the pope and chaplains of the cardinals should not loom as a critical one. The papal chaplains among the providees to Metz were not very different from those who served the cardinals.

Only six papal chaplains were in fact provided to Metz in the fourteenth century. Arnal Escharbot (Scarbotus) was provided to Metz in 1317,* described as chaplain of the pope and of Cardinal Bernard de Jarre, in addition to being *auditor causarum;* professor of law at Toulouse and *officialis* of Carcassonne, he died in 1353.[30] Guillelmus Durantis, a cleric of Nîmes, was provided in 1323 as a reward for his services on the staff of papal nuncios in Germany.* Hugo de Arpaione was provided in 1316, became dean in 1326, and resigned in 1329, when the office was provided to a local cleric. Johannes de Rostorph (Rossdorf, diocese of Mainz?) was the only curialist providee (1351) from Germany beyond Lorraine.* Audoynus de Acra was treasurer of the Comtat Venaissin when provided to Metz in 1359. Johannes de Lucembourch* was provided canon of Metz in 1358 and described in the following year as nuncio and papal *familiaris;* he was collector in the diocese of Trier and canon of St. Paulinus, Trier, in 1360 and died the following year.[31]

The collectors and subcollectors who ensured local compliance with papal fiscal assessments were frequently beneficed in the area of their activity. Nearly all were local people, and there is some question of whether they became canons before or after undertaking the duties of cameral collectors. Alero Ricciardi (see above) was a member of the *curia* active as a collector in central Europe but still held a prebend in Metz. The first known local collector was M. Humbert de Belleval in 1295, who first appears at this date as canon of Metz.* He is not known to have served the curia in any other capacity. Similarly, M. Gobert, dean of the cathedral, was mentioned in 1318 as having served as collector.[32] The only official of the camera who was actually provided to Metz in the period was Petrus Guigonis de Castronovo, who in 1329 was provided archdeacon of Vic; he had been named collector of the revenues of benefices for the provinces of Trier and Besançon in 1327. His career was not successful, and he was arrested in the *curia* in 1334 for failure to settle his accounts. The revenues of his archdeaconry were sequestered to satisfy his debts. He made a certain recovery, lamenting in 1343 that he had been litigating to get a prebend in Metz for more than six years; the provision of a successor in 1349 mentioned him as a papal chaplain.* Otto d'Avenches was subcollector in Basel from 1317 to 1319; canon and archdeacon of Basel, he was unsuccessfully provided provost of the Basel chapter in 1320 and further provided canon of Metz in 1325. He was also canon of Lausanne, Moutier, and S. Ursanne.[33] Only in 1328, however, was he finally created a papal chaplain—at the request of Jean d'Arlay, bishop-elect of Basel from 1325 to 1328 and bishop of Langres from 1328 to 1335. It is unclear whether his success was due more to papal service or family connections, but the latter is more probable.

Dominicus de Minorivilla (Domenge de Minouville), provided in 1355, was mentioned as canon of Metz in cameral accounts of 1359 and 1360 in which he figures as chaplain of Gerardus de Arbenco, collector of the revenues of vacant benefices in five provinces.[34] He had been provided in 1355,* because an earlier provision to the collegiate church of S. Maur in Hattonchâtel had turned out to be useless both because of the number of expectancies which had been granted and because of the poverty of the church. He had also been provided to the parish church of S. Euchaire in Metz. Such curial solicitude suggests that Dominicus already had some claim to official benevolence. Four other canons of Metz served as subcollectors for the camera. Jean de Heu, subcollector for Metz in 1355, by 1361 was collector for Metz, Toul, and Verdun, and in 1363 for the whole province of Trier.[35] Henri de Hombourg became canon of Metz in 1343 and by 1346 had added the duties of subcollector of Verdun and canon of Saint-Sauveur in Metz.[36] M. Alard de Thiaucourt spent several years trying to get a prebend in Metz, finally succeeded in 1351, and by the time of his death in 1359 had served as subcollector for Verdun.* A last cameral functionary with a prebend in Metz was Johannes Warini, subcollector for Lyons, who died before 20 June 1363.*

The seventy curialists who held prebends in Metz represented a substantial diversion of local revenues to curial needs, an amount comparable to that collected by papal financial levies. The common and minute services actually paid by the bishops of Metz from 1316 to 1370 amounted to an annual average of 270 florins.[37] While a simple prebend paid as much as 36 florins (see below), offices were even more lucrative: half the income of the office of treasurer in 1331 was 85 florins.[38] At least eight curialists were canons of Metz in 1345; they included the treasurer and the archdeacon of Saarbourg, who were both cardinals. Ten percent of the chapter, their number might be increased by any of the six curialist canons known in the years before or just after 1345. Such figures, of course, can only be approximations, a caution which must be borne in mind.

About 330 canons of Metz are known in the period under discussion; curial provisions account for one fifth of that total. The actual proportion was probably somewhat less, since the local sources for identifying individual canons are far better for the fourteenth century than for the thirteenth. Thus the 24 curialists in the chapter in the thirteenth century were an even smaller proportion of the chapter than the 15 percent which they form of the 158 canons known from 1211 to the end of the century. From 1250 to 1300, some 123 canons are known, of whom 22 were curial officials. There were 45 curialist canons from 1310 to 1370, more than 25 percent of the known canons. Such a proportion of the chapter's revenues, however, was certainly not consumed by the curialist canons. Nonresident canons did not receive the daily distributions, which in 1344 gave each resident canon over 80 livres tournoises. The prebendal income forwarded to canons in the *curia* by the cameral collector around the same date ranged from 22 to 36 livres tournoises (before deductions for expenses) for those who held no office in the chapter.[39]

The average length of time for which a curialist held a prebend was very likely less than the average tenure of locally recruited canons who might enter the chapter at a younger age and hardly ever exchanged their prebends for others. The impact of curial providees was not, however, significantly diminished by the lack of effect common to many provisions. Delays might and did occur, but the provisions of only two curialists are known to have failed.[40] The numbers of curialist canons given above are conservative calculations in which many more known providees to Metz might have been included. Curial practice (or perhaps the editors of the registers) never consistently gave the titles of minor curial officials when they were named in papal letters.

The most significant factor in moderating the impact of papal provisions was that not all the curialists remained at the papal court. A substantial but incalculable number of those from Lorraine returned to Metz, where they must have formed an important elite of education and experience. Henri de Fénétranges, Philippe de Floranges, M. Simon de Marville, M. Albericus, Foulque Bertrand, Hugues de Mirabel, and perhaps both Franchevilles seem to have spent fairly large parts of their careers in Metz after their provisions. A larger proportion of the thirteenth-century providees were of local origin than in the fourteenth (nine out of twenty-four as opposed to ten out of forty-five), but the smaller proportion in the fourteenth century may have been offset by an apparently greater likelihood of the curialist's returning home. The voice of caution again pleads, however, that local records are markedly better in the fourteenth century. Such veterans of the *curia* in any case were clerics who might well have acquired prebends in any case, and only their absence in the *curia* should be counted a burden on the chapter. So many other interests laid claim to prebends that it would in fact be unwise to insist at great length on the ill effects of curial provisions. The canons who never sought a bureaucratic career and stayed in Metz were a fairly undistinguished group which can however be spared criticism to the extent that such lack of distinction was the usual standard in other chapters. The promise of rewards for curial service in fact helped to increase an isolated provincial church's contacts with the world beyond Lorraine, though the price was a substantial one.

University of California. Berkeley

Notes

1. G. Barraclough, *Papal Provisions: Aspects of Church History Constitutional. Legal and Administrative in the Later Middle Ages* (Oxford, 1935), is true to its subtitle and a valuable study of the question. For more recent publications, it can be supplemented by B. Guillemain, *La Cour pontificale d'Avignon (1309–76 Étude d'une Société* (Paris, 1966).

2. J. P. Kirsch, *Die päpstlichen Kollektorien in Deutschland während des XIV. Jahrhunderts.*

Quellen and Forschungen aus dem Gebiete der Geschichte . . . von der Görres-Gesellschaft III (Paderborn, 1894), 205–9.

3. The approximately seventy members of the curia to be discussed in this essay appear in so many documents that a proper scholarly apparatus for this study might well rival the length of the text. The two most frequently used sources will therefore not be footnoted; readers are asked instead to assume that a statement of facts whose source is not footnoted is taken from a published papal register and can be verified by using the indices of the published registers (specific references will, however, be supplied for those officials who appear so frequently in the registers as to make use of the indices a time-consuming task. A convenient list of the published registers may be found in R. C. van Caenegem, *Kurze Quellenkunde des westeuropäischen Mittelalters* (Göttingen, 1964), pp. 210–11. Asterisks (*) marking certain persons and dates refer to H. V. Sauerland, *Vatikanische Urkunden und Regesten zur Geschichte Lothringens,* Quellen zur lothringischen Geschichte I–II (Metz, 1901–5), whose index s. v. *Metensis* gives ready access to his summaries of letters in the papal registers; a number of letters escaped his notice, but the work is still indispensable for entries in those registers whose publication has not yet been finished. A number of local documents are also included.

4. A. Goerz, *Mittelrheinische Regesten* (Koblenz, 1881), III: nos. 998, 1222.

5. Ibid., no. 2267.

6. G. Wolfram, "Chronica episcoporum Metensium," *Jahrbuch der Gesellschaft für lothringische Geschichte und Altertumskunde* X (1898), 296–337, at 316–17.

7. Wolfram, ibid., p. 316n. says that only later (unspecified) sources term him de Liestenberg (i.e., Lichtenberg), an important Alsatian noble family.

8. PL CCXVI: 555.

9. P. Rabikauskas, "'Auditor litterarum contradictarum' et Commissions de Juges délégués sous le Pontificat d'Honorius III," *Bibliothèque de l'École des Chartes* CXXXII (1974), 213–44 discusses, pp. 215–26, a certain M. Octavianus (and the abbreviations of his name), *auditor litterarum contradictarum,* who in 1220 heard a case about the office of scholasticus of Metz; although he does not mention the provision of someone of the same name, papal *scriptor* in 1216, the coincidence is striking.

10. *Gallia Christiana* XIII: 823. A. Paravicini Bagliani mentions all these chaplains in his *Cardinali di Curia e "familae" cardinalizie,* Italia Sacra XVIII–XIX (Padua, 1972), a work whose continuation will leave historians extremely well informed on the thirteenth-century *curia.*

11. Paris, Bibl. nat., MS 11846, fol. 49v.

12. M. Meurisse, *Histoire des Évesques de Metz* (Metz, 1634), p. 467. N. Hontheim, *Historia Treverensis* (Trier, 1750), I: 773.

13. Bar-le-Duc, Archives de la Meuse, B.2204. I have used a transcription kindly supplied by Prof. Jean Schneider.

14. Paravicini Bafliano, *Cardinali,* pp. 213–21.

15. F. Schillmann, *Die Formularsammlung des Marinus von Eboli,* Bibliothek des Deutschen Historischen Instituts in Rom XVI (Rome, 1929), I: 58, and no. 1344.

16. Kirsch, *Kollektorien,* p. XXXII.

17. E. Langlois, ed., *Les Registres de Nicolas IV,* Bibliothèque des Écoles françaises d'Athènes et de Rome, 2e série 2 vols. (Paris, 1891–93), no. 6248.

18. C. R. Cheney, *From Becket to Langton* (Manchester, 1956), pp. 180–81.

19. G. Mollat, ed., *Lettres communes de Jean XXII,* 16 vols. (Bibliothèque des Écoles françaises d'Athènes et de Rome, 3e série (Paris, 1904–47), no. 55423.

20. Sauerland, *Vatikanische Urkunden,* no. 522.

21. J.-B. Pelt, *Etudes sur la Cathédrale de Metz: Textes extraits principalement des Registres capitulaires (1210–1790)* (Metz, 1930), p. 5.

22. Cf. *Gallia Christiana,* XIII: passim.

23. Metz, Archives de la Moselle (dépôt), 2G suppl. 1, fol. 13r (1352). Fourteenth-century capitular life was not serene. Canon Thomas de Thequestorf in 1343 disturbed divine office so violently that he was still excommunicate for his unspecified offense twelve years later (ibid., fol. 15r).

24. H. V. Sauerland, *Urkunden und Regesten zur Geschichte der Rheinlande aus dem Vatikanischen Archiv,* 7 vols. Publikationen der Gesellschaft für Rheinische Geschichtskunde 23; (Bonn, 1902–13), IV, no. 500. His first mention as canon of Metz is in Metz, Archives municipales, *Bans de trefonds* 1335, no. 30.

25. Metz, Archives de la Moselle, G.492.

26. Above, n. 16. The cardinal was also granted Hugo's claim to the office of treasurer, a claim entangled in a bold bit of fraud. Cf. *Lettres communes de Jean XXII,* nos. 24538 and 26684.

27. Kirsch, *Kollektorien,* p. 166.

28. Johannes de Sancto Martino, *familiaris* of Cardinal Jean de Comminges, was provided in 1342;* Johannes de Albaperta, chaplain and *familiaris* of cardinal Pierre Bertrand, died a canon of Metz in 1348;* Egidius de Stalleghen, priest of the diocese of Liège, chaplain of cardinal Hugues Roger, was provided in 1349;* Nicolaus Caude, chaplain and *familiaris* of cardinal Etienne de Poissy, was provided in 1369;* and Johannes de Vilo (whom Sauerland, *Vatikanische Urkunden,* no. 1563) identified with a chaplain of the bishop of Metz in 1348 named Johannes de Vico, *familiaris* of cardinal Androuin de la Roche in 1370.*

29. E. Göller, ed., *Repertorium Germanicum I. Verzeichnis der in den Registern und Kameralakten Clemen' VII. von Avignon vorkommenden Personen* . . . (Berlin, 1916), p. 100.

30. He figures in E. M. Meijers, *Études d'Histoire du Droit (Leiden, 1959),* III: 193–94. The date of his death, unknown to Meijers, is in Sauerland.

31. Kirsch, *Kollektorien,* pp. 388–89; death in Sauerland, *Vatikanische Urkunden,* no. 1393.

32. Kirsch, *Kollektorien,* p. 43.

33. A Brucker, ed., *Helvetia Sacra Abt. I, Band I; Schweizerische Kardinäle. Das apostolische Gesandtschaftswesen in der Schweiz, Erzbistümer und Bistümer* (Bern, 1972), I: 280.

34. H. Hoberg, ed., *Die Einnahmen der apostolischen Kammer unter Innozenz VI.,* 2 vols., Vatikanische Quellen zur Geschichte der päpstlichen Hof- und Finanzverwaltung 1316–78 . . . von der Görres-Gesellschaft VII (Paderborn, 1955–72), I: 272, 287; Kirsch, *Kollektorian,* p. 256.

35. Hoberg, *Einnahmen,* I: 203, 317, 318.

36. Kirsch, *Kollektorien,* p. 167.

37. Sauerland, *Urkunden und Regesten,* passim (Cf. *Index rerum notabiliorum s.v. Servitia communia et minuta.*) The amounts mentioned in the documents which he published are, of course, a bare minimum. Other payments may well have escaped his notice.

38. Kirsch, *Kollektorien,* p. 129.

39. Metz, Archives de la Moselle, 2G suppl. 1, fol. 2v.; Kirsch, *Kollektorien,* pp. 166–67.

40. Romanus *natus mag.* Angeli de Insula, canon of St. Peter's but not mentioned as a curial official, was provided to Metz in 1328 (*Lettres communes de Jean XXII,* no. 43025); a successor's provision in 1348 had no effect because Romanus had never held the prebend (Kirsch, *Kollektorien,* p. 206). The provision of Johannes de Clinaco, *familiaris* of Clement VI, failed because reports of the death of the canon to whose prebend he had been provided turned out to be greatly exaggerated (ibid., p. 207).

Index

Proper Names

Legal Citations, as Contained in the Text

Biblical Citations

Matt. 19:22, 238
Matt. 26:69–75, 103
Num. 15:37–41, 3
1 Peter 2:9, 65
Prov. 28:1, 175, 179

Ps. 76:27, 167
Ps. 109:4, 65
Rev. 1:15, 4
Rom. 1, 144, 243

Manuscripts

Admont, Stiftsbibl. 7, 91–94, 220; 22,
65–66, 91, 219; 55, 219
Angers, Bibl. mun. 163(155), 161–62
Augsburg, 1, 93

Bamberg, Staatsbibl: Can. 17, 43; Can.
19, 219; Can. 20, 219; Can. 42, 91–
93; Msc. Liturg. 134, 122, 126, 128
Bar-le-Duc, Arch. de la Meuse B.2204,
322
Barcelona, Arch. de la Corona de
Aragón: Cancilleriá, pergaminos of
Raymond Berenguer IV, 223, 228–
91; Cancilleriá, Registro 1, 288;
Gran Priorato de Cataluña, Cartulary
of Gardeny, 290; 74, 117–18, 128;
perg. Alfonso I 289–91; perg. Pedro
I 291
Barcelona, Arxiu Capitular: perg.
Diversorum A.2292a,b
(15.III.1158), 292; perg.
Diversorum A.2397 (21.III.1177)
290; perg. Diversorum B.280
(7.VI.1202) 289; perg. Diversorum
B.654 (16.III.1180) 290; perg.
Diversorum B.672 (1.IV.1182) 290;
perg. Diversorum B.774
(13.III.1212), 290; perg.
Diversorum B.780 (7.VI.1202), 28
290, 292; perg. Diversorum B.137
(11.XI.1149), 289; perg.
Diversorum C, capsa 7, 388, 389
(4.V.1198), 290; S. Cubat 55, 93
Barcelona, Bibl. Central de la Diputa-
tion: Provincial 944, 118; perg.
Miret i Sans 2169, 290; perg. Miret i
Sans, 292
Berlin, Staatsbibl.: lat. f. 462, 27, 33,
45; lat. qu. 192, 45; Phillips 1732,
255–56, 264; Sav. 14, 21, 25–26,
33

Bologna, Archiginnasio A. 48, 33, 44
Bologna, Bibl. Univ. lat. 794 (1556),
118, 128
Bordeaux, Bibl. mun. 11, 127

Cambridge, Corpus Christi College: 44,
126; 289, 126
Cambridge, Gonville and Caius College
676, 29–32, 45, 92
Cambridge, Pembroke College 111,
123, 128
Cambridge, Univ. Lib.: 3321, 33, 43;
Dd.IX.38, 267; Addit. 3321, 32
Copenhagen, Kongelige Bibl. Gl. Kgl.
S.3543, 255–56, 264
Cordoba, Bibl. del Cabildo 10, 219

Dublin, Trinity College 218, 126
Durham, N.C., Duke Univ. lat. 104,
127

Erlangen, Universitätsbibl. 226, 126

Florence, Bibl. Laur., S. Croce
IV.sin.2, 219
Florence, Bibl. Naz., Conv. Soppr.
G.IV (1736), 26, 33, 45
Freiburg-im-Breisgau, Bibl. Univ. 147,
127
Fulda, Landesbibl. D.14, 218

Göttingen, iur. 159, 93
Graz, Univ. Bibl.: 106, 219; 138, 219;
374, 212; 1515, 265
Grenoble, Bibl. mun. 627, 33, 45

Hereford, Cathedral Lib. O.6.XIII, 126

Karlsruhe, Landesbibl. Aug. XL, 219–
20
Kassel, Landesbibl. iur. 11, 219